ZPG

Place
Matters

STUDIES IN GOVERNMENT AND PUBLIC POLICY

Place Matters

METROPOLITICS FOR THE TWENTY-FIRST CENTURY

SECOND EDITION, REVISED

PETER DREIER, JOHN MOLLENKOPF & TODD SWANSTROM

UNIVERSITY PRESS OF KANSAS

Published by the

University Press of Kansas

(Lawrence, Kansas 66049),

which was organized by the

Kansas Board of Regents and

is operated and funded by

Emporia State University,

Fort Hays State University,

Kansas State University,

Pittsburg State University,

the University of Kansas, and

Wichita State University.

© 2004 by the
University Press of Kansas

Library of Congress Cataloging-in-Publication Data
Dreier, Peter.
Place matters : metropolitics for the twenty-first century /
Peter Dreier, John Mollenkopf & Todd Swanstrom. —
2nd ed., rev.
p. cm. — (Studies in government and public policy)
Includes bibliographical references and index.
ISBN 0-7006-1364-1 (pbk. : alk. paper)
1. Urban poor—United States. 2. Urban policy—United
States. 3. Federal-city relations—United States.
4. Metropolitan areas—United States. I. Mollenkopf, John H.,
1946- II. Swanstrom, Todd. III. Title. IV. Series.
HV4045.D74 2004
307.76'0973—dc22
2004013599

British Library Cataloguing in Publication Data
is available.
Printed in the United States of America

10 9 8 7 6 5 4 3 2 1

The paper used in this publication meets the minimum
requirements of the American National Standard for
Permanence of Paper for Printed Library Materials
z39.48-1984.

For Bennett Harrison

Contents

Tables and Illustrations

Preface

This book grew out of our frustration with the stalemated debate about the condition of cities and our conviction that we can move beyond it. In *Place Matters,* we argue that because the problems presently facing America's cities are largely political in origin, their solution also lies in politics. We focus on how public policies and the organization of our political institutions have fostered the growth of economic segregation in metropolitan America, which in turn damages both equal opportunity and economic competitiveness. We favor moving toward forming and delivering urban policy at a broader regional context. Such steps, we believe, are a critical ingredient for transforming the politics of urban policy and broadening the coalition in support of progressive urban policies.

The thousand footnotes in *Place Matters* indicate that it is a scholarly work. Our argument derives from the most rigorous social scientific research about how place matters in people's lives and why spatial segregation of people and jobs has been increasing in the metropolitan areas of the United States. Although it is based on scientific knowledge, the reader will see that *Place Matters* has an underlying perspective and is not value-free. To paraphrase the late sociologist C. Wright Mills, "Throughout we have tried to be objective, but we do not claim to be detached." Our efforts have been motivated by the acute injustices prevailing in American metropolitan life and the certain knowledge that we can find better ways to live together.

Our analysis embraces the fundamental American beliefs that national government should be limited, that democracy rests on local participation, and that individuals must take responsibility for their actions. Yet we also rely on other basic components of the American value system, namely our sense of fair play, distaste for rules that consistently favor some groups over others, and belief that everyone should be able to engage in civic life from more or less equivalent starting points. Place matters to us because our metropolitan areas are organized in ways that increasingly undercut the American sense of fair play and equal representation. Local democracy cannot flourish when poor municipalities are beset by severe fiscal distress, and even affluent local governments chase after taxable resources while seeking to keep out moderate-income, not to mention poor, residents. The huge gap between rich and poor communities results in tremendous differences in the quality of our schools, parks, garbage collection, and police and fire protection, as well as economic and social opportunities, across our metropolitan areas. In the context of extreme local political fragmentation and autonomy, economic and racial segregation have turned local governments into privatized interest groups concerned with the narrow self-interests of their residents. For those living in ghetto neighborhoods and distressed suburbs cut off from access to jobs and decent schools — or even the same kind of shopping and household services available to most Americans — and subjected to unhealthy environments and poor health care, freedom of residential choice has little meaning. Growing economic segregation exacerbates income inequality and worsens its effects.

Given these central concerns, we were honored when the New Political Science Section of the American Political Science Association awarded *Place Matters* its 2002 Michael Harrington Award for "the book that best demonstrates how scholarship can be used in the struggle for a better world." Harrington's *The Other America,* published in 1962, was a catalyst for the nation's war on poverty. It would please us if our book, like Harrington's, inspired needed reforms in how Americans plan and govern their metropolitan areas.

We also wrote this book to fill a gap in the literature. Scholars and activists did not have a single source that provided a summary of knowledge about the power of place and the importance of economic segregation, how public policies have been transforming the shape and geography of inequality in our metropolitan areas, and what people are trying to do about this problem. Numerous book reviews and personal conversations confirm that policy makers and activists have found *Place Matters* useful.

Contrary to our hopes when the book first appeared, national politics has become less friendly toward metropolitan reform since the devastating attack on the World Trade Center on September 11, 2001. The invasions of Afghanistan and Iraq shifted national concern from domestic problems toward terrorism and international security. The Bush administration's budget and tax policies have shifted national priorities from attending to the concerns we raise in the book toward spending on the military and homeland security and tax reduction for wealthy households. The administration's proposals to reduce spending on subsidized housing vouchers and its success in limiting federal tax revenues necessary to pay for them will widen, not narrow, the economic inequalities we discuss. The redistricting of 2001 further concentrated the urban vote into fewer congressional districts rather than spreading it to districts with both urban and suburban voters.

Trends are far more promising at the state and metropolitan levels. Business leaders, foundations, unions, community groups, environmentalists, educators, policy practitioners, the news media, elected officials, and others are seeking new metropolitan approaches to sprawl, poverty, pollution, housing, and economic growth. So far, their innovative thinking has mostly taken the form of conferences, books, reports, and news articles. The business-sponsored Committee for Economic Development issued "A New Metropolitan Agenda" in 2002. Groups as diverse as the Sierra Club, the National Association of Home Builders, and the Urban Land Institute developed task forces, reports, and policy agendas dealing with sprawl and smart growth. The National League of Cities' recent report, "Divided We Fall: Inequality and the Future of America's Cities and Towns," argues that inequality is the nation's most important problem and that "local officials can make a huge difference." ACORN, the Industrial Areas Foundation, and the Gamaliel Foundation, three national networks of grassroots community organizations, have taken up the challenge of bringing people together from different neighborhoods in the same metropolitan areas to develop common regional strategies. The MacArthur Foundation is studying how to move toward equitable and competitive regions. Daily newspapers have assigned reporters to write about metropolitan-wide issues, taking up the concern pioneered by syndicated columnist Neal Peirce. Hundreds of college classes have used *Place Matters* to examine metropolitan inequality.

So far, only a few places, such as Portland and Minneapolis–St. Paul, have translated this movement into strong regional policies. But this incubation period has the potential to produce a powerful political force for national reform that will change the way we live and work in our cities and suburbs. In short, metropolitics are alive and well. September 11 may have shifted national attention toward international affairs, but it has reminded New Yorkers how much each part of the metropolis depends on the others (those who died came from all classes and all parts of the region) and launched a vigorous debate about how best to rebuild the site and the region. From these ashes, a broader debate will emerge.

Although the first edition of the book was well received, it also provoked criticism and debate.[1] A symposium in the January 2002 issue of the *Urban Affairs Review,* for example, engaged three prominent scholars to dissect the book. We welcome these criticisms. In responding to these criticisms, for this revision, we have made the argument of the book clearer and stronger. In addition, we have updated the data in the book, especially data from the 2000 census. The major criticisms made of the first edition are outlined below, along with a summary of our response.

1. *The comeback of central cities in the 1990s and the dramatic decline in concentrated poverty contradict the factual premise that economic segregation and concentrated poverty are worsening.*

It is certainly preferable to see cities as economically resilient rather than as irreparable sinkholes of social pathology. In fact, we stress that cities continue to be sources of economic dynamism even as they are burdened by a disproportionate share of the nation's poor. We reject the implication, however, that the moderate decline of concentrated poverty in central cities during the 1990s means that the problem will solve itself. Chapter 2 uses 2000 census data to detail how cities remain under stress and how only the most extreme form of concentrated urban poverty abated somewhat during the 1990s. We also outline how rising incomes for many urban residents can make matters worse for those who remain poor, especially through rising housing costs. Finally, we note that poverty concentrations are now emerging in distressed suburbs, which often have even less fiscal capacity and political clout than central cities to address their problems. The main lesson from the 1990s is that even though tight labor markets are clearly good for cities and poor people, the United States simply cannot grow its way out of the problems created by economic segregation.

2. *Social scientists do not all agree that living in areas of concentrated poverty has negative impacts on individuals. As a result, it is premature to use social science to justify government attempts to deconcentrate poverty.*

Some scholars doubt that concentrated poverty affects individual behavior after controlling for individual and family characteristics, but Chapter 3 clearly shows that residents of high-poverty neighborhoods are isolated from job opportunities, go to bad schools, suffer from unhealthy environments, and pay high grocery prices. Such factors have strong influences on individual life chances. Many studies show that people vote with their feet by leaving such places when they can, suggesting they have little doubt about the negative consequences of living in such places. Taken together, such findings clearly justify policy interventions to abate these conditions.

3. *Racial segregation and discrimination are substantially more important than economic segregation and class divisions in shaping the lives of people in our*

metropolitan areas. Racism is so entrenched in America that it prevents the formation of the broad interracial coalitions necessary for metropolitan reform.

Racial differences undoubtedly play a fundamental role in producing and reproducing metropolitan spatial inequalities in America. Our review of the evidence, however, suggests that racial segregation has declined somewhat in recent decades, while economic segregation has increased. We must continue to combat racial discrimination, but we must also address the increasingly acute problem of economic inequality across places. As metropolitan areas become more diverse, it will become more feasible to construct cross-racial coalitions focusing on common economic interests.

4. *Efforts to deconcentrate the poor throughout metropolitan areas have had somewhat positive results for those who have moved, but these experiments are too small scale to have much impact on the overall concentration of poverty. Attempts to expand "mobility" programs to achieve significant effects may backfire because suburbanites do not want the poor to move into their communities.*[2]

The current highly fragmented nature of local government, combined with local control over housing and land-use decisions, certainly does give the residents of many jurisdictions the opportunity to oppose efforts to build housing for poor people or otherwise promote the dispersion of poor urban residents to better-off neighborhoods and towns. That is why Chapter 7 argues that fundamental changes in metropolitan political arrangements must precede or coincide with broader regional efforts to deconcentrate the urban poor. We also note, however, that suburban jurisdictions do not always oppose such developments, particularly when they take place within a larger metropolitan framework that reflects a consensus about the "fair share" of such families they should house. Indeed more suburban jurisdictions are realizing that affordable housing is a suburban problem, not just an urban problem. Chicago's successful experience with this type of program suggests that, managed well and in the appropriate regional context, they could be conducted at much larger scale without political backlash.

5. *Although* Place Matters *argues persuasively that economic segregation and sprawl harm metropolitan areas, suburbanites will never support policies that limit their autonomy or shift their decision making over zoning, economic development, public education, and other matters to regional, state, or federal levels.*

The most pervasive response among our critics is that our program is not politically feasible. We understand that half of all American voters live in suburbs and that no majority coalition can be created without significant suburban support. That can happen only on the basis of interests shared by central-city and suburban residents. To date, many elected officials, particularly Republicans, have mobilized suburban voters around their differences with urban voters. But three emerging realities are tipping the balance away from the political attraction of stressing these differences and toward mobilizing efforts that stress common interests: suburbanites have a large and continuing stake in prosperous central cities; inner suburbs are becoming more like central cities than better-off outer suburbs; and metropolitan sprawl, fed by metropolitan fragmentation and competition, vexes suburbanites as well as central-city residents.

Many reviewers agreed with our policy recommendations but felt that the American electorate is not ready for them. It is true that some of our ideas push the limits of the possible, as Michael Harrington used to say, but the reader should remember that if we had been writing a hundred years ago, we would be recommending such policy innovations as a minimum wage law, old-age insurance, and subsidized housing for the poor. These ideas seemed radical and unrealistic to many observers at that time, but of course they are part of the American mainstream today. In comparison to these far-reaching social programs, our proposals are quite modest. Public opinion polls indicate that Americans generally support the ideas we outline in Chapter 7. The problem is typically not lack of public support, but lack of political will. Given the conservative influences on our political system, particularly the impact of big money on electoral politics, public opinion doesn't always get translated into public policy. Throughout the past century, significant policy shifts typically begin from the bottom up. Social movements cause ideas to percolate in local and state governments (which Justice Louis Brandeis called the "laboratories" of democracy) and then, at times of political crisis, into national policy. For example, the ideas that eventually became the heart of the New Deal were initially worked out decades before by progressive urban reformers in places like New York City and Wisconsin, motivated by popular discontent over such tragedies as the Triangle Shirt Waist fire.

Our analysis of American history makes us optimistic that new political coalitions and forces emerge unexpectedly, often behind the backs of the "experts." Chapter 8 uses 2000 census data to update our argument that the political conditions are ripe for new central city–suburban coalitions. These data show that suburbs are increasingly diverse and that more complicated multiracial ethnic patterns are gradually altering the old black-white divisions. Welfare reform has largely taken away the politically convenient but factually erroneous negative stereotype that recipients are lazy chiselers. More poor are working poor whom middle-class Americans are willing to help. Increased recognition of how public policies (especially huge tax cuts for the top end of the income distribution) have contributed to economic inequality has provided more fertile ground for political coalitions seeking economic fairness. Changing material conditions are not enough, however. Elected officials and organized citizens alike must show leadership if we are to find common ground across economic divides. We highlight how elected officials, business and labor leaders, civic and community activists, environmentalists, journalists, and philanthropists are forging new approaches that cross city lines, and we suggest ways to accelerate the pace of change.

Place Matters originated at a small conference on the future of urban America in May 1994. Sponsorship from the Spivack Program on Applied Social Research and Social Policy of the American Sociological Association (ASA) allowed us to invite some of the nation's leading scholars and practitioners to discuss the current urban conditions and how to develop political strategies for the policies needed to ameliorate them. We warmly thank the participants for their insights and candor. They include William Barnes (National League of Cities), Robert Embry (Abell Foundation), Elaine Fielding (University of Michigan), Ted Hershberg (University of Pennsylvania), Edward Hill (Cleveland State University), Mark Alan Hughes (Public/Private Ventures), Pam Karlan (Stanford University), John Logan (State University of New York at Albany), Guy Molyneaux (Peter Hart & Associates), Manuel Pastor (University of California, Santa Cruz), Neal Peirce (syndicated columnist), Nestor Rodriguez (University of Houston), Margery Austin Turner (Urban Institute), and Margaret Weir (University of California, Berkeley). None of them, of course, bear any responsibility for the contents of this book. We particularly thank our three energetic and enthusiastic ASA colleagues who made this conference a success: Felice Levine (ASA executive officer), Carla Howery (deputy executive officer), and Paula Trubisky (special assistant).

Our initial aim was to write a modest report summarizing the conference discussion. It gradually grew into a book-length study as we wrote and reconsidered drafts over several years. As a result, the first edition took much longer than we initially anticipated, but the delay allowed us to consider the remarkable resurgence of scholarly interest in regional approaches to urban issues.

Our argument builds on the work of hundreds of scholars, whose contributions we acknowledge in our many notes. A few people deserve special mention, however. On two separate occasions, Rich DeLeon read the entire manuscript and provided extensive comments that immeasurably improved it. Four scholars reviewed the first edition for the University Press of Kansas (Carl Abbott of Portland State University, Joel Rast of the University of Wisconsin Milwaukee,

Glenn Beamer of the University of Virginia, and Dennis Judd of the University of Illinois at Chicago). We are indebted to them for their penetrating suggestions for improvement.

Many other colleagues reviewed earlier versions of the manuscript, provided data and examples, and shared their thoughts about the issues we address. They include Richard Brown, Regan Carlson, Sang Chi, Frances Frisken, John Goering, David Imbroscio, Tom Kingsley, Neil Kraus, Leslie McCall, Larry Mishel, Michael Munson, Michael Leo Owens, Kathy Petit, Timothy Ross, Richard Rothstein, Richard Sauerzopf, David Schrank, Ray Seidelman, Peter Tatian, Margaret Weir, Hal Wolman, and Elvin Wyly. Research assistance was provided by Alan Lamberg, Colleen Casey, Sara Azniv Whittington, Sylvia Chico, Callie White, Mine Doyran, Victoria Hyzer, Rachel Josil, Chris Latimer, and Danielle Croce. Elizabeth McDaniel and Nicole Radmore of the Russell Sage Foundation provided critical editorial assistance in the closing stage of our work for the first edition. Fred Woodward, director of the University Press of Kansas, was enormously supportive during the entire process. We appreciate his faith in our ideas. We also benefitted from the caring professionalism of Rebecca Giusti, Larisa Martin, and Susan Schott.

A large supply of patience and love from our families helped us write this book. We thank them for their understanding. Peter wishes to thank his wife, Terry Meng, and their twin daughters, Amelia and Sarah, who were born while the book was a jumble of memos and e-mails on his computer's hard drive. John thanks his always stimulating and unfailingly supportive spouse and daughter, Kathleen Gerson and Emily Mollenkopf. Todd thanks his wife, Katie, and daughters Jessica, Madeleine, and Eleanore for their love and patience.

Just months before Bennett Harrison died in early 1999 at the age of fifty-six, he provided us with extensive comments on an early draft of our work. We will always cherish Ben's exuberant scrawls of "terrific" and "explain this" on our manuscript pages. We hope our work is informed by the insight, political commitment, and generosity that Ben radiated. We miss him dearly and dedicate this book to his memory.

I am tempted to believe that what we call necessary

institutions are often no more than institutions to which

we have grown accustomed, and that in matters of social

constitution the field of possibilities is much more extensive

than men living in their various societies are ready to imagine.

—*Recollections of Alexis de Tocqueville*

Place Still Matters

In the mid-1980s, Arletta Bronaugh and Dwight Jackson and their two children moved from Altgeld Gardens, a 1,500-apartment public housing project in Chicago's inner city, to the leafy, affluent suburb of Hoffman Estates fifty-five miles away.[1] The residents of Altgeld Gardens are mostly poor African Americans. The area is surrounded by fifty-three toxic facilities. It has many violent gangs and a high crime rate. At the time the family moved to Hoffman Estates, its median household income was $49,475, almost nine out of ten of its residents were white, and only 2 percent lived below the poverty line.[2]

The couple participated in a government program that provides federal housing vouchers to poor families so they can leave troubled neighborhoods and move to the suburbs.[3] Although Bronaugh encountered some racism and initially felt isolated, she and her family adjusted well to their new surroundings. They have a nice apartment, both adults have jobs, and their ten-year-old son Jason made the honor roll in school. In fact, they began to earn enough money so that they were no longer eligible for the rent subsidy. A former welfare recipient who now works for the phone company, Arletta observed, "I've got a job, two cars; my son goes to good schools. Whatever obstacles have been put in the way, it's worth it. I did what was best for my family and what was best for me."

Dawn Macklin made a similar journey from a public housing project in Chicago to Westmont, a western Chicago suburb with a median household income of $37,315, and where 87 percent of the residents are white and only 4.5 percent are poor. "Considering the gangs and the drugs I grew up around," she explained, "I thought it would be a much better environment for my kids." She found a job at United Parcel Service after finding that "the job market was wide open. When you're in the city, you find yourself in a trap. You can't get a job as easily. The opportunities are not there. You find you can't get yourself off public aid."

Early in 2004, in the wealthy suburb of Mission Viejo, in Orange County, California, about 100 people—ten times the usual turnout—packed a meeting of the Planning Commission to oppose a new housing development. The proposal included 168 subsidized apartments in eight three-story buildings for moderate-income families earning up to about $50,000 as well as 99 upscale single-family homes. It also called for a swimming pool, a small park, a recreation center, and tot lots.[4] Mission Viejo planning officials told the crowd that the apartments would be targeted to teachers, firefighters, nurses, and similar occupational categories, but the angry residents insisted that if they approved the development, it would destroy their community. The suburb of 98,943 people has a median household income of $78,248 and a poverty rate of 3.7 percent. The median price home is over $454,000.[5]

"We've worked too hard our entire lives to have our neighborhood changed into rentals and low-income projects," said Lin Morelic, a resident of Mission Viejo for ten years. "These projects are notoriously known for their overcrowded apartments, excess cars of friends and family, gangs, drugs and drive-by shootings. Consider what would happen to our schools and traffic, our children, or parents, grandparents and friends if this project were approved." She also said that the project would "change the complexion of our city." Others echoed that view and criticized the proposed development for being dense and reducing property values in the area. People came to the meeting in response to calls from the Committee for Integrity in Government, which circulated a leaflet saying "Stop the Nightmare Before It Starts" above a drawing of high-rise tenements and warning of "non-English speaking students," "overcrowding in local schools," "graffiti," "disease," and "crime."

Not everyone in Mission Viejo shared that view. The Planning Department staff had recommended approval of the development. One city council member in the audience walked out of the meeting in disgust, explaining to the *Los Angeles Times* that he was "embarrassed and disappointed that so many people in the community would engage in such exclusionary politics." But the Planning Commissioners that evening unanimously opposed the project.

The two Chicago families who moved to the suburbs and the opponents of the apartment complex in Mission Viejo both provide evidence for this book's thesis: place matters. Where we live makes a big difference in the quality of our individual lives. The functioning of the places where we live also has a big impact on the quality of our society. The evidence shows that places—neighborhoods, cities and suburbs, and regions—are becoming more unequal. Economic classes are becoming more distant and separate from each other as the rich increasingly live with other rich people and the poor live with other poor people. Over time, the poor have become concentrated in central cities and distressed inner suburbs, while the rich live mostly in exclusive central-city neighborhoods and outer suburbs.

This rising economic segregation has produced negative consequences that range from reinforcing disadvantage in central-city neighborhoods, to heightening the cost of suburban sprawl, to speeding the deterioration of central cities and inner suburbs. It would be bad enough if this trend resulted simply from individuals and households making choices in free markets, but it does not. Federal and state policies have favored suburban sprawl, concentrated urban poverty, and economic segregation. Only new policies for metropolitan governance that level the playing field and bring all parts of the metropolis into a dialogue with each other can stop the drift toward greater spatial inequality. Americans need a political strategy that unites central-city and suburban residents in a new coalition to support these policies.

It may seem odd to argue that place matters when technology appears to have conquered space. Americans are highly mobile. Cars and planes have made it possible for us to travel more quickly than ever before. Telephones, computers, cable networks, and, above all, the Internet enable us to engage many aspects of society without leaving our homes. With cable service, a satellite dish, or a DSL line, we can choose entertainment ranging from tractor pulls to Tolstoy, from rap to Rachmaninoff. Distance learning is growing rapidly, and "virtual" universities enable students to pursue college degrees from home. E-commerce makes it hardly necessary to drive to the mall anymore. Every day, more people work at home instead of commuting to the office. Where you live, in short, seems ever less relevant to the type of person you are and what you do. In this view, technology has eclipsed the traditional reasons why people gather in cities: to be close to jobs, culture, and shopping. Cities, some argue, are becoming obsolete.[6]

In fact, this idea is nonsense.[7] As places of intense personal interaction, cities are as important as ever. If technology were truly abolishing space and time, real estate values would flatten out. The last decade's soaring house prices in San Francisco, Boston, and New York City are proof positive that people will pay dearly to live in certain places. Indeed, over 80 percent of all of Americans have chosen to live in metropolitan areas, not the countryside.

It is true that mass ownership of automobiles has allowed people to live farther from work. If they can afford it, Americans generally prefer to live in low-density suburbs. But people still care about where they live, perhaps more than ever. The social networks of higher-income professionals extend far beyond their neighborhoods and cities, often around the globe. They use these "weak" ties for gathering information, seeking opportunities, and finding jobs.[8] But they still choose places to live depending on how much they pay in taxes, where their children go to school, who their friends are, and what connections their neighborhoods offer.

Place becomes even more important as one moves down the economic ladder. On the wrong side of the "digital divide," poor and working-class families are less likely to own a computer, have Internet access, or send and receive e-mail.[9] Local networks are more important in helping them find out about jobs and other opportunities. Often lacking a car (or even adequate mass transit), they must live close to where they work. Unable to send their children to private schools, they must rely on local public schools. Unable to afford child care, lower-income families must rely on nearby relatives and friends for informal day care.

Whether we are highly skilled professionals or minimum-wage workers, it matters where we live. Place affects our access to jobs and public services (especially education), our access to shopping and culture, our level of personal security, the availability of our medical services, and even the air we breathe. People still care deeply about where they live. The old adage still holds true: the three most important factors in real estate are location, location, location.

THE POWER OF PLACE

We can illustrate this point by looking at three different congressional districts chosen to show the range of place within metropolitan America (Table 1.1). We begin with a poor central-city district in New York City's South Bronx, proceed to an older inner-suburban district near Los Angeles, and conclude with a wealthy outer-ring suburban district west of Chicago. Although different, they all illustrate how economic segregation, concentrated poverty, and suburban sprawl have tremendous impacts on our lives.

TABLE 1.1. Comparison of Three Congressional Districts

	Median Household Income, 1999	Individuals in Poverty, 1999 (%)	Home Ownership Rate	White Population, 2000* (%)	Population per Square Mile, 2000	Democratic Vote for President 2000	Voter Turnout for President 2000
New York's Sixteenth central city	$20,451	40.2	9.8	2.4	41,875	93	132,117
California's Twenty-seventh inner ring	$48,289	12.8	48.5	51.8	1,974	53	222,762
Illinois' Thirteenth outer ring	$70,649	2.8	81.3	82.5	1,882	42	312,187

(handwritten margin note: "as % overall pop?")

Source: Demographic characteristics from U.S. Census Bureau, 2000 Census of Population and Housing, Summary Tape Files 3D, Congressional Districts of the United States; 2000 voting data from Michael Barone, Richard Cohen, and Grant Ujifsa, *The Almanac of American Politics 2004* (Washington, DC: National Journal, 2003); 2000 election results from POLIDATA, a private political and demographic research firm.
*White alone, not Hispanic or Latino.

NEW YORK'S SIXTEENTH CONGRESSIONAL DISTRICT: INNER-CITY GHETTO ON THE REBOUND

The Sixteenth Congressional District in the South Bronx is the poorest and one of the most Democratic congressional districts in the nation (Map 1.1). It was not always so. Located just north of Manhattan, the Bronx was a haven for Italian, Irish, and Jewish working- and middle-class families until about 1960. Many had moved up from the immigrant slums of the Lower East Side. Home to the New York Yankees and a thriving industrial sector, the Bronx prospered until blue collar jobs began leaving in the 1960s. Between 1969 and 1996, manufacturing jobs in the Bronx fell from 51,788 to 14,134.[10] The construction of the seven-mile-long Cross-Bronx Expressway, spearheaded by the city's urban renewal czar Robert Moses, destroyed solid neighborhoods and pushed many people out of the South Bronx. The opening of the 15,372-unit Co-op City complex in the North Bronx attracted many middle-income families out of the South Bronx. An influx of poor Puerto Ricans and the housing boom in suburbs such as Levittown, Long Island, triggered more white flight. In the 1970s, the borough's population fell by 300,000 people to 1.17 million. The exodus left

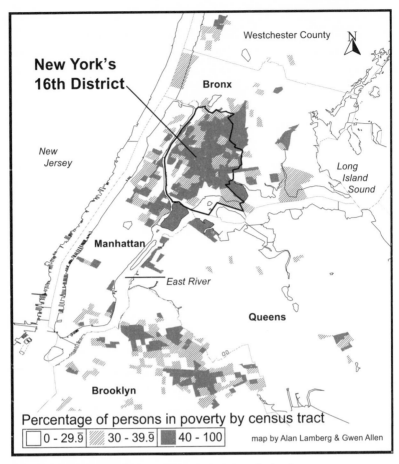

Map 1.1. New York's Sixteenth Congressional District

many apartment buildings and stores empty. The city government abandoned the neighborhood, too, failing to provide garbage collection, enforcement of housing safety laws, and fire and police protection. Crime, gang warfare, and arson for profit (when landlords burn their buildings to collect insurance payments) spiraled, accelerating a further exodus of longtime residents.

In October 1977, President Jimmy Carter made an unannounced walking tour of Charlotte Street in the South Bronx. Pictures showing him strolling through a devastated landscape resembling a bombed-out European city after World War II made the South Bronx a worldwide symbol of urban decay.[11] That night, an announcer on CBS network news declared that the South Bronx was America's worst slum. That image was reinforced by the popular 1981 Hollywood film, *Fort Apache, the Bronx,* about the neighborhood's police precinct, and by Tom Wolfe's best-selling 1987 novel, *Bonfire of the Vanities,* which depicted the area as an urban hellhole.[12] In 1999, the district's median household income ($20,451) was the lowest in the nation, and its poverty rate (40.2 percent) was the highest.[13] Less than 10 percent of its families own their own homes.

The high percentage of children in the Sixteenth Congressional District also sets it apart from others. Over one-third of its residents were under eighteen in 2000, the highest percentage of any congressional district in New York State.[14] Life has not been kind to many of these children. In *Amazing Grace,* Jonathan Kozol documented the hardscrabble life of children in Mott Haven, an area in the South Bronx. With a 1991 median household income of only $7,600, Mott Haven was and remains an area of extremely concentrated poverty. Still, most of those who could work did so. A major reason for the high poverty rate was that the city government relocated thousands of homeless families there. One formerly homeless woman bitterly observed: "Nobody thought that they was goin' to put us into fancy neighborhoods on the East Side. You're not goin' to put poor people in neighborhoods like that. But no one believed that they would concentrate us in the place that were most diseased because this would amount to a death sentence."[15]

Today the area is still beset with high rates of infectious diseases, including tuberculosis and AIDS. Lead paint poisoning, common in older apartment buildings, strikes a large number of children, who suffer brain damage and develop learning disabilities. Asthma, often triggered by cockroach droppings, is rampant. The violent crime rate was so high that parents were afraid to let their children go outside. Kozol ends his book by listing twenty-three children with whom he became acquainted who died violently between 1990 and 1994.

The odds are slim that the surviving children of Mott Haven will make it to middle-class communities. By any standard, its neighborhood schools rank near the bottom in New York City. The students come from home environments that are not conducive to educational achievement. Students often lack quiet, orderly places to study. Kozol interviewed one little boy who was forced to study with a flashlight in the closet of his brother's bedroom. Socially, economically, and psychologically isolated from the mainstream society thriving only a few miles away in Manhattan, Mott Haven sends the message to its children that they are not wanted and will not succeed. The children feel stigmatized by the squalor and the ugliness. As a school psychologist put it: "Many of the ambitions of the children are locked in at a level that suburban kids would scorn. It's as if the very possibilities of life have been scaled back."[16]

Not all the news about the South Bronx is negative. Residents of this district do not fit the stereotype that people in poor neighborhoods lack positive values and do not care for one another. Even the poorest neighborhoods have vibrant churches, immigrant associations, tenant organizations, and neighborhood associations. In the 1970s, a number of small community organizations (several based in local churches) began to sponsor community gardens, repair a handful of buildings, and organize campaigns against banks that refused to make loans in the area. Some of these groups fell by the wayside, but others expanded their know-how and political clout and pressured federal, state, and local officials to channel funds for housing and commercial development.

As a result, parts of the South Bronx enjoyed a remarkable revival in the 1980s and 1990s. Beginning in the 1980s, under Mayor Ed Koch, the city government began a ten-year, $5 billion initiative to fix up abandoned housing and construct new homes on vacant lots — the largest city-sponsored housing plan in the nation's history. Mayors David Dinkins and Rudolph Giuliani continued the program, which eventually lasted thirteen years. By 1997, it had supported the construction or rehabilitation of over 150,000 housing units in the most troubled parts of the city, including over 10,000 in the South Bronx alone.[17] The Bronx's nonprofit community development corporations (CDCs) got a significant piece of the action. One major CDC, Banana Kelly Community Improvement Association, renovated 2,000 units.[18] Two national organizations that support the work of CDCs — the Local Initiatives Support Corporation (LISC) and the Enterprise Foundation — provided technical assistance and enticed large corporations to invest in low-income rental housing built by CDCs. Another entity, the New York City Partnership, built 5,161 new housing units working with for-profit developers. Most are duplexes that include a rental unit, mixing home owners and renters. Subsidized with government money and free land, the projects inject working-class home owners into devastated neighborhoods, creating islands of renewal in the former sea of decay. They sold initially for up to $185,000, demonstrating that working families are, once again, willing to invest in the Bronx.[19]

Another community group, South Bronx Churches (an affiliate of the national Industrial Areas Foundation network), used grassroots community organizing, picketing, and protest to persuade the city government to allow it to develop 500 row houses for sale to working class families on a city-owned tract of land, a project called Nehemiah Homes after the Old Testament Prophet who rebuilt Jerusalem.[20] In 1998, it began a second phase which produced another 425 homes. As a result of this initiative, the number of vacant buildings in the Bronx plummeted from 22,596 to 4,832. The number of empty lots declined dramatically too.[21]

In addition to building housing, community groups (with foundation support) focused on improving health services, bringing new businesses (especially supermarkets) into the neighborhood, improving the schools, restoring parks and playgrounds, and reducing crime. On each front, they had some success. Violent crime declined sharply beginning in the early 1990s, as it did throughout New York City. An influx of immigrants brought new energy and entrepreneurial skills to the area and stemmed its population decline.[22] Local businesses, including grocery stores, made a comeback. The New York Yankees played in the 1998, 2000, and 2003 World Series and won twice, a source of great pride to the community.

In evaluating two successful Bronx CDCs, Mid-Bronx Desperados and Banana Kelly, urban analyst and former Albuquerque mayor David Rusk found that during the 1980s, they were able to reverse neighborhood population losses. But, he noted, poverty rates continued to rise and neighborhood buying power fell. Rusk concluded that the underlying trend toward suburbanization in the New York region will hamper neighborhood efforts to stem decay in the South Bronx, no matter how hard they work.[23] During the 1990s, however, Bronx neighborhoods increased their population even more, reflecting growing confidence and investment in the neighborhood by residents, business, and government. According to Alexander Von Hoffman:

> Today visitors to the Bronx do not see pathological urban conditions — abandoned buildings, fires left to burn, open drug markets — but rather healthy city neighborhoods.
>
> People live in archetypical New York apartment buildings or newly constructed single- and two-family houses, and on weekends, the boulevards teem with shoppers.
>
> Just as in the suburbs, Little League baseball teams, sponsored by local businesses, play safely in well-maintained parks.[24]

Thanks to the efforts of the city government, private foundations, nonprofit community groups, and allies in business, South Bronx neighborhoods are improving. But despite Von Hoffman's optimistic picture, the revitalization efforts are small scale compared with the remaining needs. The Sixteenth Congressional District remains the poorest in the nation. Unemployment, homelessness, crime, high school-dropout rates, and other social problems are still widespread. As a result, without significantly more federal and state assistance, the odds are still stacked against a larger revival for the South Bronx.

In light of both the serious problems and the signs of hope, one might think that the Sixteenth Congressional District would be a cauldron of political activism, with residents organized to demand more of their public officials. Despite the heroic efforts of community and church groups to improve the area, however, South Bronx residents do not reveal much faith in mainstream politics. Its voters cast only 132,061 ballots in the 2000 presidential election, lower than all but a dozen of the nation's other 435 congressional districts. Those who did vote gave 93 percent of their votes to Al Gore for president, the largest pro-Gore margin of any congressional district in the country. They also overwhelmingly reelected Democrat Jose Serrano to his sixth term in Congress, and two years later gave him a seventh term. Not surprisingly, Serrano is among the most liberal members of Congress, supporting programs that will bring jobs, housing, and government services to his constituents.

CALIFORNIA'S TWENTY-SEVENTH CONGRESSIONAL DISTRICT: SPREADING URBAN PROBLEMS

Every New Year's Day, millions of Americans watch the colorful floats and marching bands of the Rose Parade on TV, then settle in to view the Rose Bowl football game. Both take place in Pasadena, California, a city memorialized by Jan and Dean's song, "Little Old Lady from Pasadena." It is the heart of what was, in 2000, California's Twenty-seventh Congressional District (Map 1.2). Less than a half-mile away from where the parade route begins near Millionaires Row is northwest Pasadena, a predominantly black and Latino section with a high concentration of poor residents. This paradox symbolizes the evolution of a longtime conservative Republican stronghold into a safe Democratic district by 2000.[25]

The sprawling 4,081-square-mile area of Los Angeles County contains eighteen congressional districts. Between 1950 and 2000, its population doubled from 4.15 to 9.5 million, transforming open space into housing tracts, small towns into bedroom suburbs, and rural roads into a traffic nightmare with the nation's worst air pollution. Millions of immigrants arrived between 1980 and 2000, transforming the county into the nation's most diverse area. By 2000, a third of the county's residents were foreign born, and half did not speak English at home.[26] Latinos comprised 44.6 percent of residents, Asians, 11.9 percent, and blacks, 9.8 percent. Whites, over half the population in 1980, made up less than a third in 2000.[27] Although much of this change occurred in small towns on the county's edge, a significant part of the increase occurred in the City of Los Angeles and its older suburbs. These older suburbs continue to face pressure to add new houses and apartment buildings and to increase their density. Los Angeles County is home to both more millionaires, and more poor people, than any other metropolitan area in the nation.

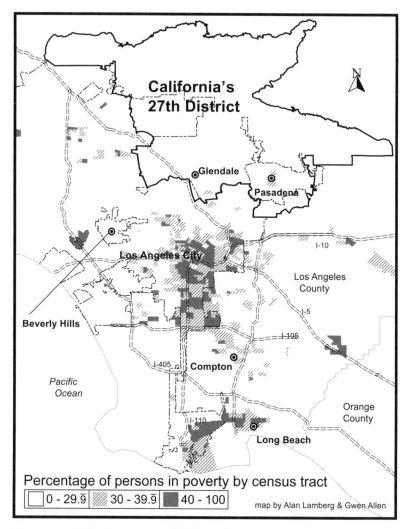

Map 1.2. California's Twenty-seventh Congressional District

These trends dramatically transformed the older suburbs that comprised the Twenty-seventh Congressional District, increasing their racial and ethnic diversity, heightening poverty, widening disparities between rich and poor, and causing growing concern about traffic congestion, pollution, crime, homelessness, and troubled schools. Home to California Institute of Technology, the Disney Company, and three other Fortune 1000 corporations as well as the Rose Bowl, the old Twenty-seventh Congressional District includes several major suburbs northeast of Los Angeles in the foothills of the Verdugo and San Gabriel Mountains. Once bedroom suburbs, Pasadena, Burbank, and Glendale are now major job centers in their own right.[28] The district also included the wealthy towns of San Marino (home of the Huntington Library) and La Canada Flintridge (home of NASA's Jet Propulsion Lab), as well as La Crescenta, Sunland, Tujunga, and Altadena. (After redistricting, the political map makers moved San Marino, La Canada Flintridge, La Crescenta, Sunland, and Tujunga out of the new twenty-ninth district and added Alhambra, Monterey Park, San Gabriel, South Pasadena, and Temple City to make it a safer seat for Democratic candidates.)

As late as 1994, the *Los Angeles Times* observed that, "Residents [of Burbank] take pride in a city that is close to Los Angeles yet insulated from big-city worries. In recent years, however, Burbank, along with Glendale and Pasadena, has begun to grapple with such issues as violent crime and growing ethnic diversity."[29] Indeed, the population of Pasadena grew from 113,327 to 133,936 between 1970 and 2000; Burbank's grew from 88,871 to 100,316, and Glendale's expanded from 132,752 to 194,973. In those years, the minority (nonwhite) population increased from 20.2 percent to 46.6 percent in Pasadena, from 1.8 percent to 36.4 percent in Glendale, and from 1.3 percent to 27.8 percent in Burbank.[30] By 2000, the Twenty-seventh District was 23 percent Hispanic, 13 percent Asian, and 7 percent black. Glendale also houses the nation's largest Armenian community—among the 40 percent who are defined as white. One-fifth of the adults in the district lacked health insurance, compared to 15 percent in Los Angeles County.[31] Despite the suburban image, less than half of the households own their home.[32] In comparative perspective, the Twenty-seventh Congressional District was predominantly middle class, with a median household income of $48,289, but the poor population grew steadily to 12.8 percent in 2000.

Wealthy midwesterners founded Pasadena as a suburban oasis in the nineteenth century, and it developed into an upper-middle-class suburb with such well-known institutions as Cal Tech and the Pasadena Playhouse, while the suburban San Fernando Valley towns of Burbank and Glendale were centers of the early aerospace and entertainment industries. Yet the combination of new development on the suburban fringe and the decline of defense spending cut into the economies of these cities. The region's larger trends brought more immigrants and more low-wage jobs. Although many parts of the district's cities retained a strong middle class, poverty grew in some neighborhoods between 1970 and 2000. The number of Pasadena census tracts where 20 percent or more of residents are poor increased from four in 1970 to seven in 2000; the seven northwest Pasadena tracts had just a third of the city's population in 2000 but almost two-thirds of its poor people, who make up one-quarter of the city's residents.[33] Burbank developed one such tract, while Glendale went from none to ten (out of its total of twenty-five tracts). These poor include newly arrived immigrants who take day laborer jobs and formerly middle-class workers at Lockheed, General Motors, and other plants who lost their good union jobs when these factories shut down.[34] Not only has the overall number of poor people increased in Pasadena, Glendale, and Burbank since 1970, but so has the geographic concentration of the poor, especially in Glendale.

Both the area's middle class and poor have a hard time finding affordable housing in a climate of rising real estate prices. In December 2003, the median sales price of a single-family home was $408,000 in Burbank, $380,000 in Glendale, and $425,000 in Pasadena.[35] Worried that its teachers, firefighters, police, secretaries, and computer programmers could not live in the city, Pasadena adopted an "inclusionary zoning" law in 2002 requiring housing developers to incorporate units affordable to low-income and moderate-income families. These rising prices have been fed by high-wage employment in technology, higher education, health care, and entertainment. Lockheed Aircraft, Cal Tech, and NASA's Jet Propulsion Lab employ many in the district, as do Disney, Warner Brothers, DreamWorks Animation, and NBC, which broadcasts the *Tonight Show with Jay Leno* from its Burbank studio.

Historically, Glendale and Burbank housed few racial minorities, but African Americans have lived in Pasadena since the late 1800s, moving there to take service jobs in its fancy hotels and plush homes. Baseball pioneer Jackie Robinson grew up in Pasadena, where his mother worked as a maid after moving from Georgia in the 1920s. He once recalled that "we saw movies from segregated balconies, swam in a municipal pool only on Tuesdays and were permitted in the YMCA one night a week."[36] This swimming pool remained segregated until 1947, when blacks were allowed to swim once a week on the day before the water was changed.[37] Blacks were barred from all but the most menial municipal jobs. When Robinson's brother Mack, a silver medalist at the 1936 Olympics, returned from college to Pasadena, the only city job he could get was cleaning sewers.[38]

Pasadena's black middle-class families, like poorer blacks, were confined to homes in northwest Pasadena and adjacent Altadena, the poorest section of the congressional district. Pasadena was run by white business and professional men from the same social clubs and civic groups, and shut out blacks from leadership roles. The growing black population began to make inroads in the 1980s, electing one member of the city council.[39] In 1984, the tradition-bound Tournament of Roses Association selected its first black woman as Rose Queen[40] and finally appointed the first black, Latino, and Asian members to its executive committee in 1993.[41] Bitter battles over court-ordered school desegregation led to white flight to private schools and other suburbs.[42] White enrollment in the public schools fell to 16 percent in 2000, even though whites comprise 53 percent of the city's population.[43]

In Burbank, a charge by the Human Relations Council in 1964 that the city had no black residents was disputed by a city official who said there were, in fact, six black families.[44] (At the time, Burbank's population was over 90,000.) In 1980, Glendale was almost entirely white, but it subsequently experienced a surge of Korean, Filipino, Mexican, Armenian, and other immigrants.[45] The rapid absorption of immigrants from abroad and other newcomers turned Glendale into a "denser, younger, and more cosmopolitan urban center."[46] By the mid-1980s, sixty-seven languages were spoken in the city's schools.[47] In 2000, the city was 30 percent Armenian and 25 percent Latino. These conditions led to new ethnic tensions. In 2000, fights broke out between Armenian and Latino gangs. Glendale High School had to cancel its annual multicultural day after fighting broke out between ethnic groups.[48] When city officials lowered the American flag at City Hall to mark the Armenian genocide, longtime residents wrote angry letters to the local newspaper. Glendale's established civic organizations — such as the Kiwanis and Rotary clubs — remain predominantly white.[49]

Before 2000, the Twenty-seventh Congressional District sent conservative Republicans to Congress. The process of demographic change gradually narrowed the Republican hold on the seat, but even in 1996, when 200,494 voters went to the polls, they gave incumbent Republican James Rogan 51 percent of their votes, although they favored Bill Clinton over Robert Dole for president by 49 to 41 percent (with 10 percent for Ross Perot and other candidates). Four years later, in 2000, Democratic state legislator Adam Schiff challenged Rogan, a member of the Judiciary Committee who had pressed for President Clinton's impeachment and had one of the House's most conservative voting records. Key Democratic groups — labor unions, women's organizations, environmental groups, and entertainment industry liberals — targeted Rogan for defeat, while business interests, prolife groups, and conservative Christian groups pledged to protect him. Rogan raised $6.8 million to Schiff's $4.3 million, making their combined total the most expensive House race in history.

Thanks to a ten percent larger voter turnout than four years earlier, fed by voter identification and mobilization efforts from unions that targeted union members, Hispanics, Armenians, and women, Schiff defeated Rogan by 53 percent to 44 percent. Voters also favored Al Gore over George Bush by 53 to 41 percent, with 4 percent going to Ralph Nader. Clearly, the political consequences of the district's social and economic transformation had made themselves felt.

As one analysis of the election noted, "the changing political and demographic fundamentals of the district outweighed the money."[50]

After the 2000 census, the state's Democratic Party, in control of the redistricting process, reconfigured the district to turn it from the swing district into a safe Democratic stronghold, now called the Twenty-ninth Congressional District. The map makers removed more affluent Republican parts of the district (including La Cañada Flintridge and San Marino) and added areas with a large number of minority residents. After redistricting changed the district's boundaries in 2002, it became 26.1 percent Hispanic, 23.7 percent Asian, and 5.9 percent black. More than half of those over five years old spoke a language other than English at home. One new part of the district, Monterey Park (61.8 percent Asian and 28.9 percent Latino), is considered the nation's first predominantly Asian suburb.[51] In this new part of the district, Asian retail stores have revitalized commercial strips with "a Filipino grocery and sandwich shop, a Vietnamese café, a Japanese bakery, an Indonesian deli and restaurants offering Taiwanese, Chinese and Japanese cuisine." Asians dominate political and civic life in these suburbs, and the schools give students flyers written in Mandarin, Cantonese, Vietnamese, and Spanish to take home to their parents.[52]

In 2002, Schiff, with a moderate voting record in Congress, was reelected without difficulty in the redrawn district, winning 63 percent of the vote. This time he spent only $712,072, while the low-profile Republican candidate raised so little money he did not even file a fund-raising report with the Federal Election Commission.[53] This outcome reflects the profound changes taking place in older suburbs throughout Los Angeles County, California, and the country—trends that some analysts believe could lay the groundwork for a new liberal coalition of urban and suburban voters.[54]

ILLINOIS' THIRTEENTH CONGRESSIONAL DISTRICT: RAPIDLY DEVELOPING SUBURBS

Illinois' Thirteenth Congressional District lies directly west of Chicago in southern DuPage County and the exurban parts of Cook and Will Counties (Map 1.3). With excellent interstate connections, the area is rich with gleaming glass corporate headquarters and research centers. AT&T built a new Bell Labs facility along the new Interstate 88 in 1966. A few years later, Amoco moved its main research and development facility there. The corporate headquarters of McDonald's, Ace Hardware, Federal Signal Corporation, and the Spiegel mail-order company are located in the area around Interstates 88, 294, and 290. Given the area's many business executives and scientists, it is not surprising that

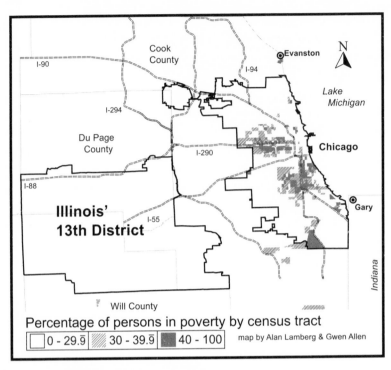

Percentage of persons in poverty by census tract

| 0 - 29.$\bar{9}$ | 30 - 39.$\bar{9}$ | 40 - 100 | map by Alan Lamberg & Gwen Allen |

Map 1.3. Illinois' Thirteenth Congressional District

the district's 1999 median family income ($70,649) was the highest in Illinois and tenth highest in the country.[55] It is also not surprising that the district was in the top 20 percent of districts in terms of voting for Republican Robert Dole in 1996 and in the top third for George Bush in 2000. It has consistently sent Republicans to Congress, including the current incumbent, Judith Biggert.

After World War II, the area's population grew rapidly as families moved out of Chicago and its inner-ring suburbs in search of communities with low crime, less congestion, and good schools. The district's most rapidly growing community is Naperville. A sleepy town of 7,000 in 1950, Naperville had a population of 128,358 in 2000.[56] Naperville is not primarily a commuter suburb for Chicago. Only about 5,000 people take the train into downtown Chicago's Loop each day. Most work in Naperville or other suburbs. Joel Garreau calls the Illinois Research and Development Corridor, including Naperville, Oak Brook, Lisle, Aurora, and the East-West Tollway, an "edge city."[57] Garreau defines an edge city as an area built up in the past thirty years that has at least 5 million square feet of office space and 600,000 square feet of retail space and that residents perceive as a destination. With its extensive office and commercial development,

Naperville is a quintessential example of the urbanization of the suburbs. The district's high levels of income and education are reflected in the relatively large number of votes cast in the 1996 presidential election (232,541) and the 2000 election (269,237).[58]

As a place to grow up in, Naperville has many strengths. A 1997 study by Zero Population Growth (ZPG) ranked Naperville the most "kid friendly" city out of 219 studied (Chicago ranked 200th). The ZPG study used twenty key statistics, including crime, teen pregnancies, school dropout rates, and the number of children living in poverty, to compute its rankings. A key difference between Naperville and Chicago was the percentage of children who lived in poverty: 1.1 percent for the former, 33.6 percent for the latter. This prompted Brian Dixon, ZPG's director of government relations, to comment, "When you have these booming edge cities, they tend to suck the life out of the inner cities." Naperville's mayor, George Pradel, disagreed: "It's not a competition. There's an interdependence between the city and Naperville."[59]

Naperville is not without problems. Rapid growth in the town and its surrounding areas requires voters to constantly pass bond issues to build new schools. The only way to pay for them without steeply raising taxes is to capture new commercial development, which provides more of a fiscal surplus than residential development can. For this reason, Thomas Scullen, superintendent of Naperville's School District 204, noted, "Some residents would like to see a moratorium on growth, but that's not going to happen."[60] So in order to enhance commercial development and tax ratables, the people who move to the Thirteenth Congressional District searching for more greenery and less congestion end up reproducing some of the urban ills they had fled. As Will County's planning director Tyson Warner put it, "The more people that come in looking for the rural atmosphere, the less rural atmosphere there is."[61]

Despite well-performing high school students, rising incomes, and soaring home values, many stresses and anxieties trouble Naperville residents. Perhaps the leading complaint is a lack of community or a sense of belonging—hardly surprising for a suburb that recently added 9,000 people in one year. Naperville is a city of transferees, with perhaps one-third of the people transferring every three years. The turnover rate in the schools is anywhere from 15 to 35 percent a year.[62] In addition, most households need two full-time incomes to afford the average house. Stories of latchkey kids abound; day care centers specialize in taking care of children after school.

In the 1950s, academic critics viewed suburbs as places of suffocating conformity. In an article on Naperville subtitled "Stressed Out in Suburbia," Nicholas Lemann argued that the new outer-ring suburbs are different.[63] "The suburban psychological force that occasionally overwhelms people," Lemann writes, "is not the need to fit in, but the need to be a success." Striving to make it in one of the most privileged suburbs in the United States takes its toll on families. The great shortage in Naperville is not money but time.

THE PROBLEM OF ECONOMIC SEGREGATION

The great variety of experiences in these three districts clearly suggests how place matters in the quality of people's lives. Their residents experience widely different living conditions, uneven access to amenities and opportunities, and disparate levels of political influence. The fundamental reality is one of growing economic segregation in the context of rising overall inequality. People of different income classes are moving away from each other not just in how much income they have but also in where they live. America is breaking down into economically homogeneous enclaves. Our argument, in a nutshell, is that although growing economic inequality is bad, it is greatly worsened by growing economic segregation. This dynamic harms the quality of life for the working and middle classes as well as for the poor, imposes costs on society as a whole (including affluent families), and lessens American society's capacity to engage in vigorous democratic debate and to act collectively to address its pressing problems.

RISING INEQUALITY

In terms of goods consumed, the United States is the richest country in the world, perhaps the richest country ever. Factoring in the low prices of consumer goods in the United States, the United States had the highest per capita income of twenty advanced industrial countries in 2000.[64] Household incomes are rising, and technological advances enable Americans to buy more and more value with each dollar.[65] After nine years of continuous economic expansion (1991–2000), the "great American job machine" had driven the unemployment rate to its lowest level since the 1960s. At the turn of the twenty-first century, the inflation rate remained low, home ownership was the highest in history, and new homes were bigger and better equipped than ever. The 1990s bull run on Wall Street and soaring corporate profits enabled those at the top to accumulate massive fortunes. The computer and telecommunications industries created new fortunes overnight (although technology stock prices began to plummet in 2000). The Internet is revolutionizing the way we do business, and the United States leads the world in information technology. In the second half of

TABLE 1.2. Household Income Inequality in Developed Countries
(Ratio of 90th Percentile of Household Income to 10th Percentile)

Country	Year	Ratio, 90th/10th
United States	2000	5.45
United Kingdom	1999	4.58
Italy	2000	4.48
Australia	1994	4.33
Ireland	1996	4.33
Canada	1998	4.13
Spain	1990	3.96
Switzerland	1992	3.62
France	1994	3.54
Austria	1997	3.37
Luxembourg	2000	3.24
Belgium	1997	3.19
Germany	2000	3.18
Denmark	1997	3.15
Netherlands	1999	2.98
Sweden	2000	2.96
Finland	2000	2.90
Norway	2000	2.80

Source: Luxembourg Income Study, Income Inequality Measures, available at http://www
.lisproject.org/keyfigures/ineqtable.htm.

the 1990s, the unusually strong U.S. economy created huge budget surpluses, and the federal government began paying down its massive debt. Americans as a whole had never been as prosperous as they were at the beginning of the twenty-first century.

This abundance did not flow proportionately to all segments of American society. In fact, the United States has the distinction of having the greatest income and wealth disparities of any advanced industrial society. Table 1.2 shows that American households in the top 10 percent make more compared with those in the bottom 10 percent than in any other advanced industrial country. By almost every other measure (Gini coefficients of inequality, wage inequality, poverty rates, and exit rates out of poverty), the United States ranks at the bottom of developed countries.[66]

In the 1980s, both *Time* and *Business Week* published articles debating whether the wage structure had a missing middle — that is, whether the low- and high-wage jobs of the new service economy were replacing the solid middle-class jobs of the fading industrial economy. The debate is now over. *Business Week*'s 1994 cover story "Inequality: How the Gap Between the Rich and the Poor Hurts the Economy" pointed out that the rich and superrich had mo-

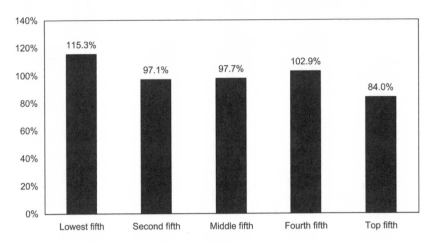

FIGURE 1.1. Income Growth by Quintiles, 1947–73

Source: Lawrence Mishel, Jared Bernstein, and Heather Boushey, *The State of Working America 2002/2003* (Ithaca, NY: Cornell University Press, 2003), 57.

nopolized most income growth and almost all wealth accumulation—a trend that persisted throughout the 1990s (Figure 1.1).[67]

Unlike previous economic expansions, during the economic boom of the mid-1990s, the real incomes of workers in the bottom half of the income scale failed to regain their previous heights. Beginning around 1995, tight labor markets finally began to pull along those at the bottom. Their wages improved, even though the gap between rich and poor continued to widen. But as unemployment rose beginning in 2001, low-wage workers fell behind again (Figure 1.2).[68]

Historically, American society has been based on an implicit social contract: if you work hard, you will get ahead. Substantiating this contract was not only the belief but also the experience that economic growth would benefit all social classes. In President Kennedy's memorable words, "A rising tide lifts all boats." Every income class of Americans benefitted from economic growth between 1947 and 1973, with those in the bottom 20 percent actually enjoying faster income growth than those above them.

From 1973 to 1979, this trend continued. But in the 1980s the foundation of the American social contract began to crumble. Bennett Harrison and Barry Bluestone called this the "great U-turn," when the country suddenly changed directions on the long road of continuously improving material conditions for most people.[69] Between 1979 and 1995, real family incomes for the bottom 20 percent of families (those making less than $22,280 in 1979 in 2001 dollars) actually fell. During the entire 1973 to 2000 period, even though each income

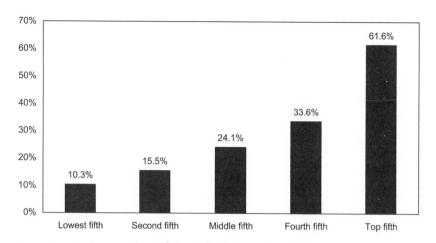

FIGURE 1.2. Income Growth by Quintiles, 1973–2000

Source: Lawrence Mishel, Jared Bernstein, and Heather Boushey, *The State of Working America 2002/2003* (Ithaca, NY: Cornell University Press, 2003), 57.

group gained, most of the gain flowed to what Robert Reich calls the "fortunate fifth." The top 20 percent of income earners (those making over $92,924 in 2000) enjoyed a healthy 61.6 percent increase in real income.[70]

By just about every measure, income inequality has increased significantly in the United States in the past twenty years.[71] The share of the nation's total income going to the bottom 80 percent of families fell from 58.6 percent in 1979 to 52.3 percent in 2001. Only the top 20 percent enjoyed an increase — from 41.4 percent to 47.7 percent of the nation's income. Those at the very top did especially well. During those years, the top 5 percent of families (those making over $164,104 in 2001) saw their share of total income increase from 15.3 to 21.0 percent; at the same time, the bottom 20 percent saw their share of total income fall from 5.4 to 4.2 percent. And as the gap between the rich and the poor widened, the middle class shrank. Between 1979 and 1998, the proportion of persons living in families making 50 to 200 percent of the median income — the broad middle class — declined from 68 to 61.5 percent.

The enormous pay increases for America's corporate chief executive officers (CEOs) are one cause of rising inequality. Between 1989 and 2000, when median hourly wages grew by just 5.9 percent, CEO compensation (including salaries, bonuses, incentive awards, stock options exercised, and stock granted) increased by 342 percent to an average of $1.7 million. In 1978, the average CEO made 37 times what the average worker made; by 2000, the average CEO made 310 times what the average worker earned. American CEOs earn between two and three times the average pay of CEOs in other developed countries. Moreover, CEO pay is not closely tied to corporate performance; CEOs often get big raises even when their firms lose money.[72]

The distribution of wealth is even more unequal than the distribution of income. The top 1 percent earned 16.6 percent of total income in 1998, but they owned 38.1 percent of all wealth (the value of assets minus debts), averaging over $10.2 million. By contrast, the middle fifth of the population held a mere 4.5 percent of wealth, and those in the bottom fifth actually owed more than they owned. Although wealth inequality increased more slowly in the 1990s than it did in the 1980s, the trend is still toward greater inequality. In the 1990s, the top 1 percent of households grew in wealth by an average of over $1 million, the middle 20 percent of households grew only marginally (from $58,800 to $61,000), and the poorest one-fifth improved significantly but still finished the decade on average $8,900 in debt. The 1990s also witnessed an explosion in the number of extremely rich households, with the number of millionaires climbing by 54 percent between 1989 and 1998; the number of decamillionaires ($10 million or more in net worth) nearly quadrupled.[73]

Unlike the other periods of sustained economic expansion in the United States, the early 1990s provided few, if any, benefits to those at the bottom. Beginning in 1995, tight labor markets finally began to pull poor people into the economic mainstream. After fifteen years of decline or stagnation, wages increased by 2.5 percent (adjusted for inflation) from 1995 to 2000.[74] Beginning in 1997, the poverty rate finally began to fall, reaching 11.3 percent in 2000, the lowest rate since 1974.[75] The poverty rate in central cities fell from 19 percent in 1990 to 16.3 percent in 2000. Meanwhile, household income grew faster in cities than in suburbs.[76]

The 1990s boom and tight labor markets had finally provided real benefits to those at the bottom of the economic ladder. But the national statistics exaggerate the progress in attacking poverty and inequality. Once again, place matters: the economic boom left many parts of the United States behind, and in prosperous regions, those at the bottom saw rising housing prices eat up their wage gains. Between October 2000 and June 2002, the unemployment rate had risen 2 percentage points to 5.9 percent, and reached 6.3 by June 2003. In September 2003, there were 2.7 million fewer jobs than there were in February 2001, the month after President George W. Bush took office. A study by the Federal Reserve Bank of New York found that the decline in the overall number of jobs that far into a "recovery" was unprecedented in the post–World War II era. The recession and the subsequent "jobless recovery" reversed previous wage gains and reductions in poverty. The nation's poverty rate climbed to 11.7 percent in 2001 and to 12.5 percent in 2003—an increase of 4.3 million people in three years. More than half of that increase occurred in suburbs, but cities also saw an increase in the number of poor people. The urban poverty rate rose to 17.5 percent.[77]

In 2000, the federal government classified one in eight cities as "doubly burdened," defined as having at least two of the following three conditions: an unemployment rate 50 percent higher than the national average, a poverty rate 20 percent or higher, and a population loss exceeding 5 percent since 1980. Although New York and Los Angeles are on this list, most are middle-sized cities located in the interior of the country, such as Dayton, Ohio, and Flint, Michigan.[78] As we will see, central-city residents continue to lag behind suburban residents in jobs and income, although the gap began to narrow in the 1990s, due as much to suburban decline as to urban recovery. Residents of disadvantaged neighborhoods—most of which are in central cities—bear substantial burdens, such as higher grocery prices and inferior schools, that do not show up in the income statistics.

The claim that the economic boom of the 1990s reduced poverty also overlooks the fact that the federal government defines poverty in a way that severely underestimates the problem. This definition, devised in the 1960s, assumes that the average family pays one-third of its income for food. The poverty formula takes the Department of Agriculture's minimum food budget for different-sized families and multiplies it by three. Since the 1960s, however, the cost of food has gone up much more slowly than other necessary expenditures, especially housing. This means that the poverty line is set too low, especially in booming regions. One study found that the actual cost of a bare-bones budget in New York City was up to five times the poverty level for families with children.[79] Similarly, in the Los Angeles area, a two-parent family with two children needs to earn at least $44,700 simply to meet basic needs such as housing, food, child care, health care, and transportation. This is almost three times the official poverty line. If the poverty rate were revised to two times the official poverty threshold, then at least one out of four workers in Los Angeles County would be "poor."[80]

The cruel irony is that the economic boom has made life harder for low-income renters, especially in overheated, high-tech regions such as New York, Boston, and San Francisco. From 1997 to 1999, rents increased by 9.9 percent nationwide, compared with the general inflation rate of 6.1 percent. But rent increases were higher in cities than in suburbs.[81] Housing planners use the standard that households should pay no more than 30 percent of their income for rent and utilities. By 1999, 41 percent of renter households paid more than that, with nearly one in five paying more than half their incomes.[82] Nowhere in the country can a family with one full-time minimum-wage worker (earning $5.15 per hour) afford the cost of a two-bedroom apartment at fair-market rent.[83] In 1999, the national two-bedroom housing wage — what a worker needed to earn to afford a typical apartment in their region — was $11.08; by 2003, the national housing wage was $15.21, a 37 percent increase. In Marin, Santa Clara, San Francisco, and San Mateo Counties in California, a worker would have to earn more than $34 per hour to afford the average apartment.[84]

So, when the economic boom of the late 1990s finally lifted the incomes of households at the bottom, it did not decrease inequality. In fact, inequality increased throughout the 1990s. Worse, many families were, and continue to be, stuck in stagnating regions or poverty-stricken neighborhoods, which handicaps their ability to advance economically. Those living in booming regions may find it easier to increase their incomes, but they usually have to spend these gains on rising housing, transportation, and other costs.

Conservative economists and commentators such as George Will and Thomas Sowell often pooh-pooh the inequality problem. They charge that the statistics on inequality exaggerate the problem, because a snapshot of inequality at one point in time overlooks the fact that people earn different incomes at different stages of their lives. (Young people always earn less.)[85] Lifetime earnings, therefore, are more equally distributed than are annual earnings. Indeed, if people were more mobile over their life spans, so that class inequalities were not so entrenched, then rising inequalities would be less worrisome. Significant mobility among classes would mean that the same people would not always be stuck in poverty or guaranteed wealth and privilege. The United States has a long tradition of offering penniless immigrants the chance to rise from rags to riches. We have always viewed ourselves as less class-bound than Europe.

The evidence shows, however, that social mobility has not compensated for the pulling apart of the income and wealth distributions. A careful review of the research found that America is indeed a mobile society, with anywhere from 25 to 40 percent of the population moving out of an income quintile (the income scale divided into five groupings of 20 percent each) every year.[86] But mobility in the United States is no higher than that in other countries and shows no signs of increasing. Economic mobility, in fact, declined after the 1960s.[87] For example, 65.9 percent of people who were in the bottom 40 percent of income distribution in 1969 remained in that group twenty-five years later. Only 5.8 percent had climbed the ladder to the richest 20 percent of the population.[88] In the United States, the "escape rate" of poor people out of poverty is second worst among the countries studied; only Canada is worse.[89] Rags-to-riches stories are rare. In short, America is becoming more of a class-bound society, and we cannot count on mobility to diminish the negative effects of rising inequality.

If we can therefore put aside the claims of some that rising inequality is exaggerated, what about those who say that although inequality may truly be rising, we do not need to worry about it? If the processes that create inequality are fair to all participants, this argument goes, then the outcomes, however unequal, are also fair. Equal opportunity is what matters, not equal results. Free-market conservatives argue that present inequalities fairly reflect people's different abilities and work efforts. As two writers for the journal of the conservative American Enterprise Institute put it, "For the most part, upper-income American families do better than lower-income families because they toil harder."[90] In this view, income differences are justifiable if they are proportional to differences in hours worked and productivity. Some have even gone so far as to argue that economic success is largely determined by IQ.[91]

The argument that increasing inequality reflects differences in work effort or productivity does not stand up to scrutiny. To give but one example, the percentage of the employable poor who worked increased from 64.8 to 70.3 percent between 1979 and 1998.[92] People at the bottom are not falling behind because they are working less; in fact, in that period, the average poor family increased its total annual working hours by 15.7 percent, to 1,112 hours.[93] Nor is it plausible to argue that the huge incomes flowing to corporate CEOs reflect disproportionately higher contributions to productivity. The average American is working longer hours and is more productive than ever, yet wage increases have not reflected this. Corporations have not shared their productivity gains through proportionate wage increases. Corporate profits were at a forty-five-year high in 1996, but wages increased at less than half the pace typical of previous economic expansions. Commenting on this wage squeeze, *Business Week* warned, "The sight of bulging corporate coffers coexisting with a continuous stagnation in Americans' living standards could become politically untenable."[94] Moreover, as we will show later, rising economic segregation has undermined equal opportunity in the United States, making it more difficult for many poor people to achieve the American dream.

Finally, many people say that we should not care about the gap between the rich and the poor, but instead focus on whether the poor are materially better off than they used to be. The availability of cheaper and better consumer goods, they argue, makes the poor better off than ever.[95] According to this view, if the American poor lived in a third world country, they would be considered well-off, at least in terms of consumption. The problem, of course, is that they actually live in a society where almost everybody makes more than they do — and this makes a big difference. Rising inequality not only has negative material effects on the poor; it also eats away at social cohesion, the foundation of our democracy. The belief that "in the long run, we are all in the same boat" holds American society together. Rising inequality sends the message that we are in different boats and that, contrary to President Kennedy's famous statement, the rising tide will lift some boats and not others. When the most negative impacts of economic change are confined to the poor and near poor, the main political effect may be growing middle-class enmity or indifference toward these poor. When the negative effects spread to the working and middle classes, however, the potential exists for an unwinding of American democracy.

Political theorists from Aristotle to the present have argued that democracies cannot survive with large inequalities. Writing in the fourth century, Aristotle warned: "It is the duty of a genuine democrat to see to it that the masses are not excessively poor. Poverty is the cause of the defects of democracy."[96] A healthy democracy depends on a strong middle class, which functions as a moderating force between the potentially divisive demands of the rich and the poor. Fearing the inequalities generated by an urban industrial society, Thomas Jefferson reflected that "an equal distribution of property is impracticable but [because of] the consequences of enormous inequality producing so much misery to the bulk of mankind, legislators cannot invent too many devices for subdividing property."[97]

Politically, the problem is not so much the existence of poverty but the gap between the rich and the poor. This gap enables the rich to dominate the poor. The possibility of blatant class legislation unfairly favoring the rich — such as unfair tax rates, more severe prison sentences for "street" crime compared with white-collar crime, weak workplace safety laws, and many others — becomes more likely. Rising inequality makes a mockery of the democratic principle of one person, one vote. The flood of billions of dollars into the 2000 presidential and congressional elections, driven by large contributions made possible in part by Wall Street's boom, demonstrates the corrupting potential of soaring inequality. Efforts to wall off the political system from the corroding effects of large contributions have been frustrated by the Supreme Court's ruling in *Buckley v. Valeo* (1976) equating campaign contributions with free speech. If the gap between the rich and the poor continues to widen, not even a carefully crafted constitutional amendment and laws constraining the influence of money on politics will be able to save our political system from the corrupting effects of concentrated wealth.

American presidents from Jefferson to Jackson, and from Teddy Roosevelt to Truman, have spoken out against that corrosive effect of economic inequality on democracy. As Franklin Roosevelt put it in his third inaugural address (January 6, 1941): "There is nothing mysterious about the foundation of a healthy and strong democracy. The basic things expected by our people of their political system are simple. They are: equality of opportunity; jobs for all those who can work; security for those who need it; the ending of special privilege for the few."[98]

PLACE-BASED INEQUALITIES

Missing from the debate about rising inequality has been an understanding of the critical role of place. The Nobel Prize–winning economist Amartya Sen provides a broader way of understanding inequality. He argues that we should understand inequality not simply in terms of income or wealth but in terms of our ability to achieve the good life, by which he means being active members of society and realizing our full potential as human beings. According to Sen, "relevant functionings can vary from such elementary things as being adequately nourished, being in good health, avoiding escapable morbidity and premature mortality, etc., to more complex achievements such as being happy, having self-respect, taking part in the life of the community, and so on."[99] Sen adds that we must also be concerned about "capabilities," or our ability to choose different activities or functionings. For example, a starving person is very different from one who has chosen to go on a hunger strike. Other things being equal, people are better off if they have real choices in life.

Sen would be the first to admit that having money, or access to jobs, services, and credit, is essential to free choice and a decent quality of life. But he argues that equality of income cannot be equated with true equality. A focus on income or wealth confuses the means to the good life with the good life itself. People's ability to convert income into the good life, Sen observes, varies tremendously. A person who suffers from severe kidney disease, for example, cannot enjoy the same quality of life as a perfectly healthy person with the same income, because of the daily monetary and emotional costs of dialysis. Thus, Sen argues, we cannot look at inequality simply in terms of income; we must take into account the actual situations and activities of people. Health, age, gender, race, education, and many other conditions besides income affect our ability to function effectively.

The thesis of this book is that where we live has a powerful effect on the choices we have and our capacity to achieve a high quality of life. Following

Sen, we examine inequality in light of how place shapes and constrains our opportunities not only to acquire income but also to become fully functioning members of the economy, society, and polity. For example, the increasing devolution of public functions from the federal government to state and local governments means that geographical location has become more important in determining what we pay in taxes and what public goods and services we enjoy. The segregation of income groups into different local governments means that supposedly equal citizens have unequal access to public goods such as schools, parks, and clean air. In Chapter 3, we show how the places we live also shape our access to jobs, retail goods and services, healthy environments, medical services, and safety (freedom from crime).

The national debate on rising income inequality has largely missed the spatial dimension of the problem. One exception has been the scholarly and media focus on the so-called underclass ghetto, often defined as areas with poverty rates of 40 percent or higher. The underclass is usually viewed as confined to minorities such as blacks and Hispanics, but the number of poor whites living in areas of concentrated poverty grew by 145 percent between 1970 and 1990.[100] Underclass areas are usually characterized by a wide range of negative conditions, including high rates of unemployment, drug use, crime, teen pregnancies, out-of-wedlock births, single-parent families, and school dropouts. Because many people at the bottom of the income distribution are increasingly forced to live in poor neighborhoods, mostly in central cities and some older and declining suburbs, they face a more negative environment and greater obstacles to mobility than if they lived among better-off neighbors.

The publication of William Julius Wilson's seminal book *The Truly Disadvantaged* in 1987 kicked off a lively scholarly debate on the causes and consequences of concentrated urban poverty.[101] This debate has shed light on how place matters for poor people, but it also has serious defects. First, it is important to remember that most poor people do not live in neighborhoods characterized by concentrated poverty. In 1990, only 17 percent of all poor people who lived in metropolitan areas lived in census tracts where the poverty rate exceeded 40 percent. By 2000, the figure had declined to 12 percent.[102] Research on these areas has often exaggerated their problems and overlooked their strengths. Most people living in such areas are hardworking, law-abiding citizens. As Katherine Newman points out, most residents of even the worst neighborhoods studied by Wilson are working, looking for work, or going to school.[103] Only a small minority engage in criminal behavior.

The research on concentrated poverty has also suffered from tunnel vision. It focuses on one extreme—concentrated poverty neighborhoods—while ignoring the broader dynamics that distribute classes across places. By so doing, research on the poor has unintentionally reinforced media stereotypes of low-income neighborhoods as basket cases whose problems stem from internal causes. Underclass neighborhoods are not distinct islands disconnected from the rest of society. Their problems are closely connected to regional and national dynamics—in particular, the migration of upper-income households and jobs to exclusive outer-ring suburbs. The problems associated with the growing spatial concentration of poverty also beset many inner-ring suburbs. Many older suburbs are in worse shape fiscally than their central cities. One study of 554 suburbs found that poverty increased in half of them, and real family income declined in a third of them, during the 1980s.[104]

The destructive factors associated with the underclass are not a world set apart from the rest of society. Problems such as single-parent families, drug use, and crime rose throughout metropolitan areas in the 1970s and 1980s. To be sure, the problems are worst in concentrated poverty areas, and the gap between "good" and "bad" neighborhoods has widened. But there was an across-the-board deterioration in many social indicators in the 1970s and 1980s. (In the 1990s, some of these social indicators, such as out-of-wedlock births and crime, improved.[105]) Areas of concentrated poverty, therefore, are merely the most pronounced and visible manifestations of problems that extend throughout society. To attribute them only to a local "subculture of poverty" in poor neighborhoods ignores the strengths of these neighborhoods and their connection to the broader society.[106] Although cities have serious problems, they also have great strengths and perform essential functions for society.

Conditions in outer-ring suburbs often appear ideal, but they are not. Wealthy outer-ring suburbs have different problems from inner-ring suburbs, central cities, and concentrated poverty neighborhoods, but they are related. In a sense, they are two sides of the same coin. The low rates of labor force participation in the South Bronx stem in part from the location of many entry-level jobs on the urban fringe, far from the inner city. In contrast, residents of outer-ring suburbs such as Naperville work long hours and commute long distances, leaving little time for family life and community responsibilities, partly because they want to live on the urban fringe far from urban problems. Their family stresses and lack of leisure time are related to the fact that an acceptable form of more urbanized living is not available to them. The environmental problems of outer suburbs and inner cities also stem from the same source. The polluted air and lack of green space in central cities may be abominable, but the flight of households to greener pastures on the urban fringe gobbles up farmland and spews additional automobile emissions into the air. In short, the problems of the different parts of metropolitan areas are interconnected; no part occupies the moral high ground. We can make progress only when the different parts of metropolitan areas work together.

Above all, discussions of concentrated poverty among researchers, public officials, and the news media have largely ignored the political causes and consequences of economic segregation. Scholars have carefully analyzed the relative contributions of economic factors, such as deindustrialization and foreign competition, and social factors, such as racial discrimination or countercultural values and underclass behaviors, to the growth of concentrated poverty. Neither side has said much, however, about how federal, state, and local policies produce and reproduce economic segregation. Nor have many researchers examined the profoundly negative effects of the geographical separation of income classes on city, state, and national politics. The growing political distance between central cities and the surrounding middle- and upper-class suburbs has made it increasingly difficult to assemble political support for policies designed to address rising inequality.

These place-based inequalities would be less worrisome if places, like people, experienced more mobility, with poor places becoming rich and vice versa. According to market economics, economic inequalities between geographical areas should have a natural tendency to correct themselves. As an area becomes poor, land prices and wages should fall until they entice entrepreneurs to come back in and take advantage of the differentials. In 1970, Edward Banfield argued in *The Unheavenly City* that this "logic of metropolitan development" would induce "the well-off" to "move from the suburbs to the cities, causing editorial writers to deplore the 'flight to the central city' and politicians to call for programs to check it by redeveloping the suburbs."[107] More than thirty-four years later, we are still waiting.

The evidence suggests, to the contrary, that the United States is facing a vicious circle of geographically rooted income inequalities. Over half a century ago, Gunnar Myrdal's magisterial study of race relations, *An American Dilemma*, developed the theory of "cumulative causation."[108] According to Myrdal, racial segregation nurtures the qualities in blacks that lead whites to discriminate against them, fueling more segregation. The idea of cumulative causation, or a vicious circle, applies to place-based inequalities in the United States today. Economic inequality leads to the concentration of poverty in certain neighborhoods. This, in turn, undermines the efforts of the residents to escape from poverty. The geographic concentration of the wealthy has the opposite effect, encasing residents in a privileged environment, especially with respect to local public education. Not only do children in rich school districts get a better education; they also make contacts (through internships, jobs, and college admission connections) that help them to succeed.

Democracies do not require perfect equality, but they do require that economic inequalities not invade and corrupt politics, or vice versa. Economic inequality should not mean that some people automatically have more political influence than others. Nor should people be able to use political power to gain privileged access to economic wealth. Political philosopher Michael Walzer calls this the "art of separation."[109] Today, growing spatial segregation means that economic, political, and social inequalities are piling on top of one another. As rich people gather in privileged places, they enhance their political power and social prestige. Poor and working people are stuck in places that society looks down on and that lack political clout. The well-off can enact policies — such as restrictive zoning and the siting of toxic facilities — whose negative consequences are borne primarily by geographically concentrated poor people who live far away from them. The development of "separate societies" for rich and poor not only directly increases income inequality by affecting access to jobs and education; it also generates dangerous stereotypes and tilts the political terrain.[110]

CITIES AS ENGINES OF PROSPERITY

Because so much attention has been given to the concentration of poverty in cities, many Americans may believe that cities are basket cases — like sick people with so few resources that they only serve to burden society. Nothing could be further from the truth. In fact, cities are economic dynamos that provide extraordinary benefits to society as a whole. Cities are both reservations for the poor (with all the burdens that entails) and centers of economic productivity and innovation. The contradictory nature of American cities is reflected in the fact that most cities have daytime working populations that are significantly higher than their nighttime residential populations. They export income to the suburbs. Ultimately, we argue, the residential concentration of poverty at the core undermines the entire region's economic efficiency and ability to innovate. Greater regional cooperation, aimed at less economic segregation and sprawl, would benefit the entire society.

Over the last half century, suburbanization, deindustrialization, and the rise of new cities in the South and West have dramatically transformed the older cities of the Northeast and Midwest. In the process, metropolitan areas became far larger, encompassing four-fifths of the nation's population, but central cities became less dominant within them. A few old cities lost half their populations, and others remained roughly the same size but lost population relative to the surrounding suburbs. Some new cities such as Phoenix and San Diego, mainly in the Sun Belt, grew dramatically. Even in these new cities, however, much of the growth took place on the periphery, leading some observers to claim that cities are now "obsolete." In their eyes, the "old" industrial economy required dense cities with many factories and much face-to-face contact, whereas the "new" information economy is more comfortable in the suburbs, where computers, the Internet, and cell phones have made the dense face-to-face interactions of the older cities unnecessary.

This view profoundly misreads the key functions that most central cities continue to play in our national economy. Regional economies are integrated wholes, with different parts of the metropolitan area specializing in different economic functions. For routine goods production and distribution activities and even many corporate headquarters, suburban locations are often preferable; however, older central cities continue to provide large pools of private assets, accumulated knowledge, sophisticated skills, cultural resources, and social networks. Cities house most of the leading global, national, and regional corporate services firms, such as banks, law firms, and management consultants. They are still centers of innovation, skill, fashion, and market exchange.

Urban density enhances economic efficiency and innovation. What economists call "agglomeration economies" are still important in the global economy. The density of employment in cities reduces the costs of transportation and increases each business's access to skilled and specialized labor. The geographical clustering of industries in certain cities further enhances productivity. In many industries, understanding ambiguous information is the key to innovation. It cannot be communicated in an e-mail message or even a phone call; it requires the kind of face-to-face interaction that cities are good at fostering. The cultural production of these cities has been just as important as their economic role.

Some maintain that American central cities are making dramatic comebacks on their own.[111] In 2003, *Business Week* described an "inner-city renaissance," but then asked "will the gains last?"[112] Harvard Business School professor Michael Porter argues that inner cities have a "competitive advantage" and will prosper if city governments simply step out of the way and promote a favorable business climate.[113] What this view ignores is that the economic dynamism of cities persists alongside crippling poverty, social exclusion, and growing inequality. Indeed, the persistent vitality of many central cities has generated the vast disparities of wealth and poverty that are sometimes located only a few zip codes from each other. As we will show in Chapter 3, concentrated poverty presents substantial barriers to market success. It is not simply a matter, as Porter implies, of government helping private-sector investors make the best of their opportunities. Moreover, as we demonstrate in Chapter 5, cities cannot capture much of the wealth generated within their borders for use in reducing concentrated poverty. As productive investments have become more mobile, even large, prosperous cities have cut back on spending for the poor. For example, New York City, with a long tradition of helping the poor, cut its per capita expenditures on the poor from $537 to $285 (in constant 1987 dollars) between 1970 and 1990.[114]

HOW THE MEDIA COMPOUND URBAN PROBLEMS

News coverage of our cities reinforces the tendency among Americans to associate "urban problems" such as crime and homelessness with cities. Images on the nightly TV news, the covers of newsweeklies, and the front pages of our daily newspapers present an unrelenting story of crime, gangs, drug wars, racial tension, homelessness, teenage pregnancy, AIDS, school dropouts, and slum housing. They typically portray government programs to combat these problems as well-intentioned but misguided failures, plagued by mismanagement, inefficiency, and, in some cases, corruption. This drumbeat of negativism wrongly leads many Americans to conclude that urban problems are intractable.

Coverage of urban crime is a good example. The public's beliefs about crime are based primarily on what they see in the media, not on personal experience. This is particularly important for how suburbanites view the condition of nearby central cities. The media bombard their audiences with news about crime, especially violent crime. The phrase "if it bleeds, it leads" characterizes the disproportionate attention paid to crime, particularly on local television news. One study of news programming in fifty-six U.S. cities found that violent crime accounted for two-thirds of all local news.[115] This coverage typically has little to do with actual crime rates. Moreover, it overrepresents minorities as violent criminals.[116]

Despite the sensationalism, our cities and metropolitan areas do reflect widening national disparities in income and wealth, racial and economic segregation, and the fraying of the social safety net. But cities are only the site in which such problems arise, not their cause. It was not inevitable that these problems would manifest themselves mostly in central cities. As we will describe in some detail, these problems result from choices about our tax code, our housing policies, our transportation practices, our economic development programs, even our military spending priorities. Cities in Canada, Western Europe, and Australia do not have nearly the same levels of poverty, slums, economic segregation, city-suburb disparities, or even suburban sprawl as does the United States. The question is not whether we can ever solve urban problems but whether we can develop the political will to adopt policies that have been shown to work.

THE PLAN OF THE BOOK

The chapters that follow are stages in developing this argument. We begin by documenting the problem of economic segregation and then go on to examine its causes in government policies that shape and reinforce market forces. We show that cities and regions cannot solve the problem by themselves as long as the playing field is tilted by federal and state policies. We end the book by proposing changes in the rules of the game and in the political strategies for implementing them. Throughout, we compare the United States with other developed countries to highlight the distinctive features of the American case.

DOCUMENTING THE PROBLEM

Chapter 2 establishes the factual premise of the book: that economic segregation is increasing both between and within regions. Not only are the rich and poor living apart, but the distances are greater than ever as the mobile middle and upper classes shift to the edges of metropolitan areas, partly to escape deteriorating conditions in central cities and inner-ring suburbs. Chapter 3 documents the costs of economic segregation and sprawl. The contexts within which people live have important effects independent of the characteristics of the individuals who live there. The contextual effects examined in Chapter 3 include jobs and income, health, consumer goods, and safety (crime). (The effect of economic segregation on access to public goods and services is covered in Chapter 5.) One of the themes of the chapter is that although most of the costs of economic segregation fall on the poor, even the rich who live on the outskirts of metropolitan areas bear substantial costs caused by economic segregation and excessive sprawl.

IDENTIFYING THE SOURCES OF THE PROBLEM

Chapter 4 challenges the view that economic segregation and sprawl are simply the products of free markets. It shows that federal and state governments could have chosen different policies that would have encouraged less segregated and more compact metropolitan development patterns. Instead, government policies encouraged spatial inequalities and low-density suburban development. Chapters 5 and 6 examine the largely failed efforts to address the problems within the current rules of the game. Chapter 5 examines how central cities have tried to revitalize themselves and cope with the costs of economic segregation. Liberal, conservative, and progressive municipal politicians have used different strategies for reversing deterioration and coping with fiscal stress. Without help from state and federal governments, however, these efforts have come up against the limits of localism.

Chapter 6 documents halting efforts at regional cooperation, efforts that have been straitjacketed by the present rules of the game. There has been a revival of interest in regional cooperation in recent years, and many valuable experiments are under way in metropolitan areas such as Portland and Minneapolis–St. Paul. The new regionalism has had some success in promoting more efficient and environmentally sound development, but it has had less success addressing the problem of economic segregation and poverty.

CHANGING THE RULES OF THE GAME

Chapter 7 outlines the policies needed to level the playing field so that metropolitan areas can halt and even reverse the trend toward greater spatial inequalities. We support policies that improve the lot of the poor and working class, but we argue that federal and state policies must also directly address metropolitan inequalities. We advocate a range of reforms, including federal programs rewarding regions that cooperate on land-use planning, reducing the bidding wars between localities by subjecting local subsidies to federal taxation, supplementing place-based community development efforts with mobility programs, and setting up elected metropolitan councils through which each region can devise democratic and workable solutions to regional problems.

Chapter 8 addresses the difficult question of how a political coalition can be assembled to support metropolitan reform with equity. We argue that these coalitions must be formed across city lines in ways that unite central-city and suburban voters. For decades, politicians have successfully used wedge issues such as affirmative action and welfare to split suburbanites from central-city voters. But the suburbs are no longer lily-white and prosperous. The increasing racial and economic diversity of suburbia and the strains on inner-ring suburbs make it more difficult to pit suburbs against central cities. The tentative success of Bill Clinton in forging city-suburban coalitions may be a harbinger of a metropolitics for the twenty-first century. We argue that even outer-ring suburban voters ultimately have an interest in more equitable regional policies. Smart growth policies are the best way to address the congestion, pollution, and loss of green space that threaten even prosperous suburbs. Finally, we maintain that public opinion can be mobilized around the moral force of regional equity. A new metropolitics for the twenty-first century can break down the walls that divide us and achieve equal opportunity for all Americans, no matter where they live.

The Facts of Economic Segregation and Sprawl

The gated community of Bear Creek lies east of Seattle, across beautiful Lake Washington. In 1995, home prices ranged from $300,000 to $600,000 in this exclusive community. It is a crime-free haven where salmon swim in the local stream. Its 500 residents like it that way and preserve it with detailed rules regulating house colors (nothing stronger than beige or gray), shrubbery heights, and basketball hoops (prohibited). Four private security guards staff the entrance gates twenty-four hours a day. The residents of Bear Creek can enjoy their environmental amenities without sharing them with the public because they own everything, even the streets and sewers, and pay steep fees to maintain them. Bear Creek's citizens like their private government and are not inclined to tax themselves to help solve Seattle's problems. One resident observed: "The citizens have moved ahead of government. The government has not kept up with what people want."[1]

Bear Creek is not exceptional. Lacking the outward signs of high status that the landed nobility of Europe once enjoyed, wealthy American families have long maintained social distance from the "common people" by withdrawing into upper-class enclaves. Often located on forested hills far from the stench and noise of the industrial districts, places like Greenwich, Connecticut; Lake Forest, Illinois; and Palm Beach, Florida, are "clear material statement[s] of status, power, and privilege."[2] Although claiming to live in a classless society, Americans are in fact acutely class conscious. Many people can scrimp and save to afford a Mercedes or a $2,000 suit, but only a few can live in exclusive neighborhoods that show one has really "made it." Indeed, a 1994 poll found that 60 percent of those making more than $400,000 a year felt that it was important to live in an exclusive neighborhood.[3] Even those recently risen above poverty into the working and lower middle classes are anxious to distance themselves socially and physically from the poor.

In a free society, where most individuals can choose where to live, economic segregation is rarely viewed as a public policy issue. Just as no one objects if someone wears a $5,000 watch or drives a $50,000 BMW, why should we be concerned if someone decides to live in an exclusive neighborhood? Living in a homogeneously upper-class neighborhood eases social intercourse and makes for tighter communities. People generally prefer to live with people similar to themselves. "Birds of a feather flock together."[4] The rich and poor will never live cheek to jowl. Every American takes for granted the right to live where one wants, subject to the limits of affordability.

According to conventional wisdom, economic segregation results naturally from free markets. Residential living patterns stem from a bidding process where the rich can bid on any location, whereas poorer families are restricted to those they can afford. (The homeless cannot even afford to participate in the auction.) In early-nineteenth-century cities, before the invention of the trolley and the automobile, the rich and poor were forced to live close to one another because everyone had to walk or ride a carriage or horse to work. (The rich often lived on the avenues and the poor on the side streets, as they do in New Orleans today.) Transportation improvements, from streetcars and subways to automobiles and freeways, have enabled people to live farther away from their work, and thus to put more distance between themselves and people they consider inferior.

The view that economic segregation should not concern policy makers because it results from a technologically driven market process is wrong. As we show in the next chapter, the quality of our lives is strongly shaped by where we live. Americans know that economic segregation is motivated not just by status concerns, but also by the knowledge that better neighborhoods offer many practical advantages. Homes appreciate more and the schools are better. Wealthy neighborhoods have cleaner air, lower property tax rates, and superior public services. Conversely, we will show that people stuck in poor neighborhoods bear the burdens of unhealthy environments, high tax rates, inferior public services, and underperforming schools. With poor access to jobs, residents of these neighborhoods are less likely to succeed. Economic segregation is thus a major barrier to achieving the fundamental American value of equal opportunity.

Americans do not want government to tell them where to live or to take away their right to move if they do not like their neighbors. We do not recommend interfering with the right of Americans to live wherever they choose. Instead, we wish to take steps to fulfill that right by overcoming ways that residential housing markets are neither free nor fair. Suburban zoning laws prevent lower-income families from moving closer to suburban job opportunities. Yet our constitutional heritage does not consider economic segregation to be as suspect as racial segregation. The Constitution prohibits communities from discriminating on the basis of skin color. The Supreme Court long ago outlawed racial zoning (*Buchanan v. Warley*, 1917). The courts have nevertheless repeatedly upheld the right of municipalities to discriminate on the basis of income by zoning out apartments or houses below a certain size.[5] This position, as Chapter 4 will show, has been reinforced by federal and state policies that have accelerated the decline of central cities and inner-ring suburbs. In short, governmental intervention has caused Americans to suffer from far more economic segregation than individuals would choose in a free market.

This chapter focuses on a deceptively simple question: what are the trends in the spatial separation of economic classes? Economic segregation can be measured in a number of different ways — for example, by using the same indices that measure trends in racial segregation.[6] But it is a greater challenge to measure economic segregation than racial segregation because economic classes are in flux and there are many more degrees of economic class than of race. Most researchers use the federal government's poverty standard to examine how the poor are segregated from the rest of society, but this captures only the bottom end of the process. Economic segregation occurs not only when the working class separates from the poor, but when the middle class separates from the working class, and so on. Results also differ by block, neighborhood, city, and region. This chapter synthesizes the literature by looking at entire regions, then moves to metropolitan areas and finally examines economic segregation among neighborhoods.

No matter what method or scale is used, economic segregation increased rapidly between 1970 and 1990. After the 2000 census, however, researchers reported a "dramatic decline" in concentrated urban poverty and an urban "comeback."[7] For reasons outlined below, this view is exaggerated. To be sure, booming regional economies and tight labor markets helped central cities and poor neighborhoods and reduced concentrated urban poverty in the late 1990s. At the same time, however, concentrated poverty remained stable in the suburbs, middle-income suburbs declined, and the gap between rich and poor suburbs widened. Affluent families continued to isolate themselves in exclusive enclaves, physically embodying a divided society in which the haves and the have-nots live in separate societies.

News from the radio, television, or newspaper often gives us statistics on the national inflation rate, growth rate, or consumer confidence index. We have gotten so used to thinking in terms of a national economy that we have almost forgotten the importance of regions. As Jane Jacobs observed, "Once we . . . try looking at the real economic world in its own right rather than as a dependent artifact of politics, we can't avoid seeing that most nations are composed of collections or grab bags of very different economies, rich regions and poor ones within the same nation."[8] Macroeconomic statistics hide tremendous variation. In 2000, for instance, commentators touted the lowest national unemployment rate in thirty years (4.0 percent), yet many cities had unemployment rates that were four times higher.

William Barnes and Larry Ledebur fault the "one-size-fits-all, 'rising tide lifts all boats,' nationalist economic framework" for obscuring the true nature of the economy, which is a "common market of regional economies."[9] Each region has one or more urban centers surrounded by an outlying area where people commute to jobs in the center. The Bureau of Labor Statistics has identified 172 economic areas in the United States with relatively unified labor and housing markets. Wages and housing prices tend to track each other within each region. These regions are the real building blocks of the American economy and the keys to its success in the global economy.[10]

For the most part, observers have viewed regional inequality as a fact of life, like the weather. Ironically, only during the administration of Richard Nixon did the country flirt briefly with a national regional growth policy. In his 1970 State of the Union Message, President Nixon asserted:

> For the past 30 years our population has . . . been growing and shifting. The result is exemplified in the vast areas of rural America emptying out of people and of promise. . . . The violent and decayed central cities of our great metropolitan complexes are the most conspicuous failure in American life today. I propose that before these problems become insoluble, the Nation develop a national growth policy. . . . If we seize our growth as a challenge, we can make the 1970s an historic period when by conscious choice we transformed our land into what we want it to become.[11]

The main issue at the time was the emptying out of small towns and rural areas. Critics attacked Nixon's attempt to get the federal government more involved in metropolitan planning as centralized planning, and after the Watergate scandal, it died in Congress.

Nixon's support for a national land-use policy would sound radical today. Since 1970, conservatives have attacked national land-use planning as an unwarranted interference in the marketplace. According to the free-market argument, inequalities among regions will correct themselves over time. Booming regions, for example, will bid up wages, prompting investors to switch to lower-wage regions. In other words, free markets have a natural tendency toward balance, or equilibrium. Regions will converge, making them more alike.[12]

For most of the twentieth century, this did in fact happen. The South had been a backward region with a disproportionate share of the nation's poverty at least since the Civil War, but it began to catch up to the rest of the country after the Great Depression of the 1930s. In defending its decision to cut federal funding for needy regions, the Reagan administration's 1982 *National Urban Policy Report* observed with satisfaction that the gap in per capita income among regions had fallen dramatically between 1930 and 1977.[13] Contrary to market theory, however, this had less to do with free markets and more to do with the federal government's huge infrastructure investments in highways, dams, and military bases in the South and West.

Vicious circles of growth and decline can cause regional fortunes to diverge. Economic growth can become self-reinforcing when successful industries cluster in certain regions, achieving higher levels of efficiency as they concentrate and boosting incomes. At the same time, poor regions can have difficulty raising the tax revenues to pay for the infrastructure needed to sustain growth. Around 1980, the century-long convergence of regional incomes stopped and regional trajectories began to diverge in complex ways.[14] Although the broad regions of the country (for example, the South and Northeast) continued to become generally more similar, exceptions began to emerge.[15] Wages converged, but a study of 315 metropolitan areas found that per capita incomes, the best measure of well-being, diverged between 1969 and 1995. Some regions experienced greater accumulations of wealth and higher levels of employment.[16] Between 1950 and 2000, the overall poverty rate evened out across regions and the "isolation" of the poor was reduced about 45 percent, but the concentration of the affluent in wealthy metro areas grew by 415 percent during this period.[17]

Personal economic success depends on the economic trajectory of the region where you live. Regions with more opportunities attract people, whereas those with few opportunities lose population. Reflecting their relative attraction, the median household income in the fifty largest metro areas in 2000 varied from $74,335 in San Jose to only $35,517 in New Orleans.[18] One study found more than twice as many "severely distressed" regions in 1990 than in 1980 or 1970.[19] The regions that become poor tend to remain poor. Of those whose median incomes ranked them in the bottom 20 percent in 1969, 60.3 percent were still at the bottom in 1995, whereas 71.4 percent of those in the top twenty percent were still there twenty-six years later.[20]

There are many reasons why some regions generate more economic opportunity than others. Economic restructuring has significantly altered the distribution of low-wage and high-wage jobs across metropolitan areas. Corporate service economies specializing in advanced producer services, such as law, finance, and accounting (Boston, San Francisco), do better than those areas that rely on manufacturing (Buffalo, Milwaukee). Between 1970 and 1990, only 35.5 percent of the new jobs created in the Boston metropolitan area paid less than $20,000 (in constant 1990 dollars), compared with 77.4 percent in Milwaukee. On the other hand, one-quarter of the net new jobs in the Boston area paid more than $40,000, compared with only about 9 percent in Detroit or Milwaukee.[21] Place matters: a person with the same education, experience, and skills will earn a very different income depending on where he or she lives.

Regions that develop clusters of cutting-edge firms acquire a competitive advantage. Although the firms in such clusters compete with each other, they also create a specialized labor force and share information on the best techniques and the latest innovations. DRI/McGraw-Hill identified 380 specialized geographical clusters driving the U.S. economy in the mid-1990s.[22] New York City specializes in law, finance, and new media (Silicon Alley); Minneapolis has Medical Alley, a center of innovation in medical instruments; Los Angeles is the worldwide center of the film industry; Portland, Oregon, has an innovative cluster in semiconductors; California's Silicon Valley and Boston's Route 128 are centers of information technology. The economic innovation nurtured by clustering creates "sticky capital." Investors in many industries do not search for the cheapest production site but rather for the richest soil in which to grow their firms, even if it is expensive. Clustering can compound inequalities across regions.

The keys to regional economic dynamism change from decade to decade. After the oil price shocks of the 1970s, the regions dominated by oil and natural resources, like Houston, did best, and New York and Boston had relatively low increases in metropolitan per capita income. This pattern changed in the 1980s and 1990s as knowledge industries, often relying on strong universities, provided the key to economic growth.[23] Quality-of-life differences, such as a pleasant climate, excellent parks, and cultural attractions, may help to attract the "creative class" that drives innovation and growth.[24] Knowledge industries also create "sticky capital" because they depend on the face-to-face exchange of cutting-edge ideas and information.

Immigration is another important factor. The Los Angeles and New York regions, whose economies grew strongly in the 1990s, also served as ports of entry for immigrants, with an astounding 1.9 million immigrants moving to those areas between 1990 and 1996 alone.[25] Immigrants provide skilled as well as unskilled labor and link cities to the global economy. Cuban immigration, for example, boosted Miami's economy by helping it become a major entrepot for imports from and exports to Latin America. Although immigration boosts growth, large numbers of unskilled, nonunion immigrants also drive down wages and increase inequality.

Inequality within regions can be both a cause and an effect of poor regional economic performance. Other things being equal, prosperous regions can reduce inequality by drawing previously unemployed workers into the labor market. Cities with rising average incomes, higher value-added economies, and tight labor markets enjoy declines in ghetto poverty.[26] As we discuss later, the booming economy of the 1990s was a major cause of the decline in concentrated poverty.

The causal relationship also works in the other direction: growing inequality within a region can hinder regional economic performance. Regions with large spatial inequalities perform less well. Ledebur and Barnes found that metropolitan areas with higher central city–suburban income disparities had lower employment growth between 1988 and 1991. Hank Savitch and colleagues found that per capita income in fifty-nine central cities was highly correlated (.59) with that of their suburbs, suggesting that central-city and suburban economic outcomes rise or fall together.[27] In Chapter 3, we examine why suburban prosperity depends, in part, on strong central cities.

Despite convergence in hourly wages, regions are becoming more unequal in important respects as advantaged regions prosper and the poor regions languish. This troubling fact alone calls for new national policies. Although interstate wage differences are only a minor cause of rising overall income inequality, it is important to address such differences.[28] For example, if Mississippi eliminated all spending inequalities among its local school districts, its students would still receive inferior educations compared to states that can afford to spend more on education. Adjusted for cost-of-living differences, per pupil spending in 1997–98 varied from $4,000 in Mississippi to more than $9,000 in New Jersey.[29]

The most important inequalities, however, are not between regions, but within them. As many analysts have observed, third world conditions prevail in the central cities of even the most prosperous metropolitan areas in America. In most other advanced industrial countries, average incomes fall as one moves outward from the city center. The opposite pattern holds in the United States: the poor live in older housing near the center, and incomes rise as you move out toward the urban fringe. This pattern has become more complex in recent years, however. Cities like Seattle, Boston, and New York have developed concentrations of high-income households at the center, pushing lower income households further out. Increasingly, poverty is moving to the suburbs, concentrating in inner-ring suburbs that are extensions of central-city ghettos.

Government planners powerfully shaped the European pattern of affluent households occupying urban centers. Baron Haussmann's massive urban renewal of Paris in the 1850s cut wide, straight boulevards through the maze of narrow streets, partly to make it easier for the army to enter Paris to put down uprisings. In the process, Haussmann displaced thousands of low-income residents and replaced their crowded quarters with luxurious apartments lining the grand Parisian boulevards, like the Champs Elysees. A government-sponsored mortgage bank provided capital for building luxury apartment houses in central Paris. (The government still subsidizes central Paris as a place for the rich to live.[30]) In the late 1860s, Vienna followed suit with its Ringstrasse, sponsoring luxury apartment houses that imitated the city's baroque palaces. The pattern spread from Paris and Vienna throughout central and eastern Europe and eventually to South America.

In the Kansas City metropolitan area, by contrast, average home prices rise steadily as one moves outward, peaking fourteen to sixteen miles from downtown.[31] This uniquely American pattern results primarily from the peculiar way that the United States has chosen to satisfy middle- and upper-class housing demand not by rehabilitating older housing near the city center, but by building new housing on the urban periphery. Oliver Byrum, former director of city planning for Minneapolis, calls the American practice of housing the poor in deteriorating areas of the city center a "de facto national housing policy."[32] The practice was so well established by the 1920s that it prompted University of Chicago sociologists to advance the "concentric zone theory" of urban development, which argued that working, middle, and upper classes would live in separate concentric rings moving outward from the city center.[33]

It is also typically American that one jurisdiction governs the center of

TABLE 2.1. The Sixteen Most Fragmented Metropolitan Areas, 2002

	Number of General-Purpose Governments	General-Purpose Governments per 100,000 Population
Pittsburgh, PA MSA	412	17.467
Louisville, KY—IN MSA	154	15.016
Rochester, NY MSA	139	12.657
Cincinnati, OH—KY—IN PMSA	197	11.966
St. Louis, MO—IL MSA	303	11.638
Columbus, OH MSA	177	11.492
Indianapolis, IN MSA	183	11.384
Boston PMSA	380	11.154
Minneapolis—St. Paul, MN—WI MSA	328	11.048
Grand Rapids—Muskegon—Holland, MI MSA	118	10.840
Kansas City, MO—KS MSA	170	9.572
Cleveland—Lorain—Elyria, OH PMSA	199	8.841
Philadelphia, PA—NJ PMSA	354	6.940
Oklahoma City, OK MSA	67	6.185
Milwaukee—Waukesha, WI PMSA	90	5.997
Chicago, IL PMSA	457	5.524

Source: Population from 2000 Census, SF3 and number of governments from Census of Governments, available at http://www.census.gov/govs/www/cog2002.html (calculations by Colleen Casey).

the metropolitan area, while many different suburban jurisdictions govern the wealthier periphery. Until the twentieth century, most central-city governments annexed adjacent territory as it was developed. Gradually, however, state legislatures passed incorporation laws enabling suburbanites to establish separate governments and avoid annexation by cities. By 1930, every state legislature had adopted such incorporation laws.[34] This split the governance of every major metropolitan area between one or two central-city governments and many suburban governments. The most fragmented metropolitan area in the nation, Pittsburgh, has 17.5 governments per 100,000 population, which means that the average municipality has less than 6,000 people (Table 2.1). In *Cities Without Suburbs,* David Rusk explores the differences between "elastic" cities, which expanded to encompass their metropolitan populations, and "inelastic" cities, which did not.[35] In 2000, the central-city proportion of metropolitan area population varied from 10 percent in Atlanta to 63 percent in Albuquerque to 100 percent in Anchorage.[36]

Keeping in mind that political decisions created the dividing lines between

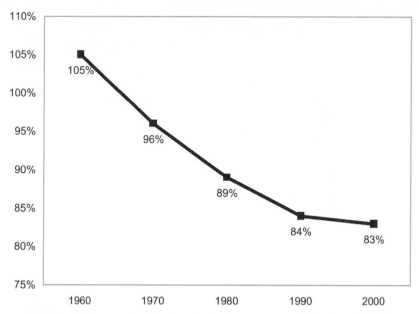

FIGURE 2.1. Central City Per Capita Income as Percentage of Suburban Per Capita Income, 85 Metropolitan Areas, 1960–2000

Source: Eighty-five metropolitan areas used in Larry C. Ledebur and William R. Barnes, *City Distress, Metropolitan Disparities and Economic Growth* (Washington, DC: National League of Cities, 1992), 2, with authors' calculation for 2000.

the central cities and their suburbs, we can trace how different economic classes became concentrated in central cities or suburbs. Figure 2.1 shows that per capita income in a sample of eighty-five cities actually exceeded that of their suburbs by 5 percent in 1960. For the next thirty years, central cities fell relative to their suburbs, reaching 84 percent in 1990. Since cities did almost as well as their suburbs in the 1990s, that gap increased by only 1 percent by 2000.

The central city–suburban income gap is a product of the exodus of the better off, the downward mobility of remaining city residents, and the influx of poorer people, including immigrants.[37] Two-parent households moved to the suburbs while single-parent, female-headed households stayed behind.[38] Only a few cities attracted relatively high-income immigrants, and they did not increase median incomes.[39] Even without this selective migration, however, city incomes would have lagged behind those of the suburbs because they attracted more new jobs, especially entry-level jobs. As manufacturing declined in the central cities, routine back office and retail jobs grew in the suburbs.

The improved condition of central cities relative to their suburbs in the 1990s substantiates the "comeback cities" thesis.[40] The release of the 2000 census data

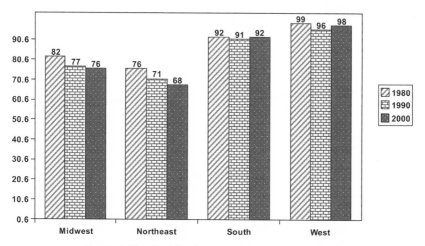

FIGURE 2.2. Central City Per Capita Income as a Percentage of Suburban Per Capita Income by Region, 1980, 1990, 2000

Source: Todd Swanstrom, Colleen Casey, Robert Flack, and Peter Dreier, "Pulling Apart: Economic Segregation in the Top Fifty Metropolitan Areas, 1980–2000" (Washington, DC: Brookings Institution Center on Urban and Metropolitan Policy, August 6, 2004), draft report.

unleashed a flood of reports about how Chicago, Memphis, Denver, and Atlanta turned population declines in the 1980s into population gains in the 1990s. Miami, San Francisco, Seattle, Chicago, and Atlanta significantly reduced their income gap with their suburbs. Although the reversal of previous patterns of urban decline is good news, cities are still much worse off than their suburbs, and many continue to fall further behind. A study of the nation's 331 metropolitan areas found that per capita income increased by about $1,000 more for suburbanites than city dwellers in the 1990s.[41] The gap between central cities and suburbs varies significantly across the country and is much more acute in the older industrial cities compared to the newer cities in the South and West. The gap is largest in the Northeast and Midwest and is still increasing in these regions. In the South and West, central cities had much smaller gaps and their income growth actually exceeded that of suburbs in the 1990s (Figure 2.2).

Cities that are much poorer than their suburbs are vulnerable to disinvestment and fiscal stress. David Rusk speculates that when city per capita income falls below 70 percent of that of its suburbs, the region reaches a "point of no return" where "economic disparities become so severe that the city, in a broad sense, no longer is a place to invest or create jobs (except in some fortress-type downtowns)."[42] Rusk updated this rule using 2000 census data to read "The Point of (Almost) No Return," because 11 out of 24 cities that were below the 70 percent standard at the beginning of the decade did manage to improve rela-

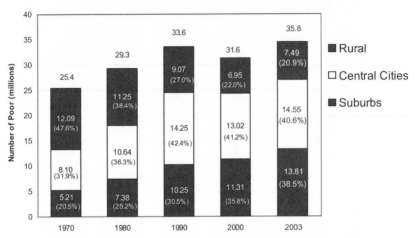

FIGURE 2.3. Suburbanization of Poverty: Percentage and Number of Poor Population Who Live in Central Cities, Suburbs, and Rural Areas, 1970–2003

Source: Decennial census; Carmen DeNovas Walt, Bernadette D. Proctor, and Robert J. Mills, *Income, Poverty, and Health Insurance Coverage in the United States: 2003* (Washington, D.C.: U.S. Bureau of the Census, August 2004).

tive to their region during the 1990s.[43] In the previous decade, all twelve cities below the 70 percent cutoff in 1980 fell further by 1990.

Although the data show that central cities did better in the 1990s than in the past, this does not mean that the metropolitan poor are doing better. As Figure 2.3 shows, the proportion of the poor living in suburbs has increased since 1970. By 2003, almost as many poor people lived in suburbs (13.8 million) as in central cities (14.5 million). Central cities may be improving their relative position simply by exporting the poor to the suburbs. This would be positive if they ended up in more supportive environments, but not if the "poor in the suburbs" live mainly in "poor suburbs" with many of the same problems as troubled cities.

ECONOMIC SEGREGATION AMONG SUBURBS

Most people now live in suburbs (Figure 2.4), but our suburban stereotypes have not caught up with the changing suburban reality. The media generally portray suburbia as white and middle class, and even boring and bland. For example, in the 1998 film *The Truman Show,* Jim Carrey played an insurance agent whose life was continuously filmed and broadcast to the world. He lived in a painfully perfect made-for-television suburb called Sea Haven, with others

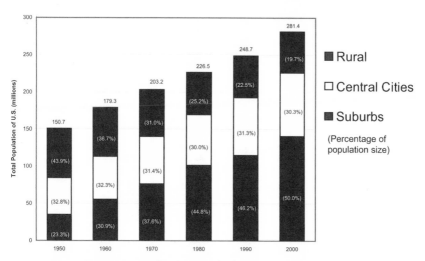

FIGURE 2.4. Percentage of U.S. Population Who Live in Suburbs, Central Cities, and Rural Areas, 1950–2000

Source: Decennial census and current population survey.

seemingly just like himself. In fact, suburbs are remarkably diverse in racial and economic makeup. Cities have considerable population diversity *within* them, whereas suburban diversity is mostly *between* suburbs. Myron Orfield has developed the most sophisticated typology of suburbs, which he classifies by their tax capacity and expenditure needs.[44] When he applies this typology to metropolitan areas, Orfield finds that half the suburban population lives in "at-risk" suburbs with high needs but low, and often declining, tax bases (Table 2.2).

Segregated, at-risk, inner-ring suburbs are basically extensions of inner-city ghettos. In most metropolitan areas, development proceeds in sectors or wedges extending like pieces of a pie from the city center. When the urban ghetto spills over the city line, it causes nearby suburbs to decline. With more than twice the regional percentage of minority residents and only two-thirds of the tax base (Table 2.2), such communities may be worse off than the central cities that they border. Harvey, Illinois, an at-risk segregated suburb outside Chicago, is a good example. Harvey's tax base is so depleted that the owner of a $100,000 house has to pay $5,000 in property taxes, three times the rate paid by homeowners in a nearby wealthy suburb.[45]

The poorest suburbs are not always located next to the central city. For that reason, the term "inner-ring suburb" is misleading. Suburban decline is concentrated not in pre–World War II suburbs, but in those built between 1945 and 1970, when the typical tract home was quite small. The typical house in the Levittown suburbs of the late 1940s was only 800 square feet. In 1954, the

TABLE 2.2. Orfield's Typology of Suburbs in Twenty-five Metropolitan Areas

Municipality Type	Percentage of Metro Area Population*	Tax Capacity as Percentage of Metro Area Average	Eligible for Free Lunch as Percentage of Metro Area Average	Percent Minority as Percentage of Metro Area Average
At-risk segregated	8	66	175	209
At-risk older	6	74	59	35
At-risk, low-density	26	66	103	65
Bedroom-developing	26	90	32	16
Affluent job centers	7	212	27	26
Very affluent job centers	<1	525	39	38

Source: Myron Orfield, *American Metropolitics: The New Suburban Reality* (Washington, DC: Brookings Institution Press, 2002), 33.

 *Does not add to 100 percent because central cities are not included.

average size of a new house was 1,140 square feet. By 2000, the average size of a new home had doubled to 2,260 square feet.[46] Older tract homes also tended to lack such standard amenities as central air conditioning, two or more bathrooms, family rooms, and nine-foot ceilings. When these postwar houses go downhill, they usually do so rapidly. After twenty-five years, roofs and furnaces need to be replaced. Upwardly mobile families usually find that it makes more sense to purchase a new home further out rather than to rehabilitate an older tract home. As Lucy and Phillips note, exurbanization is to the postwar suburbs what suburbanization was to central cities: it sucks their life out by siphoning off prosperous households.[47]

Declining suburbs are depressing places. They lack the public spaces, universities, cultural institutions, nightlife, and downtowns that make central cities exciting places, even when they house many poor people. Journalist Donna Gaines explored "suburbia's dead end kids" in Bergen County, New Jersey, and Long Island. She found they had bleak job prospects, hung out at 7-Elevens, and immersed themselves in hip-hop, goth, and raves. Gaines interprets their cultural rebellions as an understandable response to a society that has little respect for teenagers and has few opportunities for many of them.[48]

Even healthy-looking suburbs are vulnerable to decline and fiscal stress. Largely white "at-risk older" suburbs (Table 2.2) often vigorously resist racial integration. But with low tax capacity and little prospect of tax-generating development, they also risk falling into fiscal crisis. "At-risk low-density" suburbs are located on the urban fringe. With pockets of rural poverty nearby and limited tax bases, they have a hard time paying for new sewer systems and schools needed for their growth. The low-density, mostly white, "bedroom-developing" suburbs that fit the suburban stereotype are the fastest-growing category. Although they have average tax capacities, they too could find themselves in fiscal difficulty if they do not plan well for future growth.

The most privileged suburbs in Orfield's classification system contain major concentrations of office and commercial space and reap the benefits of an extraordinary tax base. These "affluent (and 'very affluent') job centers" (Table 2.2) contain four times more office space per household than any other type of suburb. Often home to massive collections of office and retail space located at major interstate highway interchanges, such as the Schaumberg area outside Chicago, these affluent suburbs need not worry about fiscal stress.[49] In the Twin Cities, the most favored suburbs, known locally as the Fertile Crescent, stretch west and south of Minneapolis, following the Interstate 494 and Interstate 35 corridors. Although their residents receive excellent local services at a reasonable tax cost, those who work in these places often cannot afford to live nearby, thus creating traffic congestion and pressures to develop open space.

It is easy to recognize exclusive suburbs. Many, like Philadelphia's mainline suburbs, were built before 1940, with housing originally constructed to the highest standards that now has historic appeal. Houses in these suburbs cost upwards of a million dollars and are situated on large lots with winding roads and tall shade trees. They may have a few apartment buildings, usually condominium complexes with swimming pools and tennis courts. Instead of Chevy Novas and Hyundais, the residents drive Mercedes and Lexuses. Their kids do not hang out at the mall. Instead, harried moms shepherd them from one enrichment activity to another. Teenagers know that they are headed for good colleges and jobs, and they are often obsessed with clothes and SAT scores.

The pattern of inequality across suburbs reflects that of American society more generally. Not only is the proportion of middle-class suburbs shrinking, but the gap between rich and poor suburbs is widening. A study of 554 suburbs found that the number in which the median family income was below 80 percent of the metropolitan area's rose from 22 to 90 between 1960 and 1990, while the number at 120 percent or more of the metropolitan median fell slightly from 148 to 142. The number of solid middle-income suburbs fell 40 percent. The average ratio between the highest- and lowest-income suburbs increased from 2.1 to 1 to 3.4 to 1.[50]

The trend toward suburban inequality continued in the 1990s, despite the tendency of tight labor markets to pull up the poorest places. Orfield reports

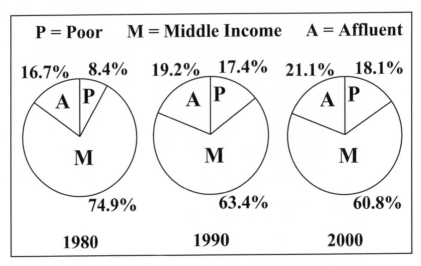

FIGURE 2.5. Percentage of Suburban Residents Who Live in Poor, Middle Income, and Affluent Suburbs, 1980, 1990, 2000 (Fifty Metropolitan Areas)

Source: Todd Swanstrom, Colleen Casey, Robert Flack, and Peter Dreier, "Pulling Apart: Economic Segregation in the Top Fifty Metropolitan Areas, 1980–2000" (Washington, DC: Brookings Institution Center on Urban and Metropolitan Policy, August 6, 2004), draft report.

that inequality in tax capacity among 4,606 suburban jurisdictions in 25 metropolitan areas increased by 8 percent from 1993 to 1998.[51] Figure 2.5 shows that the proportion of suburban residents living in "middle-income suburbs" in the 50 largest metropolitan areas declined rapidly in the 1980s and continued to decline in the 1990s. (Middle-income suburbs were defined as suburbs whose per capita incomes were between 75 and 125 percent of their region's per capita income.) The same study also showed that the gap between the top and the bottom grew. The gap between the per capita income of the suburb at the 5th percentile (better off than the other 95 percent of suburbs) and that of a suburb at the 95th percentile widened significantly between 1980 and 2000 (Figure 2.6).

Local government fragmentation and fiscal competition are the main causes of growing economic segregation among suburbs. Suburbs have become great sorting machines for separating Americans along the lines of class, race, ethnicity, religion, and lifestyle. Indeed, in 1992, the 315 metropolitan areas in the United States had an average of 104 general-purpose governments (not counting school districts and special authorities).[52] Well-to-do families want their suburban governments to protect them from the urban dangers of crime and low-performing schools. Some are small and expensive. Countryside, a Kansas City suburb, has only 134 homes, and its property taxes are three times higher

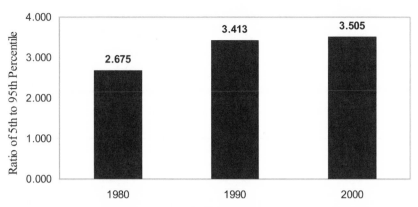

FIGURE 2.6. Per Capita Income in the Suburbs, Ratio of 5th to 95th Percentile, 1980, 1990, 2000 (Fifty Metropolitan Areas)

Source: Todd Swanstrom, Colleen Casey, Robert Flack, and Peter Dreier, "Pulling Apart: Economic Segregation in the Top Fifty Metropolitan Areas, 1980–2000" (Washington, DC: Brookings Institution Center on Urban and Metropolitan Policy, August 6, 2004), draft report.

than in neighboring jurisdictions. "People like being separate and are willing to pay more for it," says Brian Smith, former mayor of Countryside.[53] Ensconced in such enclaves, the rich are far more isolated from other income groups than are the poor.

Families also choose suburbs on the basis of their class and status aspirations. People use municipal boundaries and images as markers of where to live. They are not just buying a neighborhood, but a social rank and a school system. Over time, this sorting process makes suburban municipalities more homogeneous and more distinct from each other. The system of municipal boundaries, not neighborhood differences, thus increasingly organizes economic segregation.[54]

ECONOMIC SEGREGATION AT THE NEIGHBORHOOD LEVEL

As Paul Jargowsky has documented, the number of people living in census tracts with at least 40 percent poverty rates increased nearly 100 percent between 1970 and 1990.[55] When Jargowsky analyzed the 2000 census data, however, he reported "stunning progress." Between 1990 and 2000, the number of people living in concentrated poverty areas fell 24 percent.[56] Other researchers echoed his findings.[57] This trend suggests that poor people benefitted from the tight labor markets of the late 1990s. Contrary to the culture of poverty thesis, most poor people want to work and will do so if given the chance. For reasons outlined below, however, this news is not as good as it first appears. The neighborhood sorting of people by income is still at work.

The neighborhood-level segregation of rich and poor has fluctuated over time. Olivier Zunz's study of Detroit shows that people with different occupations (and therefore incomes) lived together in the same ethnic and immigrant neighborhoods in 1880. Pronounced spatial segregation by class emerged after the invention of the trolley. By 1920, occupational segregation had risen as ethnic segregation declined. Only in tight-knit Jewish and black communities did a wide range of occupations live on the same block.[58] Using census tract data for Chicago, Dudley and Beverly Duncan found high levels of residential segregation between the top and bottom occupational rankings in 1950.[59] In the 1960s, this segregation declined as low-status workers joined high-status workers in moving to the suburbs. One study of ten urban areas found that residential distance between managers and laborers dropped by 23 percent in the 1960s, and between professionals and laborers, it fell 19 percent.[60]

This pattern shifted once more between 1970 and 1990, as economic segregation increased rapidly, leveling off again after 1990.[61] In order to use the same methods used to study racial segregation to study economic segregation, we must divide the population into two groups.[62] Figure 2.7 uses the federal poverty standard to define the poor in comparison to households making four times the poverty level. The isolation index measures how many poor people live in the average poor person's neighborhood. Likewise, the isolation of the affluent measures how many affluent people live around the average affluent household. In 1970, the neighborhood of the average poor person was 13.6 percent poor; by 2000, that figure had risen to 24.6 percent. Similarly, in 1970, the average affluent household lived in a neighborhood where 30.8 percent of their neighbors were also affluent; but that figure rose to 33.8 percent in 2000. In both cases, economic segregation rose rapidly in the 1980s and then declined somewhat in the 1990s. At the end of this process, affluent families remain considerably more isolated from other groups than the poor.

We can also study economic segregation by measuring how many people below a certain poverty threshold live in a neighborhood. William Julius Wilson's original Chicago study defined areas with poverty rates above 30 percent as underclass or ghetto poverty neighborhoods.[63] Subsequent researchers generally used a 40 percent threshold. This standard draws on the notion that the negative effects of concentrated poverty are compounded at high levels. A 40 percent poverty neighborhood has many more negative effects than a 20 percent poverty neighborhood. Wilson calls these "concentration effects." Anyone who is familiar with big U.S. cities will immediately recognize high-poverty neighborhoods. They have abandoned houses and lots, vacant businesses, cars rotting in driveways, idle men standing on corners, and many liquor stores but

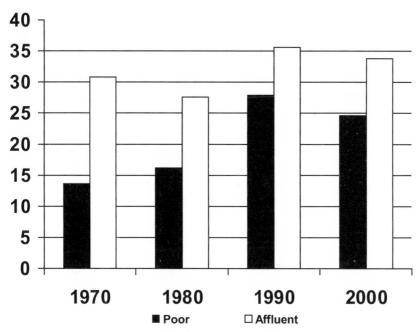

FIGURE 2.7. Isolation of Poor and Affluent Households in Sixty Metropolitan Areas, 1970–2000

Source: Douglas S. Massey and Mary J. Fischer, "The Geography of Inequality in the United States, 1950–2000," in *Brookings-Wharton Papers on Urban Affairs 2003,* ed., William G. Gale and Janet Rothenberg Pack (Washington, DC: Brookings Institution Press, 2003), 11.

few banks. Outsiders rarely venture into these areas, and surely not on foot or at night.

Even in these difficult conditions, most residents are hardworking and law abiding. Lurid media coverage and cynical politicians have fostered misleading stereotypes of ghetto residents. One is that they are lazy. In fact, more than half of all adults in high-poverty areas are working, looking for work, or in school.[64] Workforce participation in high-poverty Southern California neighborhoods increased from 39 percent in 1970 to 51 percent by 2000. Although they still lag behind nonpoverty neighborhoods (where 61 percent work), they narrowed the gap.[65] When regional labor markets were tight, as during the "Massachusetts Miracle" of the 1980s, residents of Boston's poor neighborhoods entered the labor force in droves.[66] Alas, many could only find part-time work, and many earned wages that could not lift wage earners and their families above the poverty line.

Residents of poor inner-city neighborhoods are also stereotyped as depending on government handouts. In fact, three-quarters of the income in high-poverty neighborhoods comes from wages and salaries, about the same percentage as in wealthy suburbs.[67] Residents of wealthy suburbs receive Social Security and Medicare, whereas residents of poor neighborhoods receive Medicaid and welfare. (Since the 1996 welfare reform act, the caseload has been cut 55 percent.[68]) Despite the stereotype, women on welfare do not live good lives without having to work. A study of 214 welfare recipients in Chicago, Boston, San Antonio, and Charleston found that 46 percent worked while receiving welfare, even though this was against the rules. The reason was simple: otherwise, they could not support a family.[69]

People who live in concentrated poverty areas bear significant burdens that hamper their upward mobility. That is why the "dramatic decline" in people living in concentrated poverty in the 1990s was such good news. But this decline was not universal. While the number of poor people living in concentrated poverty dropped nearly 75 percent in Detroit, it more than doubled in Los Angeles.[70] The population living in concentrated poverty increased in 91 out of 331 metropolitan areas. Moreover, the decreases elsewhere, important as they were, were tempered by these facts:

Many poor still lived in high poverty neighborhoods. With the national poverty rate falling from 13.1 percent in 1990 to 12.4 percent in 2000, enough families left the ranks of the poor to decrease neighborhood poverty rates below the 40 percent standard. But many of these neighborhoods were still quite poor. A study of all U.S. metropolitan areas found that although the proportion of poor people living in 40 percent poverty tracts dropped from 17 percent to 12 percent in the 1990s, the proportion living in census tracts with 30 to 40 percent poverty remained the same, and the proportion living in tracts with 20 to 30 percent poverty increased from 18 to 21 percent. Any neighborhood with a poverty rate over 20 percent remains a high-poverty neighborhood by national standards, and the population living in poor neighborhoods declined only 2.7 percent in the 1990s, not 24 percent.[71]

Poverty moved to the suburbs. Although the number of poor people living in central-city concentrated poverty (40 percent plus) areas dropped 21 percent, that number declined only 4 percent in the suburbs.[72] A careful examination shows that concentrated poverty is being redistributed toward inner-ring suburbs, just over the city border. This helps explain why the number of poor suburbs is increasing, as we saw in the previous section.

The federal poverty standard underestimates poverty. All of the studies cited above use the federal poverty standard to measure concentrated poverty, but that standard has serious flaws. Because the original methodology for determining the poverty cutoff has never been updated, it is set too low.[73] Updating it would substantially raise the overall poverty rate and increase the number of high-poverty neighborhoods.

Moreover, the federal poverty standard pulls poverty out of its regional context by having one poverty cutoff for all metropolitan areas, even though regions vary significantly in their wages and cost of living.[74] In 2000, the cost of living in New York City was 235 percent above the average for all metropolitan areas.[75] A poor family of three (income less than $13,738 in 2000) would have a much more difficult time making ends meet in New York than, say, Baton Rouge.

The federal poverty standard also fails to capture the relative dimension of poverty. It is more difficult to be poor when the gap with the rich is greater. The booming economy of the 1990s actually made life harder for many low-income families by enabling the middle and upper classes to bid up the cost of living, especially the cost of housing. Contextually sensitive measures of poverty would provide a more accurate measure. One study of isolation of the poor in fifty-two metropolitan areas defined poverty as less than 50 percent of the region's median household income. Even on this measure, the isolation index for the poor declined 3.8 percent in the 1990s, but this decline was much less than that calculated using the federal poverty standard.[76] The isolation index for affluent households, defined as those households making 150 percent or more of the regional median household income, increased 9.2 percent.[77]

The 2000 census is just a snapshot. It provides the best picture of what American society looked like in April 2000. With an historically low unemployment rate (4.0 percent), 2000 was not a representative year. The tight regional job markets that pulled up distressed areas in the late 1990s came to an end shortly thereafter.[78] During the 2000–2002 recession, the unemployment rate increased to 5.8 percent and the national poverty rate rose to 12.1 percent. The "jobless recovery" beginning in 2003 did not help much. Concentrated poverty has therefore probably increased since the 2000 census. Returning to tight labor markets would be one of the best things we could do to reduce concentrated poverty and economic segregation.

RACE OR CLASS?

A burning issue in the study of concentrated poverty is whether it is mainly caused by economic restructuring or racism. Wilson's initial 1987 formulation in *The Truly Disadvantaged* downplayed racial discrimination and focused instead on deindustrialization and the exodus of middle-class blacks.[79] Douglas Massey and his colleagues countered that view by asserting that racial discrimination was a central cause of concentrated poverty. Because discrimination has kept blacks in lower-paying occupations or out of the labor force altogether, racial discrimination in housing automatically heightens the concentration of disadvantage and the level of economic segregation. Massey and his colleagues argue that since African Americans in poor neighborhoods could not follow jobs out to the suburbs, the negative effects of deindustrialization were channeled into black communities. Even when blacks moved to the suburbs, they ended up in mostly black, poorer suburbs.[80]

Racial segregation not only prevents poor blacks from moving out of ghettos, it also means that middle-class blacks are more likely to live among the poor than is true of middle-class whites. Blacks moving out of concentrated poverty are not only more likely to end up living near poor neighborhoods, they also end up in lower-income, more fiscally distressed suburbs than do comparable whites. In the New York metropolitan area, for example, the median income was $3,500 lower in the places to which black people moved than in the ones to which comparable non-Hispanic whites moved.[81] Blacks need higher incomes than whites to achieve comparable social distances from the poor.

Clearly, race contributes profoundly to concentrated poverty. In 2000, only 5.9 percent of poor whites lived in concentrated poverty tracts, compared to 18.6 percent of poor African Americans and 13.8 percent of poor Hispanics. In other words, a poor black person was three times more likely to reside in a concentrated poverty neighborhood than a poor white person. But this does not mean that racial segregation is the cause of the rising economic segregation since 1970. On the contrary, racial segregation has declined while economic segregation has increased.[82] Between 1970 and 1990, the concentration of poor whites increased twice as fast as poor blacks or Hispanics. Black poverty did not rise during that period, but concentrated poverty did.[83] In the 1990s, concentrated poverty fell much more rapidly among blacks and Hispanics than among whites. In 1990, the black poor were five times more likely than whites to live in concentrated poverty; in 2000, blacks were only three times more likely to do so.[84] In a study of 60 metropolitan areas, Mary Fischer estimates that the percentage of income segregation determined by race/ethnicity fell from 81 to 65 percent between 1970 and 2000.[85]

It would be a mistake, however, to underestimate the effects of racial segregation on concentrated poverty. The countless forms of racial discrimination mean that residential segregation automatically produces economic segregation. Increasingly, however, class divisions are driving economic segregation. Those who have the resources, including middle-class blacks, are fleeing high-poverty areas, leaving behind devastating concentrations of poverty and social problems. By escaping across municipal boundaries, the affluent avoid the costs of concentrated poverty that urban governments must bear.

ECONOMIC SEGREGATION AND SPRAWL

Sprawl is a land development pattern that spreads residential units over a large area. A classic example is the single-family home built under three-acre minimum-lot zoning. Sprawl also encompasses the separation of residential from commercial land uses, the absence of clustered development or town centers, and reliance on the automobile.[86] There is no necessary logical connection between sprawl and economic segregation. If low-density developments on the urban fringe included housing options for the poor, sprawl would not promote economic segregation. In the real world, however, sprawl and economic segregation are closely intertwined.

The metropolitan United States is remarkably sprawled out. European cities are three to four times denser. The claim that American cities are sprawled out because we have so much land is countered by Canada, which has more land per person but whose cities are still twice as dense as those in the United States.[87] American cities have not always been this way. In the 1920s, they were twice as dense as they are now.[88] Suburbanization has reduced city densities to that of older suburbs, while newer suburbs are much less dense than they might have been if they had followed a clustered, mixed-use pattern surrounding commercial centers, as was true of pre–World War II suburbs like University City outside St. Louis or Shaker Heights outside Cleveland. After World War II, private developers concentrated on building large tracts of single-family homes set apart from other uses.

Over the years, scholars have debated whether suburbanization resulted mainly from "pull" factors, such as the attraction of bigger houses and yards, or "push" factors, such as deteriorating services, rising crime, and poor schools in the central cities. Free market theorists come down on the side of pull: they say changing consumer demand and technological advances led to suburbanization and sprawl, and that any attempt to constrain such trends would be inefficient. They point out that metropolitan areas are decentralizing in all wealthy nations. As incomes rise, households want bigger houses and more green space. Better-off families are willing to accept longer commutes to get cheaper land and larger houses in the suburbs, whereas the poor prefer to live in crowded conditions closer to their jobs.[89] In practice, however, this logic is questionable. Most entry-level jobs are located in the suburbs, where most poor and working-class families would prefer to live. In other countries, the rich prefer to live near the center, where they have easier access to high-paying jobs and elite culture. Something else seems to be going on in the American context to make the middle and upper classes flee to the urban fringe.

Certainly, the pull factors are real. William Fischel estimated that income growth, transportation advances, and technological changes account for about 75 percent of suburbanization. But nonmarket factors account for the other 25 percent of suburbanization.[90] Thomas Sugrue's history of postwar Detroit shows how racial change led to white flight, but the statistical evidence about white flight is contradictory.[91] Some studies show that cities with large minority populations produced more rapid suburbanization, but others show no significant effect.

There is no doubt, however, that people want to leave the social and economic deterioration of areas characterized by concentrated poverty. Crime also pushes people to the suburbs. One study estimated that more than one resident moved to the suburbs for each crime committed in moderate to large central cities.[92] (We discuss this further in Chapter 3.) Many people moved to the suburbs to gain access to higher-quality schools with high test scores. As we show in Chapter 5, the poor performance of central-city schools stems both from lower per pupil expenditures and from special needs associated with concentrated poverty. It is logical for people to leave central cities and inner-ring suburbs to escape the costs of concentrated poverty. Once households begin to do so, the process can snowball as abandonment and social decay reinforce one another.

There is no necessary reason that people moving away from concentrated poverty should settle in sprawling suburbs. One appeal seems to be distance from poverty and the attraction of a homogeneously middle class environment. As Jargowsky puts it: "Sprawl is related to poverty and inequality because sprawl puts a greater degree of separation between income classes."[93] Developers build expensive housing on large lots on the urban fringe because it is more profitable than developing housing on brownfield sites or filling in older parts of the region. But the main reason that this happens is because government policies promote it. Suburban zoning often excludes apartments, mandates large-lot single-family homes, and separates land uses (requiring households to own several automobiles).[94] Low-income households must be satisfied with the older housing left behind. Suburban "fear of falling"—a fear that a sudden influx of poor people will cause whole communities to decline—leads to public support for such policies. This fear is not entirely unwarranted in inner suburbs, because poverty rates are rising in those areas.

Sprawl thus has a complex relationship with economic segregation.[95] Although concentrated poverty does not directly create sprawl, it pushes families out of older communities and increases demand for new suburban housing—which developers meet, largely because of government policies, in a sprawled-out manner.[96] Clearly, policies that encourage development in the older parts of regions would make community development easier in poor neighborhoods. As David Rusk shrewdly observes, we need both an inside game (community development) and an outside game (limits on sprawl).[97] In Oregon, Portland's experience with its metropolitan growth boundary seems to confirm Rusk's contention. Portland's rate of concentrated poverty is low and falling, and central-city per capita income is catching up with that of the suburbs.[98] On the other hand, smart growth policies may promote economic segregation if they lead to gentrification and displacement of the poor. Precisely because there is no necessary connection between density and economic segregation, smart growth policies must include provisions to promote affordable housing and mixed-income communities.

IS THE UNITED STATES DIFFERENT?

Income inequality and spatial polarization are growing in the United States. One school of thought argues that global economic forces are driving these trends. The increasing mobility of capital, the movement of industrial jobs to third world countries, and growing immigration into first world cities undermine the middle class and polarize the wage structure between highly paid professionals and poorly paid service workers.[99] Western Europeans lament how globalization is leading to the "Americanization" of poverty and suburbanization in their cities.[100] In short, global economic forces are thought to accentuate inequality and economic segregation and to cause cities around the world to converge. Experience suggests, however, that such predictions are premature. A careful comparison between cities in the United States and other developed countries reveals stark differences, suggesting these trends are more the product of political institutions and policies than economic forces.[101]

The large public housing estates, or *grands ensembles,* located on the outskirts of French cities, particularly the *banlieux,* or inner-ring suburbs, of Paris, are frequently cited as examples of European ghettos.[102] Many contain large concentrations of poor North African immigrants. In recognition of their similarity to American ghettos, they have been called "Little Chicagos." Like concentrated poverty tracts in that city, they have high levels of poverty, crime, and social disorganization. Living in a Little Chicago stigmatizes a person as a loser; employers shun such residents, and mothers even warn their daughters against going out with boys who live there. The resurgence of the extreme right-wing Front National in the 1980s in France was based on hostility toward immigrants and their supposed threat to the French nation.

Much as the French *banlieux* may resemble American ghettos, they are also different in many ways. Generous government benefits have lifted the incomes of those at the bottom in France over the past twenty years.[103] Most government benefits are national entitlements and do not depend on where you live, as they do in the United States. For example, France has a unitary national school system. The poor in France are also less separated from the rest of society than in the United States. Clearly, race helps to explain why ghettoization is more extreme in the United States. European cities are not without economic segregation, especially when poverty status is correlated with ethnic or immigrant status, as in the case of the French *banlieux*. But the French *banlieux* usually have good public transit and do not suffer from greatly inferior public services, especially schools. Even the poorest French *banlieux* seems to have more social organization, and less violence and despair, than most American ghettos.

The experience of living in poor neighborhoods is qualitatively different across Europe and Canada. One is never in a world apart when walking through the worst neighborhoods of Amsterdam or Toronto, for example. Even cities with high levels of poverty and unemployment lack such areas. "Italy's 12 major cities cannot be characterized by a very high degree of spatial segregation of social groups."[104] Former British Prime Minister Margaret Thatcher's policy of allowing tenants to purchase their public housing units during the 1970s and 1980s meant that those who could not afford to do so clustered in less attractive estates, but their levels of ghettoization are still far lower than in the United States. The public and private sectors have not abandoned the poor neighborhoods of European cities. As one study of poor neighborhoods in Birmingham put it:

> While the levels of deprivation and disadvantage prevailing in all five inner city wards indicate a concentration of economically weak populations (especially in pockets within each ward) including high levels of concentration of racial and ethnic minorities, these neighborhoods remain vibrant and heterogeneous. Their main streets are lined with shops, restaurants, banks, churches, neighborhood offices, community centers, as well as government job centers. In addition, they are connected to the commercial city center and other wards by a large network of buses.[105]

The European poor are more integrated with the working and lower middle classes than the poor in American cities.[106] In the United States, many working-class individuals may be trapped in distressed inner-ring suburbs, but they shun the ghetto poor and view them as undeservedly absorbing government funds and threatening to spread an alleged immoral culture of poverty.[107] European poor areas have fewer working poor and more unemployed, but reliance on government benefits does not seem to arouse as much hostility from those on the next rung of the ladder, perhaps because they also benefit from these policies. European health, education, child care, and retirement policies make the quality of life less dependent on earnings. As a result, the poor are less frightening to their middle-class neighbors. By reducing inequalities, European social policies reduce resistance to economic integration.[108]

The most disturbing difference in urban poverty between Europe and the United States is that place of residence does not hamper social mobility as much in Europe. National governments fund education, so access to good schools is less dependent on living in a prosperous school district. Similarly, family assistance programs are centralized, so the rich in Europe have less fiscal incentive to move to a separate jurisdiction in order to avoid paying for programs that benefit the poor. Europe is less prone to a vicious circle in which economic segregation reinforces income inequality, which then fuels economic segregation.[109] In the United States, the evidence shows that economic segregation has a momentum of its own. The accumulating negative effects of concentrated poverty cause households to flee these areas, accentuating concentrated poverty and making it harder for those left behind to get ahead. The vicious circle of sprawl and economic segregation, we argue, imposes significant costs on all parts of the metropolitan area.

 The Costs of
Economic Segregation
and Sprawl

Every weekday, Cynthia Wiggins, a seventeen-year-old single mother, boarded the number 6 bus in her predominantly black neighborhood in Buffalo, New York. Engaged to be married, Wiggins was struggling to improve herself and dreamed of becoming a doctor. Her destination was the gleaming Walden Galleria Mall in the suburb of Cheektowaga, where she worked as a cashier at Arthur Treacher's Fish and Chips. Unfortunately, the owners of the mall refused to let city buses drive into the parking lot, and passengers had to walk 300 yards across a seven-lane highway with no sidewalks. On the morning of December 14, 1996, with mounds of snow lining the shoulder, a ten-ton dump truck struck Wiggins. She died of her injuries nineteen days later.[1]

Wiggins's tragic death highlights how place of residence can affect access to jobs and retail stores, as well as personal safety. In the Buffalo area, most job growth happens in suburban Erie County, which inner-city minorities have difficulty reaching because of poor public transit. Lacking cars, they can shop only in the inner city, where the number of retail outlets has fallen precipitously since the 1950s.[2] In Wiggins's case, she could get to her close-to-minimum-wage mall job only by public transit, which took an hour and forty minutes, ending with a dangerous hike across a busy highway. The lesson is clear: some people live in neighborhoods that provide them with all sorts of advantages; others, like Cynthia Wiggins, live in neighborhoods that impose numerous disadvantages on them.

In this chapter, we synthesize the scholarly evidence on how places affect people's life chances. In particular, we examine the negative effects of living in neighborhoods with high poverty rates. Since William Julius Wilson published

The Truly Disadvantaged in 1987, there has been an outpouring of research on the contextual effects of concentrated poverty.[3] Researchers have attempted to sort out how living in a particular kind of place may have an impact on people's lives over and above that of their individual characteristics, such as level of education. The central question is whether a poor person living in a poor neighborhood has different opportunities and achieves different outcomes than the same person living in a mixed-income neighborhood.

Like many other interesting areas of social science, the research on contextual effects is full of thorny methodological and conceptual disputes, about which a few introductory words are in order. Some scholars argue that the evidence on the contextual effects of poverty concentration is weak—too weak to serve as a guide for public policy.[4] We disagree. The evidence on the contextual effects of place is overwhelming.[5] Critics often point out that it is hard to separate the effects of individual characteristics from those of place. Good researchers take individual characteristics into account to make sure that contextual effects do not simply reflect the sorting of different kinds of people into different places. By doing so, however, one diminishes the impact of individual characteristics that are themselves affected by context, such as income or education. Urban ethnographies and firsthand accounts—such as *Manchild in the Promised Land, Tally's Corner, There Are No Children Here, Amazing Grace, The Code of the Street,* and *American Project*—provide vivid testimony to how individual and place effects are intertwined in the lives of the ghetto poor.

From a scientific point of view, the ideal way to study contextual effects would be to conduct an experiment: randomly assign essentially similar people to two different types of neighborhoods—one an area of concentrated poverty and the other a mixed-income area. Then significant differences in outcomes would be the result of the context, not individual characteristics. Fortunately, two experiments have tried to do something like this: first, the court-ordered Gautreaux program in Chicago, and second, the federally funded Moving to Opportunity (MTO) program.[6] In 1976, under the Gautreaux decision, the federal courts ordered the Chicago Housing Authority to help black families move from segregated public housing projects to integrated, usually suburban, neighborhoods. By the end of the program in 1998, about 7,100 black families had moved, and their outcomes could be compared to those who did not move.[7] MTO began in 1993 when Congress allocated $70 million for 1,400 housing vouchers to help poor families move from concentrated poverty areas (defined as having a poverty rate of 40 percent or more) to areas of low poverty (defined as areas with 10 percent or less poverty). With its emphasis on economic segregation rather than racial segregation, MTO is ideal for addressing the central question of this chapter, and we cite its findings throughout. Both experiments showed modest, but consistent and real gains of various sorts for the families who moved into neighborhoods with fewer poor people.

Even with solid experimental evidence, scholars continue to debate the extent of contextual effects. Part of their uncertainty is that researchers are focusing on behavioral outcomes — for example, does place influence teen pregnancy, drug use, or risky health behaviors such as smoking? The weight of the evidence supports the conclusion that place *does* influence behavior. In the pages ahead, however, we focus our attention not on behaviors but on *opportunity structures*. If a neighborhood has few jobs or retail outlets nearby, the contextual effect is clear. If people pay more for groceries or have worse public services, nobody can dispute that place matters.

Finally, we stress the need to look at areas of concentrated poverty in their regional context. Too often, the literature examines only the internal characteristics of neighborhoods. Areas of concentrated poverty are not islands cut off from the rest of society. Even the poorest neighborhood has many links with the regional economy. The fate of neighborhoods is determined not so much by their internal characteristics as by their relationship to the broader region. Much of the so-called underclass literature has overlooked the broader dynamics that distribute classes across space in metropolitan areas. Because concentrated poverty pushes households to the metropolitan fringe, urban sprawl, with its many costs, is the flip side of concentrated disadvantage.

In this chapter, we document the impact of economic segregation and urban sprawl on four areas of life: jobs and income, health, access to private goods and services, and crime. (We address the crucial question of the effects of concentrated poverty on the cost and quality of local public services in Chapter 5.) Although each area is examined separately, it is important to keep in mind that they are related to each other in myriad ways that compound the problems.

JOBS AND INCOME

The Personal Responsibility and Work Opportunity Reconciliation Act of 1996 (better known as welfare reform) is generally considered a success. The welfare rolls were cut from 12.3 million recipients in 1998 to 4.9 million in 2003. We know, however, that many families who left welfare are no better off than they were before.[8] Many of them had to overcome daunting obstacles. Consider Zakiya Kyle, a single mother and former welfare recipient living in South Los Angeles, who works at a nonprofit drug-abuse prevention program. She arrives at the bus stop at 6 AM with her two boys, fourteen-month-old Ishmael and five-year-old Mustafa. Two buses later, she drops Mustafa at his school in Ingle-wood, then takes two more buses to get Ishmael to his babysitter in Watts. After two more buses, Kyle finally arrives at work at 9 AM. In a masterful under-statement, Kyle sums up the problem: "In LA County, it's very difficult to live without a car."[9] The fact is, a low-wage suburban job does not make sense for many former welfare recipients because commuting is so difficult and time-consuming. Women of all classes are much more likely than men to turn down a job because it is not accessible to home or to their children's caregivers.[10]

The 1996 welfare reform act set aside money for job training and day care but made no formal provision to bridge the gap between where welfare recipi-ents live and where the jobs are. Although two-thirds of all new jobs are located in the suburbs, three-quarters of welfare recipients live in central cities or rural areas. Welfare rolls have fallen more slowly in cities than elsewhere.[11] Nation-wide, just one in twenty welfare recipients owns a car. If they do purchase a decent car, their benefits are often reduced.[12]

In 1968, Harvard economist John Kain began to write about what came to be known as the "spatial mismatch" problem. Kain used simple statistical tech-niques to show that housing segregation prevented Chicago's blacks from fol-lowing jobs out to the suburbs. As a result, they lost 22,000 to 24,000 jobs.[13] Some argue that the spatial mismatch is primarily the result of "race," not "place,"[14] but a comprehensive review of research concluded that the evidence "consistently supports" the spatial mismatch hypothesis.[15]

According to market theory, people should move closer to their jobs to mini-mize spatial mismatches. In American metropolitan areas, however, jobs and people often move in opposite directions.[16] The number of highly skilled pro-fessional jobs, such as lawyers and management consultants, has increased in central business districts. It makes sense for companies to locate their most pro-ductive workers on the most expensive land and office space at the center of metropolitan areas. A study of 101 metropolitan areas found that in 1997 aver-age annual pay for central-city jobs was 10.5 percent higher than pay for sub-urban jobs.[17] Unfortunately, most people who work at high-wage downtown jobs commute long distances from the suburbs, which they prefer not only for the lifestyle, but also to avoid the high taxes, crime, and poor city schools as-sociated with concentrated poverty in the central city.[18]

At the urban periphery, on the other hand, employment in entry-level jobs with moderate education and skill requirements, such as routine manufactur-ing, retail, and data-entry positions, is growing rapidly, but exclusionary zon-ing often prevents low-wage workers from moving closer to such jobs.[19] Sub-urbs used to be bedroom communities for workers commuting to jobs in the city. Now, many suburbs have more jobs than residents, and like central cities, suburbs have to import workers to fill them. Between 1977 and 1997, employment in Westchester County, just north of New York City, increased 21 percent, but its resident population fell slightly. In 1990, the Regional Plan Association calculated that there were 56,000 more jobs in Westchester than resident employees. Not surprisingly, the demand for housing is soaring in Westchester County. By 2003, desperate home buyers had pushed the median sales price for a single-family home to a record $570,000.[20]

Counter to market theory, housing supply has not kept pace with demand in Westchester County, primarily because local governments have adopted barriers to the building of new housing. In 1952, Westchester was zoned for 3.2 million residents. By the early 1960s, downzoning had reduced the county's population capacity to 1.8 million. Most Westchester towns simply zone out apartments. In the 1980s, apartments were permitted on less than one-half of 1 percent of the developable land in the less intensely settled areas of the county, where most development could occur.[21] At the same time, minimum lot sizes for single-family homes are being changed from one acre to three or four acres. Richard Nicholson, a town council member in Somers, a small town in northern Westchester that enacted more restrictive zoning, put it this way in 1999: "The days of one-acre zoning are over in northern Westchester."[22] Existing owners want to restrict newcomers from disturbing their lives by bringing more traffic and more children to educate in the public schools. Not coincidentally, restrictive zoning raises housing prices, handing present owners hefty profits when they sell. Those who rent do not have a place on the escalator of rising home values and inevitably fall further and further behind. In 2003, the fair market rent for a two-bedroom apartment in Westchester reached $1,294. Working 40 hours a week, a person would have to earn $24.88 an hour to afford such an apartment, nearly five times the minimum wage.[23]

Although well-to-do Westchester home owners exclude lower-income people, they still need people to tend their gardens, watch their children, and even police their streets. Many teachers, firefighters, and police officers cannot afford to live in the municipalities where they work. Most must look for houses or apartments in the older southern Westchester communities like Yonkers, Mount Vernon, or New Rochelle. Despite being the sixth richest of the nation's 3,147 counties in 1990 in per capita income, Westchester led the nation in the rate of homelessness in 1989.[24] Many of its low-wage workers make under $20,000 a year. Hispanic immigrants work as gardeners, maids, and day laborers. The demand for affordable housing pushes landlords to violate housing codes in ways that are dangerous and unhealthy. Some landlords crowd fifteen or more people into an apartment, charging them $100 to $150 each, making a windfall profit.[25] In suburban Long Island, where the housing market is as tight as Westchester, one enterprising businessman illegally converted cheap office space into housing, charging fifteen people $2,700 a month to crowd into seven tiny rooms.[26]

Given that jobs and housing are often far apart in American metropolitan areas, the crucial question becomes whether this has a significant effect on people's ability to find work. The Chicago Gautreaux program provides evidence that it does. Adults who moved to the suburbs enjoyed higher rates of employment, although not higher wages or more working hours. Children experienced more dramatic results. "Compared with the children of city movers," researchers found, "the children who moved to the suburbs were more likely to be in school, in college-track classes, in four-year colleges, employed, and in jobs with benefits and better pay."[27] Part of the reason why place matters so much is that only 18 percent of Chicago's ghetto residents have access to a car.[28]

Place also matters because neighborhoods provide networks of crucial information about jobs. More than half of all jobs are found through friends and relatives, not through want ads.[29] These networks also provide information to employers looking for good workers. More than 40 percent of Chicago firms reported that they did not advertise their entry-level openings in newspapers. Instead, they relied on informal referrals from current workers, which they felt ensured better-quality workers who would be less likely to steal or be dishonest. As one hospital official put it, "If you are just a cold applicant, chances of you getting in are almost nil."[30]

Unfortunately, if you live in a neighborhood with a high unemployment rate, your social network will be less valuable in helping you finding a job, regardless of how skilled, honest, or hardworking you are. William Julius Wilson reports that blacks in poor Chicago neighborhoods are less likely than others to have at least one employed friend.[31] In general, poor people, the less educated, and youths tend to have spatially confined social networks.[32] This is particularly problematic where entry-level jobs are located outside the central city, or inner-ring suburbs, as happens in most metropolitan areas.

The norms, values, and aspirations passed on in concentrated poverty neighborhoods may also harm labor market success. Advocates of the controversial "culture of poverty" thesis argue that poor people adopt different values from mainstream middle-class society and, for this reason, will not respond to job opportunities even when offered them. The question is not so much whether residents of concentrated poverty and minority areas differ from middle-class suburbanites (they do), but why and what this means. Conservatives like Edward Banfield and Charles Murray think that the countercultural values of the poor causes their economic failure.[33] Employers fail to locate jobs in areas of concentrated poverty, according to this view, because the residents lack a strong work ethic.

The evidence, however, contradicts this thesis. The Gautreaux program's experience shows that former residents of low-income black neighborhoods responded to new opportunities by working more and doing well in school. Even people who are stuck in the worst neighborhoods strive to enter the workforce. When Boston's economic boom produced tight labor markets in the 1980s, the ghetto unemployment rate plummeted.[34] During the sustained economic boom of the 1990s, more young black men with high school educations or less moved into the workforce, earned more, and committed fewer crimes.[35] One study of fast-food restaurants in central Harlem found that fourteen people applied for every minimum-wage job.[36] Even in high-poverty neighborhoods, most men are working or looking for work, and most household income comes from wages and salaries, not welfare or unemployment benefits.[37] These findings would not surprise William Julius Wilson. His survey of ghetto residents in Chicago found that less than 3 percent felt plain hard work was not important for getting ahead in society.[38]

Residents of high-poverty ghettos *are* different from middle-income suburbanites. They dress differently, behave differently in public, and some even speak differently.[39] They may fail to find jobs because they have simply given up. Places help to produce such attitudes. A survey of 655 Gautreaux participants found that moving to a middle-class suburb had a beneficial impact on people's sense of "efficacy," their feeling that they could control their life, plan for the future, and get ahead. In-depth interviews showed that housing project residents often took a fatalistic attitude toward life because they perceived their environment to be unpredictable and unstable. They accepted drug dealing and gang intimidation not because they approved of them but because they feared retaliation if they went to the police. In contrast, those who moved to middle-class suburbs perceived the environment as stable and predictable and thus took action to improve their lives. The fact that people's sense of efficacy could change so rapidly contradicts the culture of poverty thesis. The Chicago researchers sum up their conclusions this way: "Unlike the culture of poverty model, it has been seen that the very same individuals who report having very little efficacy over their life experiences in housing projects subsequently show considerable efficacy in middle-class suburbs. Places matter. The attributes of neighborhoods and the experiences provided by neighborhoods have profound effects on people's capabilities and their ideas about what they can accomplish."[40]

Research thus shows that where we live can determine our income, just as our income determines where we live. A vicious circle of poverty and economic isolation can result. Economists have constructed models showing how economic segregation can lead to persistent economic inequalities across generations.[41] Rising levels of economic segregation may help explain why economic mobility by Americans has declined since the late 1960s, and Americans' "escape rate" out of poverty is by far the lowest among twelve industrialized countries studied.[42]

SEGREGATION AND SPRAWL HAVE HIGH COSTS

From the viewpoint of simple fairness, it makes sense to reduce economic segregation. But if most suburbanites benefit from economic segregation, the political prospects for reform would be slim. Residents of privileged suburbs do indeed benefit from economic segregation, but economic segregation also imposes real costs on them, although these costs often go unrecognized. High-income households can pretty much live anywhere they want. When they choose to live in outer suburbs, they may maximize their personal well-being, but such choices also generate social costs that affect everyone, even the well-to-do. These include longer commutes, air pollution, and loss of green space. Long commutes are particularly difficult for parents with young children seeking to balance family and work. Most of the burden falls on women, who face longer shopping trips and spend more time transporting children to disparate destinations.

The practice of abandoning central cities and building new, low-density developments on the urban fringe drives up the cost of infrastructure for which all of us must ultimately pay. The National Research Council conducted the most comprehensive and objective research on the costs of sprawl, detailed in their 605-page report, *Costs of Sprawl—2000*.[43] It projected a growth of 24 million households from 2000 to 2025 and compared an uncontrolled growth scenario with a controlled, "smart growth" scenario.[44]

By reducing the length of water lines, sewer lines, and roads to accommodate new population, the controlled growth scenario saves taxpayers billions of dollars. For example, the controlled-growth scenario saves $12.6 billion over the twenty-five-year period by lowering demand and reducing the cost of water and sewer lines. The savings on building local roads is projected at $109.7 billion. Local government services are also less expensive under more compact development (garbage trucks and emergency vehicles don't have to travel as far, for example), resulting in an annual saving of $4 billion. Overall, the researchers conclude that more compact development would save the nation $420 billion, a 6 percent saving in total property development between 2000 and 2025.

Costs of Sprawl—2000 acknowledges that sprawl does satisfy the preferences of households for low-density living and more consumer lifestyle choices. The report also acknowledges that it is difficult, or impossible, to measure many costs and benefits and compare them systematically. Nevertheless, weighing their words carefully, the experts conclude that "there appear to be more costs than benefits" to sprawl and the additional consumption of resources is "basically unnecessary to achieve a very high quality of life."[45]

Even so, this approach understates the costs of sprawl to the older communities left behind. Communities with declining populations and disinvestment are stuck with growing social problems and shrinking fiscal resources. There are nearly 4,000 abandoned shopping centers in America's central cities.[46] Tearing down abandoned buildings is a major expense for many central-city budgets. Joseph Persky and Wim Wiewel evaluate the costs and benefits of locating a new, 1,000-employee manufacturing plant on a suburban greenfield site instead of a central-city location. They conclude that there is not much difference in overall efficiency or cost between the two sites, but the greenfield scenario places about 70 percent of the burden on low- and middle-income households, mostly central-city residents, in the form of higher public sector costs. The private sector captures most of the benefits of the greenfield site, with about 90 percent going to high-income households in the form of income from stocks and business ownership.[47] In short, central-city governments and taxpayers pick up the tab for sprawl.

SEGREGATION AND SPRAWL IMPAIR REGIONAL ECONOMIC COMPETITIVENESS

Residents of the older parts of the region bear many of the costs of sprawl. The larger question, however, is not how the costs of sprawl are divided between city and suburbs, but whether economic segregation and sprawl undermine regional economic competitiveness and diminish the potential size of the regional economy. Can suburbs prosper when their central cities decay? Many studies have documented a strong correlation between the well-being of suburbanites and central-city dwellers.[48] The incomes of city residents and those of suburban residents are highly correlated, suggesting that the economic fates of cities and suburbs are intertwined.[49]

Certainly, the relatively higher costs of regional infrastructure related to sprawl and central-city decline may harm regional competitiveness. Andrew Haughwout goes a step further and argues that massive investment in suburban infrastructure may actually reduce productivity by drawing workers away from more productive, denser urban centers.[50] Exclusionary zoning can also drive up housing costs, especially for rental housing, which in turn puts upward pressure on wages, making the region less attractive to investors. One study concluded that growth controls, including exclusionary zoning, caused housing prices in California localities to be 33 to 43 percent higher than they otherwise would have been.[51] Boston, San Francisco, and Los Angeles have clearly seen high housing prices drive up salaries. Awareness of this problem has led some corporate leaders to support efforts to expand the supply of affordable housing.[52]

More generally, economic segregation and metropolitan sprawl may reduce open space, increase traffic congestion, and harm the environment, making a region less attractive in the long run both to residents and investors. Richard Florida argues that the "creative class" — that third of all workers who generate new ideas, production processes, and strategies — is the key to regional economic growth. They are attracted to areas with a wide range of outdoor activities and urban environments "full of dense high-quality, multidimensional experiences."[53] To the extent that central-city decline and suburban sprawl undermine the metropolitan recreational environments and urban milieus that attract the creative class, regional economic growth will be harmed.

Ultimately, the claim that cities and suburbs are interdependent boils down to whether cities perform crucial functions in regional economies that the suburbs do not. One counterargument claims that information technology has rendered the need for dense face-to-face relations in cities obsolete, enabling anyone to network intensively without having to live or work in cities.[54] The evidence strongly suggests, however, that face-to-face relations are as important as ever.[55]

Another version of this argument holds that suburbs now provide the same functions traditionally performed by central cities. Palo Alto, California, and White Plains, New York, have become "mini–central cities" in the suburban realm. If they can more efficiently provide all the essential economic functions, then outer-ring suburbanites need not worry about declining cities or inner-ring suburbs. In *Edge City*, Joel Garreau notes that modern economies still require spatial concentrations of employment, but he calls downtowns "relics of the past" and argues that "edge cities . . . contain all the functions a city ever has." Edge cities may exclude the poor and minorities, but Garreau argues that they are "astoundingly efficient," able to sustain regional growth even if the urban core rots.[56]

The evidence, however, does not support Garreau's claim that central cities are no longer important. Suburban property values still depend on the availability of high-paying jobs in central cities.[57] Suburban firms rely on the rich supply of corporate services, such as banking, law, and accounting, found in city centers. One study of 5,000 large firms found that central-city firms supplied 92 percent of the professional services purchased in the region. The author of the study concluded: "Suburbia does not yet comprise an economically autonomous 'outer city' or 'edge city.'"[58]

High-paying jobs continue to locate in cities because employment density nurtures economic dynamism and productivity. On average, workers in the fifteen counties with the lowest employment densities produced less than half of the output of New York City workers.[59] The concentration of economic functions reduces transportation costs and increases access to skilled and specialized labor. Downtown companies can hire the most specialized, and therefore most productive, lawyers to represent them in complex patent or copyright cases. Dense collections of experts make for highly profitable business environments. Wichita is second only to Seattle as a center of defense and aerospace manufacturing; Charlotte has become a national banking center; Miami specializes in Latin American trade and finance; Cleveland excels in machine tooling, and Washington, DC, has a critical mass of innovative think tanks.

Jane Jacobs argues that cities are especially productive not just because of the concentration of similar businesses but also because of the mixing of *different* industries within the same geographical area. The exchange of ideas across diverse industries stimulates innovation, a key to economic development.[60] Businesses that rely on exchanging sophisticated information that cannot be encapsulated in a formula or summed up in an e-mail message benefit from dense face-to-face relations. To be on the cutting edge of fashion, you need to be in New York (or Milan or Paris). Innovation has increasingly become the key to profitability, because the first stages of the product life cycle convey monopoly-like advantages in pricing.[61] Innovation, in turn, often stems from informal collaboration between firms. In her study of Silicon Valley in California and Route 128 outside Boston, AnnaLee Saxenian showed how the superior innovation of the former depended on face-to-face networks among employees of competing firms.[62]

Density also fosters what has been termed flexible specialization.[63] Old-style manufacturing is based on low-skilled workers mass-producing identical objects in continuous assembly lines. Flexible systems produce small batches of customized goods to meet constantly changing consumer demand. Flexible specialization requires skilled, craft-type workers in smaller firms that cooperate with one another on marketing and have a network of suppliers providing just-on-time delivery of parts. The Los Angeles film industry relies on dense networks of independent contractors in cinematography, set design, computer graphics, script writing, and the like, which can be pulled together for the specialized production needs of each movie. Most film studios want to locate in Los Angeles. They are "sticky" rather than mobile.[64] Interest in "industrial clusters" as a tool of economic development has surged because it is clear that they foster a high-wage manufacturing economy. Mass production, by contrast, leads to the sweating down of labor as mobile capital seeks out the lowest-wage areas.

Although overall employment is decentralizing, idea-intensive industries continue to cluster in central cities, where they are becoming more important.[65] It is difficult to imagine cutting-edge clusters in fashion, theater, art, advertising, investment banking, or design prospering in low-density suburbs. Daniel Luria and Joel Rogers have argued that cities can nurture a "high road" to reindustrialization by competing not on low-cost, low-wage goods but on high-quality, well-designed, and better-serviced products. As they put it, "A high-road strategy must almost surely be a metro strategy because the high road generally requires the sheer density of people and firms found only in cities."[66]

In short, regional prosperity (and suburban well-being) still depends on dense clusters of business as nurtured in central cities. The connection to concentrated poverty is clear: if concentrated poverty imposes higher fiscal costs and greater disinvestment on central cities, this will either limit their ability to pay for the infrastructure and services needed by the central business district or force them to raise taxes, either way leading businesses to relocate to less productive suburban locations. Fiscally weak cities show less economic growth for both central-city and suburban residents. One study concluded that suburbanites would benefit from $2 to $4 for every dollar of aid they give to central cities.[67] When concentrated poverty and fiscal stress pull down central cities, the whole region suffers.

Ultimately, it makes no more sense to talk about suburban independence from central cities than it does to talk about the head being independent from the stomach. The parts of a region form an integral whole. Metropolitan economies drive American prosperity, producing over 85 percent of the total goods and services in 2001.[68] The different parts specialize in different functions. In his description of a pin factory in *The Wealth of Nations,* Adam Smith famously observed that a division of labor maximized efficiency. Similarly, the specialization of various parts of a region in different economic activities coherently related to one another results in greater efficiency and higher competitiveness. It is a fundamental mistake to think of these specialized functions as somehow autonomous or unrelated.

LIVING IN CONCENTRATED POVERTY NEIGHBORHOODS IS HARMFUL TO YOUR HEALTH

The growing spatial concentration and separation of poverty and wealth hurts all parts of our metropolitan regions, but they have particularly harsh effects on those consigned to live in concentrated poverty neighborhoods. In fact, it can be downright unhealthy.

In 1984, Dr. Arthur Jones founded the Lawndale Christian Health Center in one of the poorest neighborhoods of Chicago. The clinic provided decent and affordable health care for the neighborhood, but its doctors frequently complained that their patients did not follow simple directions to improve their health. In *Mama Might be Better Off Dead,* Laurie Abraham tells how Jones learned the realities of the neighborhood: "Dr. Jones told of one woman who was suffering from a severe case of hives caused by an allergic reaction to her cat, yet repeatedly refused to get rid of the animal. 'I really got kind of angry,' Dr. Jones remembered, 'and then she told me that if she got rid of the cat, there was nothing to protect her kids against the rats.'"[69]

Epidemiologists have documented a strong correlation between wealth and health at the individual level. Recently, they have uncovered a troubling paradox. Although wealthy individuals tend to live longer than the less affluent, this correlation disappears at the national (or group) level. Wealthier nations are not necessarily healthier. Although the United States, for example, had the highest gross national product (GNP) per capita (controlling for purchasing power) in 2000, it ranked fourteenth in infant mortality and twelfth in expected life span at birth in 2001.[70] Similarly, poor areas can sometimes achieve better health than richer areas. Despite having a lower per capita GNP than the rest of India, the state of Kerala achieved a life span exceeding seventy years, about the same as Saudi Arabia.[71] Black men in Harlem have a lower chance of reaching age sixty-five than do men in Bangladesh, even though the average income is many times higher in Harlem.[72]

Efforts to solve this paradox have generated an outpouring of new research on the environmental causes of death and disease. By far the most powerful explanation is that economic inequality cancels out improvements from rising

GNP. Generally speaking, a society's income distribution matters as much to health outcomes as its standard of living. Economic inequality is correlated with lower life expectancy, regardless of per capita income. One early study estimated that average life expectancy was five to ten years lower in a highly unequal country than in a relatively egalitarian country, after controlling for overall wealth.[73] Japan has the world's highest life expectancy and one of the lowest levels of income inequality. The United States, on the other hand, has a highly unequal income distribution and lower life expectancies, despite spending more per capita on health care than any other country.[74]

Spatial inequalities explain part of the strong association between inequality and health.[75] Concentrated poverty is bad for your health. Research consistently shows that socioeconomic characteristics of geographical areas are associated with death from all causes.[76] An early study comparing mortality rates of individuals in high-poverty neighborhoods in Oakland, California, with a control group living in nonpoverty areas had stunning results. White males in poverty areas were almost 50 percent more likely to die than white males in nonpoverty areas, after controlling for a wide range of individual characteristics.[77] An evaluation of the federal MTO demonstration program found that moving from a high-poverty to a low-poverty neighborhood had important mental health benefits for adults and resulted in significantly lower rates of obesity. Teenage girls had lower rates of psychological distress and engaged in fewer risky behaviors.[78]

What causes the relationship between living in concentrated poverty areas and poor health and premature death? We will examine three significant factors: poor access to health care, a harmful physical environment, and high levels of stress.

ACCESS TO HEALTH CARE

The United States is the only developed country without universal health insurance. The government does insure the poor and elderly through Medicaid and Medicare, but 45 million Americans (15.6 percent of the population), particularly the working poor, lacked health insurance in 2003.[79] For the insured as well as the uninsured, the quality of care received depends a great deal on where they live. Even though the supply of physicians has risen greatly in the past thirty years, it remains low in most low-income central-city neighborhoods. In New York City, Manhattan has the highest concentration of physicians, at 3.3 per 1,000 residents, but some poor Brooklyn neighborhoods have only 0.3 physicians per 1,000 residents. Affluent northwestern Washington and suburban Bethesda neighborhoods have one pediatrician for every 400 children, but the poor black neighborhoods of southeastern Washington have one pediatrician for every 3,700 children.[80] Even when doctors are present, many will not serve Medicaid patients. In the early 1990s, 67 percent of primary care physicians in large metropolitan areas limited the number of Medicaid patients they served, with the average practice having only 8 percent Medicaid patients.[81]

Most people believe that doctors shun Medicaid patients because the program does not pay well and burdens them with paperwork. In truth, doctors could cope by cross-subsidizing Medicaid patients with middle-income private payers. When many poor people are concentrated in a given area, however, this becomes difficult. Nine out of ten doctors are white and they prefer to practice in white areas. Crime and unpleasant conditions also discourage doctors from practicing in low-income areas, regardless of the doctor's or residents' race. Doctors in high-poverty areas complain about language difficulties, missed appointments, lack of compliance with treatment, greater tendency to sue for malpractice, and frustration over the limited ability of medical interventions to improve health when patients suffer from homelessness, substance abuse, violence, and poverty. Those who do practice in poor neighborhoods often run "Medicaid mills" that shuffle patients through as quickly as possible to collect fees. For many such doctors, this is the only place they can get a job. In the Mott Haven section of the South Bronx, described in Chapter 1, fewer than 13 percent of primary care doctors were board certified in the early 1990s.[82]

The United States spent $226 billion on Medicaid in 2000.[83] Under present circumstances, huge increases in Medicaid fees would be required to entice doctors into the poorest areas, not just because they are poor, but because wealthier suburban areas provide more profitable practices. Although nursing care for the elderly drives overall Medicaid spending, so do health problems caused by poor living conditions. If we provided excellent health care to people living in poor neighborhoods, it would improve their health and longevity. But because substandard living conditions are a big part of the problem, health disparities would remain. The United Kingdom has universal health insurance, but disease rates vary hugely from one place to another. If we really want to improve health, we need to do something about the environments in which people live.[84]

THE PHYSICAL ENVIRONMENT

More than 100 years ago, Jacob Riis shocked the nation with his photographs in *How the Other Half Lives*. Like other nineteenth-century reformers, Riis thought that crowded tenements bred disease. Poor immigrants crowded in filthy and degrading conditions were perfect for spreading cholera, typhus, smallpox, and tuberculosis. Noting that half of all clothing was made in these tenements, Riis warned that the diseases could spread: "It has happened more than once that a child recovering from small-pox, and in the most contagious stage of the disease, has been found crawling among heaps of half-finished clothing that the next day would be offered for sale on the counter of a Broadway store."[85] New York City has changed tremendously over the past century, but its slums still generate diseases from which middle-class people, even suburbanites, are not immune.[86]

Many different aspects of low-income neighborhoods make them unhealthy places to live. Houses tend to be older, crowded, dark, and dangerous, with many health and safety code violations, resulting in more accidents and fires. Poor neighborhoods often lack parks and recreational facilities, forcing children to play in the streets, where traffic presents an ever-present danger.[87] Because poor neighborhoods have fewer grocery stores and these stores charge higher prices for less healthy food, the people in these areas tend to suffer from higher rates of obesity.[88] Living in poorer areas tends to dampen physical activity. People are afraid to go outside in areas with high crime, often keeping their children locked inside after school. Tuberculosis was thought to have been controlled in the United States, but it has recently returned, nearing epidemic proportions in some inner-city neighborhoods. The emergence of multidrug-resistant strains of tuberculosis is an especially dangerous threat. As one author observed, treating it "requires proper follow-up and medical care, which is difficult for patients living in high-poverty areas. Too often they cannot afford the medicine, or follow-up appointments are impossible, as with the homeless." Of the 20 percent of toddlers who are not immunized against preventable diseases such as measles, most are poor inner-city children.[89]

Lead paint was banned in 1973, but many older homes contain high levels of lead, either in paint or in water pipes. Young children in low-income inner-city families are seven times as likely to have elevated lead levels in their blood than children in less disadvantaged environments.[90] Small children are apt to put anything in their mouths. In old houses with crumbling paint, they are prone to ingest large amounts of lead. Exposure to lead up to the age of six has been shown to impair children's IQs and their psychological and classroom performance. The damage is not reversible.[91]

Air quality is also often poor in low-income neighborhoods. Traffic, especially truck traffic, pollutes the air, as do hazardous industries or waste sites. Black and low-income households are more likely to be exposed to toxic waste dumps than are middle-class whites.[92] Garbage transfer stations and power plants are often located in low-income areas lacking the political clout to exclude them. Political leaders sited a medical incinerator in the South Bronx after residents of Manhattan's affluent East Side opposed it out of fear of cancer risks to their children. After eight years and 500 state violations, it was finally closed in May 1999.[93]

Air pollution causes elevated asthma rates in poor neighborhoods. Asthma is a chronic, incurable disease that causes swelling and constriction in the lungs, making it difficult to breathe. Asthma attacks are triggered by allergic reactions to dust, tobacco smoke, and cold air. Asthma has become much more common in recent years. Between 1980 and 1998, the number of asthma sufferers grew from 6.7 million to 17.3 million,[94] but it has reached epidemic proportions in concentrated poverty areas. While the New York State hospital admission rate for asthma was 1.8 per 1,000, it was more than three times higher in the Mott Haven area of the South Bronx.[95] Cockroaches may explain the outbreak of asthma among inner-city children. One study of eight inner-city areas found that half the children slept in areas with high levels of cockroach allergens, and they were hospitalized three times more often than other children.[96]

Nations pass through an "epidemiological transition" when deaths from infectious diseases decline rapidly and, instead, more people die from so-called lifestyle diseases, such as cancer and heart disease. At this point, health depends crucially on developing healthy lifestyles with low-fat diets, exercise, and abstinence from smoking; moderating alcohol consumption; avoiding stress; having a satisfying social life; and developing a positive self-image. The implication is that individuals largely control their health prospects. Americans are obsessed with changing their diet or behavior to live longer, healthier lives. Racks of magazines and books are devoted to giving advice on healthy lifestyles. They fail to note how powerfully our living and working environments shape our ability to lead healthy lifestyles. Americans spend billions on diets, yet we are among the fattest people in the world. Environment can overwhelm personal willpower.

Residents of concentrated poverty areas are more likely to engage in risky behaviors such as smoking, drinking, drug use, and unprotected sex.[97] Tobacco and alcohol companies target their advertising on central-city minority neighborhoods,[98] influencing the likelihood in such areas of smoking, consuming alcohol, eating fat, and failing to use seat belts. People who live with stress are more likely to do things to relieve it, such as smoking or eating junk food. Risky behaviors are also infectious.[99]

Living in areas of concentrated poverty reduces the benefits of prudent health behaviors, making them less "rational." Among seventy-seven community areas in Chicago, life expectancy at birth ranges from 54.3 to 77.4 years.[100] (The most important cause of the difference in life expectancy is the homicide rate, which ranges from 1.3 to 156 per 100,000 persons per year.) People who do not expect to live very long discount the costs of risky behaviors and engage in them more frequently.[101] Exposure to violence also stimulates risky behavior. Regardless of economic background, young people exposed to violence smoke more and feel less confident in their ability to affect their health.[102] Because risky behaviors reduce life expectancies, the result is a vicious circle of reduced life expectancies and risky behaviors.

THE "WEATHERING" EFFECTS OF STRESS

People living in poor neighborhoods often look older than their age. The most likely cause is the incredible stress they must endure day in and day out. Arline Geronimus calls the grinding stress of being poor and marginalized "weathering"—likening it to the damaging effects of exposure to wind and rain on houses.[103] Stress is the way the neighborhood literally "gets under the skin of poor people," damaging their health in myriad ways. Those living in concentrated poverty are bombarded by stress. High crime rates, noise, overcrowding, unemployment, shortages of stores, and poor public services are all stressors. Fear of becoming a victim is undoubtedly the greatest stressor, along with fear that one's children will be swept up in gangs or drugs.

Like all mammals, humans respond to stress with the "fight or flight" syndrome. The body goes through changes designed to mobilize energy and maximize the ability to run or fight, including a rush of hormones (epinephrine and nonepinephrine) that releases a second set of hormones called glucocorticoids. Because most stressors in modern life do not require, or even permit, a physical response, glucocorticoids can build up and damage our organs and immune systems.[104] Chronic stress causes cardiovascular diseases and premature death.[105] Repeated stress can result in allergic reactions to substances or conditions that were previously tolerated. (Stress is a well-known cause of asthma attacks.) Stress heightens the severity of the common cold.[106]

Everybody experiences a certain amount of stress in our fast-paced society. People who sense that they can do something about the situation experience much less debilitating stress, however, than people who feel helpless. Unfortunately, residents of high-poverty neighborhoods often develop a feeling of "learned helplessness"—the feeling that they can do little to control their environment. One benefit of moving from high-poverty to low-poverty areas is that families began to shed the fatalism that previously caused them to internalize stressful situations.[107] One fifty-two-year-old woman who moved from downtown Yonkers to a middle-class neighborhood said of her old apartment that "it was stressful just to walk out of that place. You were always scared for the kids. . . . You wake up stressed, you go to sleep stressed, you see all the garbage and the dealers. That is depressing. In a bad environment like that you say, 'What's the use of doing anything?'"[108]

Social ties can protect people from the effects of chronic stress and disease.[109] One study concludes that "the role of supportive social relationships in promoting health is one of the most thoroughly corroborated findings in social epidemiology."[110] Socially isolated people are two or three times more likely to die than people with strong networks and emotional supports. Social isolation is associated with cardiovascular disease, cancer, respiratory problems, and gastrointestinal disease, as well as smoking and drinking.[111] In *Bowling Alone,* Robert Putnam reports that deciding to join your first group will "cut your risk of dying over the next year in half."[112]

Residents of high-poverty neighborhoods have fewer social ties. Nearly half the residents of extreme-poverty areas in Chicago, for example, were not married to, living with, or steadily dating anyone. One in five had no "best friend." Two-thirds did not belong to any organization, such as a block club or fraternal group. Residents of poor neighborhoods socialize with people who are likely to have their own problems with unemployment and debts, only adding to their stress.[113]

The great public health reforms of the late nineteenth and early twentieth centuries, such as sanitary sewer and water systems, caused death rates to plummet in American cities.[114] It was thought that this would usher in a new age of health equality because everyone would benefit from the new public services and infectious disease rates would decline. It is now apparent that widening inequalities, including economic segregation, have created new health inequalities. The likelihood of being exposed to an infectious disease varies only moderately across different classes and communities. But once exposed, people's ability to fight it off varies tremendously. People living in areas of concentrated poverty find themselves particularly vulnerable.[115] Injustices in health, which Martin Luther King called "the most shocking and the most inhumane," are once again on the rise.[116]

The middle-class reformers of a century ago worried that immigrant slum diseases such as tuberculosis could easily spread to middle-class neighborhoods. As the suburban middle class has steadily distanced itself from urban ghettos over the last century, this worry has abated. Nevertheless, research shows that diseases incubated in urban ghettos can spread even to wealthy suburbs. No community is an island. The act of fleeing unhealthy conditions in inner urban areas can also exact its own toll.

Concentrated poverty can incubate epidemics of infectious diseases that we thought modern societies had nearly eliminated, like tuberculosis (TB). Known as the white plague, TB was the leading cause of death in the United States until the 1930s. In most human populations, many people are infected, but the disease remains dormant in unstressed people with healthy immune systems. Improved living and working conditions caused TB rates to drop dramatically in the twentieth century, prompting the surgeon general to call for the complete elimination of the disease in 1960. As Deborah and Rodrick Wallace show, however, TB rates soared in New York between 1978 and 1990.[117] They document how New York City cut back on fire service for the South Bronx, leading to an epidemic of fires that forced many people out of their homes. The resulting disruption of community ties and overcrowding created ideal conditions for the spread of TB (and AIDS).

Also, diseases incubated in urban ghettos spread along commuting lines to the suburbs. In a careful examination of twenty-four counties in the greater New York metropolitan area, the Wallaces found that the outward spread of TB and AIDS from the inner city was highly correlated with a county's commuting patterns into Manhattan.[118] Looking at eight metropolitan areas, they found significant variation, but Detroit, St. Louis, and Washington, DC, closely resembled the New York pattern.[119] Further research determined that infectious diseases reaching a threshold in one city can spread through migration to other metropolitan areas. The authors sum up their findings this way: "The markers of urban decay diffuse from the inner city through the suburban counties in proportion to the contacts (index of commuting) and local susceptibility (poverty rate). Even rich counties face an incidence of these markers determined by the incidence of the inner city. Essentially, the American system of apartheid (that combination of segregation and targeting of the segregated population) has turned around and bitten the middle and upper classes."[120]

Even though inner-city epidemics can spread to the suburbs, most suburbanites enjoy healthy environments with little overcrowding and plenty of greenery, sunshine, and clean air. Those with private health insurance have access to the best health care in the world. They nonetheless face health risks in their environment that often go unrecognized.

The automobile is by far the greatest threat to suburban health. The average American trip to work increased 37 percent between 1983 and 1995 (to 11.6 miles).[121] Overall use of the automobile has increased even more as spread-out destinations require more car trips. Between 1969 and 1995, total vehicle miles increased a whopping 267 percent.[122] Women do most of the family errands, often engaging in what transportation planners call "trip-chaining," zig-zag drives to do errands on the way home from work. Americans spend an average of thirty-two hours a month behind the wheel, with suburbanites driving three times as much as residents of pedestrian neighborhoods.[123] The increased vehicle miles, caused in part by suburban sprawl, harms air quality. One study found that vehicle-related air pollutants cause 20,000 to 40,000 cases of chronic respiratory illness each year.[124]

People may move to the suburbs to escape urban dangers, but twice as many people die from traffic accidents as from homicides. Traffic accidents are the leading cause of death for those aged one to twenty-four. Over 3 million people are injured in traffic accidents every year. The crash rate for teens is four times that for other drivers. Most murder victims are killed by their relatives or acquaintances, but traffic deaths are indiscriminate. A recent study of eight metropolitan areas concluded that even though rates of homicide by strangers are higher in central cities than in outer suburbs, the much higher rates of traffic fatalities in outlying areas swamps this effect — making outlying suburbs less safe than central cities and inner suburbs.[125]

Time spent in traffic jams has other health effects. Commuting seems to elevate blood pressure, heart disease, back problems, lung cancer, and self-reported stress.[126] "Road rage" is now part of the American lexicon.[127] Long commutes leave less time to relax with family and friends. The *Journal of the American Medical Association* editorialized that the American obesity epidemic stemmed partly from reliance on the car and that a solution would require "substantial changes in community or regional design."[128] Each extra degree of sprawl is associated with more weight, less walking, and higher blood pressure. Someone living in the sprawled out Geauga County outside Cleveland will weigh 6.3 pounds more than if that same person lived in compact Manhattan.[129]

The spread-out nature of suburbs also undermines the sociability that is so connected to good health.[130] The elderly and children under sixteen who cannot drive can be remarkably isolated in the suburbs. Those who do drive do not have the chance encounters made possible by the front stoop or sidewalk. As Jane Jacobs put it, "Lowly, unpurposeful, and random as they may appear, sidewalk contacts are the small change from which a city's wealth of public life may grow."[131]

ACCESS TO CONSUMER GOODS

People living in wealthy suburbs have different shopping experiences than those in poor inner-city neighborhoods. In the suburbs, people meet their day-to-day needs in stores strung out along commercial strips and make major purchases in big-box superstores or shopping centers. Shopping centers provide huge parking lots. Many stores on commercial strips have drive-up windows. The dominant chain stores are new and modern. The supermarkets are huge, use the latest technology, and offer specialized foods like sushi and live lobsters. Shopping centers include a dazzling array of stores specializing in everything from chocolate chip cookies to massage oils and athletic shoes.

Residents of poor neighborhoods shop in stores located along neighborhood commercial strips. They occupy the first floors of older buildings. With the exception of an occasional chain drugstore, gas station, or fast-food outlet, most are small and locally owned. Department stores and major appliance stores are rare. The poor usually walk or take the bus to shop. The stores look old and are often run-down. Only a few use scanners for checkout, but many have cameras to prevent shoplifting.

Concentrated poverty areas have an undersupply of retail outlets, while wealthy areas have an oversupply. One early 1990s study of retailing in ninety-eight zip codes in seven Ohio cities found that the number of retail employees per capita fell from 67 per 1,000 residents in middle-class zip codes to 16 in extreme-poverty zip codes. Department stores disappeared entirely in the poorest zip codes. The authors called the bias in locations "disturbing."[132]

Although Economics 101 teaches us that supply meets demand, the metropolitan retail sector often violates this truism. Even taking reduced consumer spending per household into account, poor areas suffer from an undersupply of grocery stores, banks, and pharmacies, while areas of concentrated wealth have an oversupply. Poor central areas thus export shoppers and rich outlying areas import them.

This was not always the case. Until the 1950s, most cities attracted people from miles around to shop at department stores and farmers markets, but the automobile freed shopping from its central location, "malling" it to death.[133] Abandoned central-city and inner-ring suburban shopping strips are now com-

TABLE 3.1. Largest Retail Gaps in
Central Cities, 1998 Estimates ($ Billion)

New York	37.1
Chicago	9.9
Los Angeles	5.4
San Jose	3.9
Long Beach	2.8
Washington, DC	2.8
San Francisco	1.5
Detroit	1.4
Baltimore	1.3

Source: U.S. Department of Housing and Urban Development, *New Markets: The Untapped Retail Buying Power in America's Inner Cities* (Washington, DC: U.S. Government Printing Office, July 1999), 21.

mon. Now, residents of these areas must travel long distances to the suburbs to shop. As Table 3.1 shows, central cities have a huge "retail gap" between their residents' purchasing power and their total retail sales. This study also uncovered a retail gap of $8.7 billion in forty-eight inner-city zip codes, with many suffering from unmet retail demand of 50 percent or more.[134]

The unfortunate result, as one pioneering book on this topic put it, is that *the poor pay more.* They not only pay more, but they have fewer choices and poorer quality goods for which they must travel farther. The middle class often looks down on the poor for buying extravagant items like expensive sneakers, and it is true that poor people often engage in what David Caplovitz labeled compensatory consumption: "Since many have small prospect of greatly improving their low social standing through occupational mobility, they are apt to turn to consumption as at least a sphere in which they can make some progress toward the American dream of success."[135]

GROCERIES: THE POOR PAY MORE

Poor people can only cut their expenditures on food so much, even when they spend considerably less than middle-class families. That is why poor families spend 30 percent of their income on food, compared to the national average of less than 13 percent.[136] What people pay for groceries depends on where they live and shop. Comparing a standard basket of food items in different parts of the metropolitan area, a 1991 New York City Department of Consumer Affairs study concluded that a family of four living in a poor zip code pays 8.6 percent more than a family in a middle-class area.[137] A 1988 study of 600 food items in 322 supermarkets in ten metropolitan areas concluded that prices were 4 percent higher in central cities than in suburban locations.[138] Monsignor William J. Linder, director of the New Community Corporation (NCC) in Newark, testified to Congress that prices in NCC's Pathmark supermarket were 35 percent lower than in local stores.[139] The small markets also presented fewer choices, and their food was inferior. Finally, shoppers who have to rely on mass transit or taxis have extra transportation costs of $400 to $1,000 a year.[140]

Why are food prices higher in poor, central-city neighborhoods? Michael Porter of the Harvard Business School argues that corporations are overlooking profitable opportunities: "At a time when most other markets are saturated, inner city markets remain poorly served."[141] He implies that if governments simply educated entrepreneurs, the inner-city retail sector would blossom. Although it is certainly true that profitable opportunities are being overlooked— the Newark Pathmark is now one of the highest grossing in the nation—NCC had to put together a complicated deal involving eight different public and foundation subsidies to get Pathmark to locate there.[142] It would be wonderful if we could solve the problem by simply educating entrepreneurs, but the causes are more deeply rooted. Costs of insurance, theft, parking, and land assembly are higher. In addition, supermarket chain executives have negative perceptions of inner-city neighborhoods and may not want to violate their images as upscale retailers.[143]

The large supermarkets in the suburbs are marvels of modern retailing, offering about 30,000 separate items and operating on a high volume that enables them to prosper with a profit margin of less than 1 percent of sales. They buy in bulk and apply the latest technology, including automated just-on-time inventory systems. Inefficient, low-volume grocery stores serving low-income (and often low-density) neighborhoods must charge higher prices to remain in business. Central cities have been losing large supermarkets for years. Between 1970 and 1992, Boston lost thirty-four out of fifty big-chain supermarkets. Supermarkets in Los Angeles County fell from 1,068 to 694 between 1970 and 1990. Chicago lost half of its supermarkets.[144] As one study noted, "Ghetto residents simply do not have access to chain supermarkets."[145]

FINANCIAL SERVICES: THE RISE OF FRINGE BANKING

Banks have also pulled out of older urban areas. In the study of seven Ohio cities, middle-class zip codes averaged 396 banking establishments in 1993; extreme-poverty zip codes averaged 39.[146] Fringe lenders—pawnshops, check-cashing outlets, payday lenders, and rent-to-own stores—have moved in to fill the vacuum. Pawnbrokers may seem like relics of a bygone era, and pawn-broking did decline from the 1930s to the 1970s. Since then, however, pawn-brokers have rebounded, doubling between 1985 and 1992. By 2002, the number of check-cashing stores had reached 11,000, doubling the number from the previous five years. Pawnshops and check-cashing outlets are spreading from poor urban neighborhoods to inner-ring suburbs, following well-traveled roads.[147] According to a Fannie Mae study, fringe lenders process 280 million transactions a year, charging $5.45 billion in unnecessarily high fees.[148]

Financial services are a necessity, not a luxury, in modern society. Workers are mainly paid by check, and they must pay their bills by check or money order. Access to credit is vital for participating in consumer culture. Most people could not buy a house, go to college, or own a car without borrowing. Families need to buy expensive items when they are young and have relatively low incomes. Most families acquire their biggest asset by taking out a mortgage to buy a house. People rely on home equity and small business loans to start up businesses. For all these reasons, banks are essential to community stability. When they pull out, the neighborhood declines.

Although most people meet their financial needs at traditional banks, those living in poverty neighborhoods often obtain financial services from more expensive alternative institutions that offer fewer services and charge higher fees. Check-cashing outlets do not offer checking accounts, mortgages, or small business loans. They specialize in cashing checks, generally charging from 1.5 to 3 percent of the amount of the check. This costs a person earning $20,000 a year about $400. (Check cashing is free to those with checking accounts.) Pawnshops offer consumer loans secured by property. Most states regulate pawnshops, but still many charge 200 percent a year for a loan. Rent-to-own shops also are springing up in low-income neighborhoods to enable customers to rent furniture or appliances for low weekly payments and then take ownership at the end of, say, ninety weeks. A New Jersey study found that they charged an average interest rate of 88 percent a year. No wonder they are called "rent-to-moan."[149]

Why do people in low-income central-city neighborhoods turn to these institutions? According to Edward Banfield, poor people are "radically improvident"—that is, they buy things on impulse and do not save for the future.[150] Statistical studies, however, show that poor families are no more wasteful than other families.[151] Most poor people do not save or bank at conventional financial institutions because their incomes are too low and unstable. People who earn near the minimum wage are forced to live hand to mouth. They cannot open up checking accounts, because checking accounts require minimum balances. The growth in the number of working poor, who find it nearly impossible to save, largely accounts for the growth of fringe banking.[152]

The problem of bank redlining has been well documented. After controlling for other factors, studies have shown that many banks discriminate against minorities and minority neighborhoods in their mortgage lending.[153] It is perfectly legal for banks to discriminate against low-income neighborhoods if they have good business reasons not to lend. Many banks have closed branches in low-income neighborhoods.[154] As conventional lenders have withdrawn, a two-tiered financial services marketplace has emerged: one for areas of concentrated poverty, and one for the rest of society. Children in poor neighborhoods grow up not even knowing what the inside of a bank looks like, reinforcing the isolation of low-income families from the economic mainstream.[155]

THE FINANCIAL BURDEN OF SUBURBAN FLIGHT

One great puzzle is why, as family incomes have grown in the past generation, more middle-class families have found themselves in financial stress, even bankruptcy. Even though wages have stagnated since the 1970s, family incomes have grown because more women are working. Between 1973 and 2001, real median family income increased 23.6 percent, from $41,900 to $51,407 (although those in the bottom half did not do nearly as well). So why are approximately 40 percent of American households spending more than they take in each year, producing rising family debt?[156] In 2001, household debt was over $8 trillion, up from $3.7 trillion in 1990, and the average household devoted one-seventh of its disposable income to debt payments.[157] If present trends persist, one out of every seven families with children will have declared bankruptcy by the end of the decade.[158] What explains "a 255 percent increase in the foreclosure rate, a 430 percent increase in the bankruptcy rolls, and a 570 percent increase in credit card debt" since 1980?[159]

A popular book argues that Americans have been infected with "affluenza," "a painful, contagious, socially transmitted condition of overload, debt, anxiety, and waste resulting from the dogged pursuit of more."[160] The implication is that Americans are spending themselves into financial disaster buying unneeded luxuries, as if a mysterious moral breakdown has swept through the middle class. A "simple living" movement has emerged to share tips on how to simplify life and live on less. If only a few families were experiencing financial stress, we could attribute it to moral failure. But when financial stress has spread to millions of families, there must be structural causes rooted in the nature of suburban middle class life, rising economic segregation, and sprawl.[161]

At first blush, economically advantaged suburbs, with their plentiful retail outlets, banks, and supermarkets, would seem to offer many advantages for keeping spending down. But suburban life also generates pressures to spend more money to meet basic needs. The main culprits are housing and transportation. The rising cost of housing is the strongest force unbalancing family budgets. As family spending on food, clothing, and appliances fell, spending on housing expenses soared, so that housing now represents one-third of all consumer expenditures. Between 1990 and 2001, residential mortgage debt doubled from $3.8 billion to $7.6 billion.[162] In 1983, the typical family comprising a married couple with children bought a house for $98,000. Fifteen years later that same family paid on average $175,000 for a house (adjusted for inflation). The proportion of *middle*-class families that are considered "house poor," spending over 35 percent of the their incomes on housing expenses, doubled over the past generation.[163]

Why is housing eating up middle-class family budgets? Some people point to increasing home sizes and expensive amenities, but this is a small part of the story. Most families buy older homes whose median size has increased only modestly over the past two decades.[164] The cost of the physical house has gone up only slightly. The real cause of soaring housing costs is the bidding war for homes in safe neighborhoods with good schools, low crime, and proximity to jobs. More dollars are chasing a relatively fixed supply. Twenty million women entered the workforce in the past generation because they recognized that living in a safe neighborhood with good schools would make a big difference in the quality of their families' lives.[165] Second incomes have become essential ammunition in the bidding wars for the best residential locations:

> Individual parents sought out homes they thought were good places to bring up kids, just as their parents had done before them. But as families saw urban centers as increasingly unattractive places to live, the range of desirable housing options began to shrink and parents' desire to escape failing schools began to take on new urgency. Millions of parents joined in the search for a house on a safe street with a good school nearby. Over time, demand heated up for an increasingly narrow slice of the housing stock.[166]

Undoubtedly, good schools are a primary motivating factor. Studies show that school quality is the single most important determinant of housing prices. The same house, located in two different school districts, can vary by tens of thousands of dollars.[167] The second most important factor is crime. As we will show in the following section, crime rates vary tremendously across communities. Although the crime rate has fallen steeply in the past decade, the fear of crime is still great, partly because the media portray cities as even more dangerous than they are.[168]

But if demand for housing in good locations has soared, why have developers not increased the supply, bringing the price back into equilibrium? Developers have responded in ways that make the overall problem worse by creating exclusive upper-middle class communities, sometimes gated, that enable families to separate themselves from the problems of concentrated poverty and urban decay. About 8 million Americans now live in gated communities.[169] The number of exclusive enclaves is limited by definition. Not everyone can live in a community where, in the words of Garrison Keillor, "all the children are above average."

Rising economic segregation drives up home prices. Wealthy and middle-class families are willing to spend more to escape the problems associated with high-poverty neighborhoods. They are moving to outlying suburbs to escape crime and bad schools. It is hard to say exactly how much of the demand for suburban housing represents "flight from blight" instead of a simple matter of taste for housing further out; whatever the reason, it clearly contributes to Americans' massive mortgage debt.[170]

The second biggest drain on family budgets is transportation, representing about one-fifth of the typical family's budget. Since the 1930s, family spending on transportation has increased an astounding 500 percent (controlling for inflation).[171] Private automobiles have become a necessity, not a luxury. As one author put it: "The shift to the suburbs, motivated in large part by the search for safe neighborhoods and decent public schools, had made the private automobile a necessity, and the emergence of the two-income family has tended to make two cars a necessity."[172] Few suburbanites can take public transit to work or shopping, and few suburbs have bike paths; many do not even have sidewalks. The average cost of owning a car was 53 cents per mile in 1997.[173] A family must shell out $10,600 to drive two cars 10,000 miles a year each. More than half of all families with car payments spend more than they earn, compared with the national average of 40 percent.[174] Urban households, in contrast, can often shed one or even two cars, saving thousands of dollars a year.[175]

Many years ago, John Kenneth Galbraith observed that booming private consumption contrasts with a starved public sector in our affluent society.[176] The lack of public amenities in the suburbs pressures families to spend more. Many suburbs have no public transit and lack community pools or parks, compelling suburban families to pay for private clubs and large backyards. Public schools are the one crucial exception. Middle-class parents pay high housing costs and property taxes to send their kids to good public schools. If they stay in the city, they often pay high private school tuition. Either way, they are putting additional strain on the family budget.

CRIME AND CONCENTRATED POVERTY

In Tom Wolfe's novel *The Bonfire of the Vanities,* Sherman McCoy, a wealthy investment banker living in a $2.6 million Park Avenue apartment, mistakenly drives his $48,000 Mercedes into the South Bronx and gets lost. The East Side and South Bronx may be only a few miles apart, but Wolfe shows that they might as well be on different planets. Wolfe brilliantly conveys the fear that envelops Sherman and his companion, Maria, as they extricate themselves from the chaotic streets of the Bronx. "Maria wasn't saying a word. The concerns of her luxurious life were now tightly focused. Human existence had but one purpose: to get out of the Bronx."[177] In a panic, they run over a young black man, setting in motion a plot that enables Wolfe to bring the separate societies of New York into crazy confrontations with each other.

Wolfe's novel assumes the well-established generalization that crime rates vary in different parts of the city. In the 1920s, University of Chicago sociologists found that juvenile delinquency rates were highest in the "zone of transition" surrounding the downtown, with crime falling as one moved farther from the center. High crime rates persisted even as the population of these areas changed from primarily Irish in 1900 to Italian and Polish in the 1920s, blacks in the 1950s, and Hispanics in the 1980s. One characteristic that did not change is that these areas always had high concentrations of poor people.

Although the dramatic drop in crime in the United States during the 1990s was good news for everyone, the relationship between place and crime remains strong. Nationwide, after peaking in 1991, the violent crime rate fell 28.9 percent by 2000. Property crime rates followed a similar pattern.[178] The experts are still debating why, but three frequent explanations are the booming economy, the decline of the crack trade, and the increased effectiveness of policing. The good news is that crime fell faster in central cities than in suburbs. The bad news is that central-city crime rates are still three times those of suburbs. Moreover, many inner-ring suburbs now suffer from higher crime rates than their central cities.

Crime damages the quality of life. High crime rates mean high rates of crime victimization. Fear of crime makes some people prisoners in their own homes. (Even in the worst neighborhoods, criminals represent only a tiny minority of the population, but they can make life miserable for the overwhelming majority of law-abiding citizens.) The risk of victimization is substantially higher in crime-prone neighborhoods.[179] In 2000, the property crime victimization rate was 35.6 percent higher in cities than in suburbs.[180] The difference is even greater for violent crime. Strangers committed less than half of all violent crimes in 2000.[181] The criminal and the victim usually know each other. Most violent crimes occur near where they both live. Violent crime typically involves people of the same race; so-called zebra crimes, black on white or white on black, are uncommon.

The issue of race and crime is a volatile topic. Young black males commit a disproportionate share of violent crimes, leading many people to think that black communities harbor a subculture of crime.[182] After controlling for other variables, such as concentrated poverty, researchers find that race alone has little effect on the likelihood of committing crimes or of being a crime victim.[183] Blacks living in higher-income census tracts, like whites in such areas, experience low rates of homicide; only blacks living in concentrated poverty areas suffer from higher levels of homicide victimization.[184] The coincidence of race and crime is partly a by-product of whites' ability to flee high-crime areas; low incomes and housing discrimination prevent blacks from doing so.[185]

If the link between concentrated poverty and crime cannot be explained by racial subcultures, then what can explain it? Research supports two main answers: blocked opportunity and social disorganization.

BLOCKED OPPORTUNITY AND CRIME

People turn to crime when limited opportunities prevent them from obtaining material goods and respect through conventional channels.[186] Residents of poor neighborhoods may be isolated from economic opportunities, but they are still enveloped by consumer culture. The average American, including the poor, sees 38,000 television commercials a year.[187] Television stimulates consumption regardless of income.[188] As Juliet Schor puts it, "For many low-income individuals, the lure of consumerism is hard to resist. When the money isn't there, however, feelings of deprivation, personal failure, and deep psychic pain result. In a culture where consuming means so much, not having money is a profound social disability."[189] Advertisers promote extravagant consumption patterns that only the middle and upper-middle classes can afford. In the 1980s, Nike conducted a sophisticated ad program using star athletes, such as Michael Jordan, to establish the desirability of expensive athletic shoes. The program was so successful that it triggered a rash of "sneaker murders" in major cities.

Deprivation in the midst of affluence may lead people to crime as a way to acquire possessions and respect.[190] Indeed, crime does pay, at least in the short run. The 1989 Boston Youth Survey calculated that crime paid an average of $19 an hour. A survey of Washington drug dealers found an average pay of $30 for the hours worked, or the equivalent of $12 per hour full-time. Legitimate jobs paid less than half as much.[191] A life of crime poses long-term risks of imprisonment or bodily harm, but as we noted earlier, the shorter life expectancies of residents of high-poverty neighborhoods may lead them to discount such risks.

People, especially young men, also turn to crime because their jobs do not command respect or decent incomes. Factories used to provide young men with jobs that valued physical strength and male bonding. Service-sector jobs now value language skills over strength and often require men to take orders from women. Feeling inferior, many minority men respond with a cool pose and heightened sensitivity to signs of disrespect.[192] Anthropologist Philippe Bourgois lived for three and a half years in Spanish Harlem, listening to Hispanic youths talk about how their service-sector bosses disrespected their street culture. One young man, Primo, turned to the crack trade, speaking bitterly about how his boss did not want him to answer the phone because of his Puerto Rican accent. His friend Caesar confirmed Primo's experiences: "I had a few jobs like that [referring to Primo's 'telephone diss'] where you gotta take a lot of shit from bitches and be a wimp. I didn't like it but I kept on working, because 'Fuck it!' you don't want to fuck up the relationship. So you just be punk [shrugging his shoulders dejectedly]."[193] Caesar later joined Primo in the crack trade.

Thwarted in achieving status through conventional channels, poor people can become obsessed with achieving respect any way they can. Some walk with an exaggerated swagger and wear clothing that calls attention to themselves (although this behavior is hardly confined to the poor). Whites often perceive this as threatening, but it is actually a defense against feeling inferior. In the words of psychologist Richard Majors, the cool pose "may be his only source of dignity and worth as a man, a mask that hides the sting of failure and frustration."[194] Sociologist Elijah Anderson describes how poor young men are hypersensitive to any signs of "dissing." They may respond violently to someone who fails to make room on the sidewalk or who maintains eye contact too long. Others must be prepared to use violence defensively in order to survive.[195] As Douglas Massey puts it, "Asking residents of poor neighborhoods to choose a less violent path or to 'just say no' to the temptation of violence is absurd in view of the threatening character of the ecological niche that they inhabit."[196]

SOCIAL DISORGANIZATION AND CRIME

The high crime rate in poor neighborhoods may also reflect inadequate or uncertain police protection. The use of computer mapping to target police resources on high-crime locations certainly suggests that police services can make a difference. At the same time, soaring expenditures for police and prisons, and a dramatic increase in prison populations, have not prevented the crime rate from remaining remarkably high in places.

A strong sense of community seems to set safer poor neighborhoods apart from the more dangerous ones. In addition to concentrated poverty, the other factor that is powerfully associated with neighborhood crime is social disorganization. In their classic 1942 work on Chicago, Shaw and McKay argued that low socioeconomic status, ethnic heterogeneity, and residential instability caused social disorganization, the key factor in high rates of delinquent crime.[197] Building on this tradition, a group of researchers funded by the MacArthur Foundation and the National Institute of Justice conducted a careful study of the role of neighborhood social organization in preventing crime in Chicago. Their work has advanced our knowledge of the contextual, or place-based, causes of crime.[198]

The central idea in the Chicago research was "collective efficacy," defined as the "ability of neighborhoods to realize the common values of the residents and maintain effective social controls."[199] Residents of 343 Chicago neighborhoods were asked questions about their neighborhood's collective efficacy, including whether they could trust their neighbors or count on them to help in threatening situations, such as when youths were hanging out on the street corner. Many Americans stereotype concentrated poverty areas as utterly lacking a sense of community. In fact, the residents of many poor communities have strong social ties. The problem is that these personal relationships may not promote social control—stopping kids from scrawling graffiti or getting into fights. Poor people do help each other to cope with situations over which they have little control.[200] But social networks in poor neighborhoods rarely connect with outside sources of influence that might help them, say, prevent a neighborhood fire station from being closed.[201]

The Chicago study found that collective efficacy was strongly associated with lower levels of violent crime, even after controlling for a wide range of other factors. Neighborhoods may have strong community organizations or numerous social service agencies, but if they lack collective efficacy, they will have elevated crime rates. The researchers warn, however, that poor neighborhoods cannot simply "bootstrap" themselves out of crime by developing collective efficacy. Concentrated disadvantage also undermines the potential for collective efficacy. Collective efficacy emerges "mainly in environments with a sufficient endowment of socioeconomic resources."[202] The researchers conclude by warning that "Recognizing that collective efficacy matters does not imply that inequalities at the neighborhood level can be ignored."[203]

CRIME IN THE SUBURBS

Moving to a far suburban location in order to live in a more secure neighborhood is rational in the short run. By moving away from criminals and avoiding high-crime areas, suburbanites substantially reduce their chances of becoming crime victims. Two factors limit this strategy, however. Crime follows people out to the suburbs, which may have weaker institutional resources for dealing with it than do central cities. And movement itself has costs. High rates of mobility can, ironically, nurture the very crime that families were trying to escape.

Fear of crime has motivated suburbanization and exaggerated suburban sprawl. Violent crime rates have a strong statistical association with increased movement out of central-city neighborhoods to the suburbs and decreased movement into high-crime areas. One study found that each additional reported crime produced roughly a one-person drop in city population.[204] Another study found that one-third of those moving from Baltimore to the suburbs "were moved to do so by their fear of crime."[205] Although the media exaggerate urban crime,[206] poor neighborhoods are more dangerous. People cannot be blamed for wanting to protect their families.

When concentrated poverty leads to high crime rates, it can wipe out home equity, leaving the elderly without the nest egg they were counting on for retirement. Declining property values reduce the fiscal capacity of central cities to address the issue. One study of Boston in the 1970s determined that a 10 percent reduction in crime would have increased property values by $95.6 million.[207]

It is difficult to put a price tag on the actions that people have taken to avoid high-crime areas, but it would certainly include the costs of moving and the destruction of social ties in the old neighborhoods. Fear of crime may even prevent suburbanites from enjoying the symphony or live theater in the city. The costs are especially great for women. Those who change their routines to avoid crime may become more fearful rather than less, setting a vicious circle in motion.[208]

Crime has moved along with poverty across city borders to the suburbs. Many inner-ring suburbs now have higher crime rates than their central cities, and they often have less ability to manage the problem. St. Louis has 123 independent police departments in the seven-county region.[209] Even though the City of St. Louis reported only 69 murders in 2003, it still had a relatively high violent crime rate. But eight suburban police departments reported even higher three-year averages.[210] Jurisdictions in the St. Louis area spent from $52 to $3,614 per capita on police. Starting pay ranged from $15,246 in Venice to $50,000 in Brentwood, which is located in the heart of the suburban retail corridor and has plenty of sales tax revenues to boost its budget. Perversely, the amount these 123 jurisdictions spend on law enforcement is inversely proportional to the crime rate. Nine of the top ten departments in terms of pay have violent crime rates of less that 2 per 1,000 population, whereas eight of the ten lowest-paying departments have violent crime rates over 26 per 1,000 population.

Needless to say, as crime rates rise in inner-ring suburbs, families want to move further out. Highly publicized crimes in well-to-do suburbs, however, have caused suburbanites to question whether distance really will insulate them. Outer-ring suburbanites are generally much safer than residents of central cities or older suburbs, but suburban crime is still a problem. In the 1990s, homicide and robbery rates fell more rapidly in cities than in suburbs, although they still remained substantially higher.[211]

The April 1999 rampage at Columbine High School in Littleton, Colorado, riveted national attention. Two alienated teenagers killed twelve students and a teacher before turning their guns on themselves. Less than a year later, two Columbine High sweethearts were shot to death in a sandwich shop. The growth of suburban gangs in the 1990s is well documented.[212] Annual crime surveys show rising rates of violence in the suburbs.[213] In the 1999 survey, 25 percent of central-city students reported the presence of gangs, but so did 16 percent of suburban students. Though 15 percent of central-city students said that they knew someone who brought a gun to school, so did 12.3 percent of suburban students. About as many suburban students (14.5 percent) reported being crime victims as urban students (14.6 percent). Many suburban schools have felt compelled to ban gang insignia, install metal detectors, and issue ID cards. Wayne Doyle, a school superintendent in suburban Pittsburgh, observed, "In some areas, people are saying, 'Well, that's happening in the city, but it won't happen here.' Others are being more realistic and realizing that it can happen anywhere."[214]

Juvenile crime is more prevalent in the suburbs than the official statistics indicate because police have discretion over vandalism, graffiti, and public drinking, and don't always make arrests for these crimes or even record them. Although the police are known to discriminate on the basis of race, they also discriminate on the basis of place. Beat police view "all persons encountered in bad neighborhoods . . . as possessing the moral liability of the area itself."[215] The Seattle Youth Survey reported that 43 percent of boys living in poor neighborhoods said they had not done what the police charged them with, compared with 25 percent of the boys from high-income areas. Boys from poor neighborhoods were significantly more likely to get a police record than boys from wealthy areas, even when they committed the same number of delinquent acts.[216]

Many people feel that suburban crime has "spread" from criminal subcultures in the inner city. Many adults find it disturbing that suburban teens imitate the clothes, speech, and mannerisms of ghetto youth, wearing baggy pants slung down low on their hips and expensive basketball shoes, listening to "gansta" rap music. Such suburban wannabes seem determined to upset their parents by bringing ghetto culture to the suburbs. Although some inner-city kids do commit crimes in the suburbs,[217] suburban crime is largely homegrown. Suburban gangs have their own distinctive profiles.[218] Teen bonding can become problematic when responsible adults set few limits. In cities and suburbs alike, sustained attachment to competent and caring adults protects teens.[219] Ghetto men, ashamed of their inability to support a family, withdraw from family life. Single mothers struggle, often without success, to control adolescent boys. In wealthy suburbs, the parents work too much instead of too little, leaving them less time to spend with their children.[220]

Ultimately, suburbanites pay for the crime they left behind in the form of higher state taxes to fund bloated state prison systems, which now have a nominal cost of $150 billion a year, or $545 per person. The National Institute of Justice estimated that the actual cost, taking into account lost earnings, legal expenses, and intangibles such as the emotional costs to a murder victim's family, is three times larger.[221] Americans also spend lavishly on private security. By 1990, 2.6 percent of the U.S. workforce had private security jobs, double the share in 1970, and more than the public security share. Fear of crime promotes gun ownership, which has increased the number of accidental deaths, suicides, and homicides rather than making society safer.[222]

THE VICIOUS CIRCLE OF INEQUALITY

The rise of income inequality in the United States has triggered much discussion, but little attention has been paid to its spatial dimension. Economic segregation has had devastating consequences. One study of 11,000 male workers in Los Angeles County calculated that statistically "moving" a person with the same education, skills, and demographic characteristics from a low-poverty area into a high-poverty area lowered his or her wages by 15 percent (from $20,000 to $17,000).[223] If that same person spent one-third of her income on groceries the 8 percent higher prices in the inner city would cost her $453 more per year. Using a check-cashing outlet would cost her another $340 (2 percent charge). And if she owned a home worth $50,000, she would pay $200 more to insure it in a low-income zip code.[224] Finally, she would pay 50 percent higher property taxes.

Although this is only a hypothetical example, the costs to a person earning $20,000 a year in a low-poverty suburb who moved to a high-poverty central-city neighborhood would be as follows: loss of wages, $3,000; more expensive groceries, $453; added cost of cashing payroll checks, $340; more expensive home owners' insurance, $200; and higher property taxes, $600, for a total of $4,593. In short, such costs represent a 23 percent tax on low-income people, not counting the many hard-to-quantify costs that we have already discussed, such as exposure to crime, unhealthy environments, inferior public services, heightened stress, and alienation from society and politics. Such costs widen already great inequalities of place.

This analysis skirts another crucial point. By discussing employment, health, retail services, and crime one by one, we have not touched on the ways in which they form a seamless web. Each is a *cause,* not just an effect, of economic segregation and suburban sprawl. Each influences the other in complex ways, generating vicious circles that widen regional inequalities. Poor fire protection can lead to neighborhood instability, causing higher rates of disease and outmigration. With fewer customers, the retail sector declines, reducing job prospects in the area. With rising unemployment, the crime rate soars, which only encourages more families to move out. To speak of these spatial effects as "externalities," as economists do, wrongly implies that they are minor problems that government can fix with short-term policy interventions. In fact, they are ubiquitous, complexly intertwined, and difficult to change.

THE POLITICAL EFFECTS OF ECONOMIC SEGREGATION

Economic segregation and sprawl also harm our political system by deforming political participation and posing major policy challenges. As spatial inequalities widen, people vote with their feet instead of getting involved to solve the problems. Economic segregation elevates the "exit" option over that of "voice" and sustained political participation.[225] The secession of the successful undermines political participation both in concentrated poverty areas and in sprawled out affluent neighborhoods. By frustrating attempts at creating effective public policies, it feeds already high levels of political cynicism.

Concentrated-poverty areas have lower levels of civic participation, including voting and belonging to voluntary organizations.[226] This may help explain why voter turnout has fallen faster in central cities than in the nation as a whole.[227] People in poor neighborhoods generally have a lower sense of collective efficacy about politics, just as they do about crime. Poor neighborhoods are less stable (turnover undermines civic participation), and fear of crime prevents people from going to public meetings. Poor neighborhoods make few campaign contributions, and they lack connections to powerful private and public actors outside the neighborhood. Capturing political office is simply not worth as much in poor neighborhoods and fiscally strapped central cities, reducing the motivation to participate in electoral politics.[228]

Economic segregation also undermines party competition, a key ingredient in a healthy democracy. There is nothing like a good political fight to get people engaged. Political parties mobilize citizens into politics around differences in class, race, and ethnicity. Economic and social inequality is a key source of political conflict. As economic classes have sorted themselves geographically, this source of political conflict has disappeared from local politics. Economic homogeneity undermines party competition, the lifeblood of politics, in both central cities and suburbs.

As central cities have become poorer and less white, the Democratic Party has become more predominant. In the 2000 presidential election, Al Gore won 80.4 percent of the vote in New York City, 82.4 percent in Chicago, and 94.8 percent in Detroit.[229] When one party becomes so entrenched, it lacks the incentive to mobilize new voters, at least in local elections.[230] One-party politics becomes almost "issueless." Mayors such as Detroit's Coleman Young and Newark's Sharpe James overstayed their welcome and became entrenched and moribund. As V. O. Key observed, the main losers in one-party politics are the have-nots, because the monopoly party has no incentive to take up their issues.[231] The fact that some of these monopolists are African Americans does not invalidate Key's generalization.[232] (Some cities have competitive mayoral politics, of course. Both New York and Los Angeles, for example, have had vigorously competitive races in recent years.)

Political theorists have long argued that democracy flourishes in small, homogeneous republics. For this reason, suburbs have often been portrayed as models of democracy. Research does show that people living in small cities participate at higher rates than those in large cities.[233] On the other hand, suburban life reduces the time people have to engage in community affairs. As

Robert Putnam noted, "each additional ten minutes in daily commuting time cuts involvement in community affairs by 10 percent."[234]

The economic and racial homogeneity of suburbs is at the root of their civic disengagement. Eric Oliver shows that, regardless of their individual characteristics, citizens in more economically homogeneous places participate less in civic affairs and vote less than citizens in more economically diverse places.[235] In some suburbs, the biggest issue is what color to paint the benches in front of city hall. Indeed, as Oliver observes, if everyone in a community is just like everyone else, there is hardly any need for representative political institutions. Anyone can represent the entire citizenry. No suburb has reached this point, but many are rapidly approaching it. If local government is a training ground for American democracy, as Tocqueville once observed, that ground is softening because it lacks the conflicts and debates necessary for producing democratic leaders and active citizens.

Economic segregation also frustrates effective public policies. Declining trust in government and in its ability to solve society's problems is well documented.[236] Some of the blame lies with the media and those on both the left and the right who have relentlessly attacked government. But some blame stems from the ways that rising economic segregation has stymied public responses to pressing social problems. Medicaid was supposed to improve the health of poor Americans, but the severe shortage of doctors in poor areas has made the program less effective than it could be, even though we spend over $226 billion a year on it. The health of people living in concentrated-poverty neighborhoods approaches third world conditions. Section 8 housing vouchers were supposed to help low-income families integrate into mainstream society, yet most voucher recipients end up in segregated low-income areas with poor schools and high crime.[237] This is like giving someone food stamps but allowing them to only choose goods placed on the bottom shelf. It's better than starvation or malnutrition, but not what it could or should be.

The debilitating effects of economic segregation are most telling in the education system. Schools with large concentrations of poor students find it difficult to achieve good results on standardized tests, even when they spend as much per pupil as better off suburban schools — which they rarely do. Demanding that low-income schools match the test scores of privileged schools is wildly unrealistic. President Bush's "No Child Left Behind" policy ignores the fact that children are left behind primarily by being isolated in areas of concentrated disadvantage. Until government policy addresses the underlying dynamics of poverty concentration, many failing public schools will not succeed.[238]

Americans trust local government more than the federal government or even the states. Many say federal responsibilities should be shifted onto the localities. Unfortunately, the governments closest to the people also experience the greatest gaps between the problems they face and the resources they can deploy to address them. Local governments have the greatest needs and the fewest resources. They cannot realistically deal with these problems until the nation commits itself to lowering the level of economic segregation.

The Roads Not Taken
How Government Policies Promote Economic Segregation and Suburban Sprawl

Martin Wuest, an electrical engineer, gets up at 3:15 every morning so he can get to work at Pericom, a semiconductor company in San Jose, California. He lives in Los Baños, an old farm town eighty-six miles from San Jose. If he leaves his house at 3:50 AM, he can usually make the drive in ninety minutes. If he leaves later, it takes a lot longer. He gets to his office by 5:30 AM. More than one-third of the residents of Los Baños join Wuest in rising before dawn to fight their way through heavy freeway traffic to commute to Silicon Valley, the high-tech region around San Jose. Many of these families moved to Los Baños because they could not afford to live any closer. The median house price in Silicon Valley rose from $397,533 in October 1999 to $530,000 a year later, and the average monthly rent for an apartment is over $1,000. To accommodate them, Los Baños has allowed developers to build large tracts of single-family homes and apartments that cost less than half the price of those in Silicon Valley. Although the people living in Los Baños pay lower housing costs, they face long commuting times, less family time together, and more family stress.[1]

Few would dispute our contention that place matters in people's lives, but some would disagree with how we interpret this claim. Some would say, "Sure, some places are better than others, but this only reflects individual preferences and ability to consume. It has always been this way. If you make money, you can afford to live in a good neighborhood. If you are poor, you can't. It is only natural that people of different economic classes sort themselves out into different neighborhoods. It is a matter of personal preferences, market forces, and cultural values." In this view, the high-technology boom caused housing prices to soar in Silicon Valley. Given his income level, Wuest chose to trade longer commuting times for lower housing costs. Some would say that this was simply a rational decision, not the result of any plot to constrain his choices.

In this chapter, we dispute the contention that sprawl and segregation simply result from rational decisions made in the marketplace. Geographic sprawl and spatial inequalities were not the inevitable result of high-tech growth in the San Jose metropolitan area. Instead, these outcomes were shaped by a whole series of government actions, ranging from freeway construction and tax policies to local zoning policies, as well as inactions, particularly the failure to build adequate supplies of moderately priced rental housing, public transit, and socially integrated communities. Although Martin Wuest undoubtedly made the best choice from among the options available to him, previous political decisions had a huge impact on what these options would be.

HOW FEDERAL POLICIES PROMOTED ECONOMIC SEGREGATION AND SUBURBAN SPRAWL

Government policies have helped to produce and aggravate metropolitan inequalities. A recent survey asked 149 leading urban scholars to identify the most important influences on American metropolitan areas since 1950. They identified "the overwhelming impact of the federal government on American metropolis, especially through policies that intentionally or unintentionally promoted suburbanization and sprawl."[2] Federal policies have had two major consequences. First, they have consistently favored investment in suburbs and disinvestment from central cities. These policies provided incentives for businesses and middle-class Americans to move to suburbs while deterring poor Americans from doing so. Government policies have also favored concentrating the poor in central cities.

Second, federal (and state) policies encouraged economic competition and political fragmentation *within* metropolitan areas, primarily by allowing "local autonomy" over taxation, land use, housing, and education, but also by failing to provide incentives for regional governance or cooperation. The power of each suburb to set its own rules and the competition among local governments for tax-generating development have powerfully promoted economic segregation and suburban sprawl. Both federal policies and the jurisdictional ground rules have created an uneven playing field that fosters segregation and sprawl.

THE FREE MARKET PERSPECTIVE

The conservative conventional wisdom has it the other way around: government policies are biased in favor of cities, wasting huge amounts of money in a futile effort to stem urban decline driven by powerful market forces. This misperception is rooted in historical amnesia and fails to appreciate the influence of government and the power of place.

Although government policies have long been biased against central cities, these biases were especially pronounced from World War II through the 1960s. Once suburban sprawl and economic segregation had gained momentum, the federal government did enact a series of policies to stem urban decline, such as urban renewal and revenue sharing with cities. But these policies were largely designed to protect central business districts, not reverse the dynamic of economic segregation and suburban sprawl. Only belatedly, and with few resources, did they even seek to address worsening conditions in central-city neighborhoods.

Many scholars have reinforced the conventional wisdom that suburbanization and economic segregation are the natural products of free marketplaces. They assume that people with similar incomes have similar preferences for lifestyles and for government services, thus confirming the folk wisdom that "birds of a feather flock together." It is only natural that rich people choose to live in the same suburban areas with other rich people. This perspective represents the way many people think about metropolitan development. Only by challenging this conventional wisdom can we overcome the widespread cynicism that government can do little to counter economic and racial segregation and metropolitan sprawl.

Those who defend economic segregation generally view it as an expression of individual choices made in a free market. In a provocative article in the conservative journal *National Review*, Llewellyn Rockwell argued that "the housing policy of a free society ought to be simple: people should be able to live where they want, using their own money and engaging in voluntary market exchanges." According to Rockwell, "markets mean choice, and with choice comes sorting. People tend to choose to work, socialize, and live with others in their own social, religious, cultural, and economic group. There's nothing wrong with that. In fact, it creates real diversity among neighborhoods." This has traditionally led to "neighborhoods centered on one group or another, whether WASP, Greek, Ukrainian, Italian, black, Chinese, or whatever."[3]

Accordingly, society actually has less economic and racial segregation than is ideal, because government has interfered in this "natural system" by engaging in "social engineering" that imposes poor people and racial minorities on communities that would otherwise choose to be more homogeneous. Those who defend segregation from this perspective view the outcome not just as maximizing efficiency and free choice but as creating a superior moral climate. Rockwell, for example, calls segregation a "natural pattern, a product of rational choice," which "makes possible strong communities."[4] Fred Siegel adds that sprawl is "an expression of the upward mobility and growth in home-ownership generated by our past half-century of economic success." Larger incomes require bigger homes on more land, forcing our metro areas to stretch out. Sprawl is "part of the price we're paying for creating something new on the face of the earth: the first mass upper-middle class."[5]

These commentators believe that economic segregation is morally just. For example, Howard Husock argues in a report for the conservative Heritage Foundation that "socioeconomic status is a universal sorting principle in American cities. People of like social rank tend to live together and apart from those of unlike rank." Moving to better neighborhoods is a mark of one's status, which, Husock argues, should be earned by hard work. Economic segregation reflects the rightful ability of those who have good values, and whose hard work and saving are rewarded by the market by allowing them to move into good neighborhoods. Those who lack good middle-class values, who are lazy and live only in the present, do not deserve to live in such neighborhoods. If left to the free market, they would not be able to afford to. Programs like the Department of Housing and Urban Development's (HUD's) Moving to Opportunity, which provides vouchers to low-income families so that they can pay for private apartments in better-off suburbs, violate this moral order. Subsidized low-income housing developments in middle-class neighborhoods are equally bad because they rob "the poor of the will and even the means to climb the neighborhood ladder on their own." They are, Husock says, an "ill-gotten gain," a "reward not commensurate with accomplishment."[6]

In a *New Republic* article entitled "Suburban Myth: The Case for Sprawl," Gregg Easterbrook acknowledges that the desire of white people to "escape contact with blacks" promotes suburbanization, but he argues that their primary motivation is the preference for "detached homes, verdant lawns [and] lower crime rates," which "represents a lifelong dream" to most Americans, regardless of race. People also move to suburbs to escape the "corruption and mismanagement" of urban governments, Easterbrook argues, especially "disastrous inner-city school systems." Acknowledging that suburban sprawl creates environmental problems, Easterbrook nevertheless believes that the benefits outweigh the costs. He associates cities with "high density tower housing" and "cramped quarters." In contrast, suburban housing tracts make widespread home ownership possible. Suburban shopping malls are a "furiously efficient means of retailing." Automobiles "promote economic efficiency and personal freedom" and, despite traffic congestion, typically get people to and from places more quickly than public transit would.[7] Freeways allow people to commute from homes in one suburb to jobs in another; subways and light railways, built along fixed corridors, do not offer nearly as much convenience and flexibility. Sprawl, he concludes, is "economically efficient."[8]

Some observers not only defend suburban sprawl but argue that central cities are becoming obsolete. In a popular book, *Washington Post* reporter Joel Garreau celebrated the emergence of "edge cities." Places such as the Gwinnett Place mall outside Atlanta, the Schaumburg area outside Chicago, the Bridgewater Mall area in central New Jersey, and Tysons Corner outside Washington, DC, constitute the "hearths of civilization," according to Garreau. "Americans are individualists," he writes. "The automobile is the finest expression of transportation individualism ever devised."[9] Thanks to cheap land, highway access, and distance from central cities, farmland and open space on the urban periphery have become attractive for development. Edge cities are now practically self-sustaining. People can live, work, shop, visit their doctors, eat at nice restaurants, and attend plays and movies in the suburbs. They no longer need a big, central urban hub. Moreover, Garreau says, none of this was planned by public officials or government bureaucrats. It came about because pioneering entrepreneurs recognized these exurban possibilities, invested in them, and attracted other entrepreneurs. What some view as ugly sprawl, sterile housing tracts, and congested highways, Garreau views as successful products of entrepreneurial innovation.

In this view, government policies that work against this logic of metropolitan growth and edge-city development are doomed to fail. Government should promote market forces, not work against them. For example, Tamar Jacoby and Fred Siegel argue that government efforts to regulate banks to lend in areas where they otherwise would not do so are misguided. Government bureaucrats, they say, create too many rules and obstacles, and do not understand how the private market works or the flexibility that individual entrepreneurs require. Government programs just thwart the entrepreneurial spirit of inner-city businesspeople.[10] Instead, Harvard Business School professor Michael Porter says, government should get out of the way and allow the "competitive advantage of the inner city" to foster economic improvements in poor urban neighborhoods.[11]

Scholars working from the free-market perspective recognize that most individual choices about where to live or locate their businesses are shaped by local government taxes, infrastructure, services, and schools. To incorporate the local public sector into their analysis, these scholars developed "public choice" theory. Its proponents view the multiplicity of local governments within metropolitan areas as creating an intergovernmental "marketplace" parallel to the private market. This promotes consumer choice. Just as shoppers can choose from among brands of towels, toothpastes, or television sets, households and businesses can choose where to live and locate from an array of cities and suburbs.[12] Each jurisdiction represents a distinct bundle of amenities and services at a distinct "price" in taxation. Because people have different tastes in cities, just as they have different tastes in clothing, public choice scholars view this arrangement as the most efficient way to allocate public goods and services.

Charles Tiebout's classic 1956 essay "A Pure Theory of Local Expenditures" provided the first systematic statement of this view: "The consumer-voter may be viewed as picking that community which best satisfies his preference pattern for public goods. . . . The greater the number of communities and the greater the variance among them, the closer the consumer will come to fully realizing his preference position."[13]

For public choice theorists, choosing a detergent and choosing a local government have much in common: "Individual choices differ for public goods and services as well as for private. Some consumers want more freeways; others want a rapid transit system instead. Some prefer local parks; others, larger private backyards."[14] Proponents of public choice theory view the competition among local jurisdictions as creating an efficient and responsive market for public services. In their view, interference by government bureaucrats and other special interests distorts the marketplace.[15]

Public choice theory justifies economic segregation on the grounds that people with similar tastes for public goods and a similar ability to pay for them will naturally congregate in local government jurisdictions that provide those goods. According to Robert Warren, public choice theory "assumes that a metropolitan area is composed of diverse communities of interests which are territorially distinct from one another and which have different preferences for goods and services in the public sector."[16] While acknowledging that regional governments may be more efficient in providing air pollution control, transportation, and hospital services, the public choice perspective argues that most services are best provided by local governments, because, according to Werner Hirsch, proximity leads to more "effective citizen-consumer feedback into the government sector," better management, less corruption, and greater efficiency.[17] In other words, competition forces each local government to be more efficient and more responsive to its citizens' concerns. If it does not meet their needs, people will move to a more responsive jurisdiction. Fragmented, competitive metropolitan areas provide a cornucopia of choices that maximize household satisfaction.

These critics believe that government can play a role in guiding metropolitan development, but that government should adapt to market trends (or, following public choice theory, imitate the market). To be sure, they recognize that unregulated markets can generate environmental problems, racial separation, and urban ghettos, but they think that any attempt to "cure" these ills will only make things worse by violating human nature and introducing inefficiencies into the market. A metropolitan-wide government, for example, would only eliminate or reduce consumer choice.

THE IMPORTANCE OF POLITICS AND GOVERNMENT IN SHAPING "FREE" MARKETS

The public choice perspective has two major flaws. The first is the assumption that markets are actually "free" of government influence. Although people do make real choices among alternatives in housing, business location, and other markets, government policies shape every aspect of how they make those choices and what they have to choose from. Indeed, government establishes the regulatory and legal framework that makes it possible to have functioning markets in the first place. The second major flaw is that public choice theory seems to work better for middle-class home owners than for the inner-city poor. It ignores all the other features of society that constrain or empower people's ability to choose. Most obviously, people with fewer means (or the wrong skin color) have a highly constricted range of choice. The market not only fails people who live in poverty; it punishes them through the negative effects of concentrated poverty.

Markets cannot be isolated from government, public policy, and politics. The "free market" is an abstraction, not a reality. For example, Husock views housing subsidies for the poor as an "ill-gotten gain" but is silent about housing subsidies for the rich. Consider an article that appeared in the *New York Times* headlined, "Expanding the Choices in Million Dollar Homes."[18] It described The Pinnacle, a cluster of new homes priced from $975,000 to $1.3 million, in Purchase, New York, a wealthy town in Westchester County. The *Times* did not describe the Pinnacle as a "subsidized" housing project, but its glowing description of the project unwittingly revealed how taxpayers underwrite the cost of luxury housing and suburbanization. The *Times* noted, "The project is on a 23-acre site, across the street from the 236-acre Silver Lake Preserve, a county-owned nature preserve." The article also gushed, "The project is only a few minutes' drive from the White Plains train station, and is within earshot of Interstate 684." (While the noise of the nearby freeway might detract somewhat from the pride of owning a million-dollar home, the convenient access to a major highway makes up for it.) Likewise, the taxpayer-subsidized Metro North commuter rail lines add significantly to The Pinnacle's value. The *Times* story did not mention another lucrative government subsidy. Pinnacle home buyers would get huge tax breaks on their property taxes and on the interest they pay on their mortgages. On a $1 million home, the home owner could expect an income tax savings (in effect, a federal subsidy) of $35,000 in the first year alone.

Similarly, in celebrating the emergence of edge cities, Garreau hardly acknowledges that they have grown up around and depend entirely on publicly funded highways and, in some cases, airports and other government facilities. Local governments do compete for residents and investors, but the rules of the game under which they do so are neither free nor fair. They do not give all people and places an equal chance to succeed. In fact, they are strongly biased away from central cities and toward suburban jurisdictions. For example, the view that suburban home ownership reflects people's cultural preferences ignores the reality that many people in post–World War II America would have preferred to remain in urban neighborhoods rather than move to suburbia. But government programs and private lenders for many years refused to provide mortgages to families who wished to purchase homes in the cities. They would provide loans to white families only if they would move to the suburbs. The white exodus from the cities was due in large part to these policies. Black families, meanwhile, often ended up renting apartments in the cities because banks refused to provide mortgages even to those who could afford to buy homes. Far from bowing to market forces, government policies have actually shaped them from the beginning.

Public choice theory's second flaw is that policy choices made at one point influence subsequent choices. It is important to recognize how the paths that were taken — or not taken — shape the options we have now. Although Easterbrook may be right that cars are now more efficient than public transit, he ignores how things would be different if, earlier in the twentieth century, we had expanded investment in public transit rather than withdrawing it. Residential development would be more compact, centered around mass transit nodes providing access to key destinations, and owning a car would be far less necessary for enjoying life. This basic decision about how to organize metropolitan life is just one way government and politics have shaped our metropolitan geography. Let us consider some others.

LOCAL GOVERNMENT FRAGMENTATION
AND LAND-USE CONTROL

Local jurisdictional arrangements propel economic segregation and suburban sprawl in the United States. Specifically, the wide latitude and autonomy that we grant to local governments has unfortunate consequences. They regulate land use, provide crucial public services (such as education and infrastructure), and finance their services with local taxes. As a result, local governments engage in a beggar-thy-neighbor competition with one another. In the competition for favored residents and investments, each jurisdiction has a strong incentive to adopt zoning and development policies that exclude potential residents with below-median incomes or who require more costly services. The better-off may view these people as "free riders" who do not pay enough taxes for the services they use. From the viewpoint of fiscal self-interest, this is a rational position. Widespread discriminatory practices in the rental, sales, and financing of housing reinforce this exclusion by price and income.[19] Similarly, each jurisdiction seeks new businesses that will pay more tax revenues than the costs of the services they will require. As the federal and state governments devolve responsibility for more programs to the local level, the fragmented nature of local government becomes even more important. This resulting dynamic strongly promotes economic segregation and suburban sprawl.

Out of this competition comes a pecking order of jurisdictions. Each tries to be more exclusive than the next. At the top end, exclusive and expensive suburbs provide their residents with excellent public services at a relatively small tax cost in relation to housing values and incomes. At the bottom, distressed suburbs and central cities provide housing of last resort for all those whom more affluent suburban jurisdictions can exclude by reason of low income, or race. Over time, the loss of well-to-do residents can undermine the ability of a city to attract commercial investments. Suburbs are arrayed according to the incomes of their residents and their commercial tax bases. Inner-ring suburbs that house working-class families with school-age children and that have little commercial wealth are not in a good position to compete in this intergovernmental marketplace. Businesses have also sought out, and sometimes even created, suburban jurisdictions to provide them with tax havens and few regulations, thus siphoning off badly needed business investment from other municipalities.[20]

Since the late 1940s, this dynamic has encouraged much of the mobile white middle class and, more recently, the black, Asian, and Hispanic middle class, to move to suburbs. Those rendered immobile by discrimination and low incomes, especially the minority poor, were constrained to live in expanding urban, and sometimes suburban, ghettos. At some distance from them, yet still within city limits, are middle-income households that, depending on local circumstances, chose to remain in the city. These include gradually shrinking white ethnic neighborhoods (whose residents may have loyalties to the local church or the neighborhood ethnic stores and culture), emerging immigrant enclaves, zones where young people seek to start their careers, and defended enclaves (such as gated communities) of the urban elite.

These ground rules also encourage towns and regions to engage in bidding wars for manufacturing plants, big-box stores like Wal-Mart and Target, shopping centers, industrial parks, luxury housing, and even sports franchises. For example, three adjacent cities in southern California (Oxnard, Ventura, and Camarillo) kept outbidding one another (with tax breaks) to attract large stores to their respective shopping centers. After several years of such maneuvering, one council member concluded, "this is not about creating new business. This is about spending $30 million to move two stores three miles."[21] The competition for business investment results in a "race to the bottom" in which the tax burden is gradually shifted from businesses to residents.[22]

The resulting development does little to help poor areas pull themselves up. After Detroit offered generous incentives for private companies to locate within the city, surrounding suburbs responded by offering the same incentives.[23]

Every other major democracy in Europe and Canada exercises greater national control over land use than does the United States.[24] Local municipalities in the United States retain great power over land use (as well as local schools). This control enables them to determine what kind of businesses and housing get built and who can afford them.[25] Of course, suburbanization could have happened in the absence of metropolitan political fragmentation. Cities could have expanded their boundaries to encompass the spreading of population and jobs. With some exceptions, this did not happen.

In the United States, local governments are not even mentioned in the U.S. Constitution. They are created by states. In the nineteenth century, state laws generally made it easy for growing central cities to annex new territory as their populations expanded. Early in the twentieth century, however, states revised their laws to make this more difficult and to enable residents of outlying areas to incorporate new suburban municipalities.[26] Although some cities (mostly in the South and West) retained the ability to annex adjacent suburban areas, most cities are trapped within their political boundaries.[27] States gave local governments the authority to tax, regulate land use, and establish their own public school systems. Instead of promoting metropolitan government and consolidation, these laws encourage balkanization.

Local governments use zoning laws, which divide localities into districts, or zones, to segregate land uses and to limit access of potential unwanted new residents and land uses. (Although free-market conservatives decry government intervention, only a few have said anything about the restrictive nature of suburban zoning laws.) Racial zoning, the American version of South Africa's apartheid system, was struck down by the Supreme Court in 1917, but the federal courts have upheld zoning based on economic distinctions.[28] Los Angeles passed the first zoning ordinance in 1909, creating zones for housing, light industry, and heavy industry. Later laws added zones for open space and retail shops. But later zoning laws went further, seeking to favor some kinds of housing over others. Some early planners described apartment buildings as "polluting" or "tainting" single-family residential areas.[29] In 1926, the U.S. Supreme Court (in *Euclid v. Ambler*) allowed the Cleveland suburb of Euclid to ban apartment buildings from neighborhoods with single-family housing. Zoning increasingly became a way for local governments to protect property values and to exclude "noxious" land uses, including apartment buildings.

States have the ultimate authority to regulate land use, but, encouraged by the federal government, they began to delegate that responsibility to local governments in the 1920s. Early state statutes were modeled on the 1924 *Standard State Zoning Enabling Act* and the 1928 *Standard City Planning Enabling Act* published by the U.S. Department of Commerce. By the late 1920s, 564 cities had zoning ordinances. The 1954 Housing Act provided federal funds for local, regional, and state planning and encouraged local zoning ordinances. By 1968, 65 percent of the 7,609 local governments in the nation's metropolitan areas had planning agencies that created and policed zoning laws.[30] Many federal task forces and commissions have recommended that Washington take a firmer stand on national land-use planning to promote efficient location of businesses and housing, to reduce geographic segregation based on income and race, and to protect the environment, but few of these recommendations have been accepted. In these and other ways, the federal government and the states have encouraged or condoned the nation's fragmented land-use practices and their social consequences.

Local zoning laws also allow municipalities to regulate the location and minimum lot size for various kinds of housing. Affluent suburbs have used "snob zoning" to limit housing for the poor. Many suburbs set minimum lot sizes (such as one-half acre per home) that increase the cost of housing and rule out the construction of dense housing—not just apartment buildings, but also bungalow-style single-family homes.[31] Intentionally or unintentionally (there is evidence of both), these zoning laws have the effect of excluding racial minorities, who generally have lower incomes than whites. Some suburbs that desire to limit school-age children, in order to avoid education costs, prohibit housing types favored by families with children.

Proponents of public choice theory believe that inequalities among local jurisdictions should balance themselves out over time as the market achieves "equilibrium." This means that land prices in the intergovernmental marketplace should rise in successful areas, reducing their attractiveness to residents and investors, who will then be attracted to poor areas, where prices have fallen. But as the previous discussion has shown, spatial inequalities have widened rather than narrowed. The competition among fragmented local governments has led to a vicious circle of rising spatial inequality.

THE EFFECTS OF FEDERAL PROGRAMS: STEALTH URBAN POLICIES

We normally think of urban policies as those directly targeted to cities or the urban poor. But virtually all federal policies, whatever their larger aims, have strong spatial effects that harm or benefit cities. (Acknowledging this, the Carter administration during the 1970s experimented with an "Urban Impact Analysis," which would enable policy makers to anticipate the negative impacts of various policies on cities and thereby lessen them.[32]) Many federal policies with profound impacts on cities and metropolitan development are implicit or indirect urban policies. Because many are invisible to people's political radar, they can be called "stealth urban policies."[33]

For example, when the New Deal initiated a large public works program during the 1930s to lift the nation out of the Depression, its primary goal was to create jobs. But a secondary effect was to lift up the cities, where most of the unemployed were located. Similarly, when the Reagan administration adopted policies to reduce inflation in the early 1980s that brought on a deep national recession, it harmed inner cities far more than other areas.[34] Because cities have a disproportionate share of low-income people, federal efforts to help poor people, such as Medicaid, food stamps, welfare, and job training programs, generally benefit cities more than suburbs. And when these programs are cut, poor urban neighborhoods are hurt the most.[35] Similarly, when the Bush administration declared a "war on terrorism" and created a "homeland security" program after the bombing of the World Trade Center on September 11, 2001, it had a disproportionate impact on American cities. The federal government required cities to dramatically increase security measures at airports, ports, and sporting events, and to improve emergency preparations around water systems, the emergency 911 telephone system, public health, and public safety, but failed to provide municipalities with adequate funds to buy equipment, or to add and train staff. Cities spent $70 million a week simply to comply with each "orange alert" security threat warning from the federal Department of Homeland Security.[36]

Here we examine four stealth urban policies: transportation, military spending, federal programs to promote home ownership, and federal efforts to reduce racial discrimination in housing. None of these policies was intended primarily to shape urban development, but each had profound urban impacts. In reality, these federal policies subsidized America's postwar suburban exodus (and still do) by pushing people and businesses out of cities and pulling them into suburbs. The idea that this happened purely as a result of the free market is a powerful myth that distorts our understanding of America's social history.

TRANSPORTATION POLICY: AN ARRANGED MARRIAGE WITH THE AUTOMOBILE

America's marriage to the automobile began early in the twentieth century. But in many ways, it was an arranged marriage, not just a love affair. Each time the nation courted mass transportation, powerful interests intervened, objecting to the arrangement. The "highway lobby," composed of the automobile, trucking, oil, rubber, steel, and road-building industries, literally paved the way to suburbia by promoting public road building over public transit and by keeping gas taxes low (by European standards).[37] By the 1920s, cars and trucks began to outstrip trolleys and trains as the major form of personal and business transportation.[38] While government officials looked the other way, the major car, truck, and bus companies purchased and dismantled many of the electric trolley lines that urban Americans relied on.[39] State governments earmarked tolls and gas taxes for road construction instead of public transit and launched major road-building programs. In 1934, Congress required states receiving federal highway funds to dedicate state turnpike tolls to road building.[40] The highway lobby was gaining momentum.

The federal Interstate Highway and Defense Act of 1956 sounded the final death knell for alternatives to the car as a major source of metropolitan mobility. Although the ostensible purpose was to promote mobility across the country and get Americans quickly out of crowded cities in case of an enemy attack (this was the height of the cold war), it would also powerfully promote suburbanization by building radial and ring freeways around the major cities. It set up the Highway Trust Fund, which used federal gas tax revenues to pay 90 percent of the freeway construction costs. Trust fund expenditures grew from $79 million in 1946 to $429 million in 1950 to $2.9 billion in 1960. It "ensured that the freeways would be self-propagating, because more freeways encouraged more automobile travel, generating more gasoline revenue that could only be used to build more highways."[41] Ultimately, it built 41,000 miles of roads.[42] Urban scholars ranked this program as the most important influence in shaping America's urban areas in the past half century.[43]

By 1997, the United States was spending $20.5 billion a year through the Highway Trust Fund.[44] But gas taxes by then covered only 60 percent of the cost of maintaining the federal highway system, so federal and state governments made up the rest. (This cost does not include the negative health consequences of pollution or the loss of economic productivity from employees stuck in traffic.) Most other industrial nations fund highways out of general revenues (as they also fund national rail systems and often regional commuter railways), forcing roads to compete with other national priorities.

America's car culture is premised on the belief that automobiles provide a degree of personal freedom and flexibility that public transit cannot. We have shown that the car culture poses many costs, including environmental damage, long commutes, and personal injuries. Even if we discount these costs, the irony of millions of Americans simultaneously exercising their personal freedom by driving their cars, only to end up in traffic jams, has been parodied in such films as *Falling Down* (1993) with Michael Douglas and Jean Luc Godard's French film *Weekend* (1967). Drivers are spending significantly more time stuck in traffic. Since 1982, traffic gridlock (the amount of time drivers spend in congestion) has more than doubled in the nation's metro areas. It has increased 580 percent in Indianapolis, 433 percent in Kansas City, 414 percent in Minneapolis, 400 percent in Salt Lake City, and 333 percent in San Antonio. Even areas with the smallest increases experienced significant traffic congestion.[45] Americans now spend 8 billion hours a year stuck in traffic.[46] According to Jane Holtz Kay, "On the coasts that hold two-thirds of all Americans, the long-suffering 'BosWash' and the newer 'Los Diegos' freeways greet their share of the day's 80 million car commuters, and, with a screech of brakes, the love song of freedom and mobility goes flat."[47]

Throughout the twentieth century, advocates for public transit argued and battled for a more balanced federal transportation strategy. They won a number of victories. In the 1970s, neighborhood groups protested federal and state plans to build a highway through Boston's working-class neighborhoods and persuaded the U.S. Department of Transportation to halt the highway and divert funds to build a subway line. In recent decades, Atlanta, Miami, Baltimore, Buffalo, Detroit, Los Angeles, Washington, DC, and San Francisco built new subway lines using federal funds shared from gas tax revenues. But federal policy had already cast the die in favor of roads and cars. Between 1975 and 1995, the United States spent $1.15 trillion for roads and highways, compared with $187 billion for mass transit and only $13 billion for Amtrak, the nation's interurban train system.[48] Highway construction continues to expand, exacerbating sprawl and undermining the economies of older cities and suburbs.[49] As a result, mass transit ridership is much lower in American cities than in Europe, Japan, and Canada, accounting for only 3 percent of all travel, one-fifth the Western European average.[50]

Our car-dominated transportation system was premised on individual choice, but in many ways it has reduced choice. Most Americans have no choice but to use the automobile. You need one to get to your job, buy groceries, or visit friends. In Canadian and European cities, households make great use of cars but also have the choice to live in pedestrian-friendly neighborhoods where they can rely on mass transit. Many live quite well without using their cars often and can even do without them. The United States chose not to take this road.

MILITARY SPENDING: MORE THAN JUST DEFENSE

Most Americans think that the search for cheaper land and lower taxes, along with the rise of truck transportation, inevitably shifted major manufacturing plants to suburban and outlying locations, or to states (mostly in the South) with lower labor costs. Obviously, government transportation policies had an enormous impact on this trend, but so did the federal government's siting of military facilities and distribution of defense contracts. Throughout the post–World War II period, military spending has accounted for the largest part of the federal budget. Pentagon decisions about where to locate military facilities and where to grant defense contracts greatly influenced regional development patterns. They are America's de facto "industrial policy," a form of government planning that has dramatically shaped the location of businesses and jobs.

Before World War II, almost all manufacturing plants were located in the nation's central cities. When the war began, the federal government took control (though not ownership) of the nation's major manufacturing industries in order to mobilize resources for the war effort. Companies that built commercial airplanes were drafted to produce military aircraft; firms that produced clothing were conscripted to manufacture uniforms; firms that turned out automobiles and freighters began making tanks and battleships for military use. America's business leaders were wary of the potential implications of this government takeover, so to appease them, President Roosevelt appointed corporate executives to run the War Production Board (WPB).

Rather than retool existing plants, many of which sat underutilized during the depression, the WPB executives decided to build new plants and to locate most of them (government funded but privately owned) in suburban areas. "In New York, Detroit, Baltimore, and Pittsburgh, for example, new investment was located outside the central cities twice or more as heavily as before the war. This pattern also held for such Sunbelt cities as Los Angeles, Dallas, Houston and San Diego." The leaders of the nation's largest industrial corporations used "government financing to reconstruct the private sector's capital base along new and more desirable lines." Suburban locations were desirable because they were "largely beyond the reach of the unions," which had a strong presence in the existing factories and were not governed by big-city mayors, who were often sympathetic to unions.[51] These location decisions had a major impact on postwar America.

Mobilization for World War II also strongly affected the regional location of employment (with disproportionate shares of wartime investment being located outside the preexisting industrial base in the urban North) and population (prompting a northward flow of blacks and a westward and southward flow of whites). The Defense Department's support for the aerospace and electronics industries continued these shifts in the cold war era.[52] After World War II, key congressmen continued to utilize the "Pentagon pork barrel" to bring jobs to firms and workers in their districts, disproportionately in suburban areas. The ripple effects of Pentagon spending dramatically changed the population and employment map of the entire country.[53]

Even in the metropolitan areas that won the Pentagon sweepstakes, most Pentagon dollars went to the suburbs, not the central cities. One study compared the military contracts and salaries coming into each city with the amount of federal taxes drained out of each city to the Pentagon. In 1990 alone, eighteen of the twenty-five largest cities suffered a loss of $24 billion. New York City alone lost $8.4 billion a year; Los Angeles, $3.3 billion; Chicago, $3.1 billion; Houston, $1.7 billion; Dallas, $731 million; and Detroit, over $900 million. In Los Angeles, taxpayers sent $4.74 billion to the Pentagon and received $1.47 billion back, for a net loss of $3.27 billion, or $3,000 per family.[54] The employment impact of this drain-off of funds is equally dramatic.

Even those cities gaining dollars and jobs from the Pentagon have discovered that depending on military contracts makes them vulnerable to "downturns in the military spending cycle."[55] Both Seattle (dominated by Boeing, the nation's largest defense contractor) and St. Louis (where defense contractor McDonnell-Douglas — recently purchased by Boeing — is the largest employer) experienced severe economic hard times when the Pentagon reduced its funding for specific weapon systems or selected another contractor. Politics influences the rise and fall of regions and cities as a result of Pentagon spending.[56]

FEDERAL HOME OWNERSHIP POLICIES: A SUBURBAN BIAS

Federal home ownership policies have also had an enormous impact on metropolitan development patterns. It is widely believed that home ownership benefits society as a whole by encouraging more stable families, higher savings rates, and greater civic participation. By their nature, home ownership policies are biased toward suburbs because, compared with cities, more suburban households own their own homes. But these programs were designed and implemented in ways that exaggerated the bias against cities and accentuated economic segregation and sprawl.

Early federal home ownership policies were shamefully racist. The federal government refused to insure loans for blacks, largely confining them to rental housing in cities and keeping them out of the great suburban migration. Although some minority families may want to live in predominantly minority neighborhoods, surveys consistently show that most minorities want to live in racially integrated neighborhoods. Self-segregation is not the major factor in their residential isolation.[57] Federal policies in some respects initially created and then exacerbated the concentration of poor blacks and Hispanics in ghettos and barrios.[58] Racist behavior and racist policies directly contradict the free-market view of metropolitan development.

In the first half of the twentieth century, overt racial discrimination in housing was widespread. Whites often resorted to violence to keep blacks out of all-white neighborhoods, a practice that persisted into the 1960s, especially in northern metropolitan areas. Local governments enacted racial zoning laws and allowed "restrictive covenants" on deeds that forbade home owners to sell to Jews, blacks, and other groups. Real estate organizations promulgated codes of ethics that sanctioned members who helped blacks buy or rent housing in white neighborhoods. Real estate agents have routinely "steered" blacks and Latinos (regardless of income) to racially segregated neighborhoods, mortgage lenders and insurance firms have redlined urban minority neighborhoods and refuse to treat minority loan applicants equally, and landlords have discriminated against minority tenants.[59] Racial segregation thus stems from the routine practices of the private real estate industry as well as from government policy. From the 1930s through the 1960s, however, the federal government generally ignored and in some cases endorsed these practices.[60]

Early in 1933, in the midst of the Depression, Congress created the Home Owners Loan Corporation (HOLC) to provide low-interest loans to home owners who were in danger of losing their homes to foreclosure. The HOLC set up a rating system to evaluate the risks associated with loans in specific urban neighborhoods. Economically well-off and racially and ethnically homogeneous neighborhoods received the highest ratings. Neighborhoods that were mostly black or were located near black neighborhoods (which typically included Jewish neighborhoods) fell into the lowest categories, which led banks to undervalue these areas and limit loans to them.[61]

The HOLC did not invent these standards. It simply embraced the general practices of the real estate industry. But it put the federal government's stamp of approval on these practices, making racial discrimination part of government policy. Banks used HOLC's system in making their own loans, compounding the disinvestment of black areas and urban neighborhoods by government and the private sector. Equally important, HOLC policy set a precedent for the later Federal Housing Administration (FHA) and Veterans Administration (VA) programs, which played a major role in changing postwar America, pumping billions of dollars into the housing industry.

The FHA was established in 1934 to promote home ownership and stimulate the construction industry, which had almost collapsed with the onset of the Depression. The FHA provided government insurance to banks lending money for approved home mortgages. (Later, a similar program was established by the VA.) With the loan guaranteed in this fashion, lenders could confidently make long-term mortgages available, thereby reducing consumers' monthly payments and stimulating the housing market. The FHA carried out its mandate in ways that promoted suburbanization and racial segregation at the expense of rebuilding central cities and promoting racial integration.

During the FHA's early years, some housing experts, civil rights groups, and public officials pushed Congress to eliminate racial segregation in federal government housing programs, but they met enormous resistance.[62] In fact, it was official FHA policy to promote racial segregation and unofficial policy to promote suburbanization. Many FHA staff came from the private lending industry, which generally refused to make loans in integrated neighborhoods. In 1938, the official FHA underwriting manual discouraged loans to neighborhoods occupied by "inharmonious racial or nationality groups." It stated that "if a neighborhood is to retain stability, it is necessary that properties shall continue to be occupied by the same social and racial classes."[63] It noted that "a change in social or racial occupancy generally contributed to instability and a decline in values." FHA staff even advised housing developers to use restrictive covenants barring sales to nonwhites before seeking FHA financing as a way to promote neighborhood stability and property values.[64]

Pent up by the Depression and World War II and then unleashed by postwar prosperity, demand for housing exploded in the 1950s and 1960s. Many returning veterans sought to gravitate away from their immigrant parents' and grandparents' neighborhoods. As a practical matter, they would find the least costly new housing in the suburban periphery, which was also removed from the growing minority populations in many older central-city neighborhoods. Much of this demand could have been satisfied within the existing city boundaries—for example, in the garden apartment complexes constructed on the outer boundaries of the prewar city. During the Truman administration, however, efforts to pass federal legislation to promote this type of middle-income rental housing in cities failed. The home-building lobby pressured Congress to make it easier to build in outlying areas.[65] The FHA and VA home loan programs became the major vehicles for expanding housing construction, home ownership, and suburbanization. "The power to award or withhold mortgage insurance gave the FHA the hidden leverage to shape the postwar metropolis."[66] The FHA and VA redlined the cities, speeding the migration of the white middle class out of the older central cities. Black families who wished to move to suburbs like Levittown, and could afford to do so, were not allowed.[67] As Robert Fishman notes, "a white home buyer who wished to stay in his old neighborhood had to seek old-style conventional mortgages with high rates and short terms. The same purchaser who opted for a new suburban house could get an FHA-insured mortgage with lower interest rates, longer terms, a lower down payment, and a lower monthly payment."[68]

During the booming 1950s, one-third of all private housing was financed with FHA or VA help.[69] Almost all these homes were built in the suburbs. FHA policy favored the construction of new homes over the remodeling of existing homes, making it "easier and cheaper for a family to purchase a new home than to renovate an older one."[70] It also favored single-family homes over multifamily (apartment) buildings. Between 1941 and 1950, FHA-insured single-family starts exceeded FHA multifamily starts by four to one. In the 1950s, the ratio was over seven to one.[71] Suburban zoning laws guaranteed that most FHA-backed apartment buildings would be located in central cities.

The vast majority of FHA and VA mortgages went to white, middle-class families in suburbs. Few went to blacks, city residents, or even whites who wanted to purchase (or renovate) city homes. The FHA underwriting manual viewed mixed-use areas or high-density areas (that is, cities) as bad credit risks. The FHA failed to make *any* loans in some cities. Between 1946 and 1959, blacks purchased less than 2 percent of all housing financed with VA and FHA help. In Miami, only one black family received FHA insurance between 1934 and 1949, and "there is evidence that he [the man who secured the loan] was not recognized as a black."[72] As late as 1966, the FHA had no mortgages in Paterson or Camden, New Jersey, older cities with declining white populations.[73] This treatment contrasts with that of Levittown, New Jersey, one of several planned suburban communities (all called "Levittown") in eastern states that featured thousands of similar single-family homes. When the development opened up in 1958, its homes were marketed and sold to whites only. The FHA went along with this practice. It took a lawsuit based on New Jersey's antidiscrimination law, seeking to prevent Levittown home buyers from getting FHA insurance, to force the developer to relent. The first black family moved into Levittown in 1960. Starting in the 1970s, under pressure from Congress, the FHA began insuring more single-family home loans in central cities and to racial minorities. But by then, the suburban momentum was well under way.

HOME OWNER TAX BREAKS: SUBSIDIZING SUBURBANIZATION

The nation's tax code allows home owners to take mortgage interest and property tax deductions that are not available to renters. These tax breaks have been in the federal tax code since it was enacted in 1912, but they were initially intended to help family farmers, not wealthy home owners. By the 1960s, they were providing billions of dollars of tax subsidies, and by the 1980s, they had become by far the largest federal housing program. Most benefits go to well-off suburban home owners. In 2002, home owner tax breaks totaled more than $106 billion, including mortgage interest deductions ($64 billion), property tax deductions ($22 billion), and exclusions of capital gains on home sales ($19 billion).[74] Between 1978 and 2000, the federal government spent $1.7 trillion (in 2001 dollars) on these breaks, compared with $640 billion on all HUD low-income housing subsidies.[75]

Today, 30 million home owners, almost one-fifth of all taxpayers, receive one or more elements of the home owner deduction. But a highly disproportionate share of these federal tax breaks flows to the highest-income taxpayers with the largest houses and biggest mortgages. For example, 59 percent of the total mortgage deduction goes to the richest 10.2 percent of taxpayers, those with incomes over $100,000.[76] Local property tax deductions are similarly regressive.

These tax breaks have significant geographic and social consequences. They clearly encourage home buyers to buy larger homes in more outlying areas than they otherwise might. Moderate-income home owners, who generally do not get much advantage from this deduction, are concentrated in older suburbs and central cities. The property tax deduction helps both suburban and central-city governments raise revenues, but suburbs get a much greater boost because more of their taxpayers claim the deduction. Tax policy thus powerfully promotes suburbanization, metropolitan sprawl, and geographic segregation by social class and race.[77]

Since the 1960s, many tax and housing experts have recommended correcting this inequity in the tax code by reducing the amount that wealthy home owners can deduct and restricting deductions to only one home. The real estate industry has successfully fought these challenges, claiming that changing the tax law would undermine the American dream of home ownership. In 1984, for example, President Reagan announced that he was planning to introduce a comprehensive tax reform plan that would simplify the tax system and reduce taxes on the well-off. One provision was to eliminate the mortgage interest deduction. The real estate industry quickly sprang into action, and when Reagan filed his bill in Congress (the Tax Reform Act of 1986), it retained the mortgage interest deduction.[78] No president since then has proposed tampering with this regressive tax break for home owners.

FEDERAL FAIR HOUSING LAWS:
LITTLE IMPACT ON SEGREGATION

It was not inevitable that American metropolitan areas would become as segregated by race and class as they now are. As early as the 1940s, advocates for racial justice and housing reformers proposed laws to challenge racial discrimination and promote racial integration. During the debate over the 1949 Housing Act, progressive members of Congress sought to ban racial segregation in public housing, but their amendment was defeated.[79] Since the 1960s, new laws have been enacted to eliminate these practices, but federal enforcement has often been halfhearted or ineffective. Even if strongly enforced, laws to limit discrimination have little impact on the patterns of residential segregation.

In 1968, the Kerner Commission, appointed by President Johnson in the wake of ghetto riots, recommended enacting a national "open occupancy" law and changing federal housing policy to build more low- and moderate-income housing outside of ghetto areas.[80] Congress passed the Fair Housing Act of 1968 a week after the assassination of Martin Luther King Jr., over the opposition of southern congressmen. This act addressed the first Kerner Commission recommendation, but not the second. The act prohibited discrimination in housing, including racial steering, redlining, and blockbusting, but it did not promote racial integration in middle-income areas.[81]

The law remains an important symbol of the civil rights movement's success, but its enforcement mechanism was glaringly weak. It gave HUD, or state and local fair housing agencies (where they existed), the right to investigate complaints of housing discrimination by individuals. (State and local governments also began enacting parallel laws during this period.) But neither HUD nor the state and local agencies had the power to issue enforcement orders. They could only refer cases to the Department of Justice for prosecution. Hampered by filing deadlines for complaints, long delays in investigations, and infrequent prosecution, the law had little impact. Many complainants bypassed HUD and these other agencies and went directly to court. Civil rights lawyers won many cases, and courts fined landlords and real estate agents. Although they helped individual victims of discrimination, these time-consuming cases rarely changed housing industry practices. In 1988, the law was amended to give HUD the power to initiate complaints and allow administrative law judges to make rulings.[82]

In the three decades since the Fair Housing Act was passed, a network of private fair housing groups, attorneys with expertise in fair housing law, and state and local government agencies has emerged to utilize the law to promote racial justice. Much money and person power have been spent by these individuals, organizations, and agencies, but the overall impact of this activity is questionable. These federal, state, and local fair housing laws "have had little effect on the overall pattern of racial segregation in most suburban housing."[83]

Only a handful of suburbs have actively and voluntarily embraced racial integration by using reduced mortgages or campaigns against "panic" selling to encourage whites to live in racially mixed neighborhoods.[84] Fair housing and fair lending laws do not challenge the basic policies and practices that lead to racial segregation. Instead, they allow individuals or organizations to seek judicial redress for individual acts of discrimination by landlords, real estate agents, or banks. Legal victories may bring monetary rewards for victims and may deter overt discrimination by landlords, lenders, real estate agents, and insurance companies, but they have not significantly changed patterns of residential segregation. Few housing discrimination cases have been brought against municipalities or major developers for the practices that lead to racial segregation. The federal government has taken some aggressive enforcement actions, but only when such violations were overt and could be proved.

FEDERAL PROGRAMS TARGETED TO URBAN AREAS

It would be wrong to suggest that all federal programs have simply been designed to promote economic segregation and suburban sprawl. The federal government has responded to these problems in two ways: promoting regional approaches and targeting aid to cities. At various times, particularly the 1930s and 1960s, the federal government has recognized the connection between the problems of cities and the problems of suburbs and has tried to craft policies to address them both. Its halting efforts to encourage regional approaches are examined in Chapter 6. Here, we review explicit urban policies targeted to cities.

Most federal policies exacerbated central-city decline and racial segregation, but the federal government also adopted another (smaller and less powerful) set of policies to improve the economic and social conditions of central cities. In truth, federal aid to cities (whether to revitalize downtowns, attract private jobs to inner-city neighborhoods, stabilize poor and working-class neighborhoods, or provide fiscal assistance to local governments) has served, in effect, to clean up the mess it created with its larger subsidies for suburbanization and urban disinvestment.[85] In Alice O'Connor's phrase, federal urban policy has been "swimming against the tide" of most federal domestic policies.[86]

Many Americans think that the federal government coddled cities and that they are worse off despite the expenditure of billions of federal dollars. Steven Hayward of the conservative Heritage Foundation observed that the federal government spent $600 billion on cities between 1965 and 1990, yet older central cities continued to decline. Such federal policies are doomed to fail, he thinks, because they ignore the "logic of metropolitan development."[87] Although conservatives overlook the improvements in urban housing and the environment, as well as the creation of a black middle class, for the most part they are correct that federal urban policies have failed. They are wrong about the reason, however. These policies did not fail because they violated the logic of the market, but because other government policies had already set powerful antiurban forces in motion. On the basis of the false belief that minimal federal help would enable cities and urban neighborhoods to bootstrap themselves out of poverty, federal policy makers almost guaranteed that urban policy would fail, opening up these programs to political counterattack.

NEW DEAL URBAN POLICY

The New Deal mounted the first serious urban policy initiatives during the Depression. America's urban population had grown dramatically in the previous fifty years. The nation's key industries—steel and iron, meatpacking, textiles, and automobiles—were centered in big cities. European immigrants flooded into these cities between 1880 and 1920, providing cheap labor. Tenement slums grew around factories, leading to serious overcrowding and public health problems. The nation's labor wars were fought on urban battlefields.

After World War I, a racist and nativist backlash led Congress to enact restrictive immigrant laws (such as the Emergency Quota Act of 1921 and the National Origins Act of 1924) and to attack immigrant culture by passing Prohibition in 1919. But America had already become an urban nation. By the late 1920s, urban voters wielded significant influence in state and national politics, symbolized by the Democratic Party's nomination of New York Governor Alfred Smith, an Irish Catholic, for president in 1928. Smith lost, and the Depression, which began in 1929 and devastated the nation's cities, became identified with Republican President Herbert Hoover. Many cities filed for bankruptcy. Cities were overwhelmed by the homeless (who constructed "Hoovervilles"), unemployed people stormed relief offices and city halls, tenants went on rent strikes, depositors rioted at bank closings, and workers organized a wave of strikes and protests.[88]

President Hoover personally opposed federal intervention but was forced politically to take some action. The Emergency Relief and Construction Act extended $300 million in loans to state and local governments so that they could provide relief to indigent people. In 1932, three years into the Depression, voters rejected Hoover's approach. Urban voters played a key role in Democrat Franklin Roosevelt's landslide victory and the election of numerous Democratic congressmen, many representing urban Catholics, Jews, and blacks. Roosevelt had no coherent plan but promised to bring the power of the federal government to address the crisis. Americans were hopeful, but urban unrest continued after Roosevelt took office. Big-city mayors set up a new organization, the U.S. Conference of Mayors, to lobby Roosevelt for help. The first wave of federal urban policy soon followed.[89]

The New Deal significantly increased federal support for public works, social insurance, business regulation, and farm policy.[90] The Social Security Act created insurance for the elderly and cash assistance (later called Aid to Families with Dependent Children [AFDC], typically referred to as "welfare") to women and children, many of whom lived in cities, but it was not specifically an "urban" policy. These two programs set the pattern for many later "people" programs such as food stamps and health insurance. New Deal public works projects put millions of unemployed Americans to work constructing urban parks, water and sewer systems, bridges, subways, airports, libraries, streets, schools, and other facilities. These programs bypassed state agencies and provided direct federal assistance to municipalities. These public works and infrastructure programs were later phased out because business groups viewed direct government involvement in job creation as an opening wedge to socialism, disappointing New Dealers who had hoped to create a permanent federal role in creating jobs for the unemployed.

The nation's mobilization for World War II drew millions more Americans into the cities to work in military installations and war production. More than half a million people moved to the San Francisco area between 1940 and 1945. The wartime migration included a substantial number of African Americans from the rural South, which led to competition with whites for housing and jobs and triggered racial tensions. This influx created serious housing shortages, especially for defense workers. During the war, the federal government funneled money for construction of public schools, playgrounds, child-care centers, and medical facilities and programs for public health and sanitation. In 1940, the Lanham Act authorized construction of 700,000 units of housing for defense workers.[91] In Oakland, California, "federal agencies built more than thirty thousand public housing units accommodating about ninety thousand war workers and their families."[92]

The unprecedented level of federal investment and planning in cities during the New Deal and World War II did not survive. These programs were all viewed as part of a wartime emergency; when the war ended, business groups pressured Congress to cancel them. The real estate industry successfully lobbied for a provision that all government-sponsored defense housing units had to be sold or demolished after the war, not converted into low-income public housing. Defense plants were sold to their operators for nominal amounts. The emerging efforts to build cross-class support for federal government intervention in urban development were uprooted.

SUBSIDIZED HOUSING FOR LOW-INCOME TENANTS

Alongside the home ownership programs described earlier, the New Deal launched a public housing program to improve housing conditions for the urban poor. The history of this program provides another example of a road not taken. Even though housing reformers played an important role in designing and implementing the initial program, it mainly served as a jobs and public works program during the Depression. Today, HUD continues to support 1.2 million units of public housing managed by local public authorities, 1.9 million households receiving Section 8 certificates and vouchers to live in private rental housing, and 1.7 million households living in privately owned units constructed or rehabilitated by federal funds under a variety of program names.[93]

Until the Depression, most Americans believed that the private market, perhaps with help from private philanthropy, could meet the nation's housing needs. Reformers who wanted government to play a major role in housing were a voice in the political wilderness. In the first decades of the twentieth century, a few unions and settlement house reformers built model housing developments for working-class families. Without government subsidies, however, poor families could not afford these apartments.[94] The Depression provided reformers with the political opening to push their idea that the federal government should build "social housing" and create a noncommercial sector free from profit and speculation. Like their European counterparts, they envisioned that the middle class as well as the poor would want to live in this housing. The reformers believed in public enterprise and the positive effect of good architecture on people and communities. Beginning in 1933, their ideas and political activism inspired two federal programs that created well-designed housing, available to a mix of income groups, sponsored by labor unions and other nonprofit groups.[95]

The reformers hoped to turn these prototypes into a permanent government program, but the real estate industry, led by the National Association of Real Estate Boards, outmaneuvered them. Fearing competition from well-designed government-sponsored housing, the industry warned about the specter of socialism. With the enactment of the Wagner Public Housing Act in 1937, the industry successfully lobbied to limit public housing to the poor and to give local governments discretion over whether to participate and where to locate such housing. The progressive social housing programs were canceled.

Since then, public housing has been restricted to the very poor. Some of these highly utilitarian, physically isolated projects became ugly warehouses for the poor, stigmatized as housing of last resort. Even today, American politicians use widely held (though often misleading) stereotypes about public housing to attack the idea of government activism. In a speech before the National As-sociation of Realtors during his 1996 presidential campaign, Senator Bob Dole labeled public housing "one of the last bastions of socialism in the world" and said that local housing authorities have become "landlords of misery."

Public housing and other federally subsidized low-income housing have generally been racially and economically segregated. This outcome was not in-evitable. These programs could have been created on a regional rather than a local basis. All communities, including suburbs, could have been required to participate. But opponents of public housing prevailed. So local participation is voluntary, localities determine where it will be situated, and state enabling laws make siting subject to local government approval and zoning laws. As a re-sult, few suburbs participate in any federally assisted low-income housing pro-gram. In fact, a few suburban areas created their own public housing authorities specifically so that city housing agencies could *not* cross their boundaries. For example, DuPage County in Illinois created a public housing authority in 1942 that intentionally declined to build a single unit for thirty years. The Fulton County Housing Authority was established to prevent the Atlanta Housing Au-thority from building public housing in unincorporated parts of the county.[96]

The business and political leaders who served on local public housing authority boards from the 1940s through the 1960s sited public housing de-velopments in segregated areas and adopted tenant selection policies that re-inforced racial separation.[97] Because whites constituted the majority of pub-lic housing residents during those decades, the projects generally excluded minorities.[98] When the large-scale postwar migration of blacks to cities and the razing of black neighborhoods for federal urban renewal programs re-quired local authorities to provide replacement housing, public housing devel-opments became overwhelmingly black. Even then, local public housing au-thorities steered black and white residents to segregated developments.[99] Most black public housing residents live in black neighborhoods, and most white public housing residents live in white neighborhoods. Public housing projects with black residents are concentrated in high-poverty areas, while those with mostly white residents are likely to be in working-class areas. The siting of fed-erally subsidized low-income housing has thus exacerbated the concentration of poverty among blacks, creating new ghettos.

From its inception, public housing was characterized by geographic, eco-nomic, and racial segregation. (Projects occupied exclusively by the elderly are less likely to be in high-poverty areas.[100]) For example, 61.4 percent of public housing units are located in central cities, 19.2 percent in suburbs, and 19.5 per-cent in nonmetropolitan areas; 68.7 percent are located in census tracts with median household incomes under $20,000, 53.6 percent in tracts with poverty rates of 30 percent or more, and 50.9 percent in tracts with a majority of minority residents. Subsequent programs, including the Section 8 new construction program and the Section 8 voucher program, are also disproportionately located in cities and low-income areas, minority areas, areas that already have a concentration of subsidized housing.[101] Section 8 vouchers and certificates provide the potential for more mobility, but low-income renters still face a shortage of affordable apartments in the suburbs and landlord resistance to the program.[102]

URBAN RENEWAL: BUILDING OFFICE DEVELOPMENTS AT THE EXPENSE OF HOUSING

In the postwar decades, the federal government's investment in highways, home ownership subsidies, and defense contracts heavily promoted suburbanization. This drew investment away from central-city business districts. In response, the federal government turned its attention to promoting private investment in urban downtowns. America's cities faced large-scale blight. As early as the 1950s, downtown department stores and other businesses worried about competition from new suburban retailers. Manufacturing firms were relocating, and so were middle-class families. Hardly any private housing had been built or repaired in the cities during the Depression and war years, leading to a severe housing shortage and widespread deterioration of existing housing. Business leaders and city officials believed that urban slums were causing property values and retail activity to decline.

Mayors, developers, business leaders, construction unions, and daily newspapers — the key components of an urban growth coalition — pressured Congress to address the worsening urban crisis.[103] Congress responded by enacting urban renewal, a key component of the 1949 Housing Act. (This law also reauthorized the federal public housing program, although it required one unit of slum housing to be torn down for every new public housing unit built.) The Urban Land Institute, the urban real estate industry lobby group, drafted the urban renewal section of the legislation.[104] The goal was to revive downtown business districts by razing the slums, bringing new businesses into the core, and attracting middle-class residents back to the cities. Urban leaders also believed that the federal highway program would reduce traffic congestion and modernize the narrow and inadequate street systems of older urban areas, thus bringing suburbanites into cities to work, shop, and attend sports and cultural events. The goal of a "slumless city," in the words of New Haven

Mayor Richard Lee, had much more to do with promoting a healthy business climate than addressing the needs of the urban poor.[105] Urban renewal began under Democratic President Harry Truman, expanded under Republican President Dwight Eisenhower, continued under Democratic Presidents John Kennedy and Lyndon Johnson, and was terminated under Republican President Richard Nixon in 1974.

Urban renewal's primary focus was to encourage private investment in central business districts and clear away neighboring "slums," which local elites and planners thought threatened downtown business districts and important institutions such as hospitals and universities. From its inception, commercial development took priority over low-cost housing. The program funded cities to use their eminent domain authority to purchase and assemble large tracts of land and sell them to developers at bargain-basement prices. Urban renewal projects were often coordinated with the construction of federally funded urban freeways. Cities often literally paved the way for private developers to build market-rate housing, commercial office buildings, and cultural complexes.

Between 1956 and 1972, urban renewal and urban freeway construction displaced an estimated 3.8 million persons from their homes.[106] In some cities, entire neighborhoods were razed or split down the middle by new highways and convention centers.[107] Some called the federal program "Negro removal" because of its focus on black neighborhoods. It pushed people out of their homes and businesses, destroyed social ties, and dispersed residents without adequate compensation for their economic and emotional losses. One-fifth of the entire population of New Haven was displaced by public projects over this period. City redevelopment agencies did a haphazard job of relocating the people and small businesses displaced by urban renewal. Public housing construction in the 1950s and 1960s was used to rehouse some of the victims of urban renewal, typically in isolated high-rise complexes.[108] Although the 1949 act authorized 810,000 units of public housing, only 320,000 units were built by 1960.[109] Freeway construction also destabilized blue-collar neighborhoods.[110] The interstate highway program damaged surrounding property, took land off city tax rolls, and created huge concrete walls separating neighborhoods from each other. The Cross-Bronx Expressway separated the South Bronx from the rest of the city, helping to turn it into one of the nation's worst ghettos. New federally funded highways cut downtown Boston and San Francisco off from their waterfronts.

The urban renewal program ignited controversy and opposition from conservatives and liberals alike. Conservatives opposed urban renewal as a misuse of "big government" social engineering. Conservative Martin Anderson described urban renewal as the "federal bulldozer."[111] Liberals viewed it as a giveaway to developers, who reaped huge profits, and as an attack on blue-collar neighborhoods and the urban poor. It soon became clear that *blight* was a term that could be used to destroy healthy neighborhoods that were in the way of major development projects.[112] The impact on black neighborhoods led many to view urban renewal as racially biased. Neighborhood groups protesting urban renewal and highway construction emerged across the country. Although few were immediately successful, they formed the basis for a growing movement of community organizing and community development beginning in the late 1960s.[113] They slowed down urban renewal projects, some of which took ten years to complete, undermining the program's credibility.

Even on its own terms, urban renewal had mixed results. It slowed down the deterioration of retail activity in some cities and may have helped a few, like Boston, Atlanta, and San Francisco, to expand office space and tourist activity. It certainly changed the skyline of some big cities by subsidizing the construction of large office buildings that housed corporate headquarters, law firms, and other corporate-oriented activity.[114] By razing slum housing, it may have removed some bad housing stock, but it destroyed far more low-cost housing than it built. Overall, urban renewal did little to stem the movement of people and businesses to the suburbs or to improve the economic and living conditions of inner-city neighborhoods. On the contrary, it destabilized many of them, promoting chaotic racial transition and white flight.

Controversy led to the demise of urban renewal in the early 1970s. Likewise, resistance to the construction of public housing, often associated with urban renewal, grew significantly during the 1960s. The program never had broad support, and Congress effectively ended new public housing construction by the mid-1970s, although it continued to fund existing developments. New public housing construction declined from 104,000 units in 1970 to 19,000 in 1974.[115]

GREAT SOCIETY URBAN PROGRAMS

As urban renewal was winding down in the mid-1960s, it was replaced by another wave of federal urban policies designed more directly to improve social, economic, and physical conditions in poor neighborhoods and to aid city budgets. These programs were adopted in response to the civil rights movement, community protests against urban renewal, and political pressure from big-city mayors. Begun in 1964, President Lyndon Johnson's Great Society and

War on Poverty initiatives continued the New Deal tradition of trying to lift the urban poor into the economic mainstream. Unlike the New Deal, Johnson's initiatives took place during a period in which rising affluence dramatized the persistence of urban poverty.

If rising affluence made a war on poverty possible, the civil rights movement and the urban unrest of the 1960s made it necessary. In the cold war battle between capitalism and communism, the conditions in America's ghettos and rural areas embarrassed the nation's political leaders as they espoused the advantages of the "American way of life."[116] And for leaders in the Democratic Party, especially in the North and Midwest, the civil rights movement catalyzed a moral force and a voting bloc they could not ignore.

Representing the left wing of the Democratic Party, United Automobile Workers (UAW) president Walter Reuther had been making proposals since World War II to renew the New Deal and engage in national economic planning. He advised Presidents Kennedy and Johnson to champion a bold federal program for full employment that would include government-funded public works and the conversion of the nation's defense industry to production for civilian needs. This, he argued, would dramatically address the nation's poverty population, create job opportunities for African Americans, and rebuild the nation's troubled cities without being as politically divisive as a federal program identified primarily as serving poor blacks. Both presidents rejected Reuther's advice. Johnson's announcement of an "unconditional war on poverty" in his 1964 State of the Union Address pleased Reuther, but the details of the plan revealed its limitations. The War on Poverty was a patchwork of small initiatives that did not address the nation's basic inequalities. Testifying before Congress in April 1964, Reuther said that "while [the proposals] are good, [they] are not adequate, nor will they be successful in achieving their purposes, except as we begin to look at the broader problems [of the American economy]." He added that "poverty is a reflection of our failure to achieve a more rational, more responsible, more equitable distribution of the abundance that is within our grasp."[117]

Although Reuther threw the UAW's political weight behind Johnson's programs, his critique was correct. Since the 1960s, federal efforts to address poverty have consistently suffered from a failure to address the fundamental underlying issues.[118] With the exception of Social Security and Medicare (health insurance for the elderly), most programs targeted at individuals provide a safety net to keep people from physical suffering, not to lift them out of poverty. For example, even at its peak, welfare benefit levels, which vary dramatically among the states, never reached the official poverty threshold, even with food stamp benefits added. Medicaid began in 1965 as a means-tested health insurance entitlement for the poor, with benefits varying by state. Housing subsidies were not an entitlement at all and have never reached more than one-third of the families who were eligible for them. The minimum wage has usually been far below the poverty threshold. Only the earned income tax credit (EITC) for the working poor, begun in the mid-1970s and expanded in the 1990s, has actually lifted some families above the poverty level.[119]

Johnson and the Democratic Congress enacted a wide range of legislation to provide assistance to the poor, promote "equal opportunity" for the poor, improve conditions in poor neighborhoods, and give poor people greater access to local political influence. The programs targeted at individuals have lasted the longest, including Head Start (early childhood education), food stamps, Medicare, and Medicaid (health insurance for the elderly and the poor). In contrast, programs targeted at cities and states for job training, neighborhood revitalization, and subsidized housing have had a more complicated history. The number and size of federal grant programs targeted at cities and states increased dramatically for about a decade, peaking during the Nixon administration. In 1960, there were 44 grant-in-aid programs for city and state governments; by 1964, there were 115 programs and 216 separate authorizations for new spending; by 1966, 399 authorizations; by 1969, almost 500. Grant-in-aid funds grew from $2.2 billion in 1950 to $7 billion in 1960 and $24 billion in 1970.[120]

Programs designed to improve urban neighborhoods tended to be poorly funded, short-lived, or both. These included the Jobs Corps, Neighborhood Youth Corps, and VISTA (Volunteers in Service to America). The Model Cities program, enacted in 1966, targeted funds for both physical improvements and social services in these neighborhoods. The War on Poverty and Model Cities legislation required that residents participate in the planning and implementation of these programs. New local antipoverty agencies, called community action agencies, were set up. Churches, community development corporations, settlement houses, and other nonprofit organizations also received federal antipoverty funds. The federal government directly funded community-based agencies, often bypassing the local government. This angered many mayors, who viewed some of these agencies and their leaders as political opponents. Indeed, some community agencies mobilized people (often in black neighborhoods) to protest against local government, including urban renewal projects, public housing authorities, and county welfare systems.

In 1965, Johnson persuaded Congress to create a new cabinet-level agency, the Department of Housing and Urban Development, to focus attention on cities.[121] HUD assumed control of the public housing program, the urban renewal program, the FHA, and the Model Cities program. Even at the height of the War on Poverty, however, HUD lacked the power to coordinate other federal agencies involved in antipoverty efforts, such as the Office of Economic Opportunity, the Labor Department, and the Commerce Department. This fragmentation continues to hamper HUD's efforts to address the economic and social problems in cities. HUD has primarily been a housing agency, not an urban development agency. Federal funding for subsidized housing has seen dramatic swings in response to political pressures, but even at its peak, HUD served less than one-third of those low-income households eligible for housing subsidies.

In the 1960s, national housing policy began to shift from a reliance on public housing authorities to use of the private sector to produce and manage subsidized housing. HUD provided private developers with low-interest mortgages, tax breaks, and rental subsidies in exchange for their renting apartments to the poor. In 1974, during the Nixon administration, Congress created the Section 8 program. It had three components: constructing new buildings in which the units were reserved for the poor, rehabilitating substandard buildings, and providing tenants with rent certificates they could use to pay for market-rate rental units.

To win congressional approval, funds were spread widely across these housing, antipoverty, and community development programs. No one city or neighborhood received sufficient funds to make a large impact on housing conditions or employment. The Model Cities program was initially supposed to be targeted to a few cities, but it eventually spread to 150.[122] It was easy to view these relatively small antipoverty programs as mere symbolism and political cooptation. "We fought a war on poverty," it was often said, "and poverty won."

In fact, the nation's poverty rate was cut in half, from 22.2 percent in 1960 to an all-time low of 11.1 percent by 1973. National economic growth, fed by the military buildup for the Vietnam War, accounts for some of this success. But the various antipoverty programs, in combination with steady increases in the minimum wage, also contributed. Most dramatic was the decline of poverty among the elderly, from 35.2 percent in 1959 to 14.6 percent in 1974. Enactment of Medicare in 1965 and the indexing of Social Security to inflation in 1972 played a significant part in this trend. The poverty rate among blacks fell from 55.1 percent in 1959 (when most blacks still lived in the rural South) to 41.8 percent in 1966 (when blacks were an increasingly urban group) to 30.3 percent by 1974.

Frustrations among the urban poor, particularly those living in black ghettos, contributed to a wave of urban rioting between 1965 and 1968. Although each urban riot had its own precipitating incident, such as an altercation with police or the assassination of Martin Luther King Jr., the underlying causes were high rates of unemployment, worsening neighborhood conditions, exclusion from national prosperity, and lack of political influence.[123] For a few years, Congress responded to the riots with increased funding for urban programs targeted at low-income neighborhoods. The riots also paved the way for the election of the first wave of black big-city mayors, starting with Richard Hatcher in Gary, Indiana, and Carl Stokes in Cleveland in 1967. But the riots also created a strong political backlash, accelerated the exodus of whites into suburbs, and created fertile ground for conservative politicians (including some big-city mayors such as Philadelphia's Frank Rizzo and Los Angeles's Sam Yorty) to use racial appeals and code words ("the silent majority") to "get tough" on urban crime while opposing funds to improve urban neighborhoods and provide assistance to the poor.

THE NEW FEDERALISM

The postriot political climate led the Nixon administration and Congress to reduce and reshape federal assistance to cities under the guise of giving cities more control over federal funds. Nixon called his approach the "New Federalism."[124] It replaced hundreds of federal urban programs, each with strings attached and specific purposes, with general-purpose funding that gave cities much greater discretion over how the money was used. One version was "general revenue sharing," begun in 1972. Congress initially authorized $30 billion over a five-year period, with one-third going to state governments and two-thirds going to local governments. The funding formula was based on cities' population, per capita income, and tax base. Cities could use the money for law enforcement, public transportation, health, social services, and environmental protection, but not for education or cash payments to welfare recipients.[125]

The Nixon administration also consolidated urban renewal, Model Cities, water and sewer facilities grants, neighborhood facilities grants, public works loans, and grants for acquisition of open-space land into the Community Development Block Grant (CDBG). Here, too, cities had discretion over its use, so long as they helped low- and moderate-income neighborhoods or helped prevent or eliminate slums. A relatively small amount of funding ($4.33 billion in 2004) was spread over many more jurisdictions than had received funding under the predecessor programs.[126] Funds were allocated according to population, poverty rate, and housing conditions, with 1,000 cities and large urban counties given entitlement status; 30 percent was channeled through states to smaller towns. Cities could use the funds for housing, public facilities, business development, child care, and other purposes.[127]

Local officials liked the flexibility of these block grant programs (although local politicians shut out many community groups from funding). During the Nixon and Ford years, the overall level of federal funding to localities increased, and it continued to grow in the first half of Jimmy Carter's administration, reaching a peak in 1978. The amount going to cities with serious poverty problems actually declined, however. Although large cities received more funds than better-off suburbs (Detroit received $28 per capita, compared with less than $4 per capita for its wealthy neighbor, Grosse Point Farms), cities actually *lost* overall funding compared with what they had been getting. Not surprisingly, the revenue-sharing program shifted federal funds away from Democratic cities and toward Republican suburbs, away from the Democratic Northeast and Midwest and toward the Republican South and West. Governors and mayors often used the funds for their own pet projects rather than helping poor neighborhoods.[128] A 1973 Brookings Institution study noted that revenue sharing was "an inefficient means of dealing with the special plight of large cities because much of the money will be distributed among suburban governments that are not facing critical fiscal problems."[129]

During the 1970s, older cities faced a worsening fiscal crisis as middle-class residents and businesses moved; this was exacerbated by a wave of factory closings in these areas, a trend that came to be called "deindustrialization."[130] President Gerald Ford took a hard line against federal aid to New York City, which was facing bankruptcy, attributing the city's problems to mismanagement. (The *New York Daily News* dramatized the conflict with a large front-page headline, "Ford to City: Drop Dead."[131])

After eight years of Republican control of the White House, big-city mayors, unions, and advocates for the poor hoped that electing Democrat Jimmy Carter and a Democratic majority in Congress in 1976 would produce a new round of federal urban programs. With a few small exceptions, however, Carter continued the urban policies of his Republican predecessors. His promise to develop a comprehensive urban initiative, and to coordinate the various federal agencies involved in urban matters, never materialized. His well-publicized visit to the South Bronx ghetto in 1977 turned out to have little follow-through.[132] Carter set up a commission to recommend ways to improve urban neighborhoods and another commission to outline a comprehensive urban strategy, but their reports had no serious impact. Carter added several worthy programs for crime control, social services, and job training (the Comprehensive Employment and Training Act), which provided some support for community organizing.[133]

The Carter administration initiated a competitive Urban Development Action Grant (UDAG) program to fund commercial, industrial, and housing development in older cities, a small-scale version of the urban renewal program. But fiscally strapped cities had to match the federal grants with their own dollars, and they could use the funds pretty much for their own priorities. In Boston, for example, Mayor Kevin White used UDAG funds to develop a downtown shopping mall with luxury housing and luxury stores such as Neiman Marcus. Even though most UDAG funds were used for commercial development, this failed to stem the decline of retail sales in most downtowns. President Carter and Congress increased funding for low-income housing during his first two years but began to cut HUD's budget in 1978, a trend that accelerated after Ronald Reagan took office in 1981.

The Carter administration revised the revenue-sharing formula to target needy communities, focusing more funds on big cities with high poverty rates. The president also pushed an antirecession stimulus package through Congress that included fiscal relief, public service jobs, and public works that flowed to big cities. Under pressure from a national network of neighborhood activist groups, Congress enacted the Community Reinvestment Act (CRA) in 1977 to combat bank redlining in minority inner-city areas, a law that has had an important long-term legacy. On the basis of evidence generated by the Home Mortgage Disclosure Act of 1975, enforcement of the CRA has significantly increased bank lending in low-income and minority neighborhoods and boosted minority home ownership, but it appears to have had little impact on increasing racial integration.

In 1980, Carter's Commission on Urban Problems released a report that viewed the decline of older industrial cities and the population shift to the suburbs and the Sun Belt as "inevitable." It argued that a national policy for revitalizing older cities was "ill-advised,"[134] providing a rationale for abandoning federal aid to such places. Rather, the report suggested, federal policy should focus on aiding poor individuals, wherever they happened to live, and encouraging them to move to areas with job opportunities.[135]

REAGAN RETRENCHMENT OF URBAN PROGRAMS

The Republican "Reagan Revolution" sought a wholesale shift in the federal government's approach to addressing domestic and urban problems. Ronald Reagan, a former actor and governor of California, came to office with what he (and the media) viewed as a mandate to reduce federal spending and federal involvement in state and local matters. Reagan owed little to big-city mayors, black or Hispanic leaders, unions, or any other Democratic constituency. He did receive support, however, from many once-Democratic blue-collar households living in older suburbs (so-called Reagan Democrats), giving the Reagan administration the political leeway to implement his conviction.[136] Reagan's vice president, George H. W. Bush, carried out the same agenda during his one term in the White House.

During the Reagan and Bush eras (1981 to 1993), cities were under attack as symbols of the failure of activist government and well-intentioned but naive liberalism. Broad electoral support and the perceived poor performance of urban programs made it possible for the Reagan and Bush administrations to slash federal assistance to cities while cutting taxes and significantly increasing military spending.[137]

Two Reagan administration task force reports released in 1982, the *Report of the President's Commission of Housing* and the *National Urban Policy Report*, explained the Reagan philosophy. Both said that the marketplace should determine social and economic conditions.[138] The housing task force, dominated by developers, landlords, and bankers, called for "free and deregulated" markets and for reliance on vouchers (instead of new construction) when government help was needed.

The Reagan and Bush administrations slashed federal programs for local governments.[139] Reagan eliminated general revenue sharing, a $1.8 billion cut to the budgets of larger cities. He slashed funding for public service jobs and job training by 69 percent (in constant dollars) and the CDBG program by 54 percent. The social services block grant and funds for urban mass transit were reduced by 37 and 25 percent, respectively. The UDAG program was cut by 41 percent. Overall, federal assistance to local governments was cut 60 percent, from $43 billion to $17 billion. The only program that survived cuts was federal aid for highways, which primarily benefitted suburbs, not cities.

These cutbacks had a particularly devastating impact on cities with high levels of poverty and limited property tax bases, many of which depended on federal and state aid for half or more of their budgets. In 1980, federal dollars accounted for 22 percent of big-city (over 300,000 population) budgets; by 1989, federal aid was only 6 percent. State governments did not step in to fill the gap, as the president had said they would. State aid constituted 16 percent of city budgets in 1980 and remained the same nine years later.

The Democrats in Congress went along with these cuts but balked at Reagan's and Bush's efforts to sharply trim federal aid to needy individuals, who disproportionately lived in America's cities. Welfare funding increased 12 percent, to $12.2 billion in 1990, but because the size of the rolls also increased during this period, real benefits per family declined from $3,506 to $3,218 during the decade.[140] Likewise, the average food stamp benefit dropped from $719 to $690, although overall federal spending on food stamps remained the same.[141]

Federal funds for Medicaid grew 86 percent, reaching $41 billion in 1990, due primarily to increasing medical costs. The Reagan administration, which opposed government price controls, did nothing to stop rising health care costs. Because states were required to match federal Medicaid funds, this put considerable strain on state budgets, leading them to cut aid to cities; this forced further local cuts in sanitation, police and fire protection, public libraries, and municipal hospitals and clinics.

The most dramatic cut in domestic spending during the Reagan and Bush years was for low-income housing subsidies. In his first year in office, Reagan halved the budget authority for public housing and Section 8 to about $17.5 billion. Each year thereafter, Reagan sought to eliminate federal housing assistance to the poor. Congress would not make such deep cuts, but it met Reagan more than halfway.[142] Federal housing assistance for the poor had never been an entitlement, but the proportion of the eligible poor who received federal housing subsidies declined during the 1980s, while urban homelessness rose dramatically. In 1970, there had been 300,000 more low-cost rental units (6.5 million) than low-income renter households (6.2 million). By 1985, the number of low-cost units had fallen to 5.6 million, and the number of low-income renter households had grown to 8.9 million, a disparity of 3.3 million units.[143] By the late 1980s, the number of homeless had swollen to 600,000 on any given night and 1.2 million over the course of a year.[144]

The nation's poverty rate increased from 11.7 percent in 1979 to 15.2 percent in 1983. The economic prosperity of the latter 1980s pushed it down to 12.8 percent in 1989, but the subsequent recession pushed it back up to 14.8 percent in 1992, when Bush left office.[145] The central-city poverty rate increased from 15.7 percent in 1979 to 21.5 percent in 1992.[146] The proportion of all poor living in central cities increased from 37 percent in 1983 to 42 percent in 1992.[147]

CLINTON URBAN POLICY: TOO LITTLE, TOO LATE

Anticipating a Democratic victory in the 1992 presidential race, many think tanks, foundations, and advocacy groups began drafting bold new urban policy agendas. The explosion of the Los Angeles ghettos in April 1992 after the Rodney King verdict hastened this flood of new prescriptions and triggered growing interest in the condition of urban areas.[148] Urban activists and big-city officials hoped that Bill Clinton's victory would usher in a new era for the nation's cities. But Clinton was elected with only 43 percent of the overall vote. Almost half of all eligible voters (disproportionately the poor and minorities) stayed away from the polls. Clinton won the vast majority of urban voters, but he owed his victory to the fact that Texas billionaire Ross Perot, running as a third-party candidate, took 19 percent of the vote, mostly from George Bush, and to the support of middle-class suburban voters who had voted for Reagan and Bush in the previous three elections. His governing agenda reflected these political realities.

President Clinton adopted a different symbolic approach to cities compared with his Republican predecessors. He visited inner-city churches and housing projects and gave stirring speeches about his personal commitment, and the nation's responsibility, to address poverty, racism, and urban blight. Presidents Reagan and Bush had refused to meet with the nation's big-city mayors, but Clinton met with them often to discuss their problems and agenda. He appointed two former big-city mayors (Federico Peña of Denver and Henry Cisneros of San Antonio) and a leading expert on urban social problems (former University of Wisconsin chancellor Donna Shalala) to his cabinet. His subcabinet included many of the nation's leading urban policy scholars and practitioners, people who had been waiting more than a decade to put their ideas into action.

Although it captured a majority of Congress, Clinton's Democratic Party was deeply divided. Many members were closely linked to business interests that opposed progressive taxation, Keynesian pump-priming, and social spending. Clinton inherited the huge federal deficit produced by the Reagan-Bush tax cuts and increased defense spending, limiting his ability to address domestic concerns without significant tax increases or dramatic cuts in military spending.

Clinton initially had bold plans to expand the New Deal and Great Society legacy. To build broad political support, he emphasized universal policies rather than means-tested programs narrowly targeted to the poor. Early in the Clinton administration, however, the Republicans (led by minority leader Senator Bob Dole) and the Democratic majority in Congress thwarted the president's efforts to enact a public investment plan to stimulate jobs, universal health insurance, and even a child immunization program, each of which would have significantly eased the problems facing cities and urban residents. After the November 1994 elections put a Republican majority in Congress, any significant progress on such matters was impossible. The Republican takeover of Congress exacerbated the political isolation of cities, symbolized by Clinton's proposal a month

later to dramatically cut the HUD budget and his willingness to consider eliminating HUD altogether.

During his eight years in office, Clinton presided over a dramatic improvement of the nation's economy, including an unprecedented combination of low
unemployment and low inflation. The nation's per capita income increased (in
2001 dollars) from $18,358 in 1992 to $22,970 in 2000. Median household income (in 2001 dollars) rose from $37,880 to $43,167; for black households it
increased from $23,190 to $30,495 and for Hispanic households, from $27,940
to $34,389. The unemployment rate dropped from 7.5 percent to 4 percent, the
lowest figure since 1969. During that period, the nation's poverty rate fell from
14.8 percent 1992 to 11.3 percent, lifting almost 6.5 million Americans out of
poverty. Half of those people lived in central cities, where the poverty rate declined from 20.9 percent to 16.3 percent. The poverty rate for blacks fell from
33.4 percent to 22.5 percent and for Hispanics from 29.6 percent to 21.5 percent. The home ownership rate rose from 64 percent to 67.5 percent, an all-time
peak, with the biggest increases among blacks and Hispanics. After a fifteen-
year decline, wages for unskilled workers increased. The crime rate reached a
three-decade low.[149]

Some trends, however, were less upbeat. Despite falling poverty and increased incomes for low-skill workers, the gap between rich and poor continued to widen. From 1992 to 2000, the proportion of all income going to the
poorest one-fifth of the population declined from 3.8 percent to 3.6 percent,
while the richest 5 percent increased its share from 18.6 percent to 22.1 percent.[150] America's gap between the rich and poor remained the widest of any
democratic industrial nation.[151] Although the Clinton administration increased
matching funds for states to provide health insurance for low-income children,
39.8 million of Americans (14.2 percent) lacked health insurance in 2000.[152]

Clinton's liberal critics believed that his administration could have done
much more to address the plight of the poor in the context of such dramatic
economic expansion. "We should be ashamed we haven't made more progress
in this economy," said Marian Wright Edelman, president of the Children's
Defense Fund. "It is totally unacceptable that with this much prosperity we
have millions of uninsured children. What's going to happen when a recession comes?" Wendell Primus, a former top official in Clinton's Department of
Health and Human Services, said, "We've clearly made gains in this administration. But I think we missed an opportunity to do even better."[153]

Unlike the Reagan and Bush view, the Clinton administration argued that
"macroeconomic policy is necessary, but not sufficient" to reduce poverty.[154]
The Clintonites did not believe that a rising tide, on its own, lifts all boats.

The improvement in the condition of cities and lives of the poor was due to both the overall economic recovery and to social policies directed at helping the poor. The most important Clinton antipoverty initiatives were not "urban" programs, even though most of those affected resided in cities. They were the expansion of the EITC, an increase in the minimum wage, and reform of AFDC (welfare reform).

Using the rhetoric of "making work pay," the Clinton administration achieved a dramatic expansion of the EITC, which provides a tax credit of up to $3,800 to the working poor; families with incomes up to $30,500 are eligible. The Clinton administration explicitly chose eligibility levels to ensure that the combination of wages, the EITC, and food stamps available to a family earning the minimum wage would lift the family out of poverty.[155] In 1998, 19.3 million families and individuals claimed the EITC, with an average benefit of $1,523.[156] In 1997, Clinton persuaded enough Republicans, then a majority in Congress, to increase the minimum wage from $4.25 an hour, where it had been since 1992, to $5.15 an hour.

Clinton's embrace of welfare reform was among the most controversial issues of his administration. During his 1992 campaign, he pledged to "end welfare as we know it." After the Republicans won a majority of seats in Congress in 1994, Clinton hoped he could forge a compromise measure that would preserve some protections for the poor while demonstrating that as a "new Democrat" he was willing to challenge his party's longstanding support for the welfare program. Despite much contention among fellow Democrats, and even within his own cabinet, Clinton signed the Personal Responsibility and Work Opportunity Reconciliation Act in August 1996. It replaced AFDC (an entitlement with no time limits) with Temporary Assistance to Needy Families (TANF), a block grant to states that ended the entitlement to federal aid and set time limits for receiving assistance.[157] During its first few years, TANF significantly reduced the number of people on the welfare rolls. Welfare caseloads fell from their peak of over 14 million persons in 1993 to less than 6 million at the end of 2000.[158] The low unemployment rate made it possible for many welfare recipients to find jobs. Many, however, simply went from the ranks of the "welfare poor" to the "working poor," with no improvement of their living standards. Sixty-four percent of those who left the welfare rolls between 1997 and 1999 were working, but their median wage was $7.15 an hour, with many working for the minimum wage. Only one-third worked for employers that provided health insurance.[159] Recipients who were concentrated in high-poverty, inner-city neighborhoods were least successful in leaving welfare.[160]

Compared with these broad antipoverty policies, the Clinton administration's overtly urban initiatives were relatively small-scale efforts. These included the empowerment zone and enterprise communities (EZ/EC) program, the "new markets" initiative, and stronger enforcement of antidiscrimination laws in housing and banking.

The EZ/EC program sought to induce private capital to invest in HUD-designated "empowerment zones" in eleven cities. Each empowerment zone city was eligible for $100 million in grants and tax breaks for businesses to create additional jobs. Another 114 cities and rural communities received a scaled-down "enterprise communities" status, with $3 million each. The goal was to entice businesses to create jobs and hire residents of these low-income areas in order to reduce poverty and unemployment.

During his final year in office, prodded by HUD Secretary Andrew Cuomo, Clinton sought to focus national attention on urban poverty. He noted that despite the nation's strong economy and the decline in poverty, many places and people had been "left behind." In 1999 there were still 32.3 million Americans (11.8 percent of the population) living in poverty. During that summer and fall, Clinton toured major cities and rural areas across the country to draw attention to persistent poverty in the midst of low unemployment and to his "new markets initiative," which was essentially an expansion of the EZ/EC program, providing tax credits, low-interest loans, and matching funds to encourage business to invest in desperately poor urban neighborhoods and rural areas.[161]

The overall impact of these EZ/EC and New Market programs was negligible. The level of funding was insufficient to induce many businesses to invest or expand operations in the zones. In most cities, economic conditions did improve in the zones, but it is difficult to attribute the improvement to the program, because many cities and neighborhoods areas without EZ/EC funding also improved during the 1990s economic expansion. It wasn't clear whether these targeted investments actually added new jobs or simply rearranged existing jobs by luring some businesses to move to the zones from elsewhere in the metropolitan areas. To win the competition for an EZ/EC designation, cities had to show that residents were actively involved, along with business, local government, and community groups, in developing the community improvement plan. The level of citizen involvement varied widely from city to city.[162]

The Clinton administration's efforts to get bank regulators to strengthen enforcement of the Community Reinvestment Act turned out to be a more successful strategy for targeting private investment in urban areas. During the Clinton years, HUD provided grants to community organizations like ACORN and local fair housing groups to audit the performance of banks with respect to discriminatory patterns in mortgage lending. HUD put online the data about each bank's track record—including the race, income, and neighborhood of consumers who applied for, were approved for, or were rejected for mortgage loans—so that community groups would utilize it. Most important, Clinton insisted that federal bank regulators scrutinize banks' lending records in low-income and minority records and use their findings in deciding whether to approve bank mergers and acquisitions. These efforts led to additional mortgage loans in inner-city neighborhoods and to minority consumers, helped increase the home ownership rate among minorities, and led banks to increase their business dealings with and philanthropic support for nonprofit community-based organizations in urban areas. Along with this progress, however, the Clinton administration failed to expand the law's scope to oversee the growing number of private mortgage brokers who are not covered by the CRA. Between 1993 and 2000, for example, home purchase loans made by CRA-regulated lenders declined from 36.1 percent to 29.5 percent of all loans.[163]

In terms of federal funding, however, Clinton did not make housing for the poor a major priority. In October 1996, toward the end of Clinton's first term, the *New York Times Magazine* ran a large story called "The Year that Housing Died," noting that the president had signed a budget with no additional subsidies for low-income housing. In fact, confronted with pressure from Republicans in Congress, Clinton even considered abolishing HUD altogether. When Carter was in office, HUD increased the supply of subsidized housing by as much as 350,000 units a year. During Reagan's two terms, the average fell to about 100,000 a year, and during Bush's term it fell further to 75,000 a year. Housing advocates expected Clinton to reverse the trend. But during the 1994 to 1999 period, the average number of new subsidized units was just over 30,000. It wasn't until Clinton's last two years that the figure jumped to over 100,000 units, mostly from the addition of 50,000 new housing vouchers committed to former welfare recipients who were making the transition to work. During Clinton's eight years in office, the gap between the need for and the supply of low-rent housing widened. Between 1991 and 1999, the number of apartments affordable to low-income families fell by 940,000 units.[164]

Clinton also implemented two tiny but potentially significant pilot programs to promote mobility for the urban poor. The Moving to Opportunity program funded six cities to provide Section 8 vouchers to about 7,500 low-income renters to escape ghettos and move to better neighborhoods.[165] The equally small ($17 million) Bridges to Work program helped poor residents of ghetto neighborhoods in five cities get access to suburban jobs through improved transportation.[166] Clinton also revised several long-standing policies on public housing. HUD began allowing local housing authorities to tear down the most distressed projects and relocate tenants by using Section 8 vouchers, a policy (called HOPE VI) that may have improved the developments but resulted in fewer subsidized units.[167] HUD also allowed local authorities to change tenant selection policies to allow more working poor families to live in public housing. Clinton's first HUD secretary, Henry Cisneros, focused public attention on the importance of building bridges between cities and suburbs. HUD sponsored research and held conferences about regional and metropolitan issues, but none of these efforts translated into policy initiatives.[168] The Clinton administration was unwilling, for example, to use the federal government's leverage to require wealthy suburbs to accept a minimal level of housing affordable to poor families.

Overall, Clinton sought to create and redefine an urban agenda, but the federal deficit, the Republican victory in 1994, the ensuing ideological attack on government activism and the relative weakness of urban constituencies inhibited the Clinton administration from promoting a bold urban policy. In particular, Clinton did not want his urban policies to threaten suburban interests that were central to his electoral victories. As a result, urban policies remained as separate targeted programs, with little effort to examine the stealth urban policies and regional dynamics that underlay the urban crisis.

GEORGE W. BUSH AND THE CITIES

George W. Bush took office in January 2001 following a close and controversial election that was ultimately decided by the U.S. Supreme Court. Vice President Al Gore won slightly more popular votes than Bush but had fewer electoral college votes after the court gave the Florida contest to Bush. Gore beat Bush convincingly among voters in cities by a 61 percent to 35 percent margin, virtually tied Bush among suburban voters by a 47 percent to 49 percent margin, and lost by a large 37 percent to 59 percent margin among rural voters. Urban voters, however, accounted for only 29 percent of the electorate. Black voters favored Gore by a 90 percent to 9 percent margin, while Hispanic voters choose Gore by a 62 percent to 35 percent margin.[169] Not surprisingly, Bush saw no reason to shape his policy agenda to appeal to urban voters.[170]

President Bush had three policy priorities: cut taxes, especially for the most affluent; reduce government regulations on business; and increase American military spending. With a Republican majority in Congress, Bush was able to accomplish all three goals. The attack on the World Trade Center on September 11, 2001, helped reverse Bush's declining favorability ratings, and made it much easier for Bush to persuade Democrats to vote to boost defense spending, invade Afghanistan and Iraq, and appropriate funds for a domestic "war on terrorism." Bush had inherited a federal budget surplus from Clinton, but the combination of huge tax cuts and increased military spending led to record budget deficits, leaving hardly any discretionary funds for social or antipoverty programs. The initial public support for Bush's focus on war and terrorism also limited the Democrats' willingness to challenge Bush's handling of the troubled economy. After the end of the previous recession in March 1991, the nation embarked on nine straight years of job growth. In contrast, the so-called Bush recession ended in November 2001, but over the next two years, the nation experienced what some economists called a "jobless recovery," with American firms sending a growing number of both blue-collar and white-collar jobs overseas. During Bush's first three years in office, the unemployment rate increased from 4 percent to 6 percent, adding more than 3 million people to the ranks of the jobless. The number of people out of work for more than six months doubled. Median household income fell from $43,848 to $43,381 between 2000 and 2003.[171] The nation's poverty rate rose from 11.3 percent to 12.5 percent. An additional 4.2 million Americans fell below the poverty line — almost 2.5 million in suburbs, 1.3 million in central cities and 517,000 in rural areas.[172] In 2003, 45 million Americans (15.6 percent of the population) lacked health insurance, an increase of 5.1 million in three years.[173]

Some of the dire predictions about Clinton's welfare reform program came to fruition during the Bush years. Robert Reich, Secretary of Labor during Clinton's first term, had warned that "when unemployment starts creeping up again, a long line of people are going to be in trouble because we've taken away a safety net."[174] For example, the proportion of families who leave welfare but could not find jobs rose from 50 percent in 1999 to 58 percent in 2002. The number of former welfare recipients still in poverty increased.[175]

In 2000, Bush had campaigned as a "compassionate conservative," but as soon as he took office he abandoned that image. His most symbolic "urban" initiative was a plan to redirect federal funds for social programs like homeless shelters, food banks, and drug rehabilitation programs to agencies sponsored by "faith-based" organizations. This idea met with substantial controversy in Congress and the press, particularly whether these organizations would be able to apply religious litmus tests in hiring staff and providing help to needy people. Many social policy experts also questioned whether religious organizations were effective at addressing these social problems. Although Bush created a faith-based office in the White House, Congress refused to enact legislation endorsing the plan.[176] The plan ran into further controversy when John DiIulio, the conservative political scientist Bush recruited to run the faith-based program, was quoted in *Esquire* magazine criticizing the president and his advisors for the "lack of even basic policy knowledge, and only casual interest in knowing more." DiIulio observed that "there were only a couple of people in the West Wing who worried at all about policy substance and analysis."[177]

Bush forged a bipartisan consensus in Congress to enact an education bill, the "No Child Left Behind Act," to require local schools to increase student testing and to issue annual "report cards" on their progress toward improving student performance. The stated goal was to force school systems—particularly schools in inner-city and minority neighborhoods—to raise standards, including the hiring of more qualified teachers, in order to improve student achievement. The bill required the federal and state governments to punish schools and school systems that failed to meet certain standards. The bill was passed with much fanfare, but Bush failed to request sufficient funds to translate its goals into real accomplishments. Education experts estimated that the nation's schools would need at least $84 billion to comply with the new federal standards, but Bush asked Congress for only $1 billion. Without adequate funds, local systems could not hire more teachers, reduce class sizes, or provide existing teachers with additional training. Schools in inner cities, which are most likely to have low-achieving students but lack the resources to add teachers or improve facilities, would be hurt most by the No Child Left Behind Act.[178]

Housing for the poor, barely on Clinton's radar screen, was even less of a priority for the Bush administration. Bush appointed Mel Martinez, a county executive in Florida and cochair of Bush's state campaign, to be HUD secretary, but *Washington Post* columnist David Broder observed that in his first two years "almost nothing has been heard" from his department.[179] Martinez told Broder that, "Housing issues are predominantly local issues. . . . The solution to meeting the nation's affordable housing needs will not come out of Washington."[180] In his first three years as president, Bush kept the HUD budget at the same level, but in 2004 he proposed major cuts to the Section 8 housing voucher program, eliminating 250,000 vouchers in 2005 and 600,000 vouchers by 2009, a 30 percent cut. Low-income tenants with vouchers would face a rent increase of about $2,000 a year.[181]

The nation's economic distress, including the spiraling federal deficit, created fiscal havoc among states and cities. Both states and cities faced their worst fiscal condition in decades. Governors and mayors, including Republicans, complained that Washington was leaving them in the lurch. The skyrocketing cost of health care strained states' ability to pay for their share of Medicaid. Governors were forced to cut funding for health care, schools, transportation, and other basic services. Nor could they cope with the cost of im-

plementing the new federal welfare-to-work mandates because rising unemployment made it nearly impossible to find jobs for former welfare recipients. Mayors and other city officials, reeling from the loss of federal and state aid, had no choice but to cut essential services, including public safety, libraries, road repair, and public schools.[182]

The cities' fiscal trauma was compounded by the Bush administration's most expensive federal mandate—complying with its homeland security and antiterrorism initiatives. Bush imposed draconian requirements on cities to increase security measures but failed to provide the funds necessary to comply with the federal mandates. It took the Bush administration and Congress a year and a half after the 9/11 attacks to enact legislation to provide states and cities with funding to improve airport security and other measures, but a year later, few cities had received the funds they were promised.[183]

The attack on the World Trade Center obviously devastated New York City more than any other city. The city and the entire metropolitan area were ravaged physically, economically, and psychologically. Bush visited the scene to help lend his sympathy to the victims and their families. With New York Mayor Rudy Giuliani at his side, Bush promised to help the city, its residents, its workforce, and its businesses rebuild and recover from the economic chaos. Bush pledged more than $20.5 billion to help New York City rebuild its subways, roads, hospitals, and other facilities, to help the city deal with the huge budget gap created by its emergency response by police, firefighters, medical personnel, and other city employees, to help business recover from the loss, and to provide financial assistance to families of people killed or injured by the attack. Three years after the tragedy, it appears that the bulk of the aid will have promoted real estate development and transit infrastructure in lower Manhattan rather than addressing broader issues like strengthening the New York City economy or that of nearby Chinatown. Much of the aid, so-called Liberty Bonds, may also go unused.[184]

Ironically, the 9/11 tragedy reminded New Yorkers and all Americans how much they depended on government, not only in emergencies, but also in normal times.[185] Even those who typically object to "big government" spending and aid to cities acknowledged that Washington had a responsibility to help New York City recover and rebuild from the physical and economic devastation caused by the attack on the World Trade Center. Moreover, for at least that moment in history, the nation's heroes were the police, firefighters, EMTs, ambulance drivers, hospital staffers, public health experts, and other public employees whose courage, commitment, and compassion helped people cope with perhaps the worst single tragedy in the nation's history.

POLITICS SHAPE MARKETS

The free-market view of urban decline and suburban sprawl is wrong. Federal policies toward metropolitan areas did not waste billions of dollars on urban programs that tried but failed to reshape cities against powerful market forces. On the contrary, federal urban policies were an outstanding "success" from a free-market perspective: they promoted powerful economic trends that resulted in greater economic segregation and more suburban sprawl, albeit with extremely high social costs.

The political, economic, and social landscape that we take for granted is a product of federal and state policies that shaped individual and corporate decision making. Each major policy initiative began with serious debates about substantially different options. Powerful interest groups (such as the highway lobby and home-building industry) got exactly what they wanted: government support for suburbanization and metropolitan segregation. Had national policy makers been prompted to make different choices—for example, to support public transportation, to provide subsidies for mixed-income housing, to invest defense dollars and other public facilities in cities—our current metropolitan landscape would look substantially different.

Looking more narrowly at the policies and programs overtly targeted at central cities and poor neighborhoods, they partly failed. Despite billions of dollars spent on bolstering central-city business districts, central cities have lost population and jobs and become poorer relative to their suburbs. These targeted policies failed partly because far more governmental resources were devoted to promoting suburbanization. Spending on home-owner subsidies was several magnitudes larger than spending on low-income housing programs; far more was spent on highways than on mass transit.

Even those urban programs most directly targeted to the urban poor were fundamentally flawed. They did not acknowledge that the problems facing poor people and poor neighborhoods are only one part of a larger dynamic of regional growth. Deeply propelled by decades of government support, this regional dynamic is hard to reshape. We have described the many ways in which it developed a self-reinforcing momentum. Compensatory programs, after the fact, are bound to have only marginal effects, especially when they do not recalibrate the institutional arrangements and incentive systems that promote economic segregation and suburban sprawl.

The federal government put its full weight behind suburbanization, refusing, for example, to insure loans in cities and integrated neighborhoods, thus encouraging redlining of cities. After governments and banks shunned eco-

nomically and racially integrated neighborhoods, this decline became a self-fulfilling prophecy. Even if governments and banks no longer discriminate, spatial inequalities have a momentum of their own. The concentration of poverty leads to fewer jobs, higher crime, unhealthier environments, and fewer shopping opportunities. As a result, those who have the wherewithal flee to better neighborhoods, accentuating the economic and social decline of inner cities and distressed suburbs.

The three congressional districts discussed in Chapter 1 illustrate these trends. The Thirteenth Congressional District in Illinois, a booming suburban area west of Chicago, was transformed by federal highway construction. Oak Brook, for example, is located near the nexus of three federally funded interstate highways (88, 294, and 290). The siting of one of the federal government's most prominent scientific facilities, the Argonne National Laboratory, with 4,500 employees, was another powerful factor in the district's growth. (Another federal facility, the Fermi National Accelerator Laboratory, is located in the adjacent district, but many of its employees reside in the Thirteenth.) New York's Sixteenth Congressional District also amply illustrates the powerful negative impact of federal policies on the urban and metropolitan fabric. Construction of the Cross-Bronx Expressway initiated the downward slump of the neighborhood, and suburban housing subsidies and the absence of federal support for urban multifamily housing drew off its population. Its numerous public housing projects tie poor people to concentrated poverty neighborhoods. Finally, the inner suburbs in what is now California's Twenty-ninth Congressional District were subsidized by a steady diet of federal funds for its aerospace industry and the highways that crisscross the area and helped create one of the most polluted areas in the nation. Today, many of the area's largest employers, including the Jet Propulsion Lab, Cal Tech, and Parsons Engineering, depend on federal funding.

This dynamic need not be perpetual and unalterable. The political dynamic will change as residents of outer suburbs recognize that current patterns have generated significant problems that they cannot solve without simultaneously addressing those of inner suburbs and central cities. As urban problems spread to thousands of suburbs, it will be more difficult to blame lazy urban poor people or incompetent and corrupt city governments. Better-off suburbs will discover that they cannot fix traffic gridlock, long commutes, environmental degradation, or skyrocketing housing costs without simultaneously addressing the interrelated problems of inner suburbs and central cities.

Urban Politics and City Limits
What Cities Can and Cannot
Do to Address Poverty

Until recently, Jose Morales, a janitor at Los Angeles International Airport, slept on flattened cardboard boxes in a garage.[1] Every day at dawn, he commuted two hours by bus to his job, then another two hours back to his makeshift home in Compton, a decaying city adjacent to Los Angeles. His eight-hour-a-day job sweeping, dusting, and dumping trash paid Morales $5.45 an hour with no health insurance. He frequently scavenged in dumpsters for food, furniture, and other items. Then, in 1997, the "living wage" law enacted by the Los Angeles City Council boosted pay and benefits to employees of private companies with city contracts or subsidies. Morales got a raise to $7.25 an hour and health insurance. He still lives frugally because housing is so expensive in Los Angeles. But he was able to move with his sister and her family into a small two-bedroom house, which he rents for $615 a month. He began to buy furniture, including a dining room table, a comfortable bed, and a six-year-old used car. With his commute time cut in half, he can now sleep until 5:00 AM.

The idea of a living wage law emerged from a coalition of unions, churches, and community groups trying to help the city's growing population of working poor. The coalition spent a year building support on the fifteen-member city council, spearheaded by councilwoman Jackie Goldberg. The Los Angeles business community fiercely opposed the law, claiming that it would damage the city's business climate. They lobbied Mayor Richard Riordan and city council members, wrote newspaper op-ed columns, and cried alarm. Responding to their pleas, Mayor Riordan, a moderate Republican, vetoed the law, but the city council overrode the veto.

The Los Angeles effort is one part of a national movement that brought labor unions together with community organizations. Baltimore passed the first living wage law in 1994, following a grassroots campaign organized by BUILD (a coalition of community groups affiliated with the Industrial Areas Foundation) and the American Federation of State, County and Municipal Employees (whose members work for local governments). This movement received a major impetus from efforts by city governments to contract public services to private firms paying lower wages and benefits than prevail in the public sector. Proponents are also motivated by the proliferation of low-wage jobs in urban areas. By 2004, community, labor, and religious coalitions have fought for and won living wage ordinances in 117 cities, including St. Louis, Boston, Tucson, San Jose, Portland (Oregon), Milwaukee, Detroit, Minneapolis, St. Paul, Miami, Detroit, San Antonio, and Oakland. Efforts were unsuccessful in some cities but are still under way in others.[2]

The living wage movement reflects both the potential and the limits of local efforts to address the problems of economic inequality and poverty. Living wage laws cover only a small proportion of a city's workforce (about 12,500 out of 1.7 million workers in the city of Los Angeles). Living wage laws typically cover only employees of employers that do business with city government.[3] In most states, cities have no authority to enact minimum wage laws that apply to all workers, but in recent years voters in San Francisco, Santa Fe, and New Orleans endorsed ballot initiatives to create citywide minimum wage laws significantly higher than the federal level.[4]

Everywhere that unions and community groups have proposed a living wage bill, business leaders have warned that it will hurt business and thwart private job creation. Like opponents of increasing the federal or state minimum wage, these foes argue that firms employing low-wage workers will be forced to close, hurting the very people the measure was designed to help. Living wage laws have not in fact had such consequences. One reason is that most of the businesses covered by these laws are immobile. Airport restaurants, private parking lots serving the city convention center, and sanitation companies under municipal contract to collect garbage are tied to the local economy. Equally important, low-wage workers typically spend everything they earn. So when their wages go up, the additional income gets pumped into the local economy (particularly in grocery stores and other retail outlets in low-income neighborhoods). Nevertheless, many local elected officials are reluctant to pass living wage laws (much less municipal minimum wage laws) for fear of costing their city jobs and themselves campaign contributions from business.

The clash over living wage and minimum wage laws reflects a larger debate over the degree to which cities can and should enact local measures to address the concentration of poor people within their borders. On the one hand, most local officials would like to improve conditions for the poor and near poor. On the other hand, they want to make their cities attractive places to do business and retain middle-class residents. Laws that regulate businesses to act in socially responsible ways—such as living wage ordinances, "linkage" fees on new commercial buildings that target the funds for affordable housing, business taxes, clean air laws, inclusionary zoning laws that require housing developers to incorporate units for low-income families, plant closing laws, and rent control—confront this dilemma. Corporations may be bluffing when they threaten to leave if cities enact such laws, but it is hard for local officials, unions, and community groups to know for certain, especially when many cities have experienced substantial job losses. Business warnings are not always empty threats. Local officials are reluctant to judge which firms are more or less likely to leave and unwilling to see just how far they can push private companies to provide more tax revenues, raise wages, reduce their pollution, or keep rents affordable. Instead, politicians tend to err in favor of promoting local businesses.[5]

Local elected officials confront a dilemma. They typically campaign for office by promising more and better jobs, more affordable housing, safer streets, more (and more efficient) public services, and better schools. Even with the best of intentions, however, local political leaders, whatever their political orientation, face overwhelming obstacles in trying to reduce poverty within their boundaries. The realities of urban finance and economics limit even the most progressive city officials. They can reduce the incidence of poverty either by lifting up the poor people in the city or by enticing more affluent people to move in. Urban politicians typically lack the brazenness to kick poor people out, although they sometimes encourage gentrification that has that effect. But they cannot require the suburbs to build affordable housing for the central-city poor. Nor can they require suburban employers to hire poor city residents or force metropolitan transportation agencies to reorganize their routes and schedules to help urban residents get to suburban jobs. Most suburbs also have an advantage in the competition to attract middle-class residents, such as better schools, lower property tax rates, and more efficient public services.

THE IRON CAGE OF MUNICIPAL FINANCE

City governments are often perched on the brink of fiscal distress. Even in cities with strong economies, local public officials compete on a playing field tilted toward their suburbs, with few mechanisms to promote city-suburb cooperation so that suburban wealth can be tapped to help reduce poverty. Urban politicians worry that higher taxes on business and the middle class, higher wages, and more regulations on employers and developers will exacerbate further flight to the suburbs. Most urban leaders, in short, are trapped in a fiscal straitjacket.

Central-city governments can tax only part of the economic rewards they generate, and these revenues fluctuate with local economic conditions. But although revenues are limited and variable, demands for services and expenditures are inexorable and often beyond municipal control (as in the case of the local share of Medicaid expenditures). As a result, even economically successful cities face chronic difficulty balancing their budgets. Since the 1930s, cities have depended on federal and state aid to help them make ends meet. Federal aid to cities rose significantly during the 1960s and 1970s, but has fallen precipitously since then. Since 1977, federal aid as a share of total city revenues has declined from 15 percent to 5 percent.[6]

In 2000, the nation's 87,525 local governments spent $996 billion, or 36 percent of all government spending in the United States.[7] They provide and finance most of the services that Americans use on a daily basis. As Robert Lineberry noted, they are "vital to the preservation of life (police, fire, sanitation, public health), liberty (police, courts, prosecutors), property (zoning, planning, taxing), and public enlightenment (schools, libraries)."[8] Cities cover most of the cost of providing these services through whatever they can raise from property, sales, and income taxes; fines; fees; and other sources. Education, public safety, and sanitation exhaust the lion's share of most municipal budgets. (Most cities also provide other services funded primarily by states or the federal government, such as welfare or public housing.)

In comparing cities' fiscal capacities, Helen Ladd and John Yinger found that most had a significant gap between their ability to raise revenue and the amounts they needed to spend to provide average-quality basic services. The typical American city has poor "fiscal health."[9] Although some cities are better managed than others, and some suffer from corruption, these factors do not explain urban fiscal stress. Corruption and inefficiency do not account for much of the cost of running cities. As Ladd and Yinger observe, "although the financial difficulties of these cities may be exacerbated by politics or management practices . . . the policy tools available to city officials are weak compared to the impact on city finances of national economic, social and fiscal trends."[10]

As the nation's economy boomed in the late 1990s, cities' fiscal condition improved. Urban poverty began to decline, residents' incomes rose, and businesses prospered, which generated more revenue.[11] But cities still could not raise enough revenue to provide everyone with good schools, public safety, and well-maintained infrastructure, or to grant raises to city employees that kept up with the rate of inflation, much less to lift the incomes of the poor. Their improved bond ratings (which allow cities to borrow money) masked the deeper reality that many cities had already tightened their belts and lowered residents' expectations during the downturns of the mid-1970s, early 1980s, and early 1990s. They closed public hospitals; reduced library hours; deferred maintenance on aging sewers, playgrounds, and parks; and reduced the numbers of public employees. If many cities were able to live within their means in the late 1990s, it is because they attempted to do less than they had done in earlier years, especially in addressing the needs of the poor.

Since 2000, urban fiscal conditions have worsened due to a national recession, rising health care and pension costs, and significant declines in federal and state aid to cities. Faced with a budget deficit approaching $500 billion in 2003 resulting from tax cuts and increased spending, the federal government significantly cut aid to states and cities. In turn, state governments—faced with $110 billion in budget deficits in 2003—cut aid to cities for the first time in more than a decade. Increasingly, cities were left to fend for themselves. Once again they were forced to trim services, lay off employees, raise taxes and fees, and postpone planned capital projects, such as construction and repair of schools, roads, sewers, and bridges.[12]

Cities generally face worse fiscal conditions than suburbs. Vast disparities of wealth and poverty are often located only a few zip codes from each other, even though they seem worlds apart. Not only do the well-off and the poor live apart from each other, but they receive strikingly unequal public services because the poor live in places that lack the fiscal capacity to provide decent public services at reasonable tax rates, while the rich live in places that can fund high-quality services at a relatively low tax rate.[13] In an extreme case, such as Camden, New Jersey, almost half of whose 85,000 residents live in poverty, the city cannot provide even minimal services despite punishingly high tax rates.[14] In Milwaukee, the per capita value of property in 1997 was $25,316 compared with $60,399 for its suburbs.[15] Residents of different communities in the same metropolitan area can pay the same tax rates but receive very different levels of public services, or pay different amounts of taxes for the same public services.

Many older inner-ring suburbs also have problems providing local services, and they lack the downtown commercial properties that generate tax revenue. Myron Orfield notes that fifty-nine Chicago suburban municipalities had a lower tax base per household than did Chicago, which was itself considerably below the regional average.[16] If the average fiscal capacity of local governments were scored 100, the city of Chicago (at 87) would be 13 percent below average, but the inner-ring suburb of Maywood would score 54, and North Chicago would score 60. At the other extreme, Winnetka would score 207 and Lake Forest 266.[17]

Suburbanization has exacerbated cities' fiscal dilemmas. Cities no longer dominate their metropolitan areas as they did fifty years ago, when they housed half or two-thirds of the population in most regions and had higher per capita incomes than did the suburbs. Almost two-thirds of the nation's twenty-five largest cities lost population after 1950.[18] Even when they grew, they did so more slowly than their surrounding suburbs. Between 1993 and 1996, central cities' share of job growth continued to fall in most metropolitan areas; almost a quarter experienced an absolute loss of employment. Half increased the number of jobs, but not as quickly as their suburbs.[19] Economic shifts and disinvestment left central-city per capita incomes considerably lower than those of suburbanites in almost every metropolitan area. They also lowered the tax base at a time when the average level of need among city residents was rising. According to Howard Chernick and Andrew Reschovsky, to compensate, cities "must increase tax rates or reduce public spending, further convincing middle-class residents to leave."[20]

Most cities are still vital centers of culture, entertainment, and other key services within their metropolitan areas. Suburbanites and tourists flock to museums, sports complexes, concert halls, and convention centers, as well as to hospitals and universities. But many of these institutions are nonprofit organizations and do not directly generate tax revenue. One-third of New York City's property value is exempt from taxes, compared with 13 percent in suburban Nassau County and 22 percent in suburban Westchester County.[21] Local efforts to lure private professional sports teams by subsidizing stadiums rarely generate enough revenues to cover costs.[22]

Enormous amounts of private wealth remain within most American cities. But city governments cannot tap much of it, in part because states restrict how cities can raise revenue. For example, only eight of the nation's twenty-four largest cities impose an income or wage tax on nonresident commuters, and at a very low rate at that.[23] In 1999, New York Governor George Pataki signed a law repealing a 0.45 percent tax on the New York City wages earned by suburban commuters. The repeal of the tax, first enacted in 1966, deprived the city of $360 million a year from the 800,000 people who work in the city but live elsewhere.[24] During the 1970s and 1980s, statewide referenda restricted the ability of municipalities to increase property taxes, such as Proposition 13 in California and Proposition 2½ in Massachusetts.

Cities also have broader service responsibilities than do most suburbs. Many serious social problems — including homelessness, AIDS, drug use, and violent crime — are concentrated in cities. City governments did not create these problems, but they have to deal with them. For example, in the 1960s and 1970s, federal and state laws deinstitutionalized mental hospital patients after the media exposed the inhumane treatment many of them received and new tranquilizers gave mental health professionals the ability to manage patients in "community" settings.[25] But the federal and state governments did not fund enough community mental health facilities, and neighborhood opposition made it hard to open those that were funded. The mental hospital patient population dropped from 558,922 in 1955 to 137,810 in 1980 and then to 118,647 in 1990. Younger schizophrenics, who previously would have been hospitalized, had no place to go for treatment. The result was a dramatic increase in mentally ill persons on America's city streets. Many became homeless, often begging and sometimes committing crimes, triggering opposition from business and neighborhood groups. At the same time, federal funding for subsidized housing also declined. Many cities used police and other personnel to manage swelling homeless populations and responded by using public funds and charitable help to provide shelter, food, and medical treatment, but in many other cities, police harassed the homeless but provided few services. By 1988, partly in response to litigation, New York City had 30,500 shelter beds and was spending $375 million in local funds to shelter the homeless.[26]

Cities' fiscal problems are compounded by many spending requirements imposed by federal and state governments and courts without providing the funds needed to carry them out. In the 1990s alone, the federal government added at least 130 mandates on cities.[27] For example, the federal government requires cities to improve the water quality, remove asbestos from old school buildings and lead paint from public housing, and make municipal buses accessible to the physically disabled (under the Americans with Disabilities Act). In 1992, Chicago estimated that it would spend more than $95 million that year for capital improvements required by federal and state environmental mandates. Atlanta had to borrow $400 million in the early 1990s to comply with federal clean water mandates.[28] Since 2001, federal mandates on cities for "homeland security" functions — such as added security at airports and protection of water supplies — have played havoc with municipal budgets, since Washington failed to provide cities with the money needed to comply with these requirements. For example, every time the Bush administration elevated the terrorist threat level to orange, Los Angeles had to spend an additional $1 million a week, and New York City spent over $5 million a week more. Similarly, President Bush's No Child Left Behind Act requires school districts to increase testing and improve student performance without providing the funds needed to meet these goals.[29]

Cities are also high-cost environments in which to provide services. Even when cities spend the same dollar amounts on public services as the suburbs, they cannot provide their residents with the same quality of services. As Anatole France bitingly observed, "The majestic egalitarianism of the law forbids rich and poor alike to sleep under the bridges, to beg in the streets, and to steal bread."[30] Treating unequals equally reinforces inequalities. The effectiveness of services provided to different neighborhoods varies tremendously because their needs vary tremendously.

Consider the world of eight-year-old Bernardo Rodriguez, who lived in the East Tremont section of the South Bronx. Bernardo was a quiet boy who did well in school. His grandmother did not let him play outside because it was too dangerous, but she thought that the hallway of their apartment building would be safe. Tragically, the elevator doors were defective, and Bernardo fell to his death. It is impossible to know whether better municipal inspection procedures would have saved his life, but it is a fact that many code enforcement inspectors refuse to go into buildings they regard as too dangerous. To protect themselves, they simply write on their report forms: "No access to building."[31]

Neighborhoods with older buildings require more frequent inspections and more rigorous enforcement. More resources may need to be committed for inspections in poor areas to achieve the level of safety expected in middle-class areas. In Los Angeles, where almost one out of six apartments is a substandard slum, the city has a huge backlog of inspections.[32] Similarly, police sometimes refuse to patrol dangerous public housing projects. Neighborhoods with many poor people need even more resources to achieve the same outcomes as better-off areas. If the goal is equal health and safety, poor neighborhoods need more housing inspectors and more police patrols and fire personnel. Their streets are more difficult to keep clean because people living in overcrowded apartments with inadequate parks use them for recreation. Poor areas also need public services that other neighborhoods do not. How many upper-middle-class suburban neighborhoods need lead paint monitoring or rat control programs?

The fact that large central-city governments spend more per capita than do middle-class suburbs is often taken as a sign that they are corrupt, inefficient, or spending too much on the undeserving poor.[33] In fact, it is largely a matter of greater need. Central cities and older inner-ring suburban municipalities often have to spend more to maintain service levels that are common in affluent suburbs, yet the average income of their taxpayers is lower.

Not surprisingly, cities with many poor people spend more on antipoverty functions. But cities with high poverty rates also spend more on nonpoverty-related services such as police, fire, courts, and general administrative functions. For every one-point increase in the poverty rate, cities spent $27.75 per capita more on nonpoverty-related services.[34] This suggests that concentrated poverty carries a substantial fiscal burden. Moreover, these expenditures typically do not achieve the same results in public security or educational achievement as their suburban counterparts. To add insult to injury, these citizens are forced to pay more of their income in taxes.[35]

Suburbanization also drives up the cost of central-city services. Suburban commuters require central cities to provide police protection and road maintenance, but they rarely pay taxes to these cities.[36] Sprawl also reduces the efficiency of central-city public services. Urban decline has reduced the population density in most areas of concentrated poverty.[37] Cleveland's population fell from 915,000 people in 1950 to less than 500,000 today. Even though it has 400,000 fewer people, and they are poorer, the city has to maintain the same number of miles of streets, sewers, and water lines.

DIFFERENCES IN FISCAL CAPACITY

Cities differ a great deal in how much leeway they have in raising their own revenues. These differences are based in part on different demographic and economic characteristics. Cities with high poverty rates, large immigrant populations, and large proportions of school-age children have a harder time raising revenue and face greater expenditure needs. Cities that have been able to annex adjacent suburban areas, incorporate the middle class within their municipal boundaries, and face less competition from surrounding communities are often in a better fiscal position.[38] Those cities whose major employers are relatively immobile and relatively profitable can impose higher taxes with less risk of promoting a business exodus.

These fiscal differences are based more on the historical and current role a city plays in the regional, national, and global economies than on how well it is managed.[39] The conventional wisdom about urban poverty rests on the experiences of old industrial cities such as Baltimore, Cleveland, Detroit, Gary, Newark, St. Louis, and Youngstown. As Table 5.1 shows, Detroit's and Cleveland's poverty rate persistently exceeds the average for all cities and for the United States. The industrial cities rapidly gained population and employment between 1880 and 1930. After World War II, they gained large minority popula-

TABLE 5.1. Poverty Rates in Selected Central Cities, 1970–2000, and for All Metropolitan Areas, Central Cities, Suburbs, and the United States, 1970–2003

Site	1970	1980	1990	1993 Estimate	1995 Estimate	2000	2003
Atlanta	19.8	27.5	27.3	35.6	33.6	24.4	NA
Boston	15.5	20.2	18.7	19.9	18.3	19.5	NA
Chicago	14.4	20.3	21.6	27.1	22.8	19.6	NA
Cleveland	17.1	22.1	28.7	37.8	29.9	26.3	NA
Detroit	14.7	21.9	32.4	39.6	33.1	26.1	NA
Indianapolis	9.2	11.5	12.5	15.6	13.3	11.9	NA
Los Angeles	13.0	16.2	18.6	29.9	28.6	22.1	NA
Minneapolis	11.6	13.5	18.5	23.7	18.7	16.9	NA
New York City	14.7	20.0	19.3	24.4	23.7	21.2	NA
Pittsburgh	15.0	16.5	21.4	23.3	20.2	20.4	NA
San Jose	8.6	8.2	9.3	11.5	11.3	8.8	NA
Seattle	10.0	11.2	12.4	15.6	13.8	11.8	NA
Metropolitan areas	10.2	11.9	12.7	14.6	13.4	10.8	12.1
Central cities	14.2	17.2	19.0	21.5	20.6	16.1	17.5
Suburbs	7.1	8.2	8.7	10.3	9.1	7.8	9.1
United States	12.6	13.0	13.5	15.1	13.8	11.3	12.5

Sources: Figures for metro areas, central cities, and suburbs from *Poverty of People, by Residence: 1959 to 1999,* U.S. Census Bureau, available at http://www.census.gov/income/histpov/histpov8.txt; national figure from *Poverty Status of People by Family Relationship, Race, and Hispanic Origins 1959 to 1999,* U.S. Census Bureau, available at http://www.census.gov/income/histpov/histpov2.txt; also from Joseph Dalaker, *Poverty in the United States: 2000* (Washington, DC: U.S. Census Bureau, September 2001). Decennial census figures for specific cities from "State of the Nation's Cities" database, Center for Urban Policy Research, Rutgers University, at http://www.supergenius.Rutgers.edu/WylyWeb/Data; 1990s estimates for specific cities from *Now Is The Time: Places Left Behind in the New Economy* (Washington, DC: U.S. Department of Housing and Urban Development, April 1999), appendix table 11, available at http://www.huduser.org. The 2003 data are from Table 8, "Poverty of People, by Residence: 1959 to 2003," U.S. Census Bureau, available at http://www.census.gov/hhes/poverty/histpov/hstpov8.html.

tions, suffered heavily from deindustrialization and the loss of corporate headquarters jobs, and became far worse off relative to their surrounding suburbs. Such cities have the least leverage over their internal problems.

A second group of old cities is better situated. They may have had a considerable amount of manufacturing, but they started out as port cities and transport nodes. Many were the first capital markets in their regions and provided the beginnings of advanced corporate services, such as corporate law firms. Typified by New York, Chicago, Boston, Pittsburgh, and San Francisco, these cities have been more prosperous than the first group. Although they lost a huge amount of blue-collar employment over the last half century, they experienced offsetting employment gains in corporate services, public services, and nonprofit services like medical centers and universities. These cities attracted black migration, but not to the extent of the first group, and they also received Hispanic and Asian newcomers, often from abroad. As a result, their minority populations are more diverse than those of the first group of cities, and their Anglo elites remain far more committed to living in the central city. As Table 5.1 shows, their poverty rates have been lower than those of Detroit, an exemplar of the first group.

Finally, relatively new cities such as Los Angeles, San Jose, San Diego, Seattle, Houston, Portland (Oregon), Phoenix, Minneapolis, Indianapolis, Charlotte, and Columbus (Ohio) have metropolitan economies based on corporate and social services, high technology, the defense industry, energy, tourism, and, sometimes, state government. Most had low levels of black immigration, although those located near the Mexican border experienced high levels of Hispanic immigration.[40] The post-1965 wave of immigration into the United States clustered in the old port cities and the newer high-tech cities, while native whites and native blacks moved away from immigrant-receiving cities toward newer, faster-growing cities with high proportions of native-born populations.[41] With the exception of Los Angeles, their poverty rates have generally been lower than those in the other two groups of cities.

All three types of cities experienced the negative impacts of concentrated urban poverty, economic segregation, and suburban sprawl. The number of high-poverty census tracts increased in almost every major U.S. city between 1970 and 1990, then declined somewhat in the 1990s as the overall poverty rate fell and more poor people moved to older suburbs.[42] Even such prosperous cities as San Jose, Seattle, Portland, Albuquerque, and San Diego have significant pockets of poverty amid the generally high family incomes surrounding them. But the negative impact of poverty has been most pronounced in the declining old industrial cities and least pervasive in the new, growing, high-technology cities. All cities have experienced a declining share of metropolitan employment, but the geographic separation between concentrated urban poverty and suburban affluence is most pronounced in the older manufacturing cities confronted with severe industrial decline, racial transition, and white flight.[43]

Public education is probably the most important service that local governments provide. (It certainly absorbs the most resources.) In 1979, the hourly wages of college graduates were 57 percent higher than those of workers without high school diplomas. By 2001, they made 138 percent more ($22.58 an hour versus $9.50 an hour).[44] In an economy characterized by shrinking manufacturing employment, rising service employment, ubiquitous information technology, and low union membership, a strong back and a willingness to work hard rarely provide a middle-class standard of living.

Public education in the United States is run by 13,506 independent school districts.[45] Their revenue capacities vary tremendously. In 1973, the Supreme Court ruled that the U.S. Constitution does not guarantee education as a fundamental right, and therefore it does not fall under the Fourteenth Amendment's equal protection clause (*San Antonio v. Rodriguez*). But eighteen state courts have ruled that fiscal inequalities across school districts violate state constitutions and have ordered action to reduce them. State equalization grants have lessened the gap in spending between the richest and poorest districts in many states, but expenditures per pupil still vary significantly. In 1997, in the New York metropolitan area, per pupil expenditures varied from $8,171 in New York City to $12,492 in suburban Nassau County and $12,760 in suburban Westchester County.[46] In 2003, a state court ruled that New York state's school financing formula had shortchanged New York City and ordered the state to provide the city's schools with sufficient funds to guarantee students equal educational opportunities. The court ruled that "New York City schools have the most student need in the state and the highest costs yet receive some of the lowest per student funding and have some of the worst results." One study estimated that the city needed an additional $4.1 billion to meet basic educational needs.[47]

Even if all school districts had the same resources, they would not produce equal educational outcomes because of social disadvantages in poor districts. Most state aid addresses fiscal disparities, not social disadvantages. Kenneth Wong estimates that only 8 percent of state aid to local school districts is specifically targeted for the socially disadvantaged.[48] Many analysts have concluded that schools simply reproduce the class inequalities that are present in American society.[49] Children from poor families typically have lower academic performance than do those from middle- and upper-class families. This has nothing to do with their intelligence but much to do with the social conditions that handicap their ability to learn, which are worse when they live in concentrated poverty neighborhoods.[50] Poor children are more likely to move frequently, and poor neighborhoods have less stability.[51] Of those children living in families with incomes below $10,000 a year, more than 30 percent have attended three or more different schools by the third grade.[52] These children lack a quiet place to study. Jonathan Kozol reports that one South Bronx boy used a flashlight to do his homework in the closet of his brother's bedroom.[53] Poor children are more likely to be malnourished and to come to school tired, and they are less likely to have books at home and parents who read with them. High crime levels in poor neighborhoods lead mothers to keep children inside for their safety and to send them to worse nearby schools rather than have them travel farther to magnet school programs.

Many residents of poor neighborhoods have supportive social networks in their immediate neighborhood, but they lack connections to opportunities outside the neighborhood. Their social networks may help them to "get by" but not to "get ahead."[54] The payoff from education may not seem real to young people who do not know anybody who has graduated from college and has a good job. As a result, they often have low expectations of what they can accomplish.

Chicago's Gautreaux program, which provides housing vouchers to help the inner-city poor rent apartments in the suburbs, provides clear evidence of the neighborhood effect on school performance. Dropout rates among poor urban students who moved to the suburbs were one-fourth the rate among those who moved to other areas within Chicago; the suburban youngsters were more likely to enroll in college-track courses, twice as likely to attend college, and more than twice as likely to attend four-year colleges as opposed to junior or community colleges.[55]

Equalizing the quality of all public services, not just education, within and across these different types of metropolitan regions, regardless of race or income, would have profound implications.[56] Confronted with the structural disparity between their revenue and their needs, and unable to bridge the gap through regional tax sharing, cities have typically looked to the federal and state governments for fiscal help. All urban leaders, regardless of political party or ideology, want more state and federal resources for their cities. But, as the next chapter discusses, cities are in a weaker political position than they were even a few decades ago. When the federal government was at its most generous in the 1970s, it filled only part of the gap. Since then, federal aid to cities has dropped dramatically, from 15 percent of municipal revenue in 1977 to less than 5 percent today. State aid did not make up the difference.[57] As a result, locally generated revenue now makes up 70 percent of city budgets.[58] "Fend-for-yourself federalism" has exacerbated cities' fiscal stress.[59]

WHO GOVERNS? URBAN POWER STRUCTURES AND URBAN REGIMES

As a result of their fiscal predicament, most cities focus on attracting new private investments, hoping that expanding tax revenues will fund programs to improve the quality of urban services. Instead of putting a high priority on antipoverty policies, they focus on enticing businesses and improving municipal services.[60] As Kurt Schmoke, the liberal mayor of Baltimore, said in 1992 (at a time when one-quarter of his city lived in poverty), "I strongly believe that if cities are to be competitive in the twenty-first century, they need to be international . . . by creating an environment that will enable international companies to use Baltimore as a gateway to the United States."[61]

Cities are not all alike in terms of their bargaining power with business—and thus their room for maneuver to address the needs of the poor.[62] Cities whose economies are dominated by high-skill industries—particularly those that do not compete directly with low-skill and low-wage industries around the world—usually have less of a problem with poverty and greater latitude in improving local economic and social conditions. Cities vary in terms of the wealth of their businesses and residents. In 2000, for example, Detroit's per capita income was $14,717, compared with $26,823 in Charlotte and $34,556 in San Francisco. In Detroit, only 11.6 percent of households earned over $81,000, in contrast to 24.1 percent in Charlotte and 33.8 percent in San Francisco.[63]

Even in economically successful cities, however, the willingness to deal with persistent poverty and inequality depends on whether the groups that have a direct stake in reducing poverty—community organizations in low-income areas, labor unions (especially those with low-wage members), minority organizations, and some religious institutions—can organize their base effectively and forge coalitions with some sectors of the middle class, the upper class, and business elites. Such coalitions are necessary to elect public officials who have the concern, support, and skill to promote an antipoverty agenda. In the late 1990s, for example, both Los Angeles and New York City experienced tremendous economic expansion. Liberal and progressive political coalitions were more successful in Los Angeles than in New York in shaping public policy, but neither city marshaled the political will to solve these problems.

If structural factors so tightly constrain cities, then what is urban politics all about? Is it all "sound and fury," as Shakespeare wrote, "signifying nothing"?

Can candidates for mayor or city councilor really have significantly different programs, not just different personalities or characters? Within the overall constraints, liberal, progressive, and conservative city governments have, in fact, pursued substantively different local strategies for dealing with the effects of concentrated urban poverty. Although all cities face some version of the same fiscal dilemmas, municipal politicians differ over how to deal with them. Three factors influence the choices local officials make about how to govern: their ideological perspective, the amount of resources the city can command, and the political coalitions that brought them into office. Public officials have different ideologies about the appropriate role of government in addressing such problems as housing, homelessness, AIDS, crime, and education. City officials are also influenced by those who helped get them into office and govern, including not only voters and campaign contributors but also business groups, the media, unions, neighborhood organizations, and other interest groups.

Conservative mayors have no qualms about attracting businesses by reducing government regulations and taxes and providing new subsidies. They expect a strong private sector to "trickle down" to the poor and near poor. Traditional liberal politicians have less sympathy for this approach and typically want businesses to hire local residents or minorities in exchange for regulatory and tax relief or for subsidies. Progressive politicians resist reducing regulations and taxes or providing subsidies in the first place. They want companies to agree to pay decent wages, contribute funds for affordable housing, or provide other long-term benefits. In other words, local officials disagree over the degree to which they are willing to test the limits and call business's bluff.

Urban politics have followed some general patterns over the last fifty years. In the period after World War II, urban politics were dominated by local pro-growth coalitions that pushed for the physical redevelopment of the downtown areas. Typically, they were preceded by the formation of organizations of corporate leaders such as the Coordinating Committee in Boston, the Committee of 25 in Los Angeles, the Bishops in Hartford, the Allegheny Conference on Community Development in Pittsburgh, the Metropolitan Fund and the New Detroit Committee in Detroit, and Central Atlanta Progress. These groups brought together the key business leaders to smooth over differences, forge a corporate consensus on public policy, marshal elite support for a progrowth agenda, and promote local involvement in the federal urban renewal program.[64] These groups usually involved an inner circle of between twenty-five and a hundred individuals with overlapping memberships on the boards of major corporations, universities, philanthropies, hospitals, museums, and social clubs.[65]

The breakthrough moment for these efforts came, however, with the election of mayoral candidates—like Richard Lee in New Haven, John Collins in Boston, Robert Wagner in New York, David Lawrence in Pittsburgh, and George Christopher in San Francisco—committed to a downtown redevelopment program, typically with support not only from real estate development interests but also from retailers, construction unions, the media, hospitals, and universities. The progrowth coalitions they built carried out urban renewal and urban freeway projects that drastically reshaped the urban fabric, modernizing business districts and providing new facilities for many of the coalition partners, including nonprofit organizations such as universities and hospitals.

Ultimately, however, urban renewal generated tremendous conflict, provoking the protest movements of the 1960s and heightening racial tensions. Low-income and minority neighborhoods bore the brunt of the costs of urban renewal, which tore down many more units of housing than it built, disrupted neighborhoods, and divided parts of the city with new highways and up-scale development projects.[66] Neighborhood activists increasingly challenged downtown-oriented development policies and advocated shifting attention to rebuilding poor neighborhoods, investing in historical preservation, and improving economic opportunities for minority residents. Occasionally, they mobilized sufficient strength to win city council seats and even to elect sympathetic mayors. As black and Hispanic populations grew, in the 1960s and 1970s, minority electoral mobilization also catapulted black and Hispanic leaders onto city councils and into mayoral offices.

As neighborhood groups and minority activists challenged the downtown business coalition from one side, economic change was undermining it from the other. Starting in the 1970s, corporate mergers and downsizing eliminated many of the corporate headquarters that once dominated major cities, as well as the local family ownership that had controlled them.[67] Local executives were no longer the top decision makers. The small elite of civic-minded bankers, lawyers, and businesspeople who once dominated cities was replaced by transient executives who were less willing to "give money for concert halls and museums, lend their names to fund-raising drives, work to build the critical mass necessary to get major projects off the ground."[68] These transformations opened up the political space for new political coalitions that put less emphasis on downtown development and more on building low- and moderate-income rental housing, enhancing neighborhood participation, and working with community-based organizations. Some cities began experimenting with new strategies to address concentrated poverty and fiscal stress.

Politicians woo voters and contributors in order to win elections, but a majority *electoral* coalition may not be enough to ensure that they can carry out their programs once they are in office. For that, they need a *governing* coalition. Holding the formal reins of power is not enough. To carry out an agenda, urban governance requires cooperation among an array of economic, civic, and political interests. Public officials need active support not only from business power centers but also from other interests, including the media, community groups, labor unions, religious leaders, and foundations. The nature of each urban regime depends on the makeup of the dominant political coalition, what resources each member brings to the coalition, and what position each holds relative to the other members, as well as on the political skills of those who put it together.[69]

In some cities, the urban regimes are quite stable over a long period of time. In other cities, new coalitions emerge and push for different policy agendas. Political regimes are not static and self-perpetuating. They can grow, decay, and be replaced by new alliances. Los Angeles had a very conservative regime under Mayor Sam Yorty from 1961 to 1973, a liberal regime for much of the 1970s and early 1980s during the first half of Mayor Tom Bradley's twenty-year reign, and then a more conservative regime during the late 1980s and 1990s, especially after the election of Mayor Richard Riordan, a Republican. In the late 1990s, a progressive coalition arose to challenge Riordan, based on the political forces that engineered the living wage law. These forces seriously contested for political power in the 2001 mayoral and city council elections. Liberal Democrat James Hahn was elected mayor, but the influence of progressives on the council, and among labor unions and community groups, led to a governing coalition that teetered between liberal and progressive.[70]

Here we discuss three different responses to the problems posed by the growing concentration of poor in central cities: traditional urban liberalism, urban progressivism, and urban conservatism.[71] Each type of regime is based on a different kind of coalition, each has a distinct philosophy about the appropriate role of government in addressing urban poverty, and each has forged different approaches to that problem. Traditional urban liberalism tries to incorporate poor and working-class people, especially minorities, by expanding government services without challenging business influence over other aspects of the urban agenda, especially downtown development. Urban progressivism seeks to challenge business dominance of development issues, empower poor neighborhoods, and distribute more resources to poor and working-class people. Urban conservatism emphasizes reducing government regulation, promoting business growth, and freeing the marketplace to create trickle-down benefits for the poor. (Naturally, these are ideal types. Actual regimes typically combine these elements and evolve, but one or another is usually predominant.)

URBAN LIBERAL REGIMES

In recent decades, urban liberalism has sought to target government benefits to ethnic and racial minorities who suffered past discrimination. More generally, urban liberalism believes in expanding government services and government employment to improve the quality of life and to provide upward mobility for working-class residents of the city. Dating from the era of big-city political machines, it seeks not so much to empower minorities as a group as to provide individual benefits (jobs, job training, housing, and health care) to group members. Urban liberals do not see the redistribution of benefits and services as antithetical to the interests or power of business. Indeed, private investment provides the tax base they can use to finance services for the poor. As the focus of urban liberalism changed from assimilating immigrants in the early part of the twentieth century to managing racial succession in the 1960s and 1970s, its efforts were often underwritten by federal grant programs. As federal aid to the cities shrank in the 1980s, many urban liberals shifted their priorities toward downtown business development, linking it with set-aside programs for minority contractors and increased employment for minority residents. Opposition sometimes came both from white ethnic groups opposed to race-targeted programs and from neighborhood organizations opposed to the renewed focus on downtown development.

The urban political machines of the twentieth century were an early manifestation of urban liberalism. They gained electoral majorities and held governing power by giving municipal jobs and other benefits to their ethnic supporters (Irish, Italians, Jews, and others) in return for votes, and by giving contracts and other special benefits to favored businesses in return for money and political support. As two historians put it, "before social security, unemployment insurance, medicare, food stamps, and aid to families with dependent children . . . machines made meaningful attempts to distribute relief and welfare."[72] Urban political machines promoted the employment of first- and second-generation immigrants by large public works projects, the municipal government, and private employers connected to the political establishment. Machines controlled as much as 20 percent of the job growth in their cities between 1900 and 1920.[73]

Urban liberalism fashioned the new immigrant groups into an organized electoral force. They made sure that immigrants could vote and mobilized reliable voters on election day, often on a block-by-block level. The regular party organizations sought to manage ethnic competition by spreading symbolic and material benefits and by recruiting candidates from different ethnic groups. (They generally excluded blacks, however, from proportionate positions of power during the first half of the twentieth century, though they did create black "submachines."[74])

In some cities in the early 1900s, immigrant-based political machines vied with and even replaced business elites as the primary force in city politics. They enhanced their power by providing select businesses with tax breaks, construction contracts, and utility franchises. Business groups often criticized machines as a corrupt and inefficient "spoils" system. They promoted various "reform" proposals to undermine the power of machines, with limited success. At the same time, they benefited from the ability and willingness of political bosses to keep immigrant workers in line, undermine unions, and oppose labor-backed political parties.

Modern urban liberalism descends from its machine predecessor. After World War II, more forward-looking urban liberal politicians formed alliances with business elites to promote urban renewal, but they also took steps to bring African Americans and later Hispanics into the circle of beneficiaries. They sought to manage and coopt the community protest and mobilization that occurred in the 1960s and 1970s. With help from the federal Great Society antipoverty programs of that period, they expanded subsidized housing, job training, public employment, and other antipoverty programs that both served and employed these formerly excluded groups. As blacks gained access to well-paying government and nonprofit jobs, the black professional and middle classes expanded, but with little positive effect on the ghetto poor.[75] In fact, they suffered most from urban renewal.

The business leaders who joined with urban liberals in forming progrowth coalitions viewed cleaning up the slums and improving central business districts as ways to bring shoppers back to the downtowns and retain new middle-class residents. Construction unions collaborated because these federal programs provided jobs for their members. Major employers viewed job training and school reform programs (such as Head Start) as a way to upgrade their potential labor pool. Private developers were eager to utilize federal funds to build low-income housing.

If one issue divided the more liberal from the more conservative variants of the progrowth coalition, it was racial integration of public schools and neighborhoods. In theory, few business and civic leaders favored racial segregation. But as civil rights activists demanded that urban liberal regimes ban housing discrimination and integrate the public schools (through busing, if necessary), political and business leaders saw that meeting these demands would trigger a serious white working-class and middle-class backlash. Similarly, demands for "community control" (which many whites perceived to mean African American control) of public schools upset white parents and teachers' unions. Controversies of this sort damaged the political careers of liberal mayors Kevin White in Boston and John Lindsay in New York.[76]

As their black populations grew rapidly in the 1950s and 1960s, urban liberal regimes clearly could not survive in most large cities without giving African Americans a greater foothold in school boards, city councils, and mayoralties. Some cities, such as Chicago under Mayor Richard Daley, clung to tokenism, giving blacks a handful of political jobs but without much real influence. However, in other cities, such as Atlanta, Los Angeles, and Cleveland, the black community mobilized to increase voter participation, while urban liberal coalition leaders actively recruited and promoted blacks.[77] In this way, a new generation of African American (and later Latino) leaders won office. The total number of black local elected officials increased from 715 in 1970 to 5,456 in 2001. (Another 1,928 blacks serve on local school boards.) Likewise, Hispanic local officeholders increased from 1,316 in 1985 to 2,197 in 1994, then fell to 1,846 in 2001. (In addition, 2,682 Hispanics serve on local school boards.[78])

The vast majority of black local officials have been in the South, primarily in small towns and middle-size cities. Mississippi alone had 607 black local elected officials in 2001, a fact that would have been hard to imagine before the civil rights movement. Similarly, most Hispanic local officials have been elected in states with large Hispanic populations, particularly California, New Mexico, Arizona, Florida, and Texas (which alone had 801 of the 1,846 Hispanic local officials in 2001).

No major American city elected an African American mayor until 1967, when Gary, Indiana, elected Richard Hatcher and Cleveland elected Carl Stokes. Maurice Ferre, a Puerto Rican, elected mayor of Miami in 1973, was the first Hispanic to become mayor of a major city.[79] He was followed by Henry Cisneros, who became mayor of San Antonio in 1981, and Federico Pena, elected mayor of Denver in 1983.[80] The number of black and Hispanic mayors of the seventy-six largest cities (those with populations over 200,000) has increased dramatically since the late 1960s. By 1997, one-third (twenty-five) of these cities had black or Latino mayors.[81] Since 2000, the number has held steady at twenty-three cities[82] (Figure 5.1).

Mobilization of minority voters has been critical for black and Hispanic candidates to win office. In the 1970s and 1980s, civil rights activism and Voting Rights Act litigation led to dramatic breakthroughs in the South, where

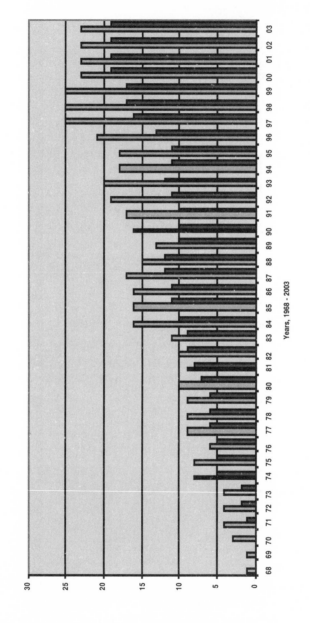

Years, 1968 - 2003

■ Minority Mayors   ■ 50% or Greater Minority Population

FIGURE 5.1. Minority Mayors, 1968–2003, U.S. Cities over 200,000 (Seventy-six Cities)

black mayoral victories occurred in Atlanta, New Orleans, Richmond, Savannah, Memphis, Birmingham, and Charlotte. The emergence of Hispanic activism in the 1970s laid the groundwork for the first generation of Latino mayors in Miami, San Antonio, and Denver, and later in Albuquerque, El Paso, Sacramento, San Jose, and Santa Ana.

Black and Latino mayoral candidates usually had to wait until their respective racial groups were a near majority of the population before they won. When Baltimore voters elected Kurt Schmoke its first black mayor in 1987, every large city with a majority black population had put a black person in the mayor's office. Even so, the first generation of black and Hispanic mayors had to attract significant white support to win and to govern. When Tom Bradley was elected mayor of Los Angeles in 1973, blacks represented only 18 percent of the city's population and an even smaller proportion of its voters. When Cisneros was elected mayor in San Antonio, Hispanics accounted for 55 percent of the population but a much smaller proportion of all voters. He defeated a white millionaire, John Steen, by getting almost 100 percent of the Hispanic vote and 45 percent of the white vote, garnering 61.8 percent of the total vote.

In a few instances, black mayors have been elected in cities with large white majorities and small black populations. Examples include Norman Rice in Seattle (elected in 1989), Emanuel Cleaver in Kansas City (1991), William Johnson in Rochester (1993), and Sharon Belton in Minneapolis (1994). Hispanics, including Martin Chavez in Albuquerque (1992) and Joseph Serna in Sacramento (1996), have also been elected in cities with white majorities and small Hispanic populations. In 1983, when Denver's population was only 12 percent Hispanic and 5 percent black, voters elected Pena as mayor and reelected him in 1987. In 1991, when Pena declined to run for reelection, Denver's minority population had grown only slightly (13 percent Hispanic and 6 percent black), but voters elected Wellington Webb, an African American, as mayor and reelected him four years later. (In 2003, when minorities represented only 30 percent of Denver's population, voters chose John Hickenlooper, a white geologist and brewpub owner, to replace Webb.) In these situations, minority candidates developed "deracialized" campaigns and policy agendas to win "crossover" votes alongside their minority political bases.[83]

As the proportion of whites in American cities declines, their importance as a voting bloc declines as well, but they remain important because they tend to have higher levels of voter turnout, they typically control the major businesses, and they are a source of campaign contributions, especially among middle-class white liberals. It is clear that in many cities, a significant number of whites—often liberal Jews, but others as well—will vote for minority candidates. In cities with a significant number of poor and working-class whites, progressive white mayors such as Ray Flynn in Boston, George Latimer in St. Paul, and Dennis Kucinich in Cleveland have forged coalitions between whites and minorities on the basis of common economic grievances and hopes, while conservative mayors such as Ed Koch and Rudolph Giuliani in New York, Frank Rizzo in Philadelphia, and Richard Riordan in Los Angeles used white resentment against minorities to win office.

Since the 1970s, each of the nation's five largest cities — where no single racial group accounted for a majority of the population — has elected a black mayor. These included David Dinkins in New York City, Tom Bradley in Los Angeles, Harold Washington in Chicago, Wilson Goode and John Street in Philadelphia, and Lee Brown in Houston. In the 1990s, whites replaced blacks as mayor in the first four cities; in 2003, the same transition occurred in Houston. In a handful of cities with black majorities or near-majorities, voters have replaced black mayors with white mayors. This occurred in Oakland (where Jerry Brown was elected in 1998), Baltimore (where Martin O'Malley was elected in 1999), Cleveland (where Jane Campbell was elected in 2001), and St. Louis (where Francis Slay was elected in 2001). These examples have led some observers to argue that there was a backlash against minority mayors.[84] But the reality is more complex.

Forging an electoral and governing coalition is difficult where no single race or ethnic group now has a majority. White, black, and Hispanic candidates have to gain significant crossover support to win election and govern. The idea that cities with "majority minority" populations will easily elect minority mayors is inaccurate. It assumes that black, Hispanic, Asian, and white liberal voters will favor the same candidates, a situation that rarely happens. Any significant split among minority groups can mean that the more conservative candidate will win, although this isn't always the case.

New York City provides an example of how this can happen. Rudy Giuliani and then Michael Bloomberg, white Republicans, won the mayoralty in 1993, 1997, and 2001 elections against significantly more liberal opponents (including the city's first African American mayor) because the city's black, Latino, and white Democrats favored different primary candidates in 1997 and 2001 and split their votes in all three general elections. In Los Angeles in 2001, James Hahn, a white liberal Democrat, defeated Antonio Villaraigosa, a Latino progressive, by winning a majority of white votes *and* a large majority of black votes.[85] In San Francisco — whose 2000 population was 44 percent white, 8 percent black, 14 percent Latino, and 31 percent Asian — crossover voters enabled Willie Brown, a liberal black state legislator, to win the mayoralty in 1995 and 1999. In 2003, he was succeeded by Gavin Newsom, a millionaire businessman and liberal Democrat on the city council, who defeated Matt Gonzalez, a progressive city councilor and Green Party member, with 53 percent of the vote. Trying to win favor with Gonzalez's more liberal constituency, Newsom's first act as mayor was to ask the city clerk to issue marriage licenses to gay couples, which provoked national controversy.

In Dallas, Laura Miller, a white former journalist and city council member, became mayor in 2002 by stitching together similar crossover support among whites (who make up about 35 percent of the city's population but more of its voters), blacks (26 percent of the population), and Latinos (36 percent of the population) to win 55 percent of the total vote. Miller had been a muckraking reporter and columnist for the two Dallas papers and the liberal weekly *Dallas Observer* (where she had written that city council members were "brain dead") before serving two terms on the city council. In print and on the council she criticized Dallas politicians — including Ron Kirk, Dallas' first black mayor — for being too cozy with the city's business elite and real estate builders. She also opposed "tax breaks for downtown developers, a city subsidy for the millionaire owners of the city's new arena called the American Airlines Center, and the [city's] bid for the 2012 Summer Olympic Games."[86] Her attacks on Kirk alienated some black leaders and voters. Her main opponent in the mayor's race, Tom Dunning, an insurance company executive, was favored by the business establishment and the two major daily papers. Despite this, Miller received about 70 percent of the white vote and 60 percent of the Hispanic vote, although only 19 percent of the black vote.[87] Once in office, her agenda focused on targeting municipal funds for housing code enforcement and street repairs. She supported a successful effort to ban smoking in restaurants, triggering the wrath of their owners, and endorsed an ordinance prohibiting discrimination on the basis of sexual orientation in employment, housing, and public accommodations. She fired the black police chief, which again angered black leaders, some of whom mounted an unsuccessful effort to have her recalled.

Dallas reflects the dilemmas of building coalitions between minority and white politicians in multiracial cities. Kirk, a black moderate, was known "for building coalitions between the city's large black community and the Dallas business establishment."[88] Miller, a white liberal upset by the business establishment's priorities, was able to build an electoral coalition of whites, Hispanics, and some blacks, but the weakness of labor unions and community organizations in Dallas and continuing difficulties with the black community handicapped her ability to create a stable governing coalition. Miller's and Kirk's priorities differed, but both pursued a careful balancing act between class and race issues in order to maintain an electoral coalition.

In cities with a black or Latino majority, the first minority mayor is typically followed by other minority mayors. This has occurred in Detroit, Washington, New Orleans, Cleveland, Atlanta, Oakland, Newark, Albuquerque, Miami, Denver, and elsewhere. The first wave of minority mayors in the late 1960s and 1970s were explicitly liberal or progressive, riding the momentum of the civil rights movement. Most of the second and subsequent wave of minority mayors consolidated the urban liberal regime, but others won office not only by mobilizing minority voters but also by accommodating business interests and white moderate voters. In cities where blacks have a large majority of the electorate, almost guaranteeing that a black politician will win the mayor's race, a liberal or progressive black candidate will often compete with a moderate or even conservative black candidate.

Once elected, minority mayors have faced the challenge of forging a robust governing coalition that could deliver to specific constituencies without undermining support from white liberals and the business elite.[89] To create a stable governing regime, mayors had to deal with the city council, whose members—regardless of race—sometimes have competing interests. Although to win election minority mayors promised black and Latino voters that they would improve opportunities and conditions for minorities, to survive in office they needed to build bridges to whites and especially to the business community, which in most cities is still dominated by white men. Minority mayors could not only reward their minority supporters. Such mayors thus had to navigate between actions that would favor African Americans (or Latinos) but anger other groups and actions that would broaden their political base but risk alienating core minority supporters, who could charge that they were watering down their campaign rhetoric or failing to deliver on their campaign promises. As a result, minority mayors had a hard time "delivering the goods" and building durable governing coalitions.[90]

Urban liberal regimes, whether head by minority or white mayors, developed strategies to incorporate minority concerns. These typically included awarding contracts to allies, reforming police practices, increasing the number of minorities on the police force, building affordable housing, and appointing minority supporters to commissions, boards, and high-level city jobs. They sought to improve snow removal, housing inspections, and police protection in previously neglected minority neighborhoods.[91] Typically, however, they failed at reforming public school systems, a major concern among minority voters.[92] They also had a hard time changing the strong organizational culture of police departments.[93] Above all, urban liberal mayors did not significantly decrease crime, which in high-poverty areas soared in the 1980s in almost every city.

Procurement programs requiring a percentage of city contracts to go to minority-owned firms offered urban liberal regimes one time-honored way to cement their position. Although increased minority representation in contracting and municipal employment is symbolically important, these mayors knew that public jobs and contracts go mostly to middle-income minorities, not the poor.[94] To address the poor's need for work, most minority mayors adopted the conventional progrowth approach. Peter Eisinger observes: "The black mayors operate on the basis of a simple equation: private economic development in the city produces jobs in the private sector and tax money that may be used for jobs and purchases in the public sector. Through the various affirmative action devices . . . a certain proportion of these jobs and purchases may be channeled to the black community."[95]

White, black, and Latino urban liberal mayors typically sought to accommodate business interests. Black Mayor Richard Hatcher discovered that U.S. Steel so dominated Gary's economy that he could do little that the company did not want.[96] White Boston Mayor Kevin White first won office in 1967 with the slogan "When landlords raise rents, Kevin White raises hell," but he soon abandoned rent control in order to promote downtown development and neighborhood gentrification. As developer contributions filled his campaign treasury, he resisted neighborhood demands for a "linkage" tax on downtown development to fund affordable housing.[97] Latino Henry Cisneros, initially elected to the San Antonio city council in 1975 with the support of the business-controlled Good Government League, sided with the management during a garbage workers' strike. After being elected mayor in 1981, he walked a tightrope between the GGL agenda (such as supporting downtown development projects like the Alamodome sports stadium and luxury hotels) and the Mexican American voting base (by increasing Hispanic appointments in government, and making some improvements in housing and infrastructure conditions in Hispanic neighborhoods).[98] In Atlanta, downtown business leaders exercised "preemptive power" over the city's agenda because mayors needed their help to build a new stadium and rebuild the airport. The day after being elected in 1981, Andrew Young, once a top aide to Martin Luther King Jr., told downtown business leaders, "I didn't get elected with your help," but "I can't govern without you."[99]

As long as federal funds flowed, urban liberal regimes could deliver some jobs, housing, and other benefits to the ghetto poor. Without federal assistance, urban liberal mayors felt that they had no choice but to promote private development, even if it led to rising rents and displacement of the poor. Some pushed for regional housing integration, but others, fearing the dispersal of their voting bases, did not.[100] Meanwhile, suburban governments, over which minority mayors had no control, continued to maintain housing barriers to the poor, though they could not keep out qualified minority buyers.

Urban liberal regimes have distributed public benefits to their core electoral supporters but have not solved, and often have not even addressed, the problem of persistent, concentrated poverty. Faced with declining federal funds and severe fiscal constraints, they could not make bold policy changes. Instead, even some who entered office as activist liberals shifted toward a more moderate approach.[101] Their successors, among them a new breed of "post–civil rights" minority mayors, relied more heavily on private investment to generate jobs and tax revenues. They focused more on downtown economic development and less on racial and economic equity.[102]

URBAN PROGRESSIVE REGIMES

Urban progressive regimes differ from urban liberal regimes by seeking to empower previously excluded groups. They seek to challenge business domination of the urban development agenda, emphasizing "economic democracy" and "equity planning."[103] Such regimes grew out of the neighborhood revolt against urban renewal and the growing concern for historic preservation and neighborhood quality of life. They also drew political support from labor unions by supporting workers' rights and expanded municipal services for poor and working-class people.[104] The urban progressive movement originated outside the electoral arena in community and union organizing, protesting, and lobbying city hall to address neighborhood improvement and empowerment. In some cases, these movements built electoral coalitions that elected progressives to city councils, school boards, or other local bodies. In a few instances, they even elected mayors.

Historically, America's cities have been the cradle of progressivism. In the first decades of the twentieth century, rapid industrialization, desperate poverty in immigrant neighborhoods, and growing inequality produced a variety of progressive reform movements. The trade union movement, housing reformers, women's rights activists, and settlement house reformers all fought to lift up poor and working-class immigrants through collective organization and new public policies. Many upper-class people (primarily women) organized to investigate and publicize the problems of the poor, often joining with working-class activists through groups such as the Women's Trade Union League. Such muckraking journalism as Lincoln Steffens's articles in *McClure's* magazine, collected in *The Shame of the Cities* (1904); Upton Sinclair's *The Jungle* (1906), a novel about the harsh conditions among Chicago's meatpacking workers; and photographs by Lewis Hine exposed these conditions to a broad public. Religious reformers crusaded to eliminate child labor and unsafe factories, clean up slum housing, build decent homes for the poor, and create municipal sanitation agencies and public hospitals.

With votes from immigrants, workers, and a rising professional middle class, reformers won election in many cities. Mayors Tom Johnson of Cleveland (1901–9), Samuel "Golden Rule" Jones of Toledo (1897–1903), and Brand Whitlock of Toledo (1906–13) fought against high streetcar and utility rates and for fair taxes and better social services. Reformers in Jersey City, Philadelphia, Cincinnati, Detroit, Los Angeles, Bridgeport, and many other cities sought to tax wealthy property owners, create municipal electricity and water utilities, and hold down transit fares.

Like the urban political machines, the progressive city officials used municipal jobs to provide employment to immigrant and working-class voters. But they also took sides in the collective struggles of these constituents. During strikes, they would not allow the local police to be used to protect strike-breaking "scabs." They pushed to enact and strengthen laws to establish and enforce building codes, moves guaranteed to make them unpopular with slum landlords.

In Detroit, Hazen Pingree, the reform mayor from 1890 to 1897, challenged the high cost of a ferry ride across the Detroit River to Belle Island Park. After Mayor Pingree threatened to revoke the company's franchise or put a municipal ferry service in operation, it reduced its fare from ten cents to five cents. In the face of opposition from businesses and even his own Baptist church (which took his family pew away), he also mobilized working-class voters to pressure the City Council to create a municipal electrical utility, to pressure the powerful private gas, telephone, and streetcar companies to reduce rates, and to increase taxes on wealthy property owners. When employees of the Detroit City Railway Company went on strike in 1891 — in part to get the company to modernize its equipment — Pingree refused the company's request to bring in the state militia to halt the strike. In his battle with the Detroit Gas Company, Pingree encouraged customers not to pay their full gas bills to put pressure on the company to lower rates. After winning four terms as mayor of Detroit — initially by beating business-backed and machine politicians by building a coalition of working-class Polish, Germans, and Irish immigrants as well as the middle class — Pingree served two terms as governor of Michigan, where he continued the fight for progressive reform.[105]

Socialists were a major component of the urban progressive movement. At its high point in 1912, about 1,200 Socialist Party members held public office in 340 cities, including seventy-nine mayors in cities such as Milwaukee, Buffalo, Minneapolis, Reading, and Schenectady.[106] Socialists recognized that they could not bring socialism to one city, but they pushed to create "public ownership of utilities and transportation facilities; increase social, recreational, and cultural services; and adopt a friendly attitude toward unions, especially in time of strikes."[107] They earned a reputation for clean government, leading some to claim that they were operating "sewer socialism."[108]

Progressive urban activists in different cities formed national organizations like the International Ladies Garment Workers Union, the National Housing Association, the National Child Labor Committee, and others to spread their message and agitate for change. By the 1920s, most major cities and some states had implemented reforms such as building codes, child labor laws, and the creation of public health departments. These urban reformers laid the foundation for national reforms during the New Deal era, which expanded urban progressivism by providing federal funds to improve conditions in cities.[109]

The New Deal benefited from and nourished urban progressivism. In Detroit, Frank Murphy won a surprise mayoral victory in 1930, a year after the Depression began, by promising unemployment relief, despite opposition from the powerful auto companies. He invited twenty-nine mayors of major cities to a conference, stating: "We have done everything humanly possible to do, and it has not been enough. The hour is at hand for the federal government to cooperate." This meeting led to the formation of the U.S. Conference of Mayors (USCM).[110] An early USCM president, New York City Mayor Fiorello LaGuardia, spoke out strongly for urban progressive measures during the Depression. New York's local public works program, slum clearance program, and low-rent public housing program became models for the New Deal's Works Progress Administration and public housing initiatives.[111]

More recent urban progressive regimes grew out of the neighborhood movements of the 1960s, 1970s, and 1980s. Many early community protests were sporadic and disorganized, but skilled organizers, often from the Industrial Areas Foundation (IAF; a national network founded by Saul Alinsky in 1940), helped neighborhood residents build strong grassroots organizations in many cities. Drawing on the experiences of the union movement, Alinsky's "people's organizations" used the threat of conflict to win concessions from local businesses and politicians.

Progressive and radical activists organized poor neighborhoods around housing, welfare, and other issues in the 1960s and 1970s. In the mid-1970s, leaders of the National Welfare Rights Organization turned to organizing low-income residents avoiding housing and other issues and formed the Association of Community Organizations for Reform Now (ACORN) to push for local reforms. Community organizing forced government agencies to shift funds to affordable housing and community-based services, halted highway projects, and promoted mass transit. In response, President Lyndon Johnson's Great Society programs required community participation and shifted public funds to community-based organizations as a major vehicle for delivering public services.[112]

By the 1970s, the "neighborhood movement" had become a stronger voice on many policy fronts.[113] Middle-class neighborhoods joined in promoting "growth control" and historic preservation of neighborhoods threatened by market forces. Responding to these new constituencies, urban liberals sought to coopt protest by community organizations by turning them into housing development and social services agencies. Churches, social services agencies, tenant organizations, and civil rights groups began delivering Head Start, child care, job training, and housing development services in the neighborhoods they served. In 1970, 100 community development corporations (CDCs) existed; a decade later, there were more than 1,000. A 1989 survey of 133 cities found that 95 percent of them had active CDCs. By the 1990s, at least 2,000 CDCs operated.[114] They received support from private foundations, local and state governments, businesses, and religious institutions. Goaded by the Community Reinvestment Act of 1977, banks also began to give more loans and grants to CDCs for affordable housing development.[115]

The neighborhood movement was strongest in older northern cities, which had the biggest battles over urban renewal. The redevelopment bulldozer was less likely to threaten residents of newer southern and southwestern cities. A study of Houston called its neighborhood groups "largely invisible."[116] In San Antonio, however, the IAF-affiliated Communities Organized for Public Service helped elect the city's first Hispanic mayor, Henry Cisneros, who redirected some city funds and public services toward poor Hispanic neighborhoods.[117] Portland, Seattle, and San Francisco all developed strong community-based organizations, but Los Angeles, San Diego, San Jose, and Phoenix, all with large Hispanic populations, had few community-based organizations and did not develop progressive-style politics through the 1980s. Although Atlanta, New Orleans, and Birmingham elected black city councilors and mayors, they, too, had little grassroots mobilization challenging the business-oriented growth agenda.

Urban progressive regimes sought to give community groups a stronger voice in government decisions that affect neighborhoods. A 1990 survey of 161 cities found that 60 percent had neighborhood councils, some officially recognized by city hall.[118] Many cities reformed their charters to provide for the election of city council members from neighborhood districts rather than at large. Many disbursed low-income-housing program money to CDCs. Some established affordable housing trust funds funded by revenue from commercial development.[119] Others adopted rent control, moratoriums on condominium conversion of rental housing, and zoning ordinances requiring developers to include affordable units in their developments.[120]

Under the rubric of "growth control," neighborhood groups asserted that policies on economic development must be more aware of the costs in air pollution, traffic congestion, loss of open space, rising rents, and a less livable city. They sought to limit new downtown office construction and downzone commercial districts. In the early 1980s, they got San Francisco and Boston to place strict limits on downtown development and to enact a "linkage" law requiring developers to contribute to a low-income-housing trust fund.[121] Many cities required new buildings to be designed in ways that fit into the existing streetscape and protected historic buildings from being altered or torn down.

In the 1970s and 1980s, veterans of the civil rights movement, the New Left, and neighborhood organizing had helped elect sympathetic city council and school board members, and even a few mayors, in dozens of cities. The most successful progressive regimes took root in small, white, middle-class cities, often university towns such as Burlington (Vermont), Cambridge (Massachusetts), Madison (Wisconsin), Berkeley, and Santa Monica (California). Progressive regimes also took power in several big cities, including Cleveland, San Francisco, Pittsburgh, Portland, Chicago, Hartford, and Boston. In most cases, organizers used concern over housing and community development issues to mobilize supporters and forge a governing regime.[122] Their coalitions sought to bring together neighborhood groups, labor unions, and poor and working-class residents, as well as residents and groups concerned about environmental and historic preservation issues. To carry out their program, however, they needed a broader base of support. Like urban liberals, progressives walked a political tightrope between the concerns of their core supporters and the constraints imposed by additional interests they needed to bring into their governing coalitions.

This tension made it difficult for urban progressive regimes to form stable and robust governing coalitions that could pursue their programs. Internal disagreement, business opposition, and economic recession undercut the perceived "antigrowth" stance of progressive activists. Racial and ethnic tensions plagued some progressive coalitions. Many progressive regimes emerged in cities with small minority populations, such as Burlington, Minneapolis, and Portland, but others faced a more complex terrain. In San Francisco, for example, activists from low-income minority communities wanted more attention paid to creating jobs for their constituents, while middle-class environmentalists sought to limit development.[123] Business leaders portrayed progressives as antibusiness zealots lacking a practical program for economic revitalization.[124] In Cleveland, banks pushed the city into default over progressive Mayor Dennis Kucinich's confrontational approach to downtown tax abatements and his opposition to the corporate takeover of the municipally owned utility, resulting in his defeat after only two years in office.

By the time urban progressivism emerged in the 1970s, the economic and demographic realities of cities had already changed dramatically. Cities had a weaker bargaining position toward business, had substantially lower average incomes than the suburbs, and were divided by racial and ethnic conflicts. In economic downturns, urban progressives become vulnerable to the charge that they are "antibusiness." In cities that are booming, however, urban progressives can push to share the prosperity with those otherwise left behind by economic growth. The economic prosperity of the 1990s provided fertile ground for urban progressivism in some cities. The momentum continued into the twenty-first century. Labor unions began to play a significant role in building progressive urban coalitions. Under energetic new leaders, some unions—particularly those with low-wage members, many of them immigrants—worked with community groups around such issues as living wage laws and affordable housing. In New Orleans, San Jose, San Francisco, Los Angeles, Milwaukee, and Stamford, among other cities, unions helped elect progressive candidates to office and pushed for laws and regulations to improve working and living conditions for poor and working-class residents. When neighborhood groups and unions become part of governing regimes, they can play a larger role in housing and economic development decisions.[125]

URBAN CONSERVATIVE REGIMES

Urban conservatives think that urban problems are caused by the misguided actions of city government, not by the larger economic and political arrangements of society. They charge that urban liberal politicians cave in to minority, union, and neighborhood demands, resulting in profligate spending, mismanagement, and corruption. From this perspective, cities can blame only themselves for their fiscal crises. Government should be run like a business instead of trying to make social change by targeting spending on minorities or poor neighborhoods. The only real solution to the problem of concentrated poverty is to cut the size and scope of city government. This will free up the private sector to invest, so the benefits of private-sector growth will trickle down to the poor.

Historically, urban conservatism has its roots in the business-backed "reform" movements of the late 1800s and early 1900s. Business leaders wanted to weaken the political machines, labor unions, and the radical and progressive urban reform movements supported by working-class immigrant voters. These mostly Protestant, middle-class conservatives viewed the mostly Catholic and Jewish immigrants as a cultural and economic threat.

In almost every city, business and professional reformers pushed to reorganize local government along more "businesslike" lines, insulating it from political pressures and eliminating corruption. They wanted to keep taxes low and deliver public services efficiently. These local "good government" groups formed national organizations such as the National Municipal League to promote their views.[126] The vast majority of the individuals who spearheaded these changes were bankers, newspaper publishers, developers, lawyers, and corporate executives.[127]

These groups also pushed for at-large elections, the elimination of partisanship from local elections, and rules requiring people to register to vote—changes that weakened working-class political influence.[128] They succeeded in many medium-sized cities during the first two decades of the twentieth century. By 1905, most states had voter registration laws. By 1920, one-fifth of all cities had a commission form of government. Nonpartisan, at-large elections were instituted in Los Angeles (1908), Boston (1909), Akron, Ohio (1915), and Detroit (1918). By 1929, more than half of all cities had adopted nonpartisan elections.[129] Where cities adopted nonpartisan elections, secret ballots, and voter registration requirements, voter turnout declined among immigrants and the poor, shifting the balance of power back into business hands.[130]

Conservatives also lobbied to shift power from elected officials to professional administrators, who, they believed, would run cities through "expertise" rather than political favoritism. They revised municipal charters so that city managers would replace strong mayors and appointive commissions would oversee departments. By the 1950s, many cities took it for granted that this was how municipal governments should work.

In addition to support from business interests, modern urban conservatism drew popular strength from the backlash of white voters against the urban liberal and progressive movements of the late 1960s. Urban conservatives have often used racial code words to solidify white support.[131] Similar to Richard

Nixon's appeal to the "silent majority" in 1968, urban conservatism has resonated with voters who resented "favoritism" toward blacks and other minorities. It also drew on fears of rising crime and frustration with "big government" common in the 1980s and early 1990s. To appeal to both business and middle-class whites, urban conservatism's rhetoric stressed reducing government regulations and taxes and providing "public order" and "keeping the peace." These slogans reflected real concerns about crime rates but also acted as code words indicating opposition to minority advancement.[132]

Urban conservatism was aided by a vibrant intellectual attack on liberal and progressive efforts to address the urban crisis. With ample funding from corporate-sponsored foundations and think tanks such as the Manhattan Institute, Heritage Foundation, American Enterprise Institute, Cato Institute, and Reason Foundation, conservative public intellectuals have blamed cities' fiscal problems on the liberal policies of the 1960s.[133] According to them, public employee unions had too much influence with local politicians, leading to bloated municipal budgets, excessively high salaries, and inefficient management.[134] They argued that the "civil rights generation" of black elected officials had simply rewarded their constituents with government jobs or contracts for which they were unqualified, subverting government efficiency and undermining the confidence of business leaders and white middle-class voters. Liberals had, in their view, created an "entitlement mentality" that was indulgent of absenteeism, tardiness, poor language skills, poor work habits, and incompetence among city workers.[135]

Edward Banfield's book *The Unheavenly City*, published in 1970, was perhaps the most influential early statement of these positions. One chapter, "Rioting for Fun and Profit," blamed liberal policies for encouraging irresponsible, even illegal, behavior among the poor. Twenty-five years later, Fred Siegel's *The Future Once Happened Here* echoed and updated Banfield's themes. He blamed the urban crisis on the "riot ideology." Banfield, Siegel, and other conservative pundits also claimed that many big-city mayors and other public officials pressured the federal government in the 1960s to expand welfare and other antipoverty programs (such as food stamps and public housing). As cities became "magnets" for the unemployed and the "undeserving" poor, the social fabric of urban neighborhoods unraveled, cities spent too much on serving the poor, and alarmed businesses and middle-class residents voted with their feet by moving to suburbia.[136]

These conservative critics also charged that liberal politicians tolerated criminal behavior and drug use and argued that low-level public nuisances (such as graffiti and other visible signs of neglect) encouraged more serious crimes. "We now believe that we can reduce crime through good policing," said Myron Magnet of the Manhattan Institute, a conservative think tank admired by New York Mayor Rudy Giuliani. "The root causes of crime are not poverty and racism. They're criminals."[137] Instead of carrying out basic "civic house-keeping" functions that would retain middle-class residents, they blamed liberal and progressive officials for frightening private investors away with rent control, subsidized low-income housing, and high business taxes.[138]

In office, urban conservatives typically seek to reduce taxes and regulations on business and to alter the social services practices that they think reward bad behavior by the poor and repel middle-class residents. They prescribe the unfettered promotion of private investment. Conservative regimes oppose height limits, zoning guidelines, hiring set-asides, rent control, environmental standards, and linked development fees.[139] They claim to address poverty by promoting private investment in the hope that benefits will trickle down. Conservatives are against protecting the poor from rising rents and displacement on the grounds that gentrification is a free-market process. They oppose local living wage laws on the grounds that they drive business out of cities.[140] Conservatives address fiscal strains by attempting to close public hospitals, increasing tuition for municipal colleges, raising fees for public transportation and other public services, and privatizing public education.[141] This has occasioned conflict with municipal unions and attacks on long-standing civil service protections.[142]

Most centrally, urban conservatives have embraced tougher police operations and crackdowns on "deviant" behavior such as public begging.[143] These measures often have a strong racial component, allowing police to stop or arrest people on the basis of their demeanor or clothing rather than on hard evidence of criminal activity. They reject civilian police monitoring boards or community involvement in crime prevention strategies while supporting more jails and tougher sentences. How such regimes operate in practice may be seen in Los Angeles and New York, where white Republicans succeeded black urban liberal mayors in 1993, and in Indianapolis, where Republican mayor Steven Goldsmith vigorously advocated downsizing government as a proponent of the new urban conservatism.[144]

The experience of some representative large cities both illustrates the actual workings of urban regimes and shows the difficulties they have in moderating the growth of income inequality, concentrated poverty, and spatial segregation — if indeed they try to address these issues at all. Before shifting attention to the politics of suburbia, we briefly examine Los Angeles, New York, Atlanta,

Detroit, Pittsburgh, Chicago, Boston, and Indianapolis. All have at one time or another illustrated the policy aims and political trajectories of urban liberal, progressive, and conservative regimes.

LOS ANGELES

Los Angeles shows how a black-led urban liberal regime can give way to a relatively conservative white-led administration (even though the white share of the city's population was shrinking) and how intraminority disagreements can hamper the emergence of a potential multiracial progressive governing coalition. When Los Angeles' Watts ghetto exploded in riots in 1965, presaging the other urban riots of the 1960s, 34 died, 1,032 were injured, and 3,952 were arrested. The riots were triggered by anger over unemployment, miserable housing conditions, exclusion from municipal jobs, and the routine mistreatment of blacks by the Los Angeles police, dramatized in the 1997 Hollywood film, *LA Confidential.* Under conservative Mayor Sam Yorty, who served from 1961 to 1973, Los Angeles was run by a small corporate elite centered on a group called the Committee of 25 and the reactionary *Los Angeles Times.* After the riots, Yorty and business leaders did little to respond to the grievances. If anything, Yorty stoked the racial tensions by encouraging stronger police measures and downplaying the social and economic causes. According to Raphael Sonenshein, "the president of the Los Angeles Chamber of Commerce sent Yorty a bound volume of letters from individual members of the Chamber, all praising the mayor and [Police] Chief [William] Parker. Letter after letter congratulated them on restoring law and order."[145]

The Watts riots energized the city's liberal forces to find an alternative to Yorty and his conservative agenda. A liberal alliance, primarily of blacks and Jews, coalesced around Tom Bradley—a police lieutenant before his election in 1963 as the first black member of the Los Angeles City Council—to replace Yorty. Bradley had been a strong critic of the Los Angeles Police Department, strengthening his own support in the black community. Backed by the liberal alliance, Bradley narrowly lost in his effort to unseat Yorty in 1969 but was successful four years later. He served as mayor for twenty years.

Although rising black voter turnout and increased black activism played a key role in his early campaigns, he maintained an electoral coalition of liberal whites (especially Jews), blacks, and, increasingly, Latinos. He did not face serious opposition after his first victory. A liberal biracial coalition, including three blacks, also controlled the fifteen-member city council. For much of Bradley's reign, the council did not have a Latino member, but Richard Alatorre won a seat from the heavily Latino east side in 1985, and it had three blacks and three Latinos by the time Bradley left office in 1993.[146]

Bradley appointed many minorities and women to city boards and commissions, increasing their share from 16 percent in Yorty's last term to 31 percent in Bradley's first year and to 49 percent in his last term. He also increased minority representation in the municipal workforce from 35.2 percent in 1973 to 49.8 percent in 1991. His modest efforts to rein in the police were hampered by the city charter, which prevented him from dismissing Chief Daryl Gates, who had served in that office for many years and whose practices angered the black community.[147]

Bradley courted developers and promoted downtown renewal. He channeled the tax revenue generated by new development (almost $750 million by the late 1980s) back into downtown development projects instead of into poor neighborhoods.[148] The city's changing skyline solidified Bradley's support from business leaders and the construction unions. He largely ignored the flight of manufacturing jobs, bank redlining in minority areas, and the shortage of low-income housing.[149] Meanwhile, the poverty rate increased steadily, especially during the recession of the early 1990s, when it jumped dramatically (Table 5.1). Poverty is far more prevalent among blacks and Latinos than Anglos and Asians.

Racial tensions had festered in Los Angeles for many years. By 1990, whites were only 37 percent of the city's nearly 3.5 million people. Latinos represented 40 percent, and blacks had fallen to 14 percent.[150] Unemployment rose to more than 10 percent during the recession of the early 1990s but was much higher in black and Latino areas. Localized conflict had been building for years between blacks and Korean store owners, between blacks and Latino immigrants for construction and other jobs, and between whites and other racial groups over the public schools. In April 1992, a major riot broke out in South Central Los Angeles, a predominantly black and Latino area, after police officers were acquitted of the beating of a black man named Rodney King. The civil unrest left fifty-five people dead and caused more than $1 billion in property damage, the most costly in the nation's history. Tensions over immigration surfaced in 1994, when the state's voters approved the anti-immigrant Proposition 187; tensions over racial issues came to a head a year later with the statewide success of Proposition 209, an initiative against affirmative action.

The response to the riots of the Los Angeles liberal political and business elites revealed how out of touch they were with everyday life in the city's neighborhoods. Bradley anointed Peter Ueberroth, who had orchestrated the business community's embrace of the 1984 Olympics, to spearhead the city's official response to the riots. The Rebuild LA program, later called simply RLA, was top-down in its structure and program. RLA promised thousands of new jobs and businesses — supermarkets, banks, assembly plants — and failed to deliver. Bradley decided not to seek reelection.

Before the 1993 election, Michael Woo, a liberal Democratic city council member with strong ties to the city's black, Latino, and Asian communities, had been considered Bradley's likely heir, but Richard Riordan, a multimillionaire Republican corporate lawyer, proved to be a wild card in the nonpartisan primary. Little known to the public, Riordan had made large campaign contributions and philanthropic donations to black and Latino community leaders and could personally finance a campaign. In the runoff, while Woo portrayed himself as a "multicultural" racial healer, Riordan campaigned on being "tough enough to turn LA around." He promised to make government more efficient, hire 3,000 additional police, and shake the city out of its economic doldrums. In the wake of the riots, a frightened electorate, worried about crime and the recession, elected Riordan, despite the fact that voter registration was two-thirds Democratic, most of the population was nonwhite, and white voters had previously strongly supported Bradley. Riordan not only drew strong support from white conservatives, but from many moderate and even liberal whites.[151]

Riordan reversed Bradley's practice of balancing his appointments from the city's varied constituencies and mainly appointed affluent whites to the city's top jobs and commissions. Even his minority appointments came from well-off neighborhoods, leading H. Eric Schockman to call his base a "neo-rainbow coalition, based on class, not on race."[152] He sought to privatize city agencies and add police officers while holding the line on taxes. He did not embrace the recommendation of the Christopher Commission, formed in the wake of the riots, that the city adopt community policing. Riordan also had little use for RLA, which he inherited from Bradley, but he offered nothing during his eight years in office to take its place as a catalyst for addressing the problems confronting the city's poor. Riordan opposed the living wage law on the grounds that it would undermine the city's business climate and lobbied the Environmental Protection Agency to relax its enforcement of the Clear Air Act on the dubious grounds that it put Los Angeles businesses at a competitive disadvantage.[153] Because Los Angeles's city council was considerably more liberal than the mayor, it stymied him on these and other issues.

Riordan paid little attention to neighborhood development and affordable housing but continued Bradley's focus on downtown development. He pushed for a new sports complex and supported a $75 million tax break for the Dream-

Works film studio. As a key member of the Metropolitan Transportation Authority, a major source of public contracts for politically connected businesses, Riordan wanted to build new subway lines rather than improve the bus system on which poor and minority riders rely. His priorities included expanding commuter rail lines, increasing the number of police, bailing out the county public health system, and repairing the damage from the 1994 earthquake.[154] None of these measures did anything to address concentrated urban poverty. As Table 5.1 reveals, poverty reached a high point in Los Angeles during the early 1990s and subsided only slightly in response to the long national expansion.

During the Riordan era, Los Angeles's business elite no longer had a coherent agenda or a cohesive network. Many of the large corporations that had once dominated the Southern Californian political landscape had been absorbed by mergers and their headquarters moved elsewhere. Smaller firms with a direct stake in local policy making filled this vacuum, making contributions to elected officials in return for access to contracts and favorable decision making from the Metropolitan Transit Authority, port, airport, and zoning and taxing authorities. Though Riordan cobbled together support from these political supplicants, his coalition was inherently unstable given its reliance on the city's declining base of white voters. By law, he could not run for a third term.

This set the stage for the 2001 mayoral contest that pitted liberal James Hahn against progressive Antonio Villaraigosa after several conservative candidates were defeated in the primary. After the 1992 riots, Los Angeles saw a groundswell of effective union and community organizing around environmental justice, housing, transportation, and labor rights, symbolized by the living wage victory. This progressive coalition came together to support Villaraigosa, a former union organizer, president of the local ACLU chapter, and speaker of the state Assembly. Villaraigosa lost to Hahn, the city attorney, by a 54 to 46 percent margin, but his campaign mobilized the city's unions, Latino and liberal white voters, and advanced a progressive policy agenda championed by grassroots activists. (Most black voters supported Hahn, whose father, a legendary local politician, had been an ardent civil rights advocate.) Within the next few years, this coalition elected several progressives (including Villaraigosa) to the city council. Hahn was torn between these progressive forces and conservative voters in the San Fernando Valley who supported a powerful, though ultimately unsuccessful, effort to break away from Los Angeles and form a separate city of 1.6 million people. To appeal to progressives, Hahn appointed key labor and community activists to important commissions and embraced an unprecedented city-funded $100 million annual housing trust fund proposed by Housing LA, a coalition of union, church, and community activists.[155] Despite the political victories of LA's liberal and progressive forces, large-scale immigration and the expansion of low-wage jobs overwhelmed the effect of these policy reforms in terms of improving conditions for most of LA's poor. In fact, Los Angeles was one of the few American cities where the number of people living in concentrated poverty neighborhoods grew in the 1990s.[156]

NEW YORK

New York has long been viewed as the quintessential liberal, even progressive, city. The city's liberal political culture was shaped by a strong trade union movement, especially among blue-collar and lower-middle-class Jews, as well as a history of cooperation between liberal whites and minority groups.[157] Two Republican mayors, Fiorello LaGuardia in the 1930s and John Lindsay in the 1960s, were among the most liberal in the nation. As early as the Depression and World War II, blacks were elected to the city council, and Puerto Ricans followed two decades later. New York had a vibrant public sector. Its city university, libraries, public transit system, hospitals, and subsidized housing projects served the poor and working class well, promoting upward mobility and a sense of common purpose.

Starting in the 1970s, however, the political coalition that forged this bastion of activist government fell apart. Ideologically, the majority of New Yorkers remain committed to a liberal and reformist agenda, but they have not translated this orientation into a stable political regime. Like Los Angeles, New York is a highly diverse city where no ethnic or racial group dominates. As a result, all successful politics must be based on coalitions. By 1980, whites were only a bare majority (51.9 percent) of the city's population, though they still cast a clear majority of its votes. Ten years later, whites comprised only 43.2 percent of all New Yorkers. By 2000, whites had declined to 35 percent of New York residents, compared with 25.6 percent black, 27 percent Latino, and 10.6 percent Asian.[158] Competition and turf battles among native-born blacks, Latinos, other immigrants (including Haitians, Dominicans, West Indians, and Asians), and liberal whites (mostly Jews) have squandered the potential of rebuilding a liberal or progressive electoral partnership and governing regime.

Three relatively conservative mayors — Ed Koch, Rudolph Giuliani, and Michael Bloomberg — have taken advantage of this situation, largely dominating the city's politics since 1977.[159] (We say "relatively conservative" because their genuinely conservative positions on crime, spending, welfare, and labor were matched by socially tolerant attitudes toward immigrants and gays that would make them seem liberal in other contexts.) Although New York's charter gives considerable power to its mayor, these three politicians were not always able to carry out their full policy agenda; they were checkmated at times by a more liberal city council (with a significant number of minority and liberal white members) and by the occasional mobilization of labor unions and protest groups.

Democratic Mayor Ed Koch (1977–89) initially responded to the severe fiscal crisis of the mid-1970s by cutting municipal services, especially services for the poor. Although the former congressman came into politics as a liberal Democrat, he repositioned himself on the death penalty, racial preferences, and low-income-housing programs in order to win the mayoralty. Black and Latino voters helped him win office in 1977, but he refocused his electoral coalition on white voters, particularly the middle class and working class who lived in the outer boroughs.[160]

During the Koch era, most big-city mayors criticized the Reagan administration's slashing federal aid to cities, but Koch echoed the Reagan's antigovernment rhetoric. During his first two terms, Koch shut down a public hospital, favored the imposition of tuition at the city university, and reduced library hours. During his last term, as the city's economy expanded and tax revenues flowed in, Koch began to spend more on city services. Exasperated by the deepening housing crisis and widespread homelessness, he initiated a ten-year, $5 billion initiative to fix up abandoned housing and construct new homes on vacant lots—the largest city-sponsored housing plan in the nation's history. Mayors David Dinkins and Giuliani continued this program, which eventually lasted thirteen years. By 1997, it had supported the construction or rehabilitation of over 150,000 housing units in the most troubled parts of the city.[161]

Municipal scandals involving close allies, Koch's narrowing electoral support, and a series of violent, racially charged incidents (dramatized in Spike Lee's film, *Do the Right Thing*) enabled Manhattan Borough president Dinkins to defeat Koch in the 1989 Democratic primary and, in a narrow victory over Republican former U.S. Attorney Rudolph Giuliani, to become New York's first African American mayor.[162] Dinkins governed as a liberal, but the severe economic recession of 1989–91 in New York made it hard for him to build a durable governing coalition or widen his electoral base. The crack cocaine epidemic, rising street crime, fiscal stress, and the perception that he could not maintain order or manage black-Korean and black-Jewish conflicts undermined his administration.

In 1993, Giuliani narrowly won his rematch with Dinkins. A former federal prosecutor and assistant attorney general, Giuliani received relatively few black or Latino votes but strengthened his position among whites compared with 1989. (A referendum on whether Staten Island should secede from New

York also raised turnout in that predominantly Republican borough.) Black turnout declined, as did that of Latinos and white liberals. Jews, who had been solidly liberal from the 1930s through the 1960s, continued their steady shift toward more conservative candidates; exit polls indicated that Jewish support for Dinkins declined from 33.8 to 31.3 percent. In 1997, Giuliani easily defeated Ruth Messinger, the very progressive Manhattan Borough president and a former social worker.

Once in office, Giuliani "terminated affirmative action programs, cut social spending, increased the size of the police department, and cracked down on 'quality of life' problems like homeless people and panhandling."[163] Minorities constituted about one-quarter of his initial appointments to commissions, but there were no minorities in his inner circle. In fact, he snubbed minority leaders and officeholders, appearing to cultivate an image as a somewhat nasty and vindictive politician. Not an archconservative, especially when compared to national conservatives such as Pat Buchanan, Newt Gingrich, and Trent Lott, Giuliani avoided socially conservative positions on abortion or gay rights that might have pushed white liberals back toward a multiracial coalition.[164] He spoke out in favor of federal and state aid to New York City, strongly defended immigrants' contributions to the city, and even endorsed Democratic Governor Mario Cuomo for reelection in 1994. In 1997, when the Republican state senate threatened to allow the state's rent control law to expire, Giuliani offered lukewarm support of rent regulation. He bolstered the city's system of monitoring child abuse and providing foster care and unsuccessfully fought Republican Governor George Pataki's move to eliminate the city's payroll tax on suburban commuters.

But Mayor Giuliani's top priorities were further expanding the city's police force, lowering the crime rate, reducing the welfare rolls, requiring welfare recipients to work for their benefits, cutting business taxes, and privatizing municipal hospitals. Like Koch, he reduced social programs for the poor. Not until 2001 did he address the growing crisis in the city's low-income-housing production, nor did he acknowledge middle-class decline and growing income inequalities as major problems facing the city.[165] Here too, as Table 5.1 shows, poverty rates climbed in recent decades and remain stubbornly high, increasing from 19.3 percent in 1990 to 21.2 percent in 2000. The mayor's policies were far more successful in reducing the welfare caseload than in reducing poverty. He cut funding to community-based organizations and opposed a living wage law pushed by ACORN, unions, and other liberal and progressive groups.

As his second term neared the end, Giuliani's popularity was waning. His problems with his marriage and his wife's charge that he had had an affair with another woman, along with his indifferent response to police brutality and racial violence, had soured many New Yorkers on him. Ironically, an event that devastated New York — the September 11, 2001, terrorist attack on the World Trade Center — saved Giuliani. His valiant efforts to coordinate the rescue of the injured and his sympathy for the dead restored New Yorkers' faith in his leadership. Not only the firefighters and policemen who lost their lives, but the upwardly striving people who worked in many of the firms in the World Trade Center were very much Giuliani's constituencies, and his response to their grief was his finest hour.

Mayor Giuliani was able to transfer some of his renewed popularity to Michael Bloomberg, a politically moderate billionaire businessman who switched parties to capture the Republican nomination for mayor in 2001. Before September 11, Bloomberg, lacking political experience and name recognition, appeared to be a long shot. He overcame the latter by spending $74 million on the race, more than any other nonpresidential campaign in American history.[166] Bloomberg also benefited from an intraparty squabble among the Democrats. Two prominent Democratic politicians — Mark Green (a progressive and the city's elected public watchdog on political corruption and consumer abuse) and Fernando Ferrer (the liberal former Bronx Borough president) — fought a close primary that became steadily more inflamed, dividing blacks and Latinos from liberal whites. Although Ferrer got the most votes in the primary, he did not win the required 40 percent. Green then narrowly won the runoff. Some of his supporters in Brooklyn used tactics that Ferrer supporters called racist, which Green denied authorizing. Ferrer's "unity" endorsement of Green as the Democratic nominee was late and half-hearted. In the general election, many Ferrer supporters, particularly Puerto Ricans in the Bronx, stayed home or voted for Bloomberg. Many Latinos saw Green as thwarting the city's chance to elect its first Latino mayor. Green won a majority of the black and Hispanic vote, but lost to Bloomberg by a 706,268 to 744,757 vote margin.[167] Like Antonio Villaraigosa in Los Angeles that same year, Green, a longtime progressive activist, suffered from splits among minority voters and insufficient support among whites.

In office, Bloomberg sought to differentiate himself from Giuliani by reaching out to liberal groups. For example, he refused to march in the first St. Patrick's Day parade held during his administration because its sponsors would not permit a gay contingent to march. (He has participated in subsequent marches.) He signed a living wage law (set at $8.60 an hour plus health benefits) covering about 50,000 employees of service firms contracting with the city, principally health care workers. He also pushed through an 18.5 percent increase in the property tax rate to forestall service cuts and enacted a ban in smoking in all public places, including bars. In other respects, Bloomberg was a gentler version of Giuliani, continuing the stress on combating crime, taking a tough position on labor negotiations, and favoring large-scale development on Manhattan's West Side and downtown. (Governor Pataki, not Mayor Bloomberg, has dominated the planning for rebuilding the World Trade Center site.)

Despite the vast growth in income received by New York City residents in both the latter 1980s and latter 1990s, severe inequality has remained a huge problem for the city, as the benefits of economic growth flowed mostly to the upper end of the income distribution, while poverty remained deeply entrenched. Indeed, the relative position of the poor worsened, as the growth of disposable income fed the gentrification of many comparatively low-rent neighborhoods. Understandably, the physical rebuilding of lower Manhattan after the devastation of 9/11, together with the broader challenge of reviving the city's economy, has preoccupied the city's business and political establishments. The Bloomberg and Pataki administrations have not responded to efforts by Chinatown residents and a community-labor coalition to use rebuilding funds to foster a wider prosperity, preferring to focus on the real estate, architectural, and symbolic aspects of the rebuilding process. As the 2005 mayoral election began to take shape, it seemed likely that government would not pay more attention to the needs of poor and working-class New Yorkers unless the city's black, Latino, and white liberal majority could overcome their past differences and coalesce around a new vision for the city.[168]

ATLANTA

Atlanta provides another example of the failure of urban liberalism to address the problem of concentrated urban poverty, even while improving conditions for some members of the city's black population. Since the 1970s, the Atlanta region has prospered, ranking near the top of metropolitan areas in terms of jobs and population growth. The city has had strong and continuous black leadership, fostered by the presence of several elite black colleges. The city of Atlanta has a significant black middle class, although they have increasingly moved to the suburbs. By the early 1970s, Atlanta had a black majority population and by 2000 it had grown to about two-thirds of all residents. Blacks constitute a majority of registered voters. Four liberal black mayors, all Democrats, have led Atlanta since 1973: Maynard Jackson (1973–81 and 1989–93), civil rights activist Andrew Young (1981–89), William Campbell (1993–2001), and Shirley Franklin (elected in 2001). Since the 1980s, Atlanta has had a black majority on the city council and school board.

Jackson was elected with strong support from black voters and black and white neighborhood activists. Riding on the momentum of the civil rights movement and community activism, Jackson and a friendly city council developed a neighborhood planning system that gave ordinary residents a voice in land-use decisions and in the allocation of some federal community development funds.[169] He entered office explicitly rejecting a "slavish, unquestioning adherence to downtown dicta."[170] Instead, he insisted that business leaders "come to City Hall to meet in his office and to ask for his support, rather than simply to inform him of their needs and assume his compliance."[171] But Jackson ultimately championed all the highly visible development projects that downtown business leaders wanted, including a light rail system that connected downtown to the Atlanta airport. Jackson's successors continued this record of support for downtown development.

Like Tom Bradley in Los Angeles, Mayors Jackson, Young, and Campbell increased black public employment, gave government contracts to minority-owned firms, and put many more African Americans on Atlanta's police force. When Jackson took office, Atlanta already had a black majority, but black-owned firms had received only a tiny fraction of the city's business. By 1988, preferential procurement had shifted 35 percent of the city's contracts to minority firms, including such major building projects as the Underground Atlanta shopping center. Jackson boasted that minority set-asides for Atlanta's airport expansion created twenty-one black millionaires. In 1996, under Mayor Bill Campbell, the corporation running the summer Olympic Games awarded one-third of its $387 million in contracts to companies owned by minorities and women.[172]

But these preferential contract awards and affirmative action hiring practices primarily benefited higher-income minorities. No such equivalent benefits were targeted to low-income blacks. As vice mayor, Jackson had joined with picketing sanitation workers, but as mayor, he fired 2,000 striking sanitation workers, most of whom were black.[173] As Stone and Pierannunzi explain, in Atlanta "there is a fault line within the African-American community between the haves and have-nots."[174] The city black political establishment has generally sided with the "haves." Although mayoral elections are contested, the black mayors have taken the votes of low-income blacks for granted. For example, when the *Atlanta Constitution* exposed widespread racial discrimination in mortgage lending in 1988, neither Young nor Jackson supported the community groups negotiating with banks to make more loans to minorities.[175] Sjoquist describes Atlanta "as a paradox of extreme racial and economic inequality—of abject poverty in a region of tremendous wealth, of a poor and economically declining city population in the face of dramatic economic growth, and of a black Mecca in a 'city too busy to hate' . . . confronting a highly racially segregated population and the substantial problems associated with racism and poverty that pervade the city."[176]

Atlanta's booming downtown and suburbs did little to help blacks trapped in low-income inner-city neighborhoods.[177] In 1950, Atlanta's median family income was 90.7 percent of its suburbs'; in 2000, it was 62.8 percent. As their white counterparts did beginning in the 1950s, many middle-class blacks have moved to the suburbs since 1980. While the black professional middle class prospered, the black poor suffered from a one-third decline in manufacturing employment between 1970 and 1985. Atlanta's poverty rate increased during the 1970s and 1980s. In fact, the number of jobs *within* Atlanta has grown, but job growth in the suburbs has increased even faster. In 1950, Atlanta accounted for three-fourths of the region's jobs; by 2000, it had declined to one-fifth. The spatial mismatch between the jobs in the sprawling suburbs and the city's low-income neighborhoods — exacerbated by an awful public transportation system — contribute to the city's persistent poverty. Atlanta's housing and job markets remained highly segregated. Unlike some cities with liberal regimes, Atlanta did little to nurture community-based organizations as sponsors of affordable housing and economic development projects.

As Table 5.1 shows, Atlanta's already high poverty rate climbed steadily during the 1970s and 1980s, and peaked during the recession of the early 1990s. By 2000, its poverty rate had declined to 24.4 percent, but this is still one of the highest among major cities. Even so, there were some signs of progress. In 1980, 18 percent of the metropolitan area's poor lived in census tracts with 40 percent or more poor people. That figure grew to 21 percent by 1990, but it declined sharply to 12 percent by 2000.[178]

In 2001, Shirley Franklin became Atlanta's first woman mayor and the first black woman mayor of a major southeastern city. Franklin had strong ties to Jackson and Young (serving as his chief administrator) as well as to the business community, having served on the regional transportation agency and as managing director of the Atlanta Committee on the Olympic Games, a bastion of the city's corporate establishment. These ties helped her raise $3.1 million for her campaign. She achieved 50.1 percent of the vote, defeating two other black candidates. Faced with $90 million budget deficit, almost 20 percent of the budget, Franklin pushed through a 50 percent increase in property taxes and job cuts, resulting in a $47 million surplus by the end of 2002.[179] With business support, she lobbied the state legislature, including suburban Republicans, to allow Atlanta to impose a sales tax to repair its crumbling sewer system.[180] These circumstances left her little room for addressing the problems facing Atlanta's poor. Between 2000 and 2002, Atlanta had the nation's highest violent crime rate.[181]

On the same day in 2001 that Franklin won the mayoral contest, Cathy Woolard, a white lesbian who had served on the council since 1997, defeated a black council member to become its president. Her background in environmental and gay rights activism made her an unusual figure in southern politics. During the 1990s, Atlanta's white population increased by 9 percent, while its black population declined by 2 percent. Her success may mark the beginning of a biracial coalition, but whether it has a liberal or a conservative character depends on the mobilization of the city's poor, the effectiveness of labor unions in attracting and mobilizing low-wage members, and the willingness of Atlanta's suburbanites — particularly the suburban black middle class — to forge regional alliances with Atlanta's poor and working-class residents. (Atlanta contains only 11 percent of the region's population.) Even if city leaders wanted to forge a regional agenda, they have little leverage outside the city limits.

DETROIT

If Atlanta typifies what urban liberals can do under good economic conditions, Detroit exemplifies what happens under bad conditions. Although some Detroit business and political leaders tried to carry out physical redevelopment, high levels of racial polarization and black poverty led most white businesses and middle-class homeowners to abandon the city.[182] From the 1930s through the 1970s, top executives of General Motors, Chrysler, and Ford had "preemptive power" over the municipal agenda.[183] The United Auto Workers also played an important role, since many members lived in the city. But as the UAW improved wages and benefits for auto industry employees, many UAW members, particularly whites, moved to Detroit's suburbs. Jerome Cavanaugh, a white attorney, served as mayor from 1962 to 1970, presiding over a liberal growth coalition that tried, unsuccessfully, to stem the white exodus. The 1967 Detroit riots accelerated white flight and increased racial segregation in the Detroit metropolitan area.[184]

The restructuring of the global auto industry badly hurt Detroit, which lost 40 percent of its jobs and its population after 1960.[185] Detroit's black population thus began to accumulate political influence just as its economy collapsed. In 1969, in the wake of the riots, a conservative white candidate, Roman Gribbs, defeated a liberal black mayoral candidate, Richard Austin, by only 1 percent of the vote, the last time white voters would play a significant electoral role. Four years later, Detroit elected Coleman Young, a onetime radical union activist, as its first black mayor. He was reelected four times, serving until 1994. Initially, he carried out the typical liberal policy agenda, reforming the police, employing more African Americans in government jobs, and pressuring private employers to hire more minorities. But as major downtown department stores closed and the middle class fled, he had an increasingly hard time pressuring employers to hire Detroit residents.

Like many of his counterparts, Young sought to bring jobs to Detroit, but he got little help from the city's corporate elite. After years of bashing business and the suburbs, he began to court business leaders in the 1980s, but most of them had little faith in the city's future or its business climate. As its suburbs boomed, the city became known as the "murder capital" of the country. Young invited General Motors to build a new plant in the white working-class neighborhood of Poletown, which triggered much neighborhood anger. His administration razed 3,600 dwellings and relocated fifty small businesses in order to expand the city airport, but to little avail in revitalizing the city's economy.

Young's confrontational style appealed to Detroit's black voters, but city council members and community organizations increasingly criticized him for ignoring the decay of residential neighborhoods. He alienated younger blacks, who had few memories of the civil rights and union struggles that had catapulted Young to political leadership. His victory margins became increasingly narrow, and after twenty years in office, he chose not to run for reelection in 1993.[186] By the time he left office, blacks accounted for 80 percent of Detroit's population.

Dennis Archer, a black corporate lawyer and state supreme court judge, succeeded Young. Archer won 57 percent of the total, splitting the black vote with another African American candidate but winning 80 percent of the white vote.[187] Archer "aggressively courted the corporate community."[188] "I have to improve the image," he said. Under Young, business "didn't feel they had a partnership they could deal with."[189] *Business Week* called Archer "a politician who has won CEOs' trust, unlike his irascible predecessor."[190] He solicited involvement from the heads of the three auto companies, the local utilities, other major businesses, the UAW, and local foundations in his new Greater Downtown Partnership.[191]

Archer convinced some suburban firms to put operations into the city and assisted those already in the city to stay. He wanted suburbanites to attend cultural and sports events in the city. Rather than "demonizing the suburbs,"[192] Archer courted them. He pushed to merge the city and suburban bus systems.

Though he failed to enact a regional tax on concert and sports tickets to provide $40 million a year for Detroit's cultural institutions, his strategy paid off politically.[193] Affluent suburbanites funded his campaigns.[194] He also earned respect from suburban business and political leaders.[195]

Archer was initially criticized for paying too little attention to poor neighborhoods, but he responded by bringing community groups together with businesses to revitalize poor neighborhoods and win a federal empowerment zone for Detroit. Developers began to build new single-family housing for middle-class families in the city.[196] He improved basic municipal services such as streetlights maintenance and trash pickup.[197] But he also reduced the municipal workforce, limiting his capacity to provide his supporters with public-sector jobs.[198] He helped lure three gambling casinos to the city, hoping they would attract suburbanites and generate additional revenues for municipal coffers. He backed the construction of a new baseball stadium for the Detroit Tigers. Detroit's two daily newspapers lauded Archer's boosterism, and he easily won reelection in 1997.

By 2000, Detroit was 82 percent black, with a substantial Arab population and a few Latino and Asian immigrants. In November 2001, Kwame Kilpatrick—a thirty-two-year-old attorney, state legislator, and son of a Detroit congressman—won office, only to face a $170 million deficit. The city also had 8,000 vacant buildings, many used by drug dealers and vagrants. Kilpatrick had pledged to knock down 5,000 of them, but he ran out of money after leveling fewer than 2,000. He also promised to attract new technology companies and rebuild the downtown. Within a year, several development projects, including a new football stadium, were underway.[199] Another post–civil rights black mayor, Kilpatrick followed Archer's example of reaching out to business and the suburbs. Compuware, a software company, spent $400 million to move its headquarters and 4,000 workers from a Detroit suburb, buying its five-acre site from the city for $1. In recent years, Detroit has seen nearly $4 billion in investments downtown and midtown, including two stadiums, corporate construction, hotels, and housing.[200]

Under Archer and Kilpatrick, such vital signs as house prices, investment, and crime rates improved, but more than one quarter of Detroit's residents remain in poverty, and its infant mortality rate is among the highest in the nation. As Table 5.1 shows, Detroit's poverty rate, already moderately high by national standards in 1970, became even higher during this period. In the late 1990s, national prosperity lifted some Detroiters out of poverty, but the poverty rate declined only to 26.1 percent in 2000—the seventh worst among the nation's 100 largest cities. The share of poor people living in neighborhoods with 30 percent poverty in metropolitan Detroit declined from 43 to 36 percent in the decade, but most of these neighborhoods are in the central city.[201]

PITTSBURGH

Pittsburgh was the country's first major city to forge a stable progrowth coalition in the years after World War II. In 1943, banker Richard King Mellon organized an elite group of corporate executives to form the Allegheny Conference on Community Development (ACCD) in order to position the city and region to prosper when World War II ended. The election of Mayor David Lawrence, a probusiness Democrat, in 1946 allowed this private-public coalition to began making big plans. Over the next several decades, Lawrence and his successors initiated many projects to redevelop downtown Pittsburgh, keep corporate headquarters in the city, link the University of Pittsburgh and Carnegie-Mellon University to business, address the need for a new airport and flood control, and keep middle-class families living within the city. Pittsburgh's elite convinced the state legislature to allow the city to acquire and clear land and borrow money for redevelopment. When the federal government passed its own urban renewal law in 1949 (modeled in part on Pittsburgh's experience), the city was in a perfect position to move quickly. When Lawrence became governor of Pennsylvania in 1959 (serving until 1963), he made sure that Pittsburgh got what it needed. Pittsburgh's resulting "renaissance" attracted national attention. *Time* magazine put Mellon on its cover and Lawrence became a national figure. Many other cities sent delegations to Pittsburgh to learn how to forge an effective growth coalition.

The city's elite could do little to halt the decline of the steel industry, which employed 80,000 workers in the 1940s but only 4,000 by 1987. As steel declined, so did other manufacturing jobs, such as machinery and primary metals. As many people with high-paying unionized jobs fell into long-term unemployment, neighborhoods and local retail businesses suffered.[202] Although the deindustrialization of Pittsburgh pointed just as inevitably toward decline as in other Rust Belt cities like Detroit, Cleveland, and Youngstown, Pittsburgh's progrowth coalition saved it from Detroit's fate.[203] Even though Pittsburgh lost half its population between 1950 and 2000, the central city continues to play a central role in the regional economy, holding 40 percent of its jobs.

The city's corporate elite and their political allies, joined by the media and universities, concentrated on promoting "specialized advanced services" serving corporate headquarters as well as the software, engineering, medicine, and higher-education sectors, turning Steel City into Software City. As the awful pollution that belched from the steel mills, ruining the air, homes, clothes, and health, disappeared, Pittsburgh has become a financial center headquartering two national banks, Mellon Bank and PNC. Pittsburgh banks hold 4 percent of the assets in the 100 largest commercial banks, ranking fifth behind New York, San Francisco, Charlotte, and Chicago.[204] Many high-paid professionals live in the city.

Unlike the central city, the steel towns on the suburban fringe suffered without benefitting from Pittsburgh's new directions. Their workers never recovered. Manufacturing jobs fell from 31.7 percent of the region's employment in 1970 to 13.8 percent in 1991. Many service-sector jobs remained in the city but paid less than the unionized manufacturing jobs that had disappeared.[205] Blacks, who were particularly hurt by the loss of manufacturing jobs, have high levels of unemployment and concentrated poverty.

Not surprisingly, not all Pittsburghers agreed with the ruling regime's downtown development agenda, including the bulldozer approach to urban renewal.[206] Neighborhood and civil rights groups challenged the progrowth coalition, occasionally prevailing. Pete Flaherty served as mayor from 1969 to 1977 without the support of business, the major unions, or the Democratic Party. He favored neighborhood participation and put several ACCD-sponsored development projects on hold, causing business elites to create a new countywide group, the Committee for Progress in Allegheny County. In the 1980s, neighborhood groups, labor unions, and churches joined in an effort to halt plant closings, challenge redlining, and pressure banks to reinvest in the city. They didn't oppose the postindustrial transformation of Pittsburgh, but they wanted to slow down the loss of manufacturing jobs and share in the benefits of the city's new face. The Pittsburgh Community Reinvestment Group was formed in 1988 to advocate for neighborhoods and organize against redlining. Its activism has resulted in over $3 billion in loans for housing and small business in Pittsburgh's neighborhoods.[207]

Since the 1980s, mayors Richard Caliguiri (1977–88), Sophie Masloff (1988–93), and Tom Murphy (since 1993) have walked the tightrope between serving proponents of corporate growth and responding to neighborhood interests. Murphy, in particular, felt he risked losing business confidence by increasing services to the poor. A former community organizer, CDC director, and state legislator, Murphy lost to Masloff in 1989 but won in 1993. Community organizations played a key role in his victory, and he named several CDC leaders and community organizers, black as well as white, to high-level positions. His administration incorporated CDCs into decision making about community development funding. Even so, community leaders opposed Murphy's plans to demolish troubled public housing projects, further redevelop downtown, and build more middle-class housing. Faulting some CDCs for not producing enough housing, Murphy turned to private developers or required CDCs to form joint ventures with them. Urban liberalism in Pittsburgh thus gave neighborhood groups more influence, but did not challenge the priorities of downtown or regional development.[208]

CHICAGO

From 1955 until his death in 1976, Mayor Richard J. Daley led the most powerful political machine in the country. Under his influence, the Cook County Democratic Party had a virtual monopoly on public office. The city and county machine distributed 30,000 public sector jobs in the early 1970s, from street cleaners to stenographers to department heads, in exchange for such political chores as working in get-out-the-vote efforts on election day. The machine's ward and precinct workers also helped people get jobs, get their apartments inspected, or get service from the police and fire departments, especially in the white neighborhoods. It ensured that most of the city's fifty council members were loyal to Daley, as were the Democrats elected to county and state offices.

Daley also used the Cook County Democratic Party to promote downtown developments that pleased the business community and employed members of the construction unions. Some business leaders disliked Daley's authoritarian style, but they applauded the new skyscrapers, convention centers, and hotels, as well as the revitalization of the Loop and the lakefront. Daley's allies in Congress were adept at getting federal funds for urban renewal and social programs. Many believe he stole the Illinois election in 1960 for fellow Democrat John F. Kennedy, making his administration a pipeline of federal funds to Chicago, the "city that works."

This machine did not work for everyone. Daley's black precinct and ward leaders were, some complained, like overseers on a plantation. Daley kept his black supporters on a short leash. In exchange for voting for Daley and his candidates, they received only the lowest-paying jobs, if any. In 1970, blacks comprised 40 percent of Chicago's population but held only 20 percent of its government jobs, mostly the least desirable.[209] Chicago was one of the most segregated cities and its police among the most racist in the country. Its public housing projects were typically all white or all black. In his quest to bring the civil rights movement north, Reverend Martin Luther King chose Chicago. The angry white mobs reacting to his protest marches for jobs and open housing led King to declare that Chicago was more racist than the South. So long as Daley was mayor, the white liberal reformers running for office and protests organized by black community groups made little headway.

After Daley died, the Democrats scrambled to keep the machine running smoothly. Several machine politicians succeeded Daley at City Hall, but they lacked his political and organizational savvy, and the machine gradually grew weaker. It was finally defeated when a coalition of organizations from black neighborhoods catapulted Congressman Harold Washington, an outspoken progressive, into the mayor's office in 1983. Washington's campaign inspired the highest ever turnout in black neighborhoods. Washington also forged ties with white liberals, radicals, and community organizers. Although rooted in the impulses of urban liberalism, Washington was ultimately more a progressive because he made neighborhood empowerment and economic redistribution central themes in his administration. His fifty-two-page election manifesto in 1983 called for balanced growth between downtown and neighborhoods, neighborhood planning, and fees on downtown development to support affordable housing. Washington battled the city council, the business community, and the Cook County Democratic machine to carry out this agenda. Above all, the white machine politicians who held a majority of the city council seats until 1986 did everything they could to thwart Washington's agenda.

Washington's neighborhood-oriented reforms were nonetheless popular, and he won reelection in 1987. With a more favorable majority on the city council, he seemed poised for new accomplishments, but unfortunately, he died from a heart attack a few months later. The hope for urban progressivism in Chicago died with him as his political coalition fragmented and many black elected officials reverted to supporting the political machine that he had sought to dismantle.

Richard M. Daley, son of the former mayor, defeated Washington's interim successor, a black Democratic regular. Reelected three times, the younger Mayor Daley has incorporated some neighborhood groups into his coalition but moved away from Washington's agenda, seeking a more traditional focus on the downtown business community, neighborhood businesses, and white ethnic voters. Blacks continue to hold countywide and statewide positions, and Hispanics have made significant inroads in public office, but Daley's regime has not sought to mobilize these groups to promote institutional change. Nevertheless, Washington's short-lived progressive regime had a lasting legacy. Daley cannot govern the way his father did. He has made significant compromises with minority and community groups that his father would have tried to quash. For example, he endorsed a significant funding increase for low-income housing and partnered with CDCs to create much of the new housing. He has incorporated Hispanics—whose share of the city population increased from 7.3 percent in 1970 to 26 percent in 2000—into his governing coalition.[210]

BOSTON

Perhaps the most successful progressive mayor in recent years was Boston's Ray Flynn, who sustained a progressive regime for almost a decade after his election in 1983. Flynn replaced Kevin White, mayor since 1968, who started off as a savvy liberal, but who had a change of heart after his first term and promoted downtown development and neighborhood gentrification. Strong economic growth in Boston sent rents and housing prices skyrocketing, owing to strong gains in income among the upper middle class. But poor and working-class residents did not think that they were sharing the benefits, which led to a surge in organizing among tenants, minorities, working-class neighborhood residents, and opponents of urban renewal. In 1981, these forces led to a charter revision increasing the city council from nine at-large members to thirteen members, nine elected from neighborhood districts. White decided not to run for reelection. In the 1983 elections, Flynn, who had been a councilman since 1978, built support among tenants' groups, neighborhood activists, and service worker unions by calling for the redistribution of downtown wealth to the neighborhoods.

In office, Flynn widened his base by including many minority leaders who had supported his opponent in the 1983 contest, black activist Mel King, and by coopting parts of the business leadership. He appointed neighborhood and progressive activists to high-level positions within the city government while promoting "managed growth" and "balanced development." Despite opposition from the real estate industry, the city enacted a "linkage" fee on downtown development to fund affordable housing and required developers to set aside 10 percent of their units for low- and moderate-income families. The city also mandated that 50 percent of the workers on downtown construction projects must be city residents, 30 percent racial minorities, and 5 percent women. The administration strengthened the city's rent-control law and limited condominium conversions. Flynn also deposited city funds in banks with a good record of lending in poor and minority neighborhoods and walked picket lines to support workers in their disputes with management.

With help from local private foundations, the United Way, and major businesses, the city formed the Boston Housing Partnership to support housing development by CDCs. It also supported the Dudley Street Neighborhood Initiative (DSNI), an innovative, comprehensive neighborhood revitalization project based in the black ghetto of Roxbury. Although one-third of the area's land was vacant, it was owned by a jigsaw puzzle of interests that prevented DSNI from assembling land for housing, businesses, or parks. The city gave DSNI the power of eminent domain to purchase property from reluctant owners, an unprecedented move in urban development.[211]

These policies improved housing conditions for average Bostonians. By 1993, linkage had raised $70 million to fund 5,000 affordable housing units, mostly sponsored by CDCs. The inclusionary housing policy added another 400 units. Pushed by the city government and community activists, banks committed $400 million to a community reinvestment loan fund for low- and moderate-income neighborhoods. The Flynn administration gave neighborhoods more power over land-use decisions through neighborhood councils and other planning innovations.

The Flynn administration nevertheless reflected the limits of localism.[212] Its innovative efforts did not compensate for severe cuts in federal housing assistance, nor did they moderate the worsening income inequality produced by Boston's growing corporate service economy and the substantial number of families who remained outside the labor market. For a time, this boom began to reduce poverty and increase incomes at the bottom of the income distribution.[213] The advent of recession in 1989, however, led the media and other opinion leaders to question Flynn's progressive policies. By the time Flynn left office in 1993 to become U.S. ambassador to the Vatican, the community organizations in his political base had fallen on hard times, hurt by funding cutbacks, staff turnover, and complacency induced by years of city hall support. Flynn's successor, city council president Tom Menino, shifted to a conventional liberal progrowth agenda. Menino was easily reelected twice and was still serving as mayor in 2004.

INDIANAPOLIS

Mayor Steven Goldsmith of Indianapolis, the nation's twelfth largest city, took office in a far more conservative environment than the other cities discussed above. Since 1970, Indianapolis has been a consolidated city-county government in which minority and low-income voters constitute a small fraction of the electorate and Republicans continuously won the mayoralty.[214] Though perhaps the most ideologically conservative mayor of a major city, Goldsmith created a policy agenda designed to include low-income and minority residents in his governing coalition.[215]

Goldsmith's predecessor, William Hudnut, had pursued a typical growth coalition focused on making Indianapolis a center for amateur and professional sports. Running in 1991, Goldsmith argued that the condition of the low-income neighborhoods surrounding downtown had undermined the city's economic health, causing firms to relocate outside the city's expanded boundary. He sought to "reduce government intervention in order to open up opportunity."[216] Once in office, he quickly reduced the municipal workforce, lowered property taxes, allowed private firms to compete with city agencies to provide municipal services such as garbage collection, and privatized some city functions.

Unlike some GOP soul mates, Goldsmith gave neighborhood groups a strong voice in municipal management. His administration targeted seven low-income neighborhoods, diverted municipal funds to neighborhood organizations, and relied on community-based organizations as the primary vehicles for neighborhood improvement efforts. City government stepped up enforcement of housing codes and took over troubled properties. Stephen McGovern argues that Goldsmith's conservative populist regime "contradicts his immediate political interests; after all, suburban neighborhoods have the heaviest concentration of GOP voters while inner-city neighborhoods continue to vote Democrat."[217] Overall, however, Goldsmith's policies made no serious impact on reducing concentrated poverty in Indianapolis. Table 5.1 shows that Indianapolis has been a relatively low-poverty city, but its poverty rate climbed gradually between 1970 and 1990, tracking the national and urban trend.

Bart Peterson was elected to succeed Goldsmith in 1999 and was reelected in 2003, the first Democrat to win that office since the city-county merger three decades earlier. From 1989 to 1995, he worked for Indiana Governor Evan Bayh, including as chief of staff. Afterward, he worked in private business and was active in various civic affairs.

During his first campaign, he issued a detailed program called the Peterson Plan, with a mix of liberal and moderate policy ideas. In 2002, the Republican-dominated city council vetoed a living wage law. But in 2003, Democrats won a majority on Indianapolis's twenty-nine-member city council, ending thirty years of Republican control. The shift gave Peterson and the council a liberal regime to promote a bolder agenda. Although Peterson is a middle-of-the-road Democrat, he is a liberal by Indianapolis standards. In March 2004—on the heels of controversies over gay marriage in San Francisco and Boston—Peterson issued an executive order prohibiting discrimination by Indianapolis city government on the basis of sexual orientation.

Indianapolis had a strong economy and relatively high per capita income.

But cities can be hurt by corporate and government decisions made in distant places. In 2003 United Airlines announced that it was closing its 1.7 million-square-foot maintenance center near Indianapolis Airport, a twenty-four-hour, state-of-the-art facility for complex heavy maintenance on Boeing and Airbus jets. At its peak in the late 1990s, it employed almost 3,000 people. Indianapolis had outbid nearly 100 cities to get the 7,500 high-paying jobs that United promised would be there by 2004. Indianapolis and Indiana paid for most of the project's $540 million cost and eliminated its property taxes. Indianapolis — along with Chicago, Denver, and other cities that United owes money — is suing United in bankruptcy court, claiming that it owes the city as much as $100 million for United's failure to create the 7,500 jobs agreed to as a condition for the investment.[218]

SUBURBAN POLITICS

Most Americans — and most voters — are now suburbanites, making them a major influence in politics at the state and national levels. But just as there is no monolithic "suburban vote," there is no single version of suburban politics. As Chapter 2 showed, America's suburbs are incredibly diverse.[219] Although many are racially homogenous, some are quite mixed. Some are bedroom suburbs, but increasingly others are job centers with office parks, shopping malls, and downtowns. Young families predominate in some, but senior citizens and empty nesters make up the majority in others.

Suburban life is supposed to provide people with greater control over their lives and political institutions, but this can often be illusory. For example, suburbanites have no more influence than central cities over whether large corporations expand or close local facilities that employ them, or the larger economic and budgetary forces that affect such decisions. A suburban government can do little on its own about metropolitan pollution or about a neighboring jurisdiction decision to permit the building of a shopping mall that creates spillover traffic.

Suburban politics focuses on schools, municipal services, and land use, areas that local authorities can largely control. Typically, suburban residents want to preserve the highest quality of neighborhood life at the lowest tax cost, which often means opposition to new development, which can bring more costs than revenues. In some areas, developers, investors, lenders, and expanding companies have forged coalitions with the media and suburban politicians to promote development. In Southern California, major defense contractors and the Pentagon joined with developers to promote growth outside Los Angeles. In a few cases, like Chicago, the big-city political machine incorporated the suburbs, limiting the friction between the two. Suburbs, too, can have liberal, progressive, and conservative regimes for addressing their policy issues.[220]

High-quality schools can be a major influence on suburban housing values. In an environment where education determines lifetime earnings and per-student spending and school quality varies tremendously between jurisdictions, families seeking first-rate education for their children are willing to pay a premium, both in housing cost and property taxes. The wealthiest suburbs can finance costly education programs even with relatively low property tax rates. In November 2003, the voters in Lower Merion, a wealthy Philadelphia suburb, "inverted the usual anti-tax logic of suburban politics by electing a new Democratic majority that would likely spend the *most* money on schools." Its strong bond rating allowed the school district to borrow $100 million at a cost of only $330 to the owner of a $330,000 house. Even after this investment, Lower Merion's wealth means that its residents have one of the lowest tax burdens of any district in Pennsylvania.[221]

In contrast to Lower Merion, most working-class suburbs lack the revenues to fund a first-rate school system and do not get enough state and federal aid to match spending in affluent districts. They end up not being able to afford as many teachers, extracurricular activities, and up-to-date equipment. Even a growing number of affluent suburbs are confronting harsh fiscal and demographic realities. In New Rochelle in suburban Westchester County, New York, where homeowners pay an average of $10,000 in property taxes, voters have twice rejected tax increase referenda to keep the $3 million-a-year public library open. Its 37,000 registered voters defeated the measure in 2002 by a 2,208 to 1,158 margin. After prolibrary residents formed Save Our Library to turn the vote around, arguing that the average property taxes would increase by only $170 a year, prolibrary forces prevailed by a 7,269 to 4,531 margin.[222]

Suburban political battles often revolve around defending suburban communities from what they consider undesirable elements. Many people move to (or stay in) the suburbs to escape problems like crime, bad schools, and congestion that they associate with cities. Suburbs can use zoning to exclude less well-off populations by favoring large homes on big lots rather than permitting low-income housing or apartment complexes. Homeowners in suburban Loudon County, Virginia, protested a plan to build 725 homes for moderate-income families selling for abut $120,000. Instead, they wanted to construct 250 $300,000 homes on the site. Nearby residents voiced fears that their children would have to attend school with children from the proposed moderate-income homes. "It was very nasty," explained a planner for the county.[223] In Pasadena,

California, homeowner associations stopped the development of 1,500 units on a forty-six-acre site. "Our wonderful suburban bedroom community is on the verge of collapsing and becoming a city we don't recognize," said one opponent.[224]

Such barriers, along with outright discrimination by real estate agents and bankers, kept African Americans from moving to the suburbs for most of the twentieth century, although a few black suburbs did emerge.[225] Black suburbanization has increased dramatically since the 1970s, but black suburbanites remain highly segregated from whites, Latinos, and Asians with comparable incomes, partly as a result of the desire among some middle-class blacks to live in a "comfort zone" among other blacks rather than to be a minority in a white community. Prince George's County, Maryland, and DeKalb County outside Atlanta have the highest African American median incomes in the country.[226] A growing number of minorities have won office in suburbs.[227] But class differences *within* black suburbs sometimes undermine blacks' ability to act cohesively, even where they are a majority.[228]

Despite this progress, subtle forms of racism continue to crop up in suburban politics. Chapter 1 noted that wealthy residents of Orange County, California, opposed a mixed-income housing development on the grounds that it would generate crime, create disruptive students, and lower property values — often code words for racial prejudice. Residents of working-class suburbs — whose economic situation can be precarious and who often live closer to urban ghettos — can be mobilized to resist racial integration, as when politicians in northeast suburbs of Baltimore roused opposition to the Moving to Opportunity program that would allow 500 of Baltimore's public housing families to move into suburban apartments.[229] Spiro Agnew rose from Baltimore County executive in the 1960s to Richard Nixon's controversial vice president, while Alphonse D'Amato, a Republican politician from Hempstead, Long Island, rose from town official to U.S. senator from 1980 to 1998. Both often made statements that resonated with the racial fears and class resentments of white suburban voters. When the *Mt. Laurel* decisions of the New Jersey Supreme Court required suburbs to open up their zoning laws to permit some low-income housing, many suburban legislators sought to hamstring implementation of the decision.[230]

This is not to say, however, that such attitudes are ingrained in the suburban political terrain. For some well-off suburbs, racial integration is not a transitional stage between the arrival of the first black residents and exit of the last white residents. Oak Park, Illinois; Shaker Heights, Ohio; and Montclair, New Jersey, have all actively encouraged racial integration through such measures as banning "for sale" signs on lawns, providing mortgage help for white families to live in integrated areas, zoning to encourage construction of apartments, and "magnetizing" public schools to draw students from a racial mix of neighborhoods.[231] Almost 100 suburbs in California have adopted "inclusionary zoning" laws requiring new housing developments to include units for low- and moderate-income families, a policy that Montgomery County, Maryland, has had in place since the 1970s. Many New Jersey municipalities, including some suburbs, adopted rent control to protect poor and middle-income tenants from skyrocketing rents.[232]

Suburban advocates for racial integration and mixed-income housing may claim that this is the morally right approach, but they also argue that it provides housing for school teachers, cops, firefighters, nurses, and service workers. A business group on Long Island, the Long Island Association (LIA), joined with labor, civic, religious, and environmental groups to advocate rental housing for low- and moderate-income families. "We are strangling ourselves," explained Matthew Crosson, LIA president, who said the lack of affordable housing made it hard for employers to recruit workers and pay salaries that met housing costs.[233] Employers in Marin County north of San Francisco, with a per capita income over $50,000, were in the same position.[234]

The negative consequences of haphazard suburban development have become an increasingly important issue within suburban politics. Residents of affluent suburbs, particularly in outlying areas, can remember when their communities were small towns and farms. Not surprisingly, such trends have triggered a backlash against sprawl. The strip malls, low-slung office complexes, and townhouses scattered along secondary highways, often in unincorporated areas monitored only by county officials, have produced what Robert Lang calls "edgeless cities."[235] Developer influence has also prompted some suburban zoning boards to allow what Lang labels "boomburbs." For example, Chandler, Arizona, a Phoenix suburb, grew from 3,799 people to 176,581 residents between 1950 and 2000, while Anaheim, California, increased from 14,556 to 328,014, and Denver suburb Aurora swelled from 11,451 to 276,393.[236] In Irvine, California, in Orange County, the population doubled from 62,134 to 143,072. One of these new residents, Lyann Collins, a mother of four who bought a $441,000 home in 2001, was assured that a new high school would open in the fall of 2003, but the city ran out of money and the state lacked the funds to make up the difference.[237]

Residents in the sprawling Gwinnett and Douglas Counties outside Atlanta complain about road congestion, air pollution, and overdevelopment, but their public officials continue to approve huge shopping malls and new highway construction.[238] To stop further development, angry homeowners in Dunkirk, a Maryland suburb, formed the Dunkirk Area Concerned Citizens Association to mobilize voters against a bond issue for new sewers. In the 1999 County Commission elections, antisewer candidates (mostly Republicans) won a majority, ousting Democrats who had controlled the board since the 1950s.[239] Residents of Loudon County, Virginia, organized "Voters to Stop Sprawl," electing all eight members of that county's Board of Supervisors, ousting incumbents who had supported developments that enabled the county's population to quadruple in twenty years, transforming it from rural farms to high-tech office complexes and residential subdivisions.[240]

The movement for "smart growth" has burgeoned since the 1980s. The main impetus has been concern about traffic congestion, pollution, and loss of open space.[241] Some affordable housing activists and developers complain that the smart growth movement can be tinged with economic elitism, using environmental rhetoric to exclude housing for poor people.[242] Yet progressive versions of smart growth have focused on mixed-income communities, reducing poverty, revitalizing low-income neighborhoods, and building housing development around transit centers.[243]

Fiscally strapped working-class and low-income suburbs that need tax revenues and jobs from new commercial development are in the weakest position to resist overdevelopment, even if it brings traffic, noise, and density. These suburbs often wind up engaging in bidding wars for new developments and are so desperate for any development — even prisons and big box stores — that they offer incentives to employers, like Wal-Mart, that pay low wages for part-time jobs.[244] In Westchester County outside New York, Mount Vernon — a predominantly black community with a $41,128 median household income — rezoned an industrial site to allow a $45 million retail complex that included a Target megastore. Officials in adjacent Pelham — a smaller village with a median household income of $82,430 — sued Mount Vernon on the grounds that traffic from the complex would endanger children as they crossed the street to Pelham's athletic fields next to the Target site. "Although we sympathize with Mount Vernon's need for economic viability," said Pelham's lawyer, "we don't want it to be on the backs of the residents of Pelham and on the schoolchildren." Mount Vernon mayor Ernest Davis replied, "People will not starve and go without jobs and let you drive your Lexus."[245]

Such battles show that development decisions made in one community inevitably spill over into others. Suburbs are more likely to be able to solve these problems if they cooperate on a regional basis. They could call a truce to bidding wars and work together on planning economic development, transportation, housing, open space, and even public safety. But many suburbs want to protect their autonomy at all costs. "Whenever I hear 'regional cooperation,'" said Peter Lund, a county official in suburban Detroit, "I grab my wallet."[246] The existing ground rules encourage each suburb to maximize its own self-interest, making battles over housing and commercial development a continuing feature of suburban politics.

Some social scientists question whether American suburbs reflect the ideals of grassroots democracy. In *Bowling Alone*, Robert Putnam argues that suburbanization undermines civic involvement, partly because suburbanites spend so much time commuting that they have less time for voluntary activities like Little League and the PTA.[247] Others claim that suburbanites favor privacy and individualism, preferring single-family homes over denser housing. Suburbs, some argue, foster social isolation and go so far as to highlight their exclusivity in the form of gated communities (or "privatopias"). It is often said that affluent Americans have withdrawn from the common institutions of democratic life. They send their children to private schools, join country clubs rather than using public parks, buy their own books rather than using the public library, and rely more on private security services and even private roads rather than government services. Indeed, the nation's wealthiest suburb—Rancho Santa Fe, California, whose 4,000 residents have a per capita income of $113,132 and where the median home price is $1.7 million on minimum two-acre lots—forbids sidewalks, street lights, and mailboxes.[248]

The truth is that only a few American families have withdrawn into a totally private world. Only 9.4 percent of all American children attend private schools, mostly (7.2 percent) church related. Only 16.2 percent of the wealthiest one-fifth of all families send their children to private schools. Affluent suburban children are more likely to attend public school than their affluent city-dwelling counterparts. As Richard Rothstein has observed, "the suburbs vote for public education."[249] Early studies of suburban life in the 1950s and 1960s found a "hyperactive social life" that included a wide range of clubs and organizations.[250] Although participation levels may have declined since then, it is not clear whether this represents a new suburban ethos or simply results from broader social trends, such as the increase of two-earner families.[251]

Some suburbs have a vibrant civic life, with participation in soccer leagues, PTA, religious institutions, Girl Scouts, Kiwanis and Rotary club, Junior League, neighborhood associations, block clubs, and community theater. People read the local paper and pay attention to the school board, city council, and planning commission. In other suburbs, though, local politics is a spectator sport, with few people paying attention or getting involved. There is much variation *within* and *between* suburbs, influenced by class, race, union membership, and many other factors, especially the presence or absence of organizations actively recruiting people to be involved.

When suburbanites realize that local measures cannot solve the problems in their communities — school funding, traffic gridlock, and inadequate public services — they may begin to rethink the go-it-alone approach. This can go in a conservative direction, as when California suburbanites revolted against high property taxes with Proposition 13 in 1978 and against immigration with Proposition 187 in 1994. But it can also have a progressive outcome, such as the growing suburban support for regional cooperation, and for state and federal solutions to suburban economic, social, and environmental problems. For example, Chapter 1 described how the inner suburbs around Pasadena, California, evolved from a Republican to a Democratic stronghold. The traditionally Republican Nassau and Suffolk Counties in suburban Long Island have both recently elected Democratic county executives. We return to this topic of suburban support for liberal and progressive policies in Chapter 8.[252]

CONCLUSION

In big central cities, urban liberals, progressives, and conservatives all formulated approaches to local government that have lasting value. Almost every city has attempted to assimilate racial minorities through such liberal strategies as public employment and contracts with community-based organizations. Even most conservative mayors now include blacks, Hispanics, and Asians among their top-level appointments. Similarly, many cities have adopted community-based approaches to economic development and the living wage laws advocated by urban progressives. Urban progressives have helped to shift the urban political debate away from appeals to racial identity toward the problem of narrowing the economic divide between races.[253] Urban conservatism can take credit for wider acceptance of the idea that municipal agencies must meet performance targets and be accountable for their results and that new policing strategies can reduce crime rates. At the same time, none of these three approaches has made much progress on reducing inequality, persistent poverty, and racial and economic segregation. Even the most well-managed and progressive cities failed to lift the incomes of their poorest residents or substantially reduce class separations. While all three types of regimes developed policy responses to these problems, none can claim significant success.

The stark limits of localism in addressing such issues seem at odds with the widely noted urban revival of the 1990s. The improvement in urban conditions during that decade was real. It was fed not only by local efforts to improve crime rates and the quality of urban life, but also by a long national economic expansion that pulled even badly-off cities into its wake. The most important fact about the nation's prosperity, however, is that it did not trickle down nearly as far as it should have. Indeed, although it reduced the number of people living in concentrated poverty, the nation's distribution of wealth and income became even more unequal. In New York City, the archetype of 1990s prosperity, the percentage of residents classified as middle class fell from 35 to 29 percent.[254] Income growth for jobs in the bottom half of the earnings distribution in central cities was too sluggish to pull many families out of poverty, while the growth of entry-level jobs was far from inner-city areas. So long as national policy subsidizes development on the urban fringe, cities and inner suburbs will find it difficult to make much headway in reducing the spatial segregation of rich and poor.[255]

The problem is even worse for distressed, inner-ring suburbs.[256] They typically lack the commercial and industrial tax base enjoyed by many cities, nonprofit institutions to address their social problems, or amenities to attract new residents. Regional elites care about central-city decline because they have substantial investments in downtown businesses, hospitals, universities, and museums. They have no such commitments to distressed suburbs. By themselves, these suburbs can do little to arrest their decline. The only way for them—as well as central cities—to remove their fiscal straitjacket is to forge regional coalitions. Yet this chapter has also shown that the leading elected officials of both central cities and inner suburbs are also deeply embedded in a game of competition with each other. They view each other with suspicion. Few have taken the lead to advocate solutions that reach beyond their own borders. We turn to this challenge in the next chapter.

Regionalisms
Old and New

Hartford is the capital of Connecticut, the richest state in the nation ($42,706 per capita income in 2002), but it has one of the highest overall poverty rates in the country (30.6 percent) and contains many large areas of concentrated poverty. In 1969, Hartford's major employers formed a new organization, the Greater Hartford Process (GHP), to address the region's problems.[1] Three years later, this elite group unveiled a plan to rebuild the city's low-income areas, create an entire new town in the suburbs, and develop new regional approaches to housing, transportation, health care, education, and social services. The plan would affect 670,000 persons in twenty-nine communities over a 750-square-mile area.

The most dramatic impact was on Coventry, a town located fifteen miles from the city. GHP had quietly begun buying land in the all-white town of 8,500 residents in order to create, from scratch, a new town of 20,000; GHP planned to set aside 15 percent of the housing units for low-income families. When they learned of this, Coventry officials refused to cooperate with the plan, which was ultimately shelved. One suburban official noted, "I don't see the problems of the central city as my responsibility." Within a few years, GHP had ceased to exist. Although most Hartford residents had responded positively, "some leaders of Hartford's black community claimed that the new-town idea was an attempt to dilute their power in the city, and others objected to the lack of citizen input into Hartford Process plans."[2]

Two decades later, a newly hired Hartford city manager, Raymond Shipman, proposed another regional plan. It would require suburbs to join a regional government that would provide some public services. Suburban commuters to

Hartford would be taxed, and three public housing projects in Hartford would be razed and their residents relocated to the suburbs.[3] Shipman was soon gone as Hartford's city manager.

Then, in 1996, the city council took a different approach: it placed a moratorium on opening new social service centers for the poor, such as soup kitchens, homeless shelters, and drug treatment centers. Within its 18.4 square miles, the city (population 140,000) already had 150 social service agencies, which city officials said attracted poor people to the city.[4] Hartford city council members claimed that these programs were "ruining the climate for urban revitalization, hurting business, shrinking the tax base, and scaring away the middle class." They also argued that a suburbs were not doing their share to address the needs of the poor — certainly an accurate statement.[5] It was almost as if Hartford officials had decided that if the suburbs refused to cooperate, the city would stop accommodating the region's poor, potentially forcing them out to the suburbs.

Memphis is another central city with many poor, minority citizens that has had an uneasy relationship with its suburbs. In 1971, suburban residents in Shelby County, Tennessee, voted two to one against merging with Memphis.[6] In 1990, suburban opposition also thwarted an attempt to merge the largely black Memphis school system with the predominantly white county school system. In 1993, Mayor W. W. Herenton, the city's first African American mayor and a former school superintendent, again proposed merging the city with suburban Shelby County. Herenton's proposal was politically courageous, because if it had succeeded, it would have diluted the black electoral power so recently gained through his election.

Between 1940 and 1980, Memphis captured 54 percent of all population growth in the region by annexing suburbs. After 1980, suburban opposition ended Memphis's expansion, and during the 1980s, Memphis lost 6 percent of its population, while that of the surrounding Shelby County suburbs more than doubled. Many African American political leaders, who had recently gained six of thirteen seats on the city council and five on the nine-member school board, argued that a merger would dilute black voting strength and cost blacks "some of the political control we have fought for for so long." Herenton, who had been elected mayor in a highly racially polarized election, countered that "blacks gain little by controlling a city that is broke."[7] Herenton garnered support from Memphis business leaders, who predicted that the merger would lessen their tax burden, but many suburbanites opposed the merger, fearing that suburban Shelby County (median household income $43,784) would face additional tax burdens when merged with Memphis (median household income $22,674). The proposal failed at the polls.

The previous chapter showed that urban leaders have a stake in forging metropolitan solutions for problems that they cannot solve on their own. The examples of Hartford and Memphis show how difficult it can be to craft and implement regional solutions to the problems of concentrated poverty and suburban sprawl. These are not the only examples—later we will point to more positive ones—nor is suburban opposition to central-city initiatives the only obstacle such initiatives face. In this chapter, we examine regional initiatives over the past 100 years and take a closer look at the "new regionalism" that has emerged since the early 1990s. While these efforts are praiseworthy, state and federal rules of the game make it difficult to forge regional cooperation and restrict what they can do.

THE PROBLEM

The competition among metropolitan jurisdictions to attract higher-income residents and exclude the less well-off has been a powerful factor promoting the concentration of poor people in central cities. In the typical metropolitan area, dozens, sometimes hundreds, of suburban towns try to establish and maintain higher positions in the metropolitan pecking order. A "favored quarter" of suburbs houses upper-income people and select business activities that pay property taxes but do not demand many services.[8] These places use large lot zoning, high housing prices, and even tacit discrimination to keep out the unwanted, or at least the less privileged. Elsewhere, less exclusive residential suburbs, suburban commercial and industrial areas, and aging inner-ring suburbs also seek to carve out their own places in the metropolitan hierarchy below these exclusive areas, but still above the central city. Even aging, economically declining inner suburbs often try to keep out inner-city residents. For those with limited means, living in the central city may be their only choice.

A similar but less keen competition takes place among central-city neighborhoods. Urban neighborhoods do not have the formal authority to exclude some residents and attract others, but factors such as housing quality and price, neighborhood amenities (particularly a good neighborhood primary school), city zoning and land-use regulations, and discrimination in the private real estate market can serve the same purpose. Unlike exclusive suburban towns, however, even well-off central-city residents pay into the city's common budget. As a result, higher-income central-city residents who do not want to pay for services for the less fortunate, or who do not use the central-city services for which they are paying (schools, public health care, public transit, and parks), have a strong monetary incentive to move to a more exclusive suburban jurisdiction.

Federal policies made suburbs more attractive relative to central-city neighborhoods by building freeways, underwriting suburban home ownership, and funding subsidized housing and social services in central cities that made them attractive to needy constituents. Suburbs often reinforce this arrangement by regulating land uses to maximize property values, by customizing their services for middle-class professional households, and by declining to build subsidized housing or sometimes even rental housing of any kind. Many central-city public officials have also contributed to this state of affairs by supporting the expansion of spending on social services. This wins favor from those who use them, enhances budgets, provides jobs for constituents, and builds political support. They are no more willing to give up responsibility for, and control over, these activities than exclusive suburbs are to embrace them. Defenders of this system draw on widely held beliefs that local autonomy, private property, and homogeneous communities are sacred parts of the American way of metropolitan living. As Harvard law professor Gerald Frug observed, fragmented metropolitan areas are not only created by law, they are also "perpetuated by the kind of person this fragmentation has nurtured."[9]

Although this deeply embedded system may seem rational to suburban residents and urban public officials, it has produced dysfunctional consequences for the larger society. Metropolitan political fragmentation has encouraged unplanned, costly sprawl on the urban fringe. As we have seen in previous chapters, it has imposed longer journeys on commuters, allowing them less time for family life. It has undermined the quality of life in older suburbs, hardened conflicts between suburbs and their central cities, hampered financing for regional public facilities such as mass transit, and encouraged disinvestment from central cities. Countries with strong national land-use regulation and regional governments have avoided or tempered many of these problems. Indeed, the United States could have avoided them if we had chosen a more intelligent path for metropolitan growth over the last one hundred years.

As these problems became increasingly evident over the last century, they drew criticism from scholars, planners, and good-government groups. These critics focused on how metropolitan political fragmentation undermines administrative efficiency, environmental quality, economic competitiveness, and social equity. As early as the 1920s, administrative experts promoted regional solutions as ways to address the overlap, duplication, lack of coordination, and waste in the provision of public services. Concern today is becoming wide-

spread. Even longtime suburban residents have expressed concern over the environmental costs of sprawl as they see their countryside being gobbled up by
new development and find themselves stuck in traffic jams even while doing
their Saturday morning shopping. They have made "smart growth" a hot-
button issue across the country. Executives of large firms, transportation planners, and economic development officials most often express concern that fragmented metropolitan areas undermine the economic competitiveness of urban
regions.

Finally, those who crusade for civil rights and racial desegregation, who
care about the plight of the inner-city poor, and who champion greater civic
participation have criticized how metropolitan fragmentation has strained the
social and economic fabric of our communities. They favor fair housing and
housing mobility programs, metropolitan administration of economic opportunity programs, tax-base sharing, and metropolitan school districts. Robert
Putnam's *Bowling Alone* documented the ways in which metropolitan fragmentation, sprawl, and inequality helped to drive the decline in community and
civic participation.[10] In the words of Frug, "The suspicion and fear that infest
our metropolitan areas threaten to generate a self-reinforcing cycle of alienation: the more people withdraw from each other, the higher percentage of
strangers that cause them anxiety, thereby producing further withdrawal."[11]

THE ORIGINS OF THE NEW REGIONALISM

The current debate over regionalism echoes the concerns of urban reform-
ers in the 1920s and 1930s. At the end of the nineteenth century, New York,
Chicago, and many other cities had moved to annex or consolidate adjacent territory likely to be developed over the next fifty years. The formation of Greater
New York from New York City, Brooklyn, the hamlets of Queens County, the
Bronx, and Staten Island in 1898 was a grand and highly successful experiment
in metropolitan government. Indeed, the current vitality of Chicago and New
York stems in considerable part from these wise actions. By the 1920s, however, middle-class urbanites, dismayed by the rapidly increasing density and
inequality of their industrial cities, and frustrated by their inability to continue
to dominate their politics, increasingly fled to the suburbs. Once they established themselves as suburbanites, they persuaded state legislatures to pass laws
hindering cities from further annexation. Metropolitan growth would hence-
forth take place largely outside the jurisdiction of the central city.

Responding to such trends in the 1920s, an early group of regionalists fore-
saw the need for new forms of metropolitan planning and cooperation. Echoing

the "garden city" idea first promulgated by Ebenezer Howard in England, Lewis Mumford and his colleagues in the Regional Planning Association of America, formed in 1923, hoped that coherent regions would gradually emerge to dissolve the problems of the industrial city. "The hope of the city," Mumford wrote in 1925, "lies outside itself."[12] Other radical (though less utopian) thinkers called for regional land-use planning as an antidote to fragmentation. In 1927, the Regional Plan Association's magisterial plan for metropolitan New York called for knitting the region together with a comprehensive system of highways and rail transit that would concentrate economic growth in Manhattan and in a few suburban centers. In 1937, the New Deal's National Resources Committee called for federal efforts to foster regional planning, including the establishment of multistate metropolitan planning agencies.[13] In the face of resistance from those who saw such measures as abrogating private property and local democracy, however, none of these visionary blueprints had much impact on the post–World War II evolution of American cities. As a result, many of the problems they anticipated did indeed come to pass.

EFFICIENCY ARGUMENTS FOR REGIONALISM

The negative consequences of unplanned metropolitan growth triggered new strains of regionalist thinking and new political constituencies that favored the creation of new regional institutions. Public administrators, city planners, and municipal reformers viewed regional planning as the best way to promote regional economic efficiency and maintain a sound environment. Writing for the National Municipal League in 1930, Paul Studentski criticized metropolitan fragmentation and called for a framework that would support "real, democratic, comprehensive, and permanent organization of the metropolitan community."[14] Prominent academics and planners such as Charles Merriam, Victor Jones, and Luther Gulick elaborated on these themes in the postwar period.[15] Robert Wood's 1961 classic *1400 Governments* argued that postwar suburbanization in metropolitan New York was irrational, inefficient, and unaccountable. The federal Advisory Commission on Intergovernmental Relations, created by Congress in 1947 (and eliminated in 1996), recommended ways to broaden the urban tax base and improve the regional distribution of services.

A common theme was that fragmented metropolitan governments promoted wasteful competition and duplication of public services, with too much variation in quality. These trenchant critiques were no more effective than the work of earlier metropolitan visionaries had been in restraining the construction of freeways, suburban shopping malls, and tract housing in the 1950s and

1960s. It nevertheless remained a key doctrine of public administration that regions required some level of metropolitan planning in order to function well. The 1960s saw the creation of many regional councils of government (often called COGs) and single-purpose regional agencies for functions such as water and sewer systems, garbage disposal, and transportation. City-county consolidation took place in Miami, Nashville, Jacksonville, and Indianapolis, but voters in many other areas rejected proposals to merge city and suburban governments into regional governments. Bucking this trend, voters in Louisville, Kentucky, and its suburbs approved (by a 54 to 46 percent margin) the consolidation of the city of Louisville with Richmond County in November 2000, the first major city-county merger to win approval in thirty years.[16] (Fast-growing cities of the South and Southwest, such as Phoenix and Albuquerque, used their control over critical water and sewage systems to continue to annex surrounding territory long after that practice ended elsewhere in the country.) Finally, voters and public officials sought to streamline and modernize the governance of suburban areas in the postwar period by enhancing county government and consolidating school districts. All these efforts, however, fell short of the goals espoused by the first and second generations of regionalists.

ENVIRONMENTAL ARGUMENTS FOR REGIONALISM

Concern for administrative efficiency motivated the early advocates of metropolitan governance. Beginning in the 1960s, a new generation of regionalists emerged, concerned about environmental protection, sustainable development, and smart growth. Development rapidly swallowed the metropolitan countryside after World War II, and the freeway construction of the 1960s and 1970s increased traffic congestion to new, more disturbing levels. Confronting these realities, suburban residents and those who represented them became less enthusiastic about unbridled metropolitan growth.

In 1974, the Council on Environmental Quality issued a report titled *The Costs of Sprawl,* calling for greater regulation of suburban development.[17] Today, national environmental organizations, including the Sierra Club, are campaigning against sprawl, Oregon and Maryland have adopted state legislation for smart growth, and many other states are actively discussing similar measures. Some approaches call for the establishment of regional growth boundaries monitored by the state; others merely provide incentives to channel new investment toward already developed areas while attempting to preserve agricultural land uses or otherwise protect undeveloped areas. Regional groups are active in the San Francisco Bay area, Washington, DC, Pittsburgh, and Suffolk County,

New York. A movement for "new urbanism" has emerged among architects and city planners who favor denser, more pedestrian- and transit-oriented forms of neighborhood development.[18]

Despite naysayers who argue that limits on growth on the metropolitan periphery will have an adverse impact on housing affordability and consumer choice, a growing consensus has emerged in many places on behalf of re-thinking older growth policies.[19] Residents of Cook County, Illinois (an old urban area), and Santa Clara County, California (the high-tech Silicon Valley), both showed overwhelming support for regional approaches to solving urban problems.[20] Voters across the country have approved ballot measures to limit suburban sprawl and preserve open spaces.[21] Responding to such senti-ments, former Vice President Al Gore made smart growth a central theme in the Clinton-Gore administration's "livability agenda," which focused on pre-serving open spaces, redeveloping brownfield areas, mitigating congestion, and improving urban air quality.[22] A recent report by the professional association of city planners found that of the 553 initiatives favoring smart growth on state or local ballots in thirty-eight states in the 2000 election, 70 percent were adopted; twenty-seven governors offered smart growth proposals in 2001.[23]

ECONOMIC COMPETITIVENESS ARGUMENTS FOR REGIONALISM

Contemporary regionalists have also argued that metropolitan areas divided against themselves cannot compete successfully in the new global economy. In particular, business leaders and regional planning organizations have recog-nized that regionally oriented planning and development policies could make metropolitan economies more competitive. Although business-supported re-gional planning groups have existed at least since the Regional Plan Associa-tion was established in New York in 1923, groups like San Francisco's Bay Area Council and Pittsburgh's Allegheny Council for Community Development be-came more common after World War II. The radical changes in technology, business organization, and global competition since the 1980s gave this per-spective new force. The high-technology companies of Silicon Valley took the lead in supporting regional approaches to the area's housing, transportation, and development issues. One scholar, AnnaLee Saxenian, found that Silicon Valley entrepreneurs' ability to collaborate in this way made that region more successful, over the long haul, than the similar technology complex along Route 128 around Boston.[24]

As we discussed in Chapter 3, social scientists who examine the interrela-tionships between central-city and suburban economies find a high correlation between the two, although in some cases, substantial central-city decline has not prevented the surrounding suburbs from prospering. Nevertheless, there are obvious linkages in the economic conditions and income growth rates of central cities and their suburbs. Central cities continue to perform functions and provide services that are critical to regional growth. The evidence suggests that cooperative regions are more likely to prosper than are more competitive, divided regions.[25]

These realities have given impetus to new efforts to form regional public-private partnerships to promote regional growth. Syndicated columnist Neal Peirce, who has given visibility to all forms of new regionalism, and his colleague Curtis Johnson have been particularly active in inspiring and advising a new generation of such organizations. They have not promoted any particular organizational forms, stressing instead the general need for collaboration, trust, dialogue, and leadership.[26] These collaborations have produced many Web sites and newsletters.[27]

Closely associated with this perspective is the growing focus on industrial clusters as a basis for urban and regional economic development. Advanced by Michael Porter's *The Competitive Advantage of Nations,* this perspective argues that a region's competitiveness is based on the quality of networks and interactions among related and often physically close firms. Even though they may compete against one another in some ways, they share technical knowledge, a skilled labor pool, and support services and spur one another to rapid technological innovation. This has led some policy makers to promote clusters as a way to address such regional needs as better-paid jobs, more rapid innovation, and a better quality of life for industrial workers. This perspective was given national prominence in the 1996 report *America's New Economy and the Challenge of the Cities.*[28]

Silicon Valley itself continues to be committed to collaborative approaches to economic growth, through the business-backed Silicon Valley Joint Venture (http://www.jointventure.org), which has been focusing on strategic planning, tax policy, and workforce development. Many state and local agencies hoping to emulate Silicon Valley's success have embraced this way of thinking about economic development, such as the Regional Technology Alliance organized by the San Diego Association of Governments. San Diego has also surveyed employers in these clusters to understand their workforce needs and has developed programs to address them.[29]

EQUITY ARGUMENTS FOR REGIONALISM

The spatial concentration of urban poverty has also motivated many new regionalists. As Michael Schill observed, "although segregating themselves in the suburbs may serve the interests of large numbers of Americans today, the long term costs of doing nothing to alleviate concentrated ghetto poverty are likely to be tremendous."[30] Distinguished public intellectuals, including Anthony Downs of the Brookings Institution, former Albuquerque mayor David Rusk, former Minnesota state legislator Myron Orfield, and his brother Harvard professor Gary Orfield, among others, have concluded that regional approaches are the only way that the problem of inner-city poverty can be solved.[31] Increasingly, they have been joined by officials representing the inner-ring suburbs who are facing the growth of "urban" problems that they cannot solve within the limits of their own jurisdictions. With foundation funding, Orfield and his associates have launched initiatives to document and remedy "growing social and economic polarization" in twenty-two metropolitan areas.[32]

Increasingly, planners are arguing that there need not be a trade-off between equality and efficiency, or growth. Indeed, regional strategies that lift up the central city can make regions more competitive. The Center on Wisconsin Strategy at the University of Wisconsin has advocated that workforce development practitioners and regional employers cooperate to train central-city residents for high-wage jobs in technologically innovative firms. This "high road" approach to regional economic development would simultaneously enhance wages, upward mobility, and employer competitiveness.[33] Through the Working Partnership USA in Silicon Valley (http://www.wpusa.org), an alliance of labor unions and community organizations has attempted to balance the strategic thinking undertaken by technology industries in that area with a number of measures to secure greater social equity, including living wage laws and the building of affordable housing. In a recent review of equity regionalism, Scott Bollens found a variety of different experiments under way in different metropolitan regions, stimulated in part by state regulations calling for balanced housing and the increasing portability of federal housing vouchers.[34]

THE PRACTICE OF METROPOLITAN COOPERATION

Although support for new, regional approaches to metropolitan problems has grown steadily over the last several decades, the actual practice of metropolitan government has made less progress. Most regions have some elements of cooperation, but they vary considerably in terms of their institutional arrangements, the political constituencies they bring into play, and their capacity to address their region's social and economic challenges. A variety of constituencies has supported regional cooperation — business leaders seeking to enhance regional economic competitiveness, program administrators concerned with better coordination, community groups seeking regional equity, and suburban advocates of slowing growth. Their aims and interests obviously diverge on many points. In contrast to this diversity, the local interest in autonomy, particularly among suburban jurisdictions, is quite consistent. This has hindered the growth of metropolitan cooperation but may not prevent it in the long run.

What experiences has the United States had with metropolitan cooperation, why have they been so ineffective, and what forms would a more effective regionalism take? In formal terms, regional cooperation ranges from limited, single-purpose activities (such as a regional sewer or transportation authority or a reverse commuting program) through multipurpose cooperative arrangements, to full-fledged regional governments. What follows is a brief review of the history and experience of metropolitan cooperation. First, we review the weak efforts that the federal government has historically made to promote regional cooperation. Then we turn to the local experience. We discuss three patterns: the typical state of affairs, which H. V. Savitch and Ronald Vogel termed "avoidance and conflict"[35]; the more ambitious forms of metropolitan governance attempted by Portland, Oregon, and Minneapolis–St. Paul; and approaches specifically designed to reduce the spatial concentration of the poor in central cities.

HALTING FEDERAL EFFORTS AT PROMOTING METROPOLITAN COOPERATION

During the Depression of the 1930s, President Franklin D. Roosevelt appointed a National Resources Committee, composed of federal administrators and academic experts, to recommend federal actions to lift the nation out of its economic crisis. In its 1937 report, *Our Cities: Their Role in the National Economy*, the committee asserted that slums and urban blight threatened economic recovery and recommended federal policies to improve the economic performance of cities. Among the key challenges it identified were real estate speculation and "uncontrolled subdivision" on the urban fringe. The "greatest obstacle," the committee said, was the "great number of conflicting and overlapping political and administrative units into which [metropolitan areas are] divided."[36] To tame these forces, the committee urged the federal government to promote metropolitan planning, limit metropolitan political fragmentation, and restrict local governments' authority to adopt their own zoning laws. Had Roosevelt and Congress taken this advice, metropolitan America would have evolved differently, but business, real estate, and suburban and rural local government interests prevailed. Even the committee's modest proposal to select nine cities for an experiment in comprehensive long-range planning was scuttled, and the National Resources Committee was eliminated in 1943.[37]

In 1961, the American Society of Planning Officials and the Ford Foundation sponsored a report by zoning lawyer Richard Babcock, *The Zoning Game,* which criticized the fragmented control of land use by local governments. "Land use planning is in chaos," he wrote. "I doubt that even the most intransigent disciple of anarchy ever wished for or intended the litter that prevails in the area of land-use regulation."[38] President John Kennedy warned that "bold programs in individual jurisdictions are no longer enough. Increasingly, community development must be a cooperative venture toward the common goals of the new metropolitan region as a whole." In 1962, Kennedy proposed a new Department of Urban Affairs, arguing, "There must be expansion, but orderly and planned expansion, not explosion and sprawl."[39] (HUD was eventually established in 1965, under President Lyndon Johnson, but it has always lacked the authority to deal with local zoning laws.)

President Johnson, too, took up the cause of metropolitan-wide planning. Unplanned growth, he said, caused "the decay of the urban centers and the despoiling of the suburbs."[40] The urban riots of the 1960s gave even greater impetus to concerns over racial and economic segregation in metropolitan areas. In 1968, the report of the National Advisory Commission on Civil Disorders (the *Kerner Report*) blamed suburban zoning practices for "restricting the area open to a growing population" and giving landlords incentives "to break up ghetto apartments for denser occupancy, hastening housing deterioration." It called for federal action to challenge suburban zoning practices that excluded the poor and racial minorities.[41] In 1969, the National Commission on Urban Problems made recommendations similar to those of the National Resources Committee thirty years earlier. It noted that "problems of air and water pollution, transportation, open space, solid waste disposal, housing, and employment do not end at municipal borders. At the same time, land-use controls, which are important factors in the creation and solution of such problems, are lodged in local governments with virtually no supervision by metropolitan or State agencies."[42]

In 1970, Senator Henry Jackson (a moderate Democrat from Washington) introduced a National Land Use Policy bill to establish uniform guidelines for state laws. Republican President Richard Nixon supported the bill, arguing that "the time has come when we must accept the idea that society as a whole has a legitimate interest in property land-use."[43] The legislation was backed by many business groups frustrated by local zoning laws that made it difficult for corporations and developers to develop office parks, manufacturing facilities, and housing developments.[44]

None of these proposals for a federal land-use policy made any headway. Despite the backing of major national political figures and business leaders, strong local opposition, which saw these proposals as infringing on local control, proved too powerful. Congress consistently failed to adopt any federal plan that would significantly trespass on local authority.

In the 1960s, the federal government did use the carrot of federal funding to encourage regional planning. Federal requirements stimulated the creation of regional COGs. There are about 500 COGs in the United States today, but for the most part, they focus on limited functions and do not address overall land-use planning. The 1962 Federal Highway Act provided matching funds to states for highways but required applicants to show that their projects were consistent with a regional plan. Especially noteworthy was the 1991 Intermodal Surface Transportation Efficiency Act (ISTEA), which required that governments in each region designate a Metropolitan Planning Organization to plan transportation improvements, including mass transit and bicycle and foot paths. This legislation has been renewed several times, as the Transportation Equity Act for the Twenty-first Century (TEA-21). Support for maintaining the role of MPOs is widespread and was reaffirmed by Congress.

In recent decades, a number of reports, some sponsored by the federal government, identified exclusionary zoning practices as obstacles to creating affordable housing, particularly in affluent suburbs.[45] For the most part, however, the federal and state governments have been reluctant to systematically challenge local zoning laws that have the effect, if not the intent, of excluding minorities and the poor. The closest HUD came was during the Carter administration in the 1970s. HUD set up metropolitan Areawide Housing Opportunity Plans (AHOPs) and created the Regional Housing Mobility Program to plan for the dispersal of Section 8 housing certificates throughout metropolitan areas, with the help of regional planning agencies and cooperating suburbs. Before these programs could be carried out, the Reagan administration took office in 1981 and canceled them. Not until the early 1990s did the federal government try this approach again, through its Moving to Opportunity program. This was a small-scale but apparently quite successful effort to replicate Chicago's Gautreaux program, which provides vouchers and housing counseling to low-income renters to help them find apartments in the suburbs on a voluntary basis.[46]

A few states have passed laws challenging exclusionary zoning. New York, New Jersey, California, and Massachusetts adopted "inclusionary zoning" laws to make it easier for developers to build affordable housing in suburban jurisdictions.[47] New Jersey's law emerged from its famous *Mt. Laurel* court cases; California and Massachusetts enacted legislation on their own.[48] These state laws have had only modest success in expanding low-income housing opportunities in suburbs. Starting in the 1980s, in response to federal housing cutbacks, some local governments adopted inclusionary zoning ordinances requiring developers of market-rate housing to set aside some units for low- and moderate-income residents or to pay fees to support affordable housing, schools, or infrastructure.[49] But neither the federal government nor these states has used the carrot-and-stick approach of withholding funds for transportation, school, infrastructure, or other programs to localities that have not complied with the law.

THE LOCAL EXPERIENCE: AVOIDANCE AND CONFLICT

In the typical metropolitan area, a region's constituent towns and cities may realize that they belong to a common region, but they seek to retain their autonomy and continue to act independently or compete with one another for economic resources. Savitch and Vogel and their colleagues found that New York, Los Angeles, and St. Louis epitomize this pattern.[50] It is common in older industrial areas with long histories of central city–suburban tension and longstanding racial, class, and social differences. David Rusk has shown that these "inelastic" central cities also have the worst race and class segregation and weak regional economic performance.[51]

The New York City consolidated metropolitan statistical area includes thirty-one counties in New York, New Jersey, Connecticut, and Pennsylvania and houses more than 21 million residents.[52] It contains some 1,787 county, municipal, town, school district, and special district governments. The nonprofit, business-backed Regional Plan Association has advocated three regional plans since 1923, most recently calling for a new emphasis on concentrated development around regional transit nodes and greater emphasis on workforce development.[53] These plans, however, have had more effect on thinking among academics and policy elites than on actual development patterns.

Efforts to create a true regional planning agency with significant authority have failed. The two public agencies that could undertake this mission have not done so. The Port Authority of New York and New Jersey, created in 1921, operates the region's seaport, its three airports, the Hudson River bridges and tunnels, and a commuter railroad. It also built the World Trade Center office complex and continues to own and oversee the site on which a memorial and new office buildings will be rebuilt in the wake of the destruction of the complex on September 11, 2001, which had a devastating impact on the organization. In recent decades, the Port Authority has responded primarily to the development agendas of the two governors who appoint its board. The agency has suffered from the need to balance any benefit to one state with an equivalent benefit to the other. It does not serve as an agent of the region's municipalities. Indeed, former Mayor Rudolph Giuliani of New York City campaigned to dissolve the Port Authority, or at least require it to return the New York airports to city control. Current New York Mayor Michael Bloomberg has little influence over how the Port Authority will rebuild lower Manhattan, despite its obvious importance to the city's future.[54] On the New York State side of the Hudson River, the Metropolitan Transit Authority operates the region's subway and bus systems, bridges and tunnels, and the commuter rail system. It, too, is a creature of compromise between the governor and mayor, the city of New York, and the adjacent counties it serves. It has had difficulty achieving agreement on new initiatives, such as providing rail service to the airports, although it has substantially upgraded the rolling stock and performance of its constituent properties.

Although New York City dominates the region and the borough of Manhattan draws more than 41 percent of the region's daily commuters, it does not dominate the region's highly fragmented politics. The surrounding states and municipalities compete vigorously to attract business investment away from the city. Since the 1970s, Westchester County and Stamford, Connecticut, have lured away many large corporate headquarters; New Jersey enticed the New York Giants and Jets football teams to the Meadowlands complex, and Jersey City has attracted many back-office operations. In response to "predatory moves" by other jurisdictions, New York City has granted large tax abatements and other concessions to attract corporations to Manhattan or to retain them. Immediately to the west of lower Manhattan, the Jersey City waterfront has used deep incentives to foster the construction of 13 million square feet of office space over the last decade, mostly tenanted by firms formerly located in New York.

Concerned about such bidding wars, the governors of New York, New Jersey, and Connecticut and New York City's mayor signed a "nonaggression" pact in

1991. They vowed to avoid negative advertising and the use of tax breaks and other incentives to steal investment from one another and agreed to cooperate on a regional development strategy. Within a year, however, the economic rivalry accelerated, all three states launched new business incentive and tax reduction programs, and the job wars continued as before. For example, New Jersey induced First Chicago Trust Company to move 1,000 jobs from lower Manhattan by subsidizing the company's office space. Bruce Berg and Paul Kantor note, "The economic competition for jobs among states and localities in the tristate region goes unregulated, to the disadvantage of almost everyone except the corporations that are the objects of subsidies."[55]

Similarly, the St. Louis region comprises twelve counties in Missouri and Illinois with a 2000 population of 2.6 million, divided by the Mississippi and Missouri Rivers.[56] In 2002, it had 795 local governments, primarily special districts. The central cities of St. Louis (in Missouri) and East St. Louis (in Illinois) suffered massive depopulation while the suburban parts of the region grew. For example, the population of St. Louis fell from 857,000 in 1950 to 348,000 in 2000. The region's poor and black residents are concentrated in the central cities and some older suburbs. Per capita taxable property among the region's municipalities ranged from $2,178 to $143,285.

The St. Louis region created a regional agency responsible for sewers, junior colleges, zoos, museums, and a regional medical center. However, these serve only St. Louis County and the city of St. Louis, not the remainder of the region. In 1949, the two states created a seven-county Bi-State Development Agency (now called Metro), but it lacks taxing authority and focuses almost exclusively on transportation matters. Twice voters in St. Charles County, the most rapidly growing area of the region, rejected ballot measures to link to the region's public transit system. Efforts to promote broader regional cooperation failed in 1926, 1955, and 1959. In 1992, voters rejected ballot measures to create a metropolitan economic development commission (funded by a 2 percent tax on nonresidential utility service) and a metropolitan park commission (to be funded by property taxes). In 2000, voters in five counties approved the creation of a bistate Metropolitan Park and Recreation District, with dedicated sales tax revenues to plan and implement a regional parks system.

Los Angeles is the quintessential "fragmented metropolis."[57] The five-county region (Los Angeles, Ventura, Riverside, Orange, and San Bernardino Counties) contains 16 million people, a land area almost the size of Ohio, and an economy that would rank the twelfth largest in the world if it were a separate country.[58] It includes more than 200 cities (33 with more than 100,000 residents) and hundreds of special district governments. The city of Los Angeles, with 3.7 million residents, holds one-fifth of the region's population, but no one center dominates this decentered region. Much of Los Angeles, including the central city, has a suburban character, reflecting the area's reliance on the automobile. Its region's population grew 25 percent during the 1980s, most dramatically among Latino and Asian immigrants, and grew another 13 percent in the 1990s. Although black ghettos and Latino barrios are disproportionately located in the city of Los Angeles, the region's minority population is dispersed throughout the region, and high-poverty census tracts have also spread across the metropolitan area. During the 1980s and 1990s, the poverty rate increased in each county.[59]

The region's many municipalities compete for private investment. After the passage of Proposition 13 in 1978, which drastically limited property taxes and forced localities to try to increase the collection of local sales taxes to expand their revenue base, this competition accelerated. Cities such as Glendale, Ventura, Pasadena, Anaheim, and Cerritos utilized redevelopment projects to reinvent themselves as office, sports, tourist, and retail centers. This competition has made efforts at regional cooperation more problematic.

The splintering of the region's media market also hampers the emergence of a regional identity. In most metropolitan areas, one daily newspaper and a few local broadcast stations constitute a single media market. Although the *Los Angeles Times* is the region's largest and most influential newspaper, most cities in the region have their own daily papers. Los Angeles television stations dominate the market, but outlying cities such as San Bernardino, Santa Ana, Ventura, and others have their own network-affiliated stations.

Los Angeles once mounted bold regional public works initiatives designed to expand the area's economy. The regional water system required complex land purchases, canals, and aqueducts that diverted water from the Owens Valley and the Colorado River. The Metropolitan Water District, a regional special district, now oversees this activity. Regional leaders also developed a port to foster regional economic growth.[60] Los Angeles and Long Beach now have separate and competing ports, however, and many smaller airports compete with Los Angeles Airport.

Business, environmental, and planning groups have frequently sought to promote regional governance. Business leaders believed that traffic congestion, polluted air, and water shortages hurt their competitive position and funded studies to encourage stronger regional coordination. In 1988, Mayor Tom Bradley appointed a Los Angeles 2000 Committee, which called for a regional planning agency to manage land use, housing, and transportation and a regional environmental agency that would consolidate the regional antipollution agency with its water control and solid waste agencies. It also proposed to strengthen the region's airport authority. Despite much debate and the filing of the necessary bills in the state legislature, municipal leaders intensified their competition during the economic downturn of the early 1990s, and support for regional approaches fell apart.

Like many areas, the region has a council of governments, the Southern California Association of Governments (SCAG). An unwieldy body, SCAG has representation from seventy elected officials (sixty-three selected by municipal elected officials, and seven by county supervisors). The city of Los Angeles has only two members. Membership is voluntary, and SCAG has no authority over its member governments. It can recommend approval or rejection of projects proposed by cities under the federal ISTEA and TEA-21 transportation programs, which allocates over $1 billion annually for the region. It can also withhold funds for local road improvements unless cities and counties develop plans to reduce auto usage. To comply, the various county-level transportation agencies embarked on such projects as a subway in Los Angeles, the imposition of tolls in Orange and Riverside Counties, and a high-speed train project.

This is one of the most polluted metropolitan areas in the nation, and the most powerful regional body is the South Coast Air Quality Management District. It has set tough standards for industry and automobile emissions, required construction of new public transportation facilities, caused county government to implement measures such as car-pool lanes, and influenced local land-use decisions. As a result, air quality has significantly improved: exposure to unhealthful ozone levels fell by half, despite population growth and constant business opposition.[61]

This improvement occurred only because federal law required it and the agency was able to set timetables and threaten sanctions. Otherwise, the region's cities still compete for investment. In 1994, for example, Los Angeles granted DreamWorks, a new film company, a $75 million tax abatement to build its headquarters in the city, even though it was unlikely to locate anywhere else. The Los Angeles region has so many separate local governments and special districts that no one local constituency, even the region's major employers, could induce all of them to cooperate or collaborate on a voluntary basis.

New York, St. Louis, and Los Angeles typify the experience of most metropolitan regions, especially the older ones. Regional cooperation is restricted to a few specific functions, parts of the region still compete for investment and advantage, and regional rivalries hamper regional planning for public improvements that would spur economic growth. Indeed, these regions have difficulty coordinating even simple functions, such as meshing the schedules of regional mass transit systems. Myriad local jurisdictions take their own approaches to federally funded activities such as the construction and management of subsidized housing, the distribution of housing vouchers, the creation of job training programs, and the like, all of which might be more effective if carried out on a regional basis.

EXPERIMENTS IN METROPOLITAN GOVERNANCE

Advocates of regional approaches consistently point to two places that have most fully developed the promise of regional government: the Twin Cities of Minneapolis and St. Paul, Minnesota, where an appointed metropolitan council carries out a number of functions and a regional tax-sharing scheme redistributes revenues from high-growth to low-growth areas; and Portland, Oregon, where an elected metropolitan government regulates suburban land development within a regional growth boundary.

The Twin Cities had a population in 2000 of 669,769 in a metropolitan area of 2.9 million people whose metropolitan per capita income is the sixteenth highest in the country.[62] In 1967, the state legislature created a seven-county Metropolitan Council to oversee planning for land use, housing, transit, sewage, and other metropolitan issues. Its members, appointed by the governor, set policy guidelines for local governments in these areas. In its first decade, the council solved a crisis in wastewater treatment. In the 1960s, the Federal Housing Administration threatened to stop insuring mortgages in burgeoning suburbs that lacked sewage treatment. In response, the state government created a Metropolitan Water Control Commission to finance and run treatment plants and build trunk sewer lines as well as creating a regional transportation system. By 1994, the Metropolitan Council not only guided planning for these functions, but had also absorbed the regional agencies for transportation and wastewater treatment. It had its own revenue streams from user fees, a small property tax, and federal grants that enabled it to undertake a substantial regional infrastructure capital program. It encouraged affluent suburbs like Golden Valley to develop low- and moderate-income housing and created regional parks where shopping centers might otherwise have been developed.

In 1971, Minnesota also adopted the Fiscal Disparities Act, which required metropolitan jurisdictions to pool 40 percent of the growth in their commercial and industrial tax bases and to allocate the proceeds according to population and level of tax capacity. This dampened competition for new development and reallocated resources from affluent, fast-growing suburbs to older, more urban parts of the region. Minneapolis and St. Paul began as beneficiaries of this system, but over time, the development of downtown Minneapolis converted it into a contributor, while St. Paul's improvement lessened its dependence on these funds. The formula only deals with revenue-raising capacity, which reflects the value of downtown construction, but does not consider spending needs generated by the relatively large poor populations of the two cities.

Despite its considerable successes, the Metropolitan Council has disappointed some early supporters. The existence of the Metropolitan Council and regional tax sharing did not prevent the Twin Cities from becoming one of the most sprawling metropolitan areas in the United States. The council did not have much impact on the major development issues of the 1980s, including the building of several sports complexes and the world's largest shopping mall. It continues to lack an independent political base (its members all serve at the pleasure of the governor, although they each represent home districts). Because the council cannot pursue policies that lack support from the governor, influential state legislators, or even some local officials, it has difficulty mobilizing support for its agenda. The council did not address neighborhood decay in the central cities or restrain the growth of central city–suburban disparities. During the 1980s and 1990s, the two cities' population rose by 4.5 percent, but the seven-county metro area grew by 25 percent. By 2000, median family income in the Twin Cities was $48,750, compared with $65,665 in the metro area; the two cities' poverty rate was 16.4 percent, compared with 6.9 percent in the metro area. Poverty had become markedly greater and more concentrated between 1970 and 1990, then less so in the 1990s. Racial minorities constituted 16.8 percent of the metro area population, but almost 37 percent of the two cities' residents in 2000. Most job growth took place in the affluent southern and western suburbs, but many central-city residents (including almost half of black households) lacked cars or public transit access to these areas. This has perhaps contributed to what some have called "Minnesota malaise," and in November 2001, a newcomer displaced the incumbent Minneapolis mayor with the slogan, "I was born in a great city, but I don't want to die in a mediocre one."[63]

Beginning in 1993, then–state legislator Myron Orfield of Minneapolis sought to give the Metropolitan Council more effective tools for addressing these disparities. He introduced a series of bills to elect the members of the Metropolitan Council, to mandate low- and moderate-income housing development goals for each suburb, to empower the council to deny sewer and highway funds to suburbs that failed to comply, to create an affordable housing trust fund by taxing residential construction valued in excess of $150,000 per home, and to give the council more power to control sprawl. After calculating that three-quarters of the region's suburbs would benefit from the housing fund and only one-quarter (including the wealthiest suburbs) would contribute, Orfield used color maps to convince city and inner suburban legislators that they had more in common than they thought, especially in terms of social problems and the distribution of state and regional funds.[64]

The legislature passed Orfield's housing bill, but the Republican governor vetoed them; the bill to elect the council failed by one vote in the state house and five in the senate. But Orfield's efforts drew public attention to the council's potential and its weaknesses and shifted the political climate toward reform. A growing number of business, civic, and political leaders, including the daily newspapers, acknowledged the need to address the region's social disparities along the lines suggested by Orfield. After Reform Party candidate Jesse Ventura was elected governor in 1998, he continued to oppose Orfield's measures. Between 2000 and 2030, the council expects the Twin Cities metropolitan area to add another million inhabitants and has developed a *2030 Regional Development Framework* that urges more compact development and denser residential development, but recognizes that successful implementation depends on cooperation from local municipalities and the rapidly growing parts of the metropolitan area outside the council's boundaries.[65] In 2003, Republican governor Tim Pawlenty appointed his council members, who in turn chose the brother of his chief of staff as the council's top administrator. At this juncture, the Metropolitan Council may be considered as much a part of the governor's administration as it is a body representing the constituent jurisdictions.

Portland, Oregon, has the nation's only directly elected regional governing body, the Metro Council.[66] It serves twenty-four cities and three counties. It has six nonpartisan members elected for four-year terms from districts containing about 200,000 constituents and a president, elected at large from the region. A chief operating office is responsible for daily management. The Metro Council formulates and implements policy on land use, growth management, solid waste, and parks and recreation and operates the region's zoo, convention center, performing arts center, and solid waste disposal system. It thus has a slightly narrower mandate than the Metropolitan Council in the Twin Cities, but it has home rule charter status and modest taxing abilities. The Oregon legislature authorized it in 1977 and the voters of Clackamas, Multnomah, and Washington Counties approved it the following year. Its initial duties were designating the urban growth boundary limit (within which new development was to be confined), planning for municipal solid waste disposal, regional transportation planning, and operating the Washington Park Zoo.

Portland was a city of 382,619 in a three-county region of 878,676 in 1970. By 2000, the city had grown to 529,121 and the region to 1.9 million. The region's economy is dominated by shipping, electronics, and manufacturing. In contrast to many cities, the city of Portland's employment base grew significantly, even though job growth has been greater in the surrounding suburbs. Many believe that the region's planning efforts, which emphasized compact development and the development of open space amenities, have been a major factor in this outcome.[67]

Until the 1970s, Portland seemed headed for decline. It lost its ability to annex suburban localities in 1906. By 1956, the three-county area had 176 governmental units, including many special districts. In 1960, the League of Women Voters published *A Tale of Three Counties*, which criticized uncoordinated services and wasteful spending and called for a new, more efficient, more accountable government structure. During the 1960s and 1970s, the state legislature and voters approved regional agencies for transportation, the zoo, and solid waste; the 1977 creation of Metro provided the occasion to consolidate these activities. In 1983, a large budget deficit in Multnomah County (which includes Portland) and the need to provide services to the unincorporated suburban areas east of Portland led the County Board of Supervisors to encourage Portland to annex some unincorporated areas, provide services to some suburbs, and create a sewer construction program for the county. These reforms created support for a metropolitan-wide governance structure. Nevertheless, heavily dependent on such troubled industries as paper and pulp, timber exports, shipbuilding, fishing, and metalworking, the Portland economy did not appear especially well positioned for future growth.

Following several blue-ribbon study commissions, the voters of the three counties approved the creation of an elected metropolitan government in May 1978. Its first task was to designate a metropolitan urban growth boundary under Oregon's land-use legislation, the nation's strongest. The state legislation authorizes Metro to compel local governments and counties to coordinate their land-use and development plans. As baby boomers moved to Portland to enjoy its environment, forest and farm product exports recovered from their slump in the 1980s, and employment surged in the region's major employers (including Intel, Tektronix, and Nike), the demand for new development grew steadily, as did the political base for managing this growth. A political alliance between Portland's business interests and residents of older neighborhoods sought to strengthen the downtown area against competition from suburban shopping malls while saving abandoned housing from the threat of large-scale land clearance and redevelopment. When Neal Goldschmidt was elected mayor in 1972, he incorporated neighborhood activists into his administration (1972–79) and continued that policy after becoming governor (1987–90). Recently, Metro was reorganized to provide for an elected president separate from a chief operating office serving alongside six council members elected from districts. At his inauguration in 2003, the new president vowed to "redeem the promise of regionalism itself. It is the promise that we can achieve more by working together than we can by being confined by arcane city and county boundaries drawn in the 19th century. It is the hope, expressed by the voters in their creation of my new post, that we set the agency on a new path that heals the feuding that eroded our effectiveness."[68]

Portland Metro largely achieved its goals for coordinating land-use planning and transportation policy, extending public transit, revitalizing older neighborhoods, and strengthening the downtown business district. Its efforts were bolstered by an urban growth boundary that preserved farmland and forests around Portland and directed urban growth into Portland and its neighboring areas. Although more office and retail development has taken place outside the city than within it, the downtown still accounts for 60 percent of the region's office space and half its upscale retail space. Several highway projects were abandoned in favor of buses and light-rail connections between the central-city, outlying neighborhoods, and nearby suburbs. By the 1990s, the region's bus and rail system carried 43 percent of downtown commuters, compared with 20 percent in Phoenix, 17 percent in Salt Lake City, and 11 percent in Sacramento. Portland shows that metropolitan government can succeed. As Orfield observed, its "regional government has been more willing than the Twin Cities' appointed Metropolitan Council to exercise its powers vis-à-vis competing authorities."[69]

At the same time, Metro has narrowly defined powers. It does not provide most public services, does not build affordable housing, and does not transcend local zoning and land-use powers. Local school districts remain distinct, eighty single-purpose special districts still have the ability to tax, and twenty cities and three counties provide a broad range of services. Key activities that might help promote mobility of the poor out of the central city—subsidized housing construction and the administration of Section 8 vouchers—are administered by the Portland city housing authority and do not operate on a metrowide basis. Two metrowide agencies with appointed boards, Tri-Met (which runs the transit system) and the Port of Portland (which runs the port, industrial parks, and the airports), operate independently of Metro. Metro's most important function is to set ground rules for development and growth—for example, by siting and building the region's $65 million convention center. It has enhanced the region's ability to resist costly and inefficient sprawl, but it is not a full-service government.

Portland suffers less from the spatial concentration of poverty than most other central cities. Portland's poverty rate (14.5 percent in 1990 and 13.1 percent in 2000) was below most other large central cities. The area's low-income residents were spread out, not highly segregated, concentrated, and isolated. The income gap between the central city and the suburbs remains one of the smallest in the nation.[70] Because Portland has a small minority population (6.5 percent African American, 6.8 percent Hispanic, and 6.6 percent Asian in 2002), the relationship between the city and its suburbs has not been racially charged. The state's "fair-share" housing mandate, along with Metro's planning efforts, have encouraged suburbs to develop more low-income housing than in other metropolitan areas. The region's housing prices did increase more than the national average during the early 1990s, but not in other periods over the last twenty years, and not as much as other growing western cities that lack Portland's growth management.[71] Cooperation between low-income housing advocates and the region's real estate developers, together with the institutional strength of regional government, has led to discussions about creating a regional housing fund. If this does occur, it would put Portland at the forefront of regional equity, as well as environmental planning. Metro has not, however, made dispersing the inner-city minority poor to the surrounding area a priority.

EFFORTS TO PROMOTE REGIONAL EQUITY

As Scott Bollens observed, even at its best, "the current state of regional governance in the United States does not effectively address issues of concentrated poverty and social equity" because it tends to focus on infrastructure rather than people and because, lacking a broad political base, it takes a narrow, technical approach to its work.[72] Recognizing the difficulty of changing this situation and the likelihood that it would not soon reduce the embedded patterns of regional inequity and constrained opportunities for the inner-city poor, many advocates have sought more direct regional solutions to the problems of concentrated urban poverty. Because the courts have generally upheld suburban jurisdictions' right to impose restrictive zoning and have found that federal law on housing discrimination does not apply to low-income households but applies only to "particular groups such as racial minorities,"[73] these advocates have generally attacked the racial dimension of exclusion. They have, for example, sought to induce suburbs to take on their fair share of housing for lower-income residents and designed programs to connect the inner-city poor with suburban job opportunities, such as reverse commuting, portable Section 8 vouchers, and new institutions that train inner-city residents and place them in suburban job openings.[74]

Because a "spatial mismatch" often prevents inner-city poor people from taking advantage of suburban job opportunities, advocates of regional equity have long sought to increase access to suburban housing. Because many urban poor are also members of federally protected minority groups, vigorous enforcement of federal fair housing and affirmative mortgage lending regulations seems to be an obvious way to provide better access. As Michael Schill has pointed out, this legal framework does not provide a way to roll back the overall framework of exclusionary zoning practices in the suburbs. Instead, it is most effective where least needed: for middle-class minority individuals who are obviously victims of discriminatory practices such as "steering" by real estate agents. Even in New Jersey, where the *Mt. Laurel* cases mandated suburban jurisdictions to do more to house the state's low-income residents, they can (and do) meet this obligation by financially supporting the construction of subsidized housing elsewhere.[75] Shifting the financing of local schools away from the property tax and toward state budgets may reduce suburbanites' fiscal incentive to exclude the less well-off, but it is not likely to lessen the propensity of middle-class whites to flee districts when the percentage of minorities in their children's classrooms begins to rise significantly.[76] Recent efforts to help central-city residents use Section 8 vouchers for suburban rental housing have shown promising results. But because these programs run up against exclusionary suburban zoning laws, it is difficult for them to help significant numbers of families.[77]

A number of metropolitan regions have adopted fair-share housing policies to provide some affordable housing in otherwise expensive housing markets that exclude low- and even moderate-income residents. One of the oldest and most successful programs is in Montgomery County, Maryland, an affluent and fast-growing area of 497 square miles adjacent to Washington, DC, with a population in 2000 of 873,341 divided among fourteen incorporated municipalities.[78] During the 1970s and 1980s, Montgomery County changed from a bedroom community of Washington to a large employment center. The population boomed, and housing costs spiraled. In the early 1970s, housing advocacy groups such as Suburban Maryland Fair Housing and the League of Women Voters began pushing to increase the supply of affordable housing. The elected county council responded by adopting an inclusionary zoning law.

Since 1974, Montgomery County has required that all new housing developments with fifty or more units include a percentage (now 12.5 to 15 percent) of moderate-priced units. In exchange, it provides developers with a "density bonus," permitting them to increase a project's density by 20 percent. The first units were built in 1976.[79] To maintain the supply of affordable housing, the county limits the resale price for ten years and the rent for twenty years, and the county's Housing Opportunity Commission or nonprofit agencies can purchase up to 40 percent of these units. By 2004, the program had created more than 10 thousand units, one-third of which may be purchased by the county's Housing Opportunity Commission (HOC), its public housing authority.[80] HOC has purchased about 1,600 units for very low-income families. It also manages another 4,700 units of its own and administers 3,500 Section 8 vouchers.

Montgomery County requires developers to integrate these affordable units within market-rate housing rather than isolate them and create mini ghettos. The county insists on high standards of design and construction for these developments. They do not look like the stereotype of government-subsidized "projects." The program is limited to people who live or work in Montgomery County. Although there has been some opposition to particular developments, "the programs have been generally well-accepted by developers and by neighbors."[81] Montgomery's program is a successful effort to address the problem of economic segregation, but it is a drop in the bucket. Indeed, because the program has a long waiting list, the families are chosen by lottery.

Recognizing the difficulties of a frontal attack on exclusion of the urban poor from suburban housing markets and school districts, proponents of greater metropolitan equity have turned to a variety of other strategies. Reverse commuting programs help low-income residents of central cities get to jobs in suburban areas. They address both the spatial mismatch dilemma and the reality that many poor workers cannot afford cars and that most public transit systems do not connect the areas where poor people live and the areas where a growing number of entry-level jobs are located.[82] Chicago's Suburban JobLink was founded in 1971 to enhance employment opportunities among low-income residents of the city's poverty neighborhoods, particularly on the West Side.[83] It had close ties to suburban employers. By the early 1990s, it operated a fleet of six buses and a car-pool service, and provided rides to employees who worked for about 150 different companies. The buses operated on multiple shifts. The program served 400 to 600 workers per day.[84] It also created a job-training and job-search facility to help inner-city residents find and apply for jobs and, in the process, "provide[d] an island of cultural, ethnic and racial familiarity in an unfamiliar world."[85]

Philadelphia, Baltimore, Detroit, and other metropolitan areas created similar programs in the 1980s and early 1990s.[86] But the number of reverse commuting efforts mushroomed in the early 1990s after the Clinton administration set up federal pilot programs modeled on these local initiatives. The U.S. Department of Transportation (DOT) created JobLinks projects in sixteen sites, including urban and rural areas; the DOT and HUD created the Bridges to Work demonstration program in Baltimore, Chicago, Denver, Milwaukee, and St. Louis. These programs give localities considerable flexibility in designing projects to help connect people to jobs: van service, jitneys (taxis), even counseling and child care.[87]

Despite these innovative reverse commuting initiatives, Margy Waller and Mark Alan Hughes warn that they will never serve more than a small fraction of the poor who need transportation from urban ghettos to suburban jobs. "In most cases," they write, "the shortest distance between a poor person and a job is along a line driven in a car."[88] They argue that the most efficient way to help the poor is to provide them with subsidies to buy cars.[89] Typically, however, state welfare and food stamp programs deny benefits to anyone with a car worth more than $1,500.[90] Now, however, five states exclude the value of at least one car from the eligibility standards to receive welfare.

Even when the poor are able to get from home to work, the jobs they go to are often inadequate to support a family. Although upgrading the job skills of the workforce will not, on its own, directly address the increasing proportion of jobs that pay poverty-level wages, it can address the immediate needs of poor people who are currently separated from decent jobs. The goal of job training programs should be to "redistribute jobs, earnings, work experience, and dignity to the residents of low-income communities."[91] Most employment training programs, however, offer poor people little more than low-wage and dead-end jobs.[92] A major obstacle to successful job training is the disconnect between training programs and employers, especially those that provide decent-paying jobs in growing industries and thus offer employees a career ladder.

Innovative employment training programs in a number of metropolitan areas have sought to overcome these hurdles by linking community-based organizations, key businesses, and educational institutions on a regional level. One of the most successful is Project Quest in San Antonio, Texas, which has utilized the tools of community organizing to connect residents of low-income neighborhoods not only with effective job training but also with good jobs in a metropolitan-wide context.[93] Two community organizations affiliated with the Industrial Areas Foundation—Communities Organized for Public Service (COPS), based primarily in Catholic congregations in the Mexican American neighborhoods, and Metro Alliance, based primarily in Protestant churches in African American neighborhoods—founded Project Quest after a wave of lay-offs in their communities. The San Antonio area had added as many as 19,000 good jobs in such fields as health care, office work, education, and mechanical repair, but "these new jobs were out of reach for most of the folks who worked or hoped to work at places like Levi's."[94] Project Quest created a new "workforce development intermediary" to package resources from a wide variety of sources and institutions. It pressured elected politicians to provide more than $6 mil-lion in local, state, and federal funds. Local businesses, particularly large firms, helped Project Quest identify occupations and sectors with growth potential and career ladders and helped design the training curricula. Between its in-ception in 1993 and the end of 1995, Project Quest enrolled more than 800 trainees in a "comprehensive, expensive package of supports, including child care, transportation assistance, medical care, tutoring, modest cash assistance for incidentals, and tuition to community colleges."[95] Programs such as Project Quest that make connections between the limited social networks of the inner-city poor and dynamic centers of growth in the regional economy are prom-ising.[96] Economic segregation and suburban sprawl, however, place huge ob-stacles in the way of successful implementation.

So far, these experiments have produced modest but promising results. Sev-eral lessons can be drawn from them. First, they have been tried only on a pilot basis. Substantial additional investments will have to be made to bring them to full scale. It appears that with sufficient counseling of tenants and careful han-dling of landlords and suburban communities, the central-city poor can find better suburban housing opportunities without bringing on the social calami-ties and political opposition that defenders of suburban exclusion predict. It appears, therefore, that deconcentrating the central-city poor is feasible at a reasonable cost and will produce desirable results. Second, it is unlikely that physical juxtaposition or spatial mobility alone will dramatically improve the access of the urban poor to suburban job opportunities. Instead, the central-city poor require not only better skills (both "soft" and "hard") but also in-corporation into networks of contact, reciprocity, and support with potential employers. In short, new labor market intermediaries may be needed. Finally, it is clear that the vast bulk of social programs are administered in a way that hinders them from functioning on a regional basis. That is, programs for sub-sidized housing, education, job training, and the like are typically adminis-tered by units of central-city governments that operate within those restricted jurisdictions. Even if they have the authority to operate outside central-city boundaries (as in the case of county public housing authorities), they generally do not. Suburban jurisdictions simply, unobtrusively, opt out. For such programs to take a regional approach to their work, they must be reorganized into a metropolitan-wide jurisdiction.

THE POLITICS OF REGIONALISM IN THE NEW MILLENNIUM

Historically, many forces have worked against a regional perspective in urban governance. Suburbs have been happy to benefit from being located in a large metropolitan area while excluding the less well-off and avoiding the payment of taxes to support services required by the urban poor. Central cities, for their part, have made a virtue of necessity by increasing spending on social services as a way of expanding the employment of central-city constituents. This spending has become an increasingly substantial part of municipal budgets and an important form of "new patronage" in city politics. As federal benefits have increasingly flowed to needy people, as opposed to needy places, it has helped to expand these functions. Legislators elected to represent areas where the minority poor are concentrated develop a stake in this state of affairs. Big-city mayors have also been reluctant to lose any of their powers within a broader metropolitan jurisdiction.

As we will see in Chapter 8, this dynamic is gradually but steadily shifting. The first wave of inner, working-class suburbs has long since been built out, their populations have aged, and their residents' incomes have stagnated since the early 1970s. Increasingly, suburbs have developed "urban" problems that they cannot solve on their own. Black and Hispanic central-city residents have increasingly moved to the suburbs. Although minority suburbs generally have significantly better conditions than inner-city minority neighborhoods, they still have higher rates of poverty and disadvantage than white suburbs and may face some of the same forces of decline that operate on inner cities. Even as metropolitan economic segregation has increased, metropolitan racial segregation has declined and suburban diversity has increased. As Myron Orfield has pointed out, these inner suburbs are coming to realize that they share significant interests with each other that are not all that dissimilar with those of their central cities. And as Juliet Gainsborough has shown, voters residing in more diverse suburbs are substantially more likely to vote like their urban neighbors.[97]

The November 2000 vote in favor of consolidation between the city of Louisville and surrounding Jefferson County shows that elite consensus can be a powerful force in promoting regionalism. After previous defeats in 1982 and 1983, the 2000 proposal was developed under the auspices of an organization of the area's leading businesses, Greater Louisville Inc. (GLI), and was backed by the sitting Louisville mayor and Jefferson county executive as well as Louisville's popular former mayor Jerry Abramson. It also received strong support from Louisville's daily newspaper. Opposition came from city and county legislators (whose offices would be abolished in favor of a twenty-six-seat county assembly), public employee unions, the local chapter of the NAACP, and other interests that thought their relatively strong position within the city would be diluted if it were merged into the county. Some African American professionals and the local black newspaper, however, favored the consolidation. Two prominent urbanists at the local university, Hank Savitch and Ron Vogel, described the backers of the merger as "a fairly tight, interlocking network of business, banking, law, and public utilities" and worried that the "suburban tilt" of the new government would mean "the city's autonomy, its power, and its unique qualities" would be "homogenized into a larger entity."[98]

The final vote was 54 percent in favor, 46 percent opposed. Proponents made much of the ways in which the new city-county consolidation would make Louisville a significantly larger city than Lexington, which was about to overtake it in size.[99] Indeed, Louisville now touts itself as the sixteenth largest city in the country (with 698,000 residents), up from its previous position as the sixty-fifth largest. (Because the new metro government does not replace all the suburban jurisdictions, Louisville remains highly politically fragmented, as described in Chapter 2.) Former city mayor Jerry Abramson, an articulate Democrat, won election as the first mayor of the new entity, along with twenty-six district council members, of whom fifteen are Democrats, six of them black. (On the former Louisville city council, all of whose members were Democrats, blacks held one-third of the seats.) Abramson led the merger of numerous municipal departments, modestly reduced the number of employees, and made development of several declining suburban commercial strips a major priority. Clearly, urban interests that had a strong position in city government under the old system now have to share that power with suburbanites and Republicans, although they are still part of the political majority coalition. Exactly how the Louisville case will play out in the coming years will be an interesting case study in the politics of regionalism.

Across the country, many powerful players, including corporations, foundations, unions, political leaders, and community organizations, have come to think that some form of regional collaboration is necessary to achieve their objectives, whether that be competitive advantage in the new global economy, more equitable access to housing and employment, or more sensible forms of land-use development that limit sprawl and preserve open space. Regions strongly divided against themselves are least able to undertake the necessary physical, human, and social capital investments. Metropolitan governance institutions—whether ad hoc regionalism focused on one objective like helping the inner-city poor to move to better suburban neighborhoods or full-blown governments like Metro Portland or Metro Louisville—are moving to carry out functions that make sense from economic, environmental, and equity perspectives.[100] These include regional capital investments, transportation, land-use planning, economic development, job training, education, and tax-base sharing. Still, we do not yet know whether these efforts will succeed in integrating metropolitan areas by following a high-productivity, high-wage high road or will instead reflect a suburban predominance that stresses new economic investments, whatever the payoff to those at the low end of the labor market.

Which path they will take may depend on the extent to which metropolitan cooperation develops a broad, democratic base and the organizational capacity to articulate the common good, not merely to sum up the individual parts of the metropolis. Cooperation of the region's constituent elements must be secured through consent, not through unwanted mandates imposed on resistant local jurisdictions. To achieve this consent, the new regional form must provide tangible benefits to all or most its constituent jurisdictions, not just an exclusive favored quarter.

Metropolicies for the Twenty-first Century

What is to be done about America's urban crisis? Critics on both the left and the right often attack the arguments about the importance of place. Many of their positions take the form of conventional wisdom, ideas so familiar that no one questions them anymore. These critics dominate what is said in the mass media and policy discussions. Rigorous debate about the conventional wisdom can expose the unexamined assumptions and questionable values embedded within it. It may be useful to sum up the views of our critics and our rejoinders, and then outline a policy agenda to address the problems facing metropolitan America.

"Free markets are the answer."[1] Many people agree with us that place matters, but they think that place-related outcomes simply stem from the operation of free markets. According to this view, some places attract jobs and investment because they do a better job of offering investors what they want. They are more efficient places for production. Free markets ensure that every parcel of land finds its "highest and best use," resulting in "the greatest good for the greatest number." Free marketers argue that if governments interfere, they only distort the fairness and efficiency of markets. They go so far as to say that local governments should be run according to free-market principles. Local government fragmentation creates a marketplace of governments in which mobile citizen-consumers can choose which bundle of taxes and services they prefer by moving into that jurisdiction. Competition between local governments ensures that the local public sector will respond to consumer preferences.

According to free-market theory, where one lives may make a big difference in the quality of one's life, but where one lives reflects market success; it does not cause it. Good neighborhoods with low crime rates and good schools are more expensive. If you work hard, get a good job, and save, then you will be able to afford a house in a good neighborhood. If you don't, you won't. Place does not determine economic success; economic success determines place.

Our rejoinder. Throughout the book, we have argued that the effects of place are not just reflections of free-market exchanges. To use the language of social science, place is an independent variable. Place has power. Chapter 3 documented the contextual effects of place and Chapter 4 showed that they are not just the result of free markets. The United States has never had a free market in land. Land markets are greatly regulated and highly influenced by federal and state policies and local political arrangements that tilt the playing field in favor of sprawl and economic segregation. The rules of this game prevent central cities and inner-ring suburbs from solving their problems themselves (Chapter 5). Local governments cannot give citizens what they want because they must compete for taxable investment. It is impossible for cities and even whole regions (Chapter 6) to reverse economic segregation and sprawl unless state and federal governments change the rules of metropolitan governance.

"A 'culture of poverty' causes the problem."[2] For many advocates of the free market, free markets in housing not only are efficient and responsive, but also reinforce a moral order. Certain moral or cultural values, such as the Protestant work ethic and family values, undergird economic success. People who possess these values succeed in job markets and congregate in more expensive neighborhoods. Their choices reflect cultural affinities as well as individual preferences. Families lacking these values generally cannot afford to rent or buy houses in such neighborhoods. The market thus protects good neighborhoods from disruptions in their cultural consensus. Disadvantaged neighborhoods suffer not because of their structural position but because the values of their residents deviate from middle-class norms. Unable to defer gratification in order to save, learn, work, and invest, the residents of disadvantaged neighborhoods live only for the moment. Those who do work hard, save, and invest are able to leave these neighborhoods. If government helps people from bad neighborhoods move into good neighborhoods, it will upset the present moral order, spreading the culture of poverty and making good neighborhoods bad.

Our rejoinder. The organization of space does not represent an underlying moral order. On the contrary, it represents a violation of core American values of equal opportunity and democratic governance. As Chapter 3 noted, most residents of so-called bad neighborhoods are hardworking and law-abiding citizens, preyed upon by a few of their neighbors who engage in antisocial behaviors such as crime and drug use. The answer is not to expand the housing choices of able-bodied people who refuse to work, use illegal drugs, or break the law. The vast majority of lower-income people who live in central cities and inner-ring suburbs hold to mainstream values but are held back by structural disadvantages, including the disadvantages of place. People with lower incomes do not have bad values — nor do rich people necessarily have good values. The culture of poverty argument is a red herring that distracts attention from the true sources of our problems.

"If the problem is poverty, the solution is jobs."[3] Moving people around is non-sense, because the fundamental causes of inequality are economic. Economic restructuring has meant a loss of well-paying industrial jobs and the rise of a service economy with a dual wage structure (high- and low-wage jobs). People in disadvantaged neighborhoods lack the education to qualify for high-wage jobs. The solution is to help people wherever they live by stimulating full employment through macroeconomic policies, investing more in education and job training, and increasing income supports such as the minimum wage and the earned income tax credit.

Our rejoinder. The nation certainly needs policies to reduce economic inequality and enhance life chances for the poor, wherever they live. Raising the quality of life for the poor through stronger social welfare policies, like those of Canada and Western Europe, would reduce people's fear of the poor and make economic integration easier. But inequality is not just a matter of incomes. Public policy should help people function effectively in American society. Place-based inequalities remain a key source of the problem. Broad social policies do not address the spatial basis of social, economic, and political inequality. As the end of Chapter 2 noted, economic segregation varies tremendously among advanced economies, suggesting that national policies and institutional practices, not the level of economic development, have the most bearing on it. The United States has significantly narrowed the educational gaps between different groups in society over the past thirty years, and during the late 1990s the economy performed better than it has in many decades; yet many places in the United States are still left behind. Place-based inequalities make it more difficult for society to recognize and deal with inequalities of all kinds. Addressing place-based inequalities will not solve the problem of inequality on its own, but it is a crucial component of any solution.

"If the problem is poverty, the answer is to increase employment in the communities where people live."[4] The predominant view among social policy analysts, practitioners, and philanthropists is that neighborhood disadvantage should be solved through neighborhood economic development. This approach brings jobs to people, rather than people to jobs. One method is enterprise zones: reduce taxes and regulatory burdens, and markets will flourish in disadvantaged neighborhoods. Another approach is community development corporations (CDCs), which are touted as expressions of American grassroots democracy with the ability to identify the particular needs of each neighborhood and act on them. Bringing together the public, private, and nonprofit sectors into neighborhood partnerships, CDCs can revitalize the worst neighborhoods and make them attractive places to live again.

Our rejoinder. The problems of low-income neighborhoods are not caused by too much regulation or too few government programs. Enterprise zones provide inequitable and inefficient subsidies that, for the most part, simply move economic activities from one place to another. CDCs do great work, but the evidence shows that they cannot revitalize neighborhoods by themselves. The reason is simple: the main source of the problem lies outside the neighborhood, within broader regional dynamics. Until we deal with the regional dynamics that continually pull higher-income households and jobs out of the central cities and toward the urban fringe, CDCs will be struggling to go up the down escalator. Regional issues must be addressed at the same time.

"The real issue is race, not class or place."[5] Talk about economic segregation distracts attention from the most important issue: racial discrimination and segregation. Even though the law forbids racial discrimination in housing, the level of racial segregation has only decreased a little in American metropolitan areas. Economic segregation is caused in large part, this view holds, by racial discrimination. Because blacks tend to be poorer than whites (because of historical discrimination), when blacks are restricted in their housing choices, the result is economic segregation. The white poor are far less segregated from middle-class society than are the black and Hispanic poor. Because racism is the primary obstacle to more economically integrated metropolitan areas, enforcing laws against discrimination is the answer.

Our rejoinder. Racial segregation is clearly an important issue and a major cause of place-based inequality. Nevertheless, as Chapter 2 shows, this problem has an important class dimension that transcends its racial aspect. We must therefore focus directly on economic segregation as well as on combating racial discrimination. Racial segregation is declining slowly, but economic segregation is still growing. Racial discrimination is illegal, but the courts have upheld the right of local governments to discriminate on the basis of income (poverty is not a constitutionally protected "suspect classification"). Indeed, economic segregation has become a crucial prop for racial segregation. Racial segregation is a problem not so much because it forces many blacks to live with other blacks, but because it forces them to live in disadvantaged, concentrated-poverty neighborhoods. Reducing place-based inequalities will not make racism go away, but it will undermine one of the pillars of black economic deprivation.

WHERE DO WE GO FROM HERE?

If one accepts the argument that place—specifically, the concentration of poverty and affluence within different parts of the metropolitan area—has negative effects not just on the inner-city poor but on the entire society, it is natural to ask the next question: what can we do about it? Unfortunately, this question is far easier to ask than to answer.

Metropolitan sprawl remains out of control in the United States. The urbanized land area of our metropolitan regions is spreading out much more rapidly than necessary to serve population growth, income growth, or housing needs.[6] In the absence of comprehensive land-use planning, metropolitan political fragmentation has encouraged suburban sprawl and economic segregation. Housing developers, businesses, upper-middle-class families, and some local politicians have a short-term stake in maintaining this system. They can benefit from regional advantages while escaping regional costs. Meanwhile, the older, lower-quality, lower-cost housing of the central cities makes them repositories of the poor, a position increasingly shared by older inner suburbs. Suburban sprawl and concentrated urban poverty are thus two sides of a single metropolitan dynamic. It provides many residents with a range of choices, but it also imposes increasing costs on many, perhaps most, participants.

This arrangement has been marked by a steady decline in urban influence. As middle-class families grew less likely to live in cities, cities have become more politically isolated and less able to win support in state legislatures or Congress.[7] Even cities with sizable middle-class populations and strong economies face growing internal conflict over whether they can afford to spend more on services to the poor, as well as growing skepticism from critics about whether these services in fact reduce poverty. Increasingly, they have come to feel that they might disadvantage themselves by trying to swim alone against national tides.

This is not a natural phenomenon: Chapter 4 documents how federal, state, and local political institutions and policies have actively promoted these outcomes during the twentieth century. Now, as we begin the twenty-first century, new approaches to public policy must play a central role in addressing these problems. We cannot, of course, turn back the clock. The United States is a suburban nation with a car-centered culture. Nevertheless, we can begin to address the problems that plague urbanites and suburbanites alike. Fortunately, a growing number of Americans are recognizing the perils of economic segregation, concentrated poverty, and metropolitan sprawl. The rise of poverty in inner-ring suburbs has made them more sympathetic to the situation of the central cities. Many suburbanites are angry about having less time for their families or leisure because they spend more time gridlocked on their way to work or even while running household errands. New leapfrog development consumes the countryside, lowering the quality of life for exurban residents.

We have also seen that other advanced industrial countries, including Canada, do far better than the United States on many of these issues. Their large cities also experience spatial segregation and social exclusion, but not nearly to the extent typical in the United States.[8] They have lower levels of class and racial segregation and more compact metropolitan development. They have narrower gaps between the rich and poor and lower overall levels of poverty, including much lower levels of child poverty. They have fewer slums and much less urban crime. Urban residents have better access to health insurance and child care, regardless of income.[9] The Netherlands made the reduction of spatial segregation and the promotion of regional integration a central part of its economic adjustment policies in the 1990s.[10]

Cities in the United States have difficulty following the European path because they are trapped in an iron cage of jurisdictional competition. Especially in light of the way federal policies favor suburbs over cities, elected officials in central cities and inner suburbs simply cannot redistribute income from the well-off to the poor or provide adequate public services within their jurisdictions without triggering a series of difficulties.

Only cities with strong economic advantages and large, politically well-organized social service establishments — for example, New York — can attempt substantial local efforts at redistributing resources. Even in these cities, most of this redistribution flows to service providers, not the poor. Although such efforts produce some tangible, positive results, they also subject these cities to chronic fiscal strain and often tether the poor to concentrated-poverty neighborhoods. As a result, even cities with a strong competitive advantage cannot solve the problem of concentrated urban poverty on their own. Indeed, their efforts to do so risk provoking the flight of those with assets and income subject to local taxation.

This is an uncomfortable conclusion for urban liberals and progressives. When Jay Forrester asserted, in his 1969 book *Urban Dynamics*, that helping the poor would only undermine urban economic growth, urban liberals countered that cities could and should provide subsidized housing, income transfers, social services, public hospitals and health clinics, and economic opportunity to needy residents. To do otherwise, they reasoned, would not only be heartless and inhumane but would renege on the cities' historic promise to help lower-income residents achieve upward mobility. When Forrester's argument was reclothed in more liberal terms, as in the 1980 national urban policy report *Urban America in the Eighties,* urban progressives countered that cities *could* fight poverty on their own.[11]

Notwithstanding the fact that cities may have enjoyed more economic leverage in 1969 than they do now, the evidence is in. Lacking national and state policies to constrain local fiscal competition and narrow differences in local fiscal capacity, central cities risk provoking capital flight when they try to engage in local income redistribution. The parameters of this risk are not known because the mobility of people and businesses is not the same in every metropolitan area, but the mere perception that large local public sectors and tax burdens contribute to economic deterioration in big cities makes such policies harder to sustain.

This does not mean that central cities or the nation should stop trying to reduce the concentration of the poor. Besides being morally imperative, reducing poverty concentrations will bolster the future of American democracy. Metropolitan polarization is more than a troubling statistical trend. It violates basic American values. The spatial and political isolation of the central-city and inner-suburban poor prevents them from forging the cross-class coalitions necessary to make their influence felt and makes blatant class legislation against the poor more likely. It threatens to dissolve the bonds of solidarity that join us as Americans. As a former president of the Federal Reserve Bank of New York observed, it forces us to ask "whether we will be able to go forward together as a unified society with a confident outlook or as a society of diverse economic groups suspicious of both the future and each other."[12] Indeed, Henry Richmond argues that the political fragmentation of metropolitan areas represents "the most important community-building challenge to face America since the adoption of the Constitution."[13]

Acting alone, cities and their regions can make only limited progress on reducing and deconcentrating poverty. In the long run, only the nation as a whole can limit, and ultimately reverse, the factors that created the current situation. It remains a sound article of faith among public finance economists that income redistribution should be left to the federal government. Because wealthy individuals subject to taxation can usually quit any local jurisdiction that engages in redistribution, only the federal government can prevent flight from obligation. (Even this scale may not be wide enough. Many observers fear that the current global economic system encourages capital to flow from more egalitarian, social democratic nations to more unequal, neoliberal nations.)

In thinking about what new policies must be adopted, we can draw on the considerable efforts of thoughtful observers to determine how best to deconcentrate urban poverty, diminish urban sprawl, and promote regional cooperation. These observers have called for breaking up existing concentrations of urban poverty; creating new metropolitan forms of tax sharing, land-use regulation, and cooperation; and reforming the underlying mechanisms that promote concentrated poverty and suburban sprawl.[14] They vary on the extent to which they stress "governance"—that is to say, new forms of cooperation among existing governmental units—and government—that is to say, the creation of new governmental institutions. We take the view that voluntary cooperative efforts will not be enough and that new metropolitan institutions must be created at the state or, more likely, federal level.

Any new federal metropolitan policy agenda that will improve the economic, social, and environmental conditions in our urban regions must marshal sufficient political support among the nation's voters and in Congress. We recognize that this is not an easy task. Place-oriented policies alone will not improve the lives of a majority of Americans, especially when larger economic trends and policies are leading to persistently high poverty rates and a widening economic divide in the United States. Any such policies must go hand in hand with national efforts to achieve full employment and insure the citizens against ill health, market failures, and business cycle swings. Achieving such policies probably requires us to reduce the influence of money in American politics and increase the power of mobilized people in our political system. At the same time, national policies that would moderate our national trend toward greater income inequality are not, on their own, sufficient to end metropolitan fragmentation and concentrated urban poverty.

Specific new steps are needed to redress the spatial dimensions of income inequality. They require us to overcome what Harold Wolman called "an ominous lack of consensus [about] how to create a viable political strategy to persuade the majority of Americans who are not poor and do not reside in cities to respond to the needs of these areas."[15] Here, we outline a metropolitan policy agenda to address the place-oriented problems discussed in this book. The next chapter addresses how a majority political coalition can be assembled in support of metropolitan reform and suggests the political appeals that might knit that coalition together.

LEVEL THE METROPOLITAN PLAYING FIELD

Federal policy makers must reverse those policies that exacerbate the economic gaps between and within metropolitan areas. As shown in Chapter 2, inequality between and within the metropolitan regions of the country has grown since the 1970s. Entire metropolitan areas have lagged far behind, even during periods of national economic prosperity. Because effective metropolitan cooperation depends partly on regional wealth, tax-base sharing alone will not help poor metropolitan areas achieve the level of per-student school spending typical of more wealthy metropolitan areas.

The disparities between metropolitan regions do not stem entirely from natural advantages. In the past, federal policies have both widened and narrowed such regional differences. The Tennessee Valley Authority, rural electrification, and the creation of national parks improved economic conditions in poor rural areas. Since World War II, military spending has advanced the economic well-being of southern California and Seattle while drawing resources out of the industrial Northeast and Midwest.[16] Given the variation across regions and the uneven impact of federal policies, Washington should distribute federal resources in ways that provide more help to less well-off regions.

The wide economic disparities *within* metropolitan areas, however, are far more pressing. Chapter 4 showed how myriad federal and state policies promote economic and racial segregation, encourage better-off people and businesses to depart the central cities for the suburbs, and tie the poor to the central cities. A first step in strengthening the capacity of metropolitan areas to address such problems would be to remove the perverse incentives that currently promote spatial inequality.[17] In short, we need to level the metropolitan playing field.

The federal government can take many steps to foster balance and promote cooperation within and between our metropolitan regions. Although we have noted that competition among local jurisdictions produces some real benefits, more balanced competition achieved through a new regionalism would *increase* the ability of local jurisdictions to realize their goals. As conservative urbanist Peter Salins has written: "Federal, state, and local politics should focus on creating a level metropolitan playing field. No longer should the well-being and service capabilities of metropolitan localities, central city or suburban, be hostage to their economic, social, or demographic profiles, nor should they be harmed by the beggar-thy-neighbor scramble of their sister municipalities for regional economic advantage."[18]

LIMIT BIDDING WARS

The federal government should repeal features of the tax code that work against cities and in favor of suburbanization, enact new provisions to dampen interjurisdictional competition, and pay more attention to equalizing its outlays within and across metropolitan regions. In particular, the federal government should prevent localities from using tax abatements and other incentives in bidding wars to draw private investment. Such incentives are extremely inefficient and damaging.[19] One option, embodied in a bill (HR 1060) introduced in Congress in 1999 by Representative David Minge of Minnesota, would impose a heavy tax on local economic development subsidies and remove the tax exemption of local development bonds.[20] This Distorting Subsidies Limitation Act deserves passage. (Although some forms of federal assistance to localities, such as the Community Development Block Grant [CDBG] program, have anti-piracy provisions, a general ban of the sort proposed by Representative Martin Meehan of Massachusetts in 1995, in HR 1842, should also be passed.) If the federal government can use its muscle to get states to raise the blood-alcohol level for drunk driving from 0.08 to 0.10, it should also be able to dampen other state practices that promote destructive forms of local economic competition. Here again, the European Union is far ahead of the United States in requiring local governments to disclose substantial local subsidies and gain EU approval for them.[21]

The federal government should also substantially reform the preferential home mortgage deduction on the personal income tax. As we noted, this deduction promotes sprawl and the exodus of better-off families from central cities and inner suburbs.[22] It should be capped at a fairly high level, with the revenue savings devoted to expanding federal housing and home ownership subsidies for families of modest means, such as a progressive tax credit to help working families purchase homes.

The federal government should also encourage jurisdictions in metropolitan areas to participate in regional tax-base sharing, as Myron Orfield has advocated. It makes no sense for a few suburbs to gain the tax benefits of a new shopping mall, amusement park, office complex, or other development while their neighbors have to live with additional traffic and air pollution. Some metropolitan areas have agreed to tax themselves to support regional sports stadiums, airports, or other facilities because the whole region clearly benefits. Only a handful have broad tax-sharing plans that distribute portions of increased property tax revenues created by new business development throughout the entire metropolitan area.[23] Instituting metropolitan-wide tax-base sharing would not only limit inefficient bidding wars but would also create the potential for more equitable distribution of tax revenues, especially for public schools.

IMPLEMENT FEDERAL AND STATE PROGRAMS
ON A METROPOLITAN BASIS

The federal government should restructure all its domestic programs so that they are carried out on a metropolitan basis. Housing markets, labor markets, transportation systems, and the interorganizational networks of modern production all operate at a regional scale. This should be (but is not) the natural unit for domestic social and economic development policies.

Federally funded programs that ought to be administered on a metropolitan basis include housing (particularly the Section 8 program), workforce development (training and job placement), welfare (job search for employable recipients), and transportation and other infrastructure investments (regulating development on the urban fringe and creating a cohesive regional transportation system). The fragmented administration of these programs currently constitutes a major obstacle to mobility out of inner-city poverty neighborhoods. Local governments administer HUD funds, local and regional Workforce Investment Boards (WIBs) allocate federal job training programs, and county social service agencies carry out welfare programs.[24] There is hardly any coordination among these agencies, although some WIBs work with regional social service agencies to administer the new welfare-to-work program.

For example, some 3,400 local housing agencies administer HUD's public housing and Section 8 housing vouchers and certificates, while separate local housing or community development departments administer the CDBG and Home Investment Partnership (HOME) programs.[25] This makes it difficult to promote mobility across city lines or to get suburbs to develop their fair share of low-income housing. At a minimum, all HUD programs should be administered by regional agencies. All local jurisdictions should be required to permit a minimum level of low-income housing, but these should not be built as 100 percent low-income developments. Rather, HUD should support only mixed-income housing developments, with no more than one-quarter or one-third of the units (for sale or for rent) targeted to low-income families. It should require suburban jurisdictions to approve the development of market-rate rental housing as well and should make some of those units available to low- and moderate-income families with Section 8 vouchers.

Section 8 vouchers should be easily carried within (and across) metropolitan areas. Policy makers have already shifted federal housing subsidies from specific units toward eligible families, but federal, state, and local officials need to pay more attention to expanding the range of choices that these families can make.[26] (It goes without saying that Congress should also expand the Section 8 voucher program to reach all eligible families, since only one-quarter of them now receive federal housing assistance.[27]) Finally, new federal legislation should ensure that federal housing programs are coordinated with federal welfare, job training, and transportation programs on a regional basis along similar lines to the requirements for regional transportation planning. For example, we should build more low- and moderate-income housing where entry-level jobs are growing.

Federal guidelines now require that federal transportation funds be administered by regional agencies, with planning and allocation by metropolitan planning organizations. Federal transportation legislation now requires regional agencies to consider all transportation options (not just highways) and to consider the links between traffic congestion, air pollution, and urban sprawl. Initially begun as ISTEA, renamed the Transportation Equity Act for the Twenty-first Century [TEA-21], the measure means that "if a suburban community wants to build a new highway interchange to alleviate congestion, before proceeding, it must demonstrate that the interchange will not increase traffic and worsen air quality."[28]

Because these provisions affect only transportation funds, regional transportation planning agencies are limited in their ability to carry out this directive. Some regional agencies are single-purpose transportation organizations; others are multipurpose organizations. The latter have been innovative and flexible in linking transportation funding with other initiatives, such as the federal government's reverse commuting Bridges to Work program, so that residents of high-poverty neighborhoods can find jobs in outlying areas.[29] Similarly, the Clean Air Act of 1990 requires regional agencies to determine whether metropolitan areas meet federal air pollution standards. In many areas, different regional bodies implement the Clean Air Act and TEA-21. These responsibilities should be combined.

In short, the federal government should require the planning, resource allocation, reporting, and evaluation functions of all federal domestic grant programs to be undertaken on a metropolitan basis. It should condition the provision of both direct funding and indirect assistance (such as FHA insurance) on regions' adopting a fair-share approach to housing (in the form of mixed-income developments or acceptance of housing vouchers), sharing the regional tax base, and balancing spending on different transportation modes, not just on new road-building projects that promote sprawl.[30]

PROMOTE METROPOLITAN COOPERATION AND GOVERNANCE

Metropolitan regions generally lack the institutional framework to carry out these functions. Federal policy should therefore help them create the necessary governance infrastructure. This infrastructure would help metropolitan regions work in a cooperative manner while leaving plenty of space for local jurisdictions to remain innovative and responsive and to debate and decide how best to utilize federal and local resources. This effort should build on the experiences of Portland, Oregon, and the Twin Cities described in Chapter 6. They exemplify how strong regional land-use planning can promote a more livable metropolitan environment and how regional tax sharing can spread the benefits of suburban growth.

By helping metropolitan regions build an institutional base that empowers localities to join in defining mutual problems, debating how to solve them, and crafting coalitions to implement these solutions, the federal government can, over the long haul, have a major impact on the perverse dynamics outlined here. During the Clinton administration, senior officials at the Office of Management and Budget and a working group involving many different departments crafted proposals to set aside funds from federal grant programs for a bonus pool that would reward regions that fashioned new metropolitan solutions to urban problems.[31] Although such a fund would be a good beginning, it is far too modest. The federal government should take the initiative by crafting model legislation for metropolitan councils, requiring that federal domestic programs be administered under their aegis, and providing matching funds for modestly sized regional support staffs.

The ad hoc metropolitan bodies now carrying out specific functions within metropolitan areas are not a good starting point. They have not led to broad-based regional cooperation, much less to a regional focus on the problem of concentrated urban poverty. They are typically undemocratic, with each jurisdiction, regardless of population, having one seat on their boards. Others include a corporatist mix of government and business leaders, with little involvement of unions or community groups.[32] To encourage a vital metropolitan voice to emerge, to enable individual jurisdictions to understand what they have in common with others, and to fairly represent each part of the metropolis, the nation must create a new level of political deliberation. Note that this is not the same as creating a new level of government, for the new regional bodies could still deliver many services through existing city and county arrangements.

Portland's Metro is the only democratically elected, multifunction regional body in the United States. Its citizens seem quite happy with how it is performing, with the main complaint being that development controls may have driven up housing costs, a view that many contest.[33] The federal government should help other regions replicate this approach. Metropolitan council members should be elected from single districts, balancing the desire to represent all parts of the metropolis with the need for a manageably sized council. Different-sized metropolitan areas would have to make this trade-off in different ways. The recent consolidation of Louisville and Jefferson County in Kentucky created a new council with twenty-six seats, each representing about 25,000 voters. In this way, both central-city neighborhoods and unincorporated areas outside the city achieved representation. In the New York and Los Angeles consolidated metropolitan areas, with populations approaching 18 million and 16 million, respectively, districts would have to be far larger, perhaps 250,000 inhabitants, to preserve this balance.

Historically, the federal government has had an enormous impact on the evolution of state and local governmental institutions and practices. Most existing regional councils of government (COGs) were created in response to Section 701 of the Housing Act of 1954, which provided federal aid for them.[34] During the Great Society programs of the 1960s, the federal government stimulated the creation of CDCs and new patterns of neighborhood participation. Long after its demise, localities continue to embrace citizen participation, CDCs, and decentralized program administration. Title 23, Section 134 of the U.S. Code, which established metropolitan planning organizations for transportation under TEA-21, shows that the federal government can stimulate the creation of new regional institutions.[35] The federal government should amend this legislation to cover other federal domestic programs, including economic development, housing, public assistance, and workforce development programs.

In addition to overseeing federal domestic programs, many of which local governments would still carry out on a day-to-day basis, metropolitan councils should be charged with identifying regional problems, debating alternative solutions, and advocating desired solutions to local and state officials. In this way, they would create new regional identities and enable parts of metropolitan regions to coalesce in new ways. In particular, they would foster coalitions among central cities and inner suburbs and between regional elites (who understand the importance of regional platforms in the global economy) and the working population of the region.

LINK COMMUNITY DEVELOPMENT TO THE REGIONAL ECONOMY

Over the last three decades, the hard truth is that neither government pro-grams for urban revitalization nor nonprofit neighborhood-based efforts have prevented the emergence of concentrated poverty neighborhoods or substan-tially improved the life conditions of their residents.[36] Cities with a shrinking job base, such as Detroit, Camden, or St. Louis, face the most difficulty in lift-ing people up where they live.[37] Such people would be more likely to find jobs and be able to send their children to decent schools if they lived in the suburbs or moved to another metropolitan area. Harsh as it may sound, it would best serve them (and the nonpoor residents of such declining cities) to help them move to places with more opportunities. But the wholesale abandonment of these areas is politically untenable. What's the alternative?

Even though neighborhood revitalization efforts have yielded only limited results, they play an important role and cities should continue to support them. Overall urban vitality depends on healthy neighborhoods that attract people who have choices about where to live. Neighborhood revitalization encour-ages a common purpose among residents from different racial, cultural, and economic backgrounds. This bond encourages them to invest in their sur-roundings rather than flee or retreat into individual coping strategies. Healthy neighborhoods provide access to employment, attractive retail services, parks, playgrounds, and other amenities, as well as decent, affordable housing. Wash-ington can help promote such neighborhoods by replacing the current top-down, functionally fragmented urban service delivery system with more ho-listic neighborhood- and family-based approaches that will build a sense of common purpose.

Various community-based organizations seek to lift low-income people out of poverty by helping them get decent-paying jobs, but it does not really matter if those jobs are located within the neighborhood. Instead, people should be helped to learn about good jobs, wherever they are, and to develop the skills and get access to the transportation necessary to obtain them. If they continue to live in the neighborhood, their higher incomes will contribute to neighbor-hood vitality. If they move, it will probably be to make life easier and better. As well as promoting mobility of the poor out of concentrated poverty neigh-borhoods, central-city development officials should seek to attract working families back into poor neighborhoods, thereby diversifying them.[38] The added clout that these working families exert on behalf of neighborhood schools and services will benefit the remaining poor. Building affordable housing, investing in housing rehabilitation, improving local schools, and providing local amenities all work toward this end.

The problem, of course, is that such strategies have had uneven results among neighborhoods. They work best in neighborhoods that already have the most going for them. They work least well in the poorest, most socially disorganized areas, whose better-off residents may be drawn to more attractive neighborhoods nearby. As a result, the current round of "comprehensive community development initiatives" is unlikely to alter the prevailing spatial concentration of the poor unless they can link the poor to wider opportunities in the regional economy.[39] The same can be said for "empowerment zones," which shift some jobs to places where poor people live instead of improving their access to job opportunities throughout the metropolitan area. Such efforts will have little impact on the matrix of forces that promote concentrated urban poverty. Much the same can be said about the other federal community development programs operating through community-based organizations and public-private partnerships.

If the overall planning, resource allocation, and program objectives are determined on a regional basis, the perspective of local community-based partners might change in a fundamental way. The community development movement has spent thirty years developing alliances and partnerships with the political and business actors who can provide the necessary resources. They have forged links with institutions outside poor neighborhoods, even outside the city limits. Some CDCs have established networks (or business alliances) with employers and community colleges at the regional level. Community developers that focus only on the neighborhood level risk becoming, in Jeremy Nowak's words, "managers of decline." In the new institutional context, they would be encouraged to develop a regional perspective on housing, business development, job training, and transportation, thus maximizing benefits to their constituents.[40]

STRENGTHEN PUBLIC SCHOOLS ACROSS THE BOARD

If educational attainment is a key determinant of individual upward mobility, greater federal support is needed to improve the primary, secondary, and postsecondary public education systems serving the urban poor and near poor. Daniel McMurrer and Isabel Sawhill found that the impact of a person's parental background on a person's life chances is decreasing while that of his or her education is increasing. That led them to conclude that federal policy makers should make decent local schooling a federal entitlement regardless of local fiscal capacity, set national standards for inner-city school performance, and expand funding for early childhood education.[41] Standards and measurement like President Bush's No Child Left Behind law are not enough; more resources have to flow to these schools.

In the long run, the poor will not achieve more economic mobility until they can achieve far better educational outcomes than they now do, especially with respect to their getting a college degree. The political isolation of central cities, the resegregation of their schools, and the poor quality of many schools in concentrated-poverty neighborhoods have had devastating consequences not only for poor neighborhoods, but for society as a whole. Many urban schools are not doing as badly as some think, especially in light of the lack of funding and the difficult situations their students come from.[42] Even so, dropout rates remain persistently high, achievement levels persistently low, and conflict and alienation pervasive. As currently configured, urban school systems systematically reinforce initial disadvantage. The problems of urban school systems not only derive from concentrated urban poverty; they also contribute to it.

As Richard Rothstein notes, most public schools do a good job at educating young people.[43] But many schools with students from low-income families do not meet basic educational goals. Student performance clearly varies tremendously across metropolitan-area school districts. In general, more money (and higher family income) makes a big difference in educational outcomes in public schools.[44] For example, smaller class sizes (better teacher-student ratios) improve student performance.[45] Schools that are in physical disrepair or lack adequate books and equipment are also less likely to reach standard educational outcomes. Students with poorly trained or poorly paid teachers do not perform as well as those with well-trained and well-paid teachers.

Simply equalizing per-student expenditures will not solve this problem. For one thing, much of the increase in public school spending in recent decades has gone toward students with physical and mental special needs or toward transportation, school meals, and other functions.[46] Comparisons of school district spending should focus on class size, teacher pay, books and equipment, and similar expenses. Because students from poor families come to school with more educational and psychological disadvantages, they need more than equalized spending on these items.[47] We need to spend *more* on the schools that teach poor students in order to provide them with a level educational playing field.

Metropolitan-wide tax-base sharing would help reduce the gap in school spending between poor and wealthy jurisdictions within the same urban area. But the wide disparities among metropolitan areas mean that geography still determines the kind of education students receive. The same holds true, to a lesser degree, with states. Legal action by parents in poorly funded central-city school districts has led to many efforts to equalize fiscal capacity for school spending within states and to break the link between the local tax base and local school expenditures. But even if every state equalized educational spending per student, students in Connecticut (with a per capita income of $42,706 in 2002) would still receive a far better education than those in Mississippi ($22,372). This is an obvious area where the federal government can level the playing field, first by requiring states to equalize spending, and second by supplementing educational spending in those states with below-average fiscal capacities.

Breaking this vicious circle must be an urgent priority in the battle against concentrated poverty. Great controversy has swirled around local school reform, and radical measures are clearly in order. Creating metropolitan school districts, increasing the financial resources flowing into them, making individual schools more accountable to students and their parents, closing failing schools, giving parents more choice among public schools, and improving the connection between schooling and employment opportunities will all broaden political support for urban schools. Increasing parental involvement is also critical to revitalizing urban schools. The work of the Industrial Areas Foundation in Texas in organizing parents to improve local schools and in pushing corporations to forge alliances with community groups to help the poor get access to jobs is a good example of the value of grassroots mobilization.[48]

Gary Orfield has argued that the resegregation and political isolation of inner-city schools have materially contributed to their poor performance and that metropolitan school districts offer important benefits.[49] Creating metropolitan school districts would help the larger society restore its stake in improving inner-city schools. Ending balkanization and equalizing metropolitan school financing would also dramatically reduce the incentives for suburban jurisdictions to exclude the relatively less well-off.

Improving public primary and secondary education is only a first step. More young people from poor families must be helped to attend and graduate from college. The urban campuses of public state college and university systems will inevitably educate the vast majority of them. Over the last several decades, most states have shifted resources away from public higher education toward prison building and shifted the burden of financing college educations onto the families of college students. States provide less tuition assistance to poor and working-class families (who are more likely to attend community colleges and second-tier state universities) than to upper-middle-class students (who are more likely to attend the more expensive and prestigious state universities).[50] Parents who can afford higher tuition at public institutions should pay it. States should offset tuition increases with more financial aid to poor and working-class families and provide more core support for urban public higher education. Typically, they have failed to do either of these things. (With higher levels of funding for these institutions should come responsibility for higher levels of performance.) The public colleges and universities that educate central-city and inner-suburban residents should also seek to build new relationships with metropolitan labor markets. Political leaders of our metropolitan areas should rally local employers to hire the graduates of these institutions. In this way, and probably only in this way, can our cities provide upward mobility to the urban poor and grow their middle-class populations.

MAKE WORK PAY

Education alone is not enough to offset the basis of concentrated urban poverty. The educational level of low-wage workers has increased substantially in the last two decades. As Jared Bernstein noted, "we now have a more skilled (at least in terms of years of education) yet lower-paid low-wage worker."[51] Regardless of how much we improve our educational system, society's dirty work always needs to get done. As the labor market increasingly polarizes wages and salaries, many people who work full-time can barely make ends meet.[52] Most of them live in America's central cities and inner suburbs.

There are as many different views about how the federal government might reduce poverty as there are diagnoses of the problem. Some even dismiss the idea that poverty is a problem. When the *New York Times* ran a seven-part series on the downsizing of America in March 1996, conservative economists and commentators lauded the overall rate of job growth, praised American flexibility in laying off workers, and dismissed the lifetime job as "more nostalgic myth than historic reality."[53] One commentator even argued that Americans' expectation that they should enjoy continuous economic betterment was a dangerous illusion.[54]

We are sympathetic with those who say that America cannot fully redress the growing spatial concentration of poverty without becoming a more egalitarian, social democratic society. Those developed countries that have centralized wage setting, strong labor unions, and more generous welfare states (especially those that support working women) also have lower rates of poverty and inequality. The United States is at the wrong end of each of these scales. It has highly decentralized wage-setting mechanisms, weak and declining labor unions, a patchwork of labor regulation, and highly decentralized and variable social welfare policies.[55] We clearly need national legislation to address these problems, but efforts to achieve these ends face enormous opposition from politically entrenched forces.

In the absence of such measures, efforts to increase labor force participation and to make work pay, even low-wage work, are vital. Although national welfare reform has substantially cut the rolls, the states have not done enough to ensure that former welfare recipients find and hold decent jobs. Many have used their fiscal windfall from welfare reform for tax relief.[56] More emphasis needs to be placed on providing support for working mothers, matching them with decent jobs and ensuring that these jobs turn into careers, not just sources of poverty wages. Much progress has been made in the last decade by increasing the earned income tax credit (EITC) and the minimum wage, but much more needs to be done.

EXPAND AND REFINE THE EARNED INCOME TAX CREDIT

The EITC, begun in 1975, is a refundable tax credit that subsidizes low-wage workers, especially those with children, by raising household income above the poverty line. It is tied to family income and household size, so it is clearly progressive. The maximum annual benefit is $4,140 for a family with two or more children and an income of $10,350 or less. It is phased out altogether at an annual income of $34,177. Even families that owe no federal income tax can receive a check from the IRS. President Clinton expanded the EITC, increasing benefit levels and expanding the number of eligible households. In 2002, 18.6 million persons claimed the EITC, costing the federal government $34 billion.[57] The EITC has definitely helped raise the incomes of the nation's poorest workers. In 1999, the EITC lifted 4.8 million people, including 2.6 million children, out of poverty.[58] Even though the average income of the bottom 40 percent of households fell by 3 percent before taxes between 1989 and 1999, after-tax income was unchanged, mostly because of the EITC.[59] The National Bureau of Economic Research found that the percentage of single mothers who worked jumped from 74 percent in 1992 to 87 percent in 1998 and concluded that the EITC had a greater effect on workforce participation than did changes in welfare law.[60]

There are several ways to make the EITC more effective. One is to expand outreach through labor unions, churches, and community-based organizations to increase the participation rate of eligible workers. The federal government could also require employers to inform employees about the EITC, as Illinois currently does.[61] Congress could increase the maximum credit by $500 or more for workers with large families and slow down the pace at which the EITC is phased out for families with two or more children. It should also take steps to decrease the penalties that two-income families pay for more earnings by raising the level at which the EITC is phased out for them. More states should adopt their own EITC programs, as sixteen states and two local governments have already done. This would help millions of hard-pressed working families, most of whom live in central cities and inner suburbs.[62] The Economic Policy Institute recommends converting the dependent exemption into a child credit and combining it with the EITC into a "universal unified child credit," which would be available to most taxpayers with children, helping many working-class families.[63]

RAISE THE MINIMUM WAGE ABOVE THE POVERTY LEVEL

About one-fifth of employees eligible for the EITC do not take it. Some friendly critics argue that the EITC subsidizes low-wage employers, perhaps lowering wage rates across the board.[64] Expanding the EITC should thus go hand in hand with raising the minimum wage, which helps the poorest workers and has an upward ripple effect on wages. The inflation-adjusted minimum wage declined substantially during the 1980s; its nominal value remained $3.35 an hour from 1981 until April 1990. Despite increases in 1991 and 1997 (to $5.15 an hour), it is still worth less than 70 percent of what it was in 1978.[65] (In 1968, it was worth nearly $8.00 an hour in today's dollars.)

In the 1960s and 1970s, the minimum wage (for a worker who worked full-time, year-round) was roughly equal to, and occasionally above, the federal poverty threshold. Today, a full-time worker earning the minimum wage earns $10,712, only 68 percent of the 2004 poverty level of $15,670 for a family of three.[66] The minimum wage today is only one-third of the average hourly earnings ($15.52 in 2004) — the lowest it has been in more than 50 years. (As noted, even this level does not guarantee that a family can meet basic necessities.[67]) This has prompted twelve states to enact their own higher minimum wages and more than 100 cities to enact living wage laws targeted to employees of firms with city contracts or subsidies.

Critics argue that the minimum wage primarily benefits teenagers (including those from wealthy families) who work part-time, as well as persons whose other family members make good incomes. In fact, the vast majority of minimum wage earners are adults; 40 percent are the sole breadwinners in their families. Most teenagers who earn the minimum wage are from low-income families. Others argue that raising the minimum wage will cause substantial job loss, but considerable evidence indicates that this is not so. States that have raised the minimum wage above the federal level have experienced no employment decline.[68] Raising the federal minimum wage to the poverty level (about $7.50 an hour) would still leave it below its 1968 peak level.

EXPAND HEALTH INSURANCE AND CHILD CARE

The United States is the only industrial country without universal health insurance. About 45 million individuals, including 8.3 million children under age eighteen, lack health insurance. The number of Americans without health insurance increased by 5.2 million between 2000 and 2003.[69] Those without health insurance are concentrated in urban areas, which helps explain their high rates of infant mortality and disease.

In recent years, some employers have cut health benefits for employees or their dependents; others require employees to pay more, which many low-wage employees cannot afford. The private-sector jobs created in the last decade, companies like Wal-Mart, the nation's largest employer, are less likely to offer insurance.[70] Also, many parents and children who were pushed off welfare have lost their Medicaid coverage and cannot afford to replace it out of pocket, leaving them worse off. Many private health maintenance organizations are dropping elderly Medicare recipients as patients.[71] The decline of union membership since the 1970s has also contributed to these trends, because workers with union contracts are more likely than others to have health insurance.

Minimally, the federal government should respond to this crisis by assuming the cost of a basic health plan for children, even those who are covered by employers. This would immediately have a dramatic impact on the well-being of the poor and near poor, reduce their out-of-pocket spending for health care, and increase their income available for other basic necessities, especially housing. Extending Medicaid-like health insurance to all 8.3 million children under eighteen without insurance would cost about $12 billion.[72] Of course, publicly subsidized preventive health care saves money in the long run by reducing the need for costly crisis medical care.

Child care is also critical. Sixty-five percent of mothers with children under age six, and 79 percent of mothers with children ages six to thirteen, are in the labor force. As more women work, the shortage of affordable child care imposes a severe economic and emotional burden on American families. Other industrial nations provide child care as a basic right.[73] In the United States, it is a privilege for those who can afford it. Quality child care also should prepare children for school. A recent study found that low-income children who received comprehensive, quality early educational intervention score higher on cognitive, reading, and math tests than a comparison group of children who did not receive the intervention. Moreover, these effects persisted into their twenties. In the long term, each dollar invested in such quality programs saved over $7, because these children were more likely to attend college and be employed and less likely to be school dropouts, dependent on welfare, or arrested for criminal activity. Nationally, only one in seven eligible children now gets assistance because funds are so limited.[74]

Affordable child care should be available to all families. This should primarily be the federal government's responsibility. Barbara Bergmann recently designed a "Help for Working Parents" program that would provide $60 billion for child care and $30 billion for health insurance.[75] It would enable all parents working at the minimum wage to reach a "basic needs budget" and would drastically reduce the child poverty that has become epidemic in recent years.[76]

DECONCENTRATE POVERTY

These general measures to lift the standard of living for the urban poor will not, by themselves, significantly reduce the spatial concentration of the less well-off in our central cities. They will continue to be hampered by the negative "neighborhood effects" associated with living in high-poverty areas unless we attack the spatial dimension of the problem head on. We must therefore adopt measures specifically aimed at deconcentrating urban poverty within metropolitan areas. Although hard to achieve, such policies are consistent with the American political tradition of decentralized federalism and are well within our reach. In place of the vicious circles that now operate, we must, as Margaret Weir has written, create "virtuous circles" in metropolitan America.[77]

Logically, there are only two ways to deconcentrate the urban poor. Either we must help the poor move out of concentrated poverty neighborhoods to more promising areas, or we must attract more opportunities and resources, and more economically diverse residents, into poor central-city neighborhoods. In practice, we must do both, because the two strategies work best together. The "people versus place" debate is a false dichotomy.

We have already discussed the importance of linking community development to the regional economy. Ironically, community development will also be aided by greater mobility. If families have greater choices, they will feel more loyalty to their neighborhoods and be more willing to engage in community-building activities. We approach the task of opening up the suburbs to poor and working people with a realistic understanding of its magnitude. Although certainly not simple, neither is it unmanageable. In 2000, 19.5 million of the nation's 31.1 million poor lived in the 100 largest metropolitan areas. According to Peter Tatian and Alisa Wilson of the Urban Institute, 6.2 million of them, or about 1.5 million households, would have to move to achieve an even distribution of the poverty population within the 100 largest metropolitan areas.[78] Over a ten-year period, that would involve only 145,000 households per year. Tatian and Wilson also calculated how many poor people would have to move in each metropolitan area. In metropolitan Houston, for example, 176,398 poor persons (in an area with a population of 4.7 million), or about 44,100 households, would need to move to spread the poor evenly throughout the metropolitan area.[79] If we devoted ten years to this task (and assuming that those who left were not replaced by new poor people), only about 4,400 poor families a year would have to move to nonpoor neighborhoods — certainly not a magnitude that would prove disruptive or administratively difficult.

A less dramatic approach would dismantle urban ghettos rather than spread the poor randomly throughout metropolitan areas. Of the 19.5 million poor persons in the nation's 100 largest metropolitan areas, 5.1 million, or 26 percent, lived in census tracts with 30 percent or more poverty.[80] Providing half of these 1.3 families with a Section 8 voucher to leave these neighborhoods would cost $3.9 billion more a year.[81] This is a serious task, but hardly overwhelming either politically or fiscally. And if these poor families move closer to jobs, like the two families described in Chapter 1, many might no longer need housing assistance after a few years.

These goals cannot be achieved solely by local measures. Promoting this kind of mobility requires federal, state, and local policies to be harmonized in ways that help poor people relocate and assist them in getting and commuting to jobs in non-poverty city neighborhoods and in the suburbs, enforce fair housing regulations, and redistribute federal housing subsidies away from current areas of poverty concentration. Federal housing mobility programs such as Moving to Opportunity offer one model for achieving these ends. Reverse commuting programs, such as the federal Bridges to Work program, should also be expanded. More vigorous enforcement of antidiscrimination laws would also help promote this type of mobility. Finally, training programs run by community colleges based in the central cities should be better linked with their regional labor markets.[82] It is not enough simply to overlay a new set of mobility programs on top of the existing administrative structure for social programs. Providing low-income central-city residents with better information about and access to suburban opportunities will require workforce development and housing programs, among others, to be reorganized along metropolitan lines.

We recognize that there is likely to be political resistance to these mobility efforts. When HUD announced its Moving to Opportunity (MTO) program in 1994, conservative politicians in several of Baltimore's working-class suburbs, fueled by right-wing radio talk-show hosts, raised the specter of masses of poor black families invading their neighborhoods. The truth is that the MTO rules prevented participating families from moving into the white working-class areas because the poverty rate was already too high there. Although the resulting clamor killed the program's expansion, it has proceeded quite successfully below the political radar screen in all five MTO pilot cities, including Los Angeles, New York, Chicago, and Boston. Like the Gautreaux program, MTO was invisible because it was small, tenants and potential landlords were both counseled, and no single suburban community got more than a few MTO families.[83]

We should recognize, however, that middle-class families resist having the poor live nearby because the income gap between them is much wider in the United States than in other advanced societies.[84] The poor in the United States are, relatively, much poorer than their counterparts in Canada and Western Europe and are thus more likely to be viewed by the middle class as "them" rather than "us." Helping to lift the poor closer to, or even slightly above, the poverty line would reduce this gap and make economic integration more acceptable and likely. That is why "making work pay" is central to our overall approach.

We do not discount the racial factors that lead middle-class whites to resist programs to deconcentrate poverty. In 2000, 18.6 percent of poor blacks and 13.8 percent of poor Hispanics lived in 40 percent plus poverty neighborhoods, but only 9.8 percent of poor Asians and 5.9 percent of poor whites did.[85] Many white (and even some black, Asian, and Latino) middle-class families fear that if "too many" people of color move into their communities, crime and other indicators of neighborhood deterioration will increase. People clearly believe that there is a "tipping point." But studies indicate that most middle-class whites would not feel uncomfortable if fewer than 15 percent of their neighbors were black.[86] Thus, efforts to deconcentrate poor families currently living in high-poverty neighborhoods — a majority of whom are black or Latino — must limit the proportion of the poor in any given neighborhood to avoid resegregation.

MOBILIZE CIVIC ENGAGEMENT ON A METROPOLITAN SCALE

Many of the problems we have discussed stem from the imbalance of political power between well-off individuals and business, on the one hand, and the poor and the working class, on the other hand. This imbalance will not change unless we change our political rules to increase popular influence and access. Reforming our voting rights and labor laws will increase the voice of urban constituencies in national political life.

Voting Rights

The civil rights movement removed many barriers to political participation. The Voting Rights Act of 1965 eliminated the poll tax, literacy tests, and other arbitrary obstacles used to deny African Americans basic rights of citizenship. Its enforcement and expansion have been instrumental in increasing the number of black elected officials, particularly in the South.[87] But serious barriers to voting remain, particularly in the poor minority and immigrant neighborhoods of urban areas. Because the poor move more frequently than others, they must constantly reregister. Registration sites, such as city halls, are often inconvenient for individuals without an car or those who cannot take time off from work to register during business hours.[88]

The National Voter Registration Act of 1993 (often called the "motor voter" law) removed some of these barriers, but others remain. Laws that require voters to register far in advance of election day depress voter turnout because many voters do not pay attention to campaigns until close to election day, "as media coverage, advertising, direct mail, and face-to-face electioneering reach their peak. The pace of registration quickens as the election approaches."[89] But because most states close registration a month before the election, many motivated voters are denied the opportunity to register.[90] Studies of presidential campaigns reveal that the closing date for registration has a major impact on the turnout rate.[91] Political analysts have also recommended adopting proportional representation to give marginalized voters a stronger voice.[92] Although some say that simply easing registration rules, without intensifying mobilization of voters by unions, community organizations, and other groups, would have little impact on voter turnout, a strong case can be made that same-day voter registration would increase turnout.[93]

Redistricting also has significant place-based consequences. As we note in the next chapter, the number of central-city congressional districts has declined significantly in recent decades. This is not only the result of the suburbanization of the population, but also of the way state legislatures and courts draw district boundaries. Since the 1965 Voting Rights Act, civil rights groups have adopted a political and legal strategy of pushing for congressional (as well as state legislative, city council, and school board) districts that will increase the odds of electing African Americans and Latinos to public office. As a result of their legal victories in the 1970s and 1980s, the number of black and Latino elected officials increased dramatically, due in great measure to the creation of more districts where African Americans and Latinos make up more than half of eligible voters. Although these districts have yielded more minority elected officials, they have also created relatively safe seats for minority candidates, which has engendered less political competition and therefore lower voter turnout. This undermines the chances of progressive candidates at the state and national levels, who rely on high turnout in low-income and minority areas. Carving out these safe minority districts also may have made other districts more white and middle class and therefore more likely to elect conservatives and Republicans. Lacking an urban constituency, these representatives have had little concern for urban problems. This undermines potential coalition building between urban and working-class suburban constituencies in Congress.[94]

A series of landmark U.S. Supreme Court decisions, beginning with *Shaw v. Reno* in 1993, nullified some of these majority minority districts on the grounds that they were so contorted as to represent an illegal form of racial segregation. Legislators were forced to redraw them, and in most cases, the districts continued to send African Americans to Congress, often with crossover support from white voters. More recently, the Supreme Court appears to be likely to uphold even middecade partisan gerrymanders put in place by new Republican majorities.

This experience suggests that urban progressives should push to create more congressional districts that straddle central cities and inner-ring suburbs, so that representatives have a stake in building bridges between poor and working-class constituents. Consider, for example, two adjacent congressional districts in California. In the 1990s, the Thirty-first Congressional District comprised predominantly low-income neighborhoods in Los Angeles, where 70 percent of residents are Latino and 13.6 percent are Asian. It is among the safest Democratic seats in the country. The seat is held by a liberal Democrat, Xavier Becerra, who won in 2002 with 81 percent of the vote.

Contiguous to the Thirty-first was the increasingly racially and economically diverse Twenty-ninth Congressional District described in Chapter 1, which included both urbanized suburbs like Pasadena, Glendale, and Burbank and more affluent suburbs like San Marino. It was represented by the far-right Republican James Rogan from 1996 to 2000. Rogan was reelected in 1998 with only 51 percent of the vote, although registered Democrats held a slight edge. In 2000, moderate Democrat Adam Schiff defeated Rogan. When redistricting shifted more Democrats into the district, it helped him win in 2002 by 30 percentage points. It would be rational to shift even more Democratic voters out of heavily Democratic districts like Becerra's into more suburban ones elsewhere in the country—in part to make both the old and new districts more competitive, thus drawing more voters to the polls. Unfortunately, as we shall see in the next chapter, the brunt of redistricting in 2001 was in the opposite direction of concentrating Democratic voters in more urban districts.

Reform Labor Law

Union strength reached a peak of 35 percent in the mid-1950s, enabling blue-collar Americans to share in the postwar prosperity and join the middle class. Unions have also been leading advocates for progressive urban policy. Union pay scales even boosted the wages of nonunion workers. Unionized workers continue to have higher wages, better pensions, longer vacations and maternity leaves, and better health insurance than their nonunion counterparts. In unionized firms, the wage gap between black and white workers is narrower than elsewhere. Whites and blacks earn roughly the same wages, and they both earn more than workers without union representation. According to the Economic Policy Institute, unionized blacks earn 12.7 percent more than blacks in comparable nonunion jobs; for whites, the union "wage premium" is 11.0 percent. It is 16.0 percent for Latinos.

The erosion of America's labor movement contributed to declining wages and living standards and the nation's widening economic disparities. Most new service-sector and light manufacturing jobs are not unionized. During the last several decades, the federal government's cold war against labor unions has made unionization more difficult to achieve. Since the 1970s, union density has declined precipitously. In 2003, only 12.9 percent of the workforce belonged to unions, with only 8.2 percent of the private workforce unionized.[95] AFL-CIO president John Sweeney has pledged to expand union organizing, and union membership has increased modestly in recent years. But successful organizing is difficult without labor law reform. Union growth would reinvigorate what has historically been the single strongest source of political support for progressive urban policies.

Union elections supervised by the National Labor Relations Board are biased in favor of management. Any employer with a clever labor attorney can stall union elections, allowing management time to intimidate potential union recruits. According to one study, one in ten workers involved in an organizing drive is fired. Employers can require workers to attend meetings where company managers and consultants give antiunion speeches, show antiunion films, and distribute antiunion literature. Unions have no equivalent right of access to employees. To reach them, organizers frequently must visit their homes or hold secret meetings. At least 40 percent of employees want union representation, but they will not vote for a union if they feel that their jobs are at stake. Reforming our nation's cumbersome labor laws will give workers elementary rights of free speech and assembly, provide a democratic voice in the workplace, and change the balance of national political influence.[96]

CONCLUSION

Our perspective is at once radical and incremental. It is radical because we propose a series of institutional innovations and policy approaches that actually address the root causes of growing spatial inequality and metropolitan political fragmentation. We can never adequately solve our national problem of growing inequality until we specifically confront its spatial dimension. Neither national policies aimed at equalizing incomes nor local efforts to reduce concentrated poverty can succeed unless this basic dynamic is confronted. National economic prosperity, for example, has increased incomes at the lower end of the distribution and reduced poverty during the 1990s, but it left the geography of inequality largely intact. In the absence of a comprehensive approach, local measures are also bound to fail.

Our perspective is also incremental because we recognize that the present arrangements have evolved over more than half a century and that many interests have developed a stake in them. It will take many decades to undo these arrangements. We call for renewed federal efforts to reduce poverty by making work pay, improving schools, assisting in the provision of housing, and helping to provide basic health and child-care services. But the centerpiece of our program is not huge tax increases, massive new spending programs, or even significant redistribution to the central cities. The missing piece in the puzzle of poverty and inequality is the need for the federal and state governments to level the playing field, encourage regional cooperation, foster closer relationships between working families and opportunities, and foster greater civic participation by the poor and working class in our metropolitan areas. By reframing the institutions of federalism, we can nurture regions that are more livable, fair, and economically successful. These measures are all worthy and laudable. Without a majority political coalition, however, they will not see the light of day. How such a political coalition can be assembled is the subject of the next chapter.

Crossing the City Line
A Metropolitics for the Twenty-first Century

The previous chapters have provided convincing evidence that metropolitan sprawl and concentrated urban poverty lie at the heart of our national urban problem, a quagmire that keeps America from being the country it would like to be. Although some might disagree about what factor is most important in promoting sprawl and concentrated urban poverty, a great deal of evidence also shows that federal, state, and local public policies interact within fragmented metropolitan political systems to worsen the urban problem, not make it better. Many would sympathize with the contention that the nation must move forcefully to increase the levels of cooperation, inclusion, and spatial mobility within our metropolitan areas in order to address these problems. The rub comes not in whether it would be desirable to move in this direction, but in whether it is politically possible.

We have highlighted the political obstacles. Many powerful interests contribute to the creation of the existing dynamic of sprawl and poverty concentration, which, once in place, reinforces their desire to maintain the status quo.[1] Residents of better-off suburbs can enjoy the benefits of strong metropolitan economies driven by vigorous central cities while they avoid paying taxes for central-city services, especially for the central-city poor. Those who reside in less exclusive suburbs have more ambiguous interests, but as CNN commentator William Schneider has argued, blue-collar suburban home owners may also seek to distance themselves — politically and socially — from the urban poor.[2] Certainly, the high degree of polarization in some metropolitan areas encourages many residents of inner suburbs to identify with wealthier people in outer suburbs rather than with the central-city poor. Finally, many central-city political leaders are heavily invested in these arrangements. They, too, show little interest in policy approaches that might dissipate their population base or dilute their authority over the place-based programs under their control.[3] Suburban representatives often resist policies that would gradually spread poor people from the central city to other parts of the metropolitan area. This is especially true when race comes into play.

This combination of circumstances leads many observers to be pessimistic about the chances for adopting programs to achieve greater metropolitan equity. Even progressive scholars who are highly sympathetic to the urban poor disagreed with Yale law professor Owen Fiss's recent proposal for a large-scale program to help urban ghetto residents to move to the suburbs (or wherever else they want).[4] Political scientist J. Phillip Thompson says, "white suburbia has already shown *in practice* where it stands on racial integration and poverty deconcentration.... Trying legally to force white Americans to integrate against their will, in a country where they are a voting majority, has not worked and it will not work. In this context, strategies focused on improving conditions where people already live such as [William Julius] Wilson's public works jobs proposal are a lot more politically realistic than housing and school integration."[5] Famed child psychologist Robert Coles doubts that "bureaucratically assisted realignment of neighborhood populations" is desirable, and Jennifer Hochschild, a gifted observer of race relations in America, worries that "absent a revolution in most Americans' preferences with regard to the race and class of their neighbors, Fiss's proposal is politically hopeless." Even Gary Orfield, one of the nation's most articulate and thoughtful advocates of metropolitan school integration, thinks that Congress will never make available the necessary housing vouchers, affordable housing, and changes in local land-use controls "when both political parties are responding to suburban majorities who are hostile to such policies."[6]

We harbor no illusions about the difficulties facing any attempt to build the broad political coalition necessary to enact the proposals outlined in the previous chapter. These difficulties include the deep divisions of interest and culture between the inner-city minority poor and white middle-class suburbanites. They also include the practical obstacles to building coalitions even among constituencies that share common interests. We understand that elected officials will only embrace measures to promote greater metropolitan equality if they are well managed, unobtrusive, and just one part of a larger package that serves, and is seen to serve, the interests of their constituents. Our political system is too prone to stalemate, and suburban opposition would be too strong, to support such measures if even a significant minority of suburbanites viewed them as a threat (even if a large majority of everybody else favored them).

Measures to deconcentrate the urban poor therefore cannot be adopted on their own. We are far more optimistic, however, that such measures can be part of a package of metropolitan reforms that also advances suburban interests. This requires dialogue, consensus building, and ultimately agreement. In other words, a new process of metropolitan civic engagement must unfold before the different parts of the metropolitan area will trust each other enough to step out of the prisoner's dilemma of metropolitan political fragmentation.[7] The current system heightens metropolitan divisions and works against the identification of common interests. If we can move toward greater metropolitan cooperation in practice, we can temper divisions and emphasize common interests. Those common interests, though latent, are real and are finding a growing number of supporters. The chances for new forms of metropolitan cooperation and new metropolitan coalitions are greater than many friendly skeptics think.

Several trends justify this optimism. Most crucially, it is simply wrong to say that suburbs are a homogeneous constituency lacking any shared interests with central cities. In fact, suburbs are highly varied and becoming more so. Perhaps a third are doing worse than central cities on such indicators as poverty rates and the incidence of crime.[8] Our discussion of Pasadena in Chapter 1 shows that poverty conditions have emerged even in well-off areas. Where suburbs are declining, suburbanites are more likely to vote like urban dwellers, except when they see that decline as emanating from adjacent central-city minority neighborhoods.[9]

More generally, most suburbanites continue to have an immediate economic interest in the central city where many of them earn their incomes. Suburban attachment to sports teams, cultural institutions, ethnic business districts in the "old neighborhood," and many other central-city institutions can also create a bond. When suburban residents see their towns losing out in the beggar-thy-neighbor game of metropolitan development, they may support our proposed reforms because they would benefit from them. Myron Orfield's efforts in metropolitan Minneapolis–St. Paul show that coalitions of mutual interest can be fashioned between central cities and inner suburbs.[10]

Even better-off suburbs are not what they used to be. As John Logan, William Frey, and a number of others have observed, white flight from increasingly black central cities to segregated white suburbs is no longer the main dynamic driving the demographic trajectories of our metropolitan areas.[11] The massive wave of immigration over the last four decades and the increased suburbanization of blacks, Latinos, and Asians have moved our metropolitan areas beyond the paradigm of "politics in black and white."[12] Although large central cities are all becoming less white, many, like New York and Los Angeles, are also becoming less black, as African Americans as well as whites suburbanize and immigrants and their children take their place. Most suburbs are also becoming more racially and ethnically diverse. Unlike in the 1960s and 1970s, these transitions are not pitting whites against blacks, but rather are creating more complex patterns. Although the full political implications of this shift have yet to play out, new forms of ethnic expression, and, in some cases, cooperation, are being overlaid on the black-white racial tensions that drove urban politics in the postwar period. The emerging politics of interethnic relations is not going to be easy, but at least it is less likely to be locked in racial polarization. More complex interracial coalitions will form. As Gary Orfield has observed, these trends surely offer "new possibilities for successful diversity."[13]

With the right leadership, sufficient dialogue, and new institutional settings, many suburbanites will come to see that our proposals serve their self-interest "rightly understood" (as Tocqueville put it). Many of us like to drive too fast or smoke cigarettes, yet most of us support the government's efforts to enforce speed limits and limit smoking. Although the present rules of the game encourage suburban jurisdictions to selfishly exclude the poor and bar multifamily rental housing, suburban residents may realize, on reflection, that the resulting high levels of economic segregation and sprawl not only harm the economic competitiveness of their metropolitan area, but saddle them with long commutes, rising congestion, and deteriorating natural environments.

Present institutional arrangements pose a classic collective action problem for any one part of the metropolis that seeks to protect the regional commons— that is, the shared interests of all members of the region. Adopting a new institutional framework that changes the rules of this game would make it easier to advance common interests. Even though narrower interests would persist, they would at least encounter claims on behalf of greater regional efficiency, environmental soundness, and equality of opportunity. Indeed, the growing movements for "smart growth," the "new regionalism," and "taking the regional high road to economic growth" show how we can move toward a broader concept of self-interest.

Metropolitan reform is politically feasible. The counterargument, in a nutshell, is that the suburbanites who constitute a majority of the national electorate are naturally conservative (owing to being small-town property owners) and will oppose aiding central cities or forming political coalitions with them. Republicans have accordingly used suburban opposition to urban policies and constituencies to attract support from working- and middle-class suburban voters who formerly identified with the Democratic Party. The differences in race, ethnicity, and class between suburban and central-city voters are large enough to overwhelm whatever they have in common.

A glance at the trends in national politics since 1960 and the current heartlands of Republican support would seem to validate this argument. We will show below, however, that Democratic presidential candidates defied conventional wisdom in 1992, 1996, and 2000 to add suburban voters to the urban base of the Democratic party. This Democratic suburban strategy enabled Bill Clinton to win twice and gave Al Gore the majority of the popular vote, if not the electoral college, in 2000. Similarly, Democratic congressional candidates have won many suburban districts outside the South. (Indeed, it was the long-term shift of white Southern Democrats to the Republican Party, not the growth of suburbia, that has given Republicans a national advantage.)

The Clinton administration did not push for the kinds of metropolitan reforms that we advocate here—although it considered a few of them in the second term. But the fact that it fashioned an urban-suburban electoral coalition demonstrates that central-city and suburban electorates are not irrevocably divided. Because suburbs are no longer lily-white middle-class enclaves, but are becoming both more diverse and more subject to economic segregation and sprawl, suburbanites are more open to appeals of the sort we outline. We use the three different congressional districts profiled in Chapter 1 to show how each might benefit from and support a metropolitan reform agenda. We end by identifying the political actors who are already pushing for a new metropolitics and clarifying what is at stake for American democracy.

THE DIVIDED METROPOLIS: SUBURBS VERSUS CENTRAL CITIES

Postwar suburbanization and rising metropolitan spatial segregation have had dramatic political consequences. The suburban component of the electorate has increased steadily since the late 1940s. By the early 1990s, national exit polls suggested that suburbanites represented over half the voters in presidential elections. The proportion of suburban seats has also increased in Congress and state legislatures. Along with the move away from parties and toward a candidate-centered, media-driven national politics, heavily dependent on corporate contributions, this has shifted the balance of national political power dramatically away from central cities. Suburban voters and congressional districts not only far outnumber their big-city counterparts; suburbanites also provide a disproportionate share of campaign contributions. As a result, we recognize that efforts to promote a metropolitan reform agenda must win support from a substantial component of the suburban electorate in coalition with central-city voters.

Some observers think this geographic shift has drawn a new fault line through American politics. Thomas and Mary Edsall argue in *Chain Reaction* (1991) that "suburbanization has permitted whites to satisfy liberal ideals revolving around activist government, while keeping to a minimum the number of blacks and the poor who share in government largess," leading toward "a national politics that will be dominated by the suburban vote."[14] William Schneider observed that suburban voters first became a majority in the 1992 election. As the center of gravity shifted to the suburbs, he argued, more voters' concerns would shift in a private, narrow direction. In this "suburban century," said Schneider, presidential candidates and congressional majorities pay no political price for ignoring urban America.[15]

Unquestionably, postwar suburbanization has altered the national political terrain. In 1944, thirty-two large old central cities cast 27 percent of the national vote in presidential elections. By 1992, their share had declined to 14 percent. Another study found that twelve large central cities cast 21.8 percent of the national vote in 1948 but only 6.3 percent in 2000 (up from 5.9 percent in 1996), even as they became more distinctly Democratic and less likely to vote compared with national patterns.[16] Residents of cities with populations over 500,000 cast only 9 percent of the vote in 2000.[17] Clearly, big-city electoral clout dwindled in the postwar years, especially in the large, old cities of the Northeast and Midwest.

Much of this loss happened because eligible voters moved from cities to suburbs. It also happened because central-city voters became less active compared with those in the suburbs. During the Depression and the New Deal, urban political machines and labor unions mobilized urban voters, enabling large cities to match the national rate of turnout. Their propensity to vote peaked in 1944 at 113 percent of the national average and remained above it through 1952. After that, urban voter turnout declined relative to the rest of the nation. In 1960, voter turnout was 62 percent in the thirty-two major central cities, compared with 64 percent in the nation. Only in two presidential elections since then, 1976 and 1984, did urban turnout exceed the national average. Otherwise, it was well below the national level. In 1992, for example, urban turnout was 47 percent compared with the overall rate of 55 percent.[18] According to Peter Nardulli, Jon Dalager, and Donald Greco, "This drop in the relative propensity to vote accounts for almost 40 percent of the loss in voting power experienced by these cities between 1944 and 1992. Based on a drop in the cities' share of the national electorate, they should have dropped only 8 points (from 27 percent to 19 percent) rather than 13 points."[19] Although the rising immigrant noncitizen and ex-offender populations in many big cities also explains this drop, the demobilization of eligible urban voters clearly compounded the trend.

This shift had a major impact on state politics as well as national politics. As the share of voters living in large central cities fell in the major states, presidential candidates, governors, and state legislators paid less attention to the needs of those cities. In 1948, New York City cast 50 percent of the votes in New York State, Chicago cast 46.5 percent of Illinois' ballots, Baltimore had 42.3 percent of the Maryland vote, and Detroit had 31.8 percent of Michigan's. Los Angeles and San Francisco combined for 51.3 percent of the California vote, while Philadelphia and Pittsburgh formed 30.7 percent of Pennsylvania's electorate. Because these were key states in the electoral college, the relative mobilization of their big-city vote could be decisive in national elections. By 2000, New York City cast only 31.6 percent of the presidential votes in New York State. The shares of Chicago (20.2 percent), Baltimore (9.6 percent), Detroit (6.5 percent), Los Angeles and San Francisco (10.6 percent), and Philadelphia and Pittsburgh (13.9 percent) fell precipitously.[20]

Similar trends have affected Congress. Harold Wolman and Lisa Marckini found that central-city districts in the U.S. House of Representatives declined 23 percent between the 1960s and the 1990s, from 121 to 93, while suburban districts rose 96 percent, from 122 to 239.[21] Excluding the more conservative cities of the South and West, urban House districts fell even more sharply, from 62 to 40. Wolman and Marckini conclude that "Congress has changed from an institution that largely reflected nonmetropolitan interests to one that is now thoroughly dominated by suburban representatives."[22] The same trends have also weakened cities' influence in state governments, where suburban politicians now dominate state legislatures.[23] As a result, the road to the political and legislative majorities necessary for enacting the programs we have proposed runs squarely through the suburbs. But which way will suburban voters lean? Will they side with the more conservative, white, middle-class Republican countryside, or with the more liberal, white, ethnic, minority, Catholic, working-class, Democratic city side? The answer depends a great deal on how parties, leaders, and the media frame the issues.

Republicans have gained a good deal of political ground since 1968 by activating the class and racial sentiments that divide residents of the suburbs from those of central cities. The "subtractive" politics of wooing white suburban Democrats away their party's nominee enabled Republican candidates to win five out of six presidential elections between 1968 and 1988. (The one exception was Jimmy Carter's 1976 post-Watergate victory.) For their part, Democrats found it difficult to forge an "additive" politics that bridged the differences between the central cities and inner suburbs. Republican candidates had long found their most supportive base in rural constituencies and white, well-to-do, predominantly Protestant suburbs. They also gained steadily in the South as whites left the Democratic Party over its commitment to civil rights and activist government. To achieve an electoral college majority, however, Republicans also had to improve their appeal to traditional Democrats in the suburbs, especially blue-collar and middle-class white Catholics. Republican presidential candidates used urban unrest, welfare dependency, and crime as wedge issues to shift these voters to their side.

Until 1994, Republicans were far less successful in applying "subtractive politics" to elections for the House of Representatives and could not defeat enough Democratic incumbents in Southern, suburban, and small town districts to gain a majority. (The senior George Bush's ability to beat Bill Clinton in 33 of the 82 Southern districts with Democratic incumbents in 1992 suggested just how ripe that body was for such an attack.) Until 1994, white voters in Southern and suburban districts evidently viewed their Democratic incumbents more favorably than they did the Democratic presidential candidate.

To win both white Southern Democratic and northern suburban Democratic districts in 1994, Speaker Newt Gingrich and his Republican team mounted a campaign to capitalize on voter resentment over paying federal taxes for programs that benefitted urban constituencies. They could make this appeal without fear of alienating nonwhite voters, because few were in their base. They sought to convince white Democrats, typically Catholics in the North and Protestants in the South, Midwest, and West, mostly in married-couple families, that they were socially and ideologically closer to the white, rural, and small-town Protestant Republican core than to the increasingly black and Latino residents of larger central cities, many of whom lived in female-headed households. Republicans portrayed themselves as occupying the moral high ground on the racial divide by asserting that liberal Democratic welfare programs perpetuated—indeed, perhaps caused—inner-city poverty. White Democrats in rural and suburban areas were receptive to claims that overly generous welfare programs were to blame for persistent urban poverty and that Republicans could get government out of their wallets by terminating these failing welfare programs.

Gingrich's "nationalization" of the 1994 House elections succeeded brilliantly. Republicans won 58 seats formerly held by Democrats while losing only 5 of their own. Soon after the election, five surviving Southern Democrats, like

Billy Tauzin of Louisiana, changed parties. This victory enabled Republicans to end six decades of Democratic control of the House. Almost all of the Republican gain occurred outside the Northeast: they scored net gains of 15 seats in the Midwest and 18 each in the South and West, mostly in suburban and mixed districts. Typical was Indiana's second district, whose biggest town is Muncie, the famous "Middletown" of the Lynds' books. The white blue-collar voters of Muncie and the district's other small cities worked at Cummins Engine, General Motors, and other manufacturers. When Philip Sharp, the moderate Democrat who had represented the area since 1975, retired in 1994, David McIntosh, a former Reagan and Bush administration official, managed to defeat his Democratic opponent by 54 to 46 percent by identifying him with the Clinton administration's crime bill; "within months [he] became one of Newt Gingrich's key political operatives."[24]

CROSSING THE LINE BY BUILDING CENTRAL CITY–SUBURBAN COALITIONS

Despite the success of the "politics of subtraction" in 1994, Democrat presidential candidate Bill Clinton won majorities in urban and suburban districts in the 1992 and 1996 presidential election on his way to pluralities of the national vote. Indeed, he won in more suburban congressional districts than either George Bush in 1992 or Robert Dole in 1996. Table 8.1 shows that Clinton won 88 of 152 suburban districts in 1992, increasing that number to 100 in 1996. His ability to win support from "Reagan Democrats" — white, ethnic, often Catholic, blue-collar and middle-class voters — provides an important lesson about how central-city and suburban voters might be united behind a metropolitan agenda — and what sorts of obstacles this effort will face.

Clinton's 1992 campaign pollster, Stanley Greenberg, spent the 1980s studying "Reagan Democrats." He argued that the Democratic Party's focus on urban blacks had "crowded out" the "forgotten middle class." These descendants of New Deal supporters told Greenberg that they believed that the urban poor lacked a work ethic and basic family values and that the federal aid they received was unwarranted. Republican candidates effectively articulated these themes. Given the gradual and perhaps permanent loss of southern whites to the Republicans, Greenberg argued that defection of northern suburbanites was the key ingredient of Republican national presidential majorities.[25] To bring this vote back into the Democratic fold while maintaining support in the Democrats' urban base, he urged candidate Clinton to develop a "common ground"

TABLE 8.1. Voting Trends by Congressional District Type

	Central City	Suburban	Rural	Mixed	Total
1990 citizen voting-age population	31,164,126	60,847,890	30,835,882	51,784,685	174,632,583
1992 presidential vote	17,485,402	37,669,244	17,770,011	31,357,616	104,279,273
1992 turnout	56.11%	61.91%	57.62%	60.55%	59.71%
Clinton vote (1992)	55.48%	41.13%	40.80%	38.98%	42.84%
Bush vote (1992)	29.43%	38.93%	43.37%	39.31%	37.60%
Clinton districts (1992)	66/82	88/152	38/74	62/127	254/435
1994 House vote	10,562,896	23,759,116	11,710,294	20,325,285	66,357,591
1994 turnout	33.89%	39.05%	37.98%	39.25%	38.00%
House Democratic vote (1994)	60.50%	44.14%	43.36%	43.74%	46.84%
House Republican vote (1994)	37.65%	53.52%	53.25%	54.20%	51.15%
Democratic districts (1994)	62/82	60/152	33/74	46/127	201/435
1996 vote	15,378,067	34,730,013	16,391,509	29,191,004	95,690,893
1996 turnout	49.35%	57.08%	53.16%	56.37%	54.80%
Clinton vote (1996)	62.18%	49.17%	45.42%	45.19%	49.4%
Dole vote (1996)	30.63%	41.47%	43.88%	44.48%	41.04%
Clinton districts (1996)	70/82	100/152	44/74	65/127	279/435
1998 House vote	9,545,946	20,722,413	10,987,871	18,796,764	60,052,994

TABLE 8.1. Continued

	Central City	Suburban	Rural	Mixed	Total
1998 turnout	30.63%	34.06%	35.63%	36.30%	34.66%
House Democratic vote (1998)	64.30%	46.23%	44.43%	43.69%	47.98%
House Republican vote (1998)	32.02%	50.54%	52.53%	53.27%	48.82%
Democratic districts (1998)	64/82	71/152	29/74	48/172	212/435
2000 citizen voting age population	28,269,112	62,896,964	33,621,136	55,933,395	180,720,607
2000 vote	16,589,906	38,404,673	17,886,981	32,187,837	105,069,392
2000 turnout	58.69%	61.06%	53.20%	57.55%	58.14%
Gore vote (2000)	62.85%	49.55%	42.06%	42.95%	48.36%
Bush vote (2000)	33.21%	46.75%	55.01%	53.19%	47.99%
Gore districts (2000)	68/82	91/152	14/74	34/127	207/435
House Democratic vote (2000)	64.22	46.46	44.33	42.57	47.50
House Republican vote (2000)	34.83	50.00	51.84	53.70	49.22
Democratic districts (2000)	65/82	74/152	28/74	46/172	213/435

Source: 1992–98 election results from U.S. Clerk of the House, "Statistics of the Presidential and Congressional Elections," available at http://clerk.house.gov/members/election _information/elections.php. Citizen Voting Age population from U.S. Census Bureau, 1990 and 2000 Censuses of Population. Districts are classified by whether the majority of their 1990 population lived in central cities with 30,000 or more, urbanized areas not in central cities, or rural areas. Where no population type was a majority, they were classified as mixed districts. Vermont's independent House member was reclassified a Democrat, and a Virginia independent was classified as a Republican. Turnout is expressed as a proportion of 1990 citizen voting age population except for 2000, where it is expressed as a proportion of 2000 citizen voting-age population.

message.[26] Even though the embers of the Los Angeles riot still smoldered in May 1992, Clinton campaigned in nearby Orange and San Diego County suburbs, linking the problems of suburbanites with those of the inner cities.[27]

In the 1992 election, the constituencies that were most likely to favor Clinton—blacks, Hispanics, Jews, white liberals, union households, and senior citizens—were also disproportionately located in cities.[28] As a southern Democratic governor elected by a biracial coalition in the South, Clinton knew that he needed black votes and was comfortable campaigning in black churches and neighborhoods. Big-city party organizations and public employee unions also provided the bulk of his field operations. But Clinton needed to project his appeal beyond city lines to achieve an electoral majority. He signaled to suburban voters that he spoke to their interests by talking about defending the middle-class standard of living (for example, health care reform), promoting middle-class values (for example, "ending welfare as we know it"), and achieving economic competitiveness (for example, balancing the budget and adopting the North American Free Trade Agreement). Although he tried to project these messages in ways that would not antagonize his urban base, he was not above distancing himself from urban blacks, as when he criticized black rap singer Sister Souljah's lyrics. Table 8.1 shows that central-city voters gave Clinton a 55–29 margin in 1992. When combined with the 41–39 margin he got in suburban districts, where he won 800,000 more votes than Bush senior, he achieved a narrow 43–38 victory over the Republican incumbent.

Clinton's ability to widen and deepen his urban and suburban support in 1996, absorbing many of those who had voted for Ross Perot in 1992, showed that advocating a middle-class politics could win support in both areas without alienating either. In 1996, his margin over Dole widened by 8 points. As Table 8.1 shows, his support surged from 55 to 62 percent in central-city districts (although central-city turnout declined more than the overall vote between the two elections), while his margin grew to 49 to 41 in suburban districts. This 1996 victory owed much to Speaker Newt Gingrich's pursuit of the "Contract with America" after the 1994 Republican takeover of the House. Many suburban voters came to perceive Republican efforts to cut federal social welfare spending as threatening not only the inner-city poor but also programs that benefited the suburban middle class. The budget conflicts of the 104th Congress swung public sentiment in Clinton's direction.

During the 2000 Democratic primaries, Al Gore and Bill Bradley both tried to meld urban and suburban supporters by advocating federal social policies that would address urban ills along with measures that would limit suburban sprawl.[29] In the controversial general election, exit polls indicated that Gore beat George W. Bush by 71 percent to 26 percent in big cities and 57 percent to 40 percent in smaller cities, but got only 47 percent of the vote to Bush's 49 percent in the suburbs. Table 8.1 shows that Democratic candidate Al Gore once again assembled a central city–suburban coalition, winning 63–33 in predominantly urban districts and 50–47 in predominantly suburban districts, while Bush got far more support than Dole in mixed and rural districts. Gore had a narrower margin of victory in predominantly urban and suburban districts than Clinton had in 1996, however. Gore beat Bush in 9 fewer suburban congressional districts than Clinton won in 1996 and 72 fewer districts overall. The geographic distribution of the Democratic vote in 2000 — specifically Gore's failure to win the cities and suburbs by as wide a margin as Clinton in 1996 — enabled George Bush to become president even without winning a majority of the popular vote. In 2002, as we shall see, redistricting, the attacks of September 11, and going to war, enabled Republicans to erase the gains Democrats had made in Congress between 1994 and 2000.

The evidence of the 1992, 1996, and 2000 presidential elections suggests that Democratic candidates can organize a central city–suburban coalition electoral majority around a program that promotes the middle-class (read suburban) quality of life while helping urban constituencies in ways that do not accentuate their differences with the suburbs. But the electoral experience of this period shows that the Clinton administration was no more successful at converting this presidential electoral coalition into a durable congressional majority than Republican presidents had been at consolidating a rural–small town–suburban alliance. The Clinton administration's metropolitan program was an ad hoc collection of policies appealing to specific constituencies, not the comprehensive approach to synthesizing urban and suburban interests recommended here.[30] Instead of reducing the cleavages between urban and suburban voters or building on the commonalities between them, President Clinton emphasized specific differences with the Republicans that enabled him to engage in symbolic populism while downplaying racially charged issues. Although members of his administration explored a metropolitan approach to domestic policy, they abandoned this effort after 1994 in order to fight such basic battles as preventing the Department of Housing and Urban Development from being dismantled.

Given the historic importance of the large Democratic House majorities for the passage of urban legislation, achieving a Democratic congressional majority is probably necessary, if not sufficient, for carrying out a new metropolitan agenda.[31] Although Democrats gained suburban seats in the 1996, 1998, and 2000 House elections and compelled Republicans to soften their stark 1994 program, they did not win back all the seats they lost in 1994. When Democrats controlled the House before 1994, southern Democrats often voted with Republicans to form a conservative majority that blocked or restrained avowedly pro-urban legislation.[32] After their historic 1994 victory, Republicans were unable to expand their numbers in the House. Their attacks on welfare and other urban programs alienated urban voters, while their attempts to alter broad-based programs like Social Security and Medicare angered suburban voters. The impeachment of the president also did not seem to please many who voted Republican in the 1994 House elections.[33]

As a result, Republicans lost a net of fifteen seats to the Democrats in the 1998 House elections, eleven in suburbs outside the South. (Their candidates won twenty-seven other House races by less than 20,000 votes.) House Democrats continued to gain in 2000, but not enough to regain control. Between 1996 and 2000, Democrats gained a net of 3 predominantly urban seats and 11 predominantly suburban seats, but lost a net of 6 rural and 1 mixed district seats. In 2000, Republicans held a slim majority of predominantly suburban House seats, 78 to 74, as well as the great majority of rural and mixed seats. In short, House Democrats never matched President Clinton's dominance of the suburban vote.

Redistricting changed the political geography of House districts for the 2002 elections. Republicans further concentrated Democratic votes in urban districts, making the remaining suburban, mixed, and rural districts more competitive for Republicans, exactly the opposite of what we recommend. The changing boundaries make it impossible to make an exact comparison between the two sets of districts, but we can classify the districts in each system according to the same density scale. A comparison of the two systems on this common scale shows that the densest districts now cast slightly more Democratic votes for House candidates. The September 11 attack on New York and Washington, the war in Afghanistan, and the conflict in Iraq also favored Republican candidates in the 2002 elections.

The Democratic share of all votes for House candidates declined from 48.8 percent in 1998 (the previous off-year election) to 45.3 in 2002. The Republican net gain of 14 House seats between 2000 and 2002 reversed the previous trend, an unusual achievement in an off-year election for the party holding the White House. The 2004 presidential and congressional elections will therefore be pivotal in determining the political climate for movement toward a metropolitan agenda. The further concentration of Democratic votes in urban districts will make this more difficult.

Table 8.1 reveals two other crucial features of the metropolitan political terrain. First, using 1990 baseline data, the voter turnout rate in central-city congressional districts lagged persistently behind those of suburban, rural, and mixed districts in the 1990s. (In 2000, new baseline data suggests that the decline of the turnout rate in urban districts was less pronounced, mainly because the eligible population of these districts declined over the decade. It remained below that of suburban areas, however.) Urban turnout was typically well below the national average. In the 1992, 1996, and 2000 presidential elections, the central city–suburban difference in turnout was 5.8 percentage points, 10.7 points, and 2.4 points. In the 1994 and 1996 off-year elections, it was 6.3 points and 4.6 points. If Democratic presidential candidates are to offset the Republican advantage in mixed and nonmetropolitan areas by building large urban majorities, they must clearly bring urban turnout rates closer to the national average. In this respect, Democrats narrowed the turnout gap substantially in the 2000 election, but they still have more to do.

Second, Table 8.1 also shows that the voting-age citizen population of urban districts declined 9.3 percent between 1990 and 2000, while that of the suburban, rural, and mixed districts increased. This reflects the ongoing movement of voting-age citizens away from central cities toward less urbanized regions of the country and the growing relative importance of winning in suburban districts.

There are many reasons why urban voters are less likely to go to the polls than their suburban and rural counterparts. We have reviewed at length how concentrated poverty depresses civic engagement, including voting. Yet the negative association between population density and turnout remains statistically strong even after controlling for income, (white) race, educational attainment, and home ownership (all of which promote turnout and Republican advantage). Urban voters are less likely to turn out not only because they are more likely to be poor than suburbanites but also because they live in overwhelmingly Democratic areas where Republicans rarely field viable candidates. It makes less sense for central-city voters to participate in general elections when the Democratic primary has determined the outcome; the votes of those who do turn out are "wasted" because Democratic candidates pile up many more votes than they need to win. For example, Democratic candidates for central-city House seats piled up almost a million more votes than they needed to win their districts comfortably in 1998. If the redistricting process had transferred these votes to suburban districts, instead of the opposite, Democratic candidates would have had a better chance in more suburban districts while the urban districts would also have become more competitive without unduly compromising Democratic representation.

TABLE 8.2. Uncontested House Seats by Party and District Density, 2002 Congressional Elections

District Density	Party of Incumbent (%)		Total (%)
	Republican	Democrat	
Lowest (least urban)	12	4	16
Low mid	19	5	24
High mid	10	8	18
Highest (most urban)	3	20	23
Total	42	39	81

Source: 2002 election results from U.S. Clerk of the House, "Statistics of the Presidential and Congressional Elections," available at http://clerk.house.gov/members/election_information/elections.php. Uncontested means one major party did not field a candidate. Density from U.S. Census 2000 108th Congressional District Summary files.

Table 8.2 uses the common density scale to examine the congressional districts drawn in 2001. It shows that one of the major parties failed to contest almost one in five House seats in 2002, but that each party's uncontested seats were located in different places. Half of the uncontested Democratic seats (20 of 39) were highly dense, urban congressional districts. The Republican uncontested seats, by contrast, may be found in all types of areas. The lack of political competition for uncontested Democratic seats is thus felt predominantly in central-city districts, while that of the Republicans is not as concentrated in that party's base area. Table 8.3 examines the Democratic margin among seats contested by both parties in 2002. It shows that Democratic voters and Democratic winning margins are heavily concentrated in the densest urban districts, while the Republican margins are greater in less dense districts, but nearly as concentrated. Even in contested elections, therefore, the Democrats' lopsided margin in urban areas probably depresses turnout. More importantly, Democratic votes are concentrated in districts that Democrats have already won. The net result is to make Republican votes count more in the less dense districts and to make the Democratic votes in dense districts count less. Making contests for the dense urban seats more competitive would not only make them more interesting to voters, resulting in higher central-city turnout, but would also improve Democratic prospects in less dense, more suburban districts by making them more winnable. This evidence strongly suggests that stretching urban districts across city lines would increase the suburban House members' support for the policy agendas of urban voters.[34] The 2001 redistricting process produced just the opposite trend, making it harder for Democrats to win con-

TABLE 8.3. Party Margin for Contested House Seats by District Density, 2002 Congressional Elections

District Density	Vote Margin (%)					
	Most Republican (R Margin ≥ 40%)	Republican (R Margin 20 to 40%)	Competitive (R Margin 20 to −20%)	Democratic (R Margin −20 to −40%)	Most Democratic (R Margin ≤ −40%)	Total
Lowest	17	29	24	18	5	93
Low mid	16	27	25	12	5	85
High mid	17	28	21	19	6	91
Highest	1	11	9	24	40	85
Total	51	95	79	73	56	354

Source: 2002 election results from U.S. Clerk of the House, "Statistics of the Presidential and Congressional Elections," available at http://clerk.house.gov/members/election _information/elections.php. Uncontested means one major party did not field a candidate. Density from U.S. Census 2000 108th Congressional District Summary files.

gressional seats in suburban districts that were redrawn to be insulated from urban voters.

The nation's 152 suburban congressional districts became significantly more diverse during the 1990s. When designed in 1991, their residents were more likely to be white, middle class, home owning, in families with children, and employed than residents of central-city districts. Even in 1992, however, the average suburban congressional district was definitely not lily-white. Their average white population was 76 percent, while their average black population was 9 percent, their Hispanic population 10 percent, and their Asian population 4 percent. But these averages mask a wide variation. The most black suburban district was 64 percent black; the most Hispanic was 84 percent Hispanic; and the most Asian was 64 percent Asian. Some suburban districts had as many as 54 percent of their population renting apartments.

In 1990, the population of suburban districts averaged 12.3 percent British ancestry, but they also averaged 9.9 percent Irish and 6.8 percent Italian ancestry, suggesting substantial Catholic populations. An average of 6 percent of their households received public assistance, 9.3 percent were poor, 10.6 percent of their young people were high school dropouts, 21 percent of the adults lacked a high school diploma, 28 percent have only a high school degree, 23 percent of the adults were in blue-collar occupations, and 25 percent of the households received Social Security benefits. The median 1990 household incomes of suburban congressional districts averaged $36,224, but one in five had a median income below that of the nation, $28,905.

Two out of five of these suburban districts had 1990 minority populations of 20 percent or more. These districts cast 24 percent of the suburban presidential vote in 1996 and 27 percent of the suburban House vote in 1998, clearly favoring the Democratic candidates. Even in the remaining predominantly white suburban districts, Clinton and House Democrats were competitive in the 1990s. This shows that a great many suburban residents, especially in increasingly diverse districts, are willing to coalesce politically with urban voters around a program favoring middle- and working-class interests.[35]

When 2000 data became available for these same districts, the average black percentage had risen above 10, the Hispanic average was up to 14, and the Asian average was above 5. Conversely, British ancestry had declined to 8.6 percent. The average foreign-born percentage was 14.7, and the suburban district average of renters was 32.5 percent. Clearly, a decade of demographic change had reshaped the suburban political terrain. Even after the Republicans did their best to turn this terrain to their advantage in redistricting, the 2002 suburban congressional districts remain socially and economically varied, although perhaps slightly less so than in 2000.

This is especially true where suburbanites continue to have ties with the central city. On average, 35 percent of employed residents of suburban congressional districts worked in central cities in 1990. The more central-city commuters, the more likely the district was to vote for Democratic candidates for Congress during the 1990s.[36] Residential density and union membership, independent of other demographic characteristics, also powerfully promote Democratic voting in suburban districts. A one percentage point increase in unionized workers produced three-quarters of a percentage point increase in the 1998 vote for the Democratic House candidate.[37] Efforts to promote union membership and to foster clustered suburban development will thus have a positive long-term impact on support for the policies we proposed. In other words, place counts in politics, as in the rest of life.

Most political analysts do not pay enough attention to this fact. They see place of residence as having only a modest influence on one's political orientation, or do not even include it in their analysis, relying instead on such individual factors as race, ethnicity, religion, gender, and income to explain values, ideological leanings, and voting patterns. How people fit into these various categories certainly does affect how they line up on the liberal-conservative and Democratic-Republican scales. But the concentration of social groups in some places and not in others also influences voting patterns. Even after controlling for individual characteristics, local context still has a big impact on how people behave politically.

Controlling for basic racial, ethnic, and religious categories and family characteristics, urban dwellers give stronger support to Democrats and liberal positions than do their suburban counterparts, who in turn are more supportive than rural dwellers. In the 1994 congressional elections, for example, the exit polls showed that married white Protestants with children living in big cities gave 61 percent of their votes to Democratic House candidates, compared with only 35 percent of similar people living in small cities and only 31 percent of those living in suburbs. Big-city white married Catholics with children gave Democrats 46 percent support in big cities, 52 percent in small cities, and 31 percent in suburbs. The 1996 exit poll showed that urban whites gave President Clinton 56 percent of their votes, suburban whites 47 percent, and rural whites 40 percent. Similar patterns hold for other racial groups. Despite the fact that pollsters routinely pluck people out of their context, their political attitudes and actions cannot be fully understood without an appreciation for the webs of political, social, and economic relations they share with their neighbors. Many aspects of the urban context promote support for Democrats. As the suburbs become more urbanized, Democrats will be increasingly able to contest any Republican advantages. This may be most pronounced in the "mini-central cities" that have emerged in the suburban realm, such as the Pasadena and Silicon Valley cases described earlier.

America's first-by-the-gate election system also makes place important. One does not win a national election with 50 percent plus one of the national vote. Instead, as the 2000 election vividly demonstrated, a presidential candidate must win pluralities in a sufficient number of states to achieve a majority in the electoral college. (This favors small states that have two senators and one House member, even when their populations fall below what would otherwise be required for a seat.) Likewise, control of the U.S. Senate is based on winning states, not a national majority. To control the House, a party must win electoral majorities in 218 of the 435 districts. In a presidential election, all votes that push a presidential candidate above a comfortable majority do not count, nor do any votes that fail to bring a candidate close to a majority. The rational candidate in such a system therefore shifts his or her attention away from noncompetitive states to competitive ones. The downside, of course, is that national presidential campaigns spend little time on local races in noncompetitive states. Local elected officials representing noncompetitive (and often uncontested) seats also have little incentive to mobilize voters to increase the statewide chances for their party and its candidates for the House, Senate, or governor.

TOWARD A METROPOLITAN POLITICAL STRATEGY

How, then, should those who advocate an urban-suburban alliance think about winning suburban majorities? We must begin by recognizing that the suburbs, despite being varied, do differ from central cities. If we array suburban House districts along several key dimensions, we find that the suburban districts were an average of 67.6 percent white in 2000, down from 76 percent in 1990. The population of suburban districts still lives predominantly in married-couple families, a large minority of whom have children under age eighteen. Most live in and own single-family homes. At the same time, two-thirds of all women, including two-thirds of all mothers with children under eighteen, work. Half of all children have two working parents, the vast majority of white adults lack a college degree, a third of all workers still commute to the central city, more than one in five work in a blue-collar occupation, a substantial minority work for government or nonprofit organizations, about 10 percent belong to unions, and a quarter of the households rely on Social Security. The members of these hardworking, middle-income families, who are mainly not highly educated managers or professionals, form the critical terrain on which American politics will be fought out.[38]

In the wake of the 2000 census, advocates of a metropolitan strategy should have convinced those responsible for redistricting to shift population from the overwhelmingly Democratic central-city House seats toward suburban House districts. Democrats held fourteen of the fifteen uncontested central-city House seats in 1998, while Republicans held twenty-six of the thirty-five uncontested suburban House seats. The 1998 Democratic vote margin over Republicans in central-city districts (more than 3 million) was far larger than the Republican margin in the suburbs (only 89,000 votes) in that off-year election. In House seats contested by both major parties, this imbalance was even more obvious (Democrats piled up 2.4 million more votes in the central cities, compared with only 34,000 for the Republicans in the suburbs).

Moving heavily Democratic precincts into suburban congressional districts would have made all districts more competitive and help forge central city–inner suburban political coalitions. Unfortunately, this did not happen. Republicans controlled redistricting in most states. The resulting districts were, according to one observer, "the most incumbent-friendly in American history" and "froze into place" a bias that gives Republicans "roughly a 50-seat head start in the battle for Congress." The combination of these factors "might prevent Democrats from regaining control of Congress in this decade, even if public opinion shifts heavily in their favor."[39]

Finally, those who wish to mobilize political support for a new metropolitan majority must develop a new political rhetoric. The urban ghetto underclass has been used as a kind of bogeyman to frighten white working-class suburbanites into supporting conservative Republicans and opposing domestic policies associated with central-city constituencies. This dynamic has produced negative consequences for metropolitan areas. Local opinion leaders can appeal to both suburban and urban constituencies on behalf of the policies proposed in the previous chapter. Such ideas as limiting sprawl, bringing housing and work closer together, improving metropolitan transportation, promoting regional cooperation, and ending destructive bidding wars for private investment will appeal to suburbanites as well as central-city residents. Smart growth policies save money by using infrastructure that is already in place instead of building expensive new roads, sewers, and water lines, by diversifying inner-city poverty concentrations, and by attracting jobs and residents back to central cities and declining suburbs.

The task of bridging the divisions between suburban and central-city voters and advancing ideas like these will not be easy, given the way political elites (Democrats as well as Republicans) have played on them in the past. The following steps can help a new metropolitan coalition overcome these divisions.

- Make clear, effective, substantive policy appeals to white, Catholic, blue-collar suburbanites, whose once strong familial attachment to progressive positions has weakened, by addressing their actual needs, which revolve around the reality that they are working harder but not gaining a higher standard of living or achieving a more family-friendly workplace.
- Communicate with and mobilize emerging black and Hispanic suburban populations with nonracial appeals that speak to the same kinds of needs.
- Emphasize issues that cross group boundaries and move them toward cooperation, rather than heightening intergroup polarization. The most potent policies would support working mothers, promote fathers' involvement in family life, improve schooling, and create new work opportunities for their children as they come of working age.
- Use existing county Democratic Party organizations, or develop new multi-county metropolitan party organizations, to strengthen working relationships between central-city political activists and suburban Democratic candidates for the House.
- Encourage all other groups mobilized in city politics, be they trade unions, church groups, or community organizations, to develop a metropolitan per-

spective on their work, following the example set by the Texas Industrial Areas Foundation and the Los Angeles County Federation of Labor.

- Follow Myron Orfield's lead in building regional coalitions of central cities and older, working-class suburbs in favor of tax-sharing schemes that would share the benefits of regional growth taking place in favored-quarter suburbs.
- Rally around existing efforts and help establish new regional efforts at collaborative planning for regional economic development, economic competitiveness, infrastructure investment, housing, labor force development, and regional environmental quality, making sure that equity remains high on the regional agenda.
- Encourage corporations with a regional perspective (through their site locations, supplier networks, employee residence base, and logistical needs) to take the lead in addressing these issues.
- Form regional legislative caucuses at the local, state, and federal levels.

It should be clear from these recommended steps that we do not expect a new metropolitan coalition to emerge from local elected officials, least of all Democratic big-city mayors. Instead, we envision a grassroots movement from below — involving unions, churches, community organizations, foundations, major employers, and others — that mounts nonpartisan campaigns around these goals. But these local efforts will ultimately be effective only if they find support with state and national political entrepreneurs — most likely but not necessarily always Democrats — who advance these coalitions by pushing for favorable legislation at the state and federal levels. Ultimately, of course, these political entrepreneurs will have to achieve legislative majorities in state houses and Congress. We now turn to the ways in which both grassroots activists and state and national political entrepreneurs can pursue such strategies, using the three congressional districts described in Chapter 1 as examples.

CROSSING THE CITY LINE: THE THREE CONGRESSIONAL DISTRICTS

Consider how the congresspersons highlighted in the first chapter — New York's Sixteenth District in the South Bronx, Illinois' Thirteenth District in suburban Chicago, and California's former Twenty-seventh District (now Twenty-ninth) in suburban Los Angeles — would respond to the ideas presented here. In the past, federal policies have profoundly shaped each district, producing local outcomes that exemplify the broader trends described in earlier chapters. Each would find ways to go beyond the limits of past trends in our proposed programs.

Federal policies had a devastating impact on New York's Sixteenth Congressional District.[40] Urban renewal and freeway construction directly assaulted its neighborhoods, and Federal Housing Administration (FHA) mortgages drained away much of its middle class to the suburbs. The construction of the Cross-Bronx Expressway displaced 15,000 people and destroyed the heart of the neighborhood, while making the South Bronx a corridor for those commuting into the city from suburbs in Westchester County, New Jersey, and elsewhere. Construction of Co-op City in the Northeast Bronx, with state subsidies, also siphoned away families from the South Bronx. Meanwhile, construction of numerous public housing projects concentrated poor families, primarily African Americans and then Puerto Ricans, in the area, with all the negative effects we examined in Chapter 3.[41] In the 1970s, an epidemic of arson for profit, bank redlining, and housing abandonment left the area increasingly depopulated.

Congressman Jose Serrano has represented the district since 1990, when he replaced a previous incumbent indicted for corruption. When he won reelection in 2002 with 62 percent of the vote, only 78,454 voters went to the polls, fewer than in all but six other contested House races. Because his district had the lowest per capita income of all 435 House districts, he naturally supports federal programs that bring jobs and benefits to the inner-city poor. Serrano has one of the most liberal voting records in Congress, overwhelmingly favorable toward unions, environmental groups, senior citizens, and other liberal constituencies.[42]

After the spiral of decline in the 1970s and 1980s, the South Bronx experienced a significant rebound in the 1990s. Although a Clinton-era federal empowerment zone covers a small part of the district, most of this improvement can be attributed to the city's Ten-Year Housing Program, begun by Mayor Koch and continued through the Dinkins and Giuliani administrations. It rebuilt much of the rental housing abandoned by private owners, often with the involvement of local community development corporations, churches, and tenant groups. In addition, the substantial reduction in crime rates during the last decade has been pivotal in encouraging reinvestment in local housing and businesses. Together, the decrease in the crime rate, the success of the new housing developments, and the rebound of the area's population provide the Bronx with good reasons to be proud.

At the same time, few working-age adults in the South Bronx benefitted from the growth of corporate service employment in the 1990s. The most important problem facing Serrano's constituents remains the lack of employment. (Only one other district, in Detroit, had fewer employed working-age men.) Although the hospitals and government agencies of the Bronx employ many of Serrano's constituents, and parts of the private sector continue to function (for example, the city's wholesale produce market), it is unlikely, the empowerment zone and Yankee Stadium notwithstanding, that many more big private employers will move into the South Bronx.

Midtown Manhattan is only a subway ride away, but most residents of the South Bronx do not have the credentials to work in the corporate service economy. The employment centers of suburban Westchester County are close by and afford employment opportunities to lower-skilled people, but they are not accessible by public transportation. It would be strongly in the interest of Serrano's constituents to be able to move closer to these opportunities, or at least to have better transportation links to them. Serrano might oppose mobility policies if they led his working-class Hispanic constituents to migrate away from his district, but he would surely favor opening up more job opportunities for them. He would also applaud policies that would lead other towns in the northern part of the New York metropolitan area to take his constituents into consideration in their housing, labor market, and transportation policies.

In the long run, therefore, Congressman Serrano would realize that increased residential choices would benefit not just those who move but also those who remain in his district. People should not feel that they are trapped in the South Bronx. If they were helped to move to suburbs or better-off parts of the city, they would have better access to jobs and other opportunities. Those who chose to stay in the Sixteenth District would do so out of a strong sense of attachment, not because it was a last resort. Further investment in the housing, economic development, and infrastructure of the South Bronx would encourage middle-class people to move in. No longer would a negative stereotype of the South Bronx as a zone of concentrated poverty be used to drive a wedge between, say, the residents of that neighborhood and the residents of Westchester.

Illinois' Thirteenth Congressional District lies at the other end of the economic spectrum from the South Bronx.[43] It includes the southern part of DuPage County, the southwest corner of Cook County, and the northern section of Will County, comprising mostly upper-middle-class suburbs of Chicago. The population of DuPage County, west of Chicago, surged from 103,000 residents in 1940 to 904,000 in 2000. Its small towns morphed into edge-city suburbs like Downers Grove, Naperville, and Oak Brook, featuring new housing subdivisions and newly built headquarters for many national corporations. Federal highway and housing programs played a key role in this transformation.

A prominent federal scientific facility, the Argonne National Laboratory, with 4,500 employees, spurred its growth and sparked the creation of many private research firms nearby.

The many well-paid business executives and professionals in the district vote consistently for Republican candidates and hold moderate to conservative ideological positions. The district can be counted on for high voter turnout. In 2000, 312,000 voters went to the polls, reelecting Republican House member Judy Biggert with 66 percent of the vote. She widened her margin to 70 percent in 2002, after redistricting. Having replaced seven-term congressman Harris Fawell, who in turn replaced Republican John Erlenborn, a twenty-year member, Biggert is poised for a long career. In 1988, George Bush garnered 69 percent of the district's vote against Democrat Michael Dukakis, but the district gave 21 percent of its vote to the Reform Party's Ross Perot in 1992, leaving Bush with 47 percent and Clinton with 32 percent. Four years later, 50 percent voted for Bob Dole, while Clinton got 41 percent and Perot 9 percent. In 2000, the Republican share climbed to 55 percent for Bush to 42 percent for Gore. It is a solidly Republican district, but not one where the issues we describe have no appeal.

Congressman Fawell took a conservative position on economic and fiscal issues, which he looked at from a businessman's point of view. He opposed organized labor, receiving low rankings from groups concerned about economic justice but somewhat higher ratings from prochoice and environmental groups. He was a cofounder of the Porkbusters Coalition, a mostly GOP organization that opposes wasteful government spending, but nevertheless was a big supporter of the Argonne lab. Congresswoman Biggert has followed in his footsteps. She has little reason to support metropolitan governance reforms that would reduce economic segregation or limit sprawl. After all, her district is part of the Chicago area's favored quarter, and her constituents are insulated from the city's concentrated poverty and the tax effort required to fund its services.

This will be the most challenging terrain for selling our program, but it may find support even here. The long-term fate of the residents of the Thirteenth Congressional District still depends to a significant degree on that of Chicago and the inner suburbs to the east. Almost half this district's residents work in the central city. The corporations that have relocated to the district acquire business services and even a significant share of their workforce from Chicago; the Argonne National Laboratory recruits educated workers from its universities. If Chicago became a less attractive place, these services would deteriorate. Chicago presents an image for the entire region that is crucial if Naperville and other suburban communities are to prosper.

Residents of the Thirteenth Congressional District have a strong interest in controlling suburban sprawl, which has been eating away at their quality of life. Sprawl is driven in part by a desire to escape the problems of concentrated poverty in Chicago. Fawell had pushed to conserve open land in metropolitan Chicago. By consolidating new development within existing built-up areas, including Chicago, the district can save substantial money and avoid the problems of excessively rapid development. Smart growth can help the suburban communities west of Chicago retain the green space that made them attractive in the first place. Controlling leapfrog development and enhancing public transit will reduce the level of highway congestion, or at least prevent it from growing worse. Moreover, as this area continues to grow economically, it too will need affordable housing and better public transportation so that it can support workers in entry-level jobs, lessen traffic jams, and address spot labor shortages. Congresswoman Biggert has stressed the importance of mass transit to her district. Shorter commutes mean more time for civic involvement and family life, including bonding with potentially troubled teens.

In between these two poles are the inner suburbs, such as those contained in California's Twenty-seventh Congressional District (now renamed the Twenty-ninth District). Stretching from the postwar San Fernando Valley suburbs of Glendale and Burbank, this district extends through the old city of Pasadena to the rapidly changing eastern suburbs of Los Angeles, such as Monterey Park. It contains the full range of experiences that are emblematic of the transformation of the inner suburbs: a build-out of available land, battles over increased density, the rise of pockets of poverty, increasing minority population, especially of Latinos and Asians, and significant threats to the quality of life from overdevelopment, congestion, and pollution. Within the district are some of the most massively overloaded freeway intersections anywhere on earth. It can boast some of the twenty-first century's finest achievements—as when the Jet Propulsion Laboratory directs NASA's rovers on Mars or the Disney studios create the latest in animation—but it also has its share of the most contemporary problems—chromium 6 in drinking water, encroachments on open space, and a severe shortage of affordable housing. As this district has shifted toward Democrat nominees—giving Al Gore a 53 to 41 percent victory in 2000 and incumbent Democratic Congressman Adam Schiff a 63 to 33 victory after redistricting in 2002—it has become more fertile territory for the new metropolitan agenda. Redistricting allowed Schiff to cast more liberal votes, gaining him a 100 percent ranking by the League of Conservation voters, 95 from Americans for Democratic Action, and 88 from the AFL-CIO.

Districts like the one Schiff represents—as well as other inner suburban dis-

tricts such as Ohio's Tenth, which straddles parts of Cleveland and its inner
suburbs and is represented by Dennis Kucinich—are key for our argument.
The relatively stable working- and middle-class suburbs in this Cleveland-area
district, such as Lakewood and Parma, have suffered in recent decades and
have experienced some deterioration. The problems motivated "leaders of nine
inner-ring suburbs to forge an alliance . . . calling themselves the First Suburbs Consortium."[44] This consortium has tried to get federal housing officials to
repair and sell FHA-insured properties, fund redevelopment of their commercial districts, and restrain the use of tax benefits and freeway construction to
promote suburban fringe development. Such older, inner-ring suburban swing
districts will be a pivotal battleground both in presidential elections and in the
search for a durable congressional majority.

THE SEEDS OF METROPOLITAN REVIVAL

In order for a new metropolitan political coalition to succeed, support must
come from public opinion, organizations and elected officials that represent
residents of central cities and inner suburbs, and political and economic elites
and opinion shapers. It must use arguments resting on efficiency and environmental reasons, as well as those of equity. And those arguments need to be made
not only by big-city mayors—who mainly have sat on the sidelines of these
issues—but also by people with broader perspectives, particularly governors
and presidential candidates. Despite the strong tradition of localism in America
and the pervasive skepticism about government's capacity to solve problems,
the seeds of a new metropolitics for the twenty-first century have been sown.
We can see evidence of their germination and growth in metropolitan areas
across the country.

Elites and opinion shapers are especially important in moving these issues
higher on the public agenda. The evident and increasing problems facing the
cities and suburbs, the growing perception that old "solutions" did not resolve
them and may even have aggravated them, and increasing understanding of
the importance of regional interdependencies have led many of these elites to
search for new metropolitan solutions. One obvious source of support can be
found among corporate leaders who are interested in improving regional economic competitiveness. Their initiatives have taken many forms in the seven
decades since the founding of the first corporate planning organization, the Regional Plan Association of metropolitan New York. Of particular interest has
been the rise of corporate-backed organizations devoted specifically to solving
problems that hamper regional economic competitiveness, such as Silicon Val-

ley: Joint Venture, the Greater Baltimore Alliance, Chicago Metropolis 2020, and the San Diego Regional Technology Alliance.[45]

As Rosabeth Moss Kanter reminds us, the rapidly changing business climate of the last several decades has undermined the old-fashioned "leading executive from the largest local corporations" form of business organization.[46] Deregulation, corporate reorganization, and a rapidly changing business environment have meant that even the core "place-bound" companies that once provided most local business leadership, such as newspapers and public utilities, are no longer locally owned, nor are their managers as focused on local public affairs. (This may be a good thing, as such elites backed some of the most destructive changes in American central cities and metropolitan regions in the postwar period, such as urban renewal and highway building.) At the same time, regions where local firms have been able to establish formal and informal ways to cooperate on common concerns often have been able to prosper through the transition from an industrial to a postindustrial economy, despite the pressures of globalization.[47] Although the conditions for organizing this constituency and the degree of leadership it requires vary considerably, it can be an important and powerful force for promoting regional cooperation to address issues of regional planning, affordable housing, transportation infrastructure investment, labor force development, and even regional equity.

The weight of this constituency will be all the more beneficial if it can meld with local labor unions and take the high road to local economic development. Instead of attempting to undercut local wages by moving production elsewhere, local employers can work with unions and local workforce development institutions (such as community colleges) to increase the skill levels of the labor pool and thereby increase regional competitiveness. The Center on Wisconsin Strategy pioneered this approach in Milwaukee.[48] In the context of tightening regional labor markets and an initiative by the Department of Labor to fund metropolitan planning for federal training programs, private-sector labor unions and employers have much to gain from such approaches. In addition, community-based organizations have begun to engage in worker training activities, often on a regional basis.[49] In southeastern Massachusetts, for example, a coalition of twenty-two churches was a significant force behind a regional improvement plan.[50] In short, although many business-led regional initiatives have focused on economic competitiveness, with only a secondary emphasis on regional environmental quality and little or no attention to regional equity, it is clear that combining these dimensions can strengthen the overall initiative. Moreover, it appears that leaders of such organizations have begun to understand the synergies among them. As a recent report by the Greater Baltimore

Committee said: "Addressing the social and economic problems that are, at the moment, largely concentrated in Baltimore City is essential to the long term vitality of the entire region. . . . We need to find policies and mechanisms and partnerships that bring the resources and capabilities of the entire region to bear on a set of problems that ultimately affect every single person living and working in the entire area."[51]

Labor unions are perhaps even more important than regionally oriented business elites for the future of a new metropolitan coalition. Although unions are usually based in central cities, the places where their members work and live stretch across the city line. Members who live in the central city often wish to move to the suburbs; workplaces where employees need union representation are also increasingly found there. As we have shown, higher levels of unionization are crucially associated with support for Democratic candidates and the creation of a sense of solidarity among workers that crosses city lines.

Because central labor councils conduct organizing drives and mobilize voters along county or multicounty lines, they are the natural locus for labor's efforts to build a new kind of regionalism. The labor movement needs to forge alliances with community organizations and other progressive forces on a regional basis. Labor-community alliances can play a central role in creating urban areas that are more humane as well as more competitive.[52] Most central labor councils have been neither as active at forging such alliances as they need to be nor as oriented toward operating on a regional basis as many metropolitan business leaders are.

Several exceptions point the way for the others, however. Particularly noteworthy is the South Bay Labor Council (SBLC), covering Santa Clara County, including Silicon Valley and the city of San Jose. The SBLC has been a national leader in promoting forms of regional growth that speak to the needs of workers, that slow the growth of inequality, and that adopt new forms of regional cooperation. Although Silicon Valley is one of the most prosperous regions in the country (when measured by indicators such as per capita income), the SBLC's affiliate, Working Partnerships, has shown that this has produced a severe housing squeeze, growing environmental problems, heightened inequality, and the threat that Latinos, a major portion of the county's population, will be excluded from these gains. In cooperation with local elected officials and academics, the SBLC has proposed a variety of creative approaches to these problems.[53]

The Los Angeles County Federation of Labor provides another notable example of the directions county labor councils should take. Over the last decade, it has become a powerful force not only for organizing new union members—especially janitors and health care workers—but also for supporting new and dynamic candidates to replace out-of-touch incumbents in Los Angeles County.[54] It is taken for granted that such candidates will be a major factor in mayoral races in Los Angeles, but they are also active in the San Gabriel Valley, the Harbor, and Glendale-Burbank. As the Los Angeles Times noted, "Los Angeles labor leaders are seeking to become key players in suburban politics."[55] With the election of new leadership in the Orange County Central Labor Council next door to Los Angeles County, this new labor activism may begin to operate on a truly regional basis. Although the Los Angeles labor federation has not yet taken up the challenge of regional economic development to the same degree as the SBLC, it is headed in that direction. If these efforts can be replicated in more metropolitan areas across the country, then labor support can be a key ingredient in a new metropolitan coalition. Given that labor and business both have a strong interest in a well-educated, highly productive, well-housed, and well-paid labor force—the high road toward regional competitiveness—the prospects for a business-labor-community alliance are brighter than some might suspect.

Opinion shapers also count. Although it is easy to scoff at the lack of political power possessed by academics, planners, and policy advocates based in nonprofit organizations, the outpouring of "new metropolitan thinking" over the last decade has been truly impressive. From the acclaimed books of David Rusk and Myron Orfield to the lucid syndicated columns and in-depth regional reports of Neal Peirce, the prescient arguments of the National League of Cities under William Barnes, the careful policy assessments of the National Academy of Science, the provocative ideas of john powell of the University of Minnesota, and the compelling studies by the Brookings Center for Urban and Metropolitan Policy led by Bruce Katz, the development of new metropolitan approaches to old urban problems has never been more squarely on the agenda of the nation's policy intellectuals. This thinking has informed new metropolitan initiatives being funded by major foundations. In the Clinton administration HUD Secretary Henry Cisneros promoted and funded regional initiatives, conferences, and reports. Fans of the free market have sought to belittle this new movement, but they have made little headway. It may take the advent of some new metropolitan crisis to provide the window of opportunity for their ideas to be put into action, but this emerging consensus is clearly an important precondition for policy innovation.

The new regionalism springing up across the country does not stem just from the words of public policy intellectuals, however. It has strong grassroots support, particularly on the environmental front. Smart growth has developed a political following among Republican as well as Democratic governors in states such as New Jersey and Maryland, and the Sierra Club has launched a successful national campaign around the need to control suburban sprawl and contain its negative environmental effects. Two dozen local communities have asked Myron Orfield and his Metropolitan Area Research Corporation to provide technical support for their efforts to understand regional inequities and develop new approaches for resolving them.[56] David Rusk has played a similar role with community organizations, churches, and business groups in several metropolitan areas.

Local elected officials are more ambivalent about regionalism. On the one hand, they understand that many of their basic problems can be solved only through regional cooperation. But they resist new metropolitan approaches when they feel that their fiefdoms might be threatened. This is true not only of those who represent the outer suburbs but also of those elected from the central city. (Indeed, in a misguided effort to win suburban support, the Democratic speaker of the New York State Assembly, Manhattan's Sheldon Silver, even abandoned his support for the relatively modest commuter tax levied by New York City.[57]) Chapter 6 detailed instances where cooperation among elected officials has been weak. In New York, former Mayor Giuliani and his predecessors vocally opposed the predatory economic development efforts of nearby jurisdictions and called for a regional cease-fire, but competition continues despite superficial agreement that it should not. Nor is this reluctance restricted to mayors; many minority elected officials fear that metropolitan approaches will dilute their power.[58] At the same time, leaders in many metropolitan areas are undertaking the hard work of overcoming these jurisdictional jealousies, as evidenced by the First Suburbs Consortium in Ohio. New institutional frameworks that would stimulate greater dialogue among local elected officials, such as regional caucuses of House members and state legislators, would be most helpful.

Proponents of a new metropolitan majority can overcome the institutional jealousies among local elected officials when these leaders finally realize that they can solve their pressing local problems only with support from political coalitions that cross city lines. Especially in the largest, most powerful jurisdictions, such as New York City, Los Angeles, and Chicago, this will be difficult to achieve, although the mayors of these cities understand the logic of regional cooperation well enough. Just as suburbs will have to look beyond their borders to see the collective interest of the region and support it in their day-to-day activities, so will the leaders of the big cities. As fate would have it, however, decades of competition from surrounding areas and other cities and decreasing support from the state and federal governments have led such big cities to become much more entrepreneurial.

The climate among elites is thus surprisingly favorable toward regionalism, particularly among the business, labor, and environmental organizations that have the most to gain from regional approaches to investing in the human and physical capital needed to promote regional competitiveness. For that matter, suburban public opinion also favors regionalism, at least insofar as regional growth management is concerned. For example, a survey of likely voters in Santa Clara County, California, found "widespread support for regional governance" among "residents of suburban areas who ostensibly covet the political independence of their suburban municipalities."[59] Clearly, successful coalitions for limiting sprawl have been forged among Democrats and Republicans; urban, suburban, and rural interests; state and local governments; and even developers in such disparate places as Oregon, Maryland, and New Jersey. In a careful review of how regional governance was successfully adopted and defended in Oregon and Minnesota, Margaret Weir concludes that "elements of an alternative approach to metropolitan problems are as yet faint and unassembled. But discontent from many quarters with the older model of metropolitan growth and urban abandonment suggests new possibilities for the future."[60]

At present, neither the rhetoric of smart growth nor that of deconcentrating urban poverty by tearing down decrepit public housing projects has been successfully coupled with the construction of affordable housing (for rent or ownership) in the middle and outer suburbs. Indeed, neither of the two "best" cases of metropolitan governance, Portland, Oregon, and the Twin Cities in Minnesota, has made much progress on this front.[61] Yet the creation of a regulatory framework for metropolitan development, when combined with the democratic representation of all the neighborhoods and constituencies within the metropolitan area, will inevitably place this issue on the agenda. In this way, the widespread suburban impulse to control growth, address traffic congestion and pollution, and (in some instances) provide more affordable housing will open the way to broader discussions of regional equity.

In the final analysis, a new metropolitan majority will be realized only if advocates of metropolitan cooperation can establish new institutional frameworks to amplify their voices. At present, many new voices can be heard speaking in favor of regional cooperation and equity. Missing is an institution that would consistently elicit such voices, provide the arena for metropolitan debate and consensus formation, and command wider public attention. Of all the recommendations in the previous chapter, therefore, establishing democratically elected metropolitan councils (stretching across state lines, where needed) is likely to have the greatest long-term impact on achieving a new metropolitan majority.

Even if such councils were no more than debating societies at first, they would serve crucial functions by representing constituencies within a common framework, articulating different views about the interests of the metropolitan region as a whole, and proposing policy solutions. (Analogous procedures for neighborhood participation within big cities have had similar impacts, even when they have not had much formal authority.[62]) The most logical source for this kind of institutional innovation is the federal government. It need not impose such forms. As the history of federal-local relations shows, the federal government can induce the adoption of metropolitan councils by prescribing how they would be organized; requiring that federal domestic programs be reviewed, if not approved or even eventually operated, by these entities; and funding a minimum level of staffing. As these metropolitan councils prove they can address serious societal problems, localities might well decide to assign them additional operating responsibilities, as has occurred in the Portland and Minneapolis–St. Paul metropolitan areas. To some, this may seem like an insufficiently dramatic response to the growth of concentrated urban poverty and the blight of uncontrolled development on the suburban fringe. We respond that these problems took fifty years to emerge, and they will take fifty years to fix. Heavy-handed solutions imposed from above would not be desirable, even if feasible. Instead, we must gradually change the basic incentive structures that produced these twin problems, which will require us to create a durable new coalition between urban and suburban voters.

THE DEMOCRATIC STAKES

Our discussion has focused on how a range of interests can be mobilized behind a new metropolitan political agenda. We should not dismiss, however, the power of the moral argument that our present system of economic segregation and sprawl is fundamentally unfair and antidemocratic. The dynamic that sustains concentrated poverty, segregated affluence, and metropolitan fragmentation is, in the words of Owen Fiss, "a moral and constitutional betrayal that demands swift and effective remedial action, not just as a matter of policy, but as a requirement of justice."[63] This betrayal has the harshest effect on those growing up in concentrated poverty, but its ramifications spread out to the entire society.

Americans believe in equal opportunity. Economic segregation violates that bedrock value. We believe that where people live in relationship to jobs and other opportunities, especially education, is an important cause of today's rising economic inequality. Moreover, place accentuates inequalities in ways that are not captured by economic statistics, such as differential access to high-quality public services and retail shopping and differential exposure to crime and unhealthy environments. Liberal democracies can tolerate a great deal of economic inequality, but they cannot tolerate the combining of economic, political, and social inequalities into a vicious circle. This is exactly what is happening in American metropolitan areas.

The "secession of the successful," as Robert Reich put it, threatens a central pillar of American democracy: the belief that we are all basically in the same boat.[64] In a metropolitan landscape characterized by economic segregation and sprawl, a rising tide does *not* lift all boats. In what is arguably the most prosperous economy ever on the face of the earth, many places (and the people who live in them) are being left behind. Not only are places becoming economically isolated from the mainstream, they are becoming politically cut off as well. The flight to the suburban fringe does not just sever social relations; it also severs political relations. Never before have economic classes sorted themselves into separate governments the way they have in the United States today. The result is a bland politics at the local level that short-circuits the normal processes of political conflict and compromise and undermines civic participation in both cities and suburbs. Stereotypes and mistrust thrive in such an environment, depleting the precious social trust that is necessary for democracy to function effectively. The revival of American democracy requires new political institutions at the metropolitan level. We all have a stake in this.

NOTES

PREFACE

1. We respond to the following reviews of *Place Matters:* Harold Henderson, *Planning* (December 2001); Neal Peirce, *Baltimore Sun* (September 6, 2001); Tom Gallagher, *East Bay Express* (November 21, 2001); James Goodno, *Urban Ecology* (Autumn 2001); Paul Jargowsky, *Urban Affairs Review* 37, no. 3 (January 2002); Fred Siegel, *Urban Affairs Review* 37, no. 3 (January 2002); J. Phillip Thompson, *Urban Affairs Review* 37, no. 3 (January 2002); Gregory Squires, *City and Community* 1, no. 1 (March 2002); Anthony Orum, *Contemporary Sociology* 31, no. 6 (November 2002); Susan Christopherson, *Economic Geography* 78, no. 4 (October 2002); Robert Stein, *Journal of Politics* 64, no. 3 (August 2002); Harold Wolman, *Housing Studies* 17, no. 5 (September 2002); Michael Tomasky, *American Prospect* (September 9, 2002); Joan Fitzgerald, Center for Urban and Regional Policy, Northeastern University, n.d; Bill Pitkin, *Critical Planning* (summer 2002); Robert Beauregard, *Choice* 39, no. 17 (March 2002); Elliott Sclar, *Dissent* (spring 2002); John Atlas, *Sunday Star-Ledger* (January 13, 2002); Kolina Vortman, *U.S. Mayor* (May 13, 2002); Margaret Pugh O'Mara, H-Urban Web site at: http://www.h-net.org/reviews/showrev.cgi?path= 164971003347228; W. Dennis Keating, *Shelterforce* (January/February 2002); David Lowery, *Perspectives on Politics* 1, no. 1 (March 2003); James Mumm, *Social Policy* (spring 2003); Karen Chapple, *Journal of the American Planning Association* 70, no. 1 (winter 2004).
2. See Edward G. Goetz, *Clearing the Way: Deconcentrating the Poor in Urban America* (Washington, DC: Urban Institute Press, 2003).

CHAPTER 1. PLACE STILL MATTERS

1. The stories of Arletta Bronaugh and Dawn Macklin are from Sharon Cohen, "Program Helps Chicago Black Families Break Out of Inner-City Despair," *Los Angeles Times,* August 23, 1992.
2. Demographic characteristics for Hoffman Estates are from the 1990 census. Information about the toxic facilities near Altgeld Gardens comes from David Naguib Pellow, *Garbage Wars: The Struggle for Environmental Justice in Chicago* (Cambridge, MA: MIT Press, 2002).
3. We discuss Chicago's Gautreaux housing mobility program, which provided these families with the housing subsidies to move to the suburbs, in more detail in Chapter 3. For more information about this program, see Leonard S. Rubinowitz and James E. Rosenbaum, *Crossing the Class and Color Lines: From Public Housing to White Suburbia* (Chicago: University of Chicago Press, 2000); and Peter Dreier and David Moberg, "Moving From the 'Hood: The Mixed Success of Integrating Suburbia," *American Prospect* 7, no. 24 (winter 1996): 75–79. For a discussion of Mov-

ing to Opportunity, a multicity federal program modeled on Gautreaux, see John Goering and Judith D. Feins, eds., *Choosing a Better Life: Evaluating the Moving to Opportunity Social Experiment* (Washington, DC: Urban Institute Press, 2003). See also Edward G. Goetz, *Clearing the Way: Deconcentrating the Poor in Urban America* (Washington, DC: Urban Institute Press, 2003).

4. Dave McKibben, "To Some, Affordable Housing Means Nightmare Neighbors; Mission Viejo Residents Denounce Plans for an Apartment Complex," *Los Angeles Times,* February 1, 2004. Additional information came from Peter Dreier's interview with Jason Ficht of the Mission Viejo Planning Department, February 17, 2004.

5. Data for December 2003 from California Association of Realtors, at http://www.car.org.

6. The growth of distance learning is profiled in Karen W. Arenson, "More Colleges Plunging into Uncharted Waters of On-Line Courses," *New York Times,* November 2, 1998. For arguments about the obsolescence of traditional dense cities, see Peter O. Muller, "Are Cities Obsolete? The Fearful Symmetry of Post-Urban America," *Sciences* (March–April 1986): 43–46; Robert Fishman, "Megalopolis," *Wilson Quarterly* (winter 1990): 25–45; Tom Morganthau and John McCormick, "Are Cities Obsolete?" *Newsweek,* September 9, 1991, 42–44.

7. For criticisms of the idea that technology is making cities obsolete, see Joseph Persky, Elliot Sclar, and Wim Wiewel, *Does America Need Cities? An Urban Investment Strategy for National Prosperity* (Washington, DC: Economic Policy Institute, 1991); Edward Glaeser, "Why Economists Still Like Cities," *City Journal* (spring 1996): 73–77. For a critical discussion of the "city obsolescence" thesis, see Manuel Castells, *The Rise of the Network Society* (Malden, MA: Blackwell Publishers, 1996), 394–98.

8. The idea of "weak ties" was introduced by Mark Granovetter in "The Strength of Weak Ties," *American Journal of Sociology* 78, no. 6 (1972): 1360–80.

9. In 2000, only 19.2 percent of households earning $15,000 or less owned a computer; only 12.7 percent were connected to the Internet. For those earning over $75,000, 86.3 percent owned a computer, and 45 percent had access to the Internet. See U.S. Department of Commerce, National Telecommunications and Information Administration, *Falling Through the Net* (Washington, DC: U.S. Government Printing Office, October 2000).

10. Figures on manufacturing employment are from *Risen from the Ashes: An All-American City Plans for Its Future* (Bronx, NY: Strategic Policy Statement for the Bronx, Borough President Fernando Ferrer, n.d.).

11. For a history of the South Bronx, see Jill Jonnes, *We're Still Here: The Rise, Fall, and Resurrection of the South Bronx* (Boston: Atlantic Monthly Press, 1986).

12. Alexander Von Hoffman, *House by House, Block by Block: The Rebirth of America's Urban Neighborhoods* (New York: Oxford University Press, 2003), 19.

13. "Income and Poverty in 1999: Census 2000; United States—Congressional Districts by State," U.S. Census, 2000.

14. "Age and Sex: 2000; United States—Congressional Districts by State," U.S. Census, American FactFinder.

15. Quoted in Jonathan Kozol, *Amazing Grace: The Lives of Children and the Conscience of a Nation* (New York: Harper Perennial, 1995), 52.

16. Quoted in ibid., 125.

17. Alex Schwartz, "New York City and Subsidized Housing: Impacts and Lessons of the City's $5 Billion Capital Budget Housing Plan," *Housing Policy Debate* 10, no. 4 (1999): 839–77; Gregg G. Van Ryzin and Andrew Genn, "Neighborhood Change and

the City of New York's Ten-Year Housing Plan," *Housing Policy Debate* 10, no. 4 (1999): 799–838; Paul Grogan and Tony Proscio, *Comeback Cities* (Boulder, CO: Westview Press, 2000); and Von Hoffman, *House by House.*

18. David Chen, "New York Is No Longer Awash in Abandoned Buildings. Now the Issue Is Supply," *New York Times,* December 21, 2003.

19. For a sympathetic, scholarly analysis of the New York City Partnership, see Charles J. Orlebeke, *New Life at Ground Zero: New York, Home Ownership, and the Future of American Cities* (Albany, NY: Rockefeller Institute Press, 1997).

20. Von Hoffman, *House by House;* Jim Rooney, *Organizing the South Bronx* (Albany, NY: SUNY Press, 1995).

21. Schwartz, "New York City," 851.

22. Despite its good work, the Banana Kelly organization fell on hard times in recent years. See Amy Waldman, "A Rebuilder In the Bronx Scales Back," *New York Times,* March 29, 2001; and Jill Grossman, "Banana Kelly U-Turn: City tells South Bronx Organizing Goliath to Pay Up, or Get Out," *City Limits,* July/August 2002.

23. As Rusk argues, only regional solutions can stem central-city decline. See David Rusk, *Cities Without Suburbs* (Washington, DC: Woodrow Wilson Center Press, 1993); and Rusk, *Inside Game/Outside Game: Winning Strategies for Saving Urban America* (Washington, DC: Brookings Institution Press, 1999).

24. Von Hoffman, *House by House,* 75.

25. After the 2000 census, California gained a congressional district and redrew its existing districts for the 2002 and subsequent elections. Most of the areas that comprised the 27th District in 2000 — including Pasadena, Glendale, and Burbank — became part of the new 29th Congressional District, still represented by Congressman Adam Schiff. The demographic and other data used in this section refer to the former 27th Congressional District unless otherwise specified.

26. *A Tale of Two Cities: Bridging the Gap Between Promise and Peril: 2003 Executive Review of the State of Los Angeles County* (Los Angeles: United Way of Greater Los Angeles, 2003).

27. U.S. Census Bureau, American FactFinder, DP-1, "Profile of General Demographic Characteristics: 2000" for Los Angeles County; *Sprawl Hits the Wall: Confronting the Realities of Metropolitan Los Angeles* (Los Angeles: Southern California Studies Center, University of Southern California, 2001).

28. Population and demographic figures for the congressional district and the cities within it are from the U.S. Census Bureau. Figures for 2000 and earlier are for the 27th Congressional District. The electoral figures come from various editions of the *Almanac of American Politics* as well as Drew A. Linzer and David Menefee-Libey, "Opening the Floodgates: Campaigning Without Scarcity in the 2000 California Twenty-Seventh Congressional District Race," in David B. Magleby, ed., *The Other Campaign: Soft Money and Issue Advocacy in the 2000 Congressional Elections* (Boulder, CO: Rowman & Littlefield, 2003), 149–65; Drew Linzer, David Menefee-Libey, and Matt Muller, "The 2002 California Twenty-Ninth Congressional District Race," *PS Online,* E-symposium, July 2003, available at http://www.apsanet.org/PS/july03/linzer.pdf.

29. "Burbank Portrait: A Small Town Moves Into Prime Time," *Los Angeles Times,* June 29, 1994; James Peltz, "Lockheed's Long Stay in Valley May be Ending," *Los Angeles Times,* August 30, 1994.

30. These are very conservative estimates in terms of the overall Hispanic populations in these three cities. There was no category "Hispanic" in the 1970 census, so some

whites who may also be Hispanic were not included in the "minority" category. To be consistent, only those Hispanics who identified themselves as "some other race" (not white, black, American Indian, Asian, or Hawaiian/Pacific Islander) were included in the minority category. The 1970 census figures are found in the report on General Population Characteristics for California places. The 2000 figures are found in the Census Bureau's American FactFinder demographic profiles for places.

31. *California's Congressional Districts: Geographic Disparities in Health Insurance Coverage: California Residents Uninsured at Any Time During the Previous 12 Months,* Los Angeles: UCLA Center for Health Policy Research, May 2003, at http://www.health policy.ucla.edu/pubs/publication.asp?pubID=69#download.

32. These figures are for 2000.

33. Authors' calculations of 2000 U.S. census data. Joseph Colletti of the Institute for Urban Research and Development in Pasadena provided a census tract map of Pasadena identifying the tracts in northwest Pasadena.

34. Myron Levin, "Rude Awakening from Suburban Dream: Life on the Poverty Line in the San Fernando Valley," *Los Angeles Times,* June 9, 1996.

35. *December 2003 Median Home Prices,* California Association of Realtors, available at *http://www.car.org.*

36. Cited in Richard Winton, "Suit Accusing Coach of Racism Stirs Bitter Memories of Pool's Past," *Los Angeles Times,* April 16, 2001.

37. Jay Mathews, "Black People Find Pasadena to Be an Island of Opportunity," *Los Angeles Times,* February 2, 1986; William Trombley, "Pasadena: Feeling Its Oats at 100," *Los Angeles Times,* June 8, 1986.

38. Patrice Gaines-Carter and Jay Mathews, "Patience Yielding Payoff in Pasadena; Suburb's Conservative Traditions Nurture Caution, Confidence," *Washington Post,* January 21, 1986.

39. Trombley, "Pasadena: Feeling Its Oats at 100."

40. Mathews, "Black People."

41. Edmund Newton, "Truce Removes Thrones from Rose Parade Diversity," *Los Angeles Times,* December 1, 1993.

42. Barry Bearak, "Revolution Incomplete: Gains Made, but Racism Runs Deep," *Los Angeles Times,* March 8, 1987.

43. Mathews, "Black People."

44. David Colker, "The Valley: 100 Years in the Making," *Los Angeles Times,* December 19, 1999.

45. Armenians are designed as white by the census.

46. Gregory Rodriguez, "Glendale's Racist Shadow Shrinks as City Transforms Itself," *Los Angeles Times,* June 16, 1996.

47. Erin Texeira, "Ethnic Friction Disturbs Peace of Glendale," *Los Angeles Times,* June 25, 2000.

48. Ibid.

49. Ibid.

50. Linzer and Menefee-Libey, "Opening the Floodgates," 149.

51. John Horton, *The Politics of Diversity: Immigration, Resistance, and Change in Monterey Park, California* (Philadelphia: Temple University Press, 1995); Wei Li, "Anatomy of a New Ethnic Settlement: The Chinese Ethnoburb in Los Angeles," *Urban Studies* 35, no. 3 (March 1998): 479–501; Max Arax, "San Gabriel Valley Asian Influx Alters Life in Suburbia," *Los Angeles Times,* April 5, 1987.

52. Arax, "San Gabriel Valley."

53. Elections data from various editions of the *Almanac of American Politics*.
54. John B. Judis and Ruy Teixeira, *The Emerging Democratic Majority* (New York: Scribner, 2002).
55. "Income and Poverty in 1999: 2000; United States—Congressional Districts by State," U.S. Census Bureau, American FactFinder.
56. U.S. Bureau of the Census Web site, at: http://www.census.gov.
57. Joel Garreau, *Edge City: Life on the New Frontier* (New York: Doubleday, 1991), 428.
58. Data from *Almanac of American Politics: 2004*.
59. The results of the Zero Population Growth study and quotes are from Dan Rozek, "Naperville Rates as No. 1 'Kid-Friendly' City," *Chicago Sun-Times,* August 27, 1997.
60. Joanne Kanter, "Naperville's Tale of Two Counties: Housing Growth in '80s Boomtown Traveling South," *Chicago Sun-Times,* April 30, 1993. In fact, nonresidential growth may not be the fiscal money winner that people believe it is. One study of rapidly developing DuPage County concluded that "nonresidential development has an impact on total tax levy increases that is over three times greater than that of residential development." DuPage County Development Department, Planning Division, "Impacts of Development on DuPage County Property Taxes" (Wheaton, IL: DuPage County Development Department, 1991), 8, as reported in Persky et al., *Does America Need Cities?,* 21.
61. Quoted in Becky Beaupre, "Suburbs Spread Further; More Residents Migrating to Kendall, Will Counties," *Chicago Sun-Times,* February 1, 1999.
62. The turnover rate in Naperville is discussed in Joanne Kanter, "Naperville Population Moves a Bit," *Chicago Sun-Times,* April 30, 1993.
63. Nicholas Lemann, "Naperville: Stressed out in Suburbia," *Atlantic* (November 1989): 34–48.
64. A cross-national comparison of per capita incomes, controlling for purchasing power, is found in Lawrence Mishel, Jared Bernstein, and Heather Boushey, *The State of Working America 2002/2003* (Ithaca, NY: Cornell University Press, 2003), 398.
65. Cox and Alm present persuasive evidence that, on average, Americans are much better off in terms of sheer consumption than they were twenty years ago. Most economists agree that the inflation rate, as low as it is, overstates inflation because it fails to take into account the technological improvements in the products we buy. See W. Michael Cox and Richard Alm, *Myths of Rich and Poor: Why We're Better Off than We Think* (New York: Basic Books, 1999). We disagree strongly, however, with Cox and Alm's argument that economic inequality is nothing to be concerned about.
66. Mishel et al., *State of Working America,* chap. 7; and Luxembourg Income Study at http://www.lisproject.org/keyfigures.htm.
67. Mishel at al., *State of Working America,* chap. 4; Edward N. Wolff, "Recent Trends in Wealth Ownership, 1983–1998," Working Paper No. 300 (Annandale-on-Hudson, NY: Jerome Levy Economics Institute, April 2000).
68. "Jobs Picture: Payrolls Up, But Growth Not Sufficient to Boost Wages" (Washington, DC: Economic Policy Institute, February 6, 2004).
69. The shift to greater inequality in the American economy is explored in Bennett Harrison and Barry Bluestone, *The Great U-Turn: Corporate Restructuring and the Polarizing of America* (New York: Basic Books, 1988).
70. Robert B. Reich, *The Work of Nations* (New York: Random House, 1991); Mishel et al., *State of Working America,* 56–57.

71. Unless otherwise noted, all figures on rising income and wealth inequality are from Mishel et al., *State of Working America*.
72. Despite drops in average CEO pay from 2000 to 2002, the wide CEO-to-worker pay gap narrowed only slightly during that period. Median CEO pay at the fifty companies with the most layoffs in 2001 rose 44 percent from 2001 to 2002. Sarah Anderson, John Cavanagh, Chris Hartman, and Scott Klinger, *Executive Excess 2003* (Cambridge: United for a Fair Economy, and Washington, DC: Institute for Policy Studies, August 26, 2003); Mishel et al., *State of Working America*, chap. 2; "Special Report: Executive Pay," *Business Week*, April 21, 2003; "Special Report: Executive Pay," *Business Week*, April 17, 2000; "Executive Pay: It's Out of Control," *Business Week*, April 21, 1997; Dean Foust, "CEO Pay: Nothing Succeeds Like Failure," *Business Week*, September 11, 2000.
73. Edward N. Wolff, "Recent Trends in Wealth Ownership, 1983–1998," Working Paper no. 300 (Jerome Levy Economics Institute, April 2000), 4; Mishel et al., *State of Working America*, chap. 4.
74. Mishel et al., *State of Working America*, 117.
75. Carmen DeNovas Walt, Bernadette D. Proctor, and Robert J. Mills, *Income, Poverty, and Health Insurance Coverage in the United States: 2003*, Current Population Report P60-226 (Washington, DC: U.S. Bureau of the Census, August 2004). U.S. Bureau of the Census, *1999 Income and Poverty Estimates Based on the March Supplement to the Current Population Survey*, available at http://www.census.gov/hhes/www/povty99 .html.
76. U.S. Department of Housing and Urban Development (HUD), *The State of the Cities 2000: Megaforces Shaping the Future of the Nation's Cities* (Washington, DC: HUD, 2000), 11; Steven A. Holmes, "Income's Up and Poverty Is Down, Data Shows," *New York Times*, September 27, 2000.
77. Mishel et al., *State of Working America*, 8; Walt, Proctor, and Mills, *Income, Poverty, and Health Insurance Coverage in the United States*; U.S. Census, Current Population Survey, "Table 8. Poverty of People, by Residence: 1959 to 2001," at http://www .census.gov/income/histpov/hstpov8.1st; Isaac Shapiro, *The Mismatch Between Federal Unemployment Benefits and Current Labor Market Realities* (Washington, DC: Center on Budget and Policy Priorities, October 15, 2003).
78. HUD, *State of the Cities 2000*, 21.
79. Nina Bernstein, "Family Needs Far Exceed the Official Poverty Line," *New York Times*, September 13, 2000.
80. *Making Ends Meet: How Much Does It Cost to Raise a Family in California?* (Sacramento: California Budget Project, October 1999); Paul More et al., *The Other Los Angeles: The Working Poor in the City of the 21st Century* (Los Angeles: Los Angeles Alliance for a New Economy, August 2000).
81. HUD, *State of the Cities 2000*, 33, ix.
82. Cushing Dolbeare, "Housing Affordability: Challenge and Context" (paper presented at Housing Policy in the New Millennium, Arlington, VA, October 2–3, 2000), table 4a.
83. The fair-market rent (FMR) is set for each metropolitan area by HUD. Currently, it is the fortieth percentile of the rental housing distribution of two-bedroom units in the region. The FMR is thus a little below the median rent in the region.
84. Cushing Dolbeare, *Out of Reach* (Washington, DC: National Low-Income Housing Coalition, September 1999); Winton Pitcoff, Danilo Pelletiere, Sheila Crowley, Kim Schaffer, Mark Treskon, Carol Vance, and Cushing N. Dolbeare, *Out of Reach 2003:*

America's Housing Wage Climbs (Washington, DC: National Low-Income Housing Coalition, 2003).

85. For conservative critiques of the literature on rising inequality, see Cox and Alm, *Myths of Rich and Poor,* and John H. Hindraker and Scott W. Johnson, "Inequality: Should We Worry?" *American Enterprise* (July–August 1996): 35–39.

86. Research on mobility is skillfully analyzed by Daniel P. McMurrer and Isabel V. Sawhill in *Getting Ahead: Economic and Social Mobility in America* (Washington, DC: Urban Institute Press, 1998).

87. Mishel et al., *The State of Working America,* 77–79, citing Panel Study of Income Dynamics data tabulated by Peter Gottschalk. For a review of studies showing declining economic mobility in America, see Aaron Bernstein, "Is America Becoming More of a Class Society?" *Business Week,* February 26, 1996, 86–91; Aaron Bernstein, "Waking Up from the American Dream: Meritocracy and Equal Opportunity Are Fading Fast," *Business Week,* December 1, 2003.

88. Mishel, et al., *State of Working America 2002/2003,* 78.

89. Greg Duncan et al., "Poverty and Social Assistance Dynamics in the United States, Canada, and Europe" (paper presented at the Joint Center for Political and Economic Studies Conference on Poverty and Public Policy, Washington, DC), as reported in Mishel et al., *The State of Working America.* See also Bernstein, "Is America Becoming More of a Class Society?"

90. Hindraker and Johnson, "Inequality: Should We Worry?", 35.

91. The argument that American society is a meritocracy in which intelligence largely determines one's class position is made in Richard J. Herrnstein and Charles Murray, *The Bell Curve: Intelligence and Class Structure in American Life* (New York: Free Press, 1994). Herrnstein and Murray greatly exaggerate the role of IQ in economic success. See Claude S. Fischer et al., *Inequality by Design: Cracking the Bell Curve Myth* (Princeton, NJ: Princeton University Press, 1996).

92. The increase in the work effort of the employable poor is found in Mishel et al., *State of Working America,* 319.

93. Ibid., 320.

94. "The Wage Squeeze," *Business Week,* July 17, 1995, 62.

95. For the case that the poor are better off than ever, see Cox and Alm, *Myths of Rich and Poor,* 14–17.

96. *The Politics of Aristotle,* ed. and trans. Ernest Barker (New York: Oxford University Press, 1962), 268.

97. Thomas Jefferson, letter to Reverend James Madison, President of William and Mary, First Bishop of the Protestant Episcopal Church in Virginia, October 28, 1785, as quoted in John P. Foley, ed., *The Jefferson Cyclopedia* (New York: Funk and Wagnalls, 1900), 727.

98. Franklin D. Roosevelt's Four Freedoms speech, in *Documents of American History,* 7th ed., ed. Henry Steele Commager (New York: Meredith, 1963), 448.

99. Amartya Sen, *Inequality Reexamined* (Cambridge, MA: Harvard University Press, 1992), 39.

100. Paul Jargowsky, *Poverty and Place: Ghettos, Barrios, and the American City* (New York: Russell Sage Foundation, 1997), 41. On white poverty concentration, see Stephen Mulherin, "Affordable Housing and White Poverty Concentration," *Journal of Urban Affairs* 22, no. 2 (2000): 139–56.

101. William Julius Wilson, *The Truly Disadvantaged: The Inner City, the Underclass, and Public Policy* (Chicago: University of Chicago Press, 1987).

102. The proportion of the metropolitan poor who live in census tracts with a poverty rate of 30 percent or more declined from 48 percent in 1990 to 38 percent in 2000. Thomas G. Kingsley and Kathryn L. S. Pettit, *Concentrated Poverty: A Change in Course* (Washington, DC: The Urban Institute, May 2003). The figure is much higher for minorities, who tend to live in more economically segregated settings. Thirty-three percent of all black poor people and 22.1 percent of all Hispanic poor lived in high-poverty census tracts in 1990, compared with only 6.2 percent of the white poor. But as we noted, the economic segregation of the white poor is increasing rapidly. Jargowsky, *Poverty and Place,* 41. By 2000, although the proportion of the poor living in high-poverty areas declined, blacks and Hispanics were still more likely than whites to live in these areas. Paul A. Jargowsky, *Stunning Progress, Hidden Problems: The Dramatic Decline of Concentrated Poverty in the 1990s* (Washington, DC: Brookings Institution, May 2003).

103. Katherine S. Newman debunks the myth that most poor people are lazy and do not want to work in *No Shame in My Game: The Working Poor in the Inner City* (New York: Knopf, 1999).

104. William H. Lucy and David L. Phillips, *Confronting Suburban Decline: Strategic Planning for Metropolitan Renewal* (Washington, DC: Island Press, 2000). See also Myron Orfield's seminal work on the problems of inner-ring suburbs in *Metropolitics: A Regional Agenda for Community and Stability* (Washington, DC: Brookings Institution Press, 1997).

105. For data on improving social trends and the difficulties conservatives are having dealing with these facts, see the special issue of *American Enterprise* (January–February 1999) entitled "Is America Turning a Corner?"

106. Our critique of the failure of the underclass literature to consider the broader regional context borrows from Mark Allen Hughes, "Misspeaking Truth to Power: A Geographical Perspective on the 'Underclass' Fallacy," *Economic Geography* 65 (1989): 187–207.

107. Edward Banfield, *The Unheavenly City: The Nature and Future of Our Urban Crisis* (Boston: Little, Brown, 1970), 38.

108. Gunnar Myrdal, *An American Dilemma: The Negro Problem in Modern Democracy* (New York: Harper and Row, 1944), 75–78.

109. The art of separation is discussed in Michael Walzer, "Liberalism and the Art of Separation," *Political Theory* 12, no. 3 (1984): 315–30; and in his *Spheres of Justice: A Defense of Pluralism and Equality* (New York: Basic Books, 1983). Similarly, democratic theorist Robert Dahl argues that pluralist democracies move from "cumulative" to "dispersed" inequalities in his classic *Who Governs? Democracy and Power in an American City* (New Haven, CT: Yale University Press, 1961), chap. 7.

110. The term "separate societies" originated in the 1968 Kerner Commission report on the urban riots of the 1960s.

111. See Grogan and Proscio, *Comeback Cities.*

112. Aaron Bernstein, "An Inner-City Renaissance: The Nation's Ghettos Are Making Surprising Strides. Will the Gains Last?" *Business Week,* October 27, 2003.

113. Michael E. Porter, "The Competitive Advantage of the Inner City," *Harvard Business Review* (May–June 1995): 55–71.

114. Edward L. Glaeser and Matthew E. Kahn, "From John Lindsay to Rudy Giuliani: The Decline of the Local Safety Net?" *Federal Reserve Board of New York Economic Policy Review* (September 1999): 128.

115. P. Klite, R. A. Bardwell, and J. Salzmann, "Local Television News: Getting Away

with Murder," *Harvard International Journal of Press/Politics* 2 (1997): 102–12, cited in Shanto Iyengar, "'Media Effects' Paradigms for the Analysis of Local Television News" (Palo Alto, CA: Department of Communication and Department of Political Science, Stanford University, 1998), available at http://pcl.stanford.edu/research/papers/effects.html.

116. Franklin D. Gilliam Jr., Shanto Iyengar, Adam Simon, and Oliver Wright, "Crime in Black and White: The Violent, Scary World of Local News," Occasional Paper no. 95-1 (Los Angeles: UCLA Center for American Politics and Public Policy, September 1995); Jeffrey D. Alderman, "Leading the Public: The Media's Focus on Crime Shaped Sentiment," *Public Perspective* 5 (1994): 26–27; Robert Entman and Andrew Rojecki, *The Black Image in the White Mind: Media and Race in America* (Chicago: University of Chicago Press, 2000); M. Freeman, "Networks Doubled Crime Coverage in '93 Despite Flat Violence Levels in U.S. Society," *Mediaweek* 4 (1994): 3–4, cited in Gilliam et al., "Crime in Black and White"; and Martin Gilens, *Why Americans Hate Welfare* (Chicago: University of Chicago Press, 1999).

CHAPTER 2. THE FACTS OF ECONOMIC SEGREGATION AND SPRAWL

1. Timothy Egan, "Many Seek Security in Private Communities," *New York Times,* September 3, 1995. Over 30 million Americans live in common-interest developments, where residents must join a community association that owns common property (e.g., streets, swimming pools) and enforces rules governing the community. For a critical analysis, see Evan McKenzie, *Privatopia: Homeowner Associations and the Rise of Residential Private Government* (New Haven, CT: Yale University Press, 1994). An estimated 8.4 million Americans also live in communities with gates that control public access. The best source on this growing trend is Edward J. Blakely and Mary Gail Snyder, *Fortress America: Gated Communities in the United States* (Washington, DC: Brookings Institution Press, 1997).

2. Stephen Richard Higley, *Privilege, Power, and Place: The Geography of the American Upper Class* (Lanham, MD: Rowman & Littlefield, 1995), 127.

3. Data on the importance of exclusive neighborhoods are from *Town and Country* magazine (1994), as reported in Blakely and Snyder, *Fortress America,* 76.

4. Miller McPherson, Lynn Smith-Lovin, and James M. Cook, "Birds of a Feather: Homophily in Social Networks," *Annual Review of Sociology,* 27 (2001), 415–44.

5. For a discussion of the court cases upholding local zoning laws that effectively exclude families based on income, see Dennis Judd and Todd Swanstrom, *City Politics: Private Power and Public Policy* (New York: Longman, 2004), 4th ed., chap. 10.

6. For a discussion of different indices of segregation, see Douglas S. Massey and Nancy A. Denton, *American Apartheid: Segregation and the Making of the Underclass* (Cambridge, MA: Harvard University Press, 1993), chap. 3.

7. Paul Grogan and Tony Proscio, *Comeback Cities* (Boulder, CO: Westview Press, 2000); Paul A. Jargowsky, *Stunning Progress, Hidden Problems: The Dramatic Decline of Concentrated Poverty in the 1990s* (Washington, DC: Brookings Institution Center for Metropolitan and Urban Policy, May 2003); Alexander von Hoffman, *House by House, Block by Block* (New York: Oxford University Press, 2003).

8. Jane Jacobs, *Cities and the Wealth of Nations: Principles of Economic Life* (New York: Random House, 1984), 32.

9. William R. Barnes and Larry C. Ledebur, *The New Regional Economies: The U.S.*

Common Market and the Global Economy (Thousand Oaks, CA: Sage Publications, 1998), 3.

10. For a discussion of the importance of regions in global competition, see Neal R. Peirce, Curtis Johnson, and John Hall, *Citistates: How Urban America Can Prosper in a Competitive World* (Washington, DC: Seven Locks Press, 1993).

11. Quoted in James L. Sundquist, *Dispersing Population: What America Can Learn from Europe* (Washington, DC: Brookings Institution Press, 1975), 1. Drawing from Europe, Sundquist makes a persuasive case for balanced regional growth policies in the United States. For an insightful analysis of why the United States failed to enact a national growth policy in the 1970s, see Sidney Plotkin, *Keep Out: The Struggle for Land Use Control* (Berkeley: University of California Press, 1987).

12. One of the earliest statements of divergence theory is Gunnar Myrdal, *Economic Theory and the Underdeveloped Region* (London: Gerald Duckworth, 1957). For a more recent statement, see Paul Krugman, *Geography and Trade* (Cambridge, MA: MIT Press, 1991).

13. The Reagan administration's touting of convergence is found in U.S. Department of Housing and Urban Development, *The President's National Urban Policy Report* (Washington, DC: U.S. Government Printing Office, 1982), 28.

14. Lynn E. Browne, "Shifting Regional Fortunes: The Wheel Turns," *New England Economic Review* (May–June 1989): 27–40. Additional evidence of regional divergence is found in Keith R. Phillips, "Regional Wage Divergence and National Wage Inequality," *Economic Review* (Federal Reserve Board of Dallas, fourth quarter 1992): 31–44; Matthew P. Drennan, Emanuel Tobier, and Jonathan Lewis, "The Interruption of Income Convergence and Income Growth in Large Cities in the 1980s," *Urban Studies* 33, no. 1 (1996): 63–82; Edward Nissan and George Carter, "Income Inequality Across Regions over Time," *Growth and Change* 24 (summer 1993): 303–19; C. Cindy Fan and Emilio Casetti, "The Spatial and Temporal Dynamics of U.S. Regional Income Inequality, 1950–1989," *Annals of Regional Science* 28 (1994): 177–96; Norman J. Glickman, "Does Economic Development 'Cause' Regional Inequality?" Working Paper No. 101 (Center for Urban Policy Research, Rutgers, March 1996). See also the Web-based presentation of inequality trends at the county level by James K. Galbraith and the University of Texas Inequality Project, available at http://utip.gov .utexas.edu/web/Web%20Presentations/usbycountiesweb/sld001.htm.

15. Janet Rothenberg Pack, *Growth and Convergence in Metropolitan America* (Washington, DC: Brookings Institution Press, 2002), 153.

16. Zhongcai Zhang, "Have Regions in the U.S. Become More Similar or More Dissimilar? An Examination of Income and Earnings Convergence of Metropolitan Areas" (Ph.D. diss., Cleveland State University, 1998).

17. Douglas S. Massey and Mary J. Fischer, "The Geography of Inequality in the United States, 1950–2000," in *Brookings-Wharton Papers on Urban Affairs 2003*, ed. William G. Gale and Janet Rothenberg Pack (Washington, DC: Brookings Institution Press, 2003), 1–29. The concentration of poverty and affluence among metropolitan areas is measured using the P isolation index.

18. "Regional Divisions Dampen '90s Prosperity," Lewis Mumford Center for Comparative Urban and Regional Research, University at Albany, June 5, 2002, 4.

19. Pack, *Growth and Convergence,* 170.

20. Zhang, "Have Regions," 167.

21. Statistics on income polarization are taken from Marc V. Levine, "Globalization and

Wage Polarization in U.S. and Canadian Cities: Does Public Policy Make a Difference?" in *Cities in a Global Society*, ed. Richard V. Knight and Garry Gappert (Newbury Park, CA: Sage Publications, 1990).

22. DRI/McGraw-Hill, *America's Clusters: Building Industry Clusters* (Sedona, AZ: DRI/McGraw-Hill, June 1995).

23. See Pack, *Growth and Convergence.*

24. Richard Florida, *The Rise of the Creative Class and How It's Transforming Work, Leisure, Community, and Everyday Life* (New York: Basic Books, 2002). The effect of amenities on regional growth is also discussed in Nissan and Carter, "Income Inequality."

25. William H. Frey, "Immigration, Domestic Migration and Demographic Balkanization in America: New Evidence for the 1990s," *Population and Development Review* 22 (December 1996): 741–63, updated by the author with U.S. census estimates released March 20, 1997.

26. The link between economic growth and declining ghetto poverty is made by Paul Jargowsky, *Poverty and Place: Ghettos, Barrios, and the American City* (New York: Russell Sage Foundation, 1997), 162; and Drennan et al., "Interruption of Income Convergence," 75–79. Tight regional labor markets draw the ghetto poor into jobs. See Richard B. Freeman, "Employment and Earnings of Disadvantaged Young Men in a Labor Shortage Economy," in *The Urban Underclass*, ed. Christopher Jencks and Paul Peterson (Washington, DC: Brookings Institution Press, 1991), 104–34; and Paul Osterman, "Gains from Growth? The Impact of Full Employment on Poverty in Boston," in *The Urban Underclass*, ed. Christopher Jencks and Paul Peterson (Washington, DC: Brookings Institution Press, 1991), 103–34; Jargowsky, *Poverty and Place*, 191–93; Richard B. Freeman and William Rodgers III, "Area Economic Conditions and the Labor Market Outcomes of Young Men in the 1990s Expansion," Working Paper W7073 (Cambridge, MA: National Bureau of Economic Research, April 1999); the study was reported in Sylvia Nasar and Kirsten B. Mitchell, "Booming Job Market Draws Young Black Men into Fold," *New York Times*, May 23, 1999.

27. The connections between regional inequality and regional growth are explored in Larry C. Ledebur and William R. Barnes, *City Distress, Metropolitan Disparities and Economic Growth* (Washington, DC: National League of Cities, 1992); Hank V. Savitch, David Collins, Daniel Sanders, and John P. Markham, "Ties that Bind: Central Cities, Suburbs, and the New Metropolitan Region," *Economic Development Quarterly* 7, no. 4 (November 1993): 341–58; Richard Voith, "City and Suburban Growth: Substitutes or Complements?" *Business Review* (Federal Reserve Bank of Philadelphia, September–October 1992): 21–33; Manuel Pastor, Peter Dreier, J. Eugene Grigsby III, and Marta Lopez-Garza, *Regions that Work: How Cities and Suburbs Can Grow Together* (Minneapolis: University of Minnesota Press, 2000).

28. One study found that only 3.3 percent of the rise in national wage inequality between 1978 and 1987 could be attributed to increased inequality in wages across states. Phillips, "Regional Wage Divergence," 37.

29. Ted Halstead and Michael Lind, "The National Debate over School Funding Needs a Federal Focus," *Los Angeles Times*, October 8, 2000.

30. Our discussion of the Haussmannization of Paris and Vienna relies on Robert Fishman, *Bourgeois Utopia: The Rise and Fall of Suburbia* (New York: Basic Books, 1987), 111–16. For a discussion of how the government in Paris is still trying to exclude immigrants, the elderly, and the poor from central Paris, see Paul White, "Ideolo-

gies, Social Exclusion and Spatial Segregation in Paris," in *Urban Segregation and the Welfare State: Inequality and Exclusion in Western Cities,* ed. Sako Musterd and Wim Ostendorf (London: Routledge, 1998), 148–67.

31. The data on housing prices in Kansas City are from Chris Lester and Jeffrey Spivak, "Buying Bigger Allows Better Housing Benefit," *Kansas City Star,* December 19, 1995. This article is part of an excellent six-part series on the costs of sprawl.

32. Oliver Byrum, *Old Problems in New Times* (Chicago: American Planning Association, 1992), 19.

33. An early statement of concentric zone theory is Ernest W. Burgess, "The Growth of the City," in Robert E. Park, Ernest W. Burgess, and Roderick McKenzie, eds., *The City* (Chicago: University of Chicago Press, 1925).

34. The best historical account of the fragmentation of American urban areas is found in Jon C. Teaford, *City and Suburb: The Political Fragmentation of Metropolitan America, 1850–1970* (Baltimore: Johns Hopkins University Press, 1979).

35. David Rusk, *Cities Without Suburbs* (Washington, DC: Woodrow Wilson Center Press, 1993).

36. Figures for Atlanta, Albuquerque, and Anchorage are from U.S. Bureau of the Census, *Statistical Abstract of the United States 2002* (Washington, DC: U.S. Government Printing Office, 2002), 32–38.

37. On the causes of the rising income gap between cities and suburbs, see Edward Hill and Harold Wolman, "Accounting for the Change in Income Disparities Between U.S. Central Cities and Their Suburbs from 1980 to 1990," *Urban Studies* 34, no. 1 (1997): 43–60; Janice Madden, "Changes in the Distribution of Poverty Across and Within the U.S. Metropolitan Areas, 1979–1989," *Urban Studies* 33, no. 9 (1996): 1581–600.

38. Data on the flight of middle-income and two-parent families out of cities is reported in John D. Kasarda, Stephen J. Appold, Stuart Sweeney, and Elaine Sieff, "Central City and Suburban Migration Patterns: Is a Turnaround on the Horizon?" *Housing Policy Debate* 8, no. 2 (1997): 307–58.

39. Kathryn P. Nelson examines migration into cities in forty metropolitan areas in *Gentrification and Distressed Cities: An Assessment of Trends in Intrametropolitan Migration* (Madison: University of Wisconsin Press, 1988).

40. Grogan and Proscio, *Comeback Cities.*

41. "The Suburban Advantage," Lewis Mumford Center for Urban and Regional Research, University at Albany, June 24, 2002.

42. David Rusk, *Cities Without Suburbs,* 3rd ed. (Washington, DC: Woodrow Wilson Center Press, 2003), 75–76.

43. Rusk, *Cities Without Suburbs,* 3rd ed., 78–79.

44. Orfield measured tax capacity based on the revenue would be forthcoming, if a municipality applied average rates to its tax base. Spending needs were evaluated using percentage of elementary students eligible for the federal free- or reduced-price lunch program; population density; population growth (1993–98); age of the housing stock; and proportion of elementary students who are non-Asian minorities. Suburbs were then grouped into categories using a statistical technique called cluster analysis. Myron Orfield, *American Metropolitics: The New Suburban Reality* (Washington, DC: Brookings Institution Press, 2002), 31–32.

45. Property tax rates in Harvey, Illinois, are reported in William H. Lucy and David L. Phillips, *Confronting Suburban Decline: Strategic Planning for Metropolitan Renewal* (Washington, DC: Island Press, 2000), 2; based on John McCarron, "Tip of the Ice-

berg: Only a Matter of Time Before Some Suburbs Come Tumbling Down," *Chicago Tribune,* April 27, 1998.

46. Tracie Rozhon, "Be It Ever Less Humble: American Homes Get Bigger," *New York Times* (October 22, 2000).

47. Lucy and Phillips, *Confronting Suburban Decline.*

48. Gaines's insightful account of teenagers in downwardly mobile suburbs is found in *Teenage Wasteland: Suburbia's Dead End Kids* (Chicago: University of Chicago Press, 1998). See also Eric Bogosian's play *Suburbia,* which takes place in a 7-Eleven parking lot and depicts the despair of teenagers in desolate suburbs.

49. Joel Garreau, *Edge City: Life on the New Frontier* (New York: Doubleday, 1992).

50. Lucy and Phillips, *Confronting Suburban Decline,* 170–77.

51. Orfield, *American Metropolitics,* 60. To measure inequality, Orfield used the GINI index, which examines differences or inequalities across the entire range of values.

52. G. Ross Stephens and Nelson Wikstrom, *Metropolitan Government and Governance: Theoretical Perspectives, Empirical Analysis, and the Future* (New York: Oxford University Press, 2000), 19.

53. The discussion of Countryside is based on Chris Lester and Jeffrey Spivak, "Divided We Sprawl," *Kansas City Star,* December 17, 1995.

54. Gregory R. Weiher, *The Fractured Metropolis: Political Fragmentation and Metropolitan Segregation* (Albany, NY: SUNY Press, 1991). Greater suburban fragmentation leads to greater socioeconomic divisions. See Eric J. Heikil, "Are Municipalities Tieboutian Clubs?" *Regional Science and Urban Economics* 26 (1996), 203–26.

55. Paul Jargowsky, *Poverty and Place: Ghettos, Barrios, and the American City* (New York: Russell Sage Foundation, 1996).

56. Jargowsky, *Stunning Progress.*

57. See Thomas G. Kingsley and Kathryn L. S. Pettit, *Concentrated Poverty: A Change in Course* (Washington, DC: Urban Institute, May 2003); and Aaron Bernstein, "An Inner-City Renaissance: The Nation's Ghettos Are Making Surprising Strides. Will the Gains Last?" *Business Week,* October 27, 2003, 64–68, reporting on data compiled by the Initiative for a Competitive City, headed by Harvard Business School professor Michael E. Porter.

58. Olivier Zunz, *The Changing Face of Inequality: Urbanization, Industrial Development, and Immigrants in Detroit, 1880–1920* (Chicago: University of Chicago Press, 1982), 342.

59. Otis Dudley Duncan and Beverly Duncan, *The Negro Population of Chicago: A Study of Residential Succession* (Chicago: University of Chicago Press, 1957), as reported in Reynolds Farley, "Residential Segregation of Social and Economic Groups Among Blacks, 1970–1980," in *The Urban Underclass,* ed. Christopher Jencks and Paul E. Peterson (Washington, DC: Brookings Institution Press, 1991), 283.

60. Albert A. Simkus, "Residential Segregation by Occupation and Race in Ten Urbanized Areas, 1950–1970," *American Sociological Review* 43 (1978): 81–93, as reported in Douglas S. Massey, "The Age of Extremes: Concentrated Affluence and Poverty in the Twenty-first Century," *Demography* 33, no. 4 (November 1996): 398.

61. Claudia J. Coulton et al., "Geographic Concentration of Affluence and Poverty in 100 Metropolitan Areas, 1990," *Urban Affairs Review* 32, no. 2 (November 1996): 186–216; Alan J. Abramson, Mitchell S. Tobin, and Matthew R. VanderGoot, "The Changing Geography of Metropolitan Opportunity: The Segregation of the Poor in U.S. Metropolitan Areas, 1970 to 1990," *Housing Policy Debate* 6, no. 1 (1995): 45–72. Peter A. Tatian and Alisa Wilson find that both the isolation and dissimilarity

indices for the poor increased in the 1980s and then fell back in the 1990s, but not back to 1980 levels. See *Segregation of the Poor in U.S. Metropolitan Areas: 1980 to 2000* (Washington, DC: Urban Institute, forthcoming).

62. For a discussion of the different quantitative techniques for measuring segregation, see Massey and Denton, *American Apartheid,* chap. 3.

63. In *When Work Disappears: The World of the New Urban Poor* (New York: Knopf, 1996), William Julius Wilson substitutes the term "ghetto poverty" for *underclass,* apparently taking to heart the criticism that the word *underclass* had been used to stereotype the residents of poor neighborhoods as the undeserving poor. See Herbert J. Gans, "Deconstructing the Underclass: The Term's Danger as a Planning Concept," *Journal of the American Planning Association* (summer 1990): 271–77.

64. Katherine S. Newman, *No Shame in My Game: The Working Poor in the Inner City* (New York: Knopf and Russell Sage Foundation, 1999), appendix 1, table 1. The source is the Chicago Urban and Family Life Survey, which was the basic source of information for Wilson's *When Work Disappears: The World of the New Urban Poor* (New York: Knopf, 1996).

65. Shannon McConville and Paul Ong, *The Trajectory of Poor Neighborhoods in Southern California, 1970–2000* (Washington, DC: Brookings Institution Press, Center for Urban and Metropolitan Policy, November 2003), 13.

66. Freeman, "Employment and Earnings"; Osterman, "Gains from Growth?"; Freeman and Rodgers, "Area Economic Conditions."

67. Jargowsky, *Poverty and Place,* 101.

68. Leslie Kaufman, "Millions Have Left Welfare, but Are They Better Off? Yes, No, and Maybe," *New York Times* (October 20, 2003).

69. Kathryn Edin and Laura Lein, *Making Ends Meet: How Single Mothers Survive Welfare and Low-Wage Work* (New York: Russell Sage Foundation, 1997), 44.

70. McConville and Ong, *Trajectory,* 4.

71. Kingsley and Pettit, *Concentrated Poverty.*

72. Jargowsky, *Stunning Progress,* 12.

73. The poverty cutoff was originally calculated in the 1960s by measuring how much it costs to purchase a minimally acceptable diet and then multiplying that figure by three (based on evidence at the time that the typical family spent one-third of its income on food). The poverty standard has been adjusted for inflation since then using the Consumer Price Index. But the typical family now spends less than one-seventh of its income on food. In 2000, the average "consumer unit," or household, devoted 13.6 percent of its expenditures to food. U.S. Bureau of the Census, *Statistical Abstract of the United States 2002,* 430. If the cost of a minimally acceptable diet was multiplied by seven instead of three, the poverty cutoff would be considerably higher, and many more families would be counted as poor. The poverty measurement was devised by Mollie Orshansky. See her "Counting the Poor: Another Look at the Poverty Profile," *Social Security Bulletin* (January 1965).

74. National Research Council, Panel on Poverty Statistics and Welfare Benefits, Committee on National Statistics, *Measuring Poverty: A New Approach,* Constance F. Citro and Robert T. Michael, eds. Washington, DC: National Academy Press (available at http://www.nap.edu/catalog/4759.html).

75. U.S. Bureau of the Census, *Statistical Atlas of the United States: 2002,* 455.

76. Using the federal poverty standard, Massey and Fisher, in "Geography of Inequality," 11, report an 11.8 percent reduction in isolation of the poor from 1990 to 2000.

77. Colleen Casey, Robert Flack, and Todd Swanstrom, "Economic Segregation in the Top Fifty Metropolitan Areas, 1980–2000," paper delivered at the Urban Affairs Association Annual Meeting, Cleveland, Ohio (March 27–29, 2003).

78. William Julius Wilson, "There Goes the Neighborhood," *New York Times* (June 16, 2003); Jargowsky, *Stunning Progress,* 13.

79. William Julius Wilson, *The Truly Disadvantaged: The Inner City, the Underclass, and Public Policy* (Chicago: University of Chicago Press, 1987). In *When Work Disappears,* Wilson gave somewhat greater weight to the role of racism.

80. The argument about the importance of race in generating concentrated poverty is found in Douglas S. Massey and Mitchell L. Eggers, "The Ecology of Inequality: Minorities and the Concentration of Poverty, 1970–1980," *American Journal of Sociology* 95 (1990): 1153–88; Massey and Denton, *American Apartheid;* Douglas S. Massey, Andrew B. Gross, and Kumiko Shibuya, "Migration, Segregation, and the Geographic Concentration of Poverty," *American Sociological Review* 59 (1994): 424–45.

81. Richard D. Alba and John R. Logan, "Analyzing Locational Attainments," *Sociological Methods and Research* 20, no. 3 (February 1992): 386. See also John R. Logan, Richard D. Alba, and Shu-Yin Leung, "Minority Access to White Suburbs: A Multiregional Comparison," *Social Forces* 74, no. 3 (March 1996): 851–81; John R. Logan, Richard D. Alba, Tom McNulty, and Brian Fisher, "Making a Place in the Metropolis: Locational Attainment in Cities and Suburbs," *Demography* 33, no. 4 (November 1996): 443–53.

82. For a more optimistic analysis of trends in racial segregation, see Edward L. Glaeser and Jacob L. Vigdor, "Racial Segregation: Promising News"; for a more pessimistic interpretation, see John R. Logan, "Ethnic Diversity Grows, Neighborhood Integration Lags." Both articles are in *Redefining Urban and Suburban America: Evidence from Census 2000,* ed. Bruce Katz and Robert E. Lang (Washington, DC: Brookings Institution Press, 2003).

83. This discussion draws heavily on Jargowsky, *Poverty and Place,* 132–43.

84. Jargowsky, *Stunning Progress,* 10.

85. Mary J. Fischer, "The Relative Importance of Income and Race in Determining Residential Outcomes in U.S. Urban Areas, 1970–2000," *Urban Affairs Review* 38, no. 5 (2003), 684. Fischer uses four income groups and measures segregation using the entropy index.

86. Sprawl is an exceedingly complex concept. Galster and colleagues have identified eight separate dimensions of sprawl. See George Galster, Royce Hanson, Michael R. Ratcliffe, Harold L. Wolman, Stephen Coleman, and Jason Reihage, "Wrestling Sprawl to the Ground: Defining and Measuring an Elusive Concept," *Housing Policy Debate* 12, no. 4 (2001), 681–718.

87. Barry Edmonton, Michael A. Goldberg, and John Mercer, "Urban Form in Canada and the United States: An Examination of Urban Density Gradients," *Urban Studies* 22 (1985): 213.

88. F. Kaid Benfield, Matthew D. Raimi, and Donald D. T. Chen, *Once There Were Greenfields: How Urban Sprawl Is Undermining America's Environment, Economy, and Social Fabric* (New York: National Resources Defense Council, 1999), 12.

89. The free-market explanation of suburbanization is based on bid-rent curves. See William Alonso, "A Theory of the Urban Land Market," in *Urban Change and Conflict: An Interdisciplinary Reader,* ed. Andrew Blowers et al. (London: Harper and Row, 1981), 63–67.

90. William A. Fischel, "Does the American Way of Zoning Cause the Suburbs of Metropolitan Areas to Be Too Spread Out?" in *Governance and Opportunity in Metropolitan America,* ed. Alan Altshuler, William Morrill, Harold Wolman, and Faith Mitchell (Washington, DC: National Academy Press, 1999), 161. For positive evidence on the push hypothesis, see William H. Frey, "Central City White Flight: Racial and Nonracial Causes," *American Sociological Review* 44 (June 1979): 425–48; Harvey Marshall and Kathleen O'Flaherty, "Suburbanization in the Seventies: The 'Push-Pull' Hypothesis Revisited," *Journal of Urban Affairs* 9, no. 3 (1987): 249–62. For contrary evidence, see David F. Bradford and Harry H. Kelejian, "An Econometric Model of Flight to the Suburbs," *Journal of Political Economy* 81 (January–June 1973): 566–89; Thomas M. Guterbock, "The Push Hypothesis: Minority Presence, Crime, and Urban Deconcentration," in *The Changing Face of the Suburbs,* ed. Barry Schwartz (Chicago: University of Chicago Press, 1976), 137–61.

91. Thomas J. Sugrue, *The Origins of the Urban Crisis: Race and Inequality in Postwar Detroit* (Princeton, NJ: Princeton University Press, 1996). See also Heather Ann Thompson, "Rethinking the Politics of White Flight in the Postwar City: Detroit, 1945–1980," *Journal of Urban History* 25, no. 2 (January 1999): 163–99.

92. Julie Berry Cullen and Steven D. Levitt, "Crime, Urban Flight, and the Consequences for Cities," *Review of Economics and Statistics* 81, no. 2 (May 1999): 159–69.

93. Paul Jargowsky, "Sprawl, Concentration of Poverty, and Urban Inequality," in *Urban Sprawl: Causes and Consequences,* ed. Gregory D. Squires (Washington, DC: Urban Institute, 2002), 51. Jargowsky's conclusion is based on data relating the decade when most of the housing in a census tract was built with the mean household income and standard deviation of incomes. The more recently the housing was built, the higher the mean income and the lower the standard deviation (or variation) in incomes.

94. Also, rigorous building codes drive up the cost of housing, make it more difficult for developers to build new low- and moderate-income housing. Thus, unlike Latin American cities, U.S. cities have no shantytowns on the urban fringe. See Anthony Downs, "Ecosystem: Suburban/Inner City," *Journal of Property Management* (November–December 1997): 62.

95. A recent study found that economic segregation actually rose as density increased across metropolitan areas—but at higher levels of density, the relationship reversed and economic segregation fell as density increased. Rolf Pendall and John I. Carruthers, "Does Density Exacerbate Income Segregation? Evidence from U.S. Metropolitan Areas, 1980–2000," *Housing Policy Debate* 14, no. 4 (2003), 541–89. On the basis of a regression analysis using 150 variables, Anthony Downs concluded that there is no statistically significant relation between urban decline and sprawl. Anthony Downs, "Some Realities About Sprawl and Urban Decline," *Housing Policy Debate* 10, no. 4 (1999): 955–74. Notwithstanding his conclusion that sprawl and urban decline are unrelated, Downs asserts that limiting sprawl would "invigorate" the urban core (972), thereby helping efforts at community revitalization in poor urban neighborhoods.

96. It is worthwhile to note that not only does concentrated poverty drive sprawl, but new housing developments on the urban fringe also undermine older neighborhoods, spreading concentrated poverty. A study of 74 metropolitan areas found that the number of new housing units built from 1980 to 2000 exceeded the number of new households by 19 percent. In those metropolitan areas where new construction exceeds new households, some housing must be abandoned. Most of that abandoned housing will be in the inner city and older suburbs. Tom Bier and Charlie Post,

Vacating the City: An Analysis of New Homes vs. Household Growth (Washington, DC: Brookings Institution Press, December 2003).

97. See David Rusk, *Inside Game/Outside Game: Winning Strategies for Saving Urban America* (Washington, DC: Brookings Institution Press, 1999).

98. Jargowsky, *Stunning Progress,* 18.

99. For accounts of economic segregation that stresses global economic forces, see Saskia Sassen, *The Global City: New York, London, Tokyo* (Princeton, NJ: Princeton University Press, 1991); and Manuel Castells, *The Informational City: Information, Technology, Economic Restructuring, and the Urban-Regional Process* (Oxford: Basil Blackwell, 1989).

100. See the special issues of *Housing Studies* on "Opportunity, Deprivation and the Housing Nexus: Trans-Atlantic Perspectives," 17, no. 1 (January 2002); and "Life in Poverty Neighborhoods," 18, no. 6 (November 2003).

101. An early advocate of the global city thesis, Castells, in a later essay written with John Mollenkopf, stressed the importance of public policy: "Occupational polarization and income inequality become translated into widespread urban dualism . . . only when public policy mirrors the naked logic of the market." In "Conclusion: Is New York a Dual City?" in *Dual City: Restructuring New York,* ed. Manuel Castells and John H. Mollenkopf (New York: Russell Sage Foundation, 1991), 413.

102. Our description of ghettos in France is based on Loic J. D. Wacquant, "Urban Outcasts: Stigma and Division in the Black American Ghetto and the French Urban Periphery," *International Journal of Urban and Regional Research* 17, no. 3 (1993): 366–83; and White, "Ideologies, Social Exclusion."

103. Sophie Body-Gendrot cites the work of Edmond Preteceille on this point in *The Social Control of Cities: A Comparative Perspective* (Oxford: Blackwell, 2000), 184. Our comparison of French and American ghettos draws heavily from Body-Gendrot's insightful analysis.

104. Ada Becchi, "The Changing Space of Italian Cities," *American Behavioral Scientist* 41, no. 3 (1997): 372. A study of Oslo, Norway, found that even though economic inequalities were widening, the residential segregation of occupational groups remained stable, primarily because of national and local public policies. Echoing our approach, the author concludes, "politics matter." Terje Wessel, "Social Polarisation and Socioeconomic Segregation in a Welfare State: The Case of Oslo," *Urban Studies* 37, no. 11 (2000): 1947–67.

105. Barbara Schmitter Heisler, "Housing Policy and the Underclass: The United Kingdom, Germany, and the Netherlands," *Journal of Urban Affairs* 16, no. 3 (1994): 212.

106. Wacquant makes the point that the ghetto poor are isolated from the rest of society in the United States, whereas in France, there has been a "closing of the economic, social, and cultural distance between immigrants and the stagnant or downwardly mobile fractions of the native working class stuck in the *banlieue*" ("Urban Outcasts," 379).

107. For an insightful if dated account of the tensions between the working class and the ghetto poor, see Jonathan Rieder, *Canarsie: The Jews and Italians of Brooklyn Against Liberalism* (Cambridge, MA: Harvard University Press, 1985).

108. The point that strong welfare policies reduce resistance to economic integration is made throughout Musterd and Ostendorf, *Urban Segregation;* and in Susan S. Fainstein, "The Egalitarian City: The Restructuring of Amsterdam," *International Planning Studies* 2, no. 3 (1997): 295–314.

109. Although the rich in Europe do not generally have the option of moving to a place

with a separate government, Jeffrey Sellers shows that when economically advantaged groups live apart from the rest of society in both Europe and America, they are less likely to support shared amenities such as parks and public transportation. See his "Public Goods and the Politics of Segregation: An Analysis and Cross-National Comparison," *Journal of Urban Affairs* 21, no. 2 (1999): 237–62.

CHAPTER 3. THE COSTS OF ECONOMIC SEGREGATION AND SPRAWL

1. Edward Barnes, "Can't Get There from Here," *Time,* February 19, 1996, 33. Under the threat of a boycott from civil rights organizations and the Buffalo Teachers Federation, the owners of the Galleria and two other malls agreed to allow bus stops on their property, with one located just a few steps from Arthur Treacher's. In November 1999, the Galleria owners agreed to a $2.55 million settlement with Wiggins's heirs (*Washington Post,* November 18, 1999).
2. Neil Kraus, *Race, Neighborhoods and Community Power: Buffalo Politics, 1934–1997* (Albany, NY: SUNY Press, 2000), 29.
3. According to one review, "the study of neighborhood effects . . . has become something of a cottage industry in the social sciences." By the late 1990s, about 100 articles a year were being published on the topic. Robert J. Sampson, Jeffrey D. Morenoff, and Thomas Gannon-Rowley, "Assessing 'Neighborhood Effects': Social Processes and New Directions for Research," *Annual Review of Sociology* 28 (2002), 443–78.
4. After a comprehensive review of the research on children, Jencks and Mayer concluded that "The literature . . . does not . . . warrant any strong generalizations about neighborhood effects." Christopher Jencks and Susan Mayer, "The Social Consequences of Growing Up in a Poor Neighborhood," in *Inner-City Poverty in the United States,* ed. Laurence E. Lynn Jr. and Michael G. H. McGeary (Washington, DC: National Academy Press, 1990), 176. Similarly, Galster and Zobel assert that the evidence that poverty concentration causes increased social problems beyond individual characteristics is "thin and contradictory." George Galster and Anne Zobel, "Will Dispersed Housing Programmes Reduce Social Problems in the U.S.?" *Housing Studies* 13, no. 5 (1998): 605. In a review of the first edition of *Place Matters,* Paul Jargowsky, one of leading researchers on concentrated poverty, criticizes us for "overstat[ing] the case for place." According to Jargowsky, "the evidence for neighborhood effects on social and economic outcomes, after controlling for family effects, is at best equivocal." Paul Jargowsky, review of *Place Matters, Urban Affairs Review* 37, no. 3 (January 2002): 443.
5. Having said this, we acknowledge that the specific social processes by which the context influences outcomes are not well understood. For an insightful discussion of the need to research the exact processes behind contextual effects, see Ingrid Gould Ellen and Margery Austin Turner, "Do Neighborhoods Matter and Why?" in *Choosing a Better Life: Evaluating the Moving to Opportunity Social Experiment,* ed. John Goering and Judith D. Feins (Washington, DC: Urban Institute, 2003), 313–38; and Sampson, Morenoff, and Gannon-Rowley, "Assessing 'Neighborhood Effects.' "
6. A third more limited experiment on the effects of poverty deconcentration was conducted in Yonkers, New York, when the federal courts ordered the city to disperse subsidized housing throughout the city. For evidence on the Yonkers case, see Michael P. Johnson, Helen F. Ladd, and Jens Ludwig, "The Benefits and Costs

of Residential Mobility Programmes for the Poor," *Housing Studies* 17, no. 1 (2002): 125–38; and Xavier de Souza Briggs, Joe Darden, and A. Aidala, "In the Wake of Desegregation: Early Impacts of Scattered-Site Public Housing on Neighborhoods in Yonkers, New York," *Journal of the American Planning Association* 65, no. 1 (1999): 27–49.

7. Although people were not randomly chosen for the program (they had to voluntarily pursue admission), their assignment to city or suburban locations was on a first-come, first-served basis, determined by the availability of units. As a result, "the city and suburban groups were highly comparable." Leonard S. Rubinowitz and James E. Rosenbaum, *Crossing the Class and Color Lines: From Public Housing to White Suburbia* (Chicago: University of Chicago Press, 2000), 77.

8. Leslie Kaufman, "Millions Have Left Welfare, But Are They Better off? Yes, No, and Maybe," *New York Times* (October 20, 2003). An Urban Institute survey of former recipients found that two-thirds were working when interviewed in 1997, but they had alarmingly low wages, averaging $6.60 an hour. Three-quarters lacked medical benefits. The Urban Institute survey of former welfare recipients is discussed in Michael M. Weinstein, "When Work Is Not Enough," *New York Times,* August 26, 1999; "AFDC/TANF Average Monthly Families and Recipients, 1936–2001," available at http://www.acf.hhs.gov/news/stats/3697.htm; 2003 caseload available at http://hhs.gov/news/press/2003/mar03_jun03.htm; Alan Weil, *Ten Things Everyone Should Know About Welfare Reform* (Washington, DC: Urban Institute, May 2002).

9. The commuting problems of single mothers in Los Angeles are described in Eric Bailey, "From Welfare Lines to Commuting Crush; Labor: Many Reentering Work Force Live Far from Jobs. Experts Fear Transit Woes May Slow Reform," *Los Angeles Times,* October 6, 1997, A1; Paul Ong and Evelyn Blumenberg, "Job Access, Commuting, and Travel Burden Among Welfare Recipients," *Urban Studies* 35, no. 1 (January 1998): 77–93.

10. Martin Wachs, "Men, Women, and Urban Travel: The Persistence of Separate Spheres," in *The Car and the City: The Automobile, the Built Environment, and Daily Urban Life,* ed. Martin Wachs and Margaret Crawford (Ann Arbor: University of Michigan Press, 1992), 86–100; Carol Lawson, "Distance Makes the Heart Skip for Commuter Moms," *New York Times,* November 7, 1991; M. A. Thompson, "The Import of Spatial Mismatch on Female Labor Force Participation," *Economic Development Quarterly* 11, no. 2 (1997): 138–45.

11. Katherine Allen and Maria Kirby, *Why Cities Matter to Welfare Reform* (Washington, DC: Brookings Institution Center for Urban and Metropolitan Policy, July 2000), available at http://www.brook.edu/es/urban/welfarecaseloads/2000report .htm. For further evidence on this point, see Sandra J. Newman, ed., *The Home Front: Implications of Welfare Reform for Housing Policy* (Washington, DC: Urban Institute, 2000), especially chap. 4 by Claudia Coulton, Laura Leete, and Neil Bania.

12. "Let Them Drive Cars: Wheels for the Poor," *New Republic,* March 20, 2000.

13. John F. Kain, "Housing Segregation, Negro Employment, and Metropolitan Decentralization," *Quarterly Journal of Economics* 82, no. 2 (1968): 175–97.

14. David T. Ellwood, "The Spatial Mismatch Hypothesis: Are There Teenage Jobs Missing in the Ghetto?" in *The Black Youth Employment Crisis,* ed. Richard B. Freeman and Harry J. Holzer (Chicago: University of Chicago Press, 1986), 147–87; Norman Fainstein, "The Underclass/Mismatch Hypothesis as an Explanation for Black Economic Deprivation," *Politics and Society* 15 (1986): 403–51. William Julius Wilson

found that racial discrimination by employers is an important factor, especially for black men; see *When Work Disappears: The World of the New Urban Poor* (New York: Knopf, 1996), chap. 5.

15. Keith Ihlanfeldt, "The Spatial Mismatch Between Jobs and Residential Locations Within Urban Areas," *Cityscape* 1, no. 1 (1994): 224. Of six literature reviews on the spatial mismatch, three find substantial support for a spatial mismatch, two find moderate support, and one finds the evidence too mixed to reach a conclusion. Gould Ellen and Austin Turner, "Do Neighborhoods Matter and Why?" 328.

16. See John D. Kasarda, "Entry-Level Jobs, Mobility, and Urban Minority Unemployment," *Urban Affairs Quarterly* 19 (1983): 21–40; "Urban Change and Minority Opportunities," in *The New Urban Reality,* ed. Paul E. Peterson (Washington, DC: Brookings Institution Press, 1985); "Urban Industrial Transition and the Underclass," *Annals, AAPSS* 501 (1989): 26–47; John Kasarda, "Industrial Restructuring and the Changing Location of Jobs," in *The State of the Union: America in the 1980s,* vol. 1, *Economic Trends,* ed. Reynolds Farley (New York: Russell Sage Foundation, 1995), 215–67; Robert Lang, *Office Sprawl: The Evolving Geography of Business* (Washington, DC: Brookings Institution Center for Urban and Metropolitan Policy, October 2000); Joseph Persky and Wim Wiewel, *When Corporations Leave Town: The Costs and Benefits of Metropolitan Job Sprawl* (Detroit: Wayne State University Press, 2000).

17. Based on U.S. Bureau of the Census, *County Business Patterns,* as compiled in U.S. Department of Housing and Urban Development (HUD), *The State of the Cities 2000: Megaforces Shaping the Future of the Nation's Cities* (Washington, DC: HUD, 2000), 2. See also Thomas Stanback, *The New Suburbanization* (Boulder, CO: Westview Press, 1991), 44, as cited in Joseph Persky, Elliott Sclar, and Wim Wiewel, *Does America Need Cities? An Urban Investment Strategy for National Prosperity* (Washington, DC: Economic Policy Institute, 1991), 12.

18. For young urban professionals, many of whom grew up in the suburbs, gentrification of historic neighborhoods around downtowns, which has surged in recent years, provides one way to address the mismatch between jobs and housing. Elvin K. Wyly and Daniel J. Hammel, "Islands of Decay in Seas of Renewal: Housing Policy and the Resurgence of Gentrification," *Housing Policy Debate* 10, no. 4 (1999), 711–71.

19. Further evidence of the spatial mismatch is that wages for entry-level jobs in outer suburbs are often higher than in central cities. Wages at a McDonald's in suburban Connecticut, for example, were found to be 19 percent higher than at a McDonald's 25 miles away in the Bronx. Not surprisingly, the suburban McDonald's offers a free McShuttle from the central city for its workers. Sam Roberts, "Migrant Labor: The McShuttle to the Suburbs," *New York Times,* June 14, 1990.

20. The figures on Westchester County jobs and residents are reported in Roberts, "Migrant Labor"; Elsa Brenner, "It's in the Numbers: Waves of New Faces," *New York Times,* October 5, 1997. Housing price information is reported in Elsa Brenner, "In the Region/Westchester; Price of Single-Family Home Up Almost 10% in Year," *New York Times,* August 10, 2003.

21. Michael N. Danielson and Jameson W. Doig, *New York: The Politics of Urban Regional Development* (Berkeley: University of California Press, 1982), 82–87.

22. Elsa Brenner, "As a Town Opts for Open Space, Not All Rejoice," *New York Times,* June 6, 1999.

23. The fair market rent is calculated by the federal government at the fortieth percentile. This means that 60 percent of the two-bedroom apartments in Westchester

rented for more than $1,294. National Low Income Housing Coalition, *Out of Reach 2003: America's Housing Wage Climbs* (Washington, DC: National Low-Income Housing Coalition, 2003).

24. Brad Kessler, "Down and Out in Suburbia," *Nation,* September 25, 1989.

25. Martin Commacho, interview with Todd Swanstrom, August 1991.

26. Dave Sheingold, "Renter's Dilemma," *Herald Statesman,* May 18, 1988; Bruce Lambert, "Raid on Illegal Housing Shows the Plight of Suburbs' Working Poor," *New York Times,* December 7, 1996.

27. Rubinowitz and Rosenbaum, *Crossing the Class and Color Lines,* 189; see also James E. Rosenbaum, "Changing the Geography of Opportunity by Expanding Residential Choice: Lessons from the Gautreaux Program," *Housing Policy Debate* 6, no. 1 (1995): 231–69. The interim evaluation of the MTO program did not find any significant employment effects. Larry Orr et al., *Moving to Opportunity Interim Impacts Evaluation* (Washington, DC: U.S. Department of Housing and Urban Development, 2003), chap. 7.

28. Wilson, *When Work Disappears,* 39.

29. Katherine M. O'Regan summarizes seven studies examining the search methods for finding jobs in "The Effect of Social Networks and Concentrated Poverty on Black and Hispanic Youth Unemployment," *Annals of Regional Science* 27 (1993): 329.

30. Quoted in Wilson, *When Work Disappears,* 133–35.

31. Ibid., 65.

32. Claude S. Fischer, *To Dwell Among Friends: Personal Networks in Town and City* (Chicago: University of Chicago Press, 1982). See also Manuel Pastor and Ara Robinson Adams, "Keeping Down with the Joneses: Neighbors, Networks, and Wages," *Review of Regional Economics* 26, no. 2 (1996): 115–45. This may help explain why another study found that blacks and whites living in Atlanta had very poor knowledge of the spatial distribution of job openings in the suburbs. Keith R. Ihlanfeldt, "Information on the Spatial Distribution of Job Opportunities in Metropolitan Areas," *Journal of Urban Economics* 41 (1997): 218–42.

33. Edward Banfield, *The Unheavenly City: The Nature and Future of Our Urban Crisis* (Boston: Little, Brown, 1970); Charles Murray, *Losing Ground: American Social Policy 1950–1980* (New York: Basic Books, 1984), 227.

34. Paul Osterman, "Gains from Growth? The Impact of Full Employment on Poverty in Boston," in *The Urban Underclass,* ed. Christopher Jencks and Paul Peterson (Washington, DC: Brookings Institution Press, 1991); and Richard B. Freeman, "Employment and Earnings of Disadvantaged Young Men in a Labor Shortage Economy," in Jencks and Peterson, *Urban Underclass,* 104–34.

35. Based on research on 322 metropolitan areas by Richard B. Freeman and William Rodgers III, "Area Economic Conditions and the Labor Market Outcomes of Young Men in the 1990s Expansion," Working Paper W7073 (Cambridge, MA: National Bureau of Economic Research, April 1999); the study was reported in Sylvia Nasar and Kirsten B. Mitchell, "Booming Job Market Draws Young Black Men into Fold," *New York Times,* May 23, 1999.

36. Katherine S. Newman, *No Shame in My Game: The Working Poor in the Inner City* (New York: Knopf and Russell Sage Foundation, 1999), 62.

37. Paul Jargowsky, *Poverty and Place: Ghettos, Barrios, and the American City* (New York: Russell Sage Foundation, 1997), 96, 101.

38. Wilson, *When Work Disappears,* 67.

39. Wilson, in *When Work Disappears,* documents that black men are particularly likely

to have attitudes and behaviors that make them less acceptable and successful in entry-level jobs, especially those that deal with the public. Wilson stresses, however, that these attitudes and behaviors are the *product* of restricted opportunities in ghetto poverty areas, not the primary cause of these restricted opportunities.

40. James E. Rosenbaum, Lisa Reynolds, and Stefanie DeLuca, "How Do Places Matter? The Geography of Opportunity, Self-Efficacy and a Look Inside the Black Box of Residential Mobility," *Housing Studies* 17, no. 1 (2002): 81.

41. Steven N. Durlauf, "A Theory of Persistent Income Inequality," *Journal of Economic Growth* 1 (March 1996): 75–93; Durlauf, "Associational Redistribution: A Defense," in *Recasting Egalitarianism: New Rules for Communities, States, and Markets,* ed. E. O. Wright (London: Verso Books, 1998), 261–84; and Roland Benabou, "Workings of a City: Location, Education, and Production," *Quarterly Journal of Economics* 108, no. 3 (1993): 619–52.

42. Lawrence Mishel, Jared Bernstein, and Heather Boushey, *The State of Working America 2002/2003* (Ithaca, NY: Cornell University Press, 2003), 78, 418.

43. Robert W. Burchell et al., *Costs of Sprawl — 2000,* TCRP Report 74 (Washington, DC: National Academy Press, 2002).

44. The controlled growth scenario is not radical. Basically, growth in outlying counties is limited to 75 percent of its upper growth limits and 20 percent of the units are developed in clusters with density twice that prevailing in undeveloped areas. Ibid., 5.

45. Ibid., preface and 21.

46. Scott Bernstein, *Using the Hidden Assets of America's Cities and Regions to Ensure Sustainable Communities* (Chicago: Center for Neighborhood Technology, 1999), part 1; as cited in Thad Williamson, David Imbroscio, and Gar Alperowitz, *Making Place for Community: Local Democracy in a Global Era* (New York: Routledge, 2002), 10.

47. Persky and Wiewel, *When Corporations Leave Town.*

48. Richard Voith, "City and Suburban Growth: Substitutes or Complements?" *Business Review* (Federal Reserve Bank of Philadelphia, September–October 1992); Larry C. Ledebur and William R. Barnes, *Metropolitan Disparities and Economic Growth* (Washington, DC: National League of Cities, 1992); H. V. Savitch, David Collins, Daniel Sanders, and John P. Markham, "Ties that Bind: Central Cities, Suburbs, and the New Metropolitan Region," *Economic Development Quarterly* 7, no. 4 (November 1993): 341–58; Larry C. Ledebur and William R. Barnes, *"All in It Together": Cities, Suburbs and Local Economic Regions* (Washington, DC: National League of Cities, February 1993); David Rusk, *Cities Without Suburbs* (Washington, DC: Woodrow Wilson Center Press, 1993); Richard Voith, "Do Suburbs Need Cities," *Journal of Regional Science* 38, no. 3 (1998): 445–64; Stephanie Shirley Post and Robert M. Stein, "State Economies, Metropolitan Governance, and Urban-Suburban Dependence," *Urban Affairs Review* 36, no. 1 (September 2000): 46–60.

49. As every social scientist knows, however, correlation does not prove causation. The association of city and suburban economic well being could be a product of a third factor, such as the regional economic mix, that is the driving force causing suburban and central city incomes to go up and down together. In order to prove a causal connection between economic segregation, sprawl, and regional competitiveness, researchers must specify the causal processes. See Edward W. Hill, Harold L. Wolman, and Coit Cook Ford III, "Can Suburbs Survive Without Their Central Cities? Examining the Suburban Dependence Thesis," *Urban Affairs Review* 31, no. 2 (November 1995): 147–74.

50. Andrew F. Haughwout, "The Paradox of Infrastructure Investment: Can a Productive Good Reduce Productivity?" *Brookings Review* 18, no. 3 (2000), 38–41.

51. William A. Fischel, "Comment on Anthony Downs's 'The Advisory Commission on Regulatory Barriers to Affordable Housing: Its Behavior and Accomplishments,'" *Housing Policy Debate* 2, no. 4 (1991): 1139–60. The question of growth controls raises a number of issues that extend beyond the scope of our discussion. Efforts by communities to protect the environment or reduce traffic may be in the public interest, but if enacted by individual communities, growth controls often cause leapfrog development, worsen sprawl, and prevent people from moving closer to their jobs. For a review of the evidence on growth controls, see Anthony Downs, *New Visions for Metropolitan America* (Washington, DC: Brookings Institution Press, 1994), 33–36.

52. Peter Dreier, David Schwartz, and Ann Greiner, "What Every Business Can Do About Housing," *Harvard Business Review* 66, no. 5 (September–October 1988): 52–58.

53. Richard Florida, "The Rise of the Creative Class," *Washington Monthly*, May 2002, 21. For a full account of Florida's theory, see *The Rise of the Creative Class and How It's Transforming Work, Leisure, Community, and Everyday Life* (New York: Basic Books, 2002).

54. See Peter O. Muller, "Are Cities Obsolete? The Fearful Symmetry of Post-Urban America," *Sciences* (March–April 1986): 43–46; Anthony Pascal, "The Vanishing City," *Urban Studies* 24 (1987): 597–603; Robert Fishman, "Megalopolis," *Wilson Quarterly* (winter 1990): 25–45; Tom Morganthau and John McCormick, "Are Cities Obsolete?" *Newsweek*, September 9, 1991, 42–44.

55. For a summary of the evidence on the continued need for face-to-face relations in the economy, see Keith Ihlanfeldt, "The Importance of the Central City to the Regional and National Economy: A Review of the Arguments and Empirical Evidence," *Cityscape* 1, no. 1 (1995): 125–50; and Edward L. Glaeser, "The Future of Urban Research: Nonmarket Interactions," in *Brookings-Wharton Papers on Urban Affairs 2000,* ed. William G. Gale and Janet Rothenberg Pack (Washington, DC: Brookings Institution Press, 2000), 101–38.

56. Joel Garreau, *Edge City: Life on the New Frontier* (New York: Doubleday, 1991), 4, 8, 25. Muller, "Are Cities Obsolete?"; and Robert Fishman, *Bourgeois Utopias* (New York: Basic Books, 1987), also argue that cities are becoming obsolete as suburbs take over their traditional functions.

57. Richard Voith, "Changing Capitalization of CBD-Oriented Transportation Systems: Evidence from Philadelphia, 1970–1988," *Journal of Urban Economics* 33 (1993): 361–76. In 1989, 46 percent of all earnings in San Francisco suburbs came from residents who worked in the central city; the figure for Denver was 41 percent, for New Orleans 39 percent. Persky, Sclar, and Wiewel, *Does America Need Cities?*, 13.

58. Alex Schwartz, "Subservient Suburbia: The Reliance of Large Suburban Companies on Central City Firms for Financial and Professional Services," *Journal of the American Planning Association* (summer 1993): 302.

59. Antonio Ciccone and Robert E. Hall, "Productivity and the Density of Economic Activity," *American Economic Review* 86, no. 1 (March 1996): 54–70.

60. Jane Jacobs, *The Economy of Cities* (New York: Random House, 1969).

61. Michael Storper, "The Limits to Globalization: Technology Districts and International Trade," *Economic Geography* 68 (1992): 60–93.

62. AnnaLee Saxenian, *Regional Advantage: Culture and Competition in Silicon Valley and Route 128* (Cambridge, MA: Harvard University Press, 1994). See also Ben-

nett Harrison, "Industrial Districts: Old Wine in New Bottles?" *Regional Studies* 26, no. 5 (1992): 469–83; Stephan Schrader, "Information Technology Transfers Between Firms: Cooperation Through Information Trading," *Research Policy* 20 (1991): 153–70; James E. Rauch, "Productivity Gains from Geographic Concentration of Human Capital: Evidence from Cities," *Journal of Urban Economics* 34 (1993): 380–400.

63. The concept of flexible specialization originated in Michael J. Piore and Charles F. Sabel, *The Second Industrial Divide: Possibilities for Prosperity* (New York: Basic Books, 1984).

64. For this reason, Mayor Richard Riordan's offer of costly incentives for the new DreamWorks studio was a waste of taxpayers' money. The studios were not about to relocate to St. Louis or any other metropolitan area.

65. Andrew F. Haughwout and Robert P. Inman, "Should Suburbs Help Their Central City?" in *Brookings-Wharton Papers on Urban Affairs 2002,* ed. William G. Gale and Janet Rothenberg Pack (Washington, DC: Brookings Institution Press, 2002), 45–88.

66. Daniel J. Luria and Joel Rogers, *Metro Futures: Economic Solutions for Cities and Their Suburbs* (Boston: Beacon Press, 1999), 13. For further support of the proposition that high-wage manufacturing can prosper in central cities, see Joel Rast, *Remaking Chicago: The Political Origins of Urban Industrial Change* (De Kalb: Northern Illinois University Press, 1999).

67. Haughwout and Inman, "Should Suburbs Help Their Central City?" 78.

68. U.S. Conference of Mayors, *The Role of Metro Areas in the U.S. Economy* (Lexington, MA: DRI/WEFA, 2002).

69. Laurie Kaye Abraham, *Mama Might Be Better Off Dead: The Failure of Health Care in Urban America* (Chicago: University of Chicago Press, 1993), 17–18.

70. U.S. Bureau of the Census, *Statistical Abstract of the United States 2002* (Washington, DC: U.S. Government Printing Office, 2002), 829, 833.

71. Amartya Sen, "The Economics of Life and Death," *Scientific American* (May 1993): 44.

72. Colin McCord and Harold P. Freeman, "Excess Mortality in Harlem," *New England Journal of Medicine* 322, no. 3 (January 18, 1990): 173.

73. G. B. Rodgers, "Income and Inequality as Determinants of Mortality: An International Cross-Section Analysis," *Population Studies* 33 (1979): 343–51.

74. National Center for Health Statistics, available at http://www.cdc.gov/nchs/releases/02news/hus02.htm.

75. Inequality also harms health within regions: a study of 282 U.S. metropolitan areas found a high correlation between regional inequality and an elevated death rate, after controlling for the overall level of income. John W. Lynch et al., "Income Inequality and Mortality in Metropolitan Areas in the United States," *American Journal of Public Health* 88, no. 7 (1998): 1074–80. Another study of 369 local authorities in England found that the greater the inequality between their neighborhoods, the higher the mortality or death rate. Yoav Ben-Shlomo, Ian R. White, and Michael Marmot, "Does the Variation in the Socioeconomic Characteristics of an Area Affect Mortality?" in *The Society and Population Health Reader: Income Inequality and Health,* ed. Ichiro Kawachi, Bruce P. Kennedy, and Richard G. Wilkinson (New York: New Press, 1999), 47–49.

76. I. H. Yen and S. L. Syme, "The Social Environment and Health: A Discussion of the Epidemiological Literature," *Annual Review of Public Health* 20 (1990): 293.

77. The increased risk of death persisted even after controlling for baseline health status, race, income, employment status, access to medical care, health insurance cover-

age, smoking, alcohol consumption, physical activity, body mass index, sleep patterns, social isolation, marital status, depression, and personal uncertainty. Because many of these conditions negatively associated with health are partly caused by residence in distressed neighborhoods, the Alameda study underestimated the effect of place on the chances of dying. Mary Haan, George A. Kaplan, and Terry Camacho, "Poverty and Health: Prospective Evidence from the Alameda County Study," *American Journal of Epidemiology* 125, no. 6 (1987): 989–98. A more recent study based on a nationally representative sample of adults found that "a person's health is associated with the SES [socioeconomic status] characteristics of the community over and above one's income, education, and assets." Stephanie A. Robert, "Community-Level Socioeconomic Status Effects on Adult Health," *Journal of Health and Social Behavior* 39 (March 1998): 18. See also George A. Kaplan, "People and Places: Contrasting Perspectives on the Association Between Social Class and Health," *International Journal of Health Services* 26, no. 3 (1996): 507–19.

78. Larry Orr et al., *Moving to Opportunity Interim Impacts Evaluation,* chaps. 4 and 5. An earlier evaluation of MTO also found lower rates of asthma rates and injuries for people who moved. See Lawrence F. Katz, Jeffery R. Kling, and Jeffrey B. Liebman, "Boston Site Findings: The Early Impacts of Moving to Opportunity," in *Choosing a Better Life,* ed. Goering and Feins, 195–96.

79. Carmen DeNovas Walt, Bernadette D. Proctor, and Robert J. Mills, *Income, Poverty, and Health Insurance Coverage in the United States: 2003,* Current Population Report P60-226 (Washington, DC: U.S. Bureau of the Census, August 2004). More central-city residents are uninsured than suburbanites. Among adults, for example, 25 percent of central-city residents are uninsured, compared with 17 percent of suburbanites. UCLA Center for Health and Policy Research, memo to the authors.

80. Data cited in James W. Fossett and Janet D. Perloff, *The "New" Health Reform and Access to Care: The Problem of the Inner City* (Washington, DC: Kaiser Commission on the Future of Medicaid, 1995), 31–32.

81. Ibid., 32.

82. Jonathan Kozol, *Amazing Grace: The Lives of Children and the Conscience of a Nation* (New York: Harper Perennial, 1995), 172.

83. U.S. Bureau of the Census, *Statistical Abstract of the United States 2002,* 344.

84. One study found that public spending on health explained "less than one-seventh of one percent" of the variation in mortality across countries. Deon Filmer and Lant Prichett, "The Impact of Public Spending on Health: Does Money Matter?" *Social Science and Medicine* 49, no. 10 (1999): 1309–23; as reported in Grace Budrys, *Unequal Health: How Inequality Contributes to Health or Illness* (Lanham, Maryland: Rowman & Littlefield, 2003), 184.

85. Jacob A. Riis, *How the Other Half Lives* (1890; reprint, New York: Hill and Wang, 1957), 81.

86. For a discussion of the parallels between New York slums in the 1890s and the 1990s, see Sam Roberts, "New York in the Nineties," *New York Times Magazine,* September 29, 1991, 35–39.

87. One study found, for example, that the rate of traffic injuries to children was four times higher in the poorest neighborhoods of Montreal compared with the least poor neighborhoods. Geoffrey Dougherty, I. Barry Pless, and Russell Wilkins, "Social Class and the Occurrence of Traffic Injuries and Deaths in Urban Children," *Canadian Journal of Public Health* 81 (May–June 1990): 204–9.

88. David Barboza, "Rampant Obesity: A Debilitating Reality for the Urban Poor," *New*

York Times, December 26, 2000. On how fear of crime prevents the poor from exercising, see Tom Farley and Deborah Cohen, "Fixing a Fat Nation," *Washington Monthly,* December 2001, 27. May Duenwald reports on a University of North Carolina study that linked the availability of supermarkets in neighborhoods to healthy diets in "Good Health Is Linked to Grocer," *New York Times,* November 12, 2002.

89. Lawrence D. Fran, Peter O. Engelke, and Thomas L. Schmid, *Health and Community Design: The Impact of the Built Environment on Physical Activity* (Washington, DC: Island Press, 2003), chap 5. Research in Great Britain confirms that poor areas lack amenities that are directly related to health, such as recreational facilities. Sally MacIntyre, Sheila MacIver, and Anne Soomans, "Area, Class and Health: Should We Be Focusing on Places or People?" *Journal of Social Policy* 22 (1993): 213–34; Anthony P. Polednak, *Segregation, Poverty, and Mortality in Urban African Americans* (New York: Oxford University Press, 1991), 139; Lauran Neegaard, "Report Urges Improvement in Immunization System," *Albany Times Union,* June 16, 2000.

90. U.S. Department of Health and Human Services, *Health, United States 1998* (Washington, DC: U.S. Government Printing Office, 1998).

91. Paul Mushak, "Defining Lead as the Premiere Environmental Health Issue for Children in America: Criteria and Their Quantitative Application," *Environmental Research* 59 (1992): 281–309; Nick Farr and Cushing Dolbeare, "Childhood Lead Poisoning: Solving a Health and Housing Problem," *Cityscape* 2, no. 3 (September 1996): 176–82.

92. A 1992 U.S. Environmental Protection Agency report on environmental equity stated that "evidence indicates that racial minority and low-income populations are disproportionately exposed to lead, selected air pollutants, hazardous waste facilities, contaminated fish tissue, and agricultural pesticides in the workplace." It concluded that this population was "more likely to actually experience harm due to these exposures." U.S. Environmental Protection Agency (EPA), *Environmental Equity: Reducing Risks for All Communities,* vols. 1 and 2 (Washington, DC: EPA Policy, Planning and Evaluation Report PM-221, EPA 230-R-92-008, 1992), letter of transmittal and 1–2. The literature on environmental equity is large and contentious. For an introduction to the issue, see Robert D. Bullard, *Dumping in Dixie: Race, Class and Environmental Quality* (Boulder, CO: Westview Press, 1990). For analyses of the literature, see J. Tom Boer, Manuel Pastor Jr., James L. Sadd, and Lori D. Snyder, "Is There Environmental Racism? The Demographics of Hazardous Waste in Los Angeles County," *Social Science Quarterly* 78, no. 4 (December 1997): 793–810.

93. Kozol, *Amazing Grace,* 7; Kemba Johnson, "Big Stack Attack," *City Limits,* July–August 1999, 5.

94. Sheryl Gay Stolberg, "Poor People Are Fighting Baffling Surge in Asthma," *New York Times,* October 18, 1999.

95. Kozol, *Amazing Grace,* 171.

96. David L. Rosenstreich et al., "The Role of Cockroach Allergy and Exposure to Cockroach Allergen in Causing Morbidity Among Inner-City Children with Asthma," *New England Journal of Medicine* 336, no. 19 (May 8, 1997): 1356–63.

97. Research has established a firm connection between poor neighborhoods and early-adolescent sexual activity and failure to use contraceptives (controlling for individual characteristics). See Karin L. Brewster, John O. G. Billy, and William R. Grady, "Social Context and Adolescent Behavior: The Impact of Community on the Transition to Sexual Activity," *Social Forces* 71, no. 3 (March 1993): 713–40; Karin L. Brewster, "Race Differences in Sexual Activity Among Adolescent Women: The Role of

Neighborhood Characteristics," *American Sociological Review* 59 (June 1994): 408–24; Karin L. Brewster, "Neighborhood Context and the Transition to Sexual Activity Among Black Women," *Demography* 31, no. 4 (November 1994): 603–14; John O. G. Billy, Karin L. Brewster, and William R. Grady, "Contextual Effects on the Sexual Behavior of Adolescent Women," *Journal of Marriage and Family* 56 (May 1994): 387–404.

98. Polednak, *Segregation, Poverty, and Mortality,* 119, 122.

99. Paula Diehr et al., "Do Communities Differ in Health Behaviors?" *Journal of Clinical Epidemiology* 46, no. 10 (1993): 1141–49.

100. Maro Wilson and Martin Daly, "Life Expectancy, Economic Inequality, Homicide, and Reproductive Timing in Chicago Neighborhoods," in Kawachi, Kennedy, and Wilkinson, *Society and Population Health Reader,* 299.

101. Geronimus argues that for poor women in poor neighborhoods who have short life expectancies and premature aging, teenage childbearing is rational because it increases the likelihood that their children will be healthy and have able-bodied caretakers. Geronimus also, however, argues that the risks and costs of teen childbearing are minimal. Arline T. Geronimus, "Teenage Childbearing and Personal Responsibility: An Alternative View," *Political Science Quarterly* 112, no. 3 (1997): 405–30.

102. Ana Correa Fick and Sarah Moody Thomas, "Growing Up in a Violent Environment: Relationship to Health-Related Beliefs and Behavior," *Youth and Society* 27, no. 2 (1996): 136–47.

103. Arline T. Geronimus, "The Weathering Hypothesis and the Health of African American Women and Infants," *Ethnicity and Disease* 2, no. 3 (1992): 222–31.

104. For an excellent nontechnical discussion of the role of stress in disease, see Budrys, *Unequal Health,* chap. 9.

105. For a review of some of this literature, see Shelley E. Taylor, Rena L. Repetti, and Teresa Seeman, "What Is an Unhealthy Environment and How Does It Get Under the Skin," in Kawachi, Kennedy, and Wilkinson, *Society and Population Health Reader,* 351–78.

106. Bruce S. McEwen, "Protective and Damaging Effects of Stress Mediators," in Kawachi, Kennedy, and Wilkinson, *Society and Population Health Reader,* 386.

107. Rosenbaum, Reynolds, and DeLuca, "How Do Places Matter?"

108. Quoted in Helen Epstein, "Enough to Make You Sick?" *New York Times Magazine,* October 12, 2003, 98.

109. Lisa Berkman and Thomas Glass, "Social Integration, Social Network, Social Support, and Health," in *Social Epidemiology,* ed. Lisa Berkman and Ichiro Kawachi (Oxford: Oxford University Press, 2000).

110. Kawachi, Kennedy, and Wilkinson, *Society and Population Health Reader,* comment by the editors, 158.

111. For an introduction to the literature, see the articles in Kawachi, Kennedy, and Wilkinson, *Society and Population Health Reader,* part 3; Robert Putnam, *Bowling Alone: The Collapse and Revival of American Community* (New York: Simon and Schuster, 2000), chap. 20.

112. Putnam, *Bowling Alone,* 331.

113. Loïc J. D. Wacquant and William Julius Wilson, "The Cost of Racial and Class Exclusion in the Inner City," *Annals of the American Academy of Political and Social Science* 501 (January 1989): 22–24.

114. Jon C. Teaford, *The Unheralded Triumph: City Government in America, 1870–1900* (Baltimore: Johns Hopkins University Press, 1984), 246; and Blake McKelvey, *The*

Urbanization of America, 1860–1915 (New Brunswick, NJ: Rutgers University Press, 1963), 90. Between 1850 and 1915, death rates in the United States fell by 55 percent. Farley and Cohen, "Fixing a Fat Nation," 29.

115. Ingrid Ellen, Todd Mijanovich, and Kerri-Nicole Dillman, "Neighborhood Effects on Health," *Journal of Urban Affairs* 23, no. 3–4 (2001): 404; Lisa F. Berkman and Ichiro Kawachi, "A Historical Framework for Social Epidemiology," in *Social Epidemiology,* ed. Berkman and Kawachi, 9.

116. Quoted in Kevin Fitzpatrick and Mark LaGory, *Unhealthy Places: The Ecology of Risk in the Urban Landscape* (New York: Routledge, 2000), 4.

117. Our discussion of inner city disease and its spread to the suburbs is based on Deborah Wallace and Rodrick Wallace, *A Plague on Your Houses: How New York Was Burned Down and National Public Health Crumbled* (New York: Verso, 1998). For a sampling of their scholarly publications, see Rodrick Wallace, "A Synergism of Plagues: 'Planned Shrinkage,' Contagious Housing Destruction, and AIDS in the Bronx," *Environmental Research* 47 (1988): 1–33; Elmer L. Streuning, Rodrick Wallace, and Robert Moore, "Housing Conditions and the Quality of Children at Birth," *Bulletin of the New York Academy of Medicine* 66, no. 5 (1990): 463–78; Rodrick Wallace, "Urban Desertification, Public Health and Public Order: 'Planned Shrinkage,' Violent Death, Substance Abuse and AIDS in the Bronx," *Social Science Medicine* 31, no. 7 (1990): 801–13; Rodrick Wallace, "A Fractal Model of HIV Transmission on Complex Sociogeographic Networks. Part 2: Spread from a Ghettoized 'Core Group' into a More General Population," *Environment and Planning A* 29 (1997): 789–804; R. Wallace, A. J. Fisher, and R. Fullilove, "Marginalization, Information, and Infection: Risk Behavior Correlation in Ghettoized Sociogeographic Networks and the Spread of Disease to Majority Populations," *Environment and Planning A* 29 (1997): 1629–45; R. Wallace and D. Wallace, "The Destruction of U.S. Minority Urban Communities and the Resurgence of Tuberculosis: Ecosystem Dynamics of the White Plague in the Developing World," *Planning and Environment A* 29 (1997): 269–91.

118. Adding in poverty in the host county with the density of commuting raised the correlation to very high levels (94%). Wallace and Wallace, *A Plague on Your Houses,* 162.

119. In the mid-1990s, Baltimore suffered an epidemic of sexually transmitted diseases, including syphilis, gonorrhea, chlamydia, herpes, and AIDS. This epidemic quickly moved from the inner city to inner-ring suburbs. A 1996 report by the National Academy of Sciences, *The Hidden Epidemic,* rang alarm bells about the fact that sexually transmitted diseases were not confined to the inner city. Sheryl Gay Stolberg, "U.S. Wakes to Epidemic of Sexual Diseases," *New York Times,* March 9, 1998.

120. Wallace and Wallace, *A Plague on Your Houses,* 165.

121. F. Kaid Benfield, Matthew D. Raimi, and Donald D. T. Chen, *Once There Were Greenfields: How Urban Sprawl Is Undermining America's Environment, Economy, and Social Fabric* (New York: National Resources Defense Council, 1999), 34.

122. U.S. Bureau of the Census, *Statistical Abstract of the United States 2002,* 677.

123. Allen Thein Durning, *The Car and the City* (Seattle: Northwest Environment Watch, 1996), 10.

124. Mark Delucchi, *Health Effects of Motor Vehicle Pollution* (Davis, CA: Institute of Transportation Standards, University of California at Davis, 1995).

125. William H. Lucy, "Mortality Risk Associated with Leaving Home: Recognizing the Significance of the Built Environment," *American Journal of Public Health* 93, no. 9 (September 2003): 1564–69. See also Durning, *The Car and the City,* 24.

126. For evidence and citations, see Meni Koslowsky, Avraham N. Kluger, and Mordechai Reich, *Commuting Stress: Causes, Effects, and Methods of Coping* (New York: Plenum Press, 1995), especially chap. 4; Steven M. White and James Rotton, "Type of Commute, Behavioral Aftereffects, and Cardiovascular Activity: A Field Experiment," *Environment and Behavior* 36, no. 6 (1998): 763–80.

127. See Gary E. McKay, *Road Rage: Commuter Combat in America* (Herculaneum, MO: Silvertip Books, 2000).

128. Jeffrey P. Kaplan and William H. Dietz, "Caloric Imbalance and Public Health Policy," *Journal of the American Medical Association* 282, no. 16 (October 27, 1999): 1579–81.

129. Research by Reid Ewing of Rutgers University, as reported in "Suburban Sprawl Adds Health Concern, Studies Say," *New York Times* (August 31, 2003). See also Jeffrey Spivak and Alan Bavley, "Expanding Suburbs, Expanding Waistlines? Some Researchers See a Connection," *Kansas City Star*, December 1, 2002.

130. Putnam, *Bowling Alone,* chap. 12.

131. Jane Jacobs, *The Death and Life of Great American Cities* (New York: Random House, 1961), 72.

132. Richard D. Bingham and Zhongcai Zhang, *The Economies of Central-City Neighborhoods* (Boulder, CO: Westview Press, 2001), 55. See also Richard D. Bingham and Zhongcai Zhang, "Poverty and Economic Morphology of Ohio Central-City Neighborhoods," *Urban Affairs Review* 32, no. 6 (1997): 766–96.

133. Part of the cause of the flight of retail out of the older parts of regions is the competition for sales tax revenues. One study found that the greater the reliance on sales taxes for municipal revenues, the more rapidly retail sprawled out to the urban fringe. Essentially, retailers, especially big box retailers like Wal-Mart and Home Depot, choose their locations on the basis of the incentives offered by competing suburban governments rather than simply responding to consumer demand—as free market theory would predict. Robert W. Wassmer, "The Influence of Local Fiscal Structure and Growth Control Choices on 'Big Box' Urban Sprawl in the American West," Graduate Program in Public Policy and Administration, California State University, Sacramento, April 3, 2002.

134. U.S. Department of Housing and Urban Development, *New Markets: The Untapped Retail Buying Power in America's Inner Cities* (Washington, DC: U.S. Government Printing Office, July 1999), 23. These inner-city areas were defined as census tracts with poverty rates above 20 percent or with median family incomes 80 percent or less of the metropolitan area median.

135. David Caplovitz, *The Poor Pay More: Consumer Practices of Low-Income Families* (Glencoe, IL: Free Press, 1963), 13.

136. *Hearing Before the Select Committee on Hunger, House of Representatives, 102nd Congress,* September 30, 1992 (Washington, DC: U.S. Government Printing Office, 1992), 17. The percentage goes down in areas with high housing costs.

137. Reported in Alix M. Freedman, "The Poor Pay More for Food in New York, Survey Finds," *Wall Street Journal,* April 15, 1991.

138. James M. MacDonald and Paul E. Nelson Jr., "Do the Poor Still Pay More? Food Price Variations in Large Metropolitan Areas," *Journal of Urban Economics* 30 (1991): 344–59; Amanda Shaffer, *The Persistence of LA's Grocery Gap* (Los Angeles: Occidental College Center for Food and Justice, May 2002).

139. As reported in *Hearing Before the Select Committee on Hunger,* 24.

140. Ibid., 1.

141. Michael E. Porter, "The Competitive Advantage of the Inner City," *Harvard Business Review* (May–June 1995): 58.

142. Testimony of Rev. Monsignor William J. Linder, in *Hearing Before the Select Committee on Hunger*, 185.

143. Personal communication to the authors by Joel Rast based on studies by the Center for Neighborhood Technology in Chicago.

144. Bill Turque, "Where the Food Isn't," *Newsweek*, February 24, 1992, 36–37.

145. Bingham and Zhang, "Poverty and Economic Morphology," 786. Bingham and Zhang report that the average grocery store in middle-class zip codes has forty-five employees, whereas the average store in extreme-poverty zip codes has fewer than seven employees (*Economies of Central-City Neighborhoods*, 56).

146. Bingham and Zhang, *Economies of Central-City Neighborhoods*, 58.

147. John P. Caskey, *Fringe Banking: Check-Cashing Outlets, Pawnshops, and the Poor* (New York: Russell Sage Foundation, 1994).

148. This figure does not include fees charged by pawnshops and auto title lenders. James H. Carr and Jenny Schuetz, "Financial Services in Distressed Communities: Framing the Issue, Finding Solutions," Fannie Mae Foundation, August 2001, as reported in Doug Dylla and Catherine A. Smith, "Fringe Lenders Gnaw Away at Personal and Community Wealth," *Bright Ideas* 21, no. 4 (fall 2002): 1–74.

149. Evelyn Nieves, "Poor Credit? Rent-to-Moan Is Wooing You," *New York Times*, January 15, 1998.

150. Edward C. Banfield, *The Unheavenly City Revisited* (Boston: Little, Brown, 1974), 61.

151. See the insightful discussion of the culture of poverty perspective in Caskey, *Fringe Banking*, 81–83. For a more realistic view of spending patterns by the poor, based on careful observation, see Elizabeth Chin, *Purchasing Power: Black Kids and the American Consumer Culture* (Minneapolis: University of Minnesota Press, 2001).

152. Bank deregulation has also contributed to the growth of fringe banking. Increasing competition has forced banks to eliminate money-losing branches and services (such as low-cost or no-cost checking accounts) that were previously cross-subsidized by more lucrative services and locations. Major banks have been ruthless about closing branches in neighborhoods where their customers are poor or even working class. Caskey, *Fringe Banking*, 89.

153. The literature on redlining is voluminous. For a summary, see Margery Austin Turner et al., *What We Know About Mortgage Lending Discrimination in America* (Washington, DC: U.S. Department of Housing and Urban Development, September 1999).

154. John P. Caskey, "Bank Representation in Low-Income and Minority Communities," *Urban Affairs Quarterly* 29, no. 4 (June 1994): 617–38.

155. A two-tiered market also exists for insurance. Many insurance companies have restrictions on writing policies for older homes or homes below a certain value. Fewer insurance agents are located in central cities. As a result of insurance redlining, it is difficult to insure a home in many city neighborhoods, and when you can, the price is often higher. See Gregory D. Squires, ed., *Insurance Redlining: Disinvestment, Reinvestment, and the Evolving Role of Financial Institutions* (Washington, DC: Urban Institute, 1997); and Gregory D. Squires, "Racial Profiling, Insurance Style: Insurance Redlining and the Uneven Development of Metropolitan Areas," *Journal of Urban Affairs* 25, no. 4 (2003): 391–410. Car insurance also costs more if you live in a poor neighborhood. According to a survey by the *Chicago Sun-Times* of the three top insurance companies, the base rate in Chicago's Austin neighborhood is more

than double that in Naperville, an outer-ring suburb. The difference can add up to $800 a year. Tim Novak and Jon Schmid, "Car Insurance Rides on Zip Codes: Cities' Rates Higher than Most Suburbs," *Chicago Sun-Times,* November 30, 1997.

156. Chandrika Jayathirtha and Jonathan Fox, "Overspending Behavior of Households with and Without Vehicle Purchases," *Consumer Interests Annual* 43 (1997): 124–30.

157. U.S. Bureau of the Census, *Statistical Abstract of the United States 2002,* 720–21.

158. Elizabeth Warren and Amelia Warren Tyagi, *The Two-Income Trap: Why Middle-Class Mothers and Fathers are Going Broke* (New York: Basic Books, 2003), 6.

159. Warren and Tyagi, *Two-Income Trap,* 20.

160. John de Graaf, David Wann, and Thomas H. Naylor, *Affluenza: The All-Consuming Epidemic* (San Francisco: Berrett-Koehler Publishers, 2001), 2. Other authors who stress that financial pressures are due to luxury overconsumption are Juliet B. Schor, *The Overspent America: Upscaling, Downshifting, and the New Consumer* (New York: Basic Books, 1998); and Robert H. Frank, *Luxury Fever: Why Money Fails to Satisfy in an Era of Excess* (New York: Free Press, 1999). In the first edition of *Place Matters,* we argued that the isolation of suburbanites in economically homogeneous enclaves heightened the status anxieties that Schor argues drive middle-class overconsumption. We have since come to the conclusion that this effect, if it exists at all, is overwhelmed by the structural pressures exerted by rising housing and transportation costs in suburbia. We are indebted to Carl Abbott for pointing out this flaw in our argument (personal communication).

161. The following section draws heavily on two books that argue, persuasively, that the financial strains in the American middle class are not primarily individual failures but are rooted in the structural conditions of middle class life. See Jerome M. Segal, *Graceful Simplicity: Toward a Philosophy and Politics of Simple Living* (New York: Henry Holt, 1999); and Warren and Tyagi, *Two-Income Trap.*

162. U.S. Bureau of the Census, *Statistical Abstract of the United States 2002,* 726. During that same period, the median sales price of existing homes increased from $92,000 to $147,800 — well beyond the inflation rate (593).

163. Warren and Tyagi, *Two-Income Trap,* 22, 133.

164. Ibid., 20–21.

165. Most women, especially those with young children, have entered the workforce out of economic necessity, not to buy luxuries or to find fulfillment. Ibid., 29–30.

166. Ibid., 28.

167. Ibid., 24.

168. Danilo Yanich, "Location, Location, Location: Urban and Suburban Crime on Local TV News," *Journal of Urban Affairs* 23, nos. 3–4 (2001): 221–41.

169. Edward J. Blakely and Mary Gail Snyder, *Fortress America: Gated Communities in the United States* (Washington, DC: Brookings Institution Press, 1997), 126.

170. William A. Fischel estimates that 25 percent of suburbanization was caused by non-market factors, such as the desire to escape urban blight. "Does the American Way of Zoning Cause the Suburbs of Metropolitan Areas to Be Too Spread Out?" in *Governance and Opportunity in Metropolitan America,* ed. Alan Altshuler, William Morrill, Harold Wolman, and Faith Mitchell (Washington, DC: National Academy Press, 1999), 161.

171. Segal, *Graceful Simplicity,* 55.

172. Ibid., 56.

173. Ibid., 640.

174. Jayathirtha and Fox, "Overspending Behavior."

175. For this reason, "location-efficient mortgages" have been proposed that allow house-holds with less automobile dependence to qualify for larger mortgages and thus buy more expensive homes. Durning, *The Car and the City,* 19.

176. John Kenneth Galbraith, *The Affluent Society* (New York: Mentor Books, 1958).

177. Tom Wolfe, *The Bonfire of the Vanities* (Toronto: Bantam Books, 1987), 87.

178. U.S. Bureau of the Census, *Statistical Abstract of the United States 2002,* 183. For a discussion of the extent of the crime drop in cities and the debate about its causes, see Paul Grogan and Tony Proscio, *Comeback Cities* (Boulder, CO: Westview Press, 2000), chap. 7; and Fox Butterfield, "Reason for Dramatic Drop in Crime Puzzles Experts," *New York Times,* March 29, 1998.

179. Robert J. Sampson and Janet L. Lauritsen, "Violent Victimization and Offending: Individual-, Situational-, and Community-Level Risk Factors," in *Understanding and Preventing Violence,* vol. 3, *Social Influences,* ed. Albert J. Reiss Jr. and Jeffrey A. Roth (Washington, DC: National Academy Press, 1994), 41–42.

180. U.S. Bureau of the Census, *Statistical Abstract of the United States 2002,* 190.

181. Ibid.

182. For a subcultural view of crime, see Murray, *Losing Ground,* chap. 8. In that chapter, Murray uses "blacks as our proxy for that group" (116) — that is, the group of people who were drawn into a culture of poverty by federal welfare spending and misguided programs to prevent crime instead of punish it.

183. Jeffrey D. Moreonoff, Robert J. Sampson, and Stephen W. Raudenbush, "Neighborhood Inequality, Collective Efficacy, and the Spatial Dynamics of Urban Violence," *Criminology* 39, no. 3 (2001), 551; Steven F. Messner and Kenneth Tardiff, "Economic Inequality and Levels of Homicide: An Analysis of Urban Neighborhoods," *Criminology* 24, no. 2 (1986), 310.

184. The evidence on this point is cited in John Hagan and Ruth D. Peterson, "Criminal Inequality in America: Patterns and Consequences," in *Crime and Inequality,* ed. John Hagan and Ruth D. Peterson (Stanford, CA: Stanford University Press, 1995), 20.

185. Allen E. Liska and Paul E. Bellair, "Violent Crime Rates and Racial Composition: Convergence over Time," *American Journal of Sociology* 101, no. 3 (November 1995): 578–610.

186. One of the first books to make this argument explicit was Richard Cloward and Lloyd Ohlin, *Delinquency and Opportunity: A Theory of Delinquent Gangs* (New York: the Free Press, 1960). Cloward and Ohlin helped establish Mobilization for Youth in New York City, which became a model of sorts for Lyndon Johnson's War on Poverty. See Nicholas Lemann, *The Promised Land: The Great Black Migration and How it Changed America* (New York: Knopf, 1991), 120–22.

187. Michiko Kakatuni, "Bananas for Rent," *New York Times Magazine,* November 9, 1997, 32.

188. Research shows that each additional hour of television watched per week decreases savings by $208. Schor, *Overspent American,* 78.

189. Ibid., 39.

190. Carol W. Kohfeld and John Sprague, "Urban Unemployment Drives Urban Crime," *Urban Affairs Quarterly* 24, no. 2 (December 1988): 215–41.

191. Studies on how much crime pays are summarized in Richard B. Freedman, "Crime and the Employment of Disadvantaged Youths," in *Urban Labor Markets and Job Opportunity,* ed. George E. Peterson and Wayne Vroman (Washington, DC: Urban Institute, 1992), 227–31.

192. Wilson, *When Work Disappears,* chap. 5.

193. Philippe Bourgois, "Office Work and the Crack Alternative Among Puerto Rican Drug Dealers in East Harlem," in *Urban Life: Readings in Urban Anthropology,* 3rd ed., ed. George Gmelch and Walter P. Zenner (Prospect Heights, IL: Waveland Press, 1996), 425.

194. Daniel Goleman, "Black Scientists Study the 'Pose' of the Inner City," *New York Times,* April 29, 1992. Dr. Majors is the coauthor of *Cool Pose: The Dilemmas of Black Manhood in America* (Lexington, MA: Lexington Books, 1992).

195. Elijah Anderson, "The Code of the Streets," *Atlantic Monthly,* May 1994, 81–94.

196. Douglas S. Massey, "The Age of Extremes: Concentrated Affluence and Poverty in the Twenty-first Century," *Demography* 33, no. 4 (November 1996): 408.

197. Clifford Shaw and Henry McKay, *Juvenile Delinquency and Urban Areas* (Chicago, IL: University of Chicago Press, 1942).

198. Their findings were initially published in the prestigious journal *Science:* Robert J. Sampson, Stephen W. Raudenbush, and Felton Earls, "Neighborhoods and Violent Crime: A Multilevel Study of Collective Efficacy," *Science* 277 (August 1997): 918–24. We use the page numbers in the article as reprinted in Kawachi, Kennedy, and Wilkinson, *Society and Population Health Reader,* 336–50. The research is extended and updated in Morenoff, Sampson, and Raudenbush, "Neighborhood Inequality."

199. Sampson, Raudenbush, and Earls, "Neighborhoods and Violent Crime," 336.

200. Wilson, *When Work Disappears,* 63–64.

201. In Robert Putnam's terms, poor neighborhoods have lots of "bonding" social capital and little "bridging" social capital. See his *Bowling Alone,* 22–23.

202. Sampson, Morenoff, and Gannon-Rowley, "Assessing 'Neighborhood Effects,'" 465.

203. Sampson, Raudenbush, and Earls, "Neighborhoods and Violent Crime," 346.

204. Julie Berry Cullen and Steven D. Levitt, "Crime, Urban Flight, and the Consequences for Cities," *Review of Economics and Statistics* 81, no. 2 (May 1999): 159–69. For evidence on the relationship between crime and population loss, see William Frey, "Central City White Flight: Racial and Nonracial Causes," *American Sociological Review* 44 (June 1979): 425–48; Robert J. Sampson and J. Wooldredge, "Evidence that High Crime Rates Encourage Migration Away from Central Cities," *Sociology and Social Research* 70 (1986): 310–14; Wesley Skogan, "Fear of Crime and Neighborhood Change," in *Communities and Crime,* ed. A. J. Reiss and M. Tonry (Chicago: University of Chicago Press, 1986), 203–29; Liska and Bellair, "Violent Crime Rates." For a review of the literature on this point, see Sampson and Lauritsen, "Violent Victimization," 75–78.

205. Mark Crispin Miller, *It's a Crime: The Economic Impact of the Local TV News in Baltimore—A Study of Attitudes and Economics* (New York: Project on Media Ownership, 1998), 17; as reported in Danilo Yanich, "Location, Location, Location: Urban and Suburban Crime on Local TV News," *Journal of Urban Affairs* 23, nos. 3–4 (2001): 238.

206. For evidence on this point see ibid.; Linda Heath and John Petraitis, "Television Viewing and Fear of Crime: Where Is the Mean World?" *Basic and Applied Social Psychology* 8, no. 1–2 (1987): 97–123; Shanto Iyengar, "'Media Effects' Paradigms for the Analysis of Local Television News" (Palo Alto, CA: Departments of Communication and Political Science, Stanford University, 1998), available at http://pcl.stanford.edu/research/papers/effects.html; Franklin D. Gilliam Jr., Shanto Iyengar, Adam Simon, and Oliver Wright, "Crime in Black and White: The Violent, Scary World of Local News," Occasional Paper 95-1 (Los Angeles: UCLA Center for

American Politics and Public Policy, September 1995); Robert Entman and Andrew Rojecki, *The Black Image in the White Mind: Media and Race in America* (Chicago: University of Chicago Press, 2000).

207. Daryl A. Hellman and Joel L. Naroff, "The Impact of Crime on Urban Residential Property Values," *Urban Studies* 16 (1979): 111.

208. Allen E. Liska, Andrew Sanchirico, and Mark D. Reed, "Fear of Crime and Constrained Behavior: Specifying and Estimating a Reciprocal Effects Model," *Social Forces* 66, no. 3 (1988): 827–37.

209. Our discussion of crime in the suburbs of St. Louis is based on an outstanding series of articles in the *St. Louis Post-Dispatch*. See especially Heather Ratcliffe and Trisha L. Howard, "The Law in Disorder," *St. Louis Post-Dispatch* (November 30, 2003).

210. It is important to note that murders in St. Louis in 2003 (69) were at their lowest in more than four decades.

211. HUD, *State of the Cities 2000*, 47. For further evidence on the converging rates of crime in cities and suburbs, see *Sourcebook of Criminal Justice Statistics* (Washington, DC: U.S. Department of Justice, Bureau of Justice Statistics, U.S. Government Printing Office, various years).

212. Dan Korem, *Suburban Gangs: The Affluent Rebels* (Richardson, TX: International Focus Press, 1994); Daniel J. Monti, *Wannabe: Gangs in Suburbs and Schools* (Cambridge, MA: Blackwell Publishers, 1994).

213. The data are based on a nationally representative sample of students reported in National Center for Education Statistics and Bureau of Justice Statistics, *Indicators of School Crime and Safety 2001*, available at http://www.ojp.usdoj.gov/bjs/pub/pdf/iscsoi.pdf.

214. Quoted in Laurel Shaper Walters, "School Violence Enters Suburbs," *Christian Science Monitor*, April 19, 1993.

215. Douglas Smith, "The Neighborhood Context of Police Behavior," in *Communities and Cities*, ed. Albert J. Reiss Jr. and Michael Tonry (Chicago: University of Chicago Press, n.d.), as reported in Robert J. Sampson, "Effects of Socioeconomic Context on Official Reaction to Juvenile Delinquency," *American Sociological Review* 51, no. 6 (1986): 877.

216. Ibid.

217. For evidence on the spread of violent crime from central cities to suburbs, see Wallace and Wallace, *A Plague on Your Houses*, chap. 8.

218. For a discussion of the differences between inner city and affluent suburban gangs, see Korem, *Suburban Gangs*, 36–39.

219. Monti, *Wannabe*.

220. See Janny Scott, "Working Hard, More or Less," *New York Times*, July 10, 1999. The reason for the time shortage is that both parents are working long hours in order to be able to afford the expensive home in the suburbs, far from the dangerous areas of concentrated poverty. Between 1989 and 1998, the average middle-income married couple with children increased the amount of hours worked by 4.5 full-time weeks per year. Women with children are working anywhere from sixty-five to eighty hours a week, including household duties. Lawrence Mishel, Jared Bernstein, and John Schmitt, *State of Working America 2000–01* (Ithaca, NY: Cornell University Press, 2001). Long commutes are common in sprawled-out suburbs, and family errands are more time-consuming because everything is spread out. The Family Research Council reported that the "total contact time" between parents and children dropped 40

percent over a twenty-five-year span. Most juvenile delinquency takes place between the time school ends and overworked parents get home, a period when children are left to fend for themselves. Reported in Sylvia Ann Hewlett, "Running Hard Just to Keep Up," *Time,* special issue, "Women: The Road Ahead" (fall 1990), 54.

221. Reported in Fox Butterfield, "Survey Finds that Crimes Cost $450 Billion a Year," *New York Times,* April 9, 1999.

222. Alan Farnham, "U.S. Suburbs Are Under Siege," *Fortune,* December 28, 1992, 43; James D. Wright, Joseph F. Sheley, and M. Dwayne Smith, "Kids, Guns, and Killing Fields," *Society* (November/December 1992).

223. Manuel Pastor Jr., Peter Dreier, J. Eugene Grigsby III, and Marta Lopez-Garza, *Regions that Work: How Cities and Suburbs Can Grow Together* (Minneapolis: University of Minnesota Press, 2000), 32.

224. Our estimate is based on a study of 1,333 zip codes in thirty-three metropolitan areas. Robert W. Klein, "Availability and Affordability Problems in Urban Homeowners Insurance Markets," in *Insurance Redlining: Disinvestment, Reinvestment, and the Evolving Role of Financial Institutions,* ed. Gregory D. Squires (Washington, DC: Urban Institute, 1997), 56.

225. Albert O. Hirschman, *Exit, Voice, and Loyalty: Responses to Decline in Firms, Organizations, and States* (Cambridge, MA: Harvard University Press, 1970).

226. Cathy J. Cohen and Michael C. Dawson, "Neighborhood Poverty and African American Politics," *American Political Science Review* 87, no. 2 (1993): 286–302; Yvette Alex-Assensoh, *Neighborhoods, Family, and Political Behavior in Urban America* (New York: Garland, 1998).

227. Richard Sauerzopf and Todd Swanstrom, "The Urban Electorate in Presidential Elections, 1920–1996," *Urban Affairs Review* 35, no. 1 (1999): 72–91; Peter F. Nardulli, Jon K. Dalager, and Donald E. Greco, "Voter Turnout in U.S. Presidential Elections: An Historical View and Some Speculation," *PS: Political Science and Politics* 29 (1996): 480–90.

228. Neil Kraus and Todd Swanstrom, "Minority Mayors and the Hollow Prize Problem," *PS: Political Science and Politics* 24, no. 1 (March 2001): 99–105.

229. Calculations by Richard Sauerzopf.

230. Steven Erie provides evidence that entrenched political machines stop mobilizing voters in *Rainbow's End: Irish Americans and the Dilemmas of Urban Machine Politics* (Berkeley: University of California Press, 1988).

231. V. O. Key Jr., *Southern Politics in State and Nation* (New York: Knopf, 1949), chap. 14.

232. Richard Keiser argues that a main reason blacks historically got the short end of the stick in urban politics was a lack of party competition. *Subordination or Empowerment? African American Leadership and the Struggle for Urban Political Power* (New York: Oxford University Press, 1997).

233. J. Eric Oliver, *Democracy in Suburbia* (Princeton, NJ: Princeton University Press, 2001).

234. Putnam, *Bowling Alone,* 213.

235. Oliver, *Democracy in Suburbia.*

236. See Putnam, *Bowling Alone,* chap. 2.

237. Laura Harris, "A Home Is More than Just a House: A Spatial Analysis of Housing for the Poor in Metropolitan America," Ph.D. diss. (State University of New York at Albany, 1999).

238. School vouchers raise complex issues that cannot be dealt with here. Suffice it to say

that if vouchers enabled poor students to attend high-performing suburban schools, they could improve the educational attainment of many low-income students. However, students would need to be able to choose from the entire region, and we doubt that suburban school districts would agree to this. If vouchers enabled students to choose private schools, they might only end up worsening the performance of urban public schools.

CHAPTER 4. THE ROADS NOT TAKEN

1. Rebecca Trouson and John Johnson, "Housing Strain Unravels Community Ties," *Los Angeles Times,* January 7, 2001; *Raising the Roof: California Housing Development Projections and Constraints 1997–2000* (Sacramento: California Department of Housing and Community Development, 2000), exhibit 45, "Housing Cost Burden by Income and Tenure for Selected California Metropolitan Areas: 1988–1995," 164; Chris Brenner, *Growing Together or Drifting Apart? A Status Report on Social and Economic Well-Being in Silicon Valley* (San Jose, CA: Working Partnerships and Economic Policy Institute, January 1998).
2. Robert Fishman, "The American Metropolis at Century's End: Past and Future Influences," *Housing Policy Debate* 11, no. 1 (2000): 199–213. The survey was conducted for the Fannie Mae Foundation among members of the Society for American City and Regional Planning History; the article can be found at http://www.fanniemae foundation.org/research/facts/wi99s1.html.
3. Llewellyn H. Rockwell Jr., "The Ghost of Gautreaux," *National Review,* March 7, 1994, 57–59.
4. Ibid.
5. Fred Siegel, "The Sunny Side of Sprawl," *New Democrat* (March–April 1999): 20–21. See also Fred Siegel, "Is Regional Government the Answer?" *Public Interest* (fall 1999): 85–98; Fred Barnes, "Suburban Beauty: Why Sprawl Works," *Weekly Standard,* May 22, 2000, 27–30.
6. Howard Husock, "Mocking the Middle Class: The Perverse Effects of Housing Subsidies," *Heritage Foundation Policy Review* (spring 1991): 96–101. Bovard agrees that federal government programs to help the poor escape the ghetto "amount to a project to dictate where welfare recipients live in every county, city and cranny across the nation." James Bovard, "Suburban Guerilla," *American Spectator* (September 1994): 26–32.
7. Nevertheless, 76 percent of transit riders had a total trip time of less than thirty minutes, 57 percent less than twenty minutes, and 25 percent less than ten minutes. David F. Schulz, "Urban Transportation System Characteristics, Condition and Performance" (paper prepared for the Conference on Transportation Issues in Large U.S. Cities, Transportation Research Board, Detroit, June 28–30, 1998).
8. Gregg Easterbrook, "Suburban Myth: The Case for Sprawl," *New Republic,* March 15, 1999, 18–21.
9. Joel Garreau, *Edge City: Life on the New Frontier* (New York: Doubleday, 1991), 242. See also Philip Langdon, *A Better Place to Live: Reshaping the American Suburb* (New York: Harper Perennial, 1995).
10. Tamar Jacoby and Fred Siegel, "Growing the Inner City?" *New Republic,* August 23, 1999.

11. Michael E. Porter, "The Competitive Advantage of the Inner City," *Harvard Business Review* (May–June 1995): 55–71. Porter's article triggered a major debate on this topic. See Thomas Boston and Catherine Ross, eds., *The Inner City: Urban Poverty and Economic Development in the Next Century* (New Brunswick, NJ: Transaction Books, 1997). Also see Bennett Harrison and Amy K. Glasmeier, "Why Business Alone Won't Redevelop the Inner City," *Economic Development Quarterly* 11, no. 1 (1997): 28–38; Timothy Bates, "Michael Porter's Conservative Agenda Will Not Revitalize America's Inner Cities," *Economic Development Quarterly* 11, no. 1 (1997): 39–44.

12. The same argument is applied to business location decisions, but here we focus on residential choice (or the lack thereof).

13. Charles M. Tiebout, "A Pure Theory of Local Expenditure," *Journal of Political Economy* 64, no. 5 (October 1956): 418.

14. Robert Bish and Robert Warren, "Scale and Monopoly Problems in Urban Government Services," *Urban Affairs Quarterly* 8 (September 1972): 99.

15. Tiebout, "Pure Theory," 416–24; Vincent Ostrom, Charles Tiebout, and Roland Warren, "The Organization of Government in Metropolitan Areas," *American Political Science Review* 55 (1961): 835–42; Vincent Ostrom, Robert Bish, and Elinor Ostrom, *Local Government in the United States* (San Francisco: Institute for Contemporary Analysis, 1988); Paul Peterson, *City Limits* (Chicago: University of Chicago Press, 1981); Mark Schneider, *The Competitive City: The Political Economy of Suburbia* (Pittsburgh: University of Pittsburgh Press, 1989). For an excellent summary of the public choice perspective, see G. Ross Stephens and Nelson Wikstrom, *Metropolitan Government and Governance: Theoretical Perspectives, Empirical Analysis, and the Future* (New York: Oxford University Press, 2000).

16. Robert Warren, "A Municipal Services Market Model of Metropolitan Organization," *Journal of the American Institute of Planners* 30 (August 1964): 198–99.

17. Werner Z. Hirsch, "Local Versus Areawide Urban Government Services," *National Tax Journal* 17 (December 1964): 331–39.

18. "Expanding the Choices in Million Dollar Homes," *New York Times,* July 6, 1990. This assumes a 10% down payment, a mortgage at 10% interest (the prevailing rate at the time), and an estimated $15,000 a year in property taxes.

19. Douglas S. Massey and Nancy A. Denton, *American Apartheid: Segregation and the Making of the Underclass* (Cambridge, MA: Harvard University Press, 1993), 96–114, 187–212. Margery Austin Turner and Ron Wienk, "The Persistence of Segregation in Urban Areas: Contributing Causes," in *Housing Markets and Residential Mobility,* ed. G. Thomas Kingsley and Margery Austin Turner (Washington, DC: Urban Institute, 1993), 193–216; Margery Austin Turner, Stephen L. Ross, George C. Galster, and John Yinger, *Discrimination in Metropolitan Housing Markets: National Results from Phase 1 Housing Discrimination Study 2000* (Washington, DC: U.S. Department of Housing and Urban Development, 2002).

20. Gary J. Miller, *Cities by Contract: The Politics of Incorporation* (Cambridge, MA: MIT Press, 1981).

21. William Fulton, *The Reluctant Metropolis: The Politics of Urban Growth in Los Angeles* (Point Arena, CA: Solano Press Books, 1997), 279.

22. *Bidding for Business and Improving Your Business Climate: A Guide to Smarter Public Investments in Economic Development* (Washington, DC: Corporation for Enterprise Development, 1996).

23. John E. Anderson and Robert W. Wassmer, *Bidding for Business: The Efficacy of Local Economic Development Incentives in a Metropolitan Area* (Kalamazoo, MI: W. E. Upjohn Institute for Employment Research, 2000).

24. See, for example, United Nations Center for Human Settlements (HABITAT), *An Urbanizing World: Global Report on Human Settlements: 1996* (London: Oxford University Press, 1996); Charles Abrams, "The Uses of Land in Cities," *Scientific American* (September 1965): 225-31.

25. See Gerald E. Frug, "The City as a Legal Concept," *Harvard Law Review* 93, no. 6 (April 1980): 1057-154; Gerald E. Frug, "Decentering Decentralization," *University of Chicago Law Review* 60, no. 2 (spring 1993): 253-73; Gerald E. Frug, "The Geography of Community," *Stanford Law Review* 48, no. 5 (May 1996): 1047-94; Gerald E. Frug, *City Making: Building Communities Without Building Walls* (Princeton, NJ: Princeton University Press, 1999); Sidney Plotkin, *Keep Out: The Struggle for Land Use Control* (Berkeley: University of California Press, 1987); Harvey M. Jacobs, "Fighting over Land," *Journal of the American Planning Association* 65, no. 2 (spring 1999): 141-49.

26. Kenneth Jackson, *Crabgrass Frontier: The Suburbanization of the United States* (New York: Oxford University Press, 1985); David Rusk, *Cities Without Suburbs,* 3rd ed. (Washington, DC: Woodrow Wilson Center Press, 2003).

27. Rusk, *Cities Without Suburbs.*

28. The Supreme Court struck down racial zoning in *Buchanan v. Warley,* 245 U.S. 60 (1917).

29. Gwendolyn Wright, *Building the Dream: A Social History of Housing in America* (New York: Pantheon, 1981), 213.

30. Mary K. Nenno and Paul C. Brophey, *Housing and Local Government* (Washington, DC: National Association of Housing and Redevelopment Officers, n.d.), 7.

31. Among many others on this topic, see Alan Mallach, *Inclusionary Housing Programs* (New Brunswick, NJ: Rutgers University Center for Urban Policy Research, 1984); and Henry R. Richmond, "Metropolitan Land-Use Reform: The Promise and Challenge of Majority Consensus," in *Reflections on Regionalism,* ed. Bruce Katz (Washington, DC: Brookings Institution Press, 2000), available at http://www.brook.edu/es/urban.

32. Ann R. Markusen, "The Urban Impact Analysis: A Critical Forecast," in *The Urban Impact of Federal Policies,* ed. Norman Glickman (Baltimore: Johns Hopkins University Press, 1979).

33. We borrow this term from Bernard H. Ross and Myron A. Levine, *Urban Politics: Power in Metropolitan America,* 5th ed. (Itasca, IL: F. E. Peacock, 1996), 434.

34. Harold Wolman, "The Reagan Urban Policy and Its Impacts," *Urban Affairs Quarterly* 21, no. 3 (March 1986): 311-35.

35. Bruce Katz and Kate Carnevale, *The State of Welfare Caseloads in America's Cities* (Washington, DC: Brookings Institution Center for Urban and Metropolitan Policy, May 1998).

36. Anya Sostek, "Orange Crush," *Governing* (August 2003): 18-23; Siobham Gorman, "Localities Short on Homeland Security Personnel, Not Equipment," *National Journal,* August 8, 2003; Ben Canada, *State and Local Preparedness for Terrorism: Policy Issues and Options* (Washington, DC: Congressional Research Service, February 5, 2002); Amy Elsbree, "Homeland Security Group Focuses on Federal Funding Flow," *Nation's Cities,* National League of Cities, July 7, 2003.

37. James Flink, *The Car Culture* (Cambridge, MA: MIT Press, 1975); Kenneth Jackson, *Crabgrass Frontier;* Jane Holtz Kay, *Asphalt Nation: How the Automobile Took over*

America and How We Can Take It Back (New York: Crown, 1997); Helen Leavitt, *Superhighway-Superhoax* (New York: Doubleday, 1970); Pietro S. Nivola, *Laws of the Landscape: How Policies Shape Cities in Europe and America* (Washington, DC: Brookings Institution Press, 1999).

38. By the mid-1920s, 56 percent of American families owned an automobile, according to Nivola, *Laws of the Landscape*, 11.

39. See Bradford C. Snell, "American Ground Transport: A Proposal for Restructuring the Automobile, Truck, Bus, and Rail Industries" (presented to the Subcommittee on Antitrust and Monopoly of the Committee on the Judiciary, U.S. Senate, February 26, 1974).

40. Nivola, *Laws of the Landscape*, 13.

41. Howard P. Chudacoff and Judith E. Smith, *The Evolution of American Urban Society*, 4th ed. (Englewood Cliffs, NJ: Prentice-Hall, 1994), 260.

42. Fishman, "American Metropolis," 3.

43. Ibid., 2.

44. U.S. Bureau of the Census, *Statistical Abstract of the United States 2000* (Washington, DC: U.S. Government Printing Office, 2000), 625.

45. David Schrank and Tim Lomax, *Urban Mobility Report* (College Station: Texas A&M University, September 2003).

46. Kay, *Asphalt Nation*, 14.

47. Ibid.

48. Nivola, *Laws of the Landscape*, 15.

49. Timothy Egan, "The Freeway, Its Cost and 2 Cities' Destinies," *New York Times*, July 14, 1999.

50. Nivola, *Laws of the Landscape*, 15.

51. John H. Mollenkopf, *The Contested City* (Princeton, NJ: Princeton University Press, 1983), 105.

52. See Mollenkopf, *Contested City*, 102–9, on World War II; Ann Markusen, Peter Hall, Scott Campbell, and Sabrina District, *The Rise of the Gunbelt: The Military Remapping of Industrial America* (New York: Oxford University Press, 1991).

53. Ann Markusen and Joel Yudken, *Dismantling the Cold War Economy* (New York: Basic Books, 1992); Markusen et al., *Rise of the Gunbelt*. Military research and development and weapons production have spawned new industries and new fields, but in doing so, much of the nation's resources and scientific expertise have been diverted from civilian production and research. Likewise, military production and research and the siting of facilities help some areas but drain others.

54. Report to the Boston Redevelopment Authority (Lansing, MI: Employment Research Associates, 1992), reported in Steven Greenhouse, "Study Says Big Cities Don't Get Fair Share of Military Spending," *New York Times*, May 12, 1992, A20, and in Marion Anderson and Peter Dreier, "How the Pentagon Redlines America's Cities," *Planners Network* (May 1993): 3–4.

55. Markusen and Yudken, *Dismantling the Cold War Economy*, 173.

56. For example, during the presidential race in September 1992, President George Bush, far behind Governor Bill Clinton in the Missouri polls, traveled to St. Louis to announce the sale to Saudi Arabia of F-15 jet fighters, which were manufactured by McDonnell-Douglas, the state's largest employer. The sale was highly questionable on defense and foreign policy grounds, but Bush made little pretense of discussing geopolitics. He emphasized the 7,000 local jobs generated by the weapon.

57. Howard Schuman, Charlotte Steeh, and Lawrence Bobo, *Racial Attitudes in America:*

Trends and Interpretations (Cambridge, MA: Harvard University Press, 1985); Massey and Denton, *American Apartheid;* Reynolds Farley, "Neighborhood Preferences and Aspirations Among Blacks and Whites," in Kingsley and Turner, *Housing Markets;* George Galster, "Research on Discrimination in Housing and Mortgage Markets: Assessment and Future Directions," *Housing Policy Debate* 3, no. 2 (1992): 639–83; David Dent, "The New Black Suburbs," *New York Times Magazine,* July 14, 1992; Reynolds Farley, Elaine L. Fielding, and Maria Krysan, "The Residential Preferences of Blacks and Whites: A Four-Metropolis Analysis," *Housing Policy Debate* 8, no. 4 (1997): 763–800; Maria Krysan and Reynolds Farley, "The Residential Preferences of Blacks: Do They Explain Persistent Segregation?" *Social Forces* 80, no. 3 (2002): 937–80.

58. Massey and Denton, *American Apartheid;* Arnold Hirsch, *Making the Second Ghetto: Race and Housing in Chicago 1940–1960* (New York: Cambridge University Press, 1983); Arnold R. Hirsch, "Searching for a 'Sound Negro Policy': A Racial Agenda for the Housing Acts of 1949 and 1954," *Housing Policy Debate* 11, no. 2 (2000): 393–442; Thomas J. Sugrue, *The Origins of the Urban Crisis: Race and Inequality in Postwar Detroit* (Princeton, NJ: Princeton University Press, 1996).

59. Margery Austin Turner, "Achieving a New Urban Diversity: What Have We Learned?" *Housing Policy Debate* 8, no. 2 (1997): 295–305; John Yinger, "Housing Discrimination Is Still Worth Worrying About," *Housing Policy Debate* 9, no. 4 (1998): 893–927; *What We Know About Mortgage Lending Discrimination in America* (Washington, DC: U.S. Department of Housing and Urban Development and the Urban Institute, September 1999); Gregory D. Squires, ed., *Insurance Redlining: Disinvestment, Reinvestment, and the Evolving Role of Financial Institutions* (Washington, DC: Urban Institute, 1997); Turner et al., *Discrimination in Metropolitan Housing Markets.*

60. Joe Darden, "Choosing Neighbors and Neighborhoods: The Role of Race in Housing Preference," in *Divided Neighborhoods: Changing Patterns of Racial Segregation,* ed. Gary Tobin (Newbury Park, CA: Sage Publications, 1987); W. Dennis Keating, *The Suburban Racial Dilemma: Housing and Neighborhoods* (Philadelphia: Temple University Press, 1994); Hirsch, "Searching for a 'Sound Negro Policy.'"

61. Rose Helper, *Racial Policies and Practices of Real Estate Brokers* (Minneapolis: University of Minnesota Press, 1969); Jackson, *Crabgrass Frontier.*

62. Charles Abrams, *Forbidden Neighbors* (New York: Harper and Brothers, 1955); Julia Saltman, *Open Housing as a Social Movement: Challenge, Conflict and Change* (Lexington, MA: Heath, 1971); Keating, *Suburban Racial Dilemma;* Hirsch, "Searching for a 'Sound Negro Policy.'"

63. Massey and Denton, *American Apartheid,* 54. See also Mara S. Sidney, *Unfair Housing: How National Policy Shapes Community Action* (Lawrence: University Press of Kansas, 2003).

64. Cited in Dennis Judd and Todd Swanstrom, *City Politics: Private Power and Public Policy,* 2nd ed. (New York: Longman, 1998), 198. The U.S. Supreme Court ruled that state courts could not enforce racial covenants in *Shelly v. Kraemer* in 1948. The FHA was forced to change its official policy. It took the FHA until 1950 to revise its underwriting manual so that it no longer recommended racial segregation or restrictive covenants. But the FHA continued to favor racial segregation. It did nothing to challenge racial steering or redlining against blacks. As a result, the Supreme Court's ruling had little impact on racial segregation in private housing. See Keating, *Suburban Racial Dilemma,* 8.

65. Barry Checkoway, "Large Builders, Federal Housing Programs, and Postwar Sub-urbanization," in *Critical Perspectives on Housing*, ed. Rachel Bratt, Chester Hart-man, and Ann Meyerson (Philadelphia: Temple University Press, 1986).
66. Fishman, "American Metropolis," 4.
67. Jackson, *Crabgrass Frontier*, 196–213; Massey and Denton, *American Apartheid*, 42–57.
68. Fishman, "American Metropolis," 4.
69. Cited in Dennis Judd and Todd Swanstrom, *City Politics: Private Power and Public Policy*, original ed. (New York: Harper Collins, 1994), 203.
70. Massey and Denton, *American Apartheid*, 53.
71. Jackson, *Crabgrass Frontier*, 207.
72. Nathan Glazer and David McEntire, eds., *Housing and Minority Groups* (Berkeley: University of California Press, 1960), 140.
73. Massey and Denton, *American Apartheid*, 55.
74. Cusling Dolbeare and Sheila Crowley, *Changing Priorities: The Federal Budget and Housing Assistance 1976–2007* (Washington, DC: National Low Income Housing Coalition, August 2002).

    Tax reform legislation passed by Congress in 1997 sweetened the capital gains provisions enormously: such home sale profits are now, under most conditions, completely untaxed up to $500,000 for a couple and $250,000 for an individual, and the benefit is available repeatedly. The previous provision, which allowed home owners to defer capital gains taxes only if they purchased a more expensive home, encouraged the purchase of larger homes, typically in suburbs farther from the central city.
75. During the 1976–2000 period, the federal government also provided $21 billion in low-income housing subsidies through the low-income housing tax credit and $104 billion in low-income housing subsidies through the Department of Agriculture. These figures, calculated from a variety of government sources, are reported and explained in Peter Dreier, "The Truth About Federal Housing Subsidies," in *Housing: Foundation of a New Social Agenda*, ed. Rachel Bratt, Chester Hartman, and Michael Stone (Philadelphia: Temple University Press, forthcoming).
76. Only 22.6 percent of the 140 million taxpayers took the mortgage interest deduction, but this varied significantly with income. For example, 70 percent of taxpayers with incomes over $200,000 took the mortgage interest deduction, with an average bene-fit of $6,293. By contrast, only 23.1 percent of those in the $40,000 to $50,000 bracket took the deduction; those who did so saved an average of $859 on their taxes. Among those in the $20,000 to $30,000 income category, only 4.6 percent took the deduc-tion and received an average benefit of only $426. Among households with incomes under $20,000, slightly more than half own their own homes. Of those that own their homes, only 28.5 percent have mortgages. Of those that have mortgages, only 6.8 percent itemize (taxpayers taking the standard deduction get no benefit from these tax breaks). Among households in the $60,000 to $100,000 income bracket, more than 80 percent own their own homes. Of those that own their homes, 78 percent have mortgages. Of those that have mortgages, 66 percent itemize. Among house-holds in the $120,000 to $140,000 income bracket, 91 percent own their homes. Of those, 82 percent have mortgages. Among this group, 92 percent itemize. Mortgage interest and property tax deductions are available for a second or vacation home as well as for one's primary residence (and until 1986 were available for as many secondary residences as the taxpayer owned, clearly adding to its regressivity).

77. Joseph Gyourko and Richard Voith, "Does the U.S. Tax Treatment of Housing Promote Suburbanization and Central City Decline?" (Philadelphia: Wharton School, University of Pennsylvania, Real Estate and Finance Departments, September 24, 1997); Thomas Bier and Ivan Meric, "IRS Homeseller Provision and Urban Decline," *Journal of Urban Affairs* 16, no. 2 (1994): 141–54; Richard Voith, "The Determinants of Metropolitan Development Patterns: Preferences, Prices, and Public Policies," in *Metropolitan Development Patterns: Annual Roundtable 2000* (Cambridge, MA: Lincoln Institute of Land Policy, 2000).
78. Jeffrey Birnbaum and Alan Murray, *Showdown at Gucci Gulch: Lawmakers, Lobbyists, and the Unlikely Triumph of Tax Reform* (New York: Random House, 1987); Christopher Howard, *The Hidden Welfare State: Tax Expenditures and Social Policy in the United States* (Princeton, NJ: Princeton University Press, 1997).
79. Abrams, *Forbidden Neighbors;* Richard Davies, *Housing Reform During the Truman Administration* (Columbia: University of Missouri Press, 1966); Nathaniel Keith, *Politics and the Housing Crisis Since 1930* (New York: Universe Books, 1973).
80. National Advisory Commission on Civil Disorders (the Kerner Commission), *Report* (New York: Bantam, 1968).
81. The housing and lending industries argue that even if they do not discriminate, consumers vote with their feet. Whites move out of a neighborhood when they perceive that it is, or could become, "too black." Surveys indicate that although whites have generally become more tolerant of racially mixed neighborhoods, they define a neighborhood as acceptably integrated when a small number of blacks (usually no more than 10 percent) live there. There is much debate about whether there are "tipping" points when whites begin to flee.
82. James Kushner, "Federal Enforcement and Judicial Review of the Fair Housing Amendments Act of 1988," *Housing Policy Debate* 3, no. 2 (1992): 537–99.
83. Keating, *Suburban Racial Dilemma,* 14.
84. Keating, in *Suburban Racial Dilemma,* discusses suburbs that have utilized these approaches. See also Philip Nyden, Michael Maly, and John Lukehart, "The Emergence of Stable Racially and Ethnically Diverse Urban Communities: A Case Study of Nine U.S. Cities," *Housing Policy Debate* 8, no. 2 (1997): 491–534.
85. For a good overview, see Robert Halperin, *Rebuilding the Inner City: A History of Neighborhood Initiatives to Address Poverty in the United States* (New York: Columbia University Press, 1995).
86. Alice O'Connor, "Swimming Against the Tide: A Brief History of Federal Policy in Poor Communities," in *Urban Problems and Community Development,* ed. Ronald Ferguson and William Dickens (Washington, DC: Brookings Institution Press, 1999). See also Raymond Mohl, "Shifting Patterns of American Urban Policy Since 1900," in *Urban Policy in Twentieth-Century America,* ed. Arnold Hirsch and Raymond Mohl (New Brunswick, NJ: Rutgers University Press, 1993).
87. Steven Hayward, "Broken Cities: Liberalism's Urban Legacy," *Policy Review* (March–April 1998): 18.
88. Frances Piven and Richard Cloward, *Poor People's Movements* (New York: Pantheon, 1977).
89. Mark Gelfand, *A Nation of Cities: The Federal Government and Urban America, 1933–1965* (New York: Oxford University Press, 1975).
90. Judd and Swanstrom, *City Politics,* 3rd ed., 121.
91. Davies, *Housing Reform.*
92. Mohl, "Shifting Patterns," 11–13.

93. *2003 Advocates Guide to Housing and Community Development Policy* (Washington, DC: National Low Income Housing Coalition, 2003), available at http://www.nlihc .org/advocates. See also "A Picture of Subsidized Households: 1998," available at http://www.huduser.org/datasets/assthsg/statedata98; and Morton J. Schussheim, *Housing the Poor: Federal Programs for Low-Income Families* (Washington, DC: Congressional Research Service, March 29, 2000). The U.S. Department of Agriculture also provides housing subsidies, but these are primarily in rural areas and account for a very small proportion of federal housing assistance.

94. Peter Dreier, "Philanthropy and the Housing Crisis: Dilemmas of Private Charity and Public Policy in the United States," in *Shelter and Society: Theory, Research, and Policy for Nonprofit Housing,* ed. C. Theodore Koebel (Albany, NY: SUNY Press, 1998), 91–137; E. L. Birch and D. S. Gardner, "The Seven Percent Solution: A Review of Philanthropic Housing, 1870–1910," *Journal of Urban History* 7 (1981): 403–38; Roy Lubove, *The Progressives and the Slums: Tenement House Reform in New York City, 1890–1917* (Pittsburgh: University of Pittsburgh Press, 1962); Gail Radford, *Modern Housing for America: Policy Struggles in the New Deal Era* (Chicago: University of Chicago Press, 1996); Wright, *Building the Dream.*

95. Radford, *Modern Housing for America.*

96. Michael Danielson, *The Politics of Exclusion* (New York: Columbia University Press, 1976), cited in Edward Goetz, *From Policy Option to Policy Problem: The Federal Government and Restrictive Housing Regulation* (Washington, DC: Fannie Mae Foundation, 1999).

97. Hirsch, *Making the Second Ghetto.*

98. Martin Meyerson and Edward Banfield, *Politics, Planning and the Public Interest: The Case of Public Housing in Chicago* (New York: Free Press, 1955).

99. Michael Schill and Susan Wachter, "The Spatial Bias of Federal Housing Law and Policy: Concentrated Poverty in Urban America," *University of Pennsylvania Law Review* 143, no. 5 (May 1995): 1285–342; Massey and Denton, *American Apartheid;* Douglas Massey and S. M. Kanaiaupuni, "Public Housing and the Concentration of Poverty," *Social Science Quarterly* 74 (1993): 109–22; Steven Holloway, Deborah Bryan, Robert Chabot, Donna Rogers, and James Rulli, "Exploring the Effect of Public Housing on the Concentration of Poverty in Columbus, Ohio," *Urban Affairs Review* 33, no. 6 (July 1998): 767–89.

100. John Goering, Ali Kamely, and Todd Richardson, *The Location and Racial Composition of Public Housing in the United States* (Washington, DC: U.S. Department of Housing and Urban Development, 1994). Most housing developments created with the federal Low Income Housing Tax Credit (a program begun in 1986) are in high-poverty neighborhoods, mostly in central cities. Preliminary research indicates that most of these developments are in predominantly minority neighborhoods, although the racial characteristics of the projects' residents is not identified. See Jean Cummings and Denise DePasquale, *Rebuilding Affordable Rental Housing: An Analysis of the Low Income Housing Tax Credit* (Boston: City Research, 1998).

101. Goering et al., *Location and Racial Composition;* Holloway et al., "Exploring the Effect of Public Housing"; Sandra Newman and Ann Schnare, "'. . . And a Suitable Living Environment': The Failure of Housing Programs to Deliver on Neighborhood Quality," *Housing Policy Debate* 8, no. 4 (1997): 755–67.

102. Only 45.3 percent of vouchers and certificates are in central cities, 32.4 percent in census tracts with median household incomes below $20,000, 14.8 percent in census tracts with poverty rates of 30 percent or more, and 21 percent in census tracts

where minorities constitute at least half the population (Newman and Schnare, "Suitable Living Environment"). Harris has documented that the affordable apartments available to Section 8 certificate holders are segregated in poor, black, central-city neighborhoods far from suburban locations with more job opportunities and good schools. Laura Harris, "A Home Is More than Just a House: A Spatial Analysis of Housing for the Poor in Metropolitan America" (Ph.D. diss., State University of New York at Albany, 1999).

103. For discussion of urban growth coalitions, see John Mollenkopf, "The Post-War Politics of Urban Development," *Politics and Society* 5, no. 2 (winter 1975): 247–96; Mollenkopf, *Contested City;* Harvey Molotch, "The City as a Growth Machine," *American Journal of Sociology* 82, no. 2 (1976): 309–32; John Logan and Harvey Molotch, *Urban Fortunes* (Berkeley: University of California Press, 1987).

104. Mohl, "Shifting Patterns," 16.

105. Cited in O'Connor, "Swimming Against the Tide," 96; Douglas W. Rae, *City: Urbanism and Its End* (New Haven, CT: Yale University Press, 2003).

106. Susan Fainstein and Norman Fainstein, eds., *Restructuring the City: The Political Economy of Urban Development* (New York: Longman, 1986), 49; Mollenkopf, *Contested City.*

107. See, for example, Herbert Gans, *The Urban Villagers* (New York: Free Press, 1965); Thomas Hines, "Housing, Baseball, and Creeping Socialism: The Battle of Chavez Ravine, Los Angeles," *Journal of Urban History* 8 (February 1982): 123–45; Chester Hartman, *Yerba Buena: Land Grab and Community Resistance in San Francisco* (San Francisco: Glide Publications, 1974); Alan Lupo, Frank Colcord, and Edward Fowler, *Rites of Way* (Boston: Little, Brown, 1971); and Jon C. Teaford, "Urban Renewal and Its Aftermath," *Housing Policy Debate* 11, no. 2 (2000): 443–65.

108. Chester Hartman, "The Housing of Relocated Families," and Herbert Gans, "The Failure of Urban Renewal," in *Urban Renewal: The Record and the Controversy,* ed. James Q. Wilson (Cambridge, MA: MIT Press, 1966).

109. Mohl, "Shifting Patterns," 15.

110. Robert Caro, *The Power Broker: Robert Moses and the Fall of New York* (New York: Random House, 1974); Mollenkopf, *Contested City.*

111. Martin Anderson, *The Federal Bulldozer* (Cambridge, MA: MIT Press, 1964).

112. Gans, *Urban Villagers,* describes the destruction of Boston's West End neighborhood by urban renewal.

113. Hartman, *Yerba Buena;* Teaford, "Urban Renewal and Its Aftermath"; Robert O. Self, *American Babylon: Race and the Struggle for Postwar Oakland* (Princeton, NJ: Princeton University Press, 2003).

114. Bruce Ehrlich and Peter Dreier, "The New Boston Discovers the Old: Tourism and the Struggle for a Livable City," in *The Tourist City,* ed. Dennis R. Judd and Susan S. Fainstein (New Haven, CT: Yale University Press, 1999); Chester Hartman, *City for Sale: The Transformation of San Francisco,* revised and updated edition (Berkeley: University of California Press, 2002); Clarence Stone, *Economic Growth and Neighborhood Discontent: System Bias in the Urban Renewal Program of Atlanta* (Chapel Hill: University of North Carolina Press, 1976).

115. Judd and Swanstrom, *City Politics,* 3rd ed., 193.

116. Mary L. Dudziak, *Cold War Civil Rights: Race and the Image of American Democracy* (Princeton, NJ: Princeton University Press, 2002).

117. Cited in Kevin Boyle, "Little More than Ashes: The UAW and American Reform in the 1960s," in *Organized Labor and American Politics, 1894–1994,* ed. Kevin Boyle

(Albany, NY: SUNY Press, 1998). See also Nelson Lichtenstein, *The Most Dangerous Man in Detroit: Walter Reuther and the Fate of American Labor* (New York: Basic Books, 1995). William Julius Wilson's *The Bridge over the Racial Divide: Rising Inequality and Coalition Politics* (Berkeley: University of California Press, 1999), updates many of Reuther's arguments.

118. Sar Levitan, Garth Mangum, and Stephen Mangum, *Programs in Aid of the Poor,* 7th ed. (Baltimore: Johns Hopkins University Press, 1998); James T. Patterson, *America's Struggle Against Poverty 1900–1980* (Cambridge, MA: Harvard University Press, 1981).

119. V. Joseph Hotz and John Karl Scholz, *The Earned Income Tax Credit* (Cambridge, MA: National Bureau of Economic Research, Working Paper No. W8078, January 2001); Alan Berube and Thacher Tiffany, *The "State" of Low Wage Workers: How the EITC Benefits Urban and Rural Communities in the 50 States* (Washington, DC: Brookings Institution Center for Metropolitan and Urban Policy, February 2004).

120. Judd and Swanstrom, *City Politics,* 3rd ed., 217.

121. During the 1950s and early 1960s, big-city mayors, the liberal National Housing Conference, and a coalition of labor unions and public housing advocates supported unsuccessful efforts by congressional Democrats to create a cabinet-level agency to deal with urban problems. The 1960 Democratic platform called for replacing the Housing and Home Finance Agency (HHFA) with a new cabinet-level agency. Upon his election, President Kennedy tried to create such a department, but he was stymied by Southern Democrats, who feared that Kennedy would appoint HHFA administrator Robert Weaver (the highest-ranking black in the federal government) to be the new secretary. Rachel Bratt and W. Dennis Keating, "Federal Housing Policy and HUD: Past Problems and Future Prospects of a Beleaguered Bureaucracy," *Urban Affairs Quarterly* 29, no. 1 (September 1993): 3–27.

122. Morton Schussheim, *The Federal Government, the Central City, and Housing* (Washington, DC: Congressional Research Service, September 29, 1992).

123. Kerner Commission, *Report.*

124. In 1970, Nixon proposed a welfare reform plan drafted by Daniel Patrick Moynihan. The Family Assistance Plan (FAP) was a guaranteed minimum income for all families with children, a radical notion at the time. Conservatives in Congress opposed it because they disagreed with the principle of a federal guaranteed income. Liberals and welfare advocacy groups opposed it because the FAP's income floor of $1,600 per family was far below the poverty line. For Moynihan's perspective, see Daniel P. Moynihan, *The Politics of a Guaranteed Income: The Nixon Administration and the Family Assistance Plan* (New York: Random House, 1973).

125. Schussheim, *Housing the Poor,* 16.

126. Ibid.

127. Ibid., 18.

128. Ibid., 17. See also Michael J. Rich, *Federal Policymaking and the Poor: National Goals, Local Choices, and Distributional Outcomes* (Princeton, NJ: Princeton University Press, 1993).

129. Cited in Mohl, "Shifting Patterns," 21.

130. This wave of plant closings and its consequences are brilliantly chronicled in Barry Bluestone and Bennett Harrison, *The Deindustrialization of America* (New York: Basic Books, 1982). See also Jefferson Crowse and Joseph Heathcott, *Beyond the Ruins: The Meaning of Deindustrialization* (Ithaca, NY: Cornell University Press, 2003).

131. "Ford to City: Drop Dead," *New York Daily News,* October 29, 1975.

132. Mohl, "Shifting Patterns," 22.

133. Carter terminated the state component of revenue sharing in 1980. See John Kincaid, "De Facto Devolution and Urban Defunding: The Priority of Persons over Places," *Journal of Urban Affairs* 21, no. 2 (1999): 135–67.

134. President's Commission on a National Agenda for the Eighties, *Urban America in the 1980s* (Washington, DC: U.S. Government Printing Office, 1980).

135. For a review of the Nixon, Ford, and Carter approaches to urban policy, see the articles in Marshall Kaplan and Franklin James, eds., *The Future of National Urban Policy* (Durham, NC: Duke University Press, 1990).

136. Reagan did not reduce federal spending in either absolute terms or as a proportion of GNP. Increases in federal military spending more than offset declines in domestic spending.

137. George Peterson and Carol Lewis, eds., *Reagan and the Cities* (Washington, DC: Urban Institute, 1986); Harold Wolman, "Reagan Urban Policy"; Frances Fox Piven and Richard Cloward, *The New Class War: Reagan's Attack on the Welfare State and Its Consequences* (New York: Pantheon, 1982); Kevin Phillips, *The Politics of Rich and Poor* (New York: Random House, 1990).

138. U.S. President's Commission on Housing, *The Report of the President's Commission on Housing* (Washington, DC: U.S. Government Printing Office, 1982); U.S. Department of Housing and Urban Development, *The President's National Urban Policy Report* (Washington, DC: U.S. Government Printing Office, 1982).

139. The figures on the Reagan and Bush administrations draw on Demetrios J. Caraley, "Washington Abandons the Cities," *Political Science Quarterly* 107, no. 1 (spring 1992): 1–30, and Demetrios J. Caraley, "Dismantling the Federal Safety Net: Fictions Versus Realities," *Political Science Quarterly* 111, no. 2 (summer 1996): 225–58.

140. The number of AFDC recipients increased from 7.4 million in 1970 to 10.6 million in 1980 to 11.5 million in 1990. See "Historical Trends in AFDC Enrollments and Average Payments, Fiscal Years 1970–96," in Committee on Ways and Means, U.S. House of Representatives, *1998 Green Book* (Washington, DC: U.S. Government Printing Office, May 19, 1998), 413.

141. Because AFDC and food stamp benefits differ from state to state, this figure is the median of all states. See "Gross Income Limit, Need Standard, and Maximum Monthly Potential Benefits, AFDC and Food Stamps, One-Parent Family of Three Persons," in Committee on Ways and Means, U.S. House of Representatives, *1992 Green Book* (Washington, DC: U.S. Government Printing Office, 1992), 636–37.

142. Actual expenditures (or outlays) for housing actually increased during the early Reagan years because of spending commitments made during the Carter administration. HUD's contracts with developers, landlords, and public housing authorities are spread out over many years. But Reagan dramatically cut HUD's ability to enter into new contracts by reducing its overall budget authority. See R. Allen Hays, *The Federal Government and Urban Housing,* 2nd ed. (Albany, NY: SUNY Press, 1995).

143. Jennifer Daskal, *In Search of Shelter: The Growing Shortage of Affordable Rental Housing* (Washington, DC: Center on Budget and Policy Priorities, June 15, 1998).

144. Joel Blau, *The Visible Poor: Homelessness in the United States* (New York: Oxford University Press, 1992); Martha Burt, *Over the Edge: The Growth of Homelessness in the 1980s* (New York: Russell Sage Foundation, 1992); Bruce Link, Ezra Susser, Ann Stueve, Jo Phelan, Robert Moore, and Elmer Struening, "Lifetime and Five-Year Prevalence of Homelessness in the United States," *American Journal of Public Health*

84, no. 12 (1994): 1907–12; U.S. Conference of Mayors, *A Status Report on Hunger and Homelessness in American Cities: 1993* (Washington, DC, December 1993).

145. "Poverty Rates for Individuals in Selected Demographic Groups, 1959–1994," in Committee on Ways and Means, U.S. House of Representatives, *1996 Green Book* (Washington, DC: U.S. Government Printing Office, November 4, 1996), 1226.

146. "Percentage of Persons in Poverty in NonMetro and Metro Areas, 1978–1994," in *1996 Green Book,* 1233.

147. William O'Hare, *A New Look at Poverty in America* (Washington, DC: Population Reference Bureau, September 1996), 14; "The Economic Crisis of Urban America," *Business Week,* May 18, 1992; "Poverty of People, by Residence: 1959 to 1998," U.S. Bureau of the Census, Current Population Survey, 1999, available at http://www.census .gov/pub/income/histpov/hstpov08.txt.

148. Billy Tidwell, *Playing to Win: A Marshall Plan for America* (Washington, DC: National Urban League, July 1991); Richard Nathan, *A New Agenda for Cities* (Washington, DC: National League of Cities, 1992); Joseph Persky, Elliott Sclar, and Wim Wiewel, *Does America Need Cities? An Urban Investment Strategy for National Prosperity* (Washington, DC: Economic Policy Institute, 1991); Urban Institute, *Confronting the Nation's Urban Crisis* (Washington, DC: Urban Institute, September 1992); "The Economic Crisis of Urban America," *Business Week,* May 18, 1992; John Mollenkopf, "Urban Policy at the Crossroads," in Margaret Weir, ed., *The Social Divide: Political Parties and the Future of Activist Government* (Washington, DC: Brookings Institution Press, 1998); Peter Dreier, "America's Urban Crisis a Decade After the Los Angeles Riots," *National Civic Review* 92, no. 1 (spring 2003): 35–55.

149. U.S. Census Bureau, Historic Income Tables — People. Table P-1, "Total CPS Population and Per Capita Money Income: 1967 to 2001," available at http://www.census .gov/hhes/income/histinc/p01.html; U.S. Bureau of the Census, *Statistical Abstract of the United States 2003,* table 684, "Money Income of Households — Median Income by Race and Hispanic Origins in Current and Constant (2001) Dollars: 1980 to 2001," available at http://www.census.gov/prod/2004pubs/03statab/income.pdf; Bureau of Labor Statistics, table 1, "Unemployment Status of the Civilian Noninstitutional Population, 1040 to Present," available at http://www.bls.gov/cps/cpsaat1.pdf; U.S. Census Bureau, Historical Poverty Tables, table 2, "Poverty Status of People by Family Relationship, Race, and Hispanic Origin: 1959 to 2002," available at http:// www.census.gov/hhes/poverty/histpov/hstpov2.html. U.S. Census Bureau, Historical Poverty Tables, table 8, "Poverty of People by Residence, 1959 to 2000," available at http://www.census.gov/hhes/poverty/histpov/hstpov8.html; U.S. Census Bureau, Housing Vacancy Survey, table 5, "Homeownership Rates for the United States: 1965 to 2003," available at http://www.census.gov/hhes/www/housing/hvs/q403tab5 .html; Jason DeParle and Steven A. Holmes, "A War on Poverty Subtly Linked to Race," *New York Times,* December 26, 2000.

150. U.S. Census Bureau, Historical Income Tables — Households. Table H-2, "Share of Aggregate Income Received by Each Fifth and Top 5 Percent of Households (All Races): 1967 to 2001," available at http://www.census.gov/hhes/income/histinc/h02 .html.

151. Daniel H. Weinberg, "A Brief Look at Postwar U.S. Income Inequality" (Washington, DC: U.S. Bureau of the Census, Current Population Reports, P60-191, June 1996); Edward N. Wolff, "Recent Trends in the Size Distribution of Household Wealth," *Journal of Economic Perspectives* 12, no. 3 (summer 1998): 131–50.

152. U.S. Census Bureau, "Numbers of Americans With and Without Health Insur-

ance Rise, Census Bureau Reports" (press release, September 1, 2003), available at http://www.census.gov/Press-Release/www/2003/cb03-154.html. See also U.S. Census Bureau, Historical Health Insurance Tables, table HI-1, "Health Insurance Coverage Status and Type of Coverage by Sex, Race, and Hispanic Origin: 1987 to 2002," available at http://www.census.gov/hhes/hlthins/historic/hihistt1.html; U.S. Census Bureau, Health Insurance Coverage: 2000, table A-3, "People Without Health Insurance for the Entire Year, Selected Characteristics: 1999 and 2000," available at http://www.census.gov/hhes/hlthins/hlthin00/hi00ta3.html.

153. Quoted in DeParle and Holmes, "War on Poverty."

154. Gene B. Sperling, "The Clinton Administration's Anti-Poverty Agenda," remarks to the National Press Club, October 1, 1999, available at http://clinton4.nara.gov/WH/EOP/nec/html/speech991001.html. Sperling was Clinton's chief economic policy adviser.

155. Rebecca Blank and David T. Ellwood, "The Clinton Legacy for America's Poor" (paper delivered at a conference on American Economic Policy in the 1990s, Cambridge, MA, Kennedy School of Government, Harvard University, June 27–30, 2001).

156. Christina FitzPatrick and Edward Lazere, *The Poverty Despite Work Handbook* (Washington, DC: Center on Budget and Policy Priorities, April 1999). For a history of the earned income tax credit, see Christopher Howard, *Hidden Welfare State*.

157. The law also made changes in federal aid for child care, food stamps, supplemental security income for children, benefits for legal immigrants, child nutrition programs, child-support enforcement, and other low-income programs.

158. Blank and Ellwood, "Clinton Legacy"; and *Change in AFDC/TANF Recipients FY1999–FY2000* (Washington, DC: U.S. Department of Health and Human Services, April 2002).

159. Alan Weil, *Ten Things Everyone Should Know About Welfare Reform* (Washington, DC: Urban Institute, May 2002). Most families leaving welfare for work earn poverty-level wages. One study found that single mothers who were working five years after leaving welfare earned an average of $10,315 a year. In eighteen of the nation's twenty largest metropolitan areas in 1995, the typical hourly wage of single working mothers who had recently received AFDC was about $6 an hour, far below the poverty line. Barbara Sard and Jennifer Daskal, *Housing and Welfare Reform: Some Background Information* (Washington, DC: Center on Budget and Policy Priorities, February 1998). Harry Holzer, *Unemployment Insurance and Welfare Recipients: What Happens When the Recession Comes?* (Washington, DC: Urban Institute, December 2000).

160. Katz and Carnevale, "State of Welfare Caseloads."

161. David Sanger, "In Visit to Northeast, Clinton Calls for Investment in Cities," *New York Times,* November 5, 1999. See also *Now Is the Time: Places Left Behind in the New Economy* (Washington, DC: U.S. Department of Housing and Urban Development, April 1999); *The New Markets: The Untapped Retail Buying Power in America's Inner Cities* (Washington, DC: U.S. Department of Housing and Urban Development, July 1999); *The State of the Cities: 1998* (Washington, DC: U.S. Department of Housing and Urban Development, June 1998).

162. Marilyn Gittell et al., "Expanding Civic Opportunity: Urban Empowerment Zones," *Urban Affairs Review* 33 (March 1998); W. Dennis Keating, "Cleveland, Ohio: The Tale of a Supplementary Empowerment Zone" and Robin Boyle and Peter Eisinger, "The U.S. Empowerment Zone Program: The Evolution of a National Urban Pro-

gram and the Failure of Local Implementation in Detroit, Michigan" (papers presented at a conference on Area Based Initiatives in Contemporary Urban Policy sponsored by the Danish building and Urban Research Institute and European Urban Research Association, Copenhagen, May 17, 2001); Winton Pitcoff, "EZ'er Said than Done," *Shelterforce* (July/August 2000); *Interim Assessment of the Empowerment Zones and Enterprise Communities Program: A Progress Report* (Washington, DC: U.S. Department of Housing and Urban Development, November 2001); Bruce K. Mulock, *Renewal Communities and New Markets Initiatives: Background, Overview and Issues* (Washington, DC: Congressional Research Service, June 5, 2001).

163. *The 25th Anniversary of the Community Reinvestment Act: Access to Capital in an Evolving Financial Services System* (Cambridge, MA: Harvard University Joint Center for Housing Studies, March 2002); Gregory D. Squires, ed., *Organizing Access to Capital: Advocacy and the Democratization of Financial Institutions* (Philadelphia: Temple University Press, 2003); Peter Dreier, "The Future of Community Reinvestment: Challenges and Opportunities," *Journal of the American Planning Association* 69, no. 4 (August 2003): 341–53.

164. Jason DeParle, "Slamming the Door: The Year That Housing Died," *New York Times Magazine*, October 20, 1996; Blank and Ellwood, "Clinton Legacy"; Rachel Bratt, "Housing for Very Low-Income Households: The Record of President Clinton, 1993–2000" (Cambridge, MA: Harvard University Joint Center for Housing Studies, n.d.).

165. The Moving to Opportunity program is based on the successful Gautreaux program in Chicago, which began in the 1970s as a result of a federal court settlement against the city's segregated public housing program. See James Rosenbaum, "Changing the Geography of Opportunity by Expanding Residential Choice: Lessons from the Gautreaux Program," *Housing Policy Debate* 6, no. 1 (1995): 231–69; Peter Dreier and David Moberg, "Moving from the 'Hood: The Mixed Success of Integrating Suburbia," *American Prospect* 7, no. 24 (winter 1996): 75–80; Jason DeParle, "An Underground Railroad from Projects to Suburbs," *New York Times*, December 1, 1993; U.S. Department of Housing and Urban Development, Office of Policy Development and Research, "Residential Mobility Programs," *Urban Policy Brief* 1 (September 1994). For an evaluation of the Moving to Opportunity program, see John Goering and Judith D. Feins, eds., *Choosing a Better Life: Evaluating the Moving to Opportunity Social Experiment* (Washington, DC: Urban Institute, 2003).

166. Bridges to Work was modeled on several successful local programs in Chicago and Philadelphia. Rochelle Stanfield, "The Reverse Commute," *National Journal*, November 23, 1996; Penelope Lemov, "The Impossible Commute," *Governing* (June 1993): 32–35; Rick Wartman, "New Bus Lines Link the Inner-City Poor with Jobs in Suburbia," *Wall Street Journal*, September 24, 1993; Mark Alan Hughes, "A Mobility Strategy for Improving Opportunity," *Housing Policy Debate* 6, no. 1 (1995): 271–97; Margaret Pugh, *Barriers to Work: The Spatial Divide Between Jobs and Welfare Recipients in Metropolitan Areas* (Washington, DC: Brookings Institution Center for Urban and Metropolitan Policy, September 1998).

167. Susan M. Vanhorenbeck, *Hope VI: The Revitalization of Severely Distressed Public Housing* (Washington, DC: Congressional Research Service, January 18, 2001).

168. Henry G. Cisneros, ed., *Interwoven Destinies: Cites and the Nation* (New York: Norton, 1993); Henry G. Cisneros, *Regionalism: The New Geography of Opportunity* (Washington, DC: U.S. Department of Housing and Urban Development, March

1995). Under Michael Stegman, assistant secretary for Policy Development and Research under Clinton, HUD sponsored several conferences on regionalism, the proceedings of which were published in HUD's former policy journal, *Cityscape*.

169. CNN exit polls, available at http://www.cnn.com/ELECTION/2000/results.

170. Darci McConnell, "Bush Alters Traditional Urban Agenda," *Detroit News*, February 18, 2001; Myron Magnet, "Solving President Bush's Urban Problem," *City Journal* (winter 2001).

171. Carmen DeNovas Walt, Bernadette D. Proctor, and Robert J. Mills, *Income, Poverty, and Health Insurance Coverage in the United States: 2003*, Current Population Report P60-226 (Washington, DC: U.S. Bureau of the Census, August 2004); Sylvia Allegretto and Andy Stettner, *Educated, Experienced, and Out of Work: Long-term Joblessness Continues to Plague the Unemployed* (Washington, DC: Economic Policy Institute, March 4, 2004).

172. U.S. Census Bureau, Historical Poverty Tables, table 8, "Poverty of People by Residence, 1959 to 2000," available at http://www.census.gov/hhes/poverty/histpov/hstpov8.html; Walt, et al., *Income, Poverty, and Health Insurance*.

173. Robert J. Mills and Shailesh Bhandari, *Health Insurance Coverage in the United States: 2002* (Washington, DC: U.S. Census Bureau, Current Population Reports, P60-223, September 2003); Walt, et al., *Income, Poverty, and Health Insurance*.

174. Quoted in DeParle and Holmes, "War on Poverty."

175. Cited in Shawn Fremstad, *Recent Welfare Reform Research Findings* (Washington, DC: Center on Budget and Policy Priorities, January 30, 2004), available at http://www.cbpplorg/1-30-04wel.htm.

176. *Faith Based Initiatives and the Bush Administration*, Pew Forum on Religion and Public Life, available at http://pewforum.org/faith-based-initiatives; Eyal Press, "Faith Based Furor," *New York Times Magazine*, April 1, 2001; Benjamin Soskis, "Act of Faith: What Religion Cannot Do," *New Republic*, February 26, 2001; Elizabeth Becker, "Bush's Plan to Aid Religious Groups is Faulted," *New York Times*, April 27, 2001; Elizabeth Becker, "Ignoring Critics, Backers of Church Aid to Offer Bill," *New York Times*, May 18, 2001; Richard Benedetto, "Bush's Faith-Based Initiative Draws Foes from Several Sides," *USA Today*, May 8, 2001; Martin Davis, "Faith, Hope, and Charity," *National Journal*, April 28, 2001; Laurie Goodstein, "Church-Based Projects Lack Data on Results," *New York Times*, April 12, 2001; Michael Goldhaber, "Compassionate Conservative Plans Assailed in Lawsuits," *National Law Journal*, January 8, 2001; Mary Leonard, "Faith-Based Hiring Bill Draws Fire," *Boston Globe*, May 6, 2001; Hanna Rosin and Thomas Edsall, "Survey Exposes Faith-Based Plan Hurdles," *Washington Post*, April 11, 2001.

177. Ron Suskind, "Why Are These Men Laughing?" *Esquire* (January 2003), available at http://www.ronsuskind.com/newsite/articles/archives/00032.html.

178. William J. Mathis, "No Child Left Behind: Costs and Benefits," Phi Delta Kappan, available at http://www.pdkintl.org/kappan/k0305mat.htm; Peter Schrag, "Bush's Education Fraud," *American Prospect* 15, no. 2 (February 2004); Richard Rothstein, "Testing Our Patience," *American Prospect* 15, no. 2 (February 2004).

179. David Broder, "Modest Man at HUD," *Washington Post*, April 3, 2002.

180. David Broder, "Housing on the Back Burner," *Washington Post*, June 9, 2002.

181. Barbara Sard and Will Fischer, *Administration Seeks Deep Cuts in Housing Vouchers and Conversion of Program to a Block Grant* (Washington, DC: Center on Budget and Policy Priorities, March 8, 2004), available at http://www.centeronbudget.org/2-12-04/hous.htm.

182. Christopher Hoene and Michael Pagano, "Fend-for-Yourself Federalism: The Impact of Federal and State Deficits on America's Cities," *Government Finance Review* (October 2003): 36–42; Michael Pagano, *Cities' Fiscal Challenges Continue to Worsen in 2003* (Washington, DC: National League of Cities, November 2003); Robert Pear, "Study By Governors Calls Bush Welfare Plan Unworkable," *New York Times*, March 3, 2002.

183. "Tracking Federal Homeland Security Funds Sent to the 50 State Governments: A 215-City/50-State Survey" (Washington, DC: U.S. Conference of Mayors, January 2004); Sostek, "Orange Crush."

184. JayEtta Z. Hecker, "Disaster Assistance: Federal Aid to the New York City Area Following the Attacks of September 11th and Challenges Confronting FEMA" (Washington, DC: U.S. General Accounting Office, September 23, 2003); Josh Rogers, "Special Report: How to Spend Downtown's Last Billion," *Downtown Express* (April 16–22, 2004).

185. Thomas Sander and Robert Putnam, "Walking the Civic Talk After September 11," *Christian Science Monitor*, February 19, 2002.

CHAPTER 5. URBAN POLITICS AND CITY LIMITS:
WHAT CITIES CAN AND CANNOT DO TO ADDRESS POVERTY

1. Nancy Cleeland, "Lives Get a Little Better on a Living Wage," *Los Angeles Times*, February 7, 1999.

2. David Reynolds, "The Living Wage Movement Sweeps the Nation," *Working USA* 3, no. 3 (September–October 1999): 61–80; Isaac Martin, "Dawn of the Living Wage: The Diffusion of a Redistributive Municipal Policy," *Urban Affairs Review* 36, no. 4 (March 2001): 470–96; Daniel Wood, "'Living Wage' Laws Gain Momentum Across U.S.," *Christian Science Monitor*, March 15, 2002; Nancy Cleeland, "Living Wage Laws Reducing Poverty Levels, Study Shows; Labor Battle Between Advocates and Business Opponents Over the Issue Has Intensified in Recent Years," *Los Angeles Times*, March 14, 2002; Robert Pollin and Stephanie Luce, *The Living Wage: Building a Fair Economy* (New York: New Press, 1998); Economic Policy Institute, *Living Wage Issue Guide* (Washington, DC), available at http://www.epinet.org/content.cfm/issue guides_livingwage_livingwage; Living Wage Resource Center, available at http:// www.livingwagecampaign.org. For a conservative critique of the living wage movement, see William Tucker, "Socialism in Every City: The Spread of the 'Living Wage,'" *Weekly Standard*, November 3, 2003.

3. States can enact minimum wage laws covering all employees. In 2000, the California minimum wage, $5.75 an hour, exceeded the federal threshold of $5.15. Although business leaders think that this puts the state at a competitive disadvantage, research suggests otherwise. David Card and Alan Krueger, *Myth and Measurement: The New Economics of the Minimum Wage* (Princeton, NJ: Princeton University Press, 1995).

4. In New Orleans in February 2002, 63 percent of voters endorsed a ballot initiative to create a citywide minimum wage that would be one dollar above the federal minimum wage, which has remained at $5.15 since 1997. The law was successfully challenged in court by business groups. In November 2003, voters in San Francisco approved a ballot measure raising the citywide minimum wage to $8.50 an hour. Santa Fe, New Mexico, adopted an $8.50 an hour minimum wage in 2003. Stewart Yerton, "N.O. Voters Approve Minimum Wage Increase," *New Orleans Times-Picayune*, Feb-

ruary 3, 2002; Robert Pollin, Mark Brenner, and Stephanie Luce, "Intended Versus Unintended Consequences: Evaluating the New Orleans Living Wage Ordinance," *Journal of Economic Issues* 36, no. 4 (December 2002); Michael Pagano, *Cities' Fiscal Challenges Continue to Worsen in 2003* (Washington, DC: National League of Cities, November 2003).

5. See Amy Ellen Schwartz and Ingrid Gould Ellen, *Cautionary Notes for Competitive Cities* (New York: New York University Wagner School of Public Service, March 1, 2000); Natalie Cohen, *Business Location Decision-Making and Cities: Bringing Companies Back* (Washington, DC: Brookings Institution Center for Urban and Metropolitan Policy, April 2000).

6. Christopher W. Hoene and Michael A. Pagano, "Fend-for-Yourself Federalism: The Impact of Federal and State Deficits on America's Cities," *Government Finance Review* (October 2003): 36–42.

7. Calculated from the following tables: U.S. Bureau of the Census, *Statistical Abstract of the United States 2003* (Washington, DC: U.S. Government Printing Office, 2003), table 434, "Government Current Receipts and Expenditures by Type: 1990 to 2002"; table 458, "Local Governments—Expenditures and Debt by State: 2000." Local governments include counties, cities, townships and towns, school districts, and special districts. See also table 431, "Number of Governmental Units by Type: 1952 to 2002."

8. Robert L. Lineberry, *Equality and Urban Policy: The Distribution of Municipal Public Services* (Beverly Hills, CA: Sage Publications, 1974), 10.

9. Helen Ladd and John Yinger, *America's Ailing Cities: Fiscal Health and the Design of Urban Policy,* updated ed. (Baltimore: Johns Hopkins University Press, 1989), 9.

10. Ibid., 292.

11. *The State of the Cities 2000: Megaforces Shaping the Future of the Nation's Cities* (Washington, DC: U.S. Department of Housing and Urban Development, 2000).

12. Hoene and Pagano, "Fend-for-Yourself Federalism"; Max B. Sawicky, *U.S. Cities Face Fiscal Crunch: Federal and State Policies Exacerbate Local Governments' Budget Shortfalls* (Washington, DC: Economic Policy Institute, June 2002); Michael Pagano, *City Fiscal Conditions in 2003* (Washington, DC: National League of Cities, 2003); Howard Chernick and Andrew Reschovsky, *Lost in the Balance: How State Policies Affect the Fiscal Health of Cities* (Washington, DC: Brookings Institution Center for Metropolitan and Urban Policy, March 2001).

13. A detailed study of the distribution of public services in San Antonio by Lineberry concluded that they were characterized by "unpatterned inequalities." Some areas got more than others, but not on the basis of race or class. See Lineberry, *Equality and Urban Policy.* Also discussing this question are Frank S. Levy, Arnold Meltsner, and Aaron Wildavsky, *Urban Outcomes* (Berkeley: University of California Press, 1974); Bryan D. Jones et al., "Service Delivery Rules and the Distribution of Local Government Services: Three Detroit Bureaucracies," *Journal of Politics* 40 (1978): 334–68; Kenneth R. Mladenka, "The Urban Bureaucracy and the Chicago Political Machine: Who Gets What and Limits to Political Reform," *American Political Science Review* 74 (1980): 991–98; and Michael J. Rich, *Federal Policymaking and the Poor: National Goals, Local Choices, and Distributional Outcomes* (Princeton, NJ: Princeton University Press, 1993).

14. Edward W. Hill and Jeremy Nowack, "Nothing Left to Lose," *Brookings Review* 18, no. 3 (summer 2000): 22–26; Neil Smith, Paul Caris, and Elvin Wyly, "The Camden Syndrome and the Menace of Urban Decline: Residential Disinvestment in Camden County, NJ," *Urban Affairs Review* 36, no. 4 (March 2001): 497–531.

15. Chernick and Reschovsky, *Lost in the Balance.*
16. Myron Orfield, *Metropolitics: A Regional Agenda for Community and Stability,* rev. ed. (Washington, DC: Brookings Institution Press, 1997), 162.
17. Robert Rafuse, "Fiscal Disparities in Chicagoland," *Intergovernmental Perspective* 17, no. 3 (1991): 14–19.
18. Losers include New York, Chicago, Philadelphia, Detroit, Baltimore, Cleveland, St. Louis, Washington, Boston, San Francisco, Pittsburgh, Milwaukee, Buffalo, New Orleans, Minneapolis, Cincinnati, Kansas City, and Newark; gainers include Los Angeles, Houston, San Antonio, Dallas, Indianapolis, Seattle, and Denver. Cities that were not in the top twenty-five in 1950 but were in 1990 include San Diego, San Jose, Jacksonville, Columbus, El Paso, Memphis, Austin, Charlotte, and Nashville. Campbell Gibson, *Population of the 100 Largest Cities and Other Urban Places in the United States: 1950 to 1999* (Washington, DC: U.S. Census Bureau, June 1998), available at http://www.census.gov/population/documentation/twps0027.html; and "Population Estimates for Cities with Populations of 100,000 and Greater (Size Rank in U.S.): July 1, 1999" (Washington, DC: U.S. Census Bureau, October 2000), available at http://www.census.gov/population/estimates/metro-city/SC100K-T1.txt.
19. John Brennan and Edward W. Hill, *Where Are the Jobs? Cities, Suburbs, and the Competition for Employment* (Washington, DC: Brookings Institution Center for Urban and Metropolitan Policy, November 1999).
20. Howard Chernick and Andrew Reschovsky, "The Long-Run Fiscal Health of Central Cities," *Chicago Policy Review* 4, no. 1 (spring 2000): 6.
21. Ibid.
22. Mark S. Rosentraub, *Major League Losers* (New York: Basic Books, 1999).
23. Chernick and Reschovsky, "Long-Run Fiscal Health," 6.
24. Richard Perez-Pena, "Court Upholds Law to Repeal Commuter Tax," *New York Times,* April 5, 2000.
25. This discussion draws on Joel Blau, *The Visible Poor: Homelessness in the United States* (New York: Oxford University Press, 1992).
26. The number of shelter beds in New York City has declined to about 25,000. Nina Bernstein, "Shelter Population Reaches Highest Level Since 1980s," *New York Times,* February 8, 2001.
27. Pietro S. Nivola, *Fiscal Millstones on the Cities: Revisiting the Problem of Federal Mandates* (Washington, DC: Brookings Institution Center for Metropolitan and Urban Policy, August 2003); General Accounting Office, *Highlights of a GAO Symposium, Addressing Key Challenges in an Intergovernmental Setting* (Washington, DC: General Accounting Office, March 2003), cited in Hoene and Pagano, "Fend-for-Yourself Federalism"; Susan MacManus, "Financing Federal, State and Local Governments in the 1990s," *Annals of the American Academy of Political and Social Science* 509 (May 1990): 22–35; Joseph Zimmerman, "Regulating Intergovernmental Relations in the 1990s," *Annals of the American Academy of Political and Social Science* 509 (May 1990): 48–59; Michael Pagano, "State-Local Relations in the 1990s," *Annals of the American Academy of Political and Social Science* 509 (May 1990): 94–105; Janet M. Kelly, *State Mandates* (Washington, DC: National League of Cities, February 1992); Timothy Conlan and David R. Beam, "Federal Mandates," *Intergovernmental Perspective* 18, no. 4 (fall 1992): 7–11; *Intergovernmental Relations: Changing Patterns in State-Local Finances* (Washington, DC: General Accounting Office, HRD-92-87FS, March 1992); *Federal Statutory Preemption of State and Local Authority: History, Inventory, and Issues* (Washington, DC: U.S. Advisory Commission on Intergovern-

mental Relations, A-121, September 1992); *Impact of Unfunded Federal Mandates on U.S. Cities: A 314 City Survey* (Washington, DC: U.S. Conference of Mayors and Price Waterhouse, October 26, 1993).

28. *Impact of Unfunded Federal Mandates.*

29. Peter Schrag, "Bush's Education Fraud," *American Prospect* 15, no. 2 (February 2004).

30. *The Oxford Dictionary of Quotations,* 3rd ed. (New York: Oxford University Press, 1979), 217.

31. Jonathan Kozol, *Amazing Grace: The Lives of Children and the Conscience of a Nation* (New York: Harper Perennial, 1995), 99–108.

32. Annette Kondo, "City Revises Code Enforcement but Adds No Staff," *Los Angeles Times,* November 29, 2000.

33. William E. Simon, *A Time for Truth* (New York: Berkeley Books, 1979), 193. See also Steven Hayward, "Broken Cities: Liberalism's Urban Legacy," *Policy Review* (March–April 1998): 14–22; Stephen Moore and Dean Stansel, "The Myth of America's Underfunded Cities," *Policy Analysis* 188 (1993): 1–20. Anthony Downs shows that urban decline is driven more by concentrated poverty and other objective conditions than by profligate spending and taxing decisions in *New Vision for Metropolitan America* (Washington, DC: Brookings Institution Press, 1994), appendix B.

34. Janet Rothenberg Pack, "Poverty and Urban Public Expenditures," *Urban Studies* 35, no. 11 (1998): 1995–2019. In their study of eighty-six cities, Ladd and Yinger showed that old housing and poverty drive up the costs of city services. A city with a poverty rate that is just one percentage point higher than that of another city will have police costs that are 5.5 percent higher, and a ten percentage point difference in the share of old housing causes a 6.9 percent increase in the cost of fire protection. Ladd and Yinger, *America's Ailing Cities,* 85–86.

35. According to data compiled by the Advisory Commission on Intergovernmental Relations in 1981, the central-city tax burden relative to income was 50 percent higher than in the suburbs. In Washington, DC, central-city residents paid 15 percent more in taxes, but creating a shared metropolitan tax base would have only a small effect on the after-tax distribution of income. Replacing local taxes with an areawide income tax would nonetheless increase the incomes of low-income households by 20 percent. See Seth B. Sacher, "Fiscal Fragmentation and the Distribution of Metropolitan Area Resources: A Case Study," *Urban Studies* 30, no. 7 (1993): 1225–39.

36. For a summary of the evidence of how suburban commuters drive up the cost of central-city services more than they contribute in taxes, see Dennis R. Judd and Todd Swanstrom, *City Politics: Private Power and Public Policy,* 2nd ed. (New York: Longman, 1998), 316.

37. Paul Jargowsky, *Poverty and Place: Ghettos, Barrios, and the American City* (New York: Russell Sage Foundation, 1997), 36.

38. David Rusk, *Cities Without Suburbs,* 3nd ed. (Washington, DC: Woodrow Wilson Center Press, 2003).

39. David Ranney, *Global Decisions, Local Collisions: Urban Life in the New World Order* (Philadelphia: Temple University Press, 2003); Saskia Sassen, *Cities in a World Economy,* 2nd ed. (Thousand Oaks, CA: Pine Forge Press, 2000).

40. John D. Kasarda, "Industrial Restructuring and the Changing Location of Jobs," in *The State of the Union: America in the 1980s,* vol. 1, *Economic Trends,* ed. Reynolds Farley (New York: Russell Sage Foundation, 1995), 215–67; William H. Frey, "The New Geography of Population Shifts," in *The State of the Union: America in the 1980s,* vol. 2, *Social Trends,* 271–336.

41. William Frey, "Immigration, Domestic Migration, and Demographic Balkanization in America: New Evidence for the 1990s," *Population and Development Review* 22, no. 4 (December 1996): 741–63.

42. Jargowsky, *Poverty and Place;* Paul Jargowsky, *Stunning Progress, Hidden Problems: The Dramatic Decline of Concentrated Poverty in the 1990s* (Washington, DC: Brookings Institution Center for Metropolitan and Urban Policy, May 2003). As we note in Chapter 2, Jargowsky's study overstates the decline in concentrated poverty. He looks at the number of census tracts with poverty rates of 40 percent or more and finds a significant decline. Kingsley and Pettit, however, find that the number of census tracts with poverty rates of 30 percent or more declined less dramatically during the 1990s. Moreover, while the *number* of poor people living in these urban high-poverty tracts (30 percent or more) declined from 7.1 million to 6.7 million, the *proportion* of all poor people living in these areas stayed the same — 21 percent. See G. Thomas Kingsley and Kathryn Pettit, *Concentrated Poverty: A Change in Course* (Washington, DC: Urban Institute, May 2003).

43. Reynolds Farley, Charlotte Steeh, Tara Jackson, Maria Krysan, and Keith Reeves, "Continued Racial Residential Segregation in Detroit: Chocolate City, Vanilla Suburbs Revisited," *Journal of Housing Research* 4, no. 1 (1993): 1–38.

44. Calculated from data in Lawrence Mishel, Jared Bernstein, and Heather Boushay, *The State of Working America, 2002/2003* (Ithaca, NY: ILR Press, 2003), 159.

45. U.S. Bureau of the Census, *Statistical Abstract of the United States 2003* (Washington, DC: U.S. Government Printing Office, 2003), 276.

46. As reported in statistical profiles of New York State school districts, New York State Education Department, April 1999, available at http://www.emsc.nysed.gov/irts/ch655/D660405.html.

47. John J. Goldman, "NYC Schools Ruled a 'Failure'; New York's High Court Finds for City Activists Who Sued the State over Funding," *Los Angeles Times,* June 27, 2003; see also Greg Winter, "State Underfinancing Damages City Schools, New York Court Finds," *New York Times,* June 27, 2003; Greg Winter, "$4 Billion More Is Needed to Fix City's Schools, Study Finds," *New York Times,* February 5, 2004.

48. Kenneth B. Wong, *Funding Public Schools: Politics and Policies* (Lawrence: University Press of Kansas, 1999), 12.

49. The controversy over the impact of spending on student achievement is reflected in two opposing studies: Eric Hanushek, "School Resources and Student Performance," in *Does Money Matter: The Effect of School Resources on Student Achievement and Adult Success,* ed. Gary Burtless (Washington, DC: Brookings Institution Press, 1996); and Richard Rothstein, *The Way We Were? The Myths and Realities of America's Student Achievement* (New York: Century Foundation Press, 1998).

50. For a good summary, see James Traub, "What No School Can Do," *New York Times Magazine,* January 16, 2000; Richard Rothstein, *Class and Schools* (Washington, DC: Economic Policy Institute, 2004).

51. Xavier de Souza Briggs, "Moving Up Versus Moving Out: Neighborhood Effects in Housing Mobility Programs," *Housing Policy Debate* 8, no. 1 (1997): 195–234.

52. As reported by the General Accounting Office in 1994 and cited in Richard Rothstein, "Inner-City Nomads Follow a Track to Lower Grades," *New York Times,* January 20, 2000.

53. Kozol, *Amazing Grace,* 216.

54. Xavier de Souza Briggs, "Brown Kids in White Suburbs: Housing Mobility and the Many Faces of Social Capital," *Housing Policy Debate* 9, no. 1 (1998): 177–221.

55. James E. Rosenbaum, "Changing the Geography of Opportunity by Expanding Residential Choice: Lessons from the Gautreaux Program," *Housing Policy Debate* 6, no. 1 (1995): 231–69.

56. In the late 1960s, black residents of the small town of Shaw, Mississippi, filed a class-action suit alleging that the town government had discriminated against them in providing city services. The town was 60 percent black, but black households accounted for 98 percent of those whose homes fronted unpaved streets and 97 percent of those not served by sanitary sewers. In 1971, a federal appeals court found that these practices violated the equal protection clause of the Fourteenth Amendment and ordered the town to correct the inequities. *Time* trumpeted the decision, saying that it would "force big as well as small cities across the U.S. to reallocate everything from police patrols to garbage pickups to park space." Subsequent to *Shaw*, however, the courts have largely withdrawn from overseeing local public service distribution. Federal courts have ruled that plaintiffs must prove racially discriminatory *intent*, not just discriminatory effects. Courts have also found it difficult to judge what level of inequality across neighborhoods is impermissible or whether equality should be measured by spending, output, or results. The courts have thus generally followed the dissenting justice in *Shaw*, who wrote, "Such problems as plaintiffs have disclosed by the evidence . . . are to be resolved at the ballot box." See "New Attacks on Discrimination," *Time,* February 22, 1971, 59; Ralph A. Rossum, "The Rise and Fall of Equalization Litigation," *Urban Interest* 2, no. 1 (1980): 2; *Hawkins v. Shaw,* 461 F.2d 1169 (1972).

57. John Kincaid, "De Facto Devolution and Urban Funding: The Priority of Persons over Places," *Journal of Urban Affairs* 21, no. 2 (1999): 136.

58. U.S. Bureau of the Census, *Finances of Municipal and Township Governments 1997* (Washington, DC: U.S. Government Printing Office, September 2000), table 1, 13.

59. Thomas R. Swartz and John E. Peck, eds., *The Changing Face of Fiscal Federalism* (Armonk, NY: M. E. Sharpe, 1990), especially Richard Child Hill, "Federalism and Urban Policy," 35–55; Hoene and Pagano, "Fend-for-Yourself Federalism."

60. Paul Peterson, *City Limits* (Chicago: University of Chicago Press, 1981).

61. Quoted in Robin Soslow, "Cleveland: A Special Report," *World Trade* (October 1992), as cited in Michael H. Shuman, *Going Local: Creating Self-Reliant Communities in a Global Age* (New York: Routledge, 2000), 1.

62. Paul Kantor and H. V. Savitch, "Can Politicians Bargain with Business? A Theoretical and Comparative Perspective on Urban Development," *Urban Affairs Quarterly,* 29, no. 2 (December 1993): 230–55.

63. Brookings Institution Center for Urban and Metropolitan Policy, Living Cities Census Series, "Income and Poverty—100 Largest Cities in the U.S.: Share of Households that are Upper-Income (Over $81,000), 2000"; U.S. Census Bureau, Per Capita Income in 1999, available at http://factfinder.census.gov.

64. For a description of these organizations, see *Taking Care of Civic Business: How Formal CEO-Level Business Leadership Groups Have Influenced Civic Progress in Key American Cities* (Grand Rapids, MI: Frey Foundation, March 1993). John Mollenkopf, Harvey Molotch, and others sought to explain how and why these alignments arose. Mollenkopf coined the phrase "pro-growth coalition" in "The Post-War Politics of Urban Development," *Politics and Society* 5, no. 3 (winter 1975): 247–96, and *The Contested City* (Princeton, NJ: Princeton University Press, 1983). Molotch used the phrase "growth machine" in "The City as a Growth Machine," *American Journal of Sociology* 82, no. 2 (1976): 309–32. See also Andrew Jonas and David Wilson, eds.,

The Urban Growth Machine: Critical Perspectives Two Decades Later (Albany: SUNY Press, 1999).

65. Michael Useem, *The Inner Circle* (New York: Oxford University Press, 1984); G. William Domhoff, *Who Rules America? Power and Politics in the Year 2000,* 3rd ed. (Mountain View, CA: Mayfield, 1998).

66. See Raymond Mohl, "Planned Destruction: The Interstates and Central City Housing," in *From Tenements to the Taylor Homes: In Search of an Urban Housing Policy in Twentieth Century America,* ed. John F. Bauman, Roger Biles, and Kristin M. Szylvian (University Park: Pennsylvania State University Press, 2000), 226–45.

67. C. H. Heying, "Civic Elites and Corporate Delocalization, *American Behavioral Scientist* 40, no. 5 (March 1997): 656–67. Joel Kotkin, "Cities Need Leaders . . . and Businessmen Are Indispensable," *American Enterprise* 9, no. 5 (September–October 1998): 12–18.

68. Rob Gurwitt, "The Rule of the Absentocracy," *Governing* (September 1991): 54. See also Nicholas Lemann, "No Man's Town: The Good Times Are Killing Off America's Local Elites," *New Yorker,* June 5, 2000.

69. This approach to urban political analysis was pioneered by Clarence Stone. See his "Urban Regimes and the Capacity to Govern: A Political Economy Approach," *Journal of Urban Affairs* 15, no. 1 (1993): 1–28, and *Regime Politics: Governing Atlanta 1946–1988* (Lawrence: University Press of Kansas, 1989). For additional discussions, see Stephen Elkin, *City and Regime in the American Republic* (Chicago: University of Chicago Press, 1987); Susan Fainstein and Norman Fainstein, eds., *Restructuring the City: The Political Economy of Urban Redevelopment* (New York: Longman, 1986); David Judge, Gerry Stoker, and Harold Wolman, eds., *Theories of Urban Politics* (Thousand Oaks, CA: Sage Publications, 1995); Mickey Lauria, ed., *Reconstructing Urban Regime Theory: Regulation and Urban Politics in a Global Economy* (Thousand Oaks, CA: Sage Publications, 1997); John Logan and Todd Swanstrom, eds., *Beyond the City Limits* (Philadelphia: Temple University Press, 1990); Adolph Reed, "Demobilization in the New Black Political Regime: Ideological Capitulation and Radical Failure in the Postsegregation Era," in *The Bubbling Cauldron: Race, Ethnicity and the Urban Crisis,* ed. Michael Peter Smith and Joe R. Feagin (Minneapolis: University of Minnesota Press, 1995). For a comparison of local government capacity in the United States and elsewhere, see Judge, Stoker, and Wolman, *Theories of Urban Politics;* Harold L. Wolman and Michael Goldsmith, *Urban Politics and Policy: A Comparative Approach* (Cambridge: Blackwell Publishers, 1992).

70. Kelly Candaele and Peter Dreier, "LA's Progressive Mosaic: Beginning to Find Its Voice," *Nation,* August 21–28, 2000, 24–29. Harold Meyerson, "Why Liberalism Fled the City . . . and How It Might Come Back," *American Prospect* 9, no. 37 (March/April 1998); Peter Dreier, "America's Urban Crisis a Decade After the Los Angeles Riots," *National Civic Review,* 92, no. 1 (spring 2003); Raphael J. Sonenshein, "Post-Incorporation Politics in Los Angeles," in *Racial Politics in American Cities,* 3rd ed., ed. Rufus Browning, Dale Rogers Marshall, and David H. Tabb (New York: Longman, 2003).

71. We borrow this typology from Judd and Swanstrom, *City Politics,* 2nd ed., chap. 13, and replace their phrase "urban populism" with "urban progressivism." Scholars have developed other typologies to describe local regimes. See Norman Fainstein and Susan Fainstein, "Regime Strategies, Communal Resistance, and Economic Forces," in Fainstein and Fainstein, *Restructuring the City;* and Elkin, *City and Regime.* Stone developed a typology of maintenance regimes, development regimes,

middle-class progressive regimes, and regimes devoted to lower-class opportunity expansion in *Regime Politics* and "Urban Regimes and the Capacity to Govern." See also Mollenkopf, "Post-War Politics."

72. Howard Chudacoff and Judith Smith, *The Evolution of American Urban Society* (Englewood Cliffs, NJ: Prentice-Hall, 1994), 156.

73. Steven P. Erie, *Rainbow's End: Irish Americans and the Dilemmas of Urban Machine Politics, 1840–1985* (Berkeley: University of California Press, 1988), 242.

74. The literature on political machines is vast. For thoughtful perspectives, see M. Craig Brown and Charles Halaby, "Machine Politics in America, 1870–1945," *Journal of Interdisciplinary History* 17, no. 3 (winter 1987): 587–612; Erie, *Rainbow's End;* Alan DiGaetano, "The Rise and Development of Urban Political Machines," *Urban Affairs Quarterly* 24, no. 2 (December 1988): 243–67; Amy Bridges, *A City in the Republic: Antebellum New York and the Origins of Machine Politics* (New York: Cambridge University Press, 1994); Martin Shefter, "The Electoral Foundations of the Political Machine: New York City, 1884–1897," in *The History of American Electoral Behavior,* ed. Joel Silbey et al. (Princeton, NJ: Princeton University Press, 1978), 263–98.

75. William Julius Wilson, *When Work Disappears: The World of the New Urban Poor* (New York: Knopf, 1996).

76. The Boston school busing wars and New York's Ocean Hill–Brownsville "community control" school controversy provide two dramatic examples of these divisions. Ralph Formisano, *Boston Against Busing: Race, Class, and Ethnicity in the 1960s and 1970s* (Chapel Hill: University of North Carolina Press, 1991); D. Garth Taylor, *Public Opinion and Collective Action: The Boston School Desegregation Conflict* (Chicago: University of Chicago Press, 1986); Alan Lupo, *Liberty's Chosen Home: The Politics of Violence in Boston* (Boston: Beacon Press, 1988); Maurice R. Berube and Marilyn Gittell, eds., *Confrontation at Ocean Hill–Brownsville: The New York School Strike of 1968* (New York: Praeger, 1969); Diane Ravitch, *The Great School Wars* (New York: Basic Books, 1974); Barbara Carter, *Pickets, Parents and Power: The Story Behind the New York City Teachers' Strike* (New York: Citation Press, 1971).

77. Harold Baron, "Black Powerlessness in Chicago," *Transaction* (November 1968): 32–38; Gregory D. Squires, Larry Bennett, Kathleen McCourt, and Phillip Nyden, *Chicago: Race, Class and the Response to Urban Decline* (Philadelphia: Temple University Press, 1987); Paul Kleppner, *Chicago Divided: The Making of a Black Mayor* (De Kalb: Northern Illinois University Press, 1985); Dianne M. Pinderhughes, "An Examination of Chicago Politics for Evidence of Political Incorporation and Representation," in *Racial Politics in American Cities,* 2nd ed., ed. Rufus Browning, Dale R. Marshall, and David Tabb (New York: Longman, 1997).

78. U.S. Bureau of the Census, *Statistical Abstract of the United States 2003,* table 417, "Black Elected Officials by Office, 1970 to 2001, and State, 2001"; and table 418, "Hispanic Public Elected Officials by Office, 1985 to 2002, and State, 2002." These figures include mayors, city council members, and county commissioners, but do not include individuals elected to local school boards or special district boards. There are no large U.S. cities with Asian American mayors.

79. Genie Stowers and Ronald Vogel, "Racial and Ethnic Voting Patterns in Miami," in *Big-City Politics, Governance, and Fiscal Constraints,* ed. George E. Peterson (Washington, DC: Urban Institute Press, 1994); Ronald Vogel and Genie Stowers, "Miami: Minority Empowerment and Regime Change," in H. V. Savitch and John Clayton

Thomas, eds., *Big City Politics in Transition* (Newbury Park, CA: Sage Publications, 1991); Christopher Warren and Dario Moreno, "Power Without a Program: Hispanic Incorporation in Miami," in Browning, Marshall, and Tabb, *Racial Politics,* 3rd ed.

80. Carlos Munoz Jr., "Mexican Americans and the Promise of Democracy: San Antonio Mayoral Elections," in Peterson, *Big-City Politics;* Rodney Hero and Susan Clarke, "Hispanics, Blacks, and Multiethnic Politics in Denver," in Browning, Marshall, and Tabb, *Racial Politics,* 3rd ed.

81. Neil Kraus and Todd Swanstrom, "Minority Mayors and the Hollow Prize Problem," *PS: Political Science and Politics* 24, no. 1 (March 2001): 99–105.

82. The 76 largest cities included in this figure are the following: Akron, Albuquerque, Anaheim, Anchorage, Arlington (Texas), Atlanta, Aurora (Colorado), Austin, Baltimore, Baton Rouge, Birmingham, Boston, Buffalo, Charlotte, Chicago, Cincinnati, Cleveland, Colorado Springs, Corpus Christi, Dallas, Denver, Detroit, El Paso, Fort Worth, Fresno, Honolulu, Houston, Indianapolis, Jacksonville, Jersey City, Kansas City (Missouri), Las Vegas, Lexington-Fayette (Kentucky), Long Beach, Los Angeles, Louisville, Memphis, Mesa (Arizona), Miami, Milwaukee, Minneapolis, Nashville-Davidson, Newark, New Orleans, New York, Norfolk, Oakland, Oklahoma City, Omaha, Philadelphia, Phoenix, Pittsburgh, Portland (Oregon), Raleigh, Richmond, Riverside (California), Rochester, Sacramento, St. Louis, St. Paul, St. Petersburg, San Antonio, San Diego, San Francisco, San Jose, Santa Ana, Seattle, Stockton, Tampa, Toledo, Tucson, Tulsa, Virginia Beach, Washington, DC, and Wichita.

83. For an analysis of the dilemmas of "deracialization," see Huey L. Perry, ed., *Race, Politics, and Governance in the United States* (Gainesville: University Press of Florida, 1996); Georgia A. Persons, ed., *Dilemmas of Black Politics* (New York: HarperCollins, 1993); Richard A. Keiser, *Subordination or Empowerment? African American Leadership and the Struggle for Urban Political Power* (New York: Oxford University Press, 1997).

84. Jim Sleeper, "The End of the Rainbow? America's Changing Urban Politics," *New Republic,* November 1, 1993, 20–25.

85. For a discussion of the 2001 mayoral elections in New York and Los Angeles, see John R. Logan and John Mollenkopf, "People and Politics in Urban America" (New York: Drum Major Institute, 2003) available at http://www.drummajorinstitute.org.

86. Susan Parrot, "Dallas Mayor Faces Texas-Size Challenge; Enemies Made During Her Stint as a Reporter Will Have to Be Handled Carefully," *Los Angeles Times,* March 3, 2002; John Nichols, "From Muckraker to Mayor," *Nation* online, February 18, 2002, available at http://www.thenation.com/thebeat/index.mhtml?bid=1&pid=18; and Paul Burka, "Sizzle and Stakes: Dallas Mayor Laura Miller is Hungry to Take on the Big Problems Facing the City," *Texas Monthly* 31, issue 9 (September 2003).

87. Jim Henderson, "Angry Alliance Seeking Recall of Dallas Mayor," *Houston Chronicle,* November 9, 2003.

88. Mary Clare Jalonick, "Accentuate the Positive: How Laura Miller was Elected Mayor of Dallas With a 'Small Things' Agenda of Change," *Campaigns and Elections,* May 2002.

89. Browning, Marshall, and Tabb, *Racial Politics,* 3rd ed.; Persons, *Dilemmas of Black Politics;* Perry, *Race, Politics, and Governance;* Sharon Wright, "The Mayoral Elections of the Nineties: An Analysis of a New Generation of Black Mayors" (paper presented to the annual meeting of the American Political Science Association, August 1996).

90. Persons, *Dilemmas of Black Politics*; Keiser, *Subordination or Empowerment?*; Browning, Marshall, and Tabb, *Racial Politics*, 2nd ed., essays by Sonenshein and Browning, Marshall, and Tabb.

91. Some urban liberal regimes changed city charters from at-large to district election of city councils, giving minority areas a greater voice.

92. Jeffrey R. Henig, "Black Leaders, White Businesses: Racial Tension and the Construction of Public-Private Partnerships" (paper presented to the annual meeting of the American Political Science Association, September 1996).

93. James Button's study of Florida cities, *Blacks and Social Change: The Impact of the Civil Rights Movement in Southern Communities* (Princeton, NJ: Princeton University Press, 1989), found that an increase in black police officers was correlated with a reduction in incidents of police misconduct and brutality. W. Marvin DeLaney, *Black Police in America* (Bloomington: Indiana University Press, 1996), found that cities with more black police officers have fewer citizen complaints against police and are more likely to institute community-based police programs.

94. Reed, "Demobilization."

95. Peter K. Eisinger, "Black Mayors and the Politics of Racial Economic Advancement," in *Urban Politics: Past, Present, and Future*, 2nd ed., ed. Harlan Hahn and Charles H. Levine (New York: Longman, 1984), 257. See also Peter K. Eisinger, "Black Employment in Municipal Jobs: The Impact of Black Political Power," *American Political Science Review* 76, no. 2 (June 1982): 380–92.

96. Edward Greer, *Big Steel: Black Politics and Corporate Power in Gary, Indiana* (New York: Monthly Review Press, 1979).

97. Peter Dreier and Bruce Ehrlich, "Downtown Development and Urban Reform: The Politics of Boston's Linkage Policy," *Urban Affairs Quarterly* 26, no. 3 (March 1991): 345–75; Barbara Ferman, *Governing the Ungovernable City: Political Skill, Leadership, and the Modern Mayor* (Philadelphia: Temple University Press, 1985); Phillip Clay, "Boston: The Incomplete Transformation," in Savitch and Thomas, *Big City Politics*; Cynthia Horan, "Coalition, Market, and State: Postwar Development Politics in Boston," in Lauria, *Reconstructing Urban Regime Theory*.

98. Howard Husock and Nancy Kates, *Battle of the Alamodome: Henry Cisneros and the San Antonio Stadium* (Cambridge: Kennedy School of Government, Harvard University, case studies in public policy, C16-89-896.0, n.d.); Munoz, "Mexican Americans"; Kemper Diehl and Jan Jarboe, *Cisneros: Portrait of a New American* (San Antonio: Corona, 1985).

99. Stone, *Regime Politics*. See also Clarence Stone and Carol Pierannunzi, "Atlanta and the Limited Reach of Electoral Control," in Browning, Marshall, and Tabb, *Racial Politics*, 2nd ed.; Adolph Reed, "A Critique of Neo-Progressivism in Theorizing About Local Development Policy: A Case from Atlanta," in *The Politics of Urban Development*, ed. Clarence N. Stone and Haywood T. Sanders (Lawrence: University Press of Kansas, 1987).

100. Douglas S. Massey and Nancy A. Denton, *American Apartheid and the Making of the Underclass* (Cambridge, MA: Harvard University Press, 1993), especially chap. 6.

101. Reed, "Critique of Neo-Progressivism"; Wilbur Rich, "Detroit: From Motor City to Service Hub," in Savitch and Thomas, *Big City Politics*; Stone, *Regime Politics*; Stone and Pierannunzi, "Atlanta and the Limited Reach of Electoral Control"; Thomas, "Detroit: The Centrifugal City"; Arnold Fleischmann, "Atlanta: Urban Coalitions in a Suburban Sea," in Savitch and Thomas, *Big City Politics*.

102. Peter Beinart, "The Pride of the Cities," *New Republic,* June 30, 1997, 16–22; Sleeper, "End of the Rainbow?"

103. Pierre Clavel, *The Progressive City* (New Brunswick, NJ: Rutgers University Press, 1986); Norman Krumholz, John Forester, and Alan A. Altshuler, *Making Equity Planning Work* (Philadelphia: Temple University Press, 1990); Norman Krumholz and Pierre Clavel, *Reinventing Cities: Equity Planners Tell Their Stories* (Philadelphia: Temple University Press, 1994).

104. For unions' recent involvement in urban progressivism, see Steven Greenhouse, "The Most Innovative Figure in Silicon Valley? Maybe This Labor Organizer," *New York Times,* November 14, 1999; David Moberg, "Union Cities," *American Prospect* 11, no. 20 (September 11, 2000); Douglas Foster, "Unions.com: Silicon Valley Isn't Exactly Known as a Stronghold of Organized Labor; Amy Dean Is Working to Change That," *Mother Jones* 25, no. 5 (September–October 2000): 74–79; and Candaele and Dreier, "LA's Progressive Mosaic."

105. This discussion of Pingree and his counterparts is summarized in Judd and Swanstrom, *City Politics,* 2nd ed., 69–70. See also Melvin G. Holli, *Reform in Detroit: Hazen S. Pingree and Urban Politics* (New York: Oxford University Press, 1969).

106. In Milwaukee, socialists were elected to the mayor's office, the city council, the school board, other city and county posts, and Congress. Milwaukee's third and last socialist mayor held office as late as 1960, but the socialists' heyday was the first two decades of the twentieth century. See James Weinstein, *The Decline of Socialism in America 1912–1925* (New York: Vintage Books, 1967), 93–108; and Sally M. Miller, *Victor Berger and the Promise of Constructive Socialism, 1910–1920* (Westport, CT: Greenwood Press, 1973).

107. Weinstein, *Decline of Socialism,* 108.

108. Gail Radford, "From Municipal Socialism to Public Authorities: Institutional Factors in the Shaping of American Public Enterprise," *Journal of American History* 90, no. 3 (December 2003); Cecilia Bucki, *Bridgeport's Socialist New Deal, 1915–1936* (Urbana: University of Illinois Press, 2001); Jeff Stansbury, "How Kilowatt Socialism Saved LA From the Energy Crisis," *Los Angeles Times,* April 29, 2001; and Jeff Stansbury, "Workers and the Municipal State: Los Angeles in the Progressive Era, 1890–1915" (paper presented at the Institute for Labor and Employment conference, Santa Cruz, CA, January 19, 2002), available at http://www.ucop.edu/ile/conferences/grad_conf/2002/stansbury.pdf.

109. On progressive urban reformers, see Roy Lubove, *The Progressives and the Slums: Tenement House Reform in New York City, 1890–1917* (Pittsburgh: University of Pittsburgh Press, 1962); John Buenker, *Urban Liberalism and Progressive Reform* (New York: Norton, 1973); Allan F. Davis, *Spearheads for Reform* (New York: Oxford University Press, 1967).

110. Mark Gelfand, *A Nation of Cities: The Federal Government and Urban America, 1933–1965* (New York: Oxford University Press, 1975), 36.

111. Thomas Kessner, *Fiorello H. LaGuardia and the Making of Modern New York* (New York: McGraw-Hill, 1989); Josh Freeman, *Working-Class New York: Life and Labor Since World War II* (New York: New Press, 2000).

112. Margaret Weir, "Power, Money, and Politics in Community Development"; and Peter Dreier, "Comment," in *Urban Problems and Community Development,* ed. Ronald Ferguson and William Dickens (Washington, DC: Brookings Institution Press, 1999).

113. Harry Boyte, *The Backyard Revolution* (Philadelphia: Temple University Press, 1980); Harry Boyte, *CommonWealth: A Return to Citizen Politics* (New York: Free Press, 1989); Gary Delgado, *Beyond the Politics of Place: New Directions in Community Organizing in the 1990s* (Oakland, CA: Applied Research Center, 1994); Peter Dreier, "Community Empowerment: The Limits and Potential of Community-Based Organizing in Urban Neighborhoods," *Cityscape* 2, no. 2 (1996): 121–59; Jeffrey M. Berry, Kent E. Portney, and Ken Thomson, *The Rebirth of Urban Democracy* (Washington, DC: Brookings Institution Press, 1993); Michael Lipsky, *Protest in City Politics* (Chicago: Rand McNally, 1970); Mary Beth Rogers, *Cold Anger: A Story of Faith and Power in Politics* (Denton: University of North Texas Press, 1990); Mark Warren, *Dry Bones Rattling* (Princeton, NJ: Princeton University Press, 2001); Peter Medoff and Holly Sklar, *Streets of Hope* (Boston: South End Press, 1994); Frances Piven and Richard Cloward, *Poor People's Movements* (New York: Pantheon, 1977).

114. Christopher J. Walker and Mark Weinheimer, *Community Development in the 1990s* (Washington, DC: Urban Institute, 1998); Edward Goetz, "Local Government Support for Nonprofit Housing: A Survey of U.S. Cities," *Urban Affairs Quarterly* 27, no. 3 (1992): 420–35; Edward Goetz, *Shelter Burden: Local Politics and Progressive Housing Policy* (Philadelphia: Temple University Press, 1993).

115. Peter Dreier, "Redlining Cities: How Banks Color Community Development," *Challenge* 134, no. 6 (1991): 15–23; Gregory D. Squires, ed., *From Redlining to Reinvestment: Community Responses to Urban Disinvestment* (Philadelphia: Temple University Press, 1992); Susan White Haag, *Community Reinvestment and Cities: A Literature Review of CRA's Impact and Future* (Washington, DC: Brookings Institution Center for Urban and Metropolitan Policy, March 2000). To ensure that the federal government will accept applications to open branches or to buy other banks, banks frequently reach agreements with community groups to expand their lending activities in poor neighborhoods. According to one estimate, more than 300 community reinvestment agreements have added $350 billion in private investment in low-income areas, primarily for housing rehabilitation and new construction. See Alex Schwartz, "From Confrontation to Collaboration? Banks, Community Groups, and the Implementation of Community Reinvestment Act Agreements," *Housing Policy Debate* 9, no. 3 (1998): 631–62.

116. Stella Capek and John Gilderbloom, *Community Versus Commodity: Tenants and the American City* (Albany, NY: SUNY Press, 1992).

117. Munoz, "Mexican Americans."

118. Carmine Scavo, "The Use of Regulative Mechanisms by Large U.S. Cities," *Journal of Urban Affairs* 15, no. 1 (1993): 100.

119. Mary Brooks, *A Status Report on Housing Trust Funds in the United States* (Washington, DC: Center for Community Change, 1997); Mary Brooks, "Housing Trust Funds: A New Approach to Funding Affordable Housing," in *Affordable Housing and Urban Redevelopment in the United States,* ed. Willem van Vliet (Thousand Oaks, CA: Sage Publications, 1997).

120. Capek and Gilderbloom, *Community Versus Commodity;* Chuck Collins and Kirby White, "Boston in the 1980s: Toward a Social Housing Policy," in *The Affordable City,* ed. John E. Davis (Philadelphia: Temple University Press, 1994); Peter Dreier, "The Landlords Stage a Rent Strike," *Nation,* June 23, 1997, 17–22; Goetz, *Shelter Burden;* Mark Kann, *Middle Class Radicalism in Santa Monica* (Philadelphia: Temple University Press, 1986); W. Dennis Keating, "Linking Downtown Development to

Broader Community Goals: An Analysis of Linkage Policy in Three Cities," *Journal of the American Planning Association* 52, no. 2 (1986): 133–46.

121. Richard DeLeon, *Left Coast City: Progressive Politics in San Francisco, 1975–1991* (Lawrence: University Press of Kansas, 1992).

122. For discussion of progressive urban regimes, see Clavel, *Progressive City;* Krumholz and Clavel, *Reinventing Cities;* Donald Rosdil, "The Context of Radical Populism in U.S. Cities: A Comparative Analysis," *Journal of Urban Affairs* 13, no. 1 (1991): 77–96; David Imbroscio, *Reconstructing City Politics: Alternative Economic Development and Urban Regimes* (Newbury Park, CA: Sage Publications, 1997). For Portland, see Carl Abbott, "The Portland Region: Where City and Suburbs Talk to Each Other and Often Agree," *Housing Policy Debate* 8, no. 1 (1997): 65–73. For Hartford, see Louise Simmons, *Organizing in Hard Times: Labor and Neighborhoods in Hartford* (Philadelphia: Temple University Press, 1994). For Chicago, see Stephen Alexander, Robert Giloth, and Joshua Lerner, "Chicago's Industry Task Forces: Joint Problem Solving for Local Economic Development," *Economic Development Quarterly* 1, no. 4 (1987): 352–57; Pierre Clavel and Wim Wiewel, eds., *Harold Washington and the Neighborhoods: Progressive City Government in Chicago* (New Brunswick, NJ: Rutgers University Press, 1991); Robert Mier, *Social Justice and Local Development Policy* (Newbury Park, CA: Sage Publications, 1993); Dianne M. Pinderhughes, "Examination of Chicago Politics"; Michael Preston, "The Politics of Economic Redistribution in Chicago: Is Balanced Growth Possible?" in *Regenerating Cities,* ed. Michael Parkinson, Bernard Foley, and Dennis Judd (Glenview, IL: Scott, Foresman, 1989); and Barbara Ferman, *Challenging the Growth Machine* (Lawrence: University Press of Kansas, 1996). For Boston, see Peter Dreier, "Ray Flynn's Legacy: American Cities and the Progressive Agenda," *National Civic Review* (fall 1993): 380–403; Dreier and Ehrlich, "Downtown Development"; Peter Dreier and W. Dennis Keating, "The Limits of Localism: Progressive Municipal Housing Policies in Boston," *Urban Affairs Quarterly* 26, no. 2 (1996); Peter Dreier, "Urban Politics and Progressive Housing Policy: Ray Flynn and Boston's Neighborhood Agenda," in *Revitalizing Urban Neighborhoods,* ed. W. Dennis Keating, Norman Krumholz, and Philip Star (Lawrence: University Press of Kansas, 1996); and Medoff and Sklar, *Streets of Hope.* For Burlington, see William Conroy, *Challenging the Boundaries of Reform: Socialism in Burlington* (Philadelphia: Temple University Press, 1990). For San Francisco, see Randy Shilts, *The Mayor of Castro Street* (New York: St. Martin's Press, 1982); DeLeon, *Left Coast City;* Richard DeLeon, "Progressive Politics in the Left Coast City: San Francisco," in Browning, Marshall, and Tabb, *Racial Politics,* 2nd ed. For Pittsburgh, see Louise Jezierski, "Neighborhoods and Public-Private Partnerships in Pittsburgh," *Urban Affairs Quarterly* 26, no. 2 (December 1990): 217–49; John Metzger, "The Community Reinvestment Act and Neighborhood Revitalization in Pittsburgh," in Squires, *From Redlining to Reinvestment;* John Metzger, "Reinventing Housing in Pittsburgh: A Former CDC Director Becomes Mayor," *Shelterforce* (March/April 1996): 13–18; John Metzger, "Remaking the Growth Coalition: The Pittsburgh Partnership for Neighborhood Development," *Economic Development Quarterly* 12, no. 1 (February 1998): 112–29; Ferman, *Challenging the Growth Machine.* For Santa Monica, see Derek Shearer, "How the Progressives Won in Santa Monica," *Social Policy* 12, no. 3 (1982): 7–14; Kann, *Middle Class Radicalism;* John Gilderbloom and Stella Capek, "Santa Monica a Decade Later," *National Civic Review* (spring 1992). For Cleveland, see Krumholz, Forester, and Altshuler, *Making Equity Planning Work;* Todd Swan-

strom, *The Crisis of Growth Politics: Cleveland, Kucinich, and the Challenge of Urban Populism* (Philadelphia: Temple University Press, 1985).

123. DeLeon, *Left Coast City;* DeLeon, "Progressive Politics in the Left Coast City."

124. DeLeon, *Left Coast City.*

125. David Reynolds, ed., *Partnering for Change: Unions and Community Groups Build Coalitions for Economic Justice* (Armonk, NY: M. E. Sharpe, 2004); Jane McAlevey, "It Takes a Community: Building Unions From the Outside In," *New Labor Forum* (spring 2003); Greg Donaldson, "With Justice for All?" *Fast Company,* 38 (September 2000), available at http://www.fastcompany.com/online/38/mcalevey.html; Daniel HoSang, "All the Issues in Workers' Lives: Labor Confronts Race in Stamford," *Shelterforce* (May/June 2000); Janice Fine, "Building Community Unions," *Nation,* January 1, 2001; Paul Saba, Amy Simon, Frank Mitchell, and Jeremy Brecher, *Forging Closer Ties: Case Studies of Labor's Role in Progressive State Coalitions* (Amherst, MA: State Strategies Fund, 2002); Immanuel Ness and Stuart Eimer, eds., *Central Labor Councils and the Revival of American Unionism: Organizing for Justice in Our Communities* (Armonk, NY: M. E. Sharpe, 2001); Jeremy Brecher and Tim Costello, eds., *Building Bridges: The Emerging Grassroots Coalition of Labor and Community* (New York: Monthly Review Press, 1990); Robert Fisher and Joseph Kling, *Mobilizing the Community: Local Politics in the Era of the Global City* (Newbury Park, CA: Sage Publications, 1993); Simmons, *Organizing in Hard Times;* Joan Fitzgerald and Louise Simmons, "From Consumption to Production: Labor Participation in Grassroots Movements in Pittsburgh and Hartford," *Urban Affairs Quarterly* 26, no. 4 (June 1991); Louise Simmons, "A New Urban Conservatism: The Case of Hartford, Connecticut," *Journal of Urban Affairs* 20, no. 2 (spring 1998); David Reynolds, *Taking the High Road: Communities Organize for Economic Change* (Armonk, NY: M. E. Sharpe, 2002).

126. At the first Conference for Good City Government in 1894, President Theodore Roosevelt urged the delegates to make local government more "practical and efficient," according to Melvin G. Holli, "Urban Reform in the Progressive Era," in *The Progressive Era,* ed. Louis Gould (Syracuse, NY: Syracuse University Press, 1974), 144. The U.S. Chamber of Commerce initially provided office space and paid the executive secretary of the City Managers Association. Judd and Swanstrom, 2nd ed., *City Politics,* 101.

127. George Mowry, *The Era of Theodore Roosevelt, 1900–1912* (New York: Harper and Row, 1958); Ernest S. Griffith, *A History of American City Government, 1900–1920* (New York: Praeger, 1974); James Weinstein, *The Corporate Ideal in the Liberal State, 1900–1918* (Boston: Beacon Press, 1968); Samuel Hayes, "The Politics of Reform in Municipal Government in the Progressive Era," in *Social Change and Urban Politics: Readings,* ed. Daniel N. Gordon (Englewood Cliffs, NJ: Prentice-Hall, 1972), 107–27.

128. Previously, voters could just show up at polling places on the day of an election. Reformers also endorsed the secret ballot. Before it was introduced in the 1880s, parties printed the ballots, and they were often cast publicly. Illiterate immigrants could ask for help in reading and filling out the ballot, something the machine's precinct captains were happy to do.

129. Willis D. Hawley, *Nonpartisan Elections and the Case for Party Politics* (New York: Wiley, 1973), 14–18.

130. Weinstein, *Decline of Socialism;* Hayes, "Politics of Reform."

131. John Mollenkopf, *A Phoenix in the Ashes* (Princeton, NJ: Princeton University Press,

1994); John Mollenkopf, "New York: Still the Great Anomaly," in Browning, Marshall, and Tabb, *Racial Politics,* 3rd ed.

132. Los Angeles Mayor Sam Yorty (elected in 1961) and Philadelphia Mayor Frank Rizzo (the city's former police chief, elected in 1971) were among the most visible big-city mayors vaulted into office by a conservative backlash. They called for "law and order," a thinly veiled call for tougher police practices in poor minority areas. Although neither Yorty nor Rizzo pretended to show concern for the plight of the poor, the urban conservatives of the 1980s and 1990s justified their policies by arguing that "big government" liberalism had trapped the poor in the welfare safety net. See Richard A. Keiser, "After the First Black Mayor: Fault Lines in Philadelphia's Biracial Coalition," in Browning, Marshall, and Tabb, *Racial Politics,* 2nd ed.

133. Edward Banfield, *The Unheavenly City: The Nature and Future of Our Urban Crisis* (Boston: Little, Brown, 1970). Heirs to Banfield include Fred Siegel, *The Future Once Happened Here: New York, DC, LA, and the Fate of America's Big Cities* (New York: Free Press, 1997); Stephen Goldsmith, *The Twenty-first Century City: Resurrecting Urban America* (New York: Rowman and Littlefield, 1999); John O. Norquist, *The Wealth of Cities: Revitalizing the Centers of American Life* (Reading, MA: Addison-Wesley, 1998); Myron Magnet, ed., *The Millennial City* (New York: Ivan Dee, 2000); Hayward, "Broken Cities"; Senator Dan Coats and Senator Spencer Abraham, "Liberalism's Mean Streets: How Conservatives Can Reverse Urban Decline," *Policy Review* (July–August 1998): 36–40; James Q. Wilson and George L. Kelling, "Broken Windows," *Atlantic Monthly* (March 1982): 29–39; Tamar Jacoby, "Mandate for Anarchy," *New Democrat* 10, no. 3 (May–June 1998): 18–23.

134. Fred Siegel and Kay Hymowitz, "Why Did Ed Rendell Fizzle Out?" *City Journal* 9, no. 4 (autumn 1999): 1–27.

135. Heather MacDonald, "Gotham's Workforce Woes," *City Journal* 7, no. 3 (summer 1997): 41–49; Sol Stern, "ACORN's Nutty Regime for Cities," *City Journal* 13, no. 2 (spring 2003), available at http://www.city-journal.org/html/13_2_acorns_nutty _regime.html. For a critique of Stern's article, see John Atlas and Peter Dreier, "Enraging the Right," *Shelterforce* (May/June 2003), available at http://www.nhi.org/ online/issues/129/ACORN.html.

136. For critiques of Siegel's book, see Elliot Currie, "The Liberals Done It," *Dissent* 45, no. 1 (winter 1998): 114–17; Adam Yarmolinsky, "Looking Backwards," *Washington Monthly* 29, no. 10 (October 1997): 59–60; and Sean Wilentz, "The Rise and Fall of Racialized Liberalism," *American Prospect* 40 (September–October 1998): 82–86.

137. Quoted in James Traub, "Giuliani Internalized," *New York Times Magazine,* February 11, 2001, 66.

138. William Tucker, whose work was funded by right-wing think tanks and published by several conservative magazines, went so far as to argue that rent control caused homelessness during the 1980s. William Tucker, "America's Homeless: Victims of Rent Control," *Heritage Foundation Backgrounder* 685 (January 12, 1989): 1–14; William Tucker, "Home Economics: The Housing Crisis that Over-Regulation Built," *Policy Review* 50 (fall 1989): 20. For a critique of Tucker's work and his backers, see Richard P. Appelbaum, Michael Dolny, Peter Dreier, and John Gilderbloom, "Scapegoating Rent Control: Masking the Causes of Homelessness," *Journal of the American Planning Association* 57, no. 2 (spring 1991): 153–64. For a conservative critique of subsidized housing, see Howard Husock, "We Don't Need Subsidized Housing," *City Journal* 7, no. 1 (winter 1997): 50–58.

139. Joe Feagin, *Free Enterprise City: Houston in Political and Economic Perspective* (New Brunswick, NJ: Rutgers University Press, 1988); Dreier, "Landlords Stage a Rent Strike"; Rob Gurwitt, "Indianapolis and the Republican Future," *Governing* (February 1994); Beinart, "Pride of the Cities."

140. Tucker, "Socialism in Every City."

141. Tracy Shryer and Marc Lacey, "Riordan Studies Privatization in Indianapolis," *Los Angeles Times*, June 22, 1993. See also Louise Simmons, "A New Urban Conservatism: The Case of Hartford, Connecticut," *Journal of Urban Affairs* 20, no. 2 (1998): 175–98; E. J. Dionne, "Saving Cities: Is 'Kojak Liberalism' the Answer?" *Washington Post*, June 28, 1993; Dan Finnigan, "Philadelphia Turnaround May Offer Lessons for LA," *Los Angeles Times*, July 15, 1993; Charles Mahtesian, "Maybe Philadelphia Is Governable After All," *Governing* (April 1993): 34–38.

142. Jonathan Walters, "Who Needs Civil Service?" *Governing* (August 1997): 17–21.

143. Evelyn Nieves, "Homeless Defy Cities' Drives to Move Them," *New York Times*, December 7, 1999. See also Elliott Currie, *Reckoning: Drugs, the Cities, and the American Future* (New York: Hill and Wang, 1993); Adele Harrell and George Peterson, eds., *Drugs, Crime, and Social Isolation* (Washington, DC: Urban Institute Press, 1992); Jeffrey Reiman, *The Rich Get Richer and the Poor Get Prison* (Needham Heights, MA: Allyn and Bacon, 1995); Wesley Skogan, *Disorder and Decline* (Berkeley: University of California Press, 1990); Michael Tomasky, "The Left and Crime," *Dissent* (fall 1997): 85–96, with comments by Elliott Currie, Ester Fuchs, and Randall Kennedy; Neal Peirce, "Community Policing that Works," *National Journal*, October 12, 1996, 2190; James Lardner, "Can You Believe the New York Miracle?" *New York Review of Books*, August 14, 1997, 54–58.

144. Goldsmith ran unsuccessfully for governor in 1996 and was George W. Bush's chief domestic policy adviser in the 2000 presidential campaign, positioning the Texas governor as a "compassionate conservative" who cares about the poor. Frank Bruni, "Bush Unveils a Proposal to Encourage Development in Struggling Neighborhoods," *New York Times*, April 19, 2000; Alison Mitchell, "Bush Draws Campaign Theme from More than 'the Heart,'" *New York Times*, June 12, 2000. On Goldsmith's tenure as mayor, see Michael Grunwald, "The Myth of the Supermayor," *American Prospect* 9, no. 40 (September–October 1998): 20–29; Beinart, "Pride of the Cities"; Rob Gurwitt, "Indianapolis and the Republican Future," 24–28; Stephen J. McGovern, "Ideology, Consciousness, and Inner-City Redevelopment: The Case of Indianapolis," *Journal of Urban Affairs*, 25, no. 1 (2003): 1–25; Sleeper, "End of the Rainbow?"; Goldsmith, *Twenty-first Century City*; Siegel, *The Future Once Happened Here*. On Mayor Rendell, see Buzz Bissinger, *A Prayer for the City* (New York: Random House, 1997); Stephen J. McGovern, "Mayoral Leadership and Economic Development Policy: The Case of Ed Rendell's Philadelphia," *Policy and Politics* 25, no. 2 (April 1997): 153–72.

145. Raphael J. Sonenshein, *Politics in Black and White: Race and Power in Los Angeles* (Princeton, NJ: Princeton University Press, 1994), 79.

146. Latino Edward Roybal was elected the city's first minority council member in 1949. He subsequently served as a congressman. In 1986, Gloria Molina won in a neighboring district created in the wake of a voting rights challenge by Latino activists. In 1993, Richard Alarcon was elected from the San Fernando Valley.

147. Raphael J. Sonenshein, "Post-Incorporation Politics in Los Angeles." In 1992, following the city's devastating riots, the voters approved a Bradley-endorsed charter reform that eliminated the police chief's civil service protection. Blacks, Lati-

nos, and white liberal voters overwhelmingly supported the measure. Bradley then forced Gates to resign and replaced him with Willie Williams, the African American police chief of Philadelphia, who pledged more cooperation between the police department and community groups. After Richard Riordan became mayor in 1993, it took him three years to force Williams to resign and to replace him with a more conservative black chief, Bernard Parks.

148. Mike Davis, *City of Quartz* (New York: Vintage, 1989); Alan Saltzstein and Raphael J. Sonenshein, "Los Angeles: Transformation of a Governing Coalition," in Hank V. Savitch and John Thomas, eds., *Big City Politics in Transition* (Newbury Park, CA: Sage Publications, 1981); Sonenshein, *Politics in Black and White;* Sonenshein, "Post-Incorporation Politics."

149. James Johnson, Jones Farrell, and Melvin Oliver, "The Los Angeles Rebellion: A Retrospective View," *Economic Development Quarterly* 6, no. 4 (November 1992): 356–72.

150. Sonenshein, "Post-Incorporation Politics."

151. "The Times Poll: Profile of the City Electorate," *Los Angeles Times,* April 10, 1997. Sixty-seven percent of all white voters supported Riordan. White conservatives, who represented a fifth of the vote and were concentrated in the San Fernando Valley area, gave him 92 percent of their votes. Moderate whites, a third of the vote, gave Riordan 75 percent of their votes, primarily over racial concerns. Riordan even made inroads into Woo's natural constituency of Bradley supporters. Several high-profile black and Latino political figures endorsed Riordan. Thirty-nine percent of Democrats and 31 percent of self-identified white liberals supported Riordan, as well as 70 percent of independents. Riordan even won 49 percent of the Jewish vote and 31 percent of the Asian vote. In addition, 43 percent of Latino voters supported Riordan. Turnout was low among Woo constituencies. Whites were only 37 percent of the population but constituted 65 percent of registered voters and 72 percent of votes cast. Although 86 percent of blacks supported Woo, blacks accounted for only 14 percent of the population, 15 percent of registered voters, and 12 percent of the mayoral vote. Latinos gave Woo 57 percent of their vote, but they represented only 10 percent of the vote. (Asians accounted for 4 percent of the total vote.) Four years later, Riordan flattened his progressive white challenger, Tom Hayden, 61 to 39 percent. Riordan improved his minority vote with 19 percent of the black vote, 60 percent of the Latino vote, and 62 percent of the Asian vote. See Karen M. Kaufman, "Racial Conflict and Political Choice: A Study of Mayoral Voting Behavior in Los Angeles and New York," *Urban Affairs Review* 33, no. 5 (May 1998): 655–85; Sonenshein, "Post-Incorporation Politics"; and Peter Dreier, "America's Urban Crisis."

152. H. Eric Schockman, "Accountability and Responsiveness: Is Los Angeles Governable?" in Michael Gear, H. Eric Schoderman, and Greg Hise, eds., *Rethinking Los Angeles* (Thousand Oaks, CA: Sage Publications, 1996), 69.

153. Marla Cone, "Smog Plan Would Harm Economy," *Los Angeles Times,* August 30, 1994; Marla Cone, "State Scales Back Clean-Air Plan in Bow to Oil, Trucking Industries," *Los Angeles Times,* November 10, 1994; Marla Cone, "Wilson, Riordan Criticize EPA's Delay on Smog Rules," *Los Angeles Times,* January 14, 1995; Marla Cone, "U.S. Unveils Scaled-Back Clean-Air Plan," *Los Angeles Times,* February 15, 1995; Marla Cone, "Economy Found Undamaged by LA Smog Rules," *Los Angeles Times,* April 3, 1995; Marla Cone, "Southland Smog Levels Are Lowest in 4 Decades," *Los Angeles Times,* October 21, 1995.

154. Riordan failed to get Los Angeles designated as a federal empowerment zone, but he

persuaded the Clinton administration to give Los Angeles federal funds to establish a community development bank to lend to inner-city businesses. He supported Clinton and Senator Dianne Feinstein for reelection, remained neutral on Proposition 187 (restricting benefits to immigrants) in 1994 and Proposition 209 (eliminating state affirmative action laws) in 1995, and marched in the city's gay pride parade.

155. Sonenshein, "Post-Incorporation Politics"; Dreier, "America's Urban"; Meyerson, "Why Liberalism Fled the City"; Candaele and Dreier, "LA's Progressive Mosaic"; Harold Meyerson, "LA Story," *American Prospect* 12, no. 12 (July 2, 2001).

156. Jargowsky, *Stunning Progress.*

157. Mollenkopf, *Phoenix in the Ashes;* John Mollenkopf, "New York: The Great Anomaly" in Browning, Marshall, and Tabb, *Racial Politics,* 2nd ed.; William Sites, "The Limits of Urban Regime Theory: New York City Under Koch, Dinkins and Giuliani," *Urban Affairs Review* 32, no. 4 (March 1997): 536–57; Jim Sleeper, *The Closest of Strangers: Liberalism and Politics of Race in New York* (New York: Norton, 1990); Freeman, *Working Class New York.*

158. John R. Logan and John Mollenkopf, *People and Politics in America's Big Cities* (New York: Drum Major Institute, April 2003).

159. John Mollenkopf, "New York: Still the Great Anomaly."

160. Mollenkopf, *Phoenix in the Ashes;* Mollenkopf, "New York: Still the Great Anomaly."

161. Alex Schwartz, "New York City and Subsidized Housing: Impacts and Lessons of the City's $5 Billion Capital Budget Housing Plan," *Housing Policy Debate* 10, no. 4 (1999): 839–77; Gregg G. Van Ryzin and Andrew Genn, "Neighborhood Change and the City of New York's Ten-Year Housing Plan," *Housing Policy Debate* 10, no. 4 (1999): 799–838; David Chen, "New York Is No Longer Awash in Abandoned Buildings. Now the Issue Is Supply," *New York Times,* December 21, 2003.

162. Mollenkopf, *Phoenix in the Ashes,* 176.

163. Mollenkopf, "New York: The Great Anomaly," 100.

164. Ibid., 111.

165. Thomas L. McMahon, Larian Angelo, and John Mollenkopf, *Hollow in the Middle: The Rise and Fall of New York City's Middle Class* (New York: Finance Division, City Council, December 1997); Kathryn Larin and Elizabeth McNichol, *Pulling Apart: A State-by-State Analysis of Income Trends* (Washington, DC: Center of Budget and Policy Priorities, December 1997); Van Ryzin and Genn, "Neighborhood Change"; Schwartz, "New York City"; Edward L. Glaeser and Matthew E. Kahn, "From John Lindsay to Rudy Giuliani: The Decline of the Local Safety Net?" *Economic Policy Review* 5, no. 3 (September 1999): 117–30.

166. Harold Meyerson, "Race Conquers All," *American Prospect* 12, no. 21 (December 3, 2001).

167. Mollenkopf, "New York: Still the Great Anomaly."

168. Some ideas about what such a vision might include are outlined in John Mollenkopf and Ken Emerson, eds., *Rethinking the Urban Agenda: Reinvigorating the Liberal Tradition in New York City and Urban America* (New York: The Century Foundation Press, 2001).

169. Michael Leo Owens and Michael J. Rich, "Is Strong Incorporation Enough? Black Empowerment and the Fate of Atlanta's Low-Income Blacks," in Browning, Marshall, and Tabb, eds., *Racial Politics,* 3rd ed.

170. Stone, *Regime Politics,* 87.

171. Reed, "Critique of Neo-Progressivism."

172. "Atlanta's Mayor Defies Threat to Affirmative Action," *New York Times,* July 16, 1999.

173. Stone, *Regime Politics*. Preferential procurement programs have been damaged by evidence that some minority-owned firms are actually "fronts" for white-owned businesses or that they do not employ more minorities than white-owned firms do. See Timothy Bates and Darrell Williams, "Preferential Procurement Programs and Minority-Owned Business," *Journal of Urban Affairs* 17, no. 1 (1995): 10–17. In 1989, in *City of Richmond v. J. A. Croson Co.,* the U.S. Supreme Court ruled that Richmond's policy requiring that 30 percent of city contracts be set aside for minority-owned businesses violated the equal protection clause of the Fourteenth Amendment. To enact a constitutional program, cities must document prior discrimination by city government and demonstrate that race-neutral approaches will not solve the problem. This decision and other rulings in the 1990s limited the ability of municipal governments to enact laws designed to expand minority participation in public employment and publicly subsidized contracts.

174. Stone and Pierannunzi, "Atlanta and the Limited Reach of Electoral Control."

175. Bill Dedman, "The Color of Money," *Atlanta Journal-Constitution,* May 1–4, 1988; Larry Keating, Lynn Brazen, and Stan Fitterman, "Reluctant Response to Community Pressure in Atlanta," in Squires, *From Redlining to Reinvestment.* Almost a decade after the initial uproar, little progress had been made in addressing racial disparities in lending. See Elvin K. Wyly and Steven R. Holloway, "'The Color of Money' Revisited: Racial Lending Patterns in Atlanta's Neighborhoods," *Housing Policy Debate* 10, no. 3 (1999): 555–600.

176. David Sjoquist, "Introduction," in David Sjoquist, ed., *The Atlanta Paradox* (New York: Russell Sage Foundation, 2000).

177. The following paragraphs draw on these sources: Stone and Pierannunzi, "Atlanta and the Limited Reach of Electoral Control"; Gary Orfield and Carole Ashkinaze, *The Closing Door: Conservative Policy and Black Opportunity* (Chicago: University of Chicago Press, 1991); Owens and Rich, "Is Strong Incorporation Enough?"; Larry Keating, *Atlanta: Race, Class, and Urban Expansion* (Philadelphia: Temple University Press, 2001).

178. Kingsley and Pettit, *Concentrated Poverty.*

179. D. L. Bennett, "Atlanta's Budget Is Out of Red; Cuts, Rise in Revenue Credited," *Atlanta Journal-Constitution,* January 17, 2003; Carrick Mollenkamp, "New Atlanta Mayor Points a Way Out of City Fiscal Hole," *Wall Street Journal,* February 14, 2003.

180. Ty Tagami, "Atlanta Mayor Balances Kudos, Critics," *Atlanta Journal-Constitution,* March 14, 2004; Rob Gurwitt, "How to Win Friends and Repair a City," *Governing* (April 2004).

181. Ellen Barry, "Chief Calls Atlanta Most Dangerous City in Nation," *Los Angeles Times,* February 21, 2004.

182. Joe Darden, Richard Child Hill, June Thomas, and Richard Thomas, *Detroit: Race and Uneven Development* (Philadelphia: Temple University Press, 1987); Richard Child Hill, "Crisis in the Motor City: The Politics of Economic Development in Detroit," in Fainstein and Fainstein, *Restructuring the City;* June Thomas, "Detroit: The Centrifugal City," in *Unequal Partnerships: The Political Economy of Urban Redevelopment in Postwar America,* ed. Gregory D. Squires (New Brunswick, NJ: Rutgers University Press, 1989).

183. Rich, "Detroit"; Marion E. Orr and Gerry Stoker, "Urban Regimes and Leadership in Detroit," *Urban Affairs Quarterly* 30, no. 1 (September 1994): 48–73.

184. Heather Ann Thompson, *Whose Detroit? Politics, Labor, and Race in a Modern American City* (Ithaca, NY: Cornell University Press, 2001).

185. Bill Vlasic, "Motown in Motion," *Business Week,* April 21, 1997. Japanese and European competition and the shift of U.S. production to the "global assembly line" meant layoffs and plant closings in Detroit, according to Hill, "Crisis in the Motor City," and Richard Child Hill and Joe R. Feagin, "Detroit and Houston," in *The Capitalist City,* ed. Michael Peter Smith and Joe R. Feagin (Cambridge: Basil Blackwell, 1987). In the mid-1960s, manufacturing accounted for 42.4 percent of the area's jobs; by 1988, it represented only 24.2 percent. Blacks constituted 43 percent of Detroit's population in 1970, rising to 76 percent in 1990, and 82 percent in 2000. Middle-class black professionals and auto workers began leaving Detroit to escape its property taxes, schools, and crime. The city poverty rate increased dramatically during the 1970s and 1980s, becoming the highest among the nation's 100 largest cities. Banks redlined the city, landlords and home owners abandoned their buildings, and many residential neighborhoods came to resemble bombed-out areas. In 1993, only one building permit was taken out for a new house, as reported in Vlasic, "Motown." Detroit's downtown core hollowed out as businesses closed or fled. Meanwhile, federal funds, as a percentage of Detroit's general revenue, declined from 27.5 percent in 1976 to 5.9 percent in 1988, according to Rich, "Detroit."

186. Rich, "Detroit."

187. Frank Washington and Bill Turque, "New Deal in Detroit," *Newsweek,* September 12, 1994.

188. Vlasic, "Motown."

189. John King, "Whining Doesn't Work Any More, Mayors Learning," *San Francisco Chronicle,* June 27, 1996.

190. Vlasic, "Motown."

191. Jon Pepper, "Power Elite Designing a New Downtown," *Detroit News,* March 10, 1996. Chrysler agreed to invest $2.1 billion in the city, about half in a new engine plant on the decaying East Side, for which the city granted an $87 million tax abatement. General Motors pledged to spend $250 million to upgrade its facilities and $72 million to purchase the Renaissance Center, a partly vacant riverfront office complex that had been a failure from the time it was built in 1976. Archer supported the construction of new professional football and baseball stadiums downtown to keep the Lions and Tigers in Detroit, according to Vlasic, "Motown." The UAW agreed to move its education and training program, run in collaboration with General Motors, from suburban Oakland County into Detroit. See also Gary Heinlein and Suzette Hackney, "City on the Rebound," *Detroit News,* January 5, 1997. Business support helped the city improve its junk bond rating, according to Tom Henderson, "Calculating the Archer Effect," *Corporate Detroit Magazine* (June 1994): 34–43. Archer gave minority entrepreneurs a share in the private economic growth. The Detroit Tigers agreed to award 20 percent of the construction work on their new $235 million stadium to minority businesses, at least one-quarter based in Detroit, and half the construction workers will be Detroit residents, as reported in Washington and Turque, "New Deal." See also Valarie Basheda and Tricia Serju, "Minority Firms Will Get Share of Stadium Work," *Detroit News,* November 21, 1995.

192. Washington and Turque, "New Deal."

193. Ibid.

194. Melinda Wilson, "Archer's Biggest Donors Are in the 'Burbs," *Detroit News,* March 9, 1997.

195. Tim Kiska, Judy DeHaven, and Suzette Hackney, "Archer Win Strengthens City's

Ties with Suburbs: Tricounty Leaders Praise Mayor's Ability to Reach Out, Create Coalition," *Detroit News,* September 10, 1997.

196. Robyn Meredith, "Demand for Single-Family Homes Helps Fuel Inner-City Resurgence," *New York Times,* July 5, 1997.

197. Suzette Hackney, "Archer Gets Chance to Take a Bow," *Detroit News,* January 27, 1997.

198. Washington and Turque, "New Deal."

199. Alexandra Starr, "We Shall Overcome, Too: A Cadre of Young, Centrist African Americans is Redefining Black Politics," *Newsweek* (July 15, 2002); Kevin Chappell, "Kwame Kilpatrick," *Ebony* (December 2002); Jeremy Grant, "Hip Hop Mayor Upbeat on Detroit Revival," *Financial Times* (February 21, 2004).

200. Jeffrey Ghannam, "Motor City Paves Road to a Renaissance," *Boston Globe,* December 7, 2003.

201. Kingsley and Pettit, *Concentrated Poverty.*

202. Louise Jezierski, "Pittsburgh: Partnerships in a Regional City," in H. V. Savitch and Ronald K. Vogel, eds., *Regional Politics: America in a Post-City Age* (Thousand Oaks, CA: Sage Publications, 1996).

203. Hyung Je Jo, "Regional Restructuring and Urban Regimes: A Comparison of the Pittsburgh and Detroit Metropolitan Areas" (Office for the Study of Automotive Transportation, University of Michigan Transportation Research Institute, July, 2002).

204. Stanley Lowe and John T. Metzger, "A Citywide Strategy: The Pittsburgh Community Reinvestment Group," in Gregory D. Squires, ed., *Organizing Access to Capital: Advocacy and the Democratization of Financial Institutions* (Philadelphia: Temple University Press, 2003).

205. Jezierski, "Pittsburgh."

206. Dan Fitzpatrick, "The Story of Urban Renewal," *Pittsburgh Post-Gazette,* May 21, 2000.

207. Lowe and Metzger, "Citywide Strategy."

208. See Ferman, *Challenging the Growth Machine.* Information on political trends in Pittsburgh was provided by John Metzger in a personal communication, August 11, 1997.

209. Erie, *Rainbow's End.*

210. Pinderhughes, "Examination of Chicago Politics," 113; Dianne Pinderhughes, "Chicago Politics: Incorporation and Restoration," in Browning, Marshall, and Tabb, *Racial Politics,* 3rd ed.

211. Medoff and Sklar, *Streets of Hope.*

212. Dreier and Keating, "Limits of Localism."

213. Paul Osterman, "Gains from Growth? The Impact of Full Employment on Poverty in Boston," in *The Urban Underclass,* ed. Christopher Jencks and Paul E. Peterson (Washington, DC: Brookings Institution Press, 1991).

214. When the consolidation law took effect in 1970, Indianapolis's jurisdiction swelled from 82 to 402 square miles and its population from 480,000 to 740,000. The consolidation occurred over opposition from Democrats and African Americans, who feared that the inclusion of a large segment of suburban Republicans in the local electorate would undermine their influence. See McGovern, "Ideology, Consciousness."

215. McGovern, "Ideology, Consciousness"; Grunwald, "The Myth of the Supermayor."

216. McGovern, "Ideology, Consciousness," 8.

217. Ibid., 17–18.
218. Rob Gurwitt, "Bart Peterson: Hoover Surprise," *Governing* (December 1999); "Peterson's Radical City Restructuring Plan," *Indianapolis*, August 8, 2004; "United Airlines Officials Confirm Departure from Indy." *USA Today*, May 5, 2003.
219. For a discussion of the different types of suburbs, see Myron Orfield, *American Metropolitics: The New Suburban Reality* (Washington, DC: Brookings Institution Press, 2002).
220. Andrew E. G. Jonas, "Regulating Suburban Politics: Suburban-Defense Transition, Institutional Capacities, and Territorial Reorganization in Southern California," in Lauria, *Reconstructing Urban Regime Theory;* John Logan and Kyle Crowder, "Political Regimes and Suburban Growth," *City and Community* 1, no. 1 (March 2002): 113–36.
221. Matthew Blanchard, "A New Regime Takes on a Fiery Issue," *Philadelphia Inquirer*, December 1, 2003.
222. Lydia Polgreen, "City in Suburbs Faces a Choice: More Property Tax or Loss of Its Libraries," *New York Times*, May 30, 2003 and George M. Eberhart, "Referenda Roundup, 2003," *American Libraries* 35, no. 1 (January 2004).
223. Kristin Downey, "Suburbs Support Cheaper Housing, but in Someone Else's Back Yard," *Washington Post*, November 12, 1991.
224. Gary Scott, "Ambassador Project Is Groups' Rallying Point," *Pasadena Star-News*, February 24, 2004.
225. Andrew Wiese, *Places of Their Own: African American Suburbanization in the Twentieth Century* (Chicago: University of Chicago Press, 2004); Andrew Wiese, "Racial Cleansing in the Suburbs: Suburban Government, Urban Renewal, and Segregation on Long Island, New York, 1945–1960," A. Scott Henderson, "A Better Home in a Nice Neighborhood: Housing, Race, and Residential Conflict," and Ellen J. Skinner, "The War Against the Housing of the Minority Poor: White Plains, New York," in Marc L. Silver and Martin Melkonian, eds., *Contested Terrain: Power, Politics, and Participation in Suburbia* (Westport, CT: Greenwood Press, 1995).
226. Haya el Nasser, "Minorities Make Choice to Live with Their Own," *USA Today*, July 8, 2001; Ellen Barry, "Atlanta Suburbs Boom for Blacks," *Los Angeles Times*, February 27, 2004; David Dent, "The New Black Suburbs," *New York Times Magazine*, June 14, 1992. Surveys suggest that most blacks want to live in integrated neighborhoods, meaning one-third to one-half black. That proportion of blacks, however, makes most whites uncomfortable, so they leave, ultimately resulting in a mostly black area. See Massey and Denton, *American Apartheid;* Ron French, "Mistrust Keeps Races Living Apart: Subtle Perceptions Shade Decisions on Where to Live, Reinforcing Racial Divide," *Detroit News*, January 14, 2002. A few suburbs have engaged in what some call "managed integration."
227. Sharon Sutker McGowen, "Suburban Town Halls No Longer for Whites Only," *Chicago Reporter*, July/August 1993.
228. Valerie Johnson, *Black Power in the Suburbs: The Myth or Reality of African American Suburban Political Empowerment* (Albany: State University of New York Press, 2002); J. Eric Oliver, *Democracy in Suburbia* (Princeton, NJ: Princeton University Press, 2001).
229. Peter Dreier and David Moberg, "Moving From the 'Hood: The Mixed Success of Integrating Suburbia," *American Prospect* 7, no. 24 (winter 1996).
230. David L. Kirp, John P. Dwyer, and Larry A. Rosenthal, *Our Town: Race, Housing, and the Soul of Suburbia* (New Brunswick, NJ: Rutgers University Press, 1997).

231. Richard D. Kahlenberg, *All Together Now: Creating Middle Class Schools Through Public School Choice* (Washington, DC: Brookings Institution Press, 2001); Isabel Wilkerson, "One City's 30-Year Crusade for Integration," *New York Times,* December 30, 1991; Evan McKenzie and Jay Ruby, "Reconsidering the Oak Park Strategy: The Conundrums of Integration" (Chicago: University of Illinois, Political Science Department, n.d.).

232. Dennis Keating and Mitch Kahn, "Rent Control in the New Millennium," *Shelterforce* (May/June 2001).

233. Bruce Lambert, "Housing Pinch on L.I. Causes New Group to Push for More Rentals," *New York Times,* April 25, 2002.

234. Rone Tempest, "In Marin County Plenty, a Poverty of Service Workers, Jobs: As Booming Economy Creates Openings, High Cost of Living Puts Area out of Reach for Low-Paid Employees," *Los Angeles Times,* October 25, 1999.

235. Robert E. Lang, *Edgeless Cities: Exploring the Elusive Metropolis* (Washington, DC: Brookings Institution Press, 2003).

236. Robert E. Lang and Patrick A. Simmons, "Boomburbs: The Emergence of Large, Fast-Growing Suburban Cities," in Bruce Katz and Robert E. Lang, eds., *Redefining Urban and Suburban America: Evidence From Census 2000* (Washington, DC: Brookings Institution Press, 2003).

237. Milton Carrero Galarza, "4,000 Homes, No Schools in Sight," *Los Angeles Times,* April 22, 2002.

238. David Firestone, "In Atlanta, Suburban Comforts Thwart Plans to Limit Sprawl," *New York Times,* November 21, 1999.

239. Lyndsey Layton, "Sewer Bans Become a Weapon in the War on Sprawl," *Washington Post,* February 22, 1999.

240. John J. Fialka, "Campaign Against Sprawl Overruns a County in Virginia, and Soon Perhaps Much of Nation," *Wall Street Journal,* January 4, 2000.

241. Mark Baldassare, *Trouble in Paradise* (New York: Columbia University Press, 1986).

242. Richard A. Oppel, "Efforts to Restrict Sprawl Find New Resistance from Advocates for Affordable Housing," *New York Times,* December 26, 2000.

243. Danielle Arigoni, "Common Ground: Smart Growth and Affordable Housing Advocates Start a Dialogue," *Shelterforce* (November/December 2001); Dennis Hevesi, "Antidotes to Sprawl Taking Many Forms," *New York Times,* October 6, 2002.

244. Nancy Cleeland and Abigail Goldman, "The Wal-Mart Effect: Grocery Unions Battle to Stop Invasion of the Giant Stores," *Los Angeles Times,* November 25, 2003; Anthony Bianco and Wendy Zellner, "Is Wal-Mart Too Powerful?" *Business Week* (October 6, 2003).

245. Lisa Foderaro, "Affluent Town Seeks to Curb Development Outside Its Borders," *New York Times,* March 11, 2000.

246. "Us Vs. Them: Too Many Roadblocks Impede Regional Progress," *Detroit Free Press,* December 23, 2003.

247. Robert D. Putnam, *Bowling Alone: The Collapse and Revival of American Community* (New York: Simon and Schuster, 2000).

248. Phillip Langdon, *A Better Place to Live: Reshaping the American Suburb* (New York: Harper Perennial, 1995); James Kunstler, *The Geography of Nowhere* (New York: Simon and Schuster, 1993); Evan McKenzie, *Privatopia: Homeowner Associations and the Rise of Residential Private Government* (New Haven, CT: Yale University Press, 1994); Tony Perry and Louis Sahagan, "Rich Enclave Values Privacy, Money," *Los Angeles Times,* June 5, 2002.

249. Richard Rothstein, "The Suburbs Vote for Public Education," *New York Times,* March 15, 2000. Rothstein provided the authors with census data on public and private school enrollment (including church-related and non-church-related private school attendance) by income groups.

250. Bennet Berger, *Working Class Suburb* (Berkeley: University of California Press, 1960), 6.

251. For a discussion of civic and political participation in suburbs, see Oliver, *Democracy in Suburbia;* Theda Skocpol and Morris P. Fiorina, eds., *Civic Engagement in American Democracy* (Washington, DC: Brookings Institution Press, 1999); and Juliet B. Schor, *The Overworked American: The Unexpected Decline of Leisure* (New York: Basic Books, 1992).

252. Bruce Lambert, "Suburban Democrats Undercut Myth of Republican Stronghold," *New York Times,* November 6, 2003; John B. Judis and Ruy Teixeira, *The Emerging Democratic Majority* (New York: Scribner, 2002).

253. See William Julius Wilson, *The Bridge over the Racial Divide: Rising Inequality and Coalition Politics* (Berkeley: University of California Press, 1999).

254. McMahon, Angelo, and Mollenkopf, *Hollow in the Middle,* 5.

255. Booming urban economies have had a downside for the poor: the housing burden has soared. Since 1975, median renter income (adjusted for inflation) in New York City went up 3 percent, while median rent increased 33 percent. Bruce Lambert, "Housing Crisis Confounds a Prosperous City," *New York Times,* July 9, 2000.

256. The best analysis of distressed suburbs is William H. Lucy and David L. Phillips, *Confronting Suburban Decline: Strategic Planning for Metropolitan Revival* (Washington, DC: Island Press, 2000). It concentrates more on documenting suburban decline than on analyzing how distressed suburban governments are responding to the crisis. See also, William Hudnut, *Halfway from Anywhere: A Portrait of America's First-Tier Suburbs* (Washington, DC: Urban Land Institute, 2003).

CHAPTER 6. REGIONALISMS OLD AND NEW

1. Kenneth Neubeck and Richard Ratcliff, "Urban Democracy and the Power of Corporate Capital," in *Business Elites and Urban Development,* ed. Scott Cummings (Albany, NY: SUNY Press, 1988).

2. Ibid., 322.

3. Shipman's plan is described in Vicki Kemper, "Operation Urban Storm," *Common Cause Magazine,* July–August 1991, 10–16, 39–40.

4. At the time, at least thirty cities across the country had adopted zoning laws to restrict social service agencies. A growing number of cities, responding to the increase in homelessness, adopted laws to restrict homeless people from panhandling or from sleeping in public places. Evelyn Nieves, "Homeless Defy Cities' Drives to Move Them," *New York Times,* December 7, 1999; William Claiborne, "From Champion to Chief Critic of the Homeless," *Washington Post,* December 9, 1997.

5. Michael Matza, "Social Service Groups Caught in the Middle," *Houston Chronicle,* August 22, 1996; "Hartford Restricts Social Services to Stem Flow of Poor People," *New York Times,* August 14, 1996; Colman McCarthy, "Heartless Go After Services for Homeless," *Washington Post,* May 14, 1996.

6. Ronald Smothers, "City Seeks to Grow by Disappearing," *New York Times,* October 18, 1993; Woody Baird, "Memphis' Black Mayor Fears a Bleak Future: Leader

Wants to Merge City with Majority-White Suburbs to Relieve the Strain on Tax Base," *Los Angeles Times*, October 3, 1993.

7. Baird, "Memphis' Black Mayor Fears a Bleak Future."

8. The term "favored quarter" is from Myron Orfield, *Metropolitics: A Regional Agenda for Community and Stability*, rev. ed. (Washington, DC: Brookings Institution Press, 1997), 5.

9. Gerald Frug, *City Making: Building Communities Without Building Walls* (Princeton, NJ: Princeton University Press, 1999), 80.

10. Robert D. Putnam, *Bowling Alone: The Collapse and Revival of American Community* (New York: Simon and Schuster, 2000), chap. 12; J. Eric Oliver, "The Effects of Metropolitan Economic Segregation on Local Civic Involvement," *American Journal of Political Science* 43 (January 1999): 186–212; J. Eric Oliver, "City Size and Civic Involvement in Metropolitan America," *American Political Science Review* 94, no. 2 (June 2000): 361–73.

11. Frug, *City Making*, 137.

12. Carl Sussman, ed., *Planning the Fourth Migration: The Neglected Vision of the Regional Planning Association of America* (Cambridge, MA: MIT Press, 1976), 89.

13. Regional Plan Association, *Regional Plan of New York and Its Environs* (1927); National Resources Committee, *Our Cities: Their Role in the National Economy* (Washington, DC: U.S. Government Printing Office, 1937).

14. Paul Studentski, *The Government of Metropolitan Areas in the United States* (New York: National Municipal League, 1930), 64.

15. An overview of their work is provided by G. Ross Stephens and Nelson Wikstrom, *Metropolitan Government and Governance: Theoretical Perspectives, Empirical Analysis, and the Future* (New York: Oxford University Press, 2000), chap. 2. That volume, together with David K. Hamilton, *Governing Metropolitan Areas: Response to Growth and Change* (New York: Garland, 1999), and Alan Altshuler, William Morrill, Harold Wolman, and Faith Mitchell, eds., *Governance and Opportunity in Metropolitan America* (Washington, DC: National Academy Press, 1999), offer the most thorough reviews of the history, theory, and contemporary practice of metropolitan government.

16. Neal R. Peirce, "Louisville Votes Merger — First Since Indy in 1969," syndicated column, December 3, 2000.

17. The report reflected a new sophistication among environmentalists regarding urban fragmentation. Real Estate Research Corporation, *The Costs of Sprawl* (Washington, DC: U.S. Government Printing Office, 1974), prepared for the Council on Environmental Quality, HUD, and the Environmental Protection Agency, executive summary, available at http://www.smartgrowth.org/pdf/costs_of_sprawl.pdf.

18. See Peter Calthorpe, *The Next American Metropolis: Ecology, Community, and the American Dream* (New York: Princeton Architectural Press, 1993), and Andres Duany, Elizabeth Plater-Zyberk, and Jeff Speck, *Suburban Nation: The Rise of Sprawl and the Decline of the American Dream* (New York: North Point Press, 2000).

19. A representative critique is Alex Anas, "The Costs and Benefits of Fragmented Metropolitan Governance and the New Regionalist Policies" (paper presented to the symposium "Regionalism: Promise and Problems," SUNY Buffalo Law School, March 6, 1999), available at http://www.pam.usc.edu. For a review of the evidence on the costs and benefits of sprawl, see Robert W. Burchell, George Lowenstein, William R. Dolphin, Catherine C. Gelley, Anthony Downs, Samuel Seskin, Katherine Gray Still, and Terry Moore, *Costs of Sprawl—2000 Revisited*, Transit Coopera-

tive Research Program Report 74 (Washington, DC: National Academy Press, 2002). Robert W. Burchell, "State of the Cities and Sprawl" (paper presented to the U.S. Department of Housing and Urban Development conference "Bridging the Divide," Washington, DC, December 8, 1999), estimates that a more consolidated form of metropolitan growth would generate $250 billion in savings over ten years. A good short statement of this consensus is Bruce Katz and Jennifer Bradley, "Divided We Sprawl," *Atlantic Monthly* (December 1999): 26–42.

20. Metro Chicago Information Center, 1998 annual survey; Larry N. Gerston and Peter J. Haas, "Political Support for Regional Government in the 1990s: Growing in the Suburbs?" *Urban Affairs Quarterly* 29, no. 1 (September 1993): 154–63.

21. Todd Purdum, "Suburban Sprawl Takes Its Place on the Political Landscape," *New York Times,* February 6, 1999; Daniel Pedersen, Vern E. Smith, and Jerry Adler, "Sprawling . . . ," *Newsweek,* July 19, 1999; Bruce Katz and Jennifer Bradley, "Divided We Sprawl"; Julie Cart, "Rapidly Growing Phoenix Finds Dust Unsettling," *Los Angeles Times,* September 7, 1999; William Fulton and Paul Shifley, "Operation Desert Sprawl," *Governing* (August 1999); Mark Arax, "Putting the Brakes on Growth," *Los Angeles Times,* October 6, 1999; Rob Gurwitt, "The Quest for Common Ground," *Governing* (June 1998); Rob Gurwitt, "The State vs. Sprawl," *Governing* (January 1999); Alan Ehrenhalt, "The Czar of Gridlock," *Governing* (May 1999); *Smart Growth, Better Neighborhoods: Communities Leading the Way* (Washington, DC: National Neighborhood Coalition, 2000); Neal R. Peirce, "Smart Growth, Smart Regions, Smart Politics?" syndicated column, January 16, 2000; Neal R. Peirce, "Sprawl Debate Warms Up," syndicated column, March 5, 2000; Neal R. Peirce, "Smart Growth 2000, Bumps and Breakthroughs," syndicated column, December 31, 2000.

22. For documentation, see http://www.smartgrowth.org.

23. American Planning Association, "Planning for Smart Growth State of the States 2002" (Washington, DC, February 2002), 7.

24. AnnaLee Saxenian, *Regional Advantage: Culture and Competition in Silicon Valley and Route 128* (Cambridge, MA: Harvard University Press, 1994).

25. Pivotal statements in this discussion include Joel Garreau, *Edge City: Life on the New Frontier* (New York: Doubleday, 1991); David Rusk, *Cities Without Suburbs* (Washington, DC: Woodrow Wilson Center Press, 1993); Neal Peirce, Curtis Johnson, and John Hall, *Citistates* (Washington, DC: Seven Locks Press, 1993); Henry Cisneros, ed., *Interwoven Destinies: Cities and the Nation* (New York: Norton, 1993); H. V. Savitch et al., "Ties that Bind: Central Cities, Suburbs, and the New Metropolitan Region," *Economic Development Quarterly* 7, no. 4 (1993): 341–58; Edward W. Hill, Harold L. Wolman, and Coit Cook Ford III, "Can Suburbs Survive Without Their Central Cities? Examining the Suburban Dependence Thesis," *Urban Affairs Review* 31, no. 2 (November 1995): 147–74; H. V. Savitch, "Straw Men, Red Herrings, and Suburban Dependence," *Urban Affairs Review* 31, no. 2 (November 1995): 175–79; Keith Ihlanfeldt, "The Importance of the Central City to the Regional and National Economy: A Review of the Arguments and Empirical Evidence," *Cityscape* 1, no. 1 (1995): 125–50; Todd Swanstrom, "Ideas Matter: Reflections on the New Regionalism," *Cityscape* 2, no. 2 (May 1996): 5–23; Manuel Pastor, Peter Dreier, Eugene Grigsby III, and Marta Lopez-Garza, *Regions that Work: How Cities and Suburbs Can Grow Together* (Minneapolis: University of Minnesota Press, 2000); William R. Barnes and Larry C. Ledebur, *The New Regional Economies* (Thousand Oaks, CA:

Sage Publications, 1998); David Rusk, *Inside Game/Outside Game: Winning Strategies for Saving Urban America* (Washington, DC: Brookings Institution Press, 1999).

26. Neal Peirce and Curtis Johnson, *Boundary Crossers: Community Leadership for a Global Age* (College Park, MD: Academy of Leadership, University of Maryland, 1997), synthesize lessons from a number of case studies included in Bruce Adams, et al., *Boundary Crossers: Case Studies of How Ten of America's Metropolitan Regions Work* (College Park, MD: Academy of Leadership, University of Maryland, 1997), available at http://civicsource.org/KLFP/boundary.htm. Peirce and Johnson's Web site is available at http://www.citistates.com/index.htm. Other important regionalism sites include http://www.cnt.org/mi/index.htm, the Metropolitan Initiative of the Center for Neighborhood Technology, and http://www.brookings.edu/es/urban/urban.html, the Brookings Institution Center on Urban and Metropolitan Policy. See also Allan Wallace, "The Third Wave: Current Trends in Regional Governance," *National Civic Review* 83 (summer–fall 1994): 292–93; he characterizes the trends of the 1990s as stressing governance and business-government partnerships as opposed to purely public initiatives, with collaboration, process, and networks of trust more important than formal structure.

27. See the National Association of Regional Councils, at http://narc.org; and the Alliance for Regional Stewardship, at http://regionalstewardship.org.

28. Michael Porter, *The Competitive Advantage of Nations* (New York: Basic Books, 1990); ICF Kaiser Consulting, *America's New Economy and the Challenge of the Cities* (Washington, DC: U.S. Department of Housing and Urban Development, October 1996). A summary of this report can be found at http://www.hud.gov/nmesum.html. But see Bennett Harrison, Jon Gant, and Maryellen R. Kelly, "Specialization vs. Diversity in Local Economies: The Implications for Innovative Private Sector Behavior" (Heinz School of Public Policy and Management, Carnegie Mellon University, January 1995), for an argument that diversity of proximate companies and urbanization shape innovation, whereas proximity of like firms does not.

29. http://www.sdrta.org/sdrta/clusterdata/industriescluster.html.

30. Michael H. Schill, "Deconcentrating the Inner City Poor," *Chicago-Kent Law Review* 67, no. 3 (1992): 852.

31. In addition to Rusk's previously cited work, see Anthony Downs, *New Visions for Metropolitan America* (Washington, DC: Brookings Institution Press, 1994); Gary Orfield and Carole Ashkinaze, *The Closing Door: Conservative Policy and Black Opportunity* (Chicago: University of Chicago Press, 1991); Myron Orfield, *American Metropolitics: The New Suburban Reality* (Washington, DC: Brookings Institution Press, 2002).

32. For a description of these activities, see the Web site of the Metropolitan Area Research Corporation at http://www.metroresearch.org/; and Orfield, *American Metropolitics*.

33. Midwest Consortium for Economic Development Alternatives, *Metro Futures: A High-Wage, Low-Waste, Democratic Alternative Development Strategy for America's Cities and Inner Suburbs* (New York and Madison: Sustainable America and Center on Wisconsin Strategy, 1996); Daniel D. Luria and Joel Rogers, *Metro Futures: Economic Solutions for Cities and Their Suburbs* (Boston: Beacon Press, 1999), 11–39 (also available at http://www.bostonreview.mit.edu/BR22.1/ and http://www.cows.org).

34. Scott Bollens, "In Through the Back Door: Social Equity and Regional Governance," *Housing Policy Debate* 13, no. 4 (2003): 631–57.

35. H. V. Savitch and Ronald K. Vogel, eds., *Regional Politics: America in a Post-City Age* (Thousand Oaks, CA: Sage Publications, 1996).

36. National Resources Committee, *Our Cities: Their Role in the National Economy* (Washington, DC: U.S. Government Printing Office, 1937).

37. Alice O'Connor, "Swimming Against the Tide: A Brief History of Federal Policy in Poor Communities," in *Urban Problems and Community Development,* ed. Ronald Ferguson and William Dickens (Washington, DC: Brookings Institution Press, 1999).

38. Cited in Sidney Plotkin, *Keep Out: The Struggle for Land Use Control* (Berkeley: University of California Press, 1987), 160.

39. Cited in ibid., 160–61.

40. Ibid., 161.

41. Cited in ibid., 162.

42. National Commission on Urban Problems, *Building the American City* (Washington, DC: U.S. Government Printing Office, 1969), 211.

43. Plotkin, *Keep Out,* 26.

44. In 1960, for example, the Committee for Economic Development (CED), a business-sponsored policy group, issued a report calling for greater metropolitan coordination and national laws to regulate local land use and zoning. The CED noted that "most American communities lack any instrumentality of government with legal powers, geographic jurisdiction, and independent revenue sources necessary to conduct self-government in any valid sense." See Plotkin, *Keep Out,* 155–59. See also Shelby Green, "The Search for a National Land Use Policy: For the Cities' Sake," *Fordham Urban Law Journal* 26, no. 1 (November 1998): 69–119.

45. See Advisory Commission on Regulatory Barriers to Affordable Housing, *"Not in My Back Yard": Removing Barriers to Affordable Housing* (Washington, DC: U.S. Department of Housing and Urban Development, July 1991).

46. Chicago's Gautreaux program is the best known of several local housing "mobility" programs that sought to help poor and minority residents find rental housing in suburban areas. It resulted from a 1966 lawsuit brought by attorney Alexander Polikoff on behalf of public housing tenants (led by Dorothy Gautreaux) against the city's housing authority for siting public housing projects in segregated black neighborhoods. In 1969, U.S. District Court judge Richard Austin ordered the Chicago Housing Authority to build low-rise, scattered-site public housing throughout the city, but the housing authority failed to comply. In response, the U.S. Supreme Court ordered HUD in 1976 to create a Section 8 rent subsidy program throughout the six-county Chicago area and to fund the nonprofit Leadership Council for Metropolitan Open Communities to manage it. This pathbreaking decision defined the metropolitan area, not just the city of Chicago, as the relevant context for remedying the city's practices. Five years later, a consent decree required HUD to continue the rent subsidy program until 7,100 black families had been placed in areas with less than 30 percent black population. Originally, participants could move to predominantly white neighborhoods in Chicago or to the suburbs; since 1991, however, all participants have been required to move to the suburbs. Smaller Gautreaux-like programs exist in Cincinnati, Memphis, Dallas, Milwaukee, Hartford, and a few other cities, often brought about by court order. The success of the Gautreaux program led Congress in 1992 to create a federal version, called Moving to Opportunity. HUD selected five cities in 1994 to test the program, which included providing tenants with housing search and

counseling services, but congressional opposition forced HUD to scale back the program.

47. In 1968, New York State created an urban development corporation (UDC) to develop new towns and mixed-income housing (mostly for middle-income families) on a major scale. The legislature gave it the authority to override local zoning codes, if necessary, to construct its projects. Suburban political opposition led the legislature to revoke the UDC's zoning override authority. In 1969, Massachusetts passed an antisnob zoning law. If localities denied permits to developers of low- and moderate-income housing, the developers could, under certain circumstances, appeal to a state appeals board, which could order the municipality to issue the permit. Massachusetts was one of the few states with its own low-income rental housing construction program, as well as a major conduit for federally subsidized housing. State officials assumed that the antisnob zoning law would promote the siting of developments in suburbs and open them up to minorities. After more than two decades, the state claimed that the law had facilitated the construction of 20,000 units. Critics argued that many of these developments were targeted for the elderly, not families, and that the number was still relatively small. By the late 1980s, the city of Boston had 20 percent of the metropolitan population but 40 percent of its poor people and 42 percent of the subsidized housing.

California requires local governments to develop and periodically update a comprehensive master plan, including a so-called housing element, that is subject to review by state agencies. As part of the housing element, every city and county must show how it will comply with a regional "fair-share" allocation for low-income housing. The state has failed to enforce this law. In fact, under Republican governors Deukmejian and Wilson in the 1980s and 1990s, it opposed local inclusionary housing programs. Most municipalities with such policies have favored moderate-income over low-income housing.

New Jersey has the most expansive state program, resulting from a series of court cases known as *Mt. Laurel, Mt. Laurel II,* and *Mt. Laurel III.* In 1971, the NAACP sued the small suburb of Mt. Laurel on the grounds that its zoning regulations excluded housing that was affordable to poor minorities. (Discrimination against the poor is not a violation of the Fair Housing Act, but discrimination against racial minorities is.) In 1975, the state supreme court unanimously ruled that Mt. Laurel and every municipality in the state were obligated by the state constitution to allow all economic groups access to housing. The decision declared a "fair share" doctrine, requiring each region to assess its housing needs and, in effect, set a quota for each municipality to meet. When the state government and municipalities dragged their feet, the state supreme court ruled in *Mt. Laurel II* in 1983 that the state government had a responsibility to monitor and enforce the decision. A Council on Affordable Housing (COAH) was set up to implement the policy. *Mt. Laurel III* in 1986 added new provisions to the policy. The COAH had an original goal of adding 145,000 affordable housing units by 1993. By 1992, only 25,000 Mt. Laurel units had been approved, but fewer than 10,000 had actually been started or completed. Moreover, few occupants of Mt. Laurel units were racial minorities or low-income families. In other states, a few metropolitan areas adopted voluntary fair-share housing policies without the impetus of court orders or state legislation. In the 1970s, the Dayton, Ohio, region did so, using federal housing programs to build about 8,000 units and reducing the central city's share of the region's low-income housing inventory. The Minneapolis–St. Paul metropolitan area adopted a similar policy in the early 1970s with modest success. Other voluntary fair-share plans during the 1970s—in Chicago, San Francisco, and Washington, DC—failed, in part because of the Nixon administration's moratorium on federally assisted developments and in part because suburban areas were reluctant to cooperate. In 1988, Connecticut created a pilot program for voluntary regional fair-share housing compacts. Two years later, twenty-six of the twenty-nine municipalities in the greater Hartford region approved the Capital Region Fair Housing Compact on Affordable Housing, with a goal of creating at least 5,000 units of affordable housing over a five-year period. To assist this plan, HUD let Hartford use its Section 8 subsidies in the suburbs, and local foundations (drawing on the Gautreaux program model) provided funds to counsel low-income Hartford residents about the program. In the 1990s, the Twin Cities adopted another regional fair-share plan, this time with the support of state legislation. See W. Dennis Keating, *The Suburban Racial Dilemma: Housing and Neighborhoods* (Philadelphia: Temple University Press, 1994); Nico Calavita, Kenneth Grimes, and Alan Mallach, "Inclusionary Housing in California and New Jersey: A Comparative Analysis," *Housing Policy Debate* 8, no. 1 (1997): 109–42; and Orfield, *Metropolitics.*

48. Calavita, Grimes, and Mallach, "Inclusionary Housing in California and New Jersey"; David L. Kirp, John P. Dwyer, and Larry A. Rosenthal, *Our Town: Race, Housing, and the Soul of Suburbia* (New Brunswick, NJ: Rutgers University Press, 1995).

49. *Removing Regulatory Barriers to Affordable Housing: How States and Localities Are Moving Ahead* (Washington, DC: U.S. Department of Housing and Urban Development, Office of Policy Development and Research, December 1992); Dwight Merriam, David Brower, and Philip Tegeler, *Inclusionary Zoning Moves Downtown* (Chicago: American Planning Association, 1985); Alan Altshuler and Jose A. Gomez-Ibanez, *Regulation for Revenue: The Political Economy of Land Use Exactions* (Washington, DC: Brookings Institution Press, 1993).

50. Savitch and Vogel, *Regional Politics.*

51. David Rusk, *Cities Without Suburbs,* 3rd ed. (Washington, DC: Woodrow Wilson Center Press, 2003).

52. This section draws on Bruce Berg and Paul Kantor, "New York: The Politics of Conflict and Avoidance," in Savitch and Vogel, *Regional Politics;* U.S. Bureau of the Census at http://www.census.gov.

53. Robert D. Yaro and Tony Hiss, *A Region at Risk: The Third Regional Plan for the New York–New Jersey–Connecticut Metropolitan Area* (Washington, DC: Island Press, 1996).

54. John Mollenkopf, "Who Decides and How? Government Decision-Making After 9/11," *Properties,* Special Issue on 9/11 (April 2002): 392–409.

55. Berg and Kantor, "New York," 42.

56. The St. Louis discussion draws on Donald Phares and Claude Louishomme, "St. Louis: A Politically Fragmented Area," in Savitch and Vogel, *Regional Politics;* and Andrew Glassberg, "St. Louis: Racial Transition and Economic Development," in *Big City Politics in Transition,* ed. H. V. Savitch and John Clayton Thomas (Newbury Park, CA: Sage Publications, 1991). Number of governments calculated from U.S. Census Breau, *2003 Census of Governments,* vol. 1, no. 1, Government Organization (Washington, DC: U.S. Government Printing Office, 2002).

57. This term was coined by Robert Fogelson, *The Fragmented Metropolis: Los Angeles 1850–1930* (Cambridge, MA: Harvard University Press, 1967).

58. The Los Angeles discussion draws on Alan Saltzstein, "Los Angeles: Politics Without Governance," in Savitch and Vogel, *Regional Politics;* Scott A. Bollens, "Fragments of Regionalism: The Limits of South California Governance," *Journal of Urban Affairs* 19, no. 1 (1997): 105–22; Charles Lockwood and Christopher Leinberger, "Los Angeles Comes of Age," *Atlantic Monthly* (January 1988); Pastor et al., *Regions that Work;* William Fulton, *The Reluctant Metropolis: The Politics of Urban Growth in Los Angeles* (Point Arena, CA: Solano Press Books, 1997).

59. James P. Allen and Eugene Turner, *The Ethnic Quilt: Population Diversity in Southern California* (Northridge: Center for Geographical Studies, California State University–Northridge, 1997); U.S. Census Bureau, "Income and Poverty Status in 1989" for the five counties.

60. Steven Erie, "How the West Was Won: The Local State and Economic Growth in Los Angeles, 1880–1932," *Urban Affairs Quarterly* 27, no. 4 (June 1992): 519–54.

61. Marla Cone, "State Scales Back Clean-Air Plan in Bow to Oil, Trucking Industries," *Los Angeles Times,* November 10, 1994; Marla Cone, "U.S. Unveils Scaled-Back Clean-Air Plan," *Los Angeles Times,* February 15, 1995; Linda Wade and Gail Ruderman Feuer, "'Good News' that Means Dirtier Air," *Los Angeles Times,* August 5, 1996; James Lents and William Kelly, "Clearing the Air in Los Angeles," *Scientific American,* October 1993.

62. John J. Harrigan, "Minneapolis–St. Paul: Structuring Metropolitan Government," in Savitch and Vogel, *Regional Politics;* Orfield, *Metropolitics.* The Metropolitan Council Web site is http://www.metrocouncil.org.

63. Rob Gurwitt, "Minneapolis: Mysteries of Urban Momentum," *Governing* (April 2002). The 2000 data were provided by Reagan Carlson and Michael Munson of the Metro Council staff. Poverty concentration data are from G. Thomas Kingsley and Kathryn Pettit, *Concentrated Poverty: A Change in Course* (Washington, DC: Urban Institute, May 2003).

64. Orfield gives a detailed description of his efforts in *Metropolitics.* See also Rusk, *Inside Game/Outside Game,* 222–48.

65. Metropolitan Council, "2030 Regional Development Framework" (Minneapolis, January 14, 2004).

66. This discussion draws on Arthur Nelson, "Portland: The Metropolitan Umbrella," in Savitch and Vogel, *Regional Politics,* 253–74; Carl Abbott, "The Portland Region" (and comments by Henry Richmond and William Fischel), *Housing Policy Debate* 8, no. 1 (1997): 11–73; Christopher Leo, "Regional Growth Management Regime: The Case of Portland, Oregon," *Journal of Urban Affairs* 20, no. 4 (1998): 363–94; Orfield, *Metropolitics,* 157–59; Rusk, *Inside Game/Outside Game,* 153–77. See also Timothy Egan, "Urban Sprawl Strains Western States," *New York Times,* December 29, 1996; Timothy Egan, "Drawing the Hard Line on Urban Sprawl," *New York Times,* December 30, 1996; Kim Murphy, "Portland Struggles to Draw Line on Growth," *Los Angeles Times,* December 10, 1997. The Metro Web site is http://www.metro-region.org.

67. Arthur C. Nelson, "Smart Growth Equals Central City Vitality and a Higher Quality of Life" (paper presented to the U.S. Department of Housing and Urban Development conference "Bridging the Divide," Washington, DC, December 8, 1999).

68. Metro President David Bragdon's inaugural address, January 6, 2003, available at http://www.metro-region.org.

69. Orfield, *Metropolitics,* 102.

70. Abbott, "Portland Region," 24.

71. Ibid., 35.

72. Scott A. Bollens, "Concentrated Poverty and Metropolitan Equity Strategies," *Stanford Law and Policy Review* 8, no. 2 (summer 1997): 13.

73. Schill, "Deconcentrating," 836.

74. Considerable attention has also been paid to equalizing the financial basis for school systems and creating metropolitan school districts, as discussed in Schill, "Deconcentrating," 847–52. In general, spending per pupil has become more equal within states but has increased across states, according to William J. Hussar and William Sonnenberg, "Trends in Disparities in School District Level Expenditures per Pupil" (Washington, DC: National Center for Education Statistics in Early Childhood, 1999). High levels of disparities among districts within states and within districts have persisted in many cases, however. The trend on school desegregation and district consolidation has been toward what Gary Orfield has described as "resegregation." See Gary Orfield, Susan Eaton, and the Harvard Project on School Desegregation, *Dismantling Desegregation: The Quiet Reversal of Brown v. Board of Education* (New York: New Press, 1996).

75. Schill, "Deconcentrating," 845–47.

76. Charles T. Clotfelter, *Are Whites Still 'Fleeing'? Racial Patterns and Enrollment Shifts in Urban Public Schools, 1987–1996* (Working Paper W7290, National Bureau of Economic Research, August 1999), found that "white losses appear to be spurred both by interracial contact in districts where their children attend school and by the opportunities available in metropolitan areas for reducing that contact."

77. These efforts were inspired by the successes of the Gautreaux program in Chicago (see note 46, as well as the discussion in Chapter 3). In 1994, HUD launched a five-city, ten-year social experiment in which 4,610 families were randomly assigned to an "MTO [Moving to Opportunity] treatment group," which moved to more suburban settings (1,820 families); a "Section 8 comparison group," which moved out of projects but remained in central-city settings (1,350 families); and an "in place control group" (1,440 families). A preliminary report on the project (John Goering, Joan Kraft, Judith Feins, Debra McInnis, Mary Joel Holin, and Huda Elhassan, *Moving to Opportunity for Fair Housing Demonstration Program: Current Status and Initial Findings* [Washington, DC: U.S. Department of Housing and Urban Development, Office of Policy Development and Research, September 1999], available at http://www.huduser.org) found that counseling played an important role in the success of the program, and those who moved out of the projects experienced improved security from crime and more support for finding jobs (32–33). All the mobility programs report positive results, but the numbers involved are tiny compared with the need. The most comprehensive report is John Goering and Judith D. Feins, eds., *Choosing a Better Life: Evaluating the Moving to Opportunity Social Experiment* (Washington, DC: Urban Institute Press, 2003).

78. Discussion of the Montgomery County program is drawn from Alexander Polikoff, ed., *Housing Mobility: Promise or Illusion?* (Washington, DC: Urban Institute, 1995); George E. Peterson and Kale Williams, eds., *Housing Mobility: What Has It Accomplished and What Is Its Promise?* (Washington, DC: Urban Institute, October 1994); David Rusk, *Inside Game/Outside Game;* Christie I. Baxter, *Moderately Priced Dwelling Units in Montgomery County, Maryland* (Cambridge, MA: Kennedy School of Government, Case Program, c16-91-1043.0, 1991). Data were also drawn from the Web sites of Montgomery County (http://www.co.mo.md.us), the Montgomery County Planning Board (http://www.mc-mncppc.org), the Montgomery County

Housing Opportunity Commission (http://www.hocweb.org), and the Innovative Housing Institute (http://www.inhousing.org/MPDUNarr.htm), as well as from a telephone interview with Erik Larsen, section chief with the Moderately Priced Dwelling Units program, October 11, 2000.

79. These income targets increased steadily over the years, parallel to changes in the county's median household income, as did the sales prices and rents of the units.

80. In 1974, Maryland enacted legislation to create a Montgomery County Housing Opportunity Commission to acquire, own, lease, and operate housing. The seven-member board is appointed by the county executive and approved by the county council.

81. Polikoff, *Housing Mobility,* 74.

82. Brian D. Taylor and Paul M. Ong, "Spatial Mismatch or Automobile Mismatch? An Examination of Race, Residence, and Community in U.S. Metropolitan Areas," *Urban Studies* 32 (1995): 1453–73; Evelyn Blumenburg and Paul Ong, "Job Access, Commuting, and Travel Burden Among Welfare Recipients," *Urban Studies* 35, no. 1 (1998): 77–93; Martin Wachs and Brian D. Taylor, "Can Transportation Strategies Help to Meet the Welfare Challenge?" *Journal of the American Planning Association* 64, no. 1 (1998): 15–19; Margy Waller and Mark Alan Hughes, "Working Far from Home: Transportation and Welfare Reform in the Ten Big States" (Washington, DC: Progressive Policy Institute, August 1, 1999); Carol Harbaugh and Theresa Smith, "Welfare Reform and Transportation: There Is a Connection," *Public Roads* (January–February 1998), available at http://www.bts.gov/NTL/DOCS/Welfare/HS Reform.htm.

83. Discussion of this program draws on Mark Alan Hughes and Julie E. Sternberg, *The New Metropolitan Reality: Where the Rubber Meets the Road in Antipoverty Policy* (Washington, DC: Urban Institute, December 1992); Rochelle Stanfield, "The Reverse Commute," *National Journal,* November 23, 1996, 2546–49.

84. Stanfield, "Reverse Commute," 2547–48.

85. Ibid., 2548.

86. Ibid.; Rick Wartzman, "New Bus Lines Link the Inner-City Poor with Jobs in Suburbia," *Wall Street Journal,* September 24, 1993.

87. Descriptions and initial evaluations of JobLinks can be found at http://www.ctaa.org/ntrc/atj/joblinks; for Bridges to Work, see http://www.huduser.org/publications/pvosoc/btw.html.

88. Waller and Hughes, "Working Far from Home," 1.

89. See also the editorial "Let Them Drive Cars," *New Republic,* March 20, 2000.

90. In October 2000, the Clinton administration proposed increasing the car and housing allowances used to calculate food stamp eligibility. The proposal lifts the $4,650 limit that a family is allowed to deduct for the value of its car. See Janet Hook, "Food Stamp Expansion Gets Surprising Boost," *Los Angeles Times,* October 11, 2000.

91. Bennett Harrison and Marcus Weiss, *Workforce Development Networks: Community-Based Organizations and Regional Alliances* (Thousand Oaks, CA: Sage Publications, 1998), 2.

92. Mark Drayse, Dan Flaming, and Peter Force, *The Cage of Poverty* (Los Angeles: Economic Roundtable, September 2000); Nicholas Riccardi, "Post-Welfare Jobs No Cure for Poverty, Study Finds," *Los Angeles Times,* September 7, 2000; Kate Shatzkin, "Study Finds Workers Off Welfare Often Remain in Need of Assistance," *Baltimore Sun,* October 6, 2000.

93. This discussion of Project Quest draws on Jay Walljasper, "A Quest for Jobs in San Antonio," *Nation,* July 21, 1997, 30–32; and Harrison and Weiss, *Workforce Development Networks.*

94. Walljasper, "Quest for Jobs," 30.

95. Harrison and Weiss, *Workforce Development Networks,* 72.

96. See also Harrison and Weiss, *Workforce Development Networks;* Marcus Weiss, "Regional Workforce Development Networks" (paper presented to the U.S. Department of Housing and Urban Development conference "Bridging the Divide," Washington, DC, December 8, 1999); Bennett Harrison, "It Takes a Region (or Does It?): The Material Basis for Metropolitanism and Metropolitics," in *Urban-Suburban Interdependencies,* ed. Rosalind Greenstein and Wim Wiewel (Cambridge, MA: Lincoln Institute of Land Policy, 2001).

97. See Orfield, *American Metropolitics;* and Juliet F. Gainsborough, *Fenced Off: The Suburbanization of American Politics* (Washington, DC: Georgetown University Press, 2001).

98. H. V. Savitch and Ronald K. Vogel cast a critical eye on this event in "Suburbs Without a City: Power and City-County Consolidation," *Urban Affairs Review* 39, no. 5 (May 2004).

99. Rick McDonough, "Merger Wins with Solid Majority," *Louisville Courier-Journal,* November 8, 2000. See http://www.louky.org, the Metro web site. The Brookings Institution Center on Urban and Metropolitan Policy, *Beyond Merger: A Competitive Vision for the Regional City of Louisville* (Washington, DC, 2002) presents a wealth of data on the emerging regional city and advocates a smart growth agenda for it. The *Courier-Journal*'s first-year roundup on the merger may be found at http://www.courier-journal.com/cjextra/2003projects/mergeryear/.

100. Douglas R. Porter and Allan D. Wallis, *Exploring Ad Hoc Regionalism* (Lincoln Institute of Land Policy, December 2002); Scott A. Bollens, "In Through the Back Door."

CHAPTER 7. METROPOLICIES FOR THE TWENTY-FIRST CENTURY

1. For a defense of free markets in housing and a critique of government interference, see Peter D. Salins, *The Ecology of Housing Destruction: Economic Effects of Public Intervention in the Housing Market* (New York: New York University Press, 1980); and Peter D. Salins and Gerard C. S. Mildner, *Scarcity by Design: The Legacy of New York City's Housing Policies* (Cambridge, MA: Harvard University Press, 1992). For a general argument that poor areas can be revitalized by markets with little help from government, see Michael E. Porter, "The Competitive Advantage of the Inner City," *Harvard Business Review* (May–June 1995): 55–71. For the free-market defense of fragmented local governments, see the works cited in Chapter 4 by Charles Tiebout, Elinor Ostrom, Robert Bish, and others.

2. The classic statement of an urban culture of poverty is found in Edward Banfield, *The Unheavenly City: The Nature and Future of Our Urban Crisis* (Boston: Little, Brown, 1970). Charles Murray argues that welfare policies are a major cause of the culture of poverty. See his influential *Losing Ground: American Social Policy 1950–1980* (New York: Basic Books, 1984). For a recent statement that enhancing the mobility of poor households would spread the culture of poverty, see Howard Husock, "Let's End Housing Vouchers," *City Journal* (autumn 2000): 84–91.

3. The classic statement that the problems of concentrated poverty are caused mainly

by deindustrialization and should be addressed primarily by economic policies is William Julius Wilson's *The Truly Disadvantaged: The Inner City, the Underclass, and Public Policy* (Chicago: University of Chicago Press, 1987). In *When Work Disappears: The World of the New Urban Poor* (New York: Knopf, 1996), Wilson emphasizes spatial policies as well as macroeconomic policies.

4. The literature on enterprise zones and CDCs is voluminous. One of the first advocates for enterprise zones was Stuart Butler in his *Enterprise Zones: Greenlining the Inner City* (New York: Universe, 1981). See also Karen Mossberger, *The Politics of Ideas and the Spread of Enterprise Zones* (Washington, DC: Georgetown University Press, 2000). Congress created the Enterprise Zone/Empowerment Community program in 1993; many states have enacted enterprise zone programs of their own. For a sampling of the literature on CDCs, see Rachel G. Bratt, *Rebuilding a Low-Income Housing Policy* (Philadelphia: Temple University Press, 1989); Avis Vidal, "CDCs as Agents of Neighborhood Change: The State of the Art," in *Revitalizing Urban Neighborhoods,* ed. W. Dennis Keating, Norman Krumholz, and Philip Star (Lawrence: University Press of Kansas, 1996), 149–63; C. Theodore Koebel, ed., *Shelter and Society: Theory, Research, and Policy for Nonprofit Housing* (Albany, NY: SUNY Press, 1998); Herbert J. Rubin, *Renewing Hope Within Neighborhoods of Despair: The Community-Based Development Model* (Albany, NY: SUNY Press, 2000). The National Congress for Community Economic Development (NCCED) is the trade organization for CDCs and publishes an annual survey of their accomplishments (http://www.ncced.org). For a critical history of the movement, see Robert Halpern, *Rebuilding the Inner City: A History of Neighborhood Initiatives to Address Poverty in the United States* (New York: Columbia University Press, 1995).

5. The classic argument for the importance of race in causing problems of concentrated poverty is Douglas D. Massey and Nancy A. Denton, *American Apartheid: Segregation and the Making of the Underclass* (Cambridge, MA: Harvard University Press, 1993).

6. William A. Fischel, "Does the American Way of Zoning Cause the Suburbs of Metropolitan Areas to Be Too Spread Out?" in *Governance and Opportunity in Metropolitan America,* ed. Alan Altshuler, William Morrill, Harold Wolman, and Faith Mitchell (Washington, DC: National Academy Press, 1999).

7. Harold L. Wolman, Todd Swanstrom, and Margaret Weir with the assistance of Nicholas Lyon, *The Calculus of Coalitions: Cities and States and the Metropolitan Agenda* (Washington, DC: Brookings Institution Center for Urban and Metropolitan Policy, April 2004).

8. See, for example, Pietro S. Nivola, *Laws of the Landscape: How Policies Shape Cities in Europe and America* (Washington, DC: Brookings Institution Press, 1999). See also John Mollenkopf, "Assimilating Immigrants in Amsterdam: A Perspective from New York," *Netherlands Journal of Social Science* 36, no. 2 (2000), with comments from Malcolm Cross, Susan Fainstein, Robert Kloosterman, Enzo Mingione and Enrico Pugliese, Kees van Kerksbergen, and Hans Vermeulen and Tijno Venema; Sako Musterd and Wim Ostendorf, eds., *Urban Segregation and the Welfare State: Inequality and Exclusion in Western Cities* (London: Routledge, 1998).

9. Timothy Smeeding, "Why the U.S. Anti-Poverty System Doesn't Work Very Well," *Challenge* (January–February 1992): 30–36; Janet Gornick and Marcia Meyers, "Support for Working Families: What the United States Can Learn from Europe," *American Prospect* 12, no. 1. (January 1–15, 2001): 3–7; Peter Dreier and Elaine Bernard, "Kinder, Gentler Canada," *American Prospect* 12 (winter 1992): 85–88; Lee Rainwater

and Timothy Smeeding, *Poor Kids in a Rich Country: America's Children in Comparative Perspective* (New York: Russell Sage Foundation, 2003).

10. Jacques van de Ven, "Urban Policies and the 'Polder Model': Two Sides of the Same Coin" (Amsterdam Center for the Metropolitan Environment, University of Amsterdam, May 1998).

11. Jay Forrester, *Urban Dynamics* (Cambridge, MA: MIT Press, 1969); President's Commission on a National Agenda for the Eighties, *Urban America in the 1980s* (Washington, DC: U.S. Government Printing Office, 1980). Paul Peterson's *City Limits* (Chicago: University of Chicago Press, 1981) reflects a similar perspective.

12. William McDonough, "Opening Remarks," *Economic Policy Review,* Federal Reserve Bank of New York, January 1995, 2. See also Mark Rank, *One Nation, Underprivileged: Why American Poverty Affects Us All* (New York: Oxford University Press, 2004).

13. Henry R. Richmond, "Metropolitan Land-Use Reform: The Promise and Challenge of Majority Consensus," in *Reflections on Regionalism,* ed. Bruce Katz (Washington, DC: Brookings Institution Press, 2000), 36, available at http://www.brook.edu/es/urban.

14. For representative agendas, see Alan Altshuler, William Morrill, Harold Wolman, and Faith Mitchell, eds., *Governance and Opportunity in Metropolitan America* (Washington, DC: National Academy Press, 1999), chaps. 4 and 5 (see http://www .nap.edu/html/governance/HSopportunity/); David Rusk, *Inside Game/Outside Game: Winning Strategies for Saving Urban America* (Washington, DC: Brookings Institution Press, 1999), chaps. 12 and 14; Myron Orfield, *Metropolitics: A Regional Agenda for Community and Stability,* rev. ed. (Washington, DC: Brookings Institution Press, 1997), chap. 6; Katz, *Reflections on Regionalism* (http://www.brook.edu/ ES/Urban/), has been particularly effective in stimulating discussion of these issues. See also the Metropolitan Initiative of the Center for Neighborhood Technology at http://www.cnt.org/mi/, the Citistates site at http://www.citistates.com, and Myron Orfield's Metropolitan Area Research Corporation site at http://www.metroresearch .org.

15. Harold Wolman and Elizabeth Agius, eds., *National Urban Policy and the President's National Urban Policy Report* (Detroit: Wayne State University Press, 1996), 26.

16. Ann Markusen, Peter Hall, Scott Campbell, and Sabina Deitrick, *The Rise of the Gunbelt: The Military Remapping of Industrial America* (New York: Oxford University Press, 1991); Steven Greenhouse, "Study Says Big Cities Don't Get Fair Share of Military Spending," *New York Times,* May 12, 1992.

17. Our thinking on these matters has been influenced by Scott Bollens, "Concentrated Poverty and Metropolitan Equity Strategies," *Stanford Law and Policy Review* 8, no. 2 (summer 1997): 11–23; Michael Schill, "Deconcentrating the Inner City Poor," *Chicago-Kent Law Review* 67, no. 3 (1992): 795–853; the work of Bruce Katz and his colleagues at the Brookings Center for Urban and Metropolitan Policy; and the writings of Neal Peirce. For parallel discussions, see Bruce Katz, *The Limits of Urban Revival: The Case for Metropolitan Solutions to Urban Problems* (Washington, DC: Brookings Center for Urban and Metropolitan Problems, March 1998); the Forum on Forging Metropolitan Solutions to Urban and Regional Problems, May 28, 1997, available at http://www.brook.edu/es/urbancen/metnif.htm; Bruce Katz, "Beyond City Limits: A New Metropolitan Agenda" in *Setting National Priorities: The 2000 Election and Beyond,* ed. Henry Aaron and Robert Reischauer (Washington, DC: Brookings Institution Press, 1999). For the views of Peirce and his col-

league Curtis Johnson, see *Boundary Crossers: Community Leadership for a Global Age* (College Park, MD: Academy of Leadership, University of Maryland, 1997). Additional perspectives are provided in Tony Hiss, "Outlining the New Metropolitan Initiative" and Clement Dinsmore, "The Federal Role in Metropolitan Cooperation" (Chicago: Center for Neighborhood Technology, March 1997), both available at http://www.cnt.org/mi; DeWitt John et al., *Building Stronger Communities and Regions: Can the Federal Government Help?* (Washington, DC: National Academy of Public Administration, April 1998), available at http://www.napawash.org. For an analysis of the link between regional economic inequality and urban poverty, see Manuel Pastor, Peter Dreier, J. Eugene Grigsby III, and Marta Lopez-Garza, *Regions that Work: How Cities and Suburbs Can Grow Together* (Minneapolis: University of Minnesota Press, 2000).

18. Peter D. Salins, "Metropolitan Areas: Cities, Suburbs, and the Ties that Bind," in *Interwoven Destinies: Cities and the Nation,* ed. Henry Cisneros (New York: Norton, 1993), 147–66.

19. For a discussion of how the federal government can limit bidding wars, see Melvin Burstein and Arthur Rolnick, "Congress Should End the Economic War for Sports and Other Business," *Region* 10, no. 2 (June 1996): 35–36. This issue of the Federal Reserve Bank of Minneapolis publication was devoted to the topic of bidding wars. It is available at http://minneapolisfed.org/sylloge/econwar.

20. For the text of the Minge bill, see http://minneapolisfed.org/sylloge/econwar/HR 1060.html.

21. See William Schwenke, "Curbing Business Subsidy Competition: Does the EU Have an Answer?" *Accountability: The Newsletter of the Business Incentives Clearinghouse* 2, no. 9 (September 2000): 1–4. This newsletter is an excellent source of ideas and information about this issue.

22. Joseph Gyourko and Richard Voith, "Does the U.S. Tax Treatment of Housing Promote Suburbanization and Central City Decline?" (Philadelphia: Wharton School, University of Pennsylvania, Real Estate and Finance Departments, September 24, 1997); Joseph Gyourko and Todd Sinai, "The Spatial Distribution of Housing-Related Tax Benefits in the United States" (Philadelphia: University of Pennsylvania, Wharton School, Real Estate Department, April 11, 2000).

23. John et al., *Building Stronger Communities.*

24. Mark Alan Hughes, "The Administrative Geography of Devolving Social Welfare Programs" (Joint Occasional Paper 97-1, Center for Public Management and Center for Urban and Metropolitan Policy, Brookings Institution Press, 1997), available at http://www.brook.edu/ES/Urban/admgeo.htm.

25. There have been a few efforts to administer the Section 8 voucher and certificate program on a regional basis. For one good approach to this problem, see Bruce Katz and Margery Austin Turner, "Who Should Run the Housing Voucher Program? A Reform Proposal," *Housing Policy Debate* 12, no. 2 (2001): 239–62.

26. Many studies have shown that Section 8 households tend to be clustered in established zones of concentrated poverty; see Hughes, "Administrative Geography." One way to expand choices may be through the "split subsidy" approach advocated by Jill Khadduri, Marge Martin, and Larry Buron, "Split Subsidy: The Future of Rental Housing Policy?" (paper presented to the annual meeting of the American Political Science Association, Washington, DC, September 2, 2000).

27. For ideas on how best to do this, see Center on Budget and Policy Priorities (CBPP), *Section 8 Utilization and the Proposed Housing Voucher Success Fund* (Washing-

ton, DC: CBPP, March 22, 2000), available at http://www.cbpp.org/3-22-00hous2
.htm; and Barbara Sard, "Housing Vouchers Should Be a Major Component of
Future Housing Policy for Low Income Families," *Cityscape* 5, no. 2 (2001): 89–110.

28. David K. Hamilton, *Governing Metropolitan Areas: Response to Growth and Change*
(New York: Garland, 1999), 160.

29. See John et al., *Building Stronger Communities;* Robert Puentes, *Flexible Funding for
Transit: Who Uses It?* (Brookings Institution Center for Urban and Metropolitan
Policy, May 2000).

30. This echoes points made in Rusk, *Inside Game/Outside Game;* and Katz, "Beyond
City Limits."

31. Christopher Edley, "The Next Phase of the Clinton Urban Policy: Metropolitan Empowerment Zones" (draft memorandum, Office of Management and Budget, Executive Office of the President, October 1993).

32. Paul G. Lewis, "Regionalism and Representation: Measuring and Assessing Representation in Metropolitan Planning Organizations," *Urban Affairs Review* 33, no. 6
(July 1998): 839–53.

33. Anthony Downs, "Have Housing Prices Risen Faster in Portland than Elsewhere?"
Housing Policy Debate 13, no. 1 (2002): 7–31; and comments by Arthur Nelson and
William Fischel.

34. Hamilton, *Governing Metropolitan Areas,* 232.

35. U.S. Code, Title 23, Section 134, available at http://www4.1aw.cornell.edu/uscode/
23/134.text.html.

36. See Rusk, *Inside Game/Outside Game,* for an evaluation of the limited role that community development efforts have played in reducing concentrated poverty.

37. Edward Hill and Jeremy Nowak recommend a program of federally funded tax relief,
administrative reform, massive land acquisition and clearance, and wage subsidies
for such cities in "Nothing Left to Lose," *Brookings Review* 18, no. 3 (summer 2000):
22–26.

38. For a discussion of the experiences of racially and economically diverse neighbor-
hoods, see the following articles, all contained in a special issue of *Housing Policy
Debate* 8, no. 2 (1997): Margery Austin Turner, "Achieving a New Urban Diversity:
What Have We Learned?"; Roberto G. Quercia and George C. Galster, "Threshold
Effects and the Expected Benefits of Attracting Middle-Income Households to the
Central City"; Robert E. Lang, James W. Hughes, and Karen A. Danielsen, "Targeting
the Suburban Urbanite: Marketing Central-City Housing"; Philip Nyden, Michael
Maly, and John Lukehart, "The Emergence of Stable Racially and Ethnically Diverse
Urban Communities: A Case Study of Nine U.S. Cities."

39. For varying perspectives on these initiatives, see Joan Walsh, *Community Building
and the Future of Urban America* (New York: Rockefeller Foundation, January 1997),
available at http://www.Rockfound.Org/Reports/community/renewal.html; Karen
Fulbright-Anderson, Anne C. Kubish, and James P. Connell, eds., *New Approaches to
Evaluating Community Initiatives* (Washington, DC: Aspen Institute, 1998); Rebecca
Stone and Benjamin Butler, *The Core Issues in Comprehensive Community-Building
Initiatives: Exploring Power and Race* (Chicago: Chapin Hall Center for Children,
February 2000).

40. Jeremy Nowak, "Neighborhood Initiative and the Regional Economy," *Economic
Development Quarterly* 11, no. 1 (February 1997): 3–11; Pastor et al., *Regions that Work;*
Edwin Melendez and Bennett Harrison, "Matching the Disadvantaged to Job Op-
portunities: Structural Explanations for the Past Successes of the Center for Em-

ployment Training," *Economic Development Quarterly* 12, no. 1 (February 1998): 3–11; Bennett Harrison and Marcus Weiss, *Workforce Development Networks: Community-Based Organizations and Regional Alliances* (Thousand Oaks, CA: Sage Publications, 1998).

41. Daniel P. McMurrer and Isabel V. Sawhill, *Getting Ahead: Economic and Social Mobility in America* (Washington, DC: Urban Institute Press, 1998). See also Richard Rothstein, *Class and Schools* (Washington, DC: Economic Policy Institute, 2004).

42. Richard Rothstein, "The Myth of Public School Failure," *American Prospect* 13 (spring 1993); Richard Rothstein, "LA's School District Doesn't Deserve to Be Called a Failure," *Los Angeles Times,* May 11, 1997; Richard Rothstein, "Testing Our Patience," *American Prospect* 12, no. 2 (February 2004).

43. Rothstein, "Myth of Public School Failure."

44. Robert A. Levine, "Schools: Standards Are Important, but Money Is Vital," *Los Angeles Times,* May 21, 2000.

45. Nick Anderson, "Smaller Classes Aid Test Schools, Results Show," *Los Angeles Times,* December 29, 1998.

46. Richard Rothstein with Karen Hawley Miles, *Where's the Money Gone? Changes in the Level and Composition of Education Spending, 1967–1991* (Washington, DC: Economic Policy Institute, 1995); Richard Rothstein, *Where's the Money Going? Changes in the Level and Composition of Education Spending 1991–96* (Washington, DC: Economic Policy Institute, 1997); Richard Rothstein, *The Way We Were? The Myths and Realities of America's Student Achievement* (New York: Century Foundation Press, 1998); Richard Rothstein, "Does Money Not Matter? The Data Suggest It Does," *New York Times,* January 17, 2001; Abby Goodnough, "New York Is Shortchanged in School Aid, State Judge Rules," *New York Times,* January 11, 2001; John Goldman, "NY's School Funding Illegal, Judge Rules," *Los Angeles Times,* January 11, 2001.

47. James Traub, "What No School Can Do," *New York Times Magazine,* January 16, 2000.

48. Dennis Shirley, *Community Organizing for Urban School Reform* (Austin: University of Texas Press, 1997); Harrison and Weiss, *Workforce Development Networks;* Jay Walljasper, "A Quest for Jobs in San Antonio," *Nation,* July 21, 1997; Eva Gold and Elaiger Simon, "Successful Community Organizing for School Reform," March 2002, available at http://comm-org.utoledo.ued/papers2003/goldsimon/goldsimon .htm.

49. Gary Orfield, Susan Eaton, and the Harvard Project on School Desegregation, *Dismantling Desegregation* (New York: New Press, 1996); Gary Orfield with Jennifer Arenson, Tara Jackson, Christine Bohrer, Dawn Gavin, Emily Kalejs, and many volunteers for the Harvard Project on School Desegregation, "City-Suburban Desegregation: Parent and Student Perspectives in Metropolitan Boston" (report of a research conference sponsored by the Harvard Civil Rights Project, September 1997).

50. See, for example, Stephen Burd, "In Some Federal Aid Programs, Not all Campuses Are Treated Alike," *Chronicle of Higher Education* 46, no. 41 (June 16, 2000): A27; and David Leonhardt, "As Wealthy Fill Top Colleges, Concerns Grow over Fairness," *New York Times,* April 22, 2004.

51. Jared Bernstein, "Two Cheers for the Earned Income Tax Credit," *American Prospect* 11, no. 15 (June 19–July 3, 2000): 64. The original study is Jared Bernstein and Heidi Hartmann, "Defining and Characterizing the Low-Wage Labor Market," in *The Low-Wage Labor Market: Challenges and Opportunities for Economic*

Self-Sufficiency (Washington, DC: Urban Institute, December 1999), available at http://aspe.hhs.gov/hsp/lwlm99/index.htm.

52. Jared Bernstein, Chauna Brocht, and Maggie Spade-Aguilar, *How Much Is Enough: Basic Family Budgets for Working Families* (Washington, DC: Economic Policy Institute, 2000).

53. "Is America's Economy Really Failing? The Backlash Against the *New York Times* Scare," *American Enterprise* (July–August 1996): 26–31, excerpting op-ed pieces by Robert J. Samuelson, Jonathan Marshall, Irwin Stelzer, John Cassidy, James K. Glassman, and Herbert Stein.

54. Robert J. Samuelson, *The Good Life and Its Discontents: The American Dream in the Age of Entitlement, 1945–1995* (New York: Times Books, 1995).

55. Janet C. Gornick, Marcia K. Meyers, and Katherin E. Ross, "Supporting the Employment of Mothers: Policy Variation Across Fourteen Welfare States," *Journal of European Social Policy* 7, no. 1 (1997): 45–70.

56. For the case of New York, see the *New York Times* series on welfare reform: Alan Binder, "Evidence Is Scant that Workfare Leads to Full Time Jobs," April 12, 1998; Rachel Swarns, "Mothers Poised for Workfare Face Acute Lack of Day Care," April 14, 1998; Vivian Toy, "Tough Workfare Rules Used as a Way to Cut Welfare Rolls," April 15, 1998.

57. For a history of the EITC, see Christopher Howard, *The Hidden Welfare State: Tax Expenditures and Social Policy in the United States* (Princeton, NJ: Princeton University Press, 1997). For recent EITC experience, see Bernstein, "Two Cheers"; "Earned Income Tax Credit and Other Tax Benefits," available at http://www.makingwageswork.org.

58. See previous note.

59. Bernstein, "Two Cheers."

60. Bruce Meyer and Dan Rosenbaum, "Welfare, the Earned Income Tax Credit, and the Labor Supply of Single Mothers" (Working Paper 7363, National Bureau of Economic Research, September 1999).

61. Peter Dreier, "Low-Wage Workers Miss a Tax Break," *Los Angeles Times*, January 24, 1999.

62. See Robert Greenstein, *Should EITC Benefits Be Enlarged for Families with Three or More Children?* (Washington, DC: Center for Budget and Policy Priorities, July 10, 2000), available at http://www.cbpp.org/3-14-00tax.htm; Robert Greenstein, *Should the EITC for Workers Without Children Be Abolished, Maintained, or Expanded?* (Washington, DC: Center for Budget and Policy Priorities, July 7, 2000), available at http://www.cbpp.org/6-22-00eitc.htm.

63. Max Sawicky and Robert Cherry, *Giving Credit Where Credit Is Due: A 'Universal Unified Child Credit' that Expands the EITC and Cuts Taxes for Working Families* (Washington, DC: Economic Policy Institute, April 2000).

64. See Bernstein, "Two Cheers," for this critique.

65. "The Minimum Wage," on the Web site of Making Wages Work, available at http://www.makingwageswork.org/minimum.htm; Lawrence Mishel, Jared Bernstein, and Heather Boushay, *The State of Working America, 2002/2003* (Ithaca, NY: ILR Press, 2003).

66. Oren M. Levin-Waldman, *Automatic Adjustment of the Minimum Wage: Linking the Minimum Wage to Productivity,* Public Policy Brief 42 (Annandale-on-Hudson, NY: Jerome Levy Economics Institute of Bard College, 1998); Amy Chasanou and Jeff

Chapman, *A Long Overdue Increase in the Minimum Wage Is Needed to Restore Lost Ground* (Washington, DC: Economic Policy Institute, April 28, 2004).

67. Kathryn Porter, "Proposed Changes in the Official Measure of Poverty" (Washington, DC: Center on Budget and Policy Priorities, November 15, 1999); Bernstein, Brocht, and Maggie Spade-Aguilar, *How Much Is Enough.*

68. This paragraph draws on the following: Owen M. Levin-Waldman and George McCarthy, *Small Business and the Minimum Wage* (Annandale-on-Hudson, NY: Jerome Levy Economics Institute of Bard College, 1998); Jared Bernstein and John Schmitt, *Making Work Pay: The Impact of the 1997 Minimum-Wage Increase* (Washington, DC: Economic Policy Institute, 1998); *Raising the Minimum Wage: Talking Points and Background* (Washington, DC: AFL-CIO, July 1999); David Card and Alan Krueger, *Myth and Measurement: The New Economics of the Minimum Wage* (Princeton, NJ: Princeton University Press, 1995).

69. Jennifer Campbell, *Health Insurance Coverage: 1998* (Washington, DC: U.S. Census Bureau, Current Population Reports, October 1999); Robert J. Mills, *Health Insurance Coverage: 1999* (Washington, DC: U.S. Bureau of the Census, Current Population Reports, P60-211, September 2000); Carmen DeNovas Walt, Bernadette D. Proctor, and Robert J. Mills, *Income, Poverty, and Health Insurance Coverage in the United States: 2003* (Washington, DC: U.S. Census Bureau, Current Population Reports, P60-226, August 2004).

70. Walt, Proctor, and Mills, *Income, Poverty, and Health Insurance Coverage.*

71. Sharon Bernstein and Robert Rosenblatt, "More Recipients of Medicare to Be Cut from HMOs," *Los Angeles Times,* July 25, 2000.

72. Calculated and updated from 1995 figures found in Gary Burtless, "Growing American Inequality," in *Setting National Priorities: The 2000 Election and Beyond,* ed. Henry Aaron and Robert Reischauer (Washington, DC: Brookings Institution Press, 1999).

73. See Steven Greenhouse, "Why Paris Works," *New York Times Magazine,* July 19, 1992; Smeeding, "Why the U.S. Anti-Poverty System Doesn't Work Very Well"; Rainwater and Smeeding, *Poor Kids in a Rich Country.*

74. All the information in the previous two paragraphs is drawn from the Children's Defense Fund, "Overview of Child Care, Early Education, and School-Age Care" (1999).

75. Barbara R. Bergmann, "Reducing Poverty Among American Children Through a 'Help for Working Parents' Program" (Foundation for Child Development Working Paper Series, November 1997); Barbara R. Bergmann, "Decent Child Care at Decent Wages," *American Prospect* 12, no. 1 (January 1–15, 2001): 8–9.

76. Center for the Future of Children, David and Lucile Packard Foundation, "Children and Poverty," *Future of Children* 7, no. 2 (summer–fall 1997).

77. Margaret Weir, "Coalition-Building for Regionalism," in Katz, *Reflections on Regionalism.*

78. According to the March 1999 Current Population Survey of the Bureau of the Census, the median central-city poor person lives in a household with four people in it. Thus, these calculations assume that there are four persons in each low-income household.

79. These data were provided by Peter Tatian and Alisa Wilson of the Urban Institute from their forthcoming report *Segregation of the Poor in U.S. Metropolitan Areas,* updating the 1990 data in Alan J. Abramson, Mitchell S. Tobin, and Matthew R.

VanderGoot, "The Changing Geography of Metropolitan Opportunity: The Segregation of the Poor in U.S. Metropolitan Areas, 1970 to 1990," *Housing Policy Debate* 6, no. 1 (1995).

80. Kingsley and Pettit, *Concentrated Poverty.*

81. A typical Section 8 voucher—which allows low-income families to pay for apartments in the private rental market by paying the difference between 30 percent of a family's income and market-level rents—costs about $6,000 per year.

82. See Harrison and Weiss, *Workforce Development Networks.*

83. According to HUD's evaluation report, except for Baltimore, "there was no further political opposition in low-poverty areas we are aware of, and few instances of suspected discrimination were reported." John Goering, Joan Draft, Judith Feins, Debra McInnis, Mary Joel Holin, and Hudu Elhassan, *Moving to Opportunity for Fair Housing Demonstration Program: Current Status and Initial Findings* (Washington, DC: U.S. Department of Housing and Urban Development, Office of Policy Development and Research, September 1999), 53. See also John Goering, Helene Stebbins, and Michael Siewert, *Promoting Housing Choice in HUD's Rental Assistance Programs: A Report to Congress* (Washington, DC: U.S. Department of Housing and Urban Development, Office of Policy Development and Research, April 1995); John Goering and Judith Feins, *Choosing a Better Life?;* Thomas Waldron, "Parading Politicians Hear Critics of Housing Program," *Baltimore Sun,* September 12, 1994; Larry Carson, "City Vows to Proceed on Housing," *Baltimore Sun,* September 21, 1994; Peter Dreier and David Moberg, "Moving from the 'Hood: The Mixed Success of Integrating Suburbia," *American Prospect* 7, no. 24 (winter 1996): 75–80; Llewellyn H. Rockwell Jr., "The Ghost of Gautreaux," *National Review,* March 7, 1994; Margery Austin Turner, Susan Popkin, and Mary Cunningham, *Section 8 Mobility and Neighborhood Health: Emerging Issues and Policy Challenges* (Washington, DC: Urban Institute, April 2000).

84. Timothy M. Smeeding and Peter Gottschalk, "Cross-National Income Inequality: How Great Is It and What Can We Learn From It?" *Focus* (Institute for Research on Poverty, University of Wisconsin–Madison) 19, no. 3 (summer–fall 1998): 15–19.

85. Paul Jargowsky, *Poverty and Place: Ghettos, Barrios, and the American City* (New York: Russell Sage Foundation, 1997); Paul Jargowsky, *Stunning Progress, Hidden Problems* (Washington, DC: Brookings Institution, May 2003).

86. These studies are summarized in Massey and Denton, *American Apartheid.*

87. See Richard Engstrom, "The Voting Rights Act: Disfranchisement, Dilution, and Alternative Election Systems," *PS: Political Science and Politics* 27, no. 4 (December 1994): 685–88; Frances Fox Piven and Richard Cloward, *Why Americans Don't Vote* (New York: Pantheon, 1998).

88. A study of turnout in 5,400 electoral districts in New York City concluded that neighborhood instability depressed turnout even more than concentrated poverty (though poor neighborhoods tend to be more unstable than middle-income areas). This is not just because of low registration rates but because unstable neighborhoods lack the social capital to link citizens to the political process. David Olson, "Place Matters: Explaining Turnout in New York City Elections, 1988–1994," Ph.D. diss. (Department of Political Science, State University of New York at Albany, 1997).

89. Raymond Wolfinger, "Improving Voter Registration" (unpublished paper, University of California at Berkeley, March 1994).

90. According to the Federal Election Commission (FEC), most states require voters to

register at least twenty-eight days before an election. See the FEC Web site, available at http://www.fec.gov/pages/faqs.htm.

91. Raymond E. Wolfinger and Steven J. Rosenstone, *Who Votes?* (New Haven, CT: Yale University Press, 1980); Jan Leighley and Jonathan Nagler, "Individual and Systemic Influences on Turnout: Who Votes?" *Journal of Politics* 54 (1992): 718–40; Glen Mitchell and Christopher Wlezien, "The Impact of Legal Constraints on Voter Registration, Turnout, and the Composition of the American Electorate" (paper presented at the annual meeting of the Midwest Political Science Association, 1989), cited in Wolfinger, "Improving Voter Participation."

92. See Douglas Amy, *Real Choices, New Voices: The Case for Proportional Representation Elections in the United States* (New York: Columbia University Press, 1993); Robert Richie and Steven Hill, *Reflecting All of Us: The Case for Proportional Representation* (Boston: Beacon Press, 1999); Lani Guinier, *Tyranny of the Majority: Fundamental Fairness in Representative Democracy* (New York: Free Press, 1994).

93. Ruy Teixeira, *The Disappearing American Voter* (Washington, DC: Brookings Institution Press, 1992); David Callahan, "Ballot Blocks: What Gets the Poor to the Polls?" *American Prospect* 9, no. 39 (July–August 1998): 68–76; Robert Dreyfuss, "The Turnout Imperative," *American Prospect* 9, no. 39 (July–August 1998): 76–82; Marshall Ganz, "Motor Voter or Mobilized Voter?" *American Prospect* 7, no. 28 (September–October 1996): 41–50.

94. See, for example, Carol Swain, *Black Faces, Black Interests: The Representation of African Americans in Congress* (Cambridge, MA: Harvard University Press, 1993).

95. Bureau of Labor Statistics, "Union Members in 2003," January 21, 2004, available at http://stats.bls.gov/news.release/union2.nr0.htm.

96. Richard Rothstein, "Toward a More Perfect Union: New Labor's Hard Road," *American Prospect* 7, no. 26 (May–June 1996): 47–54; Richard Freeman, ed., *Working Under Different Rules* (New York: Russell Sage Foundation, 1994); Kate Bronfenbrenner, Sheldon Friedman, Richard Hurt, Rudolph Oswald, and Ronald Seeber, *Organizing to Win: New Research on Union Strategies* (Ithaca, NY: ILR Press, 1998); Mishel, Bernstein, and Boushay, *State of Working America 2002/2003;* Peter Dreier and Kelly Candaele, "Canadian Beacon," *Nation,* December 16, 1996, 20.

CHAPTER 8. CROSSING THE CITY LINE: A METROPOLITICS FOR THE TWENTY-FIRST CENTURY

1. See Christopher R. Conte, "The Boys of Sprawl," *Governing* (May 2000): 28–33; David Rusk, *Inside Game/Outside Game: Winning Strategies for Saving Urban America* (Washington, DC: Brookings Institution Press, 1999).

2. William Schneider, "The Suburban Century Begins," *Atlantic,* July 1992, 33–43. See also Juliet F. Gainsborough, *Fenced Off: The Suburbanization of American Politics* (Washington, DC: Georgetown University Press, 2001), chap. 5. Lee Sigelman and Lars Willnat, "Attitudinal Differentiation Between African-American Urbanites and Suburbanites: A Test of Three Accounts," *Urban Affairs Review* 35, no. 5 (May 2000): 677–94, suggest that the urban-suburban differences among blacks are relatively minor, however.

3. Harold L. Wolman, Todd Swanstrom, Margaret Weir, and Nicholas Lyon, in *The Calculus of Coalitions: Cities and States and the Metropolitan Agenda* (Washington, DC:

Brookings Institution Center for Urban and Metropolitan Policy, April 2004), conclude that "one of our most striking findings is that big city mayors are not leading the way in metropolitan reform" (20).

4. Owen Fiss, *A Way Out: America's Ghettos and the Legacy of Racism,* edited by Joshua Cohen, Jefferson Decker, and Joel Rogers (Princeton, NJ: Princeton University Press, 2003).

5. J. Phillip Thompson, "Beyond Moralizing," in Fiss, *A Way Out,* 65.

6. Robert Coles, "Better Neighborhoods," 58, Jennifer Hochschild, "Creating Options," 68, and Gary Orfield, "Exit and Redevelopment," 75, in Fiss, *A Way Out.*

7. Robert Axelrod, *The Evolution of Cooperation,* New York: Basic Books, 1984.

8. David R. Harris, "All Suburbs Are Not Created Equal: A New Look at Racial Differences in Suburban Location" (Research Report 99–440, Population Studies Center, Institute for Social Research, University of Michigan, September 1999); William H. Lucy and David L. Phillips, *Confronting Suburban Decline: Strategic Planning for Metropolitan Renewal* (Washington, DC: Island Press, 2000).

9. Gainsborough, *Fenced Off,* chap. 6.

10. For an insightful discussion of the types of metropolitan coalitions formed in state legislatures and the manner in which they came about, see Wolman et al., *Calculus of Coalitions.*

11. For the case of New York City, see Richard D. Alba, John R. Logan, and Brian Stults, "The Changing Neighborhood Contexts of the Immigrant Metropolis" *Social Forces* 79 (December 2000): 587–621; more generally, see William H. Frey and Douglas Geverdt, "Changing Suburban Demographics: Beyond the 'Black-White, City-Suburb' Typology" (Research Report 98–422, Population Studies Center, Institute of Social Research, University of Michigan, June 1998).

12. For a discussion of New York and Los Angeles, see John Logan and John Mollenkopf, *People and Politics in Urban America* (New York: Drum Major Institute, 2003).

13. Orfield, "Exit and Redevelopment"; William Julius Wilson, *The Bridge over the Racial Divide* (Berkeley: University of California Press, 1999); Mark R. Warren, *Dry Bones Rattling* (Princeton, NJ: Princeton University Press, 2001).

14. Thomas Byrne Edsall and Mary D. Edsall, *Chain Reaction: The Impact of Race, Rights, and Taxes on American Politics* (New York: Norton, 1991), 228, 229.

15. Schneider, "Suburban Century Begins."

16. Richard Sauerzopf and Todd Swanstrom, "The Urban Electorate in Presidential Elections, 1920–1996," *Urban Affairs Review* 35, no. 1 (September 1999): 72–91; 2000 figures updated by the authors.

17. Gerald M. Pomper, "The Presidential Election," in *The Elections of 1992,* ed. Michael Nelson (Washington, DC: CQ Press, 1993), 139; "Who Voted: A Portrait of American Politics, 1976–2000," *New York Times,* November 12, 2000, 4.

18. Peter F. Nardulli, Jon K. Dalager, and Donald E. Greco, "Voter Turnout in U.S. Presidential Elections: An Historical View and Some Speculation," *PS: Political Science and Politics* 29 (1996): 480–90.

19. Ibid., 484.

20. Sauerzopf and Swanstrom, "Urban Electorate," 78; 2000 figures updated by the authors.

21. Harold Wolman and Lisa Marckini, "Changes in Central City Representation and Influence in Congress Since the 1960s," *Urban Affairs Review* 34, no. 2 (November 1998): 294. See also Gainsborough, *Fenced Off,* chap. 7.

22. Wolman and Marckini, "Changes in Central City Representation," 310.

23. Margaret Weir, "Central Cities' Loss of Power in State Politics," *Cityscape* 2, no. 2 (May 1996): 23–40, and Wolman et al., *Calculus of Coalitions*.

24. Robert S. Lynd and Helen M. Lynd, *Middletown: A Study in Contemporary American Culture* (New York: Harcourt, Brace, and Company, 1929); *Middletown: A Study in Cultural Conflicts* (New York: Harcourt Brace, 1937); Michael Barone and Grant Ujifusa, *The Almanac of American Politics 1996* (Washington, DC: National Journal, 1995), 479.

25. Stanley B. Greenberg, *Middle Class Dreams: The Politics and Power of the New American Majority* (New York: Times Books, 1995), 278–83. See also Al From, "The Next Battleground: Suburbs Are the Key to Democratic Victories in 2000," *New Democrat* (March–April 1999): 35–36.

26. Greenberg extends this analysis in his most recent book, *The Two Americas: Our Current Political Deadlock and How to Break It* (New York: Thomas Dunne Books, 2004).

27. Chris Black, "Clinton Links Suburbanites to Solutions for Urban Ills," *Boston Globe,* May 10, 1992, 9; David Lauter, "Clinton Tells Orange County Not to Ignore Cities," *Los Angeles Times,* May 31, 1992, A1.

28. Pomper, "Presidential Election," 138–39.

29. Neal Peirce, "Sprawl Control: A Political Issue Comes of Age" (syndicated column, November 15, 1998); Todd Purdum, "Suburban Sprawl Takes Its Place on the Political Landscape," *New York Times,* February 6, 1999; Margaret Kriz, "The Politics of Sprawl," *National Journal,* February 6, 1999.

30. John Mollenkopf, "Urban Policy at the Crossroads," in Margaret Weir, ed., *The Social Divide: Political Parties and the Future of Activist Government* (Washington, DC: Brookings Institution Press, 1998). For an analysis of how to attract suburban voters into an alliance with urban voters, see John Judis and Ruy Teixeira, *The Emerging Democratic Majority* (New York: Scribner, 2002).

31. John H. Mollenkopf, *The Contested City* (Princeton, NJ: Princeton University Press, 1983), 48–52. Arguably, the Nixon administration launched or proposed some of the most important urban policies, but this happened when nonsouthern Democrat strength in the House was at a post–New Deal high.

32. See Wolman and Marckini, "Changes in Central City Representation," for a discussion of the limited circumstances under which a cohesive urban delegation was able to influence contested House votes in this period. See also Nicol C. Rae, *Southern Democrats* (New York: Oxford University Press, 1994).

33. For an excellent discussion of the interplay of policy and politics in this period, see Weir, *Social Divide.*

34. See Charles Cameron, David Epstein, and Sharyn O'Halloran, "Do Majority-Minority Districts Maximize Substantive Black Representation in Congress?" *American Political Science Review* 90, no. 4 (December 1996): 794–812, for a related argument concerning the concentration of black voters in majority-black districts.

35. For a well-documented argument to this effect, see Ruy Teixeira and Joel Rogers, *America's Forgotten Majority: Why the White Working Class Still Matters* (New York: Basic Books, 2000).

36. The correlation is .134 with 1996 Democratic presidential votes and .262 with 1998 Democratic votes in contested House races, according to our analysis of Mollenkopf's Congressional District Database, constructed from 1990 census population statistics (Summary Tape Files 1D and 3D, Census of Population and Housing, 1990, Congressional Districts of the United States, 104th Congress, on CD-ROM) and elec-

tion results from various editions of Michael Barone and Grant Ujifusa, *Almanac of American Politics* (Washington, DC: National Journal), as confirmed by data compiled from official sources by Robin H. Carle, clerk of the House of Representatives, available at http://clerkweb.house.gov/elections/elections.htm.

37. The unstandardized coefficient between the percentage voting for the House Democratic candidate in 1998 and the unionized percentage of the labor force was .759 after controlling for the log of density, median household income, and percentage black, according to our analysis of Mollenkopf's Congressional District Database. The standardized coefficient was .228, and the standardized coefficient for density vote was .452. These variables were significant at the .05 level, and the adjusted R squared for the model was .368.

38. Teixeira and Rogers, *America's Forgotten Majority;* and Judis and Teixeira, *Emerging Democratic Majority.*

39. Sam Hirsch, "The United States House of Representatives: What Went Wrong in the Latest Round of Congressional Redistricting," *Election Law Journal* 2, no. 2 (2003): 179–216.

40. This discussion draws on Michael Barone and Richard Cohen, *Almanac of American Politics, 2004* (Washington, DC: National Journal, 2003), 1145–47.

41. Asher Arian, Arthur Goldberg, John Mollenkopf, and Edward Rogowsky, *Changing New York City Politics* (New York: Routledge, 1991), 145. See also Robert Caro, *The Power Broker: Robert Moses and the Fall of New York* (New York: Random House, 1974).

42. In 2000 and 2002, Serrano had a 100 percent voting record in rankings by the National Council of Senior Citizens, the National Education Association, and National Abortion and Reproductive Rights Action League; he had a 93 percent rating from the League of Conservation Voters; 90 percent from the ADA and AFL-CIO, and 86 percent from the ACLA. Project Vote-Smart (http://www.vote-smart.org) and David Hawkins and Brian Nutting, eds., *CQ's Politics in America 2004* (Washington, DC: Congressional Quarterly Press, 2003).

43. Barone and Ujifusa, *Almanac of American Politics, 1998,* 502–3.

44. Alan Achkar, "Suburbs' Plight: Inner-Ring Communities Fight Loss of Funds, People to Outlying Cities," *Cleveland Plain Dealer,* March 23, 1998, 1A.

45. See http://www.jointventure.org, http://www.greaterbaltimore.org, http://www.chicagometropolis2020.org, and http://www.sdrta.org.

46. Rosabeth Moss Kanter, "Business Coalitions as a Force for Regionalism," in *Reflections on Regionalism,* ed. Bruce Katz (Washington, DC: Brookings Institution Press, 2000), 154–81.

47. AnnaLee Saxenian, *Regional Advantage: Culture and Competition in Silicon Valley and Route 128* (Cambridge, MA: Harvard University Press, 1994), compares the former favorably to the latter, noting that Silicon Valley benefitted from a network of specialized firms that, while competing intensely, also collaborated in formal and informal ways with one another and with local universities and governments. See also Stephen S. Cohen and Gary Fields, "Social Capital and Capital Gains in Silicon Valley," *California Management Review* 41, no. 2 (1999): 108–26, available at http://socrates.berkeley.edu/~brie/www/pubs/wp/wp132.htm; Rosabeth Moss Kanter, *World Class: Thriving Locally in the Global Economy* (New York: Simon and Schuster, 1995). Louise Jezierski, "Political Limits to Development in Two Declining Cities: Cleveland and Pittsburgh," *Research in Politics and Society* 3 (1993): 173–89, makes a similar point regarding these two cities.

48. For the Milwaukee case, see David Wood, Josh Whitford, and Joel Rogers, *At the Center of It All* (Center on Wisconsin Strategy, University of Wisconsin, June 2000), available at http://www.cows.org/pdf/metro/mvp-report.pdf. More generally, see Eric Parker and Joel Rogers, "Building the High Road in Metro Areas: Sectoral Training and Employment Projects" (Center on Wisconsin Strategy, University of Wisconsin, May 2000).

49. Bennett Harrison and Marcus Weiss, *Workforce Development Networks: Community-Based Organizations and Regional Alliances* (Thousand Oaks, CA: Sage Publications, 1998).

50. Kanter, "Business Coalitions," 159.

51. The Greater Baltimore Committee, "'One Region, One Future': A Report on Regionalism" (July 1997), at http://www.gbc.org/reports/regionalism.htm.

52. For more extended discussion, see Peter Dreier, "Labor's Love Lost? Rebuilding Unions' Involvement in Federal Housing Policy," *Housing Policy Debate* 11, no. 2 (2000): 327–92, especially 366–81; and David Reynolds, ed., *Partnering for Change: Unions and Community Groups Build Coalitions for Economic Justice* (Armonk, NY: M. E. Sharpe, 2004).

53. For a perspective on Silicon Valley developed by the Working Partnerships program of the South Bay Labor Council, see Chris Benner, *Growing Together or Drifting Apart: Working Families and Business in the New Economy—A Status Report on Social and Economic Well Being in Silicon Valley* (San Jose, CA: Working Partnerships USA and Economic Policy Institute, 1998), available at http://www.atwork.org/wp/cei/gtda.pdf.

54. For a discussion of both the Los Angeles County Labor Federation and the South Bay Labor Council, see Harold Meyerson, "Rolling the Union On: John Sweeney's Movement Four Years Later," *Dissent* (winter 2000), available at http://www.dissentmagazine.org/archive/wi00/meyerson.html; Steven Greenhouse, "The Most Innovative Figure in Silicon Valley? Maybe This Labor Organizer," *New York Times,* November 14, 1999; Kelly Candaele and Peter Dreier, "LA's Progressive Mosaic: Beginning to Find Its Voice," *Nation,* August 21–28, 2000; Douglas Foster, "Unions.com: Silicon Valley Isn't Exactly Known as a Stronghold of Organized Labor; Amy Dean Is Working to Change That," *Mother Jones* 25, no. 5 (September–October 2000).

55. Antonio Olivo and Jean Merl, "Unions Seeking to Increase Clout in Suburban Races," *Los Angeles Times,* March 12, 2000.

56. See the Metropolitan Area Research Corporation Web site, available at http://www.metroresearch.org/about.html. Its report, "An Activist's Guide to Metropolitics," is available there. For a variety of case studies of progressive smart-growth initiatives, see *Smart Growth, Better Neighborhoods: Communities Leading the Way* (Washington, DC: National Neighborhood Coalition, 2000). See also Sheryll Cashin, *The Failures of Integration: How Race and Class are Undermining the American Dream* (New York: Public Affairs Books, 2004); and Mark Rank, *One Nation, Underprivileged: Why American Poverty Affects Us All* (New York: Oxford University Press, 2004).

57. Ester R. Fuchs, "The City Already Pays More Than Its Fair Share," *New York Times,* May 22, 1999.

58. John A. Powell, "Addressing Regional Dilemmas for Minority Communities," in Katz, *Reflections on Regionalism,* 218–46. For an eloquent defense of this perspective, see John O. Calmore, "Racialized Space and the Culture of Segregation: 'Hewing a Stone of Hope from a Mountain of Despair,'" *University of Pennsylvania Law Review* 143 (1995): 1233–71.

59. Larry N. Gerston and Peter J. Haas, "Political Support for Regional Government in the 1990s: Growing in the Suburbs?" *Urban Affairs Quarterly* 29, no. 1 (September 1993): 154. See also "Sprawl: The Revolt in America's Suburbs," *New Democrat* 11, no. 2 (March–April 1999); "Crossing the Line: The New Regional Dynamics," *Governing* (January 2000): 44–50; "Smart Growth," *Planning* (January 2000): 5–29.

60. Margaret Weir, "Coalition Building for Regionalism," in Katz, *Reflections on Regionalism,* 148.

61. Thomas Kamber, "The Politics of Section 8 in Portland and New York City" (Ph.D. diss., Political Science Program, CUNY Graduate Center, 2000); Edward G. Goetz, "The Politics of Poverty Concentration and Housing Demolition," *Journal of Urban Affairs* 22, no. 2 (2000): 157–73.

62. Jeffrey M. Berry, Kent E. Portney, and Ken Thomson, *The Rebirth of Urban Democracy* (Washington, DC: Brookings Institution Press, 1993).

63. Owen Fiss, "A Task Unfinished," symposium on "Moving Out," *Boston Review* (summer 2000).

64. Robert B. Reich, *The Work of Nations* (New York: Random House, 1991).

INDEX

economic, xi, 219, 226, 231, 256, 279, 297, 302, 303; metropolitan, xvi, 218, 247, 256; political, 273; regional, 213, 223–24, 305, 307, 332n49; sprawl and, 72–76, 279

Comprehensive Employment Training Act, 137–38

Compuware, 200

Concentrated poverty, 3, 59, 163, 166, 178, 239, 262; addressing, 167, 183, 261, 264, 308; decrease in, xiv, 33, 56, 57, 61, 207, 225, 226, 253, 275; described, 4, 7, 101, 151, 162, 276; increase in, xiv, 30, 56, 186, 190; negative effects of, 55, 60, 63, 109; problems with, 91, 215, 259, 276, 308; promoting, 218, 276; regional context for, 66, 218; research on, 28–29, 30, 65; spatially, 265; sprawl and, 251, 252, 326n96

Concentric zone theory, 44

Conflict, 229–34

Congestion, 36, 151, 209, 212, 214, 220, 258, 279; addressing, 73, 307; decreased, 301; increased, 116, 222

Consumer choice, 108, 109

Consumer demand, 59, 74–75

Consumer goods, 18, 25, 34, 85

Contract with America, 287

Cook County, 15, 299; regional approaches in, 223

Cook County Democratic Party, 203

Cooperation; competitiveness and, 224; metropolitan, 154, 220–21, 225–26, 255, 278; promoting, 226–29, 255; regional, 31, 35, 167–68, 213, 214, 226, 231, 233, 254, 259, 275, 276, 296, 303, 306; stalling, 226–29

Coordinating Committee, 166

COPS. *See* Communities Organized for Public Service

Corporate growth, 18, 202

Corporate services, 42, 74, 161, 162, 298–99

Corruption, 33, 183, 184, 194

Costs of Sprawl, The (Council on Environmental Quality), 222

Costs of Sprawl 2000, 71, 72

Council on Affordable Housing (COAH), 389n47

Council on Environmental Quality, 222

Councils of government (COGs), 222, 228, 233, 260

Coventry, GHP and, 216

Cox, W. Michael, 315n65

CRA. *See* Community Reinvestment Act

Crime, 1, 6, 17, 33, 34, 62, 66, 78, 90, 99, 164, 166, 191, 200, 209, 210, 248, 309; blocked opportunity and, 93–94; concentrated poverty and, 67, 92–93, 96, 151, 186; decrease in, 9, 47, 92, 96, 137, 142, 176, 193, 215, 252, 298; fear of, 92–93, 96, 271; increase in, 29, 59, 94–95, 96, 98, 101, 185, 344n217; juvenile, 97–98; pay for, 93–94; place and, 95; protection from, 28, 53, 186; sprawl and, 96; street, 26, 192; suburban, 96–98; urban, 92, 252;

violent, 7, 12, 33, 92–93, 95, 96, 97, 158, 198, 344n217; as wedge issue, 283

Crime bill, 284

Cross-Bronx Expressway, 5, 131, 151, 298

Crosson, Matthew, 211

Culture, 42, 112, 180, 200; car-centered, 116, 251–52; cities and, 4, 157; consumer, 88, 93; elite, 60; political, 191

Culture of poverty thesis, 54, 63, 69–70, 340n151, 394n2; criticism of, 248–49

Cummins Engine, 284

Cumulative causation, theory of, 30

Cuomo, Andrew, 144

Cuomo, Mario, 193

Dalager, Jon, 281

Daley, Richard J., 171, 203, 204

Daley, Richard M., 204–5

Dallas Observer, 175

D'Amato, Richard, 210

Davis, Ernest, 212

Death, 334n75, 338n114; accidental, 98; premature, 77; risk of, 334n77; *See also* Homicides

Debts, 19, 82, 89, 90

Decentralization, 60, 75

Defense industry, 74, 117, 133, 162, 208

Deindustrialization, 30, 31, 58, 137; impact of, 160–61

DeKalb County, minorities in, 210

Democracy, xii, xvi, 26; economic, 178; equality and, 31; foundation of, 27; participation and, xi; poverty and, 26

Democratic Party, 126, 281, 283, 296; central cities and, 100, 280, 284; House seats for, 289; suburban vote and, 280, 288, 289, 293; urban vote and, 289, 294, 295; voter turnout gap and, 290; war on poverty and, 133; welfare and, 143; *See also* California Democratic Party; Cook County Democratic; Party

Density, 220, 241, 291, 332n44; economic efficiency and, 33; economic segregation and, 61, 326n95; employment, 74; specialization and, 74–75; suburban, 293

Department of Agriculture, 23

Department of Commerce, 113, 135

Department of Defense, 118–19, 208

Department of Health and Human Services, 142

Department of Homeland Security, 115

Department of Housing and Urban Development (HUD), 144, 148, 228, 257, 288; antipoverty efforts and, 135; Bridges to Work and, 242; cuts at, 138; discrimination and, 124; elimination of, 142; establishment of, 227; FMR and, 316n83; MTO and, 106, 270, 271; public housing and, 128, 134, 145–46; regional initiatives and, 305; Section 8 program and, 388n46; subsidies from, 122

Department of Justice, 124

Department of Labor, 135, 303

Department of Transportation (DOT), 117, 242

Ford, 198
Ford, Gerald, 137
Ford Foundation, 227
"Ford to City: Drop Dead" (*New York Daily Review*), 137
Forrester, Jay, 252, 253
Fort Apache, the Bronx (movie), 6
Fortune 1000 companies, 11
Foundations, 9, 168, 245
1400 Governments (Wood), 221
Fourteenth Amendment, 163, 366n56, 379n173
Fragmentation, 135, 221–22, 231–32, 245, 385n17; criticism of, 219–20; limiting, 221, 227; local government, 247; metropolitan, xvi, 219, 220, 254, 278, 308; political, 219, 251, 253, 275, 276; suburban, 323n54
France, Anatole: on inequality, 159
Franklin, Shirley, 195, 197, 198
Freedom of assembly, 270
Freedom of speech, 270
Free markets, 25, 41, 105–9, 115, 247, 248, 305, 339n133; shaping, 109–11; sprawl and, 34, 150; support for, 247
Freeways. *See* Highways
Frey, William, 278
Front National, immigrants and, 62
Frug, Gerald, 219, 220
Fulton County Housing Authority, 129
Future Once Happened Here, The (Siegel), 185

Gainsborough, Juliet, 244
Galbraith, John Kenneth, 91
Gamaliel Foundation, xiii
Gangs, 1, 2, 6, 14, 70; media and, 33; suburban, 97
Garreau, Joel, 73, 74; on edge cities, 16, 107, 110
Gated communities, 37, 91, 319n1
Gates, Daryl, 188, 377n147
Gautreaux, Dorothy, 388n46
Gautreaux program, 65, 69, 70, 164, 229, 311n3, 359n165, 388n46, 390n47, 392n77
Gays, 175, 191, 193, 198, 378n154
Geauga County, 84
General Motors, 13, 198, 284, 380n191; Poletown and, 199
General Population Characteristics for California Places, 314n30
Gentrification, 154, 177, 186, 195, 205, 330n18
Geronimus, Arline: on weathering, 81
Gerrymandering, 274
GGL. *See* Good Government League
Ghettos, 44, 49, 83, 109, 129, 133, 135–36, 210, 232, 327n102; culture of, 98; dismantling, 270; European, 62; expansion of, 112; French/American compared, 327n103; grocery stores and, 87; high-poverty, 70; levels of, 62; media and, 55; mini, 241; race and, 62
GHP. *See* Greater Hartford Progress
Gingrich, Newt, 193, 283–84, 287
Gini coefficients, 19, 323n51
Girl Scouts, 213

Giuliani, Rudy, 149, 191, 298; affirmative action and, 193; on crime, 186; economic development and, 306; housing plans and, 192; popularity of, 193–94; Port Authority and, 230; South Bronx and, 8; vote for, 174, 192–93
Glendale, 11, 12, 301, 305; minorities in, 13; poverty in, 13; redevelopment in, 232
Glendale City Hall, Armenians and, 14
Glendale High School, tensions at, 14
Global economy, 33, 40, 43, 320n10, 327n99
Globalization, 61, 223, 245, 260, 303, 380n185; social democratic/neoliberal nations and, 254
GNP. *See* Gross national product
Godard, Jean Luc, 116
Goldberg, Jackie, 152
Goldschmidt, Neal, 237
Goldsmith, Steven, 186
Goldsmith, William, 206–7
Gonzalez, Matt, 174–75
Goode, Wilson, 174
Good government groups, 177, 184
Good Government League (GGL), 177
Gore, Al, 14, 100, 300, 301; central cities and, 287–88; livability agenda and, 223; suburbs and, 288; vote for, 10, 146, 280, 287
Gottschalk, Peter, 317n87
Governments, 52, 105, 387n26; special district, 231, 368n78; splitting, 45; state, xvi, 162; streamlining, 222; trust in, 101–2; *See also* City governments; Local governments; Metropolitan; governments; Regional governments; Suburban governments; Urban; governments
Grands ensembles, 61
Grants, 134, 163, 234
Grassroots movements, 8, 181, 213, 250, 264, 297, 305–6
Great Depression, 41, 128, 191, 226; political machines during, 281; urban policy and, 126
Greater Baltimore Alliance, 303
Greater Baltimore Committee, 303–4
Greater Downtown Partnership, 199
Greater Hartford Progress (GHP), 216
Greater Louisville Inc. (GLI), 245
Greater New York, 220
Great Society, 141, 170, 181, 260; urban programs of, 132–36
Great U-turn, 20
Greco, Donald, 281
Green, Mark, 194
Greenberg, Stanley, 284
Greenfield site, 72
Green Party, 174
Green space. *See* Open space
Gribbs, Roman, 198
Grocery stores, 9, 89; healthy diets and, 336n88; in middle-class areas, 340n145; in poor areas, 86–87, 340n145
Grosse Point Farms, 137

Hughes, Mark Alan, 242
Human Relations Council, 14
Huntington Library, 12
Husock, Howard, 106

IAF. *See* Industrial Areas Foundation
Illinois Research and Development Corridor, 16
Illinois 13th Congressional District, 151, 297, 299, 300; described, 15–18; map of, 16; and others compared, 5 (table); sprawl and, 301
Immigrants, 9, 13, 14, 68, 78, 112, 160, 191, 232; assimilating, 169, 170; associations, 8; Cuban, 43; diseases and, 82; high-income, 46; North African, 62; opposition to, 184, 188, 214; voting by, 179
Immigration, 10, 162, 282; economy and, 43; laws on, 126; suburbanization and, 278–79; unskilled labor and, 43; *See also* Migration
Income, 17, 34, 334n77, 402n83; African American, 210; children and, 164; decline in, 147; distribution of, xvii, 22, 24, 28, 77, 195, 206, 215, 252, 364n35; increase in, 18, 20 (fig.), 21, 21 (fig.), 22, 43, 44, 47, 60, 142, 157, 195, 215, 224, 251; jobs and, 66–71; life expectancy and, 77; median, 46, 89, 197, 326n93, 339n134, 392n79; place and, 42, 71; regional, 57; suburban, 46 (fig.), 47 (fig.), 53 (fig.), 292, 332n49; urban, 23, 46 (fig.), 47 (fig.), 332n49; *See also* Minimum wage; Wages
Income inequalities, 19, 20–21, 43, 46, 47, 52, 61, 98, 206, 239, 254; in developed cities, 19 (table); economic segregation and, 63; geographically rooted, 30; increase in, 21, 31, 186, 254, 316n71
Indianapolis, coalitions in, 206–8
Indianapolis Airport, 208
Industrial Areas Foundation (IAF), xiii, 8, 180, 264; COPS and, 242; living wage laws and, 153
Industrial economy, 19–20, 32, 303
Industrialization, 178
Inequalities; economic segregation and, 61; health, 77, 82; increase in, 18–27, 30, 43, 61, 255, 275, 304, 317n85; metropolitan, 33, 34, 35, 104; persistence of, 98–99, 165; place-based, 3, 27–31, 30, 99, 249, 250, 309; political, 31, 249, 309; poverty and, 33, 275; racial segregation and, 196, 250; regional, 40, 44, 99, 321n27, 334n75; social, 31, 100, 236, 249, 309; spatial, xv, 3, 35, 76, 77, 104, 114, 151, 255, 275; suburban, 34, 51–52; *See also* Economic inequalities; Income inequalities
"Inequality: How the Gap Between the Rich and the Poor Hurts the; Economy" (*Business Week*), 19
Infant mortality, 200, 268
Inflation, 40, 142, 156, 315n65, 341n162
Information economy, suburbs and, 32
Infrastructure, 111, 297, 299; creating, 259; funds for, 229; investing in, 257; regional,

72–73, 234; smart growth and, 296; suburban, 72–73
Initiative for a Competitive City, 323n57
Inner-ring suburbs, 34, 44, 61, 69, 111, 214, 218; central cities and, 283; competitive advantages for, 33, 107; congressional districts of, 273; crime in, 96, 97; decline of, 3, 39, 49; European, 62, 63; problems in, 156, 157, 215, 225, 248, 252; revival of, 302; services in, 159
Institute for Urban Research and Development, 314n33
Insurance, 87, 99, 120, 340n153; car, 340n155; discrimination in, 120; home owners', 99; social, 127; unemployment, 169; *See also* Health insurance
Integration, 121, 151, 382n226; economic, 63, 249, 271, 327n108; housing, 177–78; poverty deconcentration and, 277; promoting, 123, 252; racial, 124, 138, 210, 211, 277; regional, 252
Intel, 237
Intermodal Surface Transportation Efficiency Act (ISTEA) (1991), 228, 233, 258
Internal Revenue Service (IRS), 266
International Ladies Garment Workers Union, 180
Internet, 3, 18–19, 32; connection to, 4, 312n9
Interstate 35, 51
Interstate 88, 15, 151
Interstate 290, 15, 151
Interstate 294, 15, 151
Interstate 494, 51
Interstate 684, 110
Interstates. *See* Highways
Interstate Highway and Defense Act (1956), 115
Investments, 72, 157, 303; physical/human/social capital, 246; private, 232; public, 141
Iraq, war in, xii, 289
IRS. *See* Internal Revenue Service
Irvine, growth of, 211
Isolation, 54, 55 (fig.), 57, 220, 323n61, 324n76, 341n160; economic, 71, 89, 309; political, 141–42, 253, 263; of poor, 41, 55 (fig.), 71, 324n76; social, 82, 335n77; spatial, 253
ISTEA. *See* Intermodal Surface Transportation Efficiency Act

Jackson, Andrew, 27
Jackson, Dwight, 1
Jackson, Henry, 227–28
Jackson, Jason, 1
Jackson, Maynard, 195, 196, 197
Jacobs, Jane, 40, 74, 84
Jacoby, Tamar, 107
James, Sharpe, 100
Jan and Dean, 10
Jargowsky, Paul, 53, 60, 326n93, 328n4, 365n42
Jefferson, Thomas, 26, 27
Jefferson County, Louisville and, 244–45, 260
Jersey City, businesses in, 230
Jet Propulsion Laboratory (NASA), 12, 13, 151, 301

Rogan, James, 14, 273
Rogers, Joel, 75
Roosevelt, Franklin D., 126; on democracy, 27; mayors and, 127; metropolitan America and, 227; National Resources Committee and, 226; WPB and, 118
Roosevelt, Theodore, 27, 374n126
Rose Bowl/Parade, 10, 11, 13
Rotary Club, 14, 213
Rothstein, Richard, 213, 263, 382–83n249
Route 128, 42, 74, 223
Rural areas; percentage population in, 49 (fig.); poor in, 48 (fig.)
Rusk, David, 48, 229, 305, 306; on CDCs, 9; on central-city decline, 313n23; on community development/sprawl, 61; on elastic cities, 45; on per capita income, 47; regional approach and, 225
Rust Belt, decline in, 201

Safety, 33, 34, 160; access to, 28; codes, 79; equal, 159; housing, 6; public, 115, 149, 155, 212
SAFTEA, 228
St. Charles County, 231
St. Louis County, 231
St. Louis Post-Dispatch, 344n209
St. Patrick's Day parade, Bloomberg and, 194
St. Paul, development in, 234–35
Salins, Peter: on playing field, 255
San Antonio v. Rodriguez, 163
San Bernardino, 232
San Bernardino County, fragmentation and, 231
San Diego Association of Governments, 224
San Diego County, Clinton and, 287
San Diego Regional Technology Alliance, 303
San Fernando Valley, 12, 190, 301, 376n146, 377n151
San Gabriel, 12, 305
Sanitation, 6, 79, 155, 179, 200, 207, 227, 233; regional, 222; strike by, 196
San Marino, 12, 15, 273
Santa Clara County, regional approaches in, 223
Save Our Library, 209
Savitch, Hank, 43, 226, 229, 245
Sawhill, Isabel, 262
Saxenian, AnnaLee, 74, 223
SBLC. *See* South Bay Labor Council
SCAG. *See* Southern California Association of Governments
Schaumberg, 51, 107
Schiff, Adam, 14, 273, 313n25; vote for, 301–2; voting record of, 15
Schill, Michael, 225, 240
Schmoke, Kurt, 165, 173
Schneider, William, 276, 281
Schockman, H. Eric, 189
School systems; financial basis for, 391n74; metropolitan, 263, 391n74; private/public, 4;

statistical profiles of, 365n46; turnover rate at, 17; *See also* Education
Schor, Juliet, 93
Scullen, Thomas, 17
Seattle Youth Survey, 97
Section 8 program, 101, 128, 130, 135, 140, 145, 146, 148, 228, 238, 240, 241, 257–58, 271; administering, 397n25; affordable apartments and, 354n102; comparison group, 392n77; creation of, 388n46
Security, xii, 4, 149
Segregation, 83, 263–64, 271, 392n74; class, 123, 229; costs of, 71–72; ethnic, 54; geographic, 113, 123, 129; housing, 350n64, 359n165; income, 28, 59; measuring, 319n6, 324n62, 325n85; occupational, 54; residential, 59, 124, 125, 327n104; self-, 119; social, 39; spatial, xi, 54, 62, 186, 215, 252, 280; suburban, 225; support for, 104, 120, 150; *See also* Economic segregation; Racial segregation
Sen, Amartya, 27
Separate societies, 31, 318n110
September 11th, xii, xiii, 146, 230; big government and, 149; Giuliani and, 193–94; impact of, 115, 149, 195, 288, 289
Serna, Joseph, 173
Serrano, Jose, 10, 298, 299, 406n42
Services. *See* Public services
Service sector, 61, 202, 274
SES. *See* Socioeconomic status
Set-asides, 169, 186
Settlement houses, 178
Sewer socialism, 180
Sewer systems, 212, 234, 235, 296; regional, 222, 226; sales tax for, 197
Sexually transmitted diseases (STDs), 338n19
Shaker Heights, 59, 210
Shakespeare, William, 165
Shalala, Donna, 141
Shame of the Cities, The (Steffens), 178
Sharp, Philip, 284
Shaw v. Reno (1993), 273, 366n56
Shelby County, Memphis and, 217–18
Shelly v. Kraemer (1948), 350n64
Shelter beds, 158, 363n26
Shipman, Raymond, 216–17
Shopping centers, 4, 107, 112, 208, 221; abandoned, 72; concentrated poverty and, 85
Siegel, Fred, 106, 107, 185
Sierra Club, xiii, 222, 306
Silent majority, 136, 184
Silicon Valley, 74, 294, 304, 407n53; commuting to, 103; information technology and, 42; regionalism in, 223, 225; specialized firms in, 406n47; success in, 224; technology companies in, 223
Silicon Valley Joint Venture, 224, 302–3
Silver, Sheldon, 306
Silver Lake Preserve, 110
"Simple living" movement, 89
Sinclair, Upton, 178

membership in, 295; metropolitan governments and, 259; municipal, 186; political culture and, 191; progressive urban coalitions and, 183; progrowth coalitions and, 170; public employee, 185, 245, 287; service worker, 205; suburban membership of, 293; teachers, 171; urban conservatism and, 184; voting by, 272

United Airlines, 208

United Auto Workers (UAW), 133, 198, 199

United Parcel Service, 2

U.S. Census Bureau, 313n28

U.S. Chamber of Commerce, 374n126

U.S. Conference of Mayors (USCM), 127, 180

U.S. Constitution, 112, 163

U.S. Steel, 177

U.S. Supreme Court, 113, 350n64

United Way, 205

University City, 59

University of Pittsburgh, 201

Upper class, 37, 91

Urban abandonment, model for, 307

Urban Affairs Review, xiv

Urban America in the Eighties, 253

Urban areas; federal programs for, 125–26; fragmentation of, 322n34

Urban conservative regimes, 168, 375n132; described, 183–86; local government and, 214

Urban crisis, 105, 146; concentrated poverty and, 364n33; free-market view of, 150; riot ideology and, 185; sprawl and, 326n95

Urban Development Action Grant (UDAG) program, 138

Urban development corporation (UDC), 388–89n47

Urban Dynamics (Forrester), 252

Urban fringe, 51, 66, 202, 250, 308, 326n94; flight to, 60; income and, 44; subdivision on, 226

Urban governments; cooperation in, 167–68; corruption/mismanagement of, 106; regional perspective on, 244

Urban Impact Analysis, 114

Urban Institute, 270, 329n8

Urban Land Institute, xiii, 130

Urban liberal regimes, 168, 184, 187, 203, 204; African Americans and, 171; concentrated poverty and, 195; described, 169–71, 173–78; local government and, 214; minorities and, 169, 176

Urban policy, xi, 356n135; federal, 125, 127; New Deal, 126–27; problems with, 140–46; stealth, 114–15, 146

Urban power structures, 165–68

Urban problems; corruption and, 33; media and, 33–34; spread of, 10–15, 151

Urban programs, 150, 132–36, 138

Urban progressive regimes, xi, 168, 184, 204, 367n71, 371n104; antigrowth stance of, 182; described, 178–83; local government and, 214

Urban regimes, 165–68

Urban renewal, 130–32, 134, 138, 303, 354n112; controversy over, 131–32, 167, 205; demise of, 132–33; federal, 129; focus of, 131; funds for, 203; Haussmann on, 44; highways and, 131; impact of, 298; poor and, 170; programs for, 166; promoting, 170

Urban-suburban alliances, 295

Urban unrest, 133, 283

Urban voters, xiii, 15, 141–42, 290; demobilization of, 281–82; Democratic Party and, 289; interests of, 293; policy agendas of, 291; Roosevelt and, 126; suburban voters and, xvi, 281, 288, 289, 296, 308, 405n30

USCM. *See* U.S. Conference of Mayors

Utilities, 180

VA. *See* Veterans Administration

Values, xi, 248, 249, 287

Ventura, redevelopment in, 232

Ventura, Jesse, 236

Ventura County, fragmentation and, 231

Veterans Administration (VA), 120, 121, 122

Vienna, apartments in, 44

Vietnam War, 135

Villaraigosa, Antonio, 174, 190, 194

Violence, 78, 81, 193; *See also* Crime, violent

VISTA. *See* Volunteers in Service to America

Vogel, Ronald, 226, 229, 245

Voluntary organizations, 99–100

Volunteers in Service to America (VISTA), 134

Von Hoffman, Alexander, 9

Voter registration laws, 184

Voters to Stop Sprawl, 212

Voter turnout, 14, 173, 184, 300; African American, 175, 187, 287; depressed, 272, 273, 291, 402n90; Hispanic, 287; suburban, 290; urban, 281, 287, 289–90, 291

Voting; barriers to, 272; patterns, 293; reforming, 272; trends, by district type, 285–86 (table)

Voting Rights Act (1965), 171, 272

Vouchers, 139, 353n102; housing, 1, 145, 164, 225, 228, 229, 234, 238, 240, 241, 257–58, 271, 277; school, 345–46n238

Wages, 40, 267; gap in, 19, 267, 321n28; poverty, 265, 268, 357n159; *See also* Income

Wagner, Robert, 166

Wagner Public Housing Act (1937), 128

Walden Galleria Mall, 64, 328n1

Wallace, Deborah and Rodrick, 83

Waller, Margy, 242

Wall Street, boom on, 26

Wal-Mart, 112, 212, 339n133

Walzer, Michael, 31

Warner, Tyson, 17

Warner Brothers, 13

War on poverty, 133, 134, 135, 342n186

War on terrorism, 114, 147

War Production Board (WPB), 118

Warren, Robert, 108

Washington, Harold, 174, 204
Washington County, metropolitan government and, 236
Washington Park Zoo, 236
Washington Post, 107, 148
Water, 115, 179, 222, 233, 296; problems with, 158, 227, 301
Watergate, 40
Watts, riots in, 187
Wealth; access to, 20, 31; concentrated, 26; disparities in, 19, 22, 33, 316n71; distribution of, 22, 205, 215; health and, 76–77; poverty and, 156; separation of, 76
Wealth of Nations, The (Smith), 75
Weathering, 81–82
Webb, Wellington, 173
Wedges, 49, 283
Weekend (movie), 116
Weir, Margaret, 269, 307
Welfare, 35, 70, 114, 127, 136, 155, 185, 191, 257, 265, 269; attacks on, 289; county, 134; decrease in, 67, 143, 147, 193, 287, 357n159; federal, 258; fighting for, 180; funding, 140; reform of, 56, 66, 67, 143, 147, 266, 355n124, 400n56; social, 249; state, 242; as wedge issue, 283
Welfare recipients, 67, 149, 242, 329n8, 346n6
Welfare-to-work programs, 149, 257
Westchester County, 212, 298; corporate headquarters in, 230; employment in, 68, 299; housing in, 68, 69, 109; per pupil spending in, 163; taxation in, 157, 209
West Side, 195, 241
White, Kevin, 138, 171, 177, 205
White flight, 115, 132, 278; desegregation and, 13–14; financial burden of, 89–91; racial change and, 60; riots and, 136, 198
Whitlock, Brand, 179
WIBs. *See* Workforce Investment Boards
Wiewel, Wim, 72
Wiggins, Cynthia, 64, 328n1
Will, George, 24
Will County, 15, 17, 299
Wilson, Alisa, 270
Wilson, William Julius, 28, 69, 70; on concen-

trated poverty, 55, 64–65; on ghetto poverty, 324n63; public works and, 277
Wolfe, Tom, 7, 92
Wolman, Harold, 254, 282
Women's Trade Union League, 178
Wong, Kenneth, 163
Woo, Michael, 189, 377n151
Wood, Robert, 221
Woolard, Cathy, 198
Workforce Investment Boards (WIBs), 257
Workforces, development of, 224, 229, 243, 257, 260, 297, 303
Working class, 327nn106, 107; African American, 198; voting by, 179
Working Partnerships, 225, 304, 407n53
Works Progress Administration, 180
World Trade Center, 230; attack on, xii, 115, 146, 149; Giuliani and, 193–94; rebuilding at, 195
World War I, racism/nativism after, 126
WPB. *See* War Production Board
Wuest, Martin, 103–4

Yankee Stadium, 299
"Year that Housing Died" (*New York Times Magazine*), 145
Yinger, John, 155
YMCA, 13
Yonkers, 68, 81–82
Yorty, Sam, 136, 168, 187, 375n132
Young, Andrew, 177, 195, 196, 197
Young, Coleman, 100, 199

Zero Population Growth (ZPG), 17, 315n59
Zoning, 104, 111, 129, 155, 182, 190, 209, 218, 227; boards, 211; costs and, 73; exclusionary, 67, 73, 228, 229, 240; inclusionary, 13, 154, 211, 229, 240; local, 113–14, 228; low-income housing and, 210; minimum-lot, 59; opposition to, 186; racial, 39, 113, 119; regional, 238; restrictive, 31, 68, 239; snob, 113; suburban, 39, 60–61, 113, 122, 240
Zoning Game, The (Babcock), 227
ZPG. *See* Zero Population Growth
Zunz, Olivier, 54